THE *Art* OF LIVERPOOL FC

THE Art OF LIVERPOOL FC

A CELEBRATION OF **LIVERPOOL FC** CREATIVE CULTURE

Reach Sport

Hardback edition first published in Great Britain in 2023

www.reachsport.com
@reach_sport
Reach Sport is a part of Reach PLC Ltd, 5 St Paul's Square, Liverpool, L3 9SJ
One Canada Square, Canary Wharf, London, E15 5AP

Thanks to Stephen Done from The Liverpool FC Story Museum for 'Anfield gallery' images.
Additional reporting for 'Frank's flag' and 'Peter the great' by Davey Brett.
Image of Audubon's cormorant courtesy of the John James Audubon Center at Mill Grove, Montgomery County Audubon Collection, and Zebra Publishing.
Inspiration...courtesy of the LFC Family.

Editor: David Cottrell
Production Editor: Michael McGuinness
Design: Lee Ashun, Rick Cooke
Cover design: Lee Ashun

Photography: Liverpool FC Getty Images, Mirrorpix, Alamy, Courtney Neary/MurWalls, Jack Finnigan, Tony Woolliscroft

Printed and bound by Bell & Bain.

FSC www.fsc.org MIX Paper | Supporting responsible forestry FSC® C007785

Contents

Red

FLAGS AND BANNERS

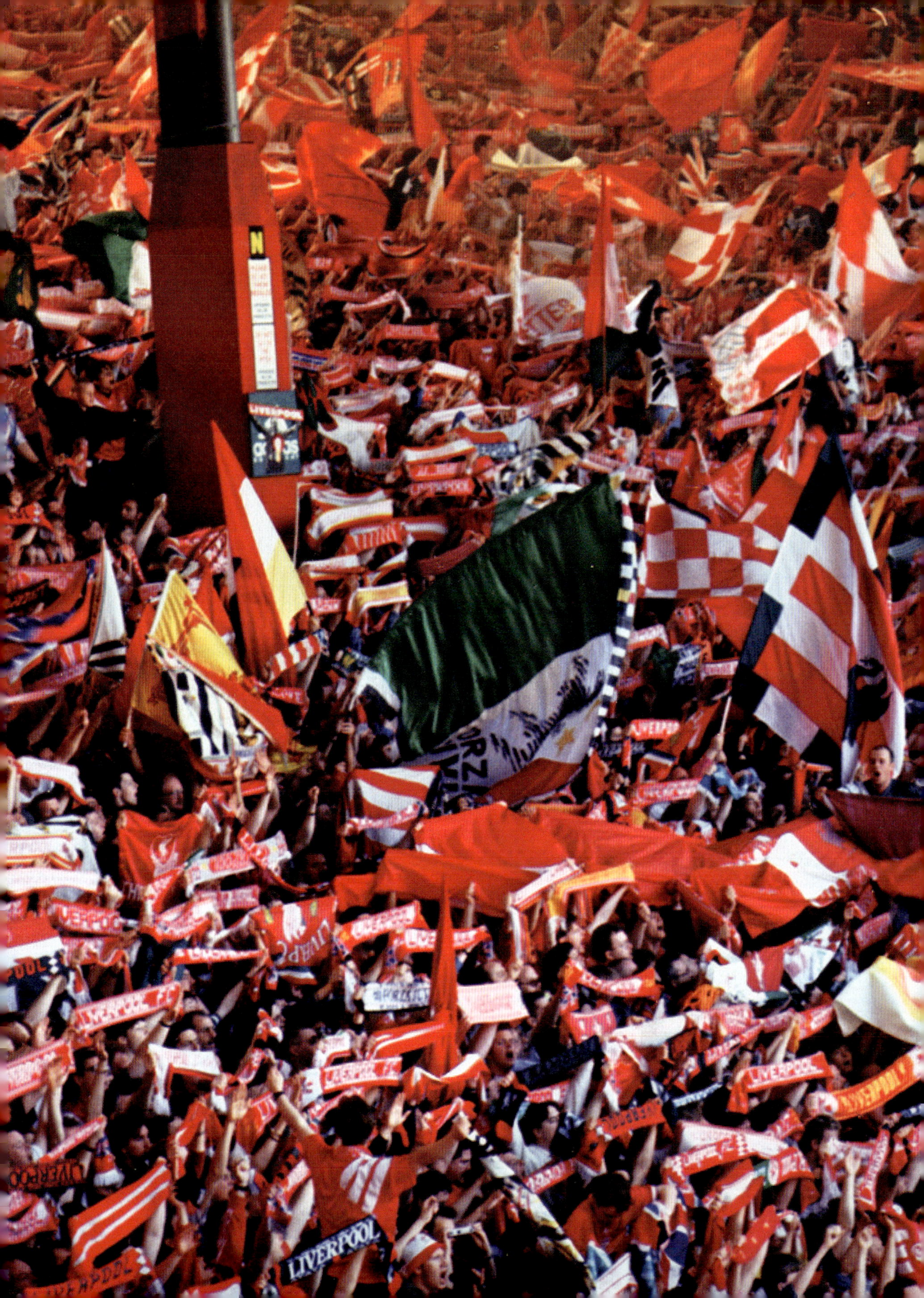
LIVERPOOL
LIVERPOOL
LIVERPOOL
LIVERPOOL

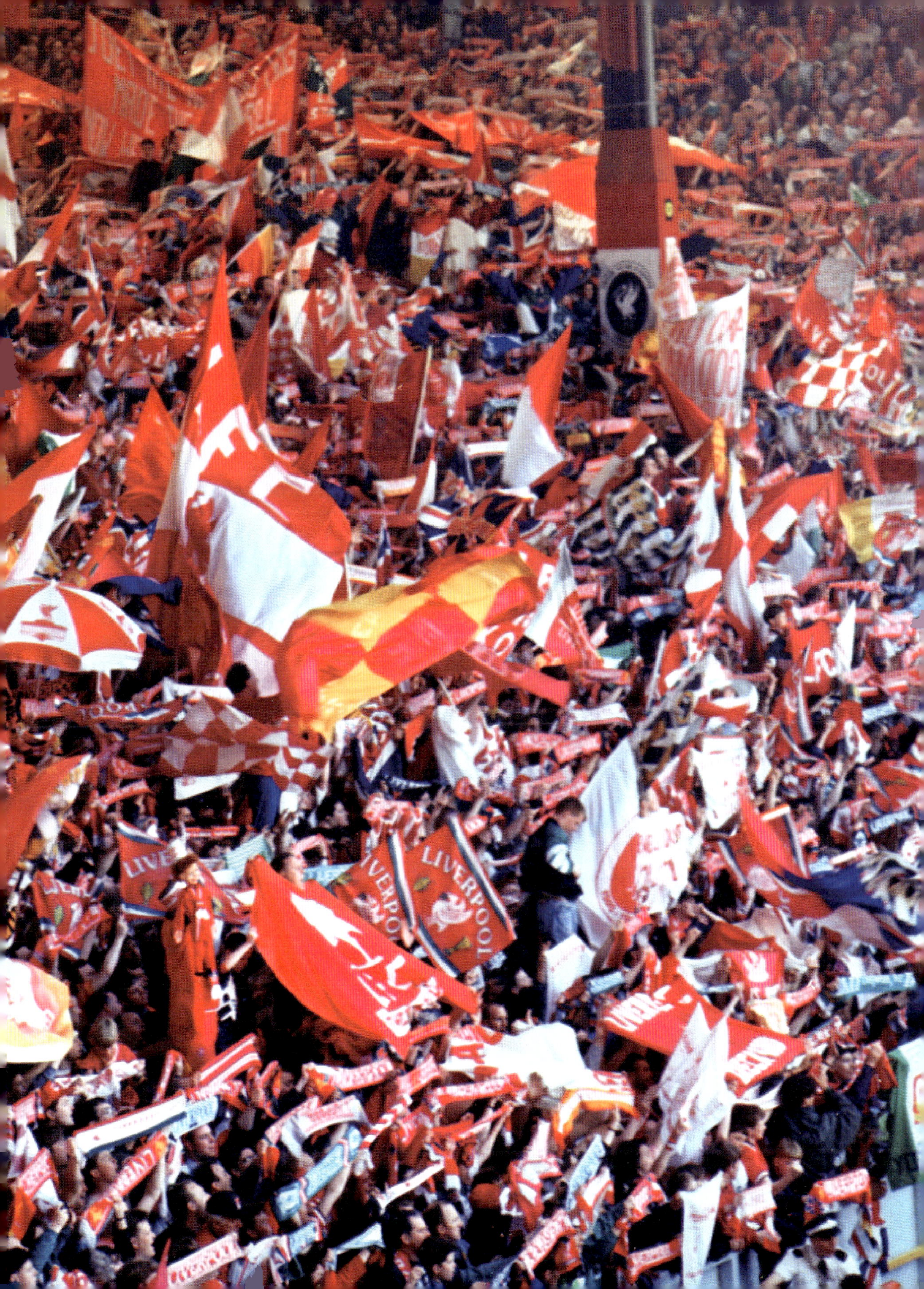
LIVERPOOL

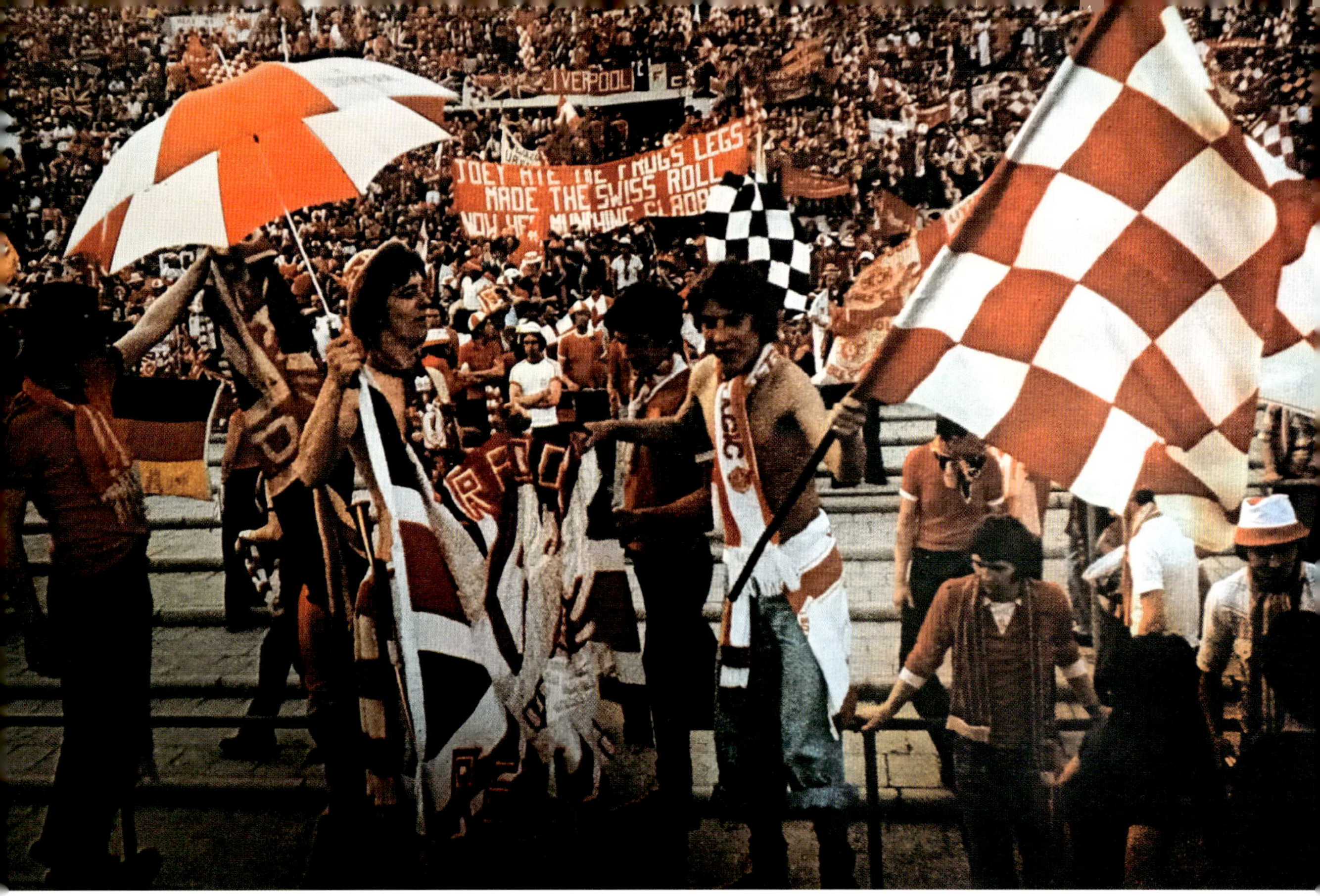
LIVERPOOL
JOEY ATE THE FROGS LEGS
MADE THE SWISS ROLL

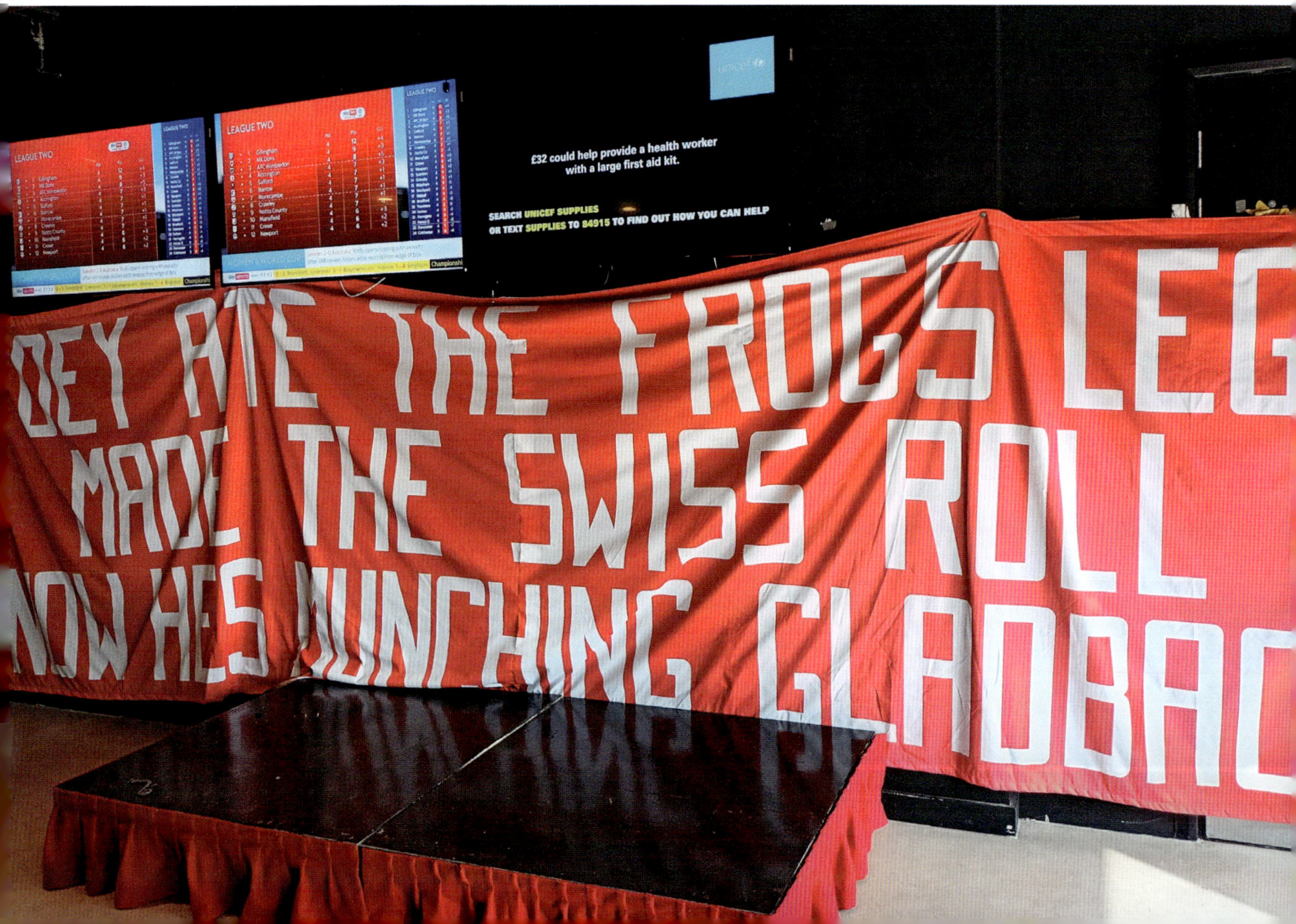
LEAGUE TWO
LEAGUE TWO
£32 could help provide a health worker
with a large first aid kit.
SEARCH UNICEF SUPPLIES
OR TEXT SUPPLIES TO 84915 TO FIND OUT HOW YOU CAN HELP
OEY ATE THE FROGS LEG
MADE THE SWISS ROLL
NOW HES MUNCHING GLADBAC

Munching Gladbach and *all that*

Early Kop colour and a famous banner for Rome

It started with a wiry-framed, hard-as-nails, tenacious-tackling, tattooed Welsh son of Liverpool called Joey Jones who'd built up a rapport with the Spion Kop at Anfield with his clenched-fist salutes before kick-off. Left-back Joey was part of the team which would go on to win the European Cup for the first time in the club's history – and both he and that 1976/77 season were immortalised by a banner which is part of LFC fan folklore.

By the mid-Seventies, banners with wisecracks and puns had become a tradition at Wembley FA Cup finals, with Kopites providing their fair share. Europe, though, was another matter, and when the Reds reached the final of the Continent's premier competition, a pair of Scouse wits had come up with something truly special: 'JOEY ATE THE FROGS LEGS, MADE THE SWISS ROLL, NOW HE'S MUNCHING GLADBACH.'

Originally, ahead of the second leg of the titanic quarter-final with French side St Etienne, supporters Phil Downey and Jimmy Cummings created a 6ft x 4ft banner with the words 'JOEY EATS FROGS LEGS'. When FC Zurich were swept aside in the semis, he'd also 'MADE THE SWISS ROLL'. But it took Phil's mum to come up with the piece-de-resistance in time for the final against reigning German champions Borussia Moenchengladbach in Rome's Stadio Olimpico: 'NOW HE'S MUNCHING GLADBACH'. A new 24ft x 8ft banner was born and the rest is history.

In his 1977 book *Champions Of Europe*, author John Keith wrote: "Rome had seen many sights in its long, colourful history but surely nothing to compare with the Scouse invasion that swelled the streets...an estimated 26,000 Liverpool supporters travelled for the game, vastly outnumbering Borussia fans and making their presence felt inside the stadium hours before kick-off.

"The legends on their banners reached new heights of ingenuity, their singing and chanting of such passion and intensity that it was as if the Kop had been moved *en bloc*. When in Rome do as the Romans do, goes the old saying, but

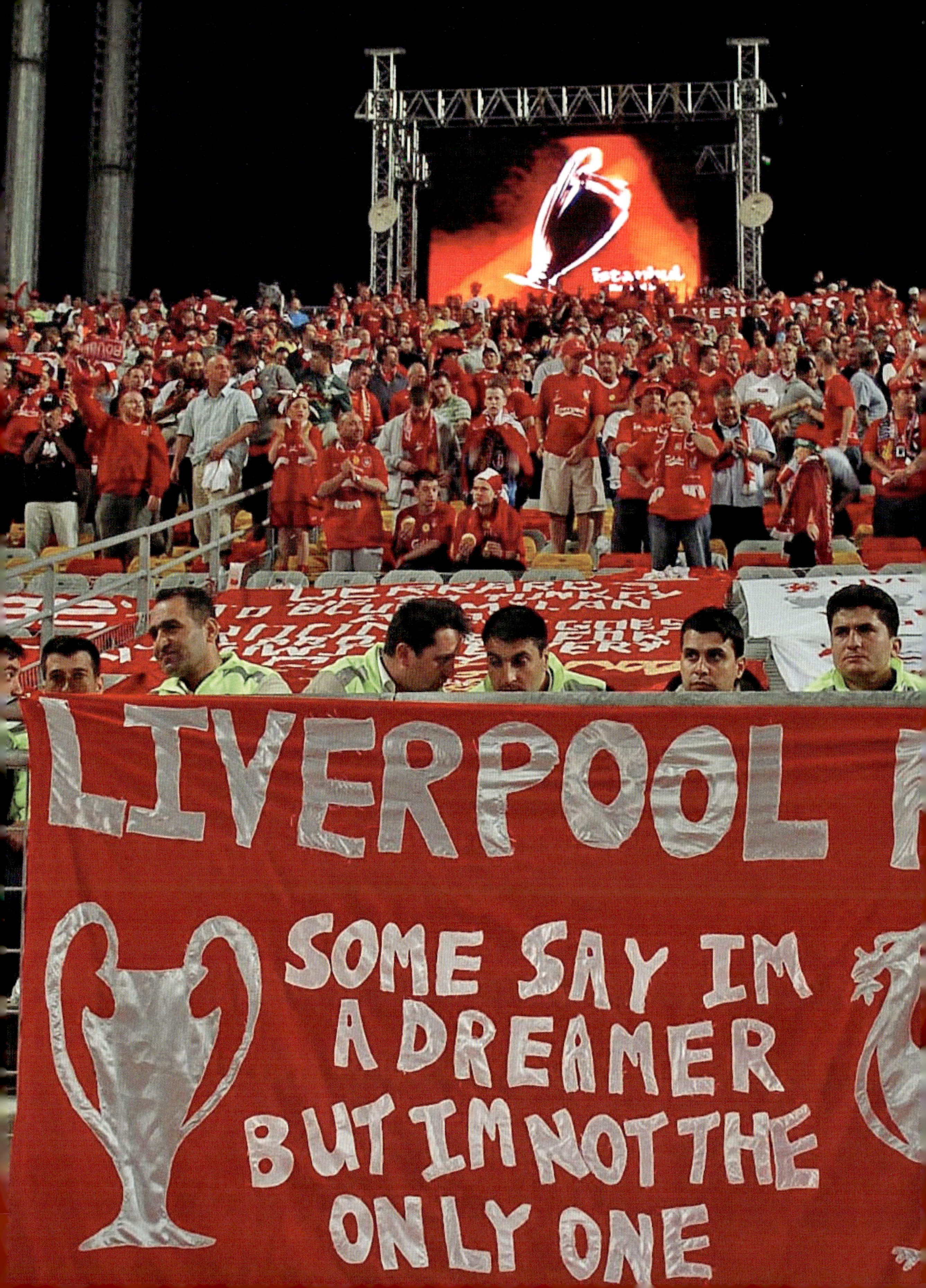
LIVERPOOL
SOME SAY IM
A DREAMER
BUT IM NOT THE
ONLY ONE

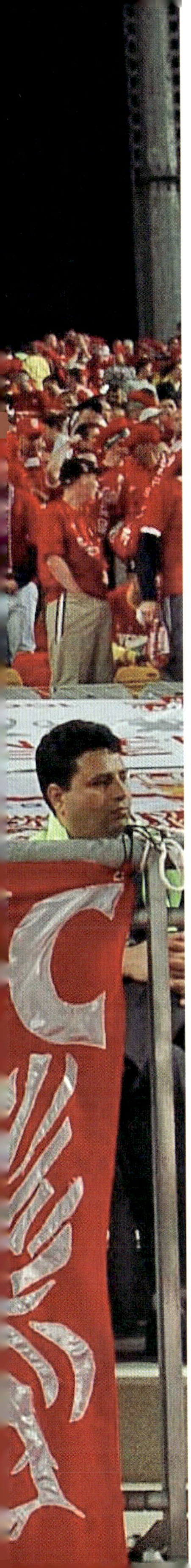

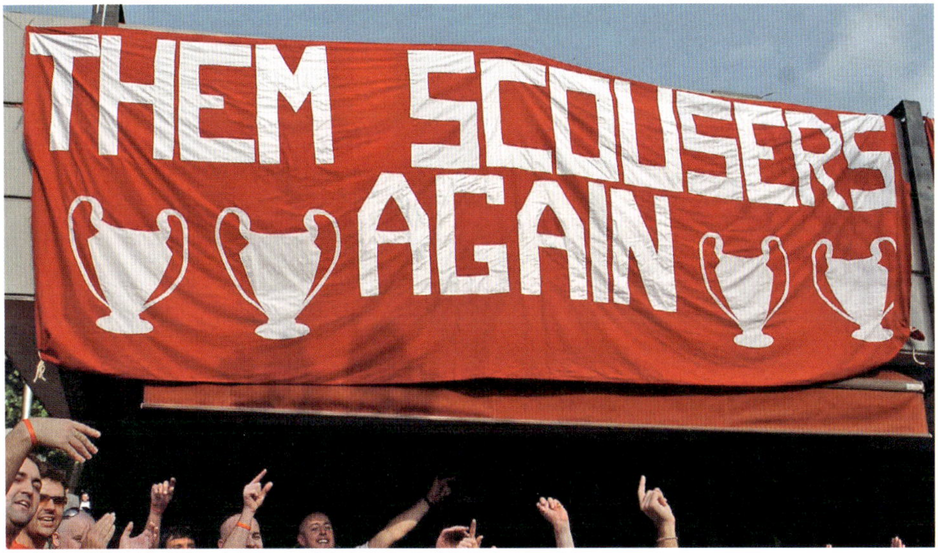

as far as they were concerned they were doing as Liverpudlians do and as the players emerged for a pre-kick-off stroll around the stadium their appreciation of their followers was made crystal-clear. The first blow, albeit psychological, had been struck. And it had been struck for Liverpool."

Years later Joey himself recalled: "When I left Liverpool, Jimmy and Phil gave it to me and I kept it for years in my house. A few years ago I loaned it back to Liverpool's club museum because they wanted to display it and that is the only place I would've let it go back to, because for me it is a supporters' banner.

"It's nice to be reminded about it because they could have made that banner about any player in that team, not one of the lesser-known ones like myself. So I have always appreciated that and I feel honoured that they made it in my name – I think as much of that banner as I do of my medal."

The original was back on the Kop in February 2019 for the Champions League last-16 first leg against Bayern Munich, 42 years since it was first unfurled on that famous night in Rome, and a replica is behind the stage in Anfield's Kop Bar.

Continuity is a big thing among LFC's generations – on forthcoming pages witness the periodic reincarnation of another banner proclaiming: 'LIVERPOOL CREAM OF EUROPE', first captured on camera before the 1966 European Cup Winners' Cup final against Borussia Dortmund at Glasgow's Hampden Park, then in 1976 on the Kop at the second leg of the UEFA Cup semi-final versus Barcelona, and more recently at Anfield in 2021 for the Champions League group game with AC Milan.

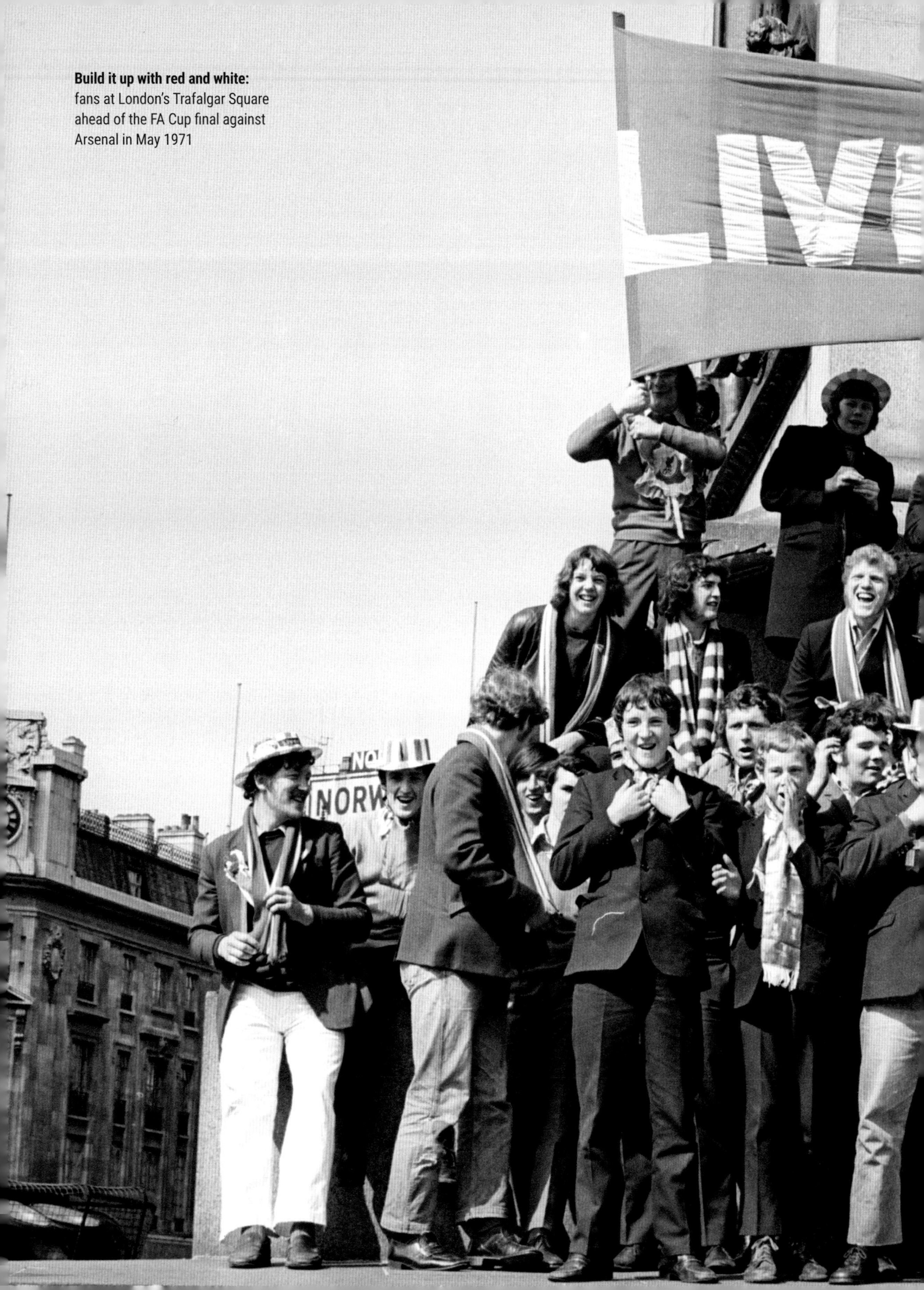

Build it up with red and white: fans at London's Trafalgar Square ahead of the FA Cup final against Arsenal in May 1971

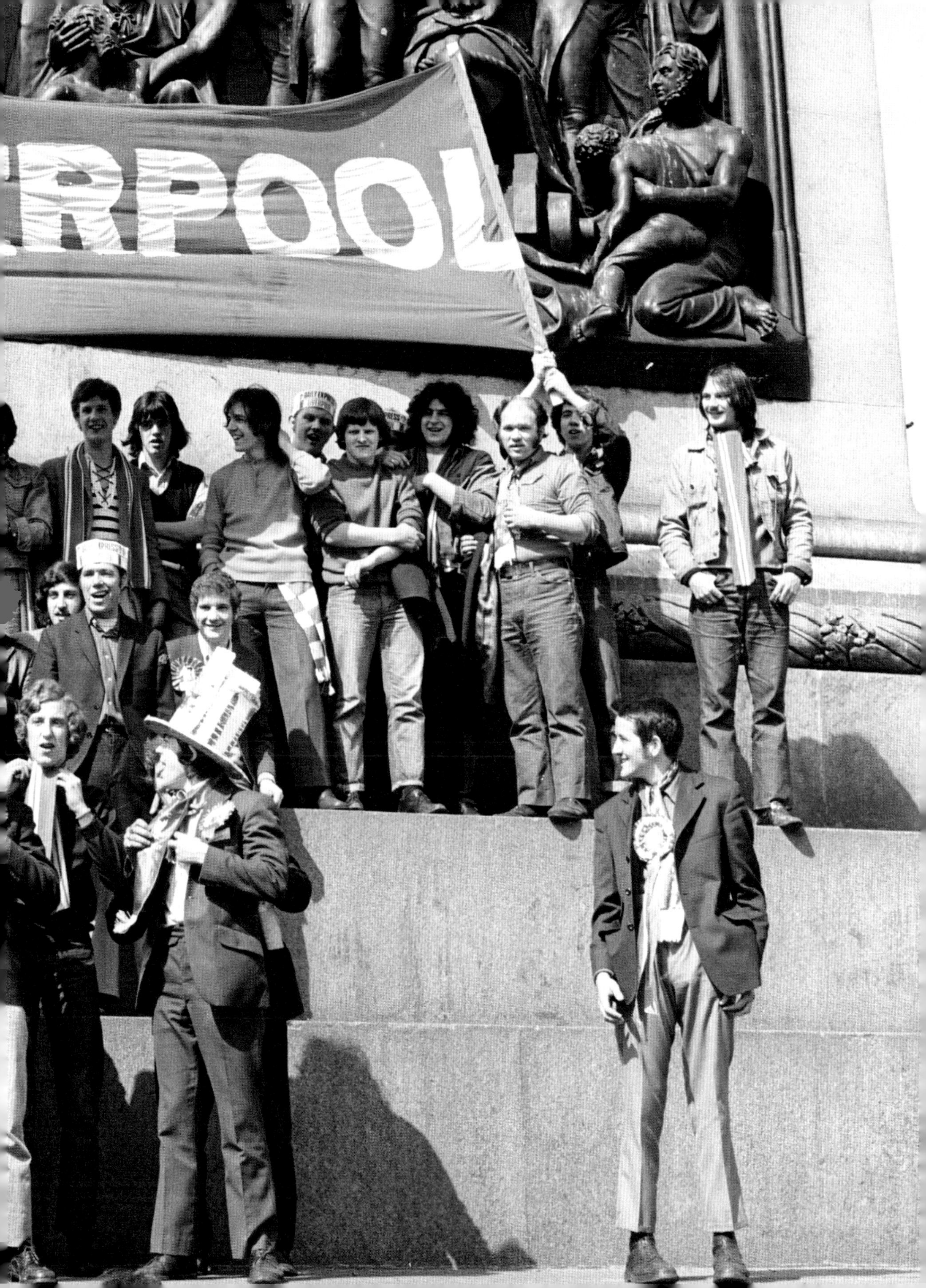
RPOOL

Below: young flag-wavers outside Goodison in 1966 before the derby
Opposite: the 'Cream of Europe' banner in various incarnations

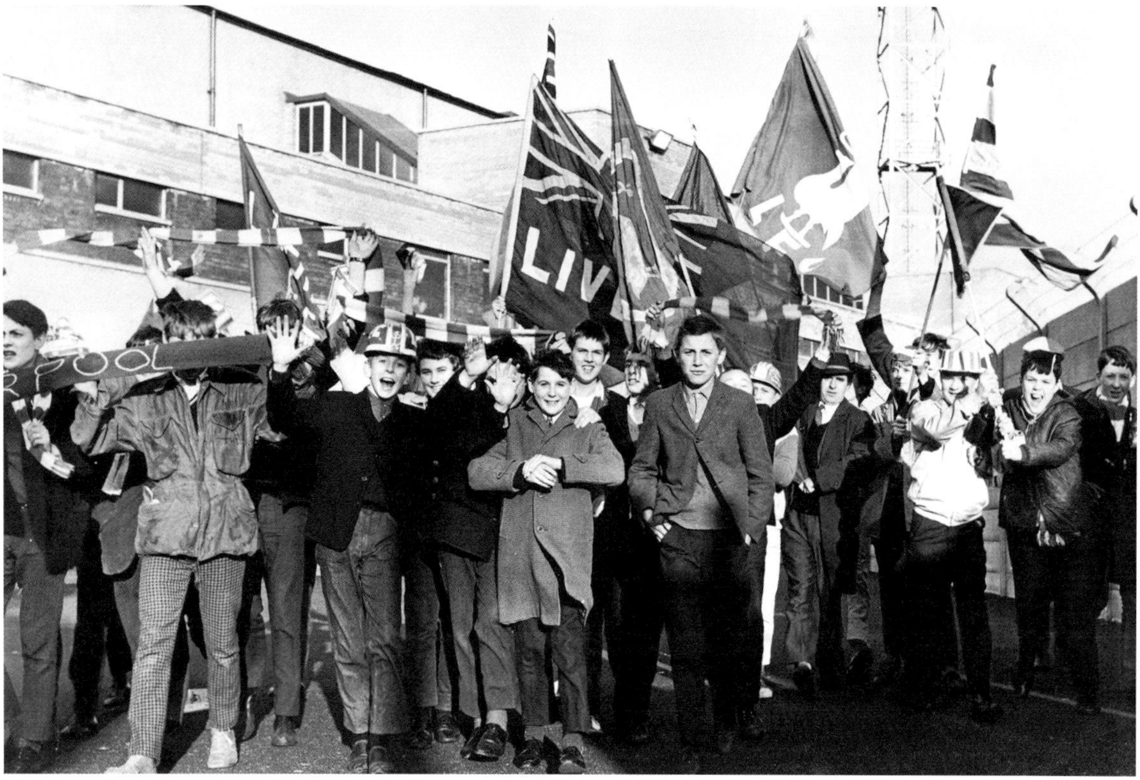

In the late Sixties, junior supporters were photographed with LFC flags outside Goodison Park before a Merseyside derby, and today it's a point of principle that younger fans get to wave the regular flags on the Kop today. One other thing we'll just leave here: whisper it in some quarters, but Union Jacks often formed the backdrop for simple 'LIVERPOOL' flags in the 1970s and into the 80s.

At the end of the 1993/94 season, following the post-Hillsborough recommendations of the Taylor Report, the Kop enjoyed a defiant 'Last Stand' before it became all-seater. Its sea of colour that day (see pages 8 and 9), for the final home game against Norwich City, was unforgettable. The following decade, in a new era of 'Flag Days' kick-started by fans to rekindle the old Anfield atmosphere, travelling banners were again all the rage in Dortmund for the 2001 UEFA Cup final and in Istanbul for the 2005 Champions League final.

Then along came Jürgen Klopp...and whole new works of art on the Kop.

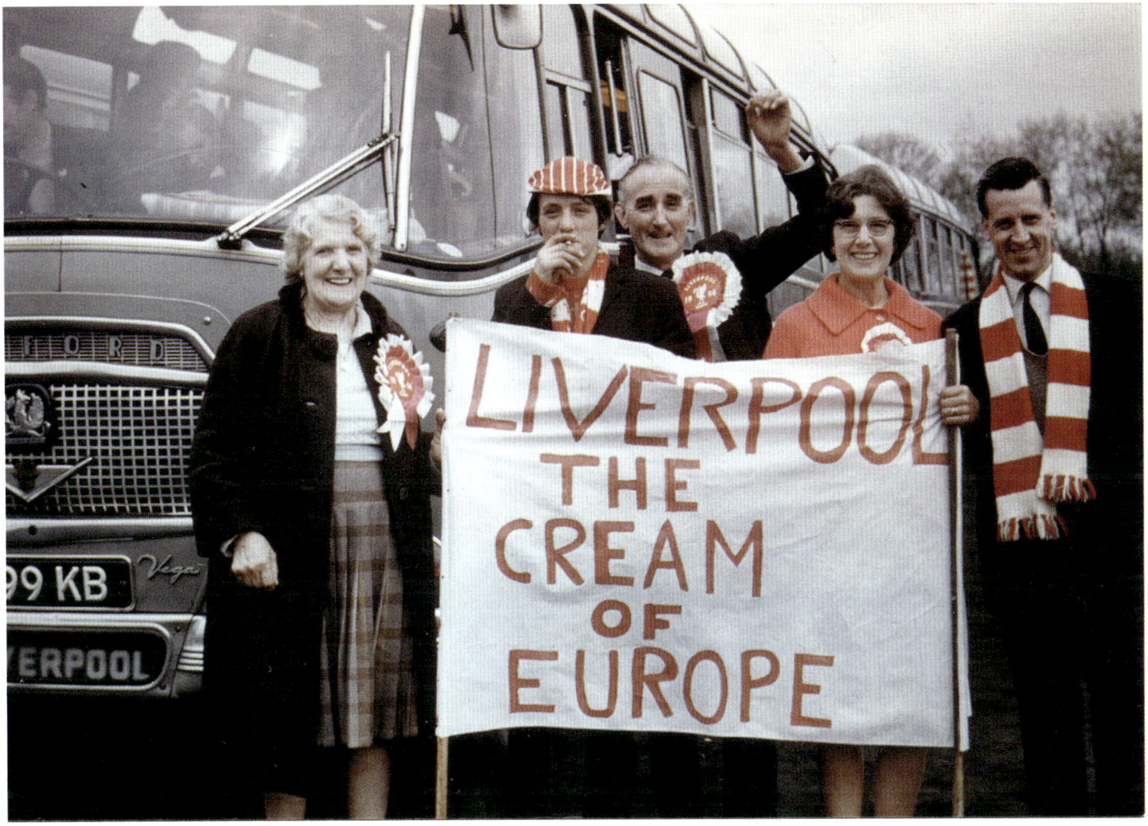
LIVERPOOL
THE
CREAM
OF
EUROPE
99 KB
VERPOOL

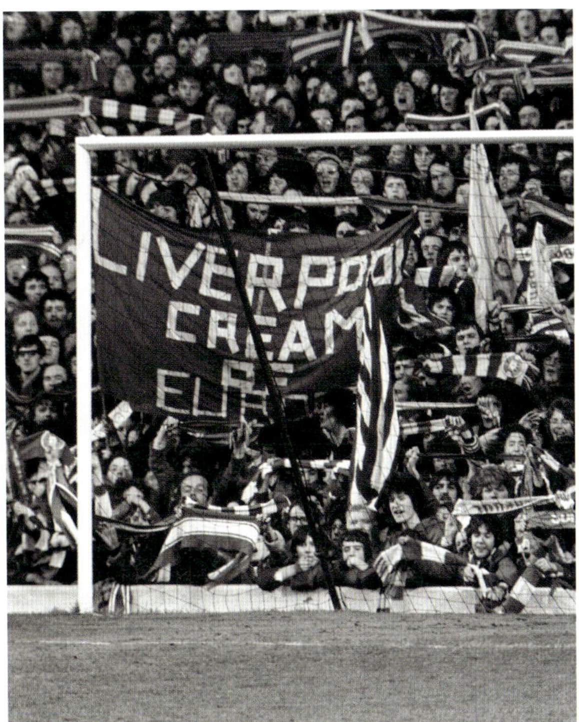
LIVERPOO
CREAM

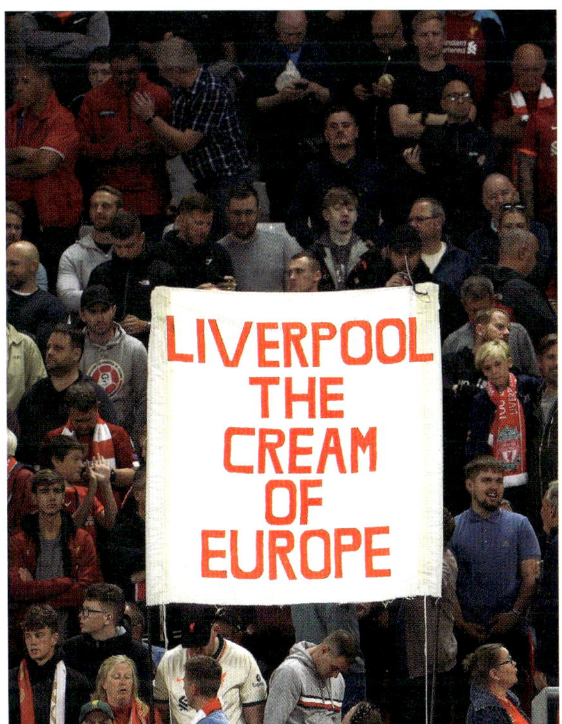
LIVERPOOL
THE
CREAM
OF
EUROPE

Never gonna stop

A wealth of new flags and banners worthy of a magical modern era

Fans of other top-flight clubs may have caught on but Kopites remain in a league of their own when it comes to flags and banners. They've given Anfield a colour and vibrancy all of its own, drawn from an unparalleled history of success at home and abroad.

It remains as much as part of modern LFC culture as the street-art scene and the trend for young Scouse troubadours, embraced by Liverpool's new legion of bright, savvy boy-and-girl supporters who'd sensed, ever since the Jürgen Klopp juggernaut began to gather pace, that this was their time. We've conquered all of Europe, we're never gonna stop.

Heroes come and go, of course. Departing star Roberto Firmino made his tearful exit at the end of season 2022/23 with a farewell banner on the Kop, while the LFCTV documentary *Bobby* took a flag – specially made by fan Peter Carney – all the way to his home country Brazil where it was filmed with pupils from his old school in the city of Maceio.

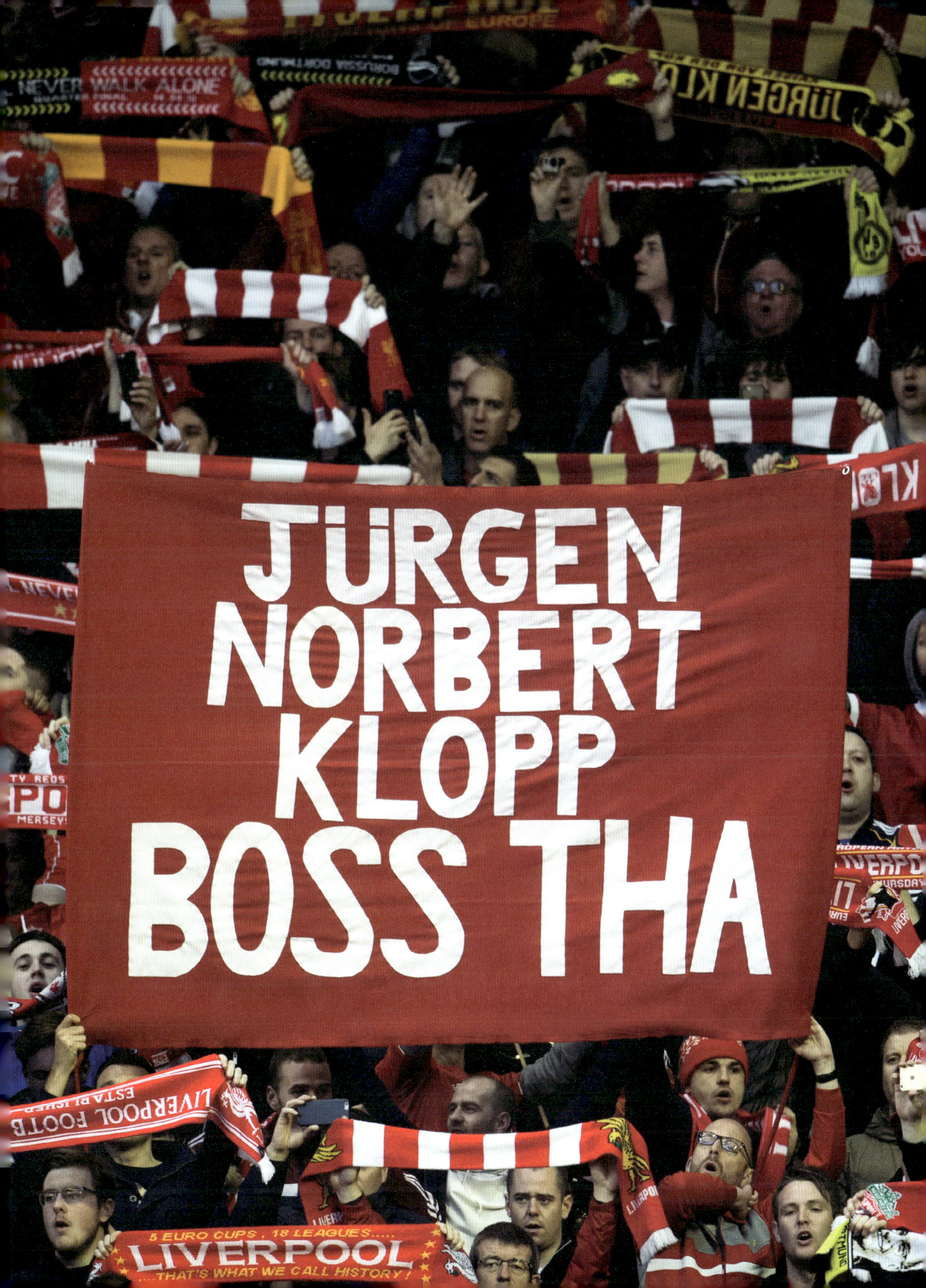
JÜRGEN
NORBERT
KLOPP
BOSS THA
WALK ALONE
5 EURO CUPS . 18 LEAGUES.....
LIVERPOOL
...THAT'S WHAT WE CALL HISTORY!

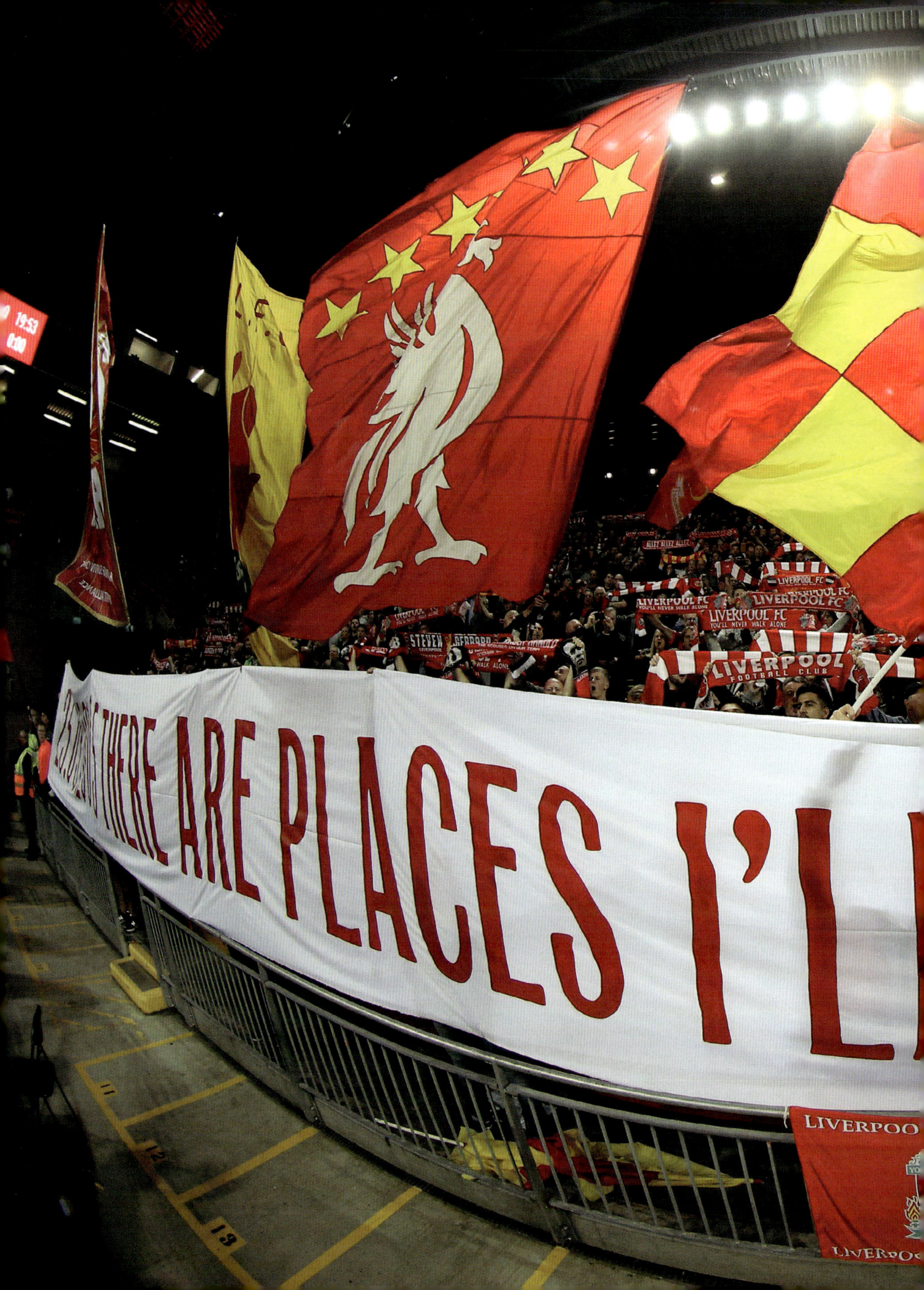
THERE ARE PLACES I'L
LIVERPOOL FC
YOU'LL NEVER WALK ALONE
LIVERPOOL
FOOTBALL CLUB
STEVEN
LIVERPOO
LIVERPOO

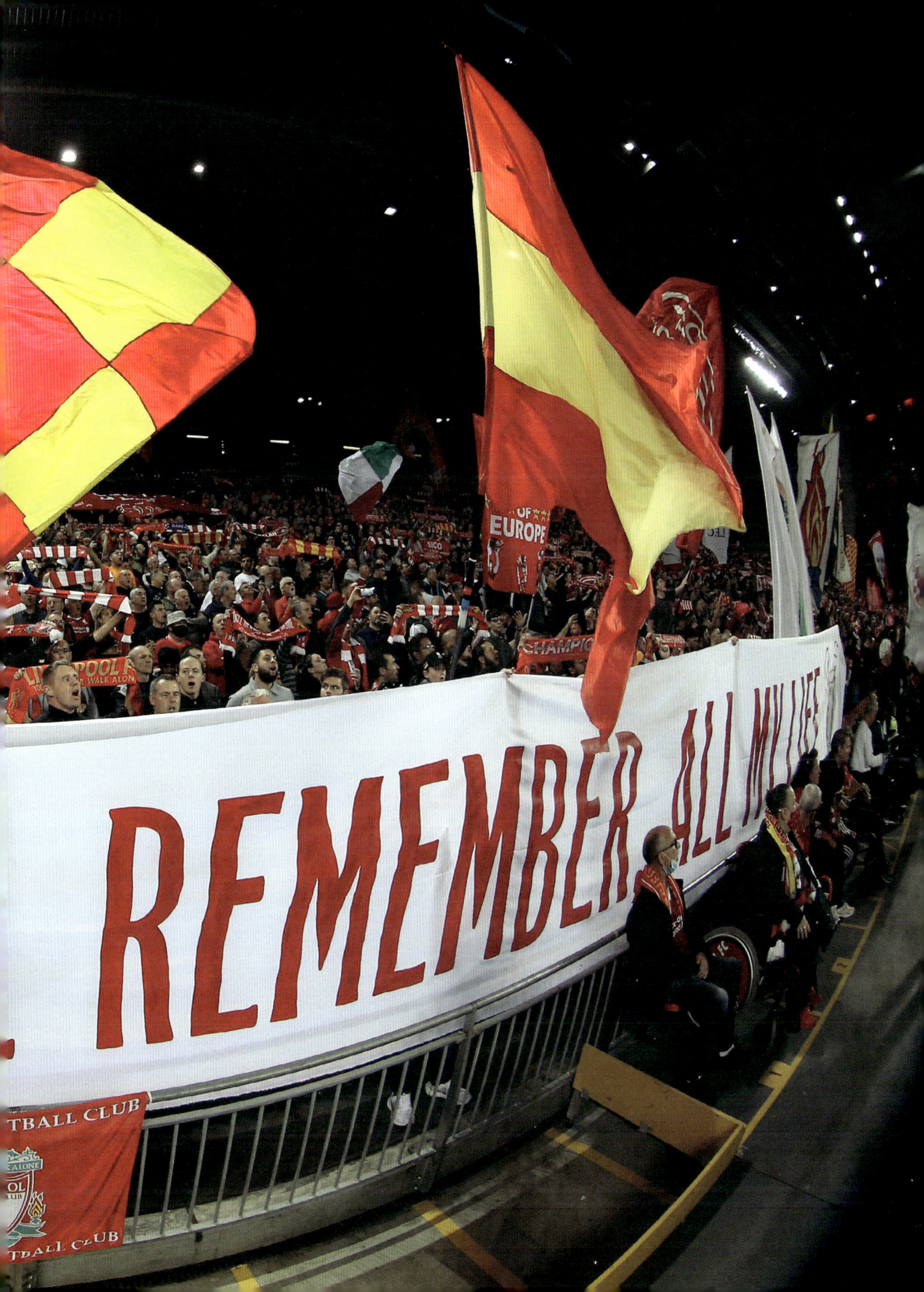
REMEMBER
EUROPE
TBALL CLUB
TBALL CLUB

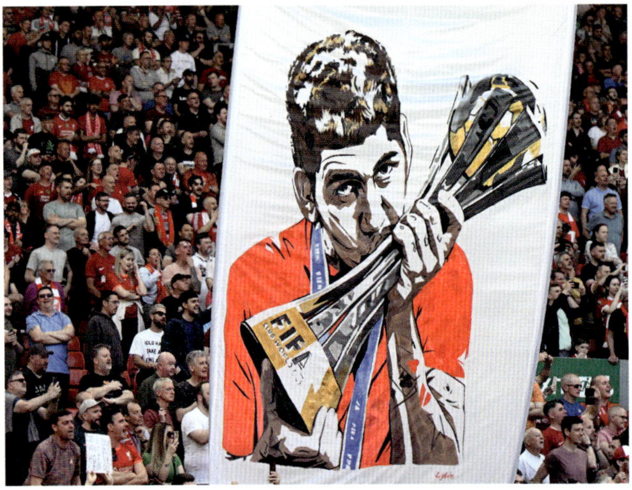
FIFA

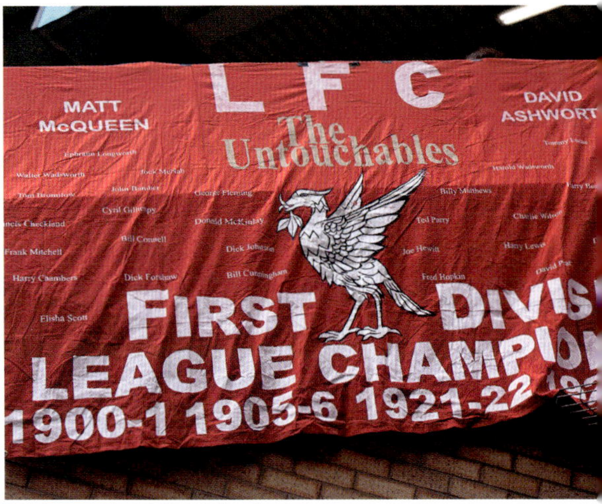
L F C
MATT McQUEEN
DAVID ASHWORT
The Untouchables
FIRST DIVIS
LEAGUE CHAMPIO
1900-1 1905-6 1921-22

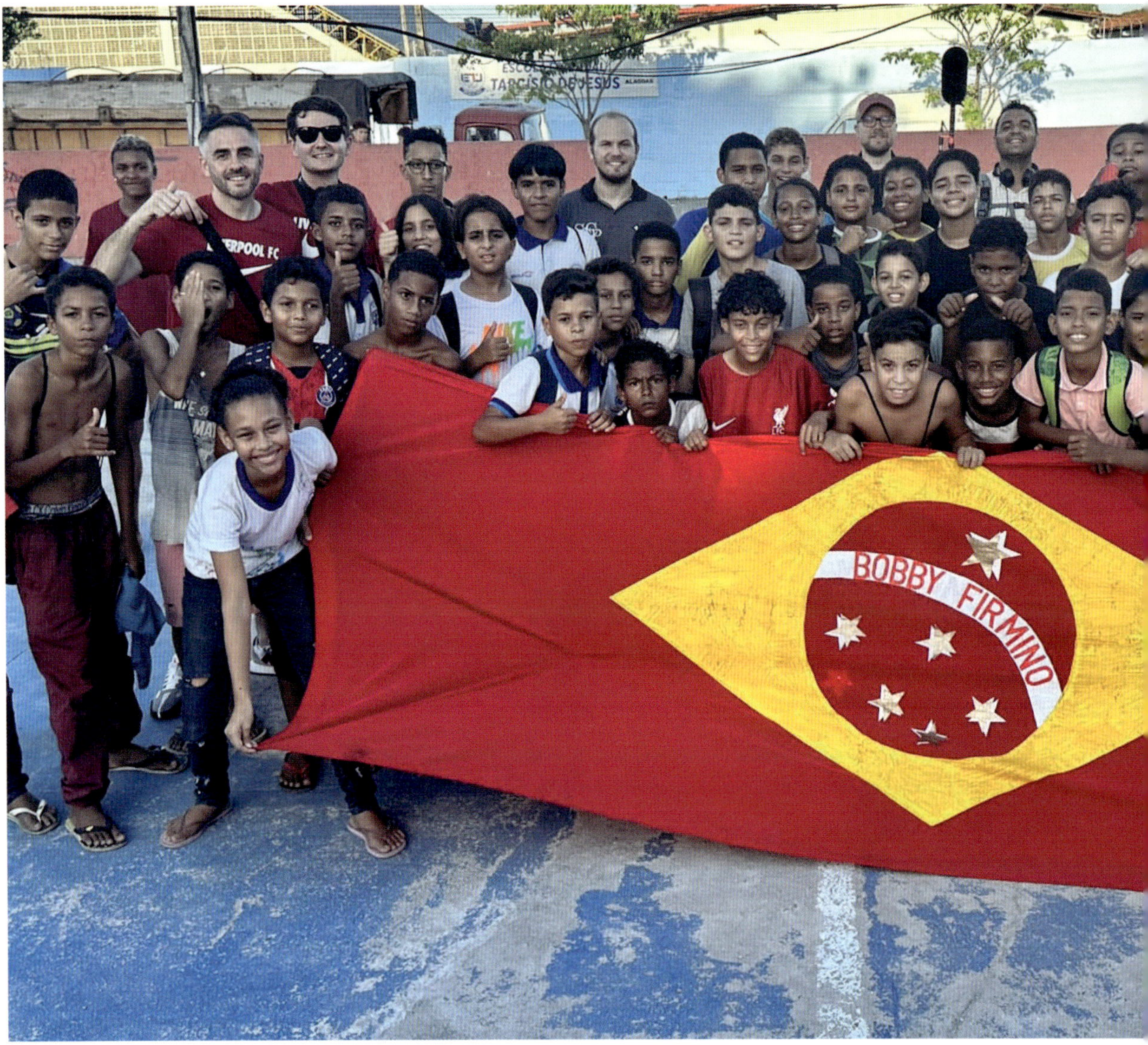
TARCISIO DE JESUS
BOBBY FIRMINO

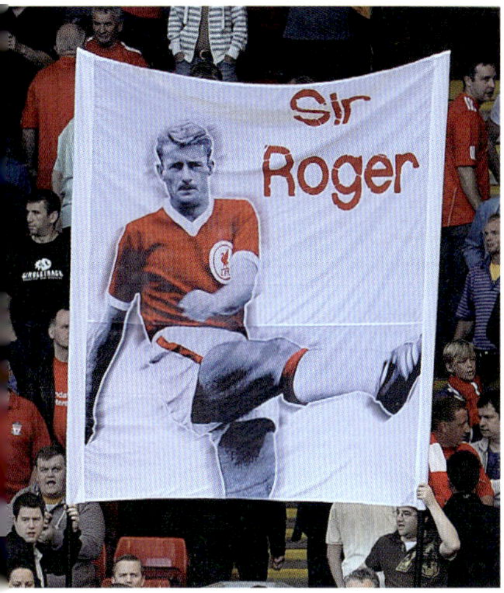

Top from left to right: Roberto Firmino's send-off banner on the Kop; a modern replica of the 1921-22-23 champions flag; tribute to Roger Hunt
Below left: Maceio schoolchildren with the special Firmino flag

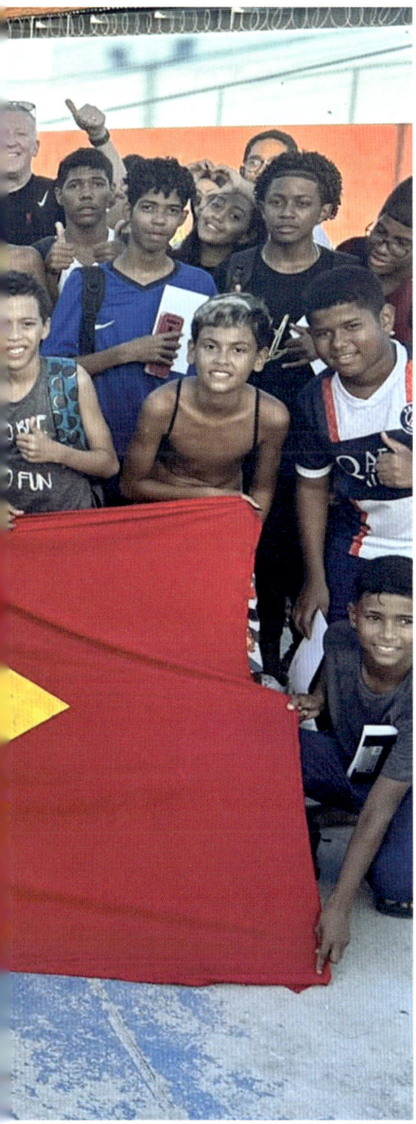

Peter was also behind the tribute to the double title-winning Reds side of the early Twenties which was displayed at the corner of the Kop and Sir Kenny Dalglish Stand almost exactly a century after the second championship was clinched on 21 April 1923. The banner was a close replica of an original from back in the day which was photographed and featured in the local press.

Regular sights on the Kop are banners for Sixties goalscoring legend Roger Hunt, former club captain Jordan Henderson, winger Mohamed Salah, goalkeeper Alisson and left-back Andy Robertson, with another recent addition being a banner for current skipper Virgil van Dijk to commemorate his first five years as a Liverpool player.

Unveiled at the end of 2022 and the work of the Spion Kop 1906 collective, it depicts a victorious Virgil in June 2019, holding the Champions League trophy after the victory over Spurs in Madrid. The money spent on creating the banner, as well as the cost of filming a special piece with LFCTV, was donated to two local charities.

The previous season, Spion Kop 1906 created a tribute to erstwhile Reds manager Gerard Houllier and his former assistant (and skipper in his playing days) Phil Thompson – and Thommo himself beamed with pride when he saw it while recording with LFCTV prior to Liverpool's Premier League match with Norwich City in February 2022.

Depicting the duo with the five trophies they won with Liverpool in the calendar year of 2001 (page 27), the banner had been commissioned and paid for by lifelong fan and Spirit of Shankly member Keith Sorrell who sadly passed away in 2021.

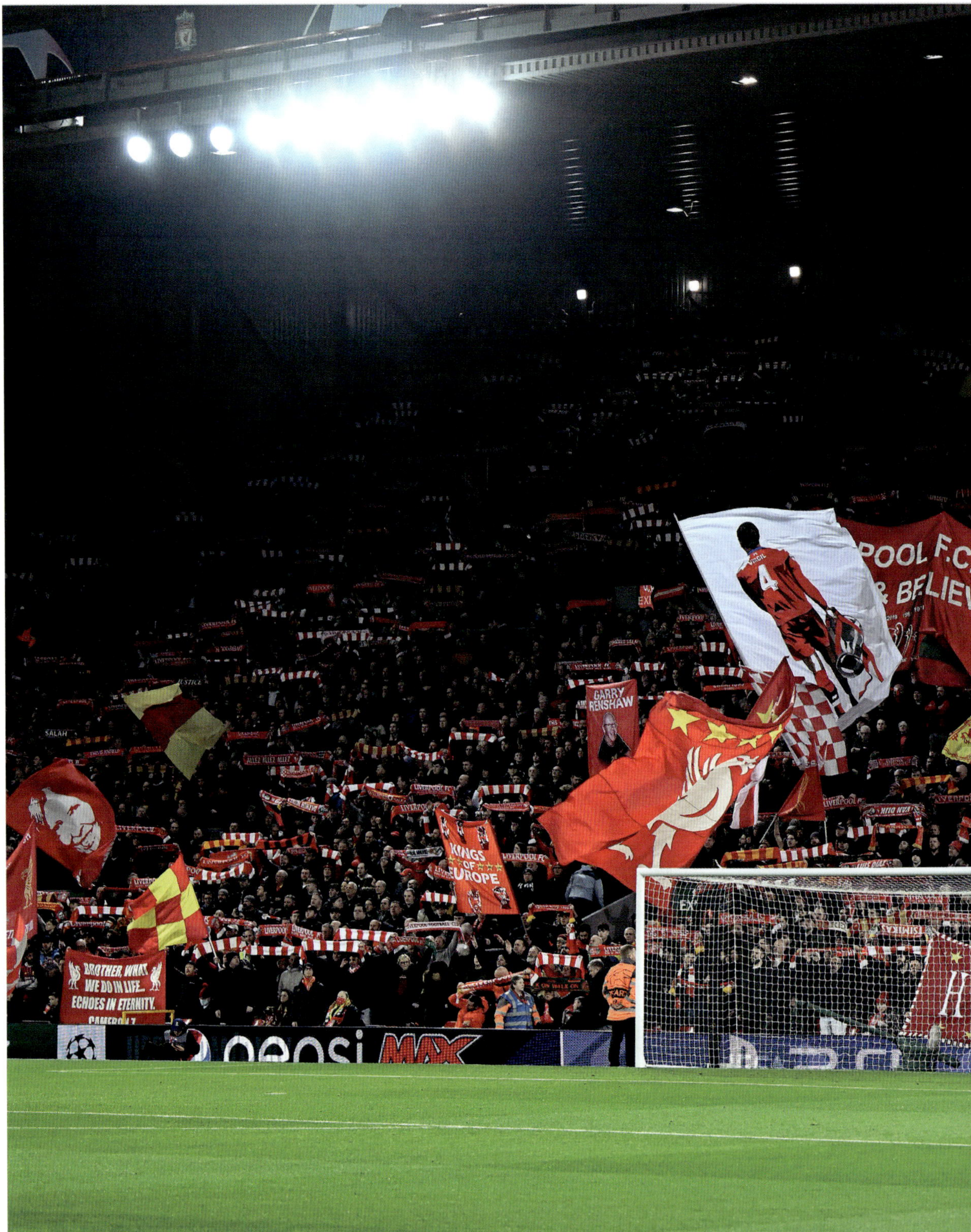
POOL F.C.
& BELIEV
GARRY RENSHAW
KINGS OF EUROPE
BROTHER, WHAT WE DO IN LIFE... ECHOES IN ETERNITY.
pepsi MAX

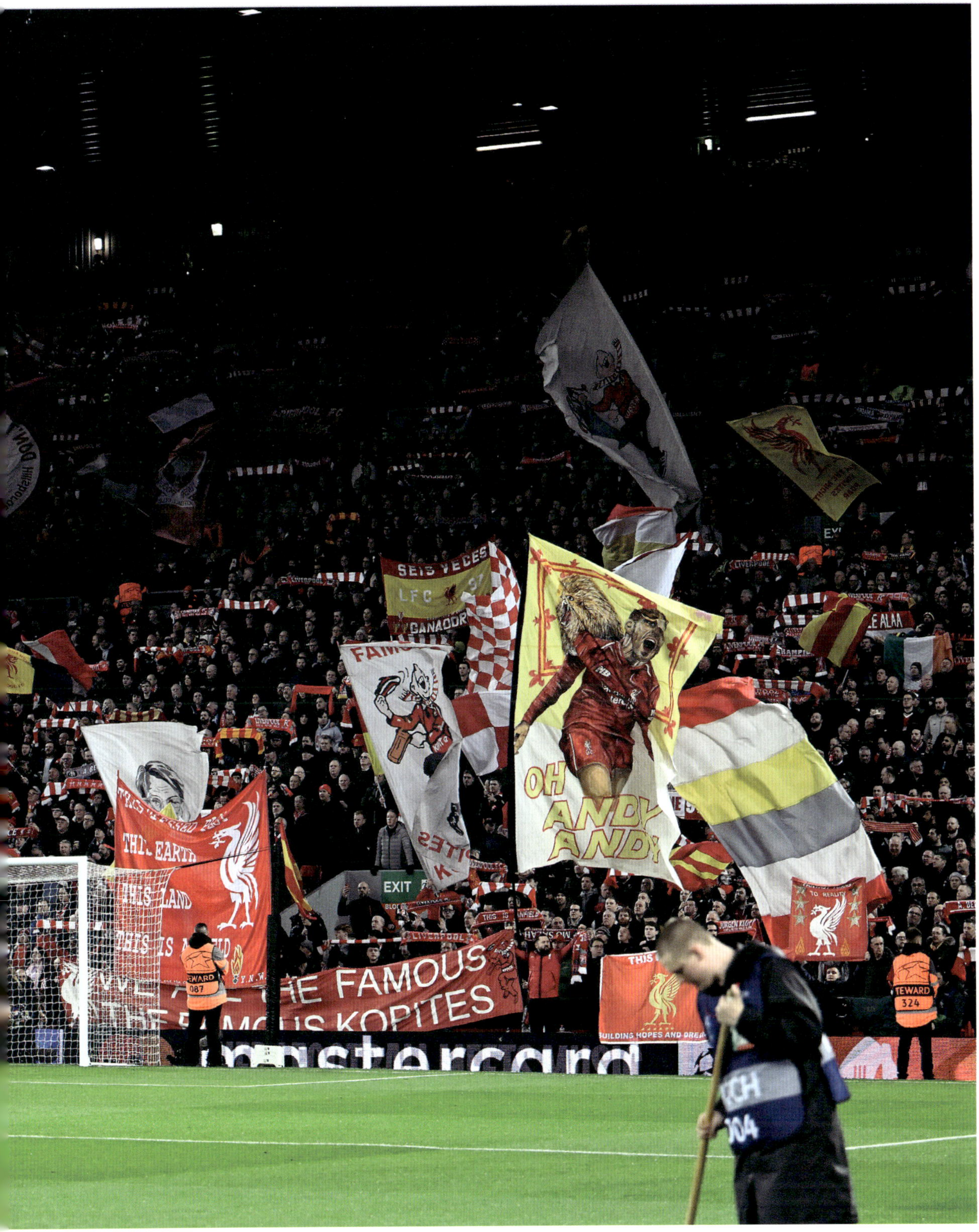
SEIS VECES
LFC
OH
ANDY
ANDY
THIS EARTH
THIS LAND
EXIT
THE FAMOUS
TEWARD
324
BUILDING HOPES AND DREA

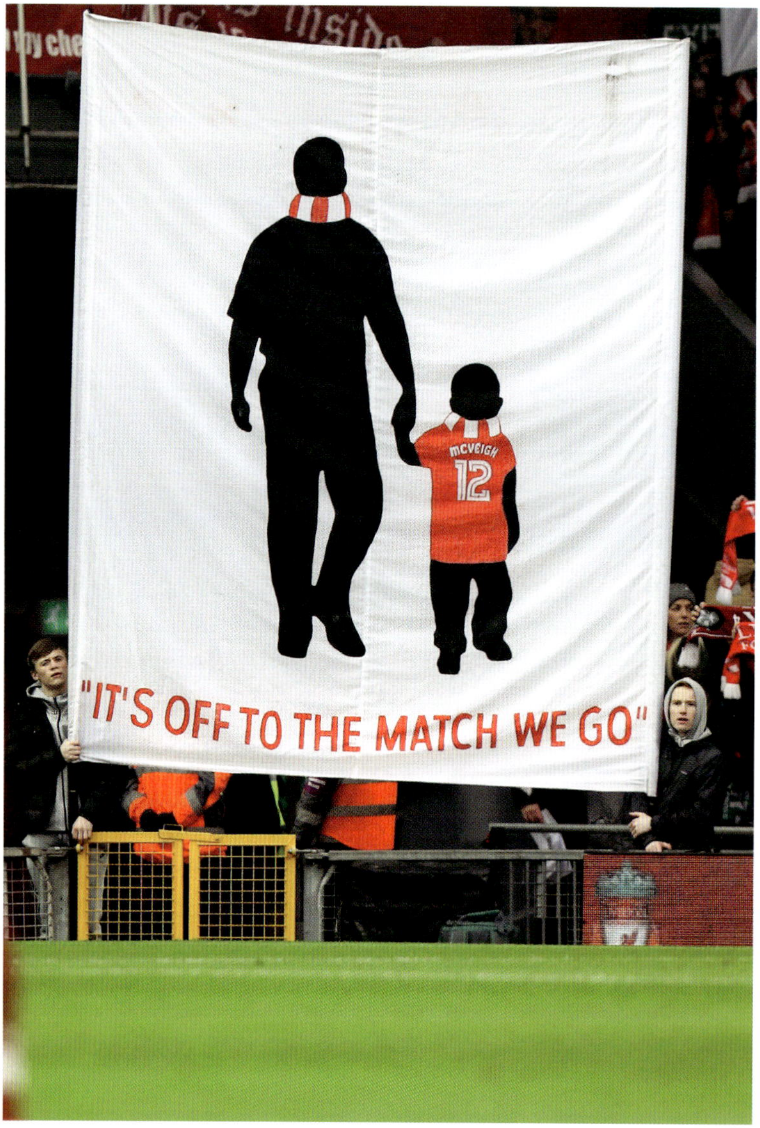

Owen's banner: the moving tribute to a young Liverpool fan who passed away, with a line from the classic Kop song 'Every Other Saturday' **Opposite:** just some of the pomp and pageantry displayed on the Kop

Back at the start of 2016 a poignant banner for young fan Owen McVeigh made its Kop debut. Eleven-year-old Owen had passed away the previous December, having been diagnosed with leukaemia. His dad Mark, who subsequently set up a foundation in Owen's name, revealed: "I approached the Spion Kop 1906 group about doing something on behalf of Owen and the response was fantastic. I was completely blown away by the flag they came up with and will take great pride in seeing Owen there at every game."

Three years earlier, Spion Kop 1906 had re-made the Anne Williams 'Iron Lady' flag originally flown by Indonesian fans for Liverpool's pre-season friendly in Jakarta then presented to her family.

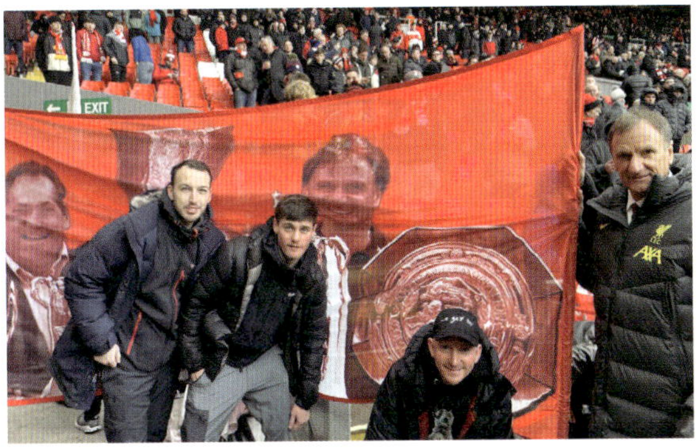

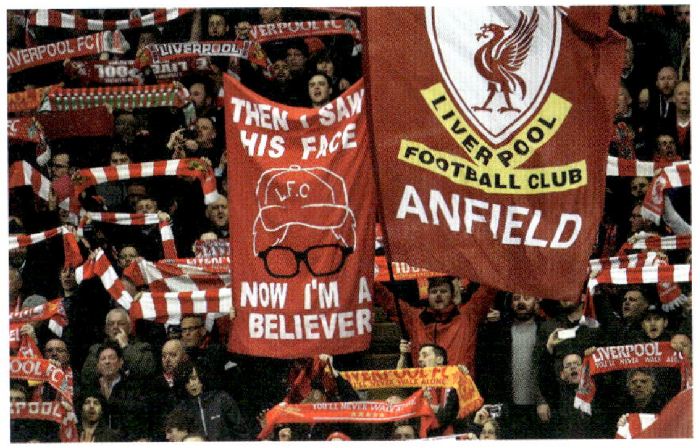
THEN I SAW
HIS FACE
NOW I'M A
BELIEVER
LIVERPOOL
FOOTBALL CLUB
ANFIELD

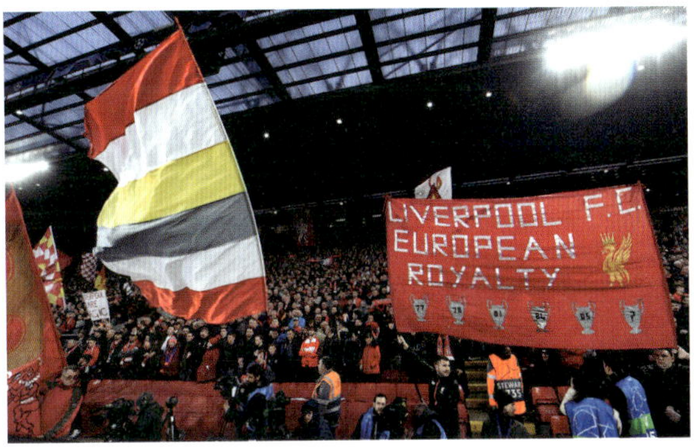
LIVERPOOL F.C.
EUROPEAN
ROYALTY

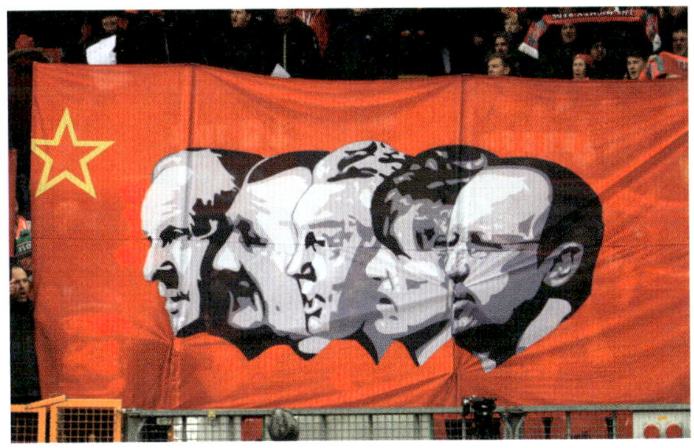

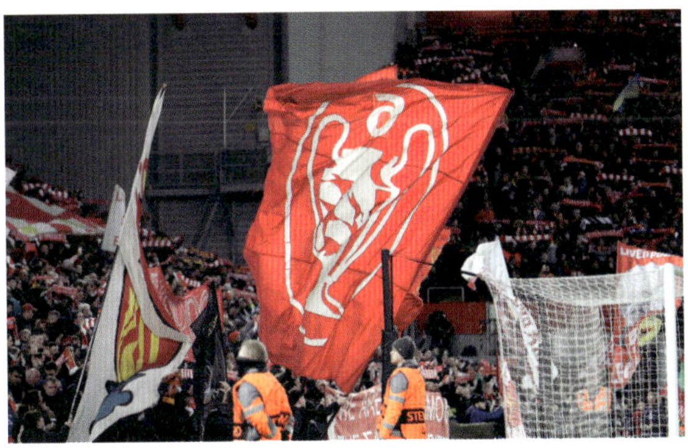

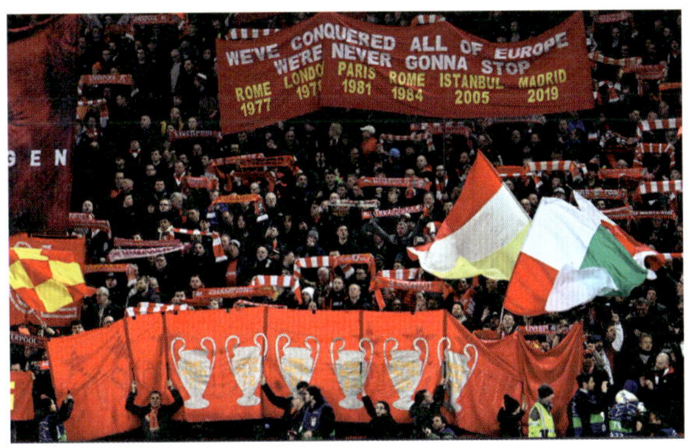
WE'VE CONQUERED ALL OF EUROPE
WE'RE NEVER GONNA STOP
ROME 1977
PARIS 1981
ROME 1984
ISTANBUL 2005
MADRID 2019

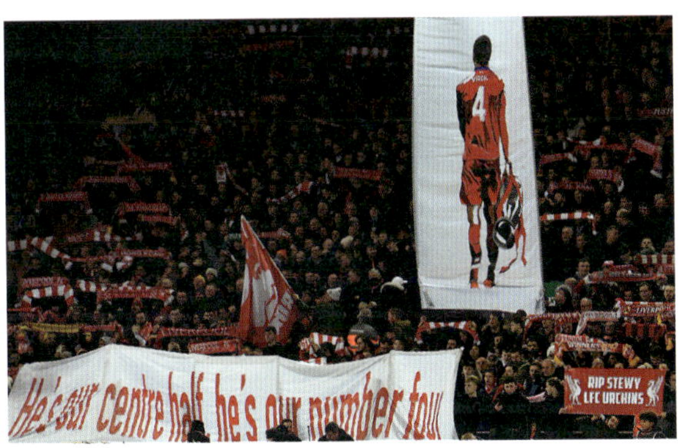
He's our centre half, he's our number four
RIP STEWY
LFC URCHINS

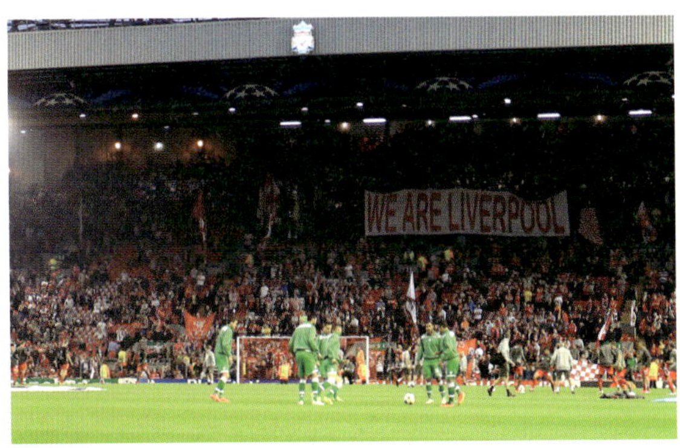
WE ARE LIVERPOOL

Frank's flag

They don't come any bigger or better than the one which passes over the Spion Kop prior to kick-off

Frank Graceffa and his Kop-surfing super-flag has made two guest appearances in the LFC matchday programme in recent times: first as the subject of a long-read feature in an issue for a Champions League group game; then as part of a tribute to extra-special supporters in the 'Born and Red' fans section of the Premier League champions souvenir edition against Chelsea in July 2020.

'South-ender' Frank, very much Scouse but born in Sicily, had the idea for the flag two decades ago. Back then it was a 'modest' 30ft by 30ft club crest. It simply grew and grew, and now it's a 130ft by 80ft masterpiece, almost the height of ten double-decker buses, detailing Liverpool FC's successes down the years. Since there were no hands to help it glide across the Kop before kick-off when football resumed after lockdown in the early summer of 2020, instead it was the centrepiece of the Kop backdrop when the Reds returned to action behind-closed-doors at Anfield.

Frank worked at the King's Leadership Academy in Dingle Vale in South Liverpool and it was there that, with the help of pupils one lunchtime, he unfurled the flag for a drone photograph for the matchday programme.

A flag of this size is a constant work-in-progress. Even when Liverpool aren't winning trophies, repairs are needed to fix the inevitable wear-and-tear, and every time a change is required he takes the flag apart section-by-section before reassembling it again for matchday.

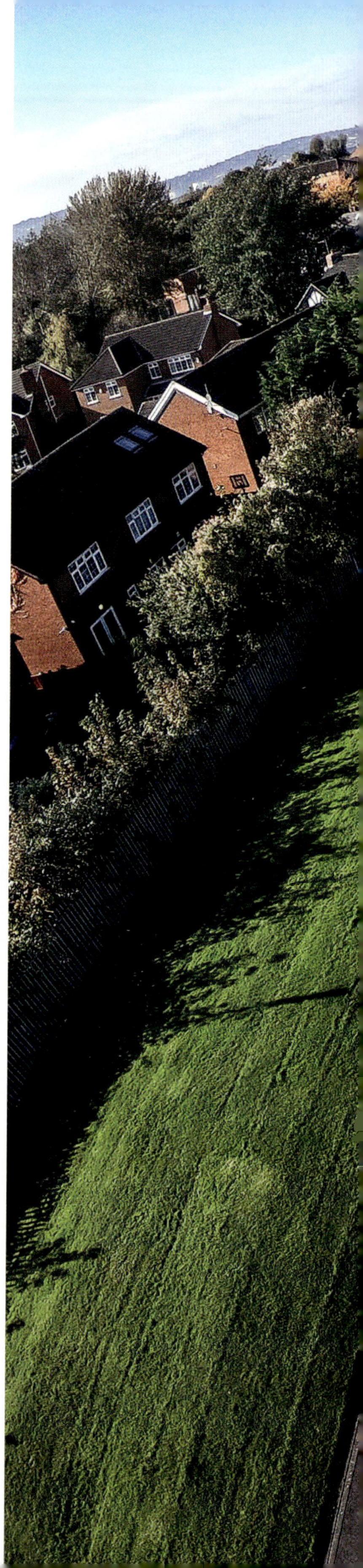

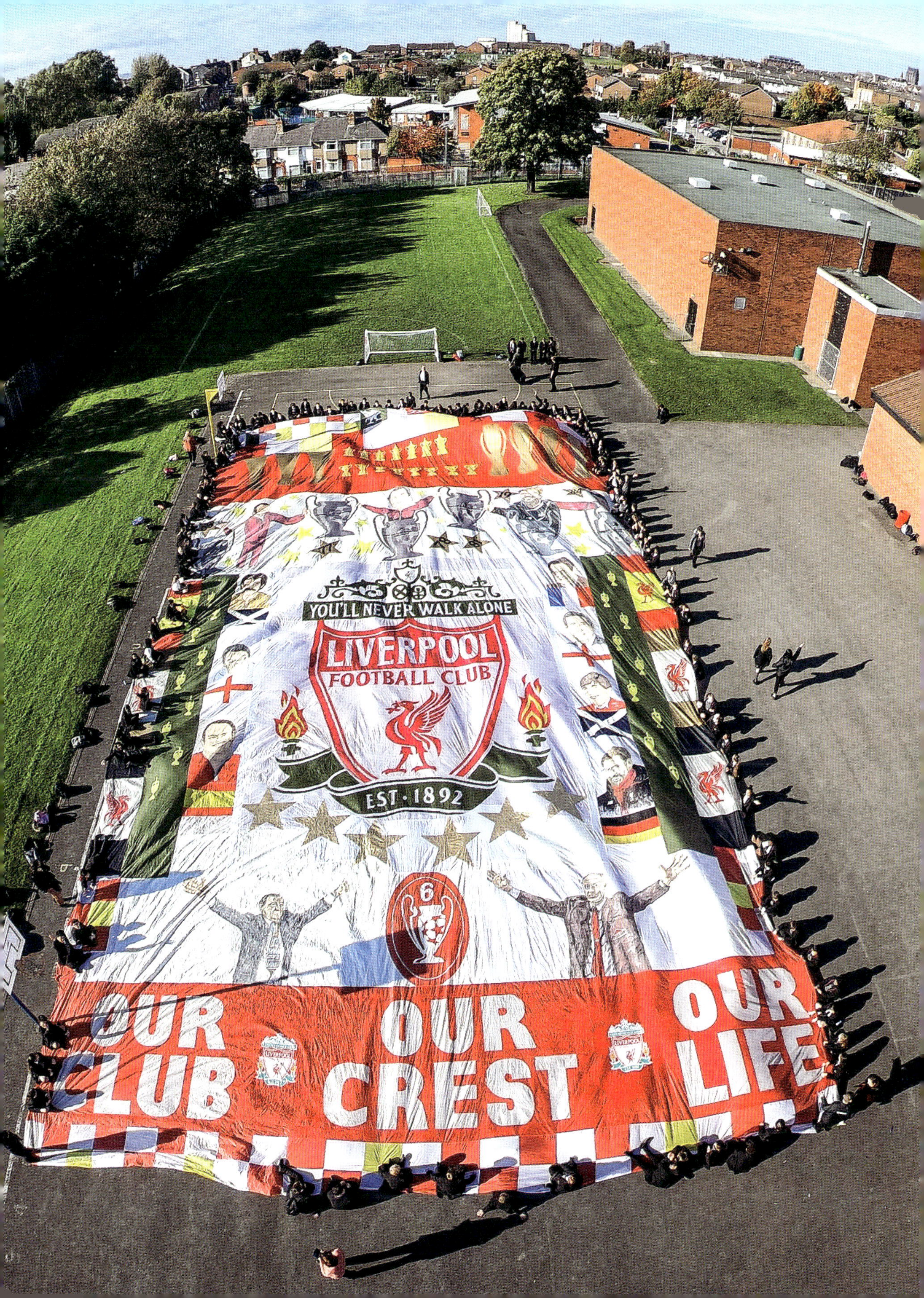

YOU'LL NEVER WALK ALONE
LIVERPOOL
FOOTBALL CLUB
EST · 1892
6
OUR CLUB
OUR CREST
OUR LIFE

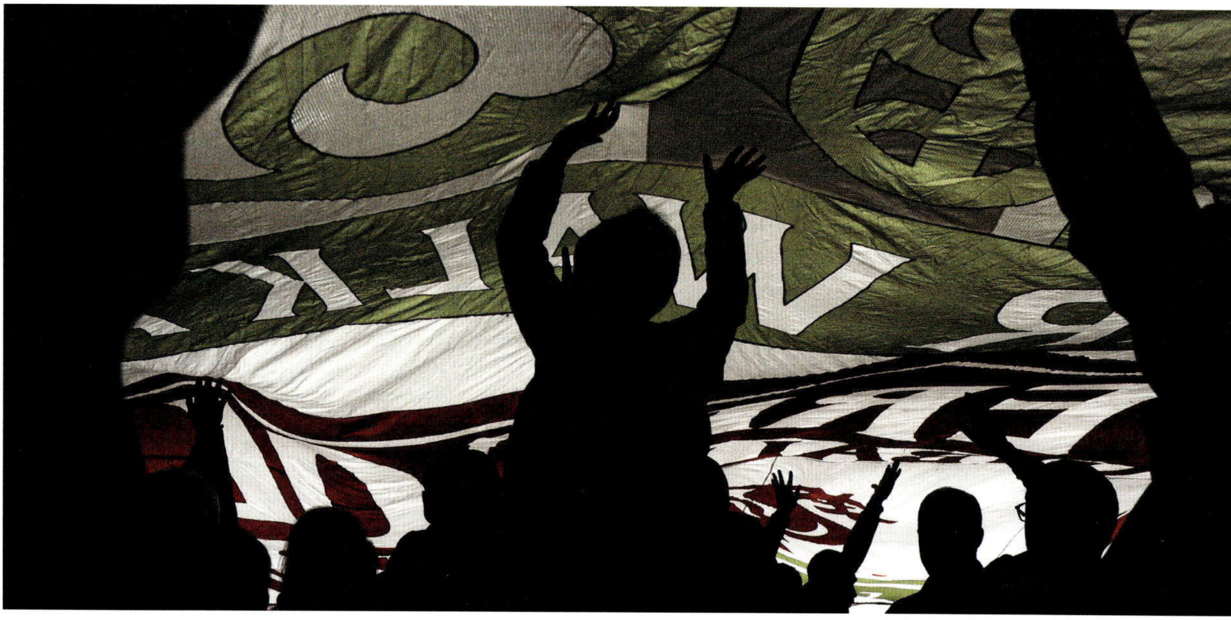

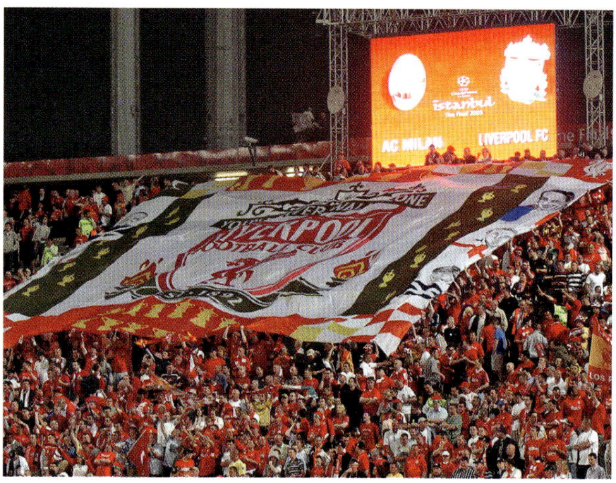
AC MILAN
LIVERPOOL FC

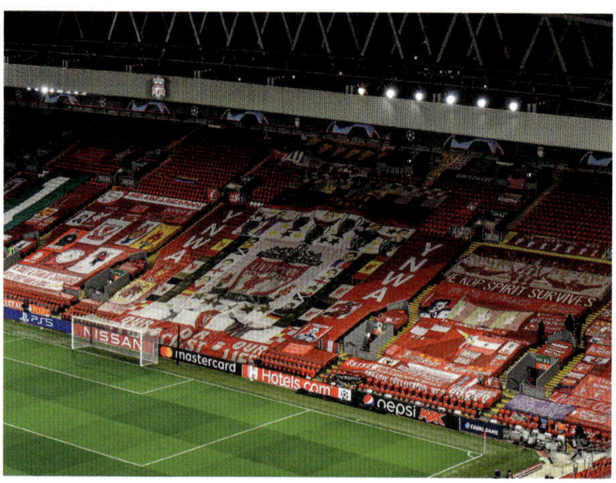
THE KOP SPIRIT SURVIVES
NISSAN
mastercard
Hotels.com

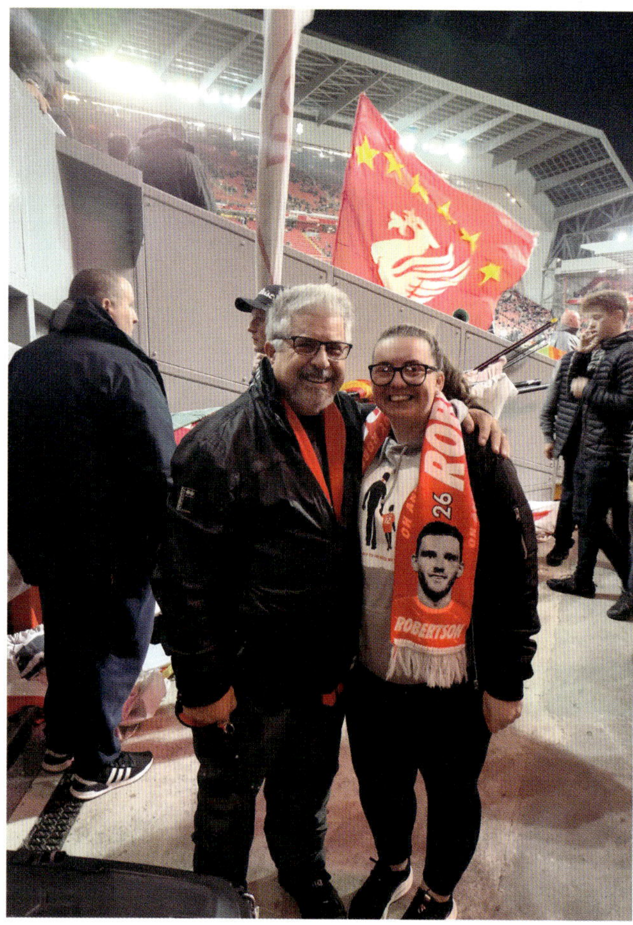
ROBERTSON

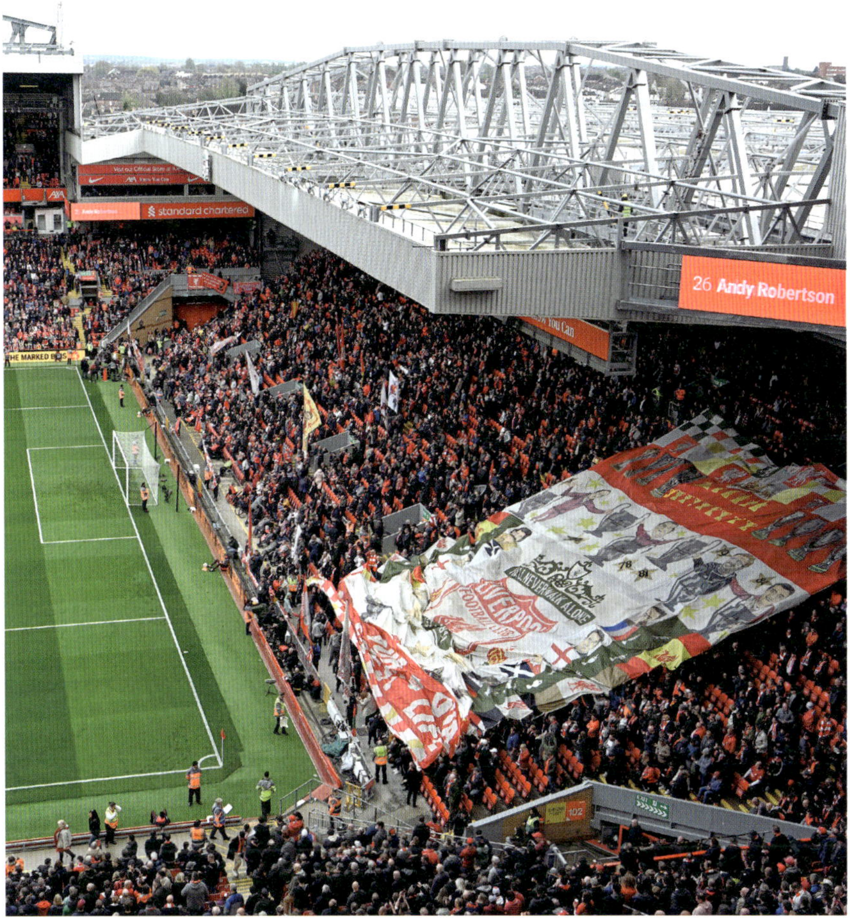

Countdown to kick-off: the flag begins its customary voyage across the Kop

Opposite page clockwise from top: fans passing the flag overhead; Frank with niece Amy; the flag on the Kop for a behind-closed-doors fixture; back when it was still a 'baby' in Istanbul for the 2005 Champions League final

Before every home game a loyal crew of matchgoing mates helps him to take the concertina-folded flag out of its substantial storage bag and send it on its way. From thereon the fans do the rest, hauling it reverently across the Kop in their droves while the pre-match excitement builds.

Aside from continuous maintenance between matchdays, every year the flag has to go through rigorous fire-safety tests which means more disassembling and assembling, separating each part into its various components.

Also Frank's work: a flag for Mo Salah, one for Andy Robertson, the Hillsborough flame as well as a 'Ring of Fire'.

Why does he do it? You only need to look around his old school workshop, a shrine to Liverpool FC, for the answer. "It's a sacrifice you have to make," he says. "You have to do these things for the love of the club.

"If it's a headache, then I love having headaches because for me that means success for Liverpool Football Club. It doesn't get any better than that."

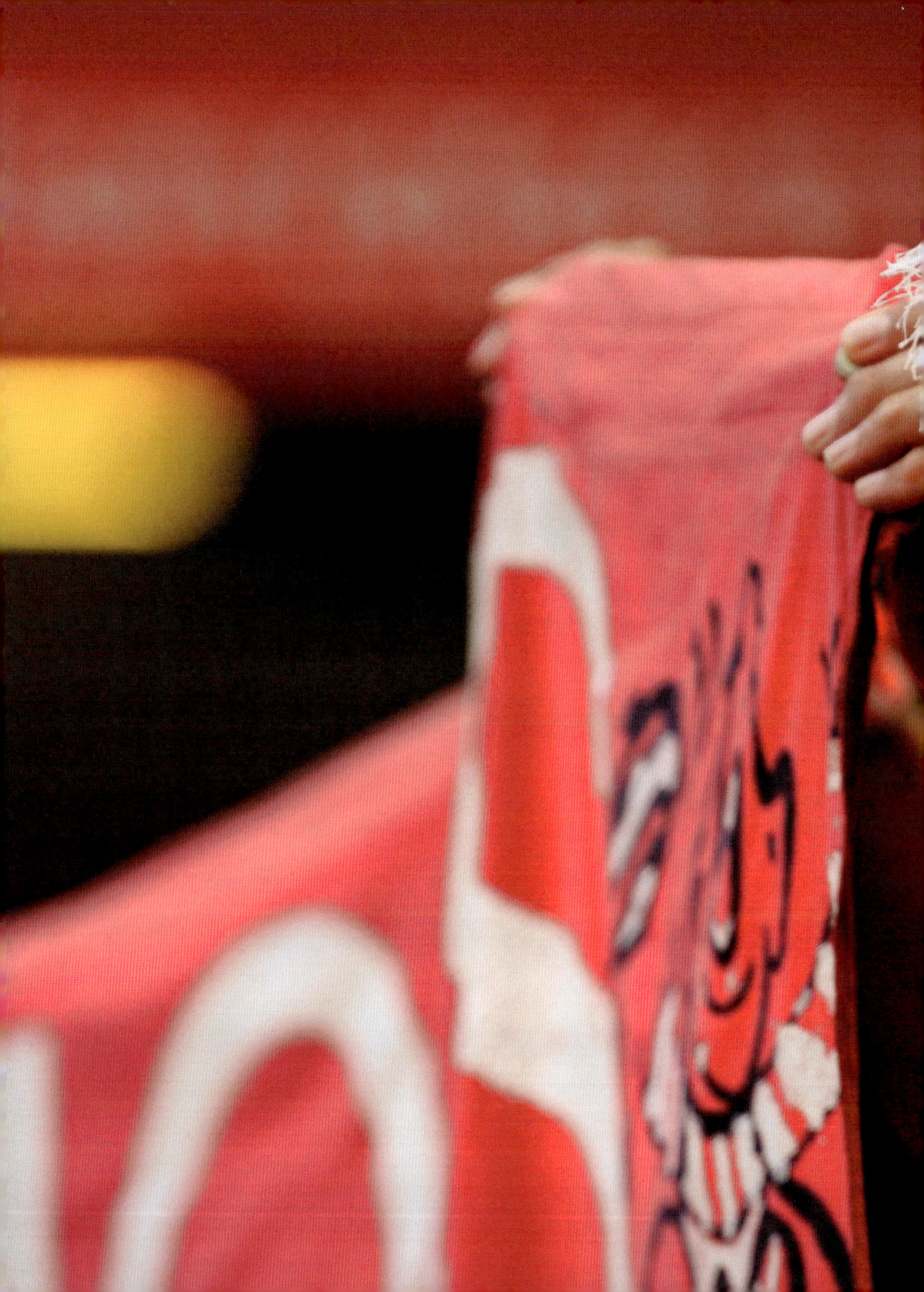

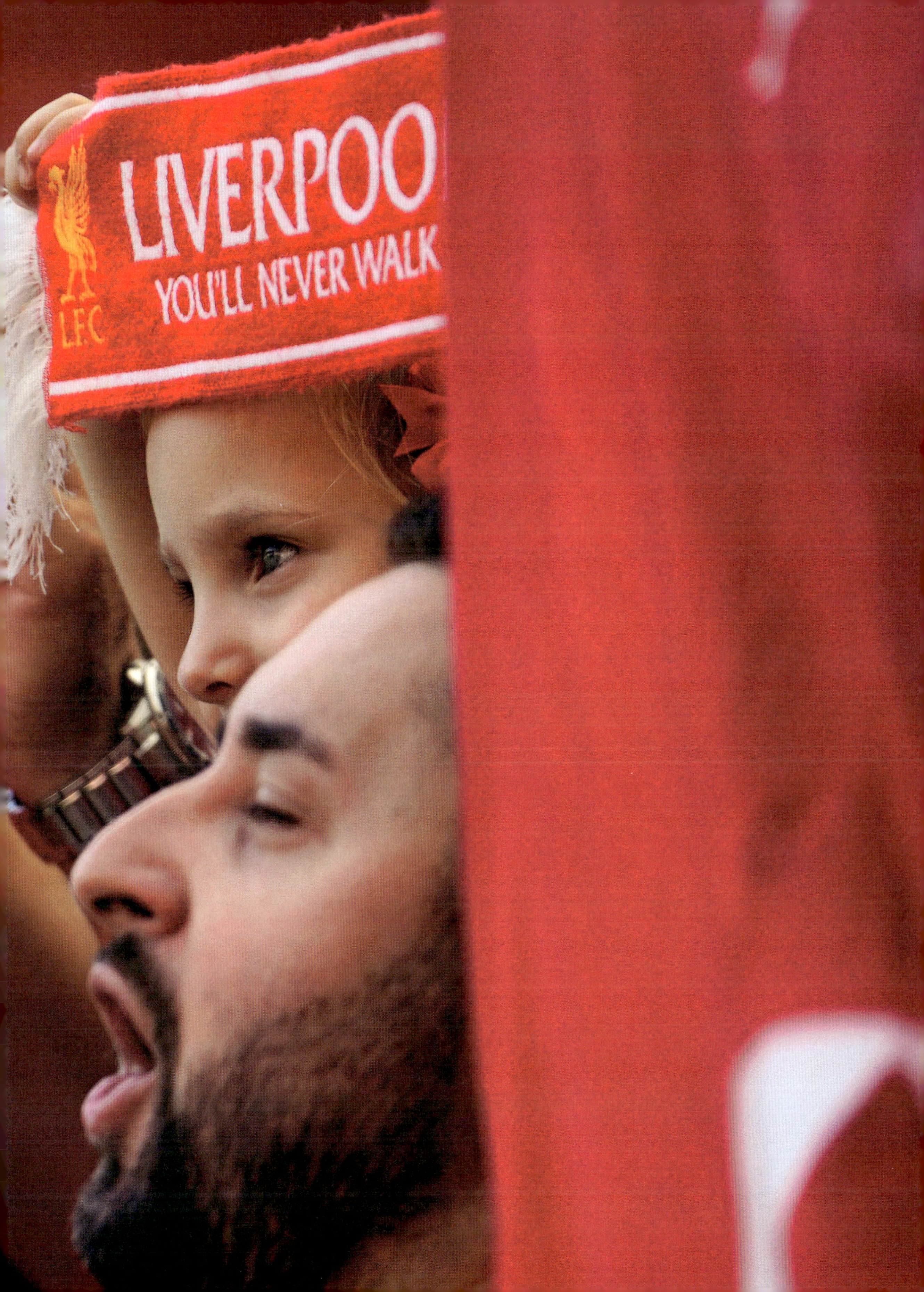
LIVERPOO
YOU'LL NEVER WALK
L.F.C

Peter the great

For one dedicated Kopite, making flags and banners is nothing short of a passion

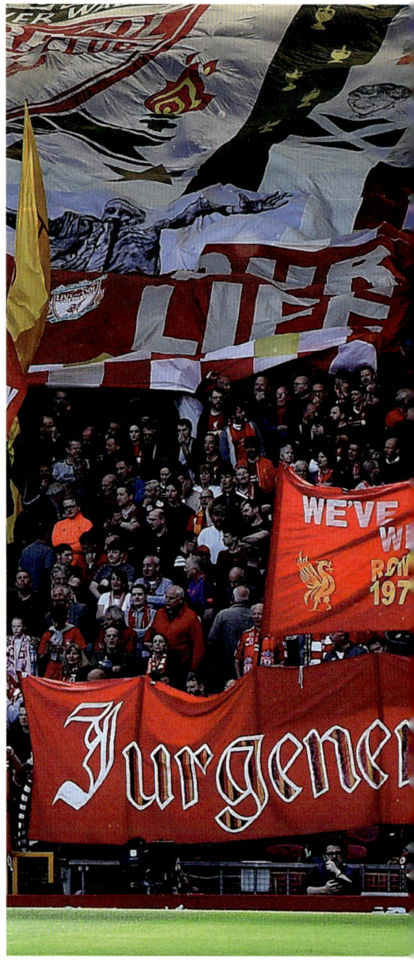

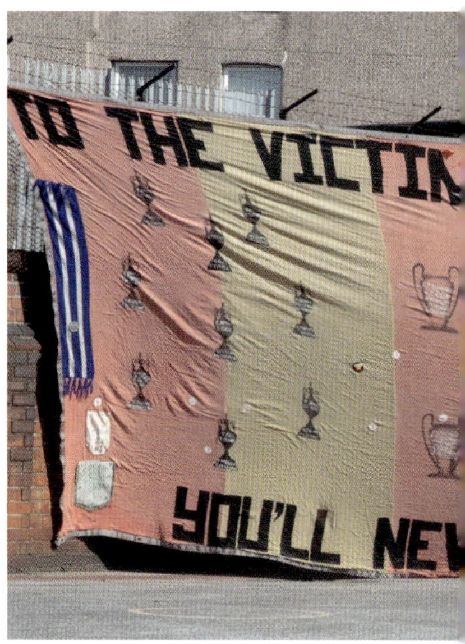

Matchgoers will have seen Peter Carney's many flags and banners at Anfield, even if they weren't aware who was behind them. At the start of the 2019/20 season he was in the LFC matchday programme, having previously appeared in *Mundial* magazine, and he also runs the acclaimed Soccer In The City minibus tours taking in Liverpool's footballing history and landmarks.

Perhaps Peter's most famous creations are his Hillsborough banners. The original version has been described by one cultural historian as "unique and irreplaceable." A second changes the words from 'You'll Never Walk Alone' to 'We Never Walk Alone' and includes the names of some of the survivors as well as those who were lost. At its centre is a white Liver Bird in padded material and there are eternal flames in silk and even pockets to hold bouquets of flowers.

He also made a flag for Sean Cox, the Irish supporter who suffered life-changing injuries in an unprovoked attack outside Anfield stadium before the Champions League semi-final first leg against AS Roma in April 2018 – the players posed with it after the second leg in the Italian capital.

Others include 'Welcome To Wonderland' ("What's our keeper called?" Peter asks, "think about it!") and 'Robertson: Sweeter Than Jam'.

"For me, it's about being able to express my support for the team," he says.

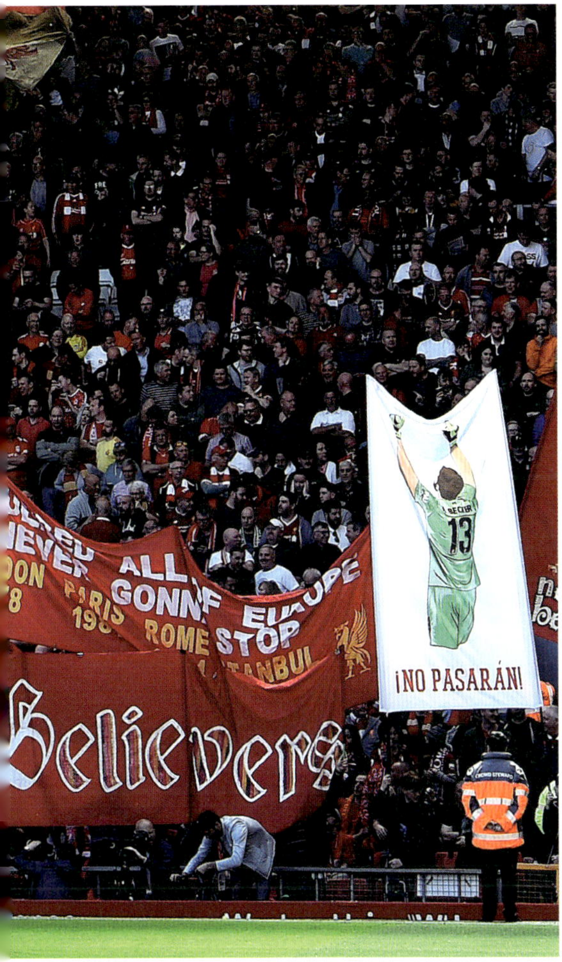
¡NO PASARÁN!
Believers

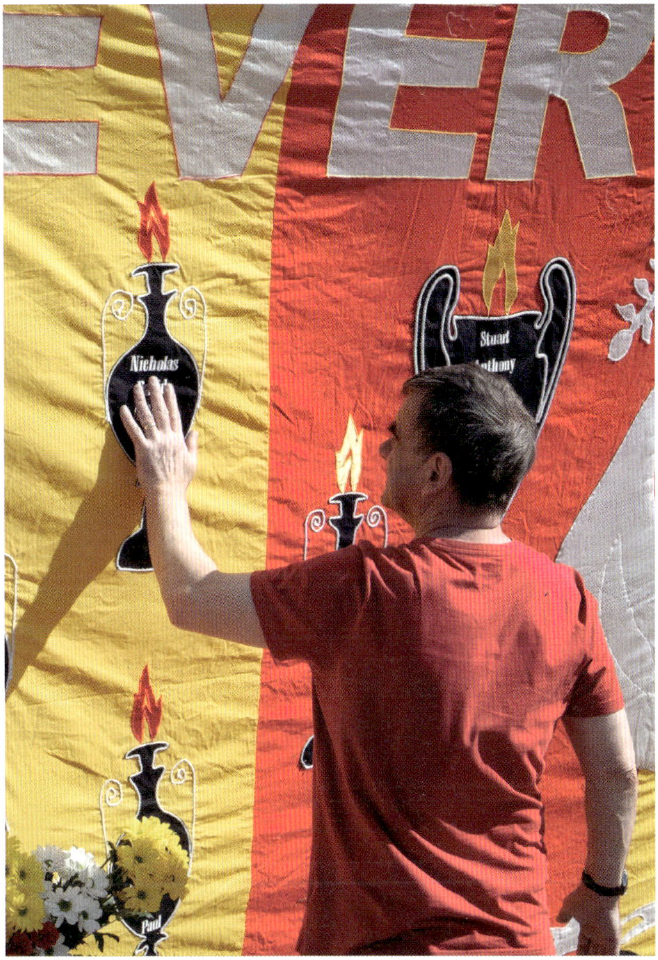
Nicholas
Stuart

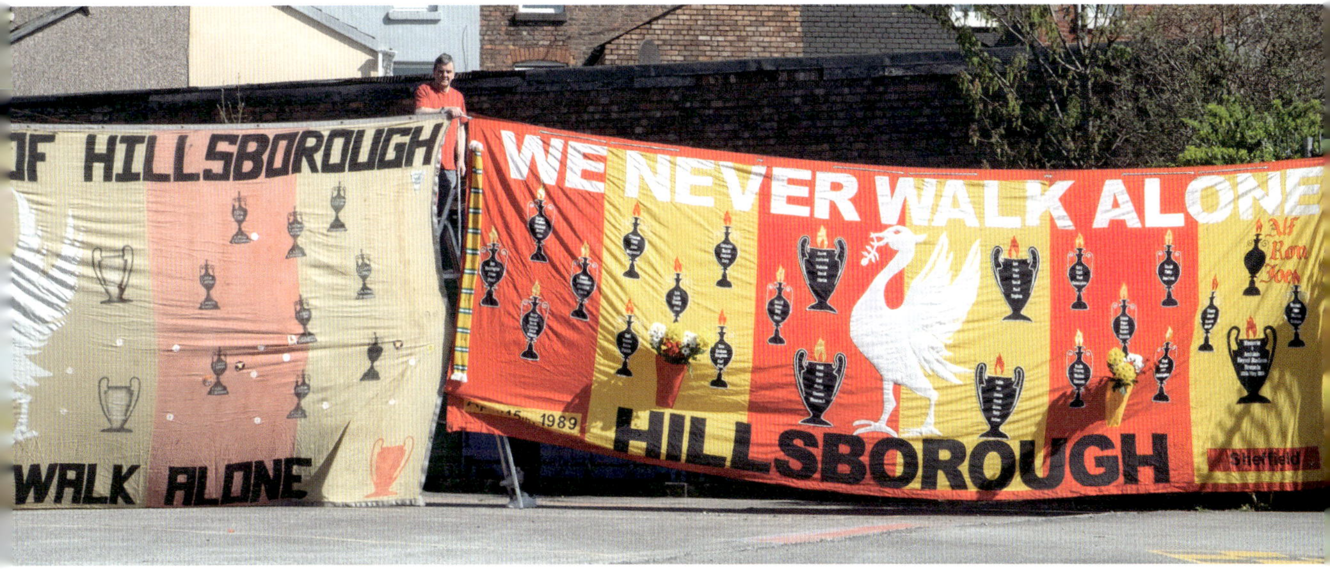
HILLSBOROUGH
WALK ALONE
WE NEVER WALK ALONE
1989
HILLSBOROUGH

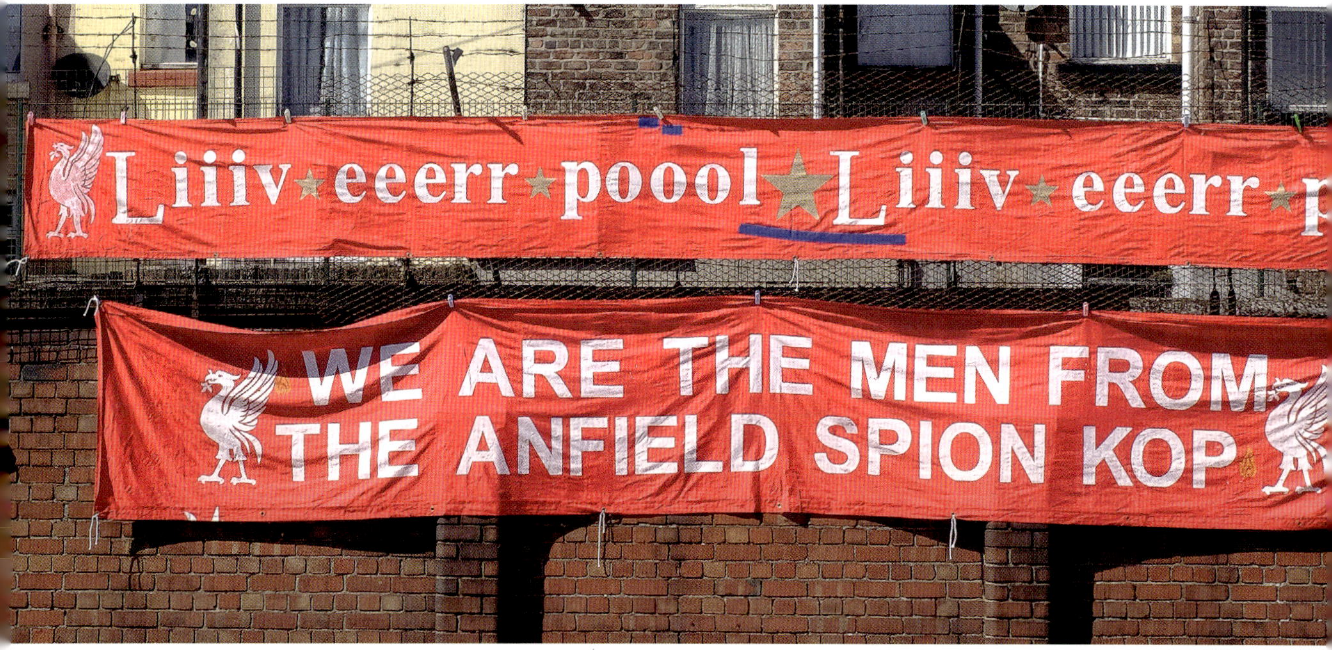
Liiiv eeerr poool Liiiv eeerr
WE ARE THE MEN FROM
THE ANFIELD SPION KOP

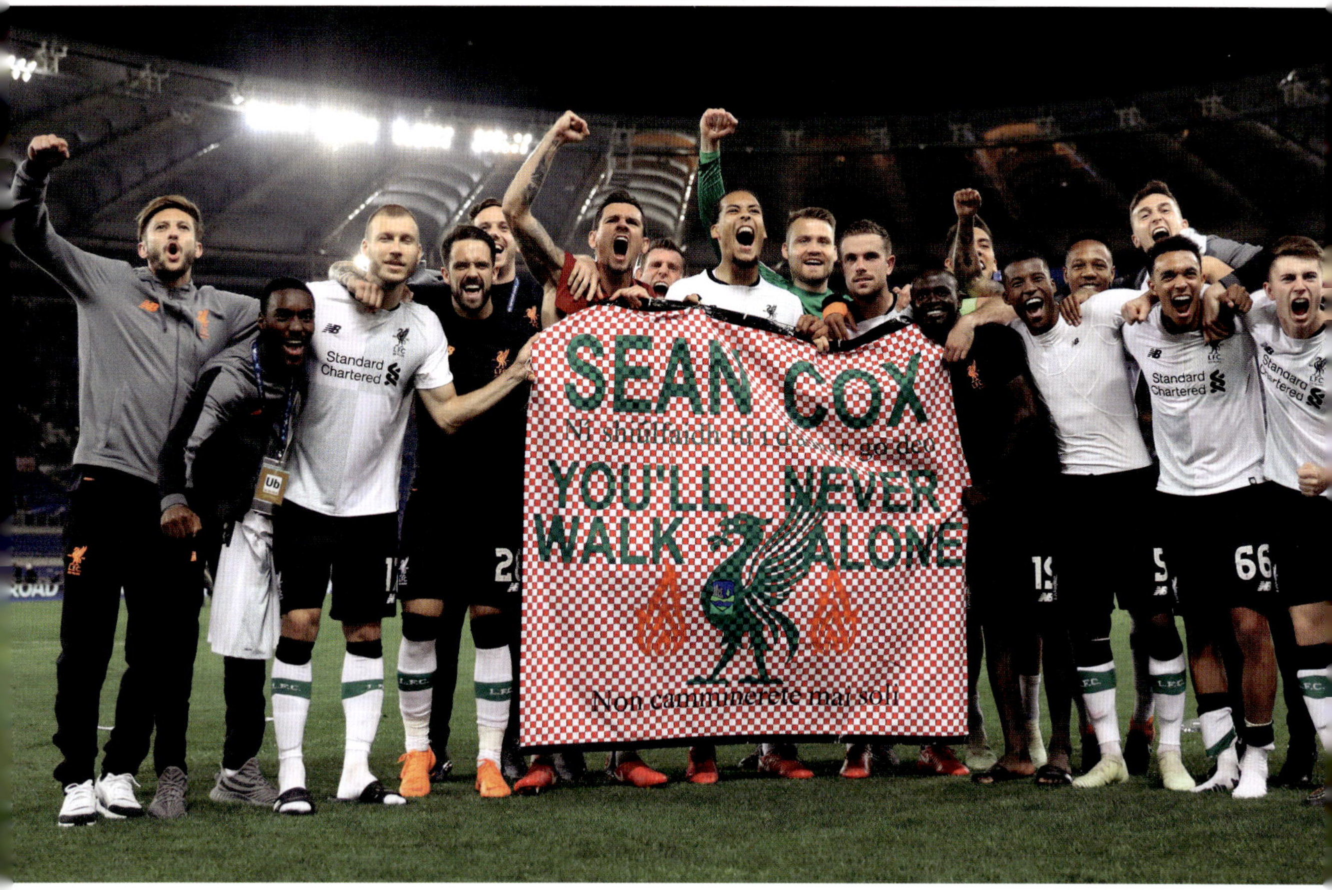
SEAN COX
YOU'LL NEVER
WALK ALONE
Standard Chartered

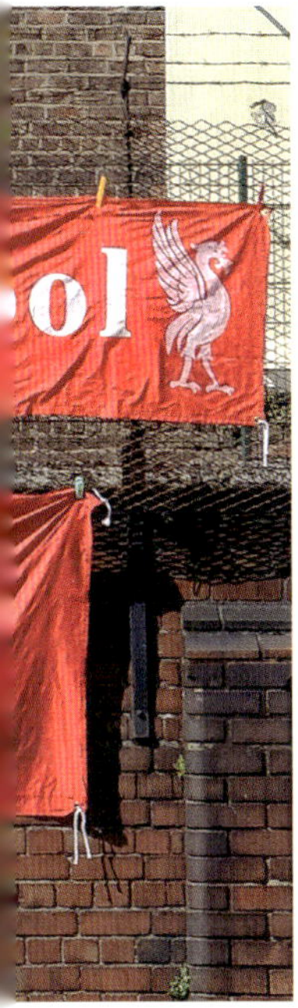

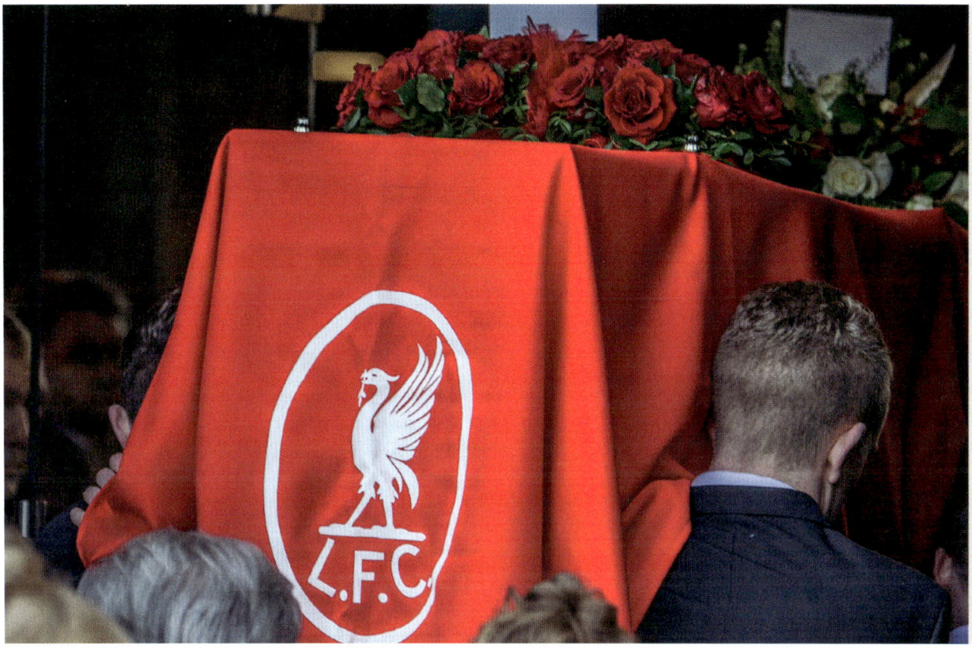

A flag for Tommy: the funeral for a goalkeeping legend in January 2018 featured Peter Carney's red flag with the Shankly-era club crest

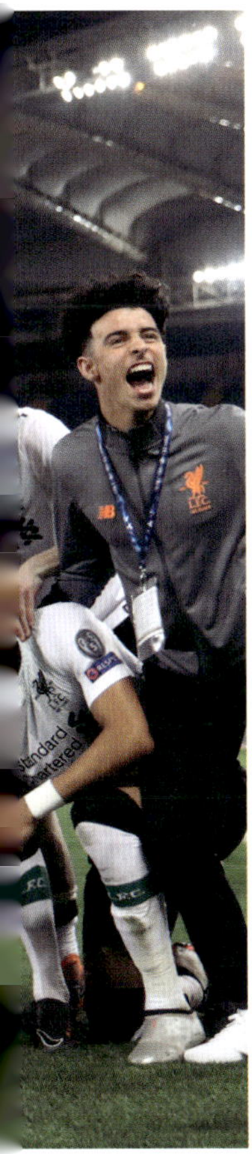

"It's about expressing my belonging to the club, my vision for what's going on and my ideas."

Peter Hooton, lifelong Liverpool follower and member of the Spirit of Shankly fan group, describes him as "an artist. The Hillsborough banner is the best one for me. Every name was embroidered on to it.

"He's recording history in a way – it's the Scouse Bayeux Tapestry. Peter will go down in posterity. If I wanted someone to make a banner for my funeral, it'd be Peter Carney. He did one for Tommy Lawrence and Peter Thompson when they passed away and the families were made-up with them.

"They're magnificent. He takes his time. He knows what he's doing."

Carney's devotion was evident for the funeral of former Reds goalkeeper Lawrence in January 2018. The Scot was Bill Shankly's last line of defence and helped the Reds to win two top-flight titles, in 1964 and 1966, plus a first-ever FA Cup for the club in 1965. His coffin was draped in a flag which had been made by Peter and was later displayed outside Homebaked, the community-owned bakery on Anfield's Oakfield Road, then inside the ground at the corner of the Kop and Sir Kenny Dalglish Stand.

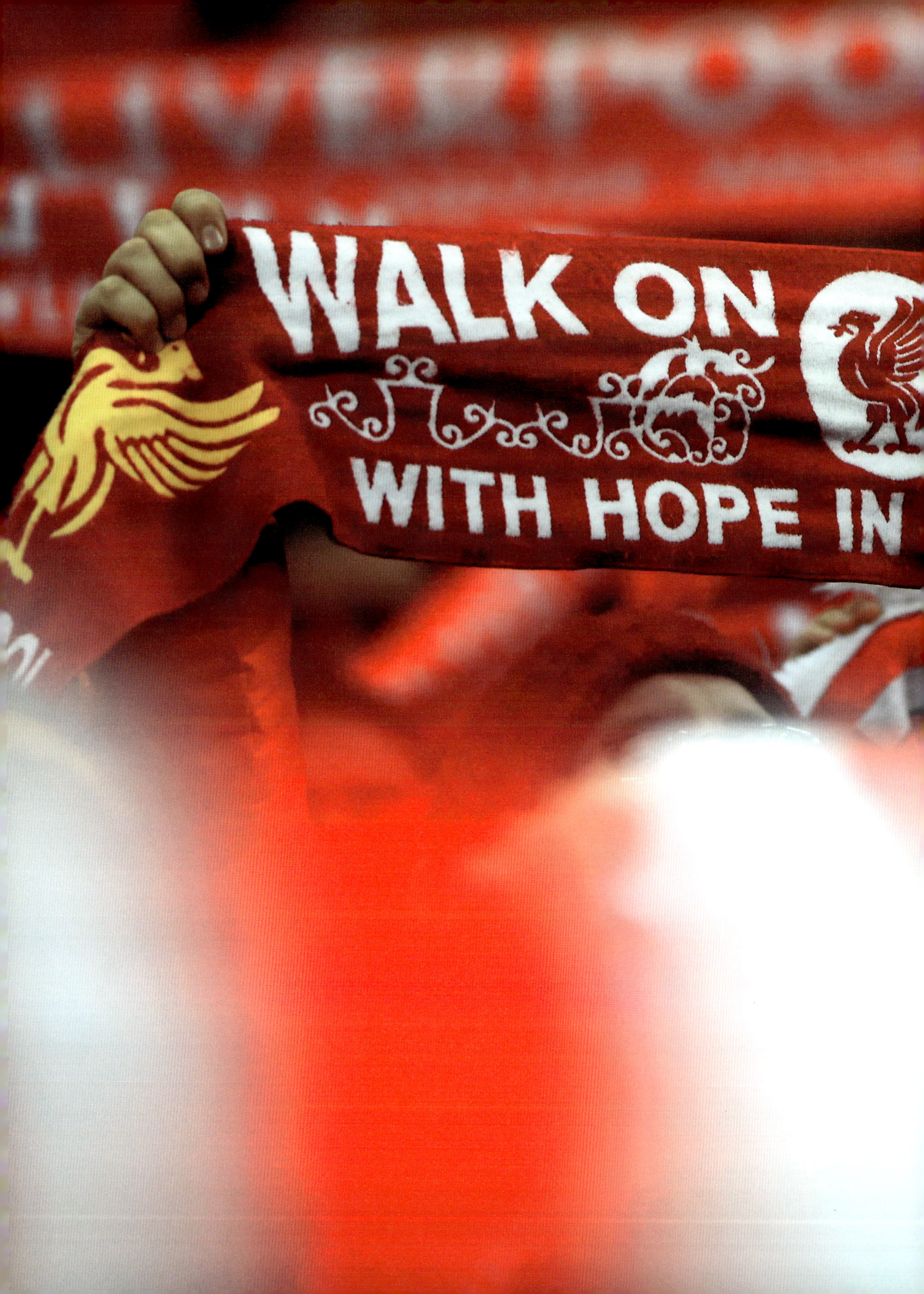
WALK ON
WITH HOPE IN

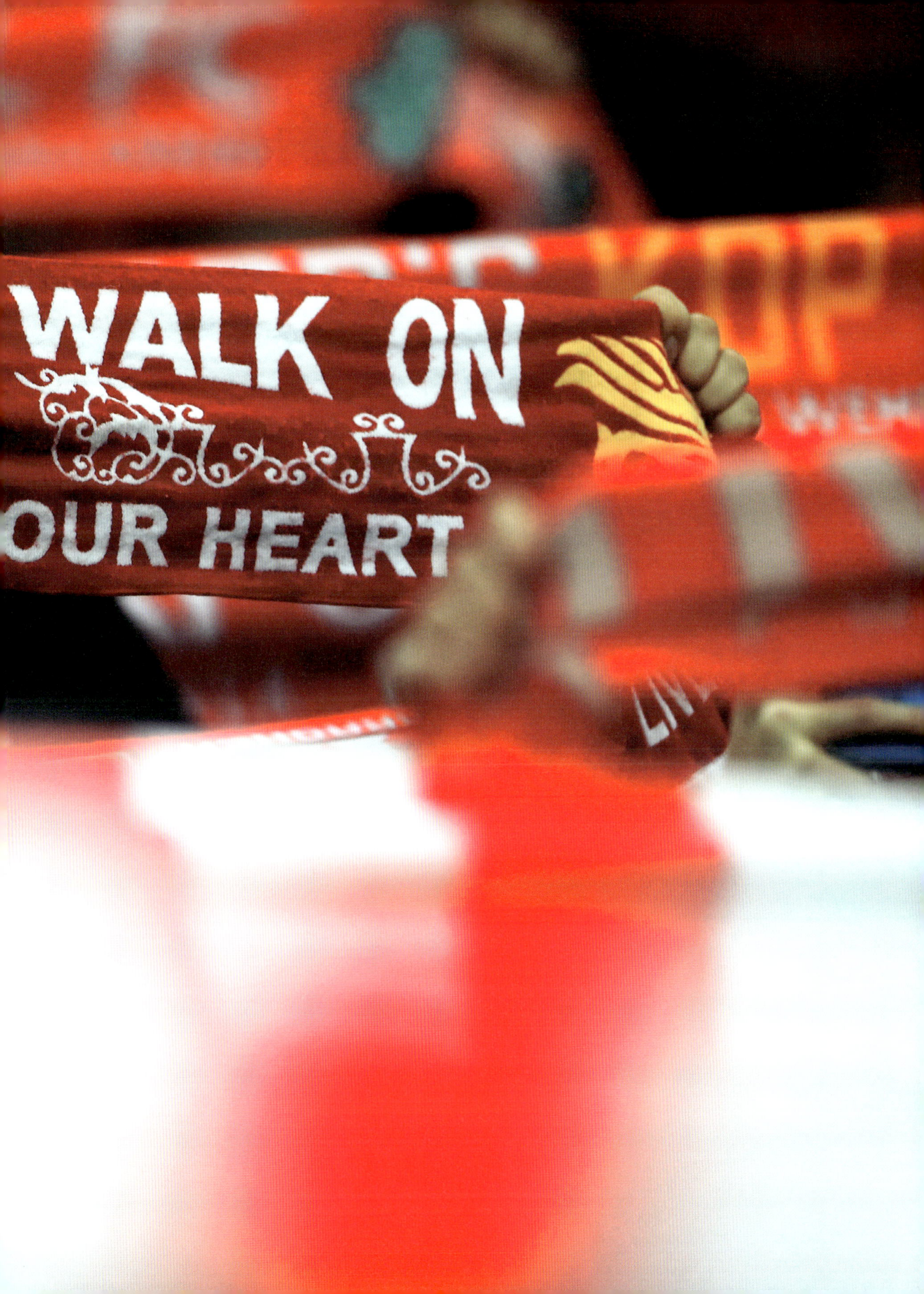
WALK ON
OUR HEART

The 12th Man

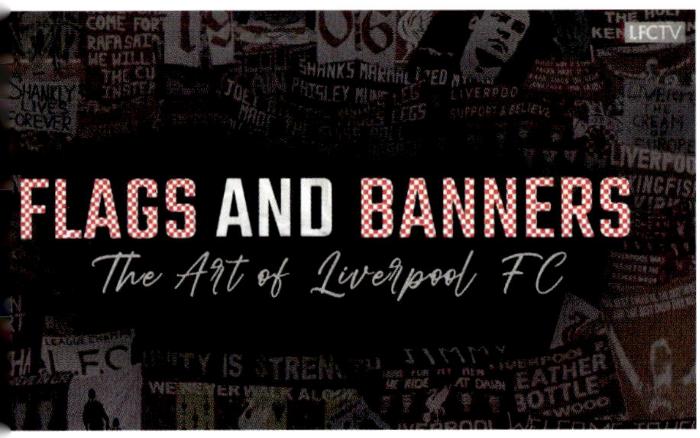

Liverpool FC paid tribute to the fans behind the flags when lockdown brought their Anfield absence into sharper focus

Late December 2020 saw the release of a feature-length documentary on LFCTV and LFCTV GO entitled *Flags and Banners: The Art of Liverpool FC*. Taking viewers on a trip through the history of LFC terrace art, the 70-minute film was a tribute to those who have decorated the Kop – as well as stadiums and city-centres across the Continent – in support of their beloved Reds.

It spanned a century, from the early 1920s, when the club unfurled the first known Liverpool FC banner, to the summer of 2020 when COVID brought life as we knew it to a standstill and fans like Peter Carney, Frank Graceffa and the Spion Kop 1906 group laid their flags inside the stadium to show their support was still there. In the film they shared their story alongside fellow banner-makers and experts like historian Frank Monaghan, collector Adrian Killen and LFC matchday programme writer Chris McLoughlin.

Viewers could watch how banners became 'comfort blankets' in the aftermath of the Hillsborough tragedy in 1989, and how they festooned Anfield on the day of the Kop's 'Last Stand' five years later; into the 2000s when successive managers Gerard Houllier and Rafael Benitez stoked supporters' passions who brought their artistic qualities to the fore once again; then onto the modern era and more insight from artist Emma Norbury, maker of more than 250 flags.

Joe Connolly from Spion Kop 1906 reflected at the time: "This lockdown situation has meant that we're all pretty committed to making sure that when we can all be back in the ground, it'll be pretty special." It certainly was.

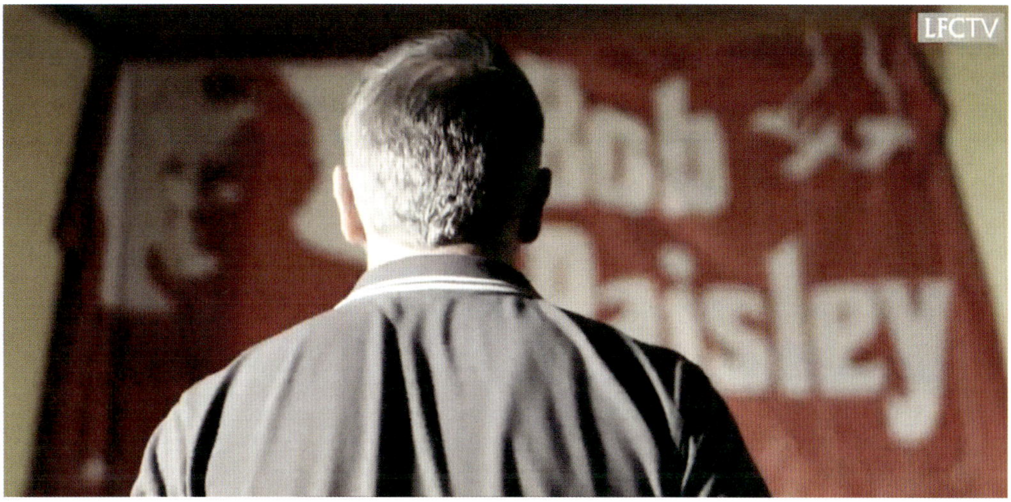
LFCTV
Bob
Paisley

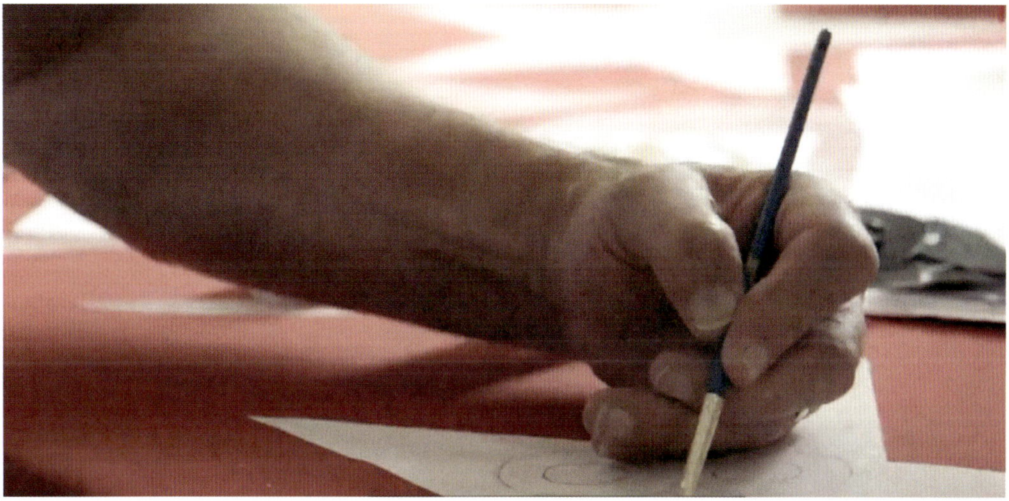

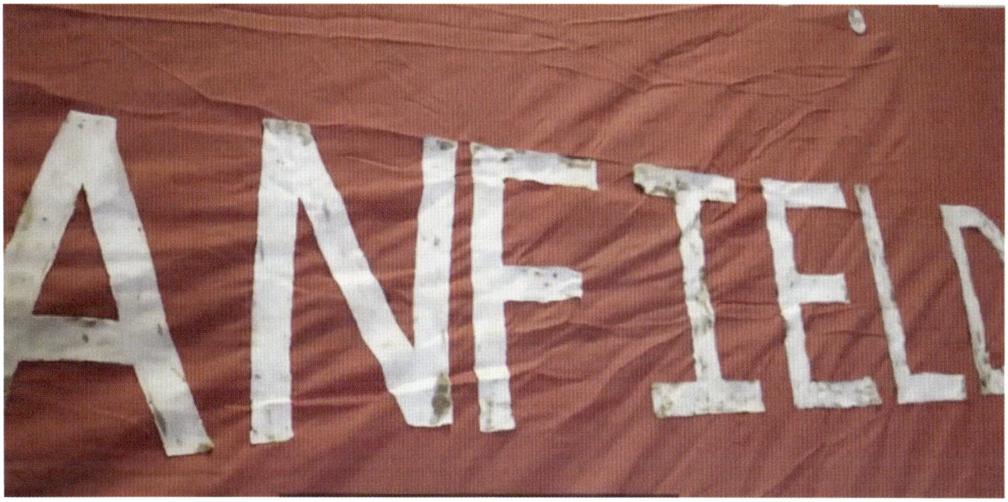
ANFIELD

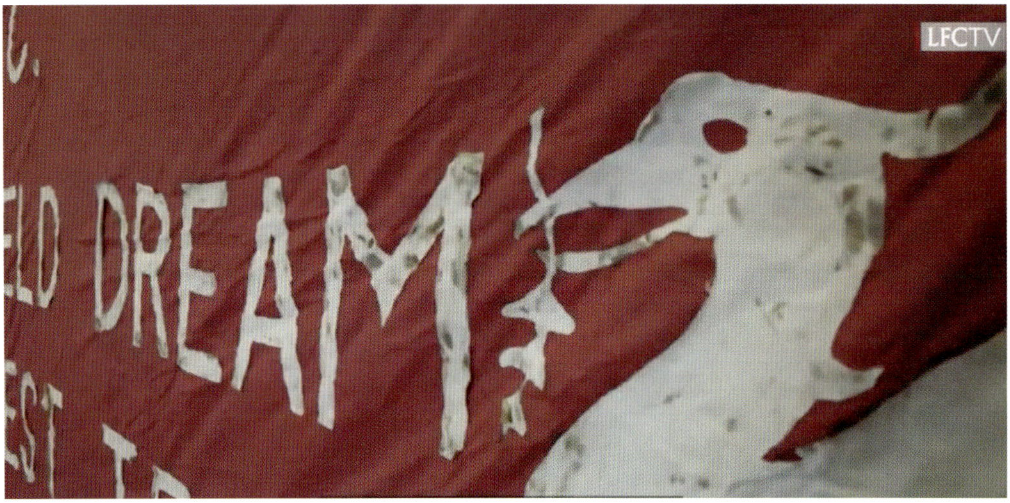
LFCTV
DREAM

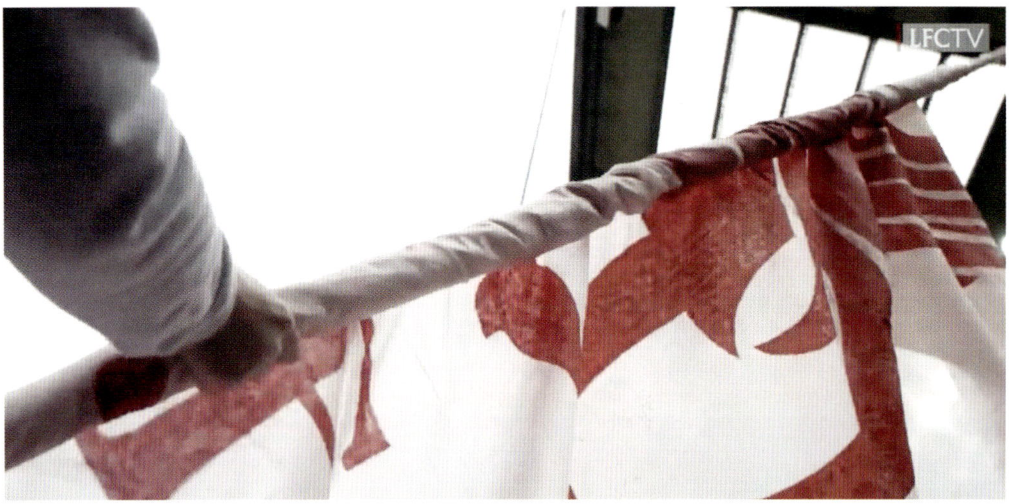
LFCTV

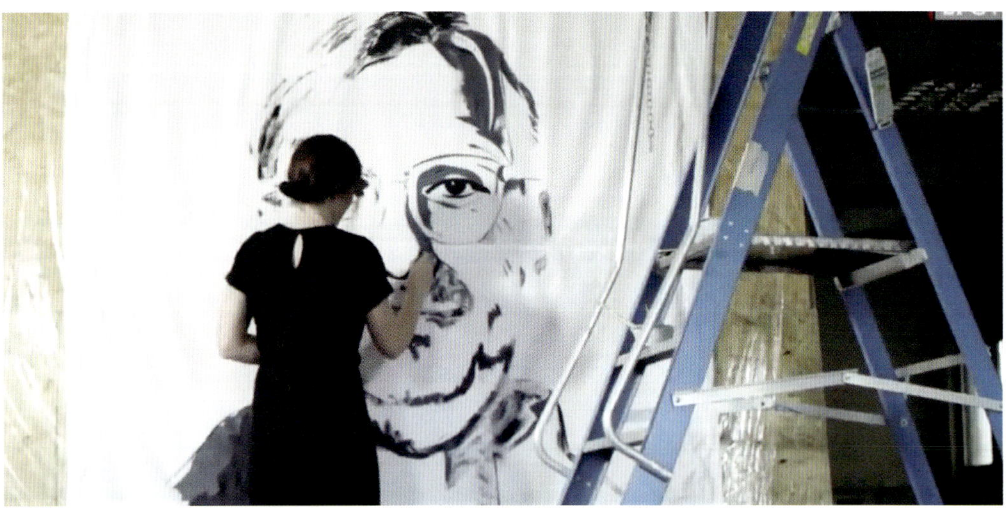

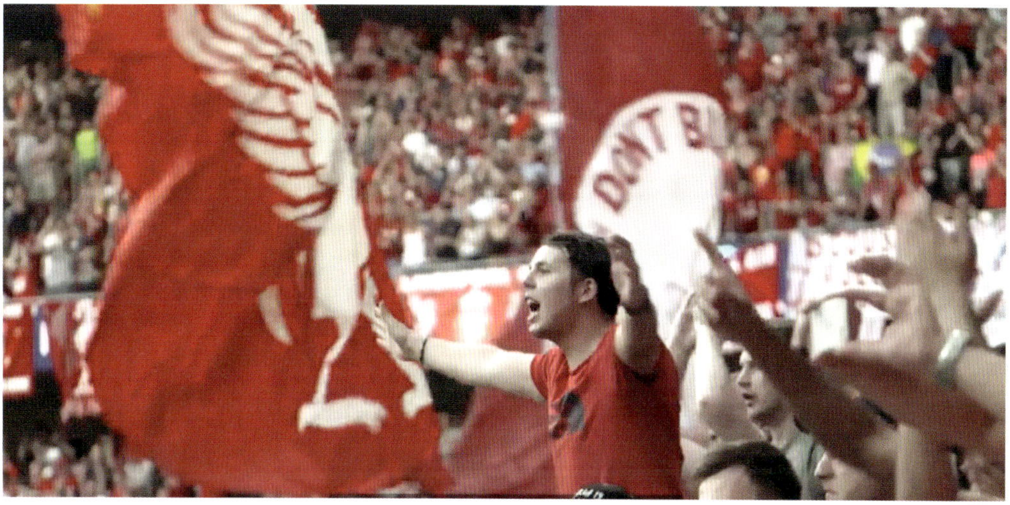

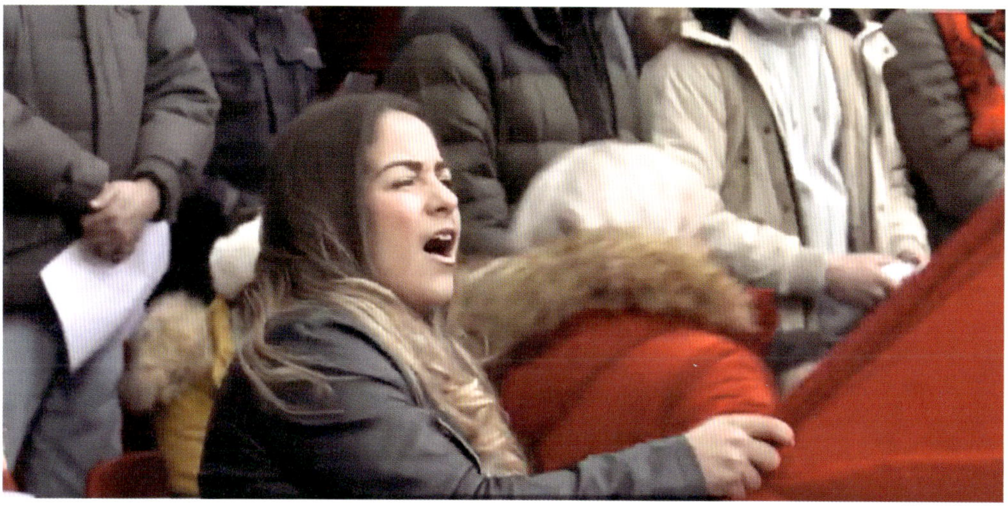

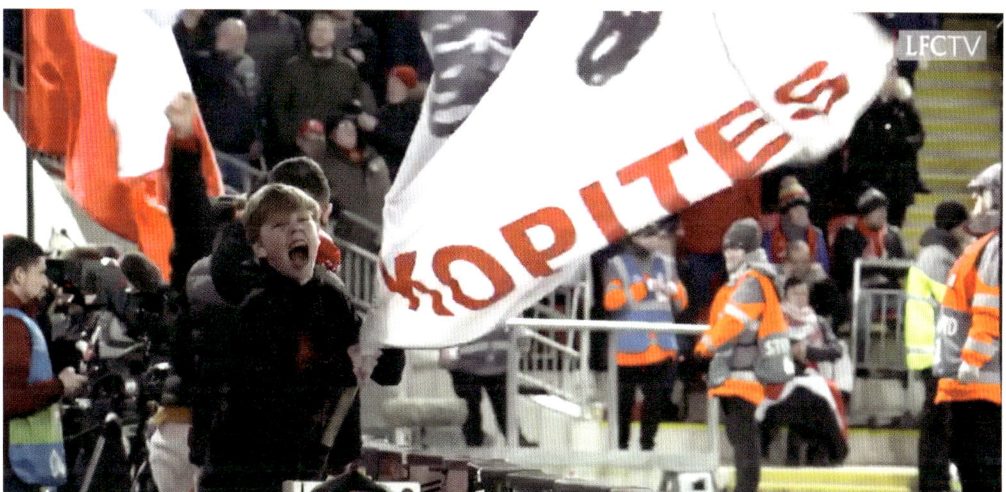
LFCTV
KOPITES

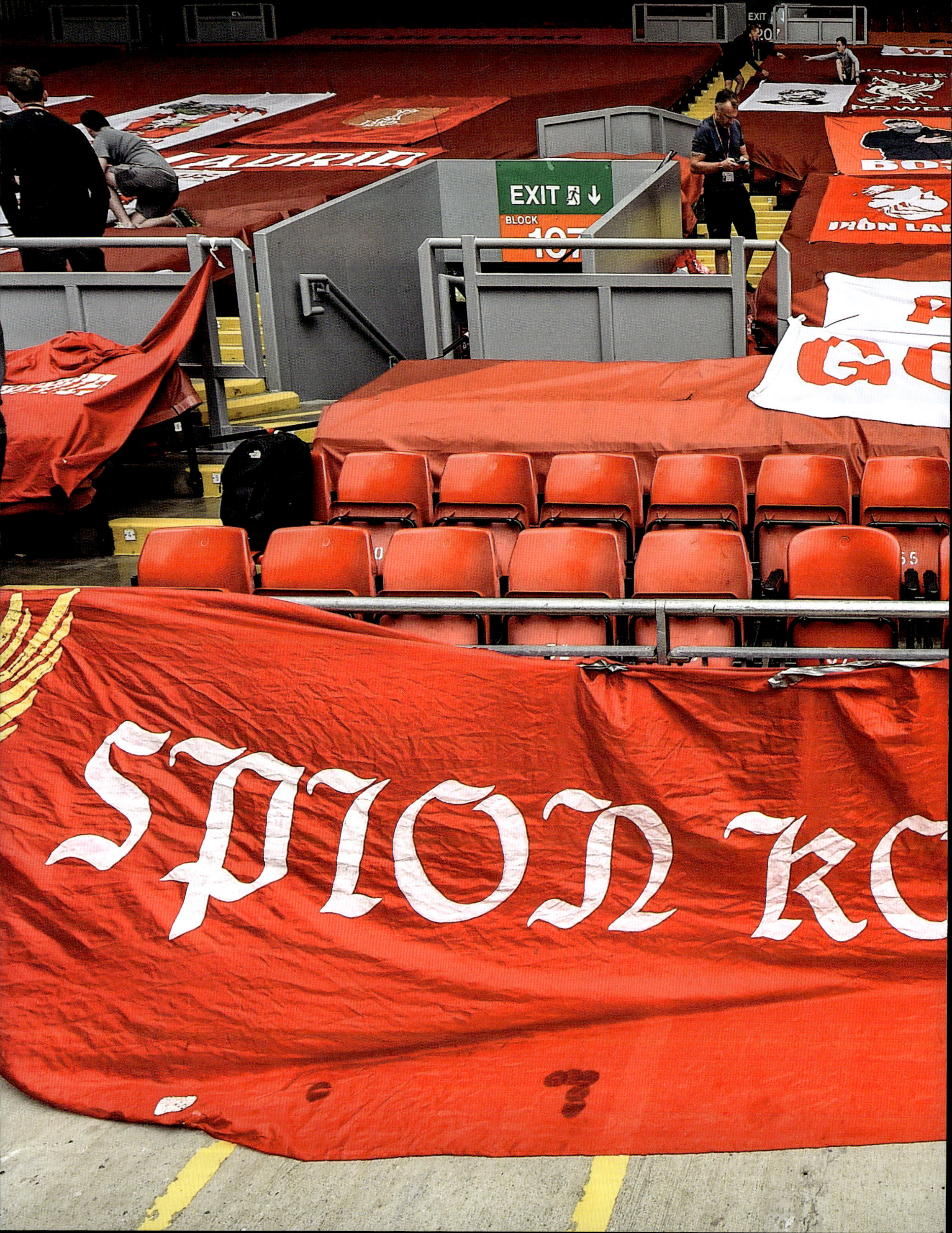
EXIT
BLOCK
SPION KO

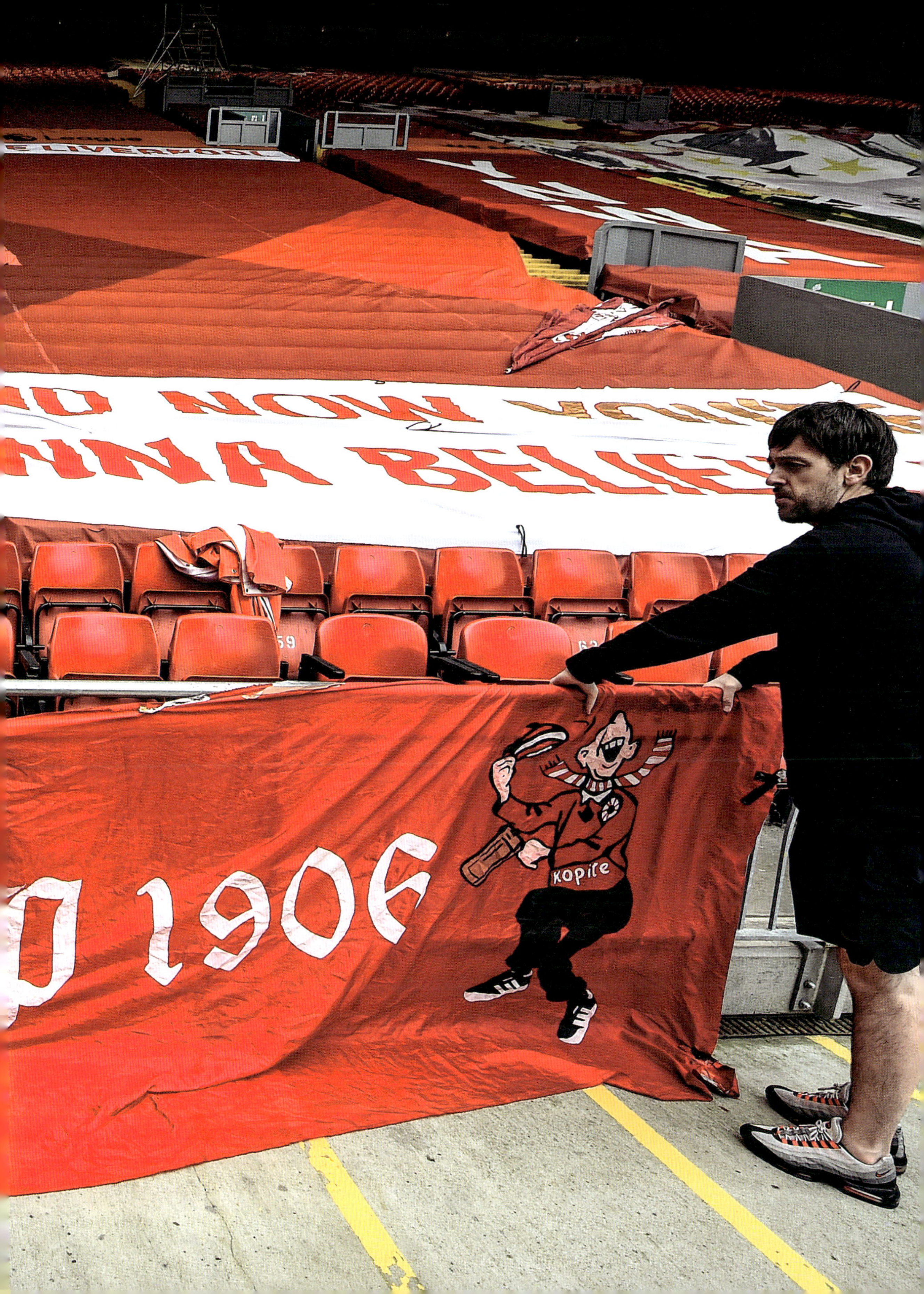
1906
kopite

The Kop Spirit survives

Anfield's soulful backdrop to a title-clinching finale

That was exactly what one of the banners said, and that was how everyone felt when the COVID pandemic kept fans away from football but couldn't stop them adorning Anfield's famous stand in red-and-white reminders instead.

Liverpool v Crystal Palace on Wednesday 24 June 2020 was the first home fixture after lockdown and supporters made sure there would still be a passionate welcome for the players despite the empty stadium, with flags and banners laid all over the Kop. It stayed that way until the end of the season.

In his matchday programme notes Jürgen Klopp had this message for the supporters: "You are still with us today."

He went on: "We know what our club and this group of players in particular means to you. We know the joy it brings. We know you kick every ball and shout still as if you were in the middle of the Kop. We know the impact of what we do now will be as big as anything we have ever done, because you are making sacrifices for us by staying in your homes.

"We may be apart physically, but we are always together."

The Kop still looked spectacular thanks to the dedication of fan group Spion Kop 1906 and their friends. LFCTV had made a short film of them at work with this special message from the manager: "When I sit in my spot in the stadium before the game starts, I always look to the Kop and it's always incredible because we have all these common experiences and memories.

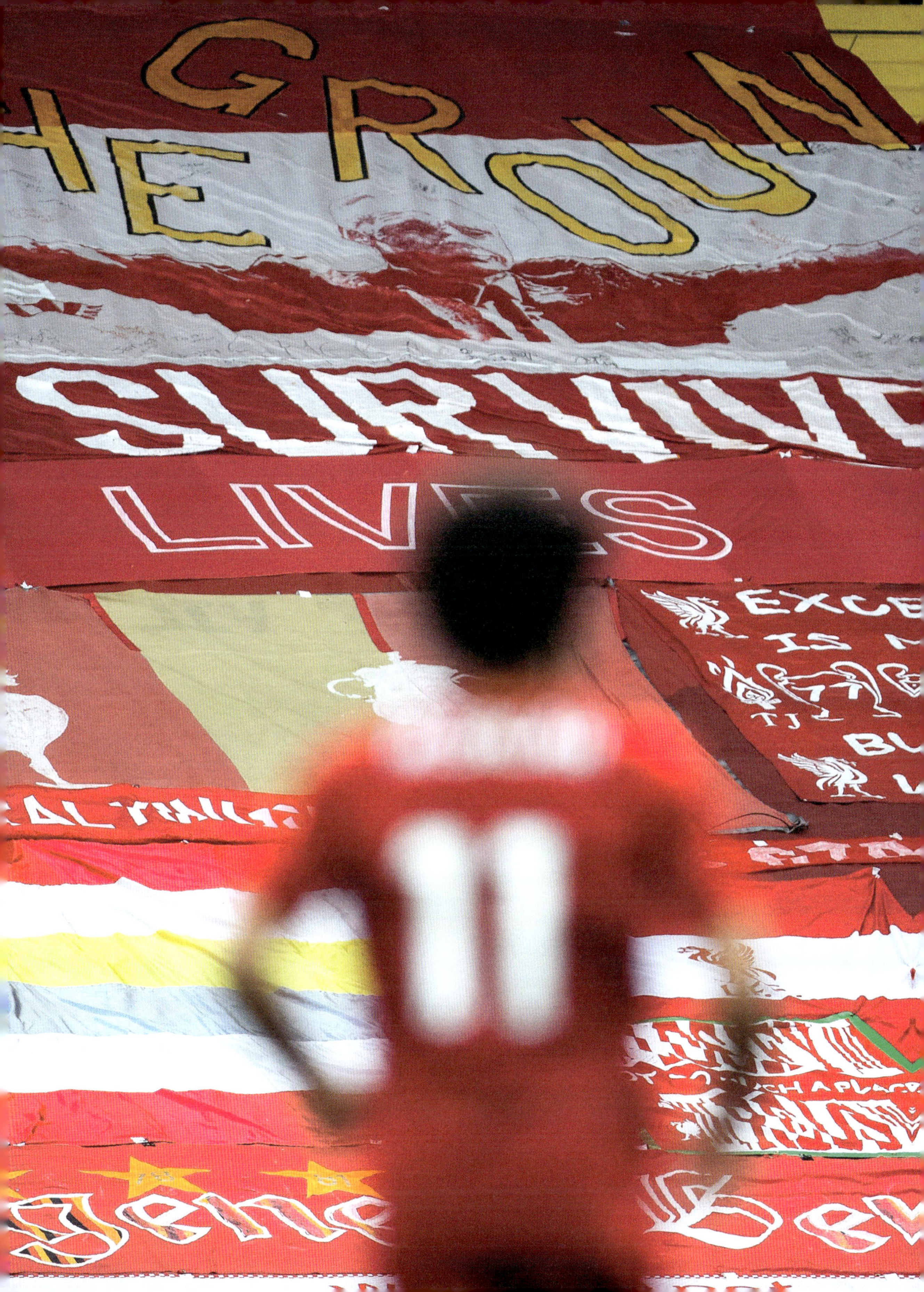
LIVES
11

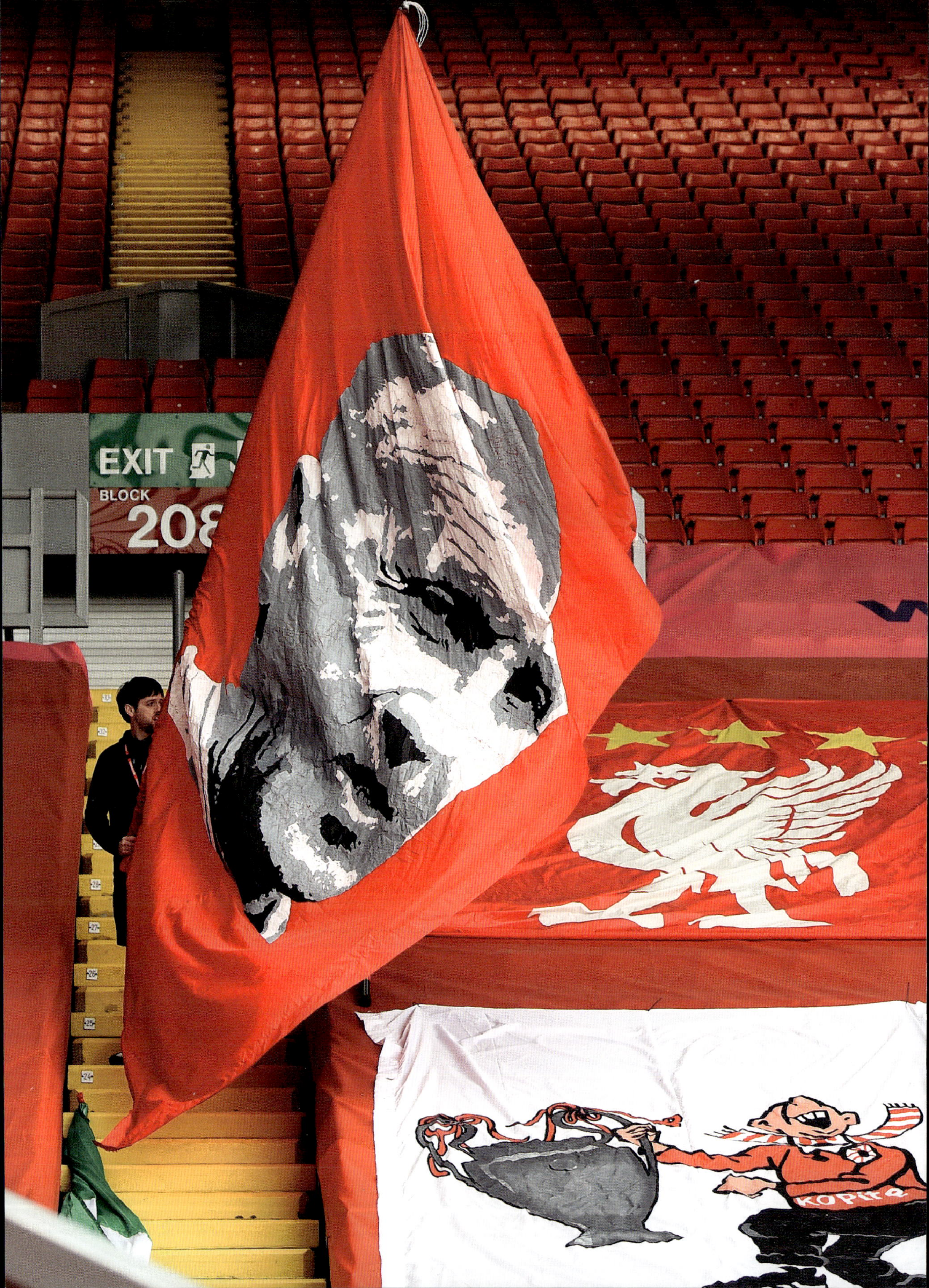
EXIT
BLOCK
208
KOPite

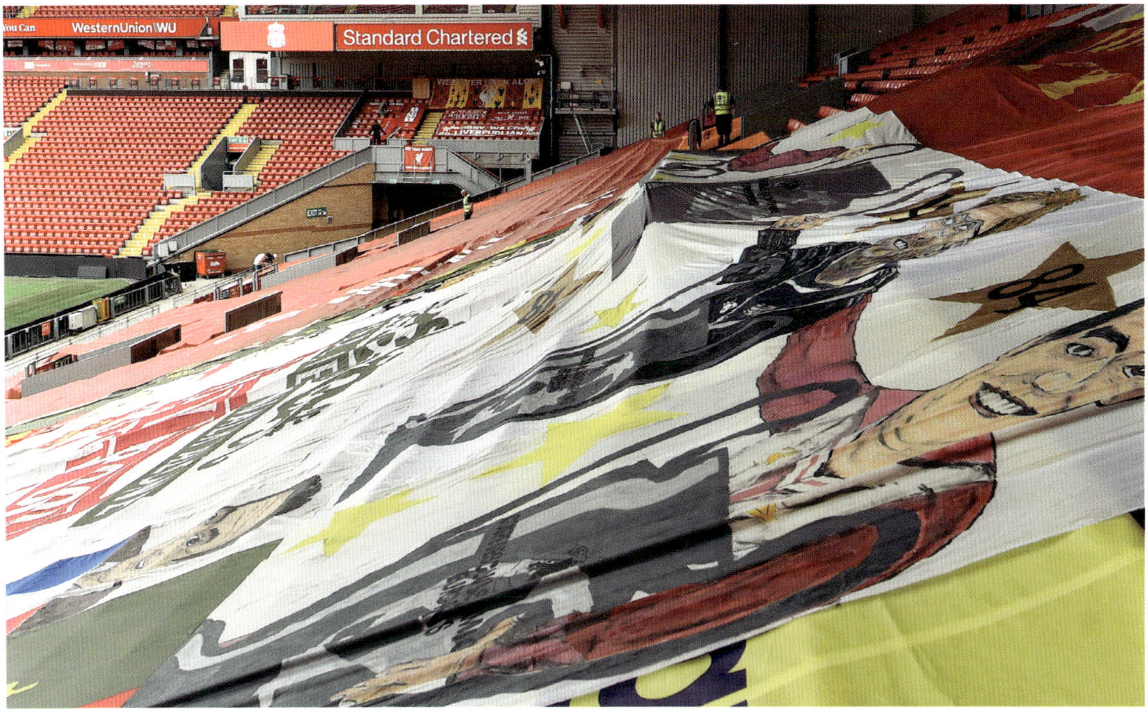
WesternUnion WU
Standard Chartered

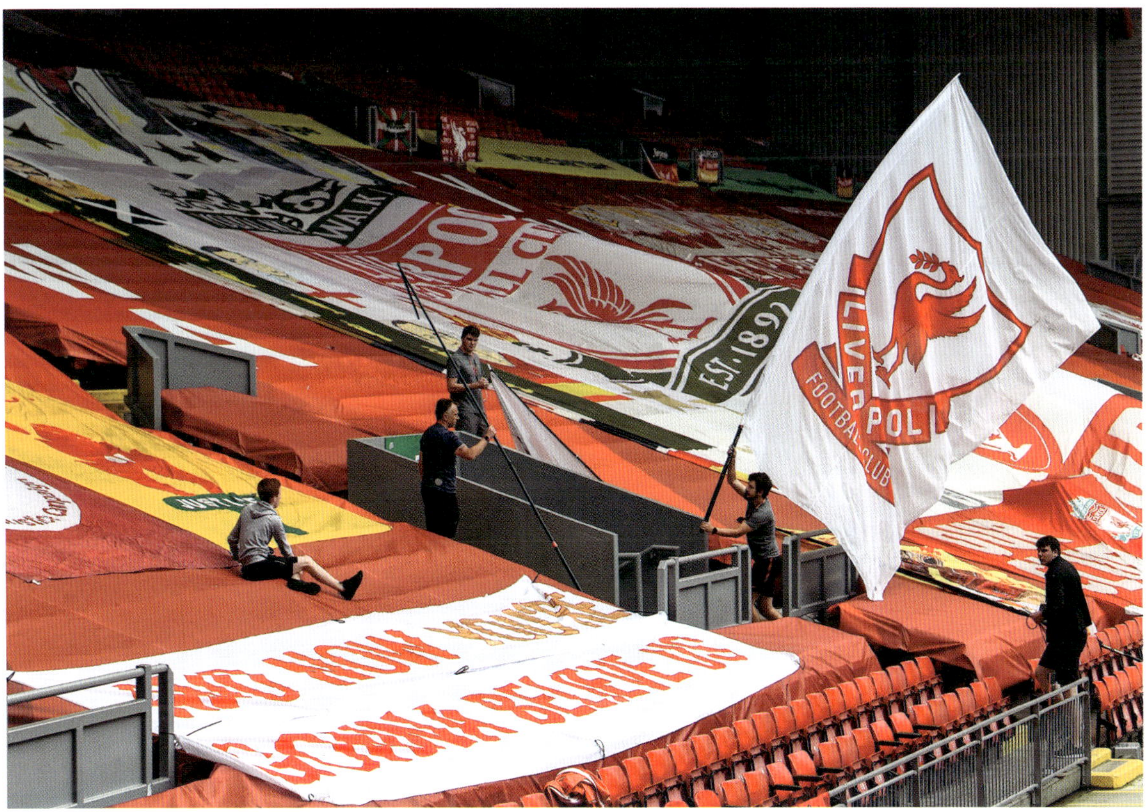
EST. 1892
LIVERPOOL
FOOTBALL CLUB

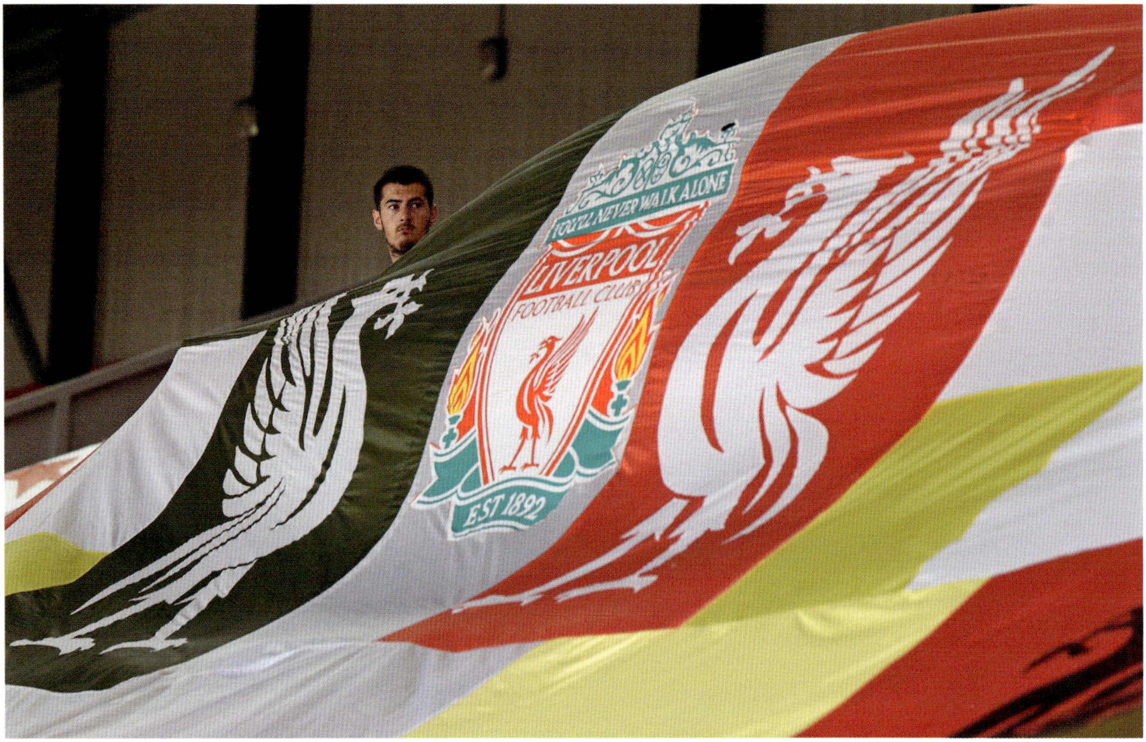
LIVERPOOL
FOOTBALL CLUB
EST 1892

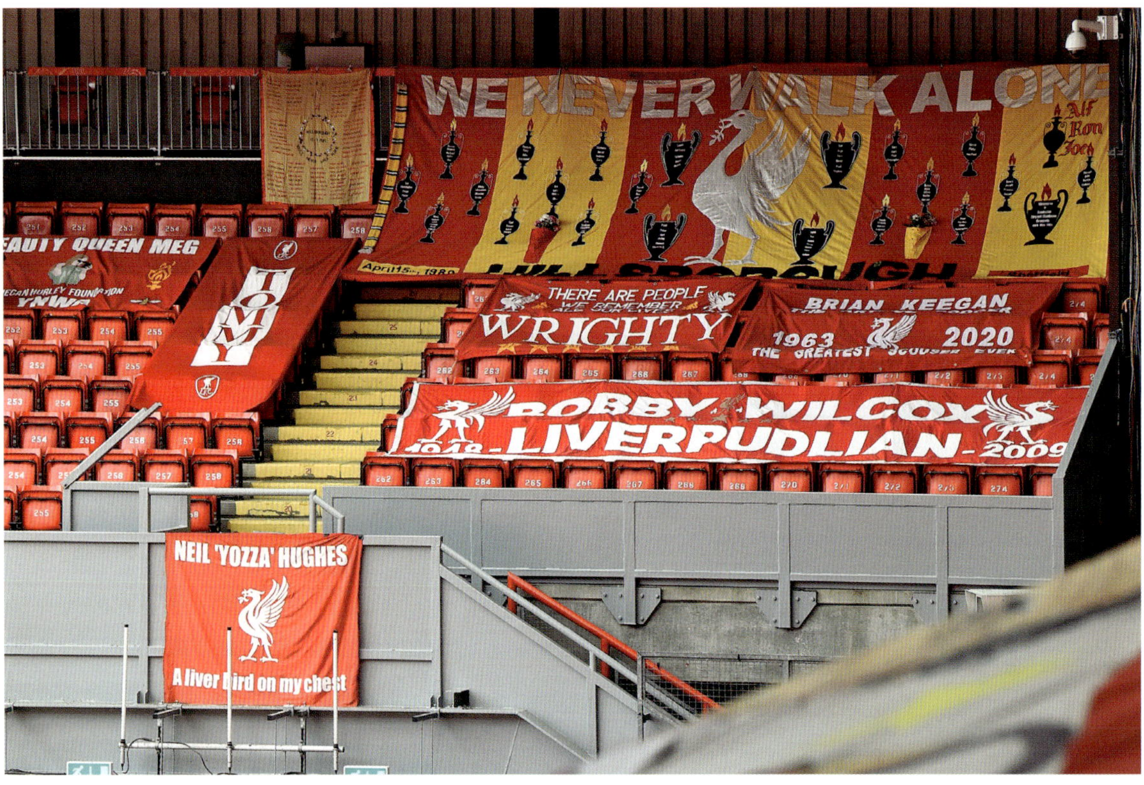
WE NEVER WALK ALONE
TOMMY
THERE ARE PEOPLE
WRIGHTY
BRIAN KEEGAN
1963 2020
ROBBY WILCOX
LIVERPUDLIAN
NEIL 'YOZZA' HUGHES
A liver bird on my chest

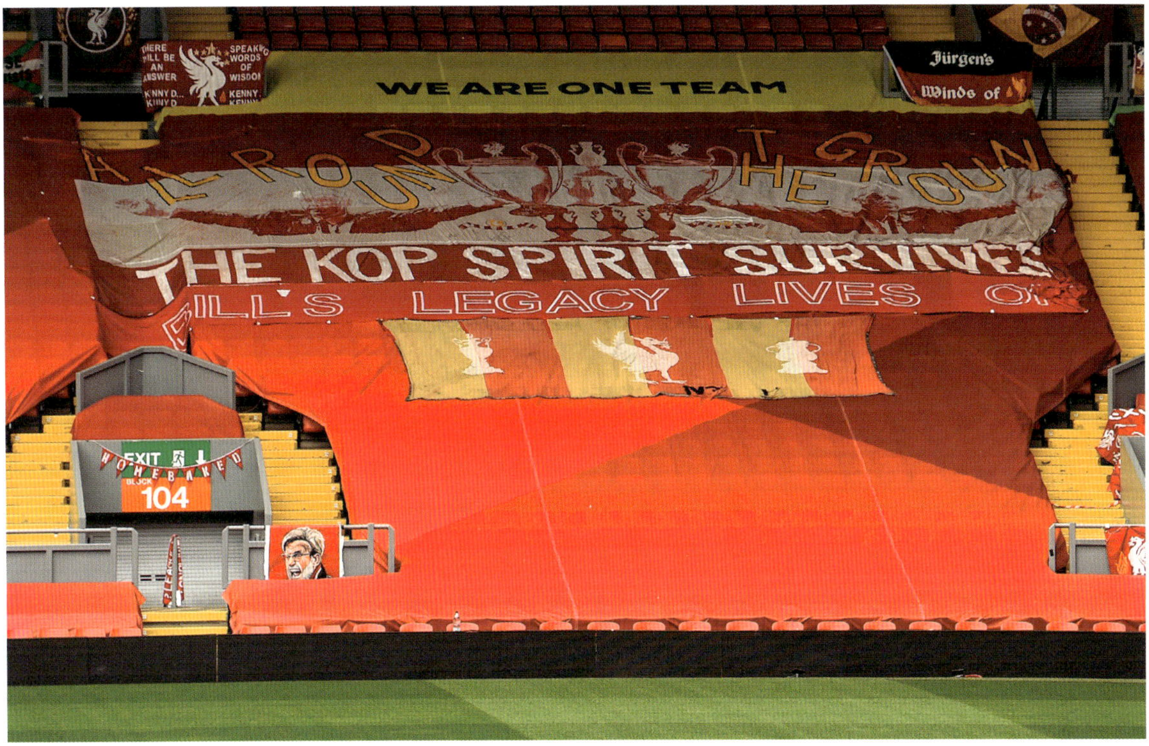
WE ARE ONE TEAM
THE KOP SPIRIT SURVIVES
LEGACY LIVES
Jürgen's
Winds of
EXIT
104

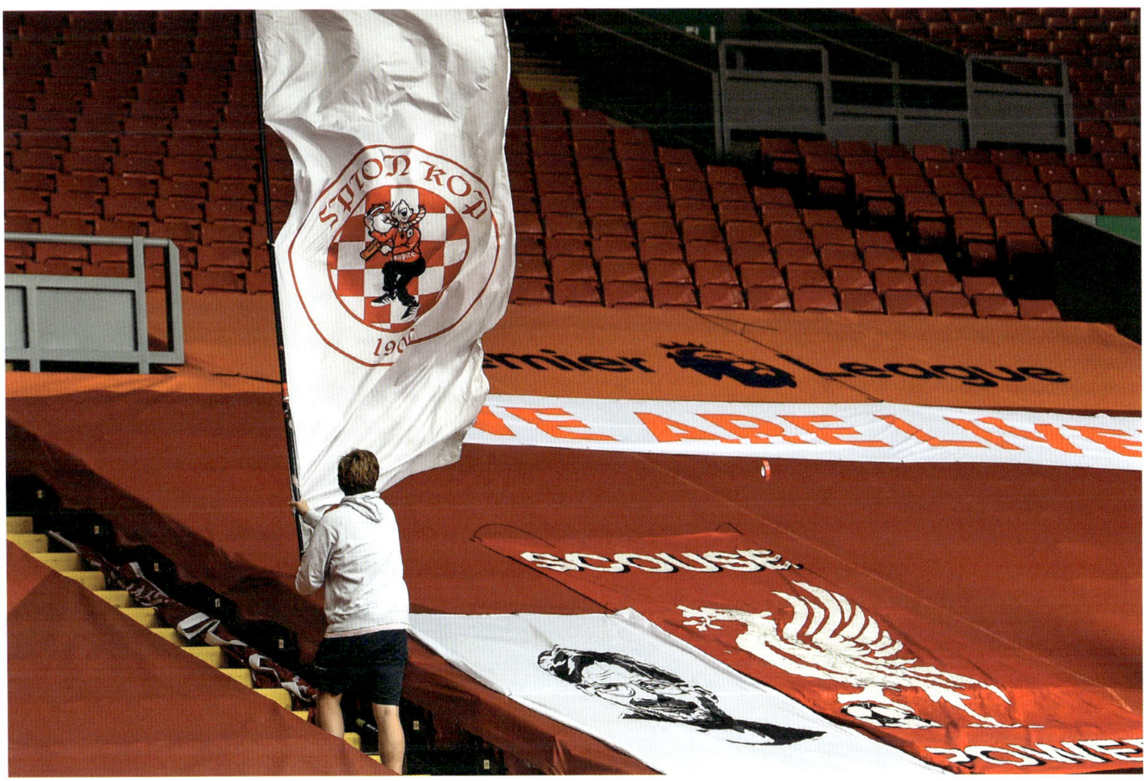
SPION KOP
League
SCOUSE

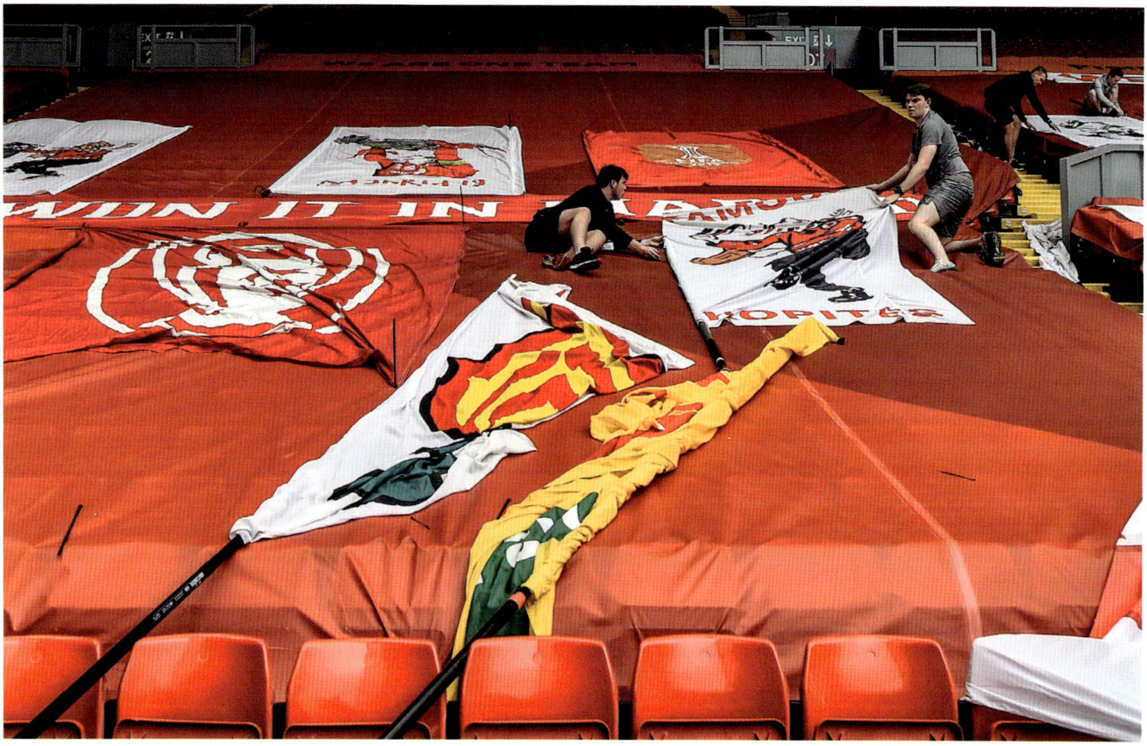

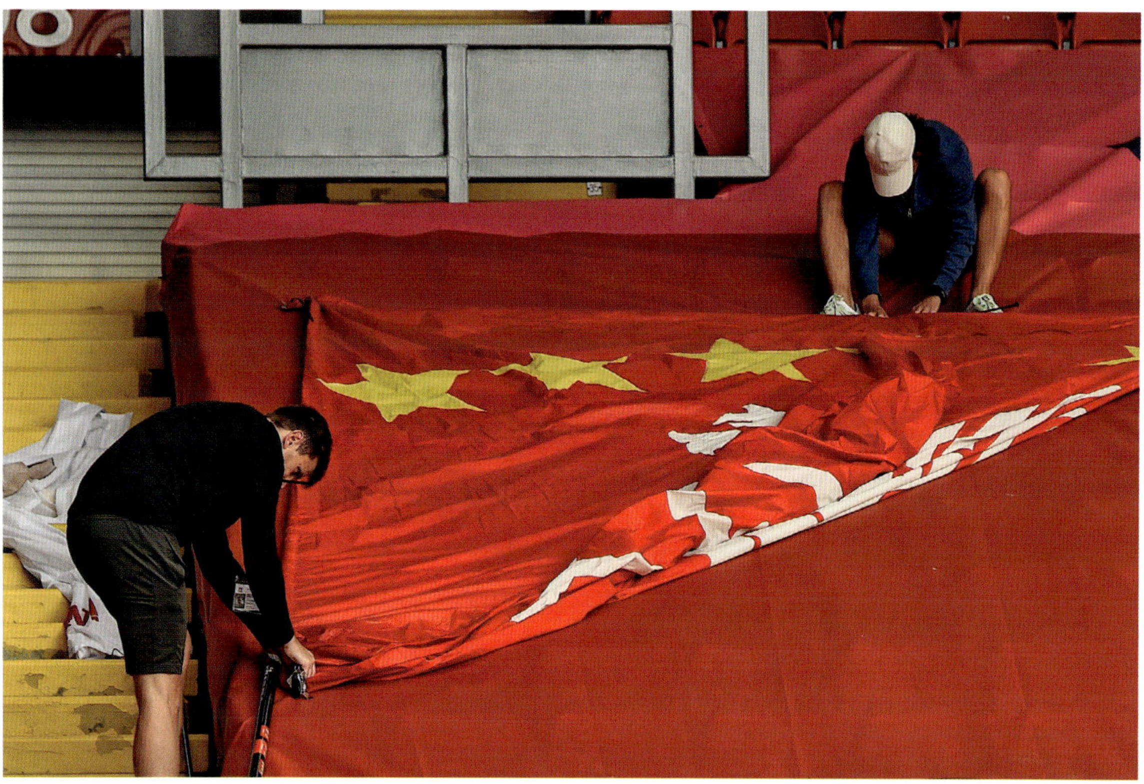

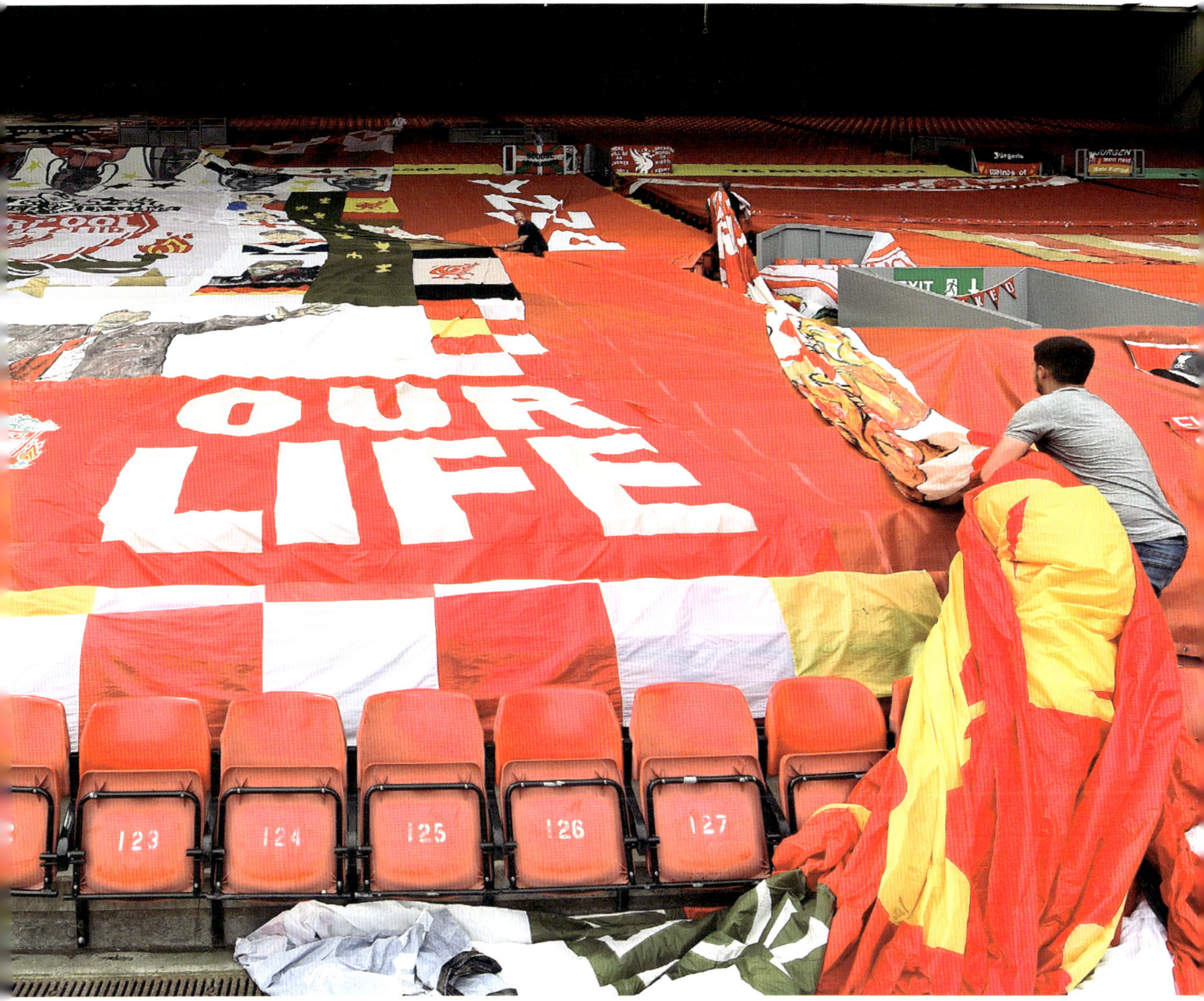

The boss continued: "Thank you very much to everybody who puts so much soul into it – it's incredible."

Midfielder James Milner, who must have thought he'd seen everything in his footballing career, admitted that he was "gutted for the supporters more than us as players" about clinching the Premier League title behind-closed-doors. But he insisted: "They'll be with us even if they're not there."

His view was echoed by defender Virgil van Dijk who said: "We have a strong enough connection to our fans to know they'll be with us for every kick, header, pass, shot and save. It's not that Liverpool fans aren't around anymore – they just have to watch from home. I think we can still make this cool if we all really give our best and we'll do that as players.

"The supporters know we feel them still."

Say it *Loud*

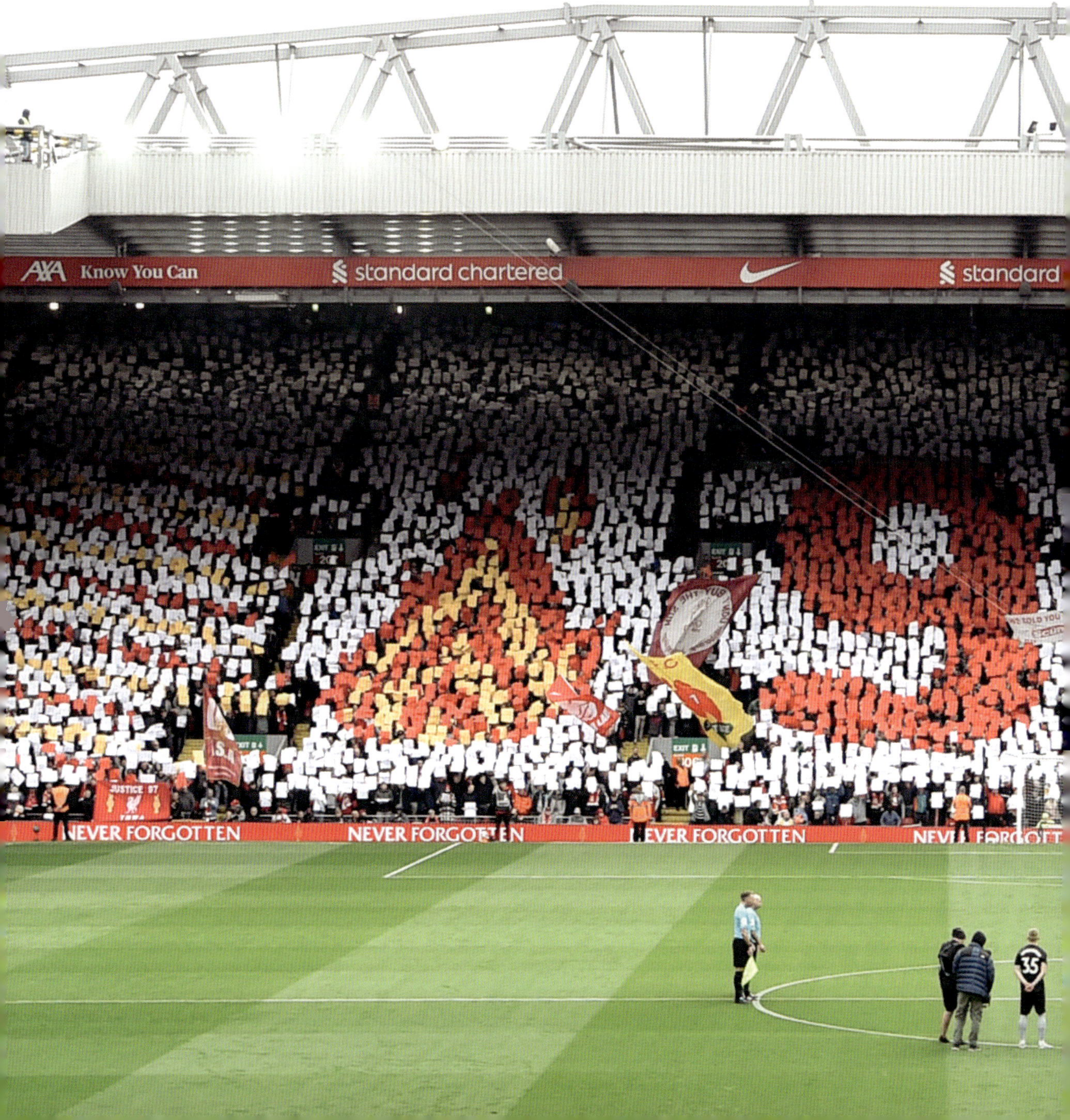
AXA Know You Can
standard chartered
standard
NEVER FORGOTTEN
NEVER FORGOTTEN
NEVER FORGOTTEN
JUSTICE 97

say it Clear

How the Kop honours its Liverpool heroes

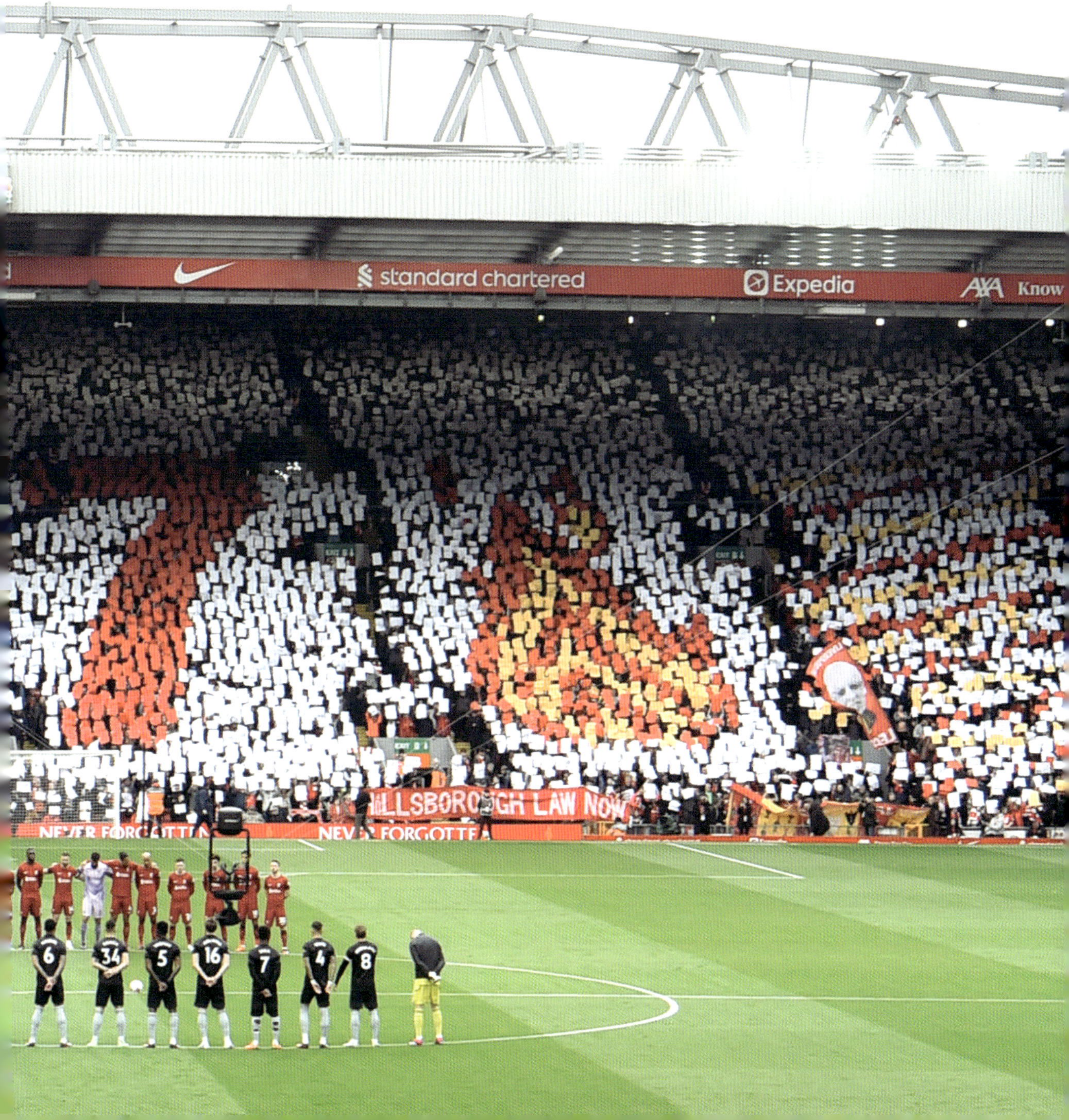

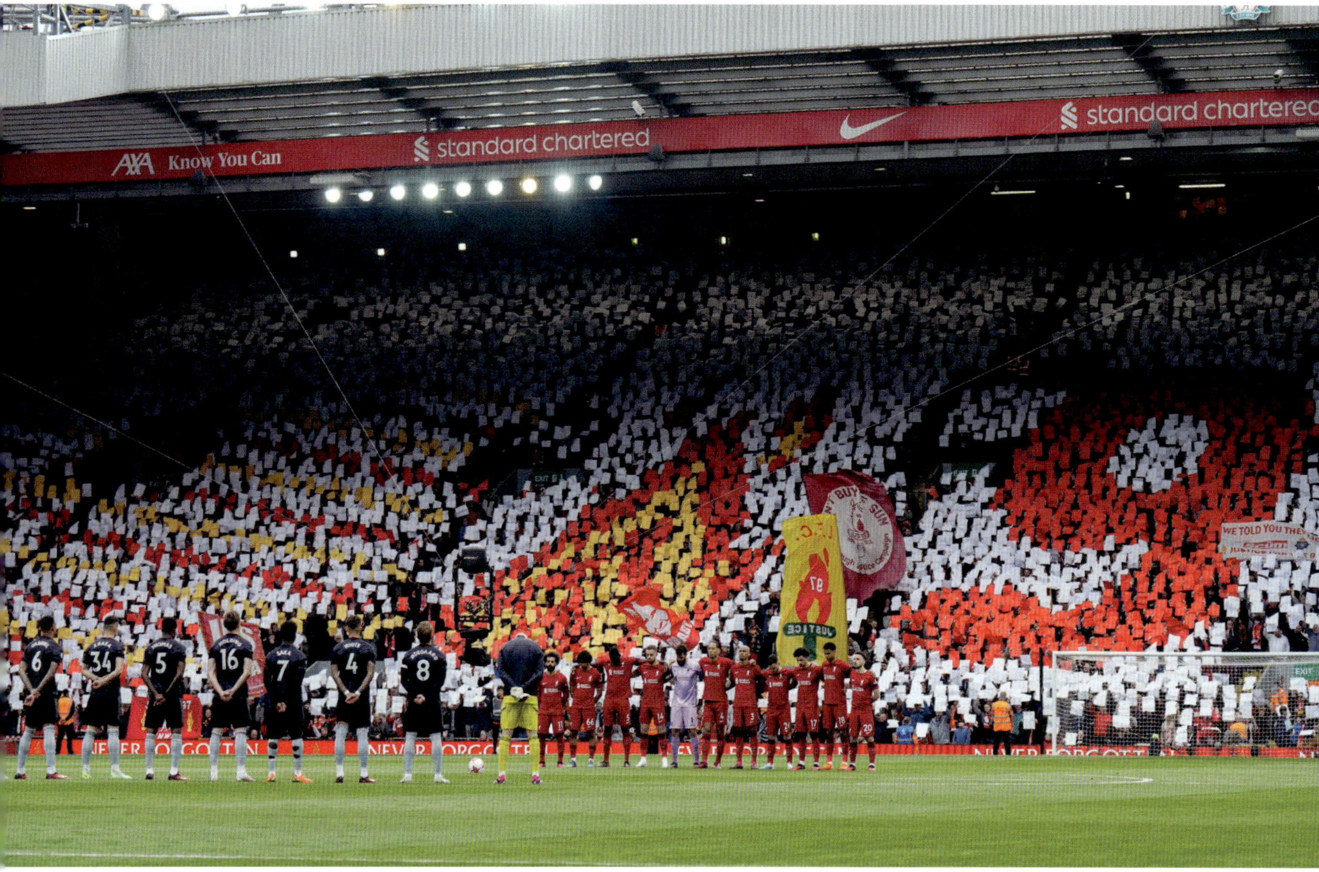

Has a minute's silence in remembrance of Hillsborough ever been more impeccably observed than before the Liverpool v Arsenal game on Sunday 9 April 2023? What made the moment even more poignant that day was the simple but spectacular mosaic on the Kop: the number '97' in red flanked by two eternal flames and streaks of red and yellow.

Down the years the tragedy's anniversary and the pursuit of justice have been commemorated at Anfield several times in similar fashion – along with tributes to LFC legends – thanks to one hugely talented Reds fan and a team of volunteers who work closely with the club. It takes creativity, ingenuity, no little effort and bags of dedication, and we have graphic designer Andy Knott to thank for a good 20 of these striking creations – each composed of thousands of individual coloured A3-sized cards – over the last two decades or so.

The design and colour-coding for each mosaic is mapped out digitally with each separate sheet – and there are 12,500 of them in total – assigned to a seat on the Kop. Among the most recent were tributes for Liverpool's record league goalscorer Roger Hunt and Seventies midfield maestro Ray Kennedy, both of whom passed away in late 2021. Often the club's matchday programme features a special front cover to coincide with the occasion, with Jürgen Klopp paying his own respects in his manager's notes inside.

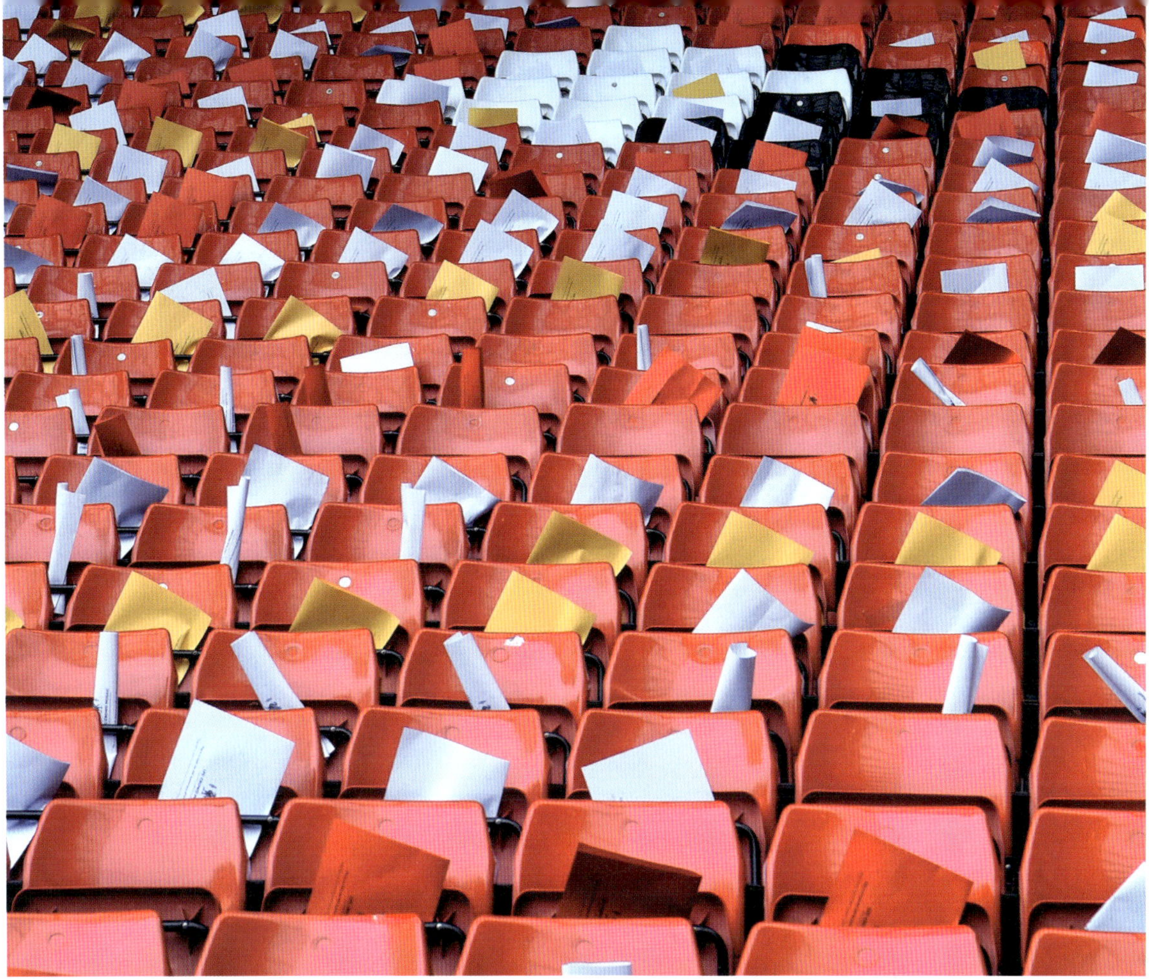

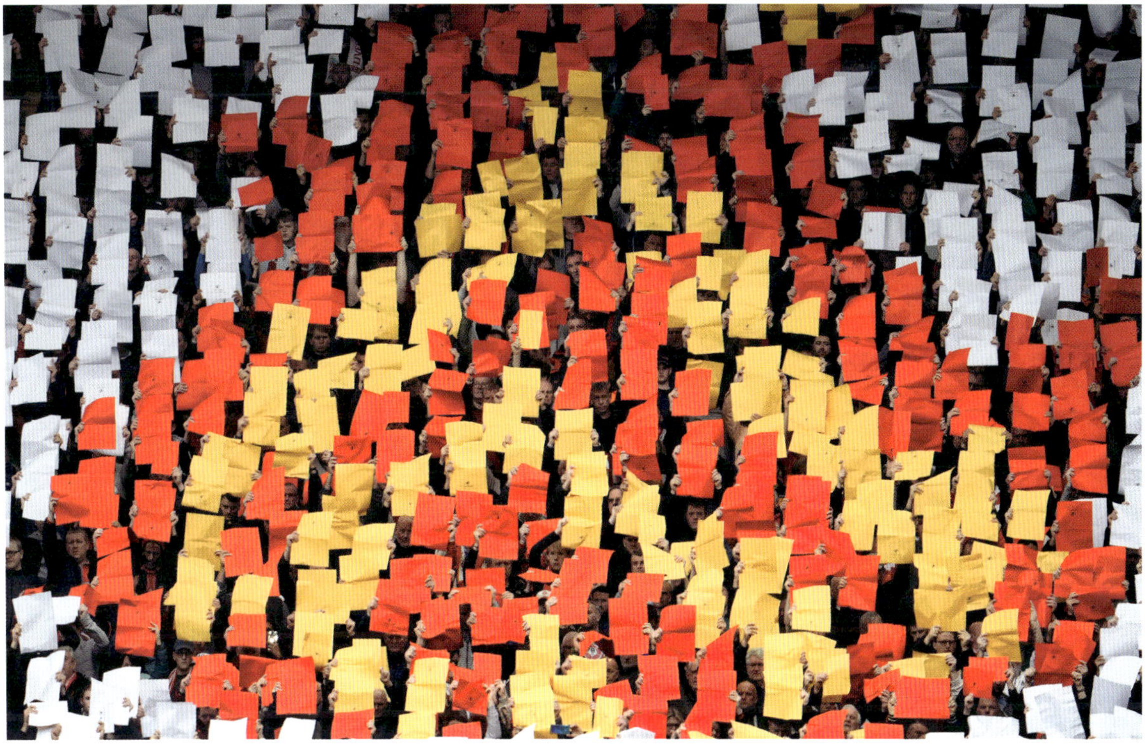

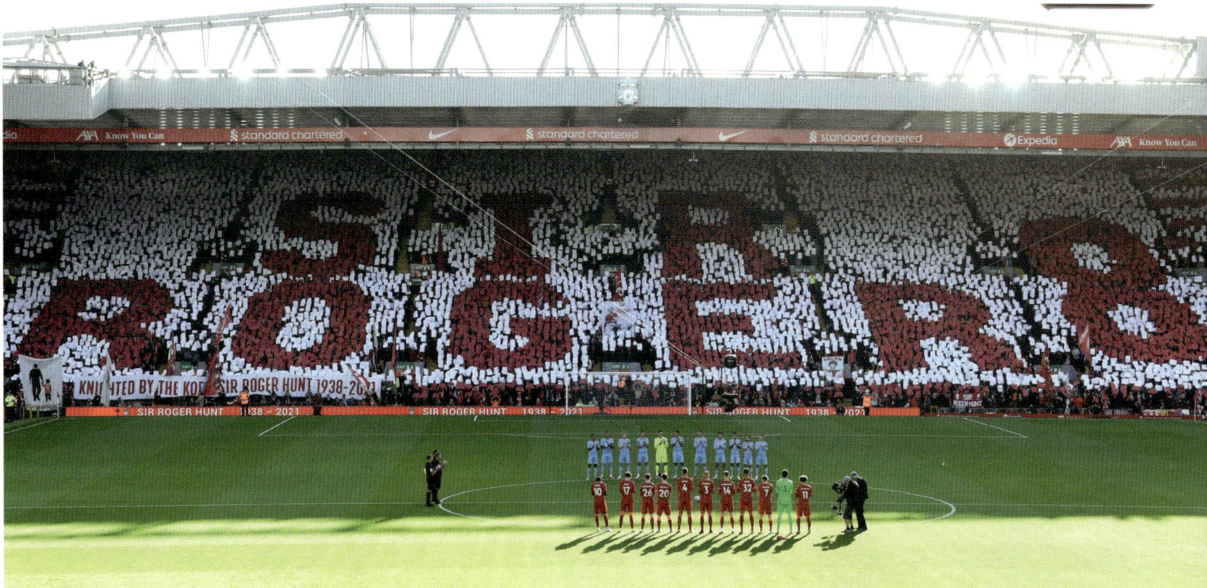

Before Liverpool's big match with Manchester City kicked off on Sunday 3 October 2021, the Kop mosaic spelt out the words 'SIR ROGER' and Hunt's shirt number '8' both in red on a white background, and Klopp wrote in his notes: "I hope the outpouring of love and appreciation brings comfort to his family. I hope they again see why the Liverpool fans choose to honour him as a 'Sir'.

"I saw a quote from him saying that honour coming from the Kop meant more than it ever could coming from any establishment or organisation. We stand to remember and pay tribute and then we try to play in a way he would have been proud of: be selfless, committed and adventurous."

Ray Kennedy's mosaic, on Saturday 11 December 2021 for the visit of Steven Gerrard's Aston Villa, was a simple number 5 in white on an all-red background and just as impactful.

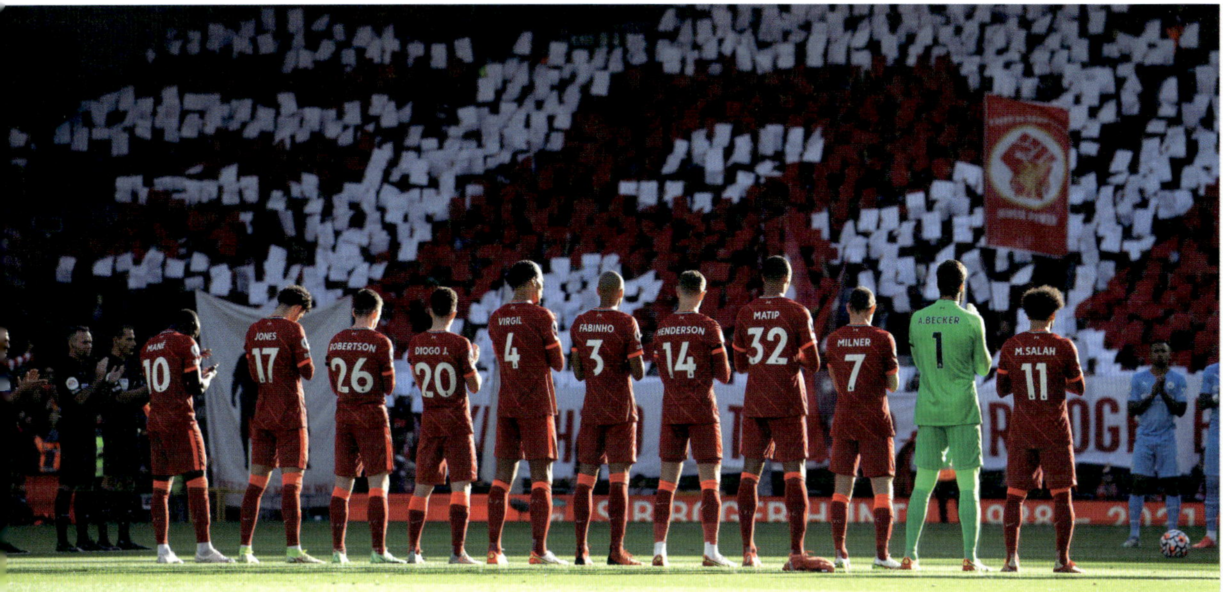
MANÉ
10
JONES
17
ROBERTSON
26
DIOGO J.
20
VIRGIL
4
FABINHO
3
HENDERSON
14
MATIP
32
MILNER
7
A.BECKER
1
M.SALAH
11

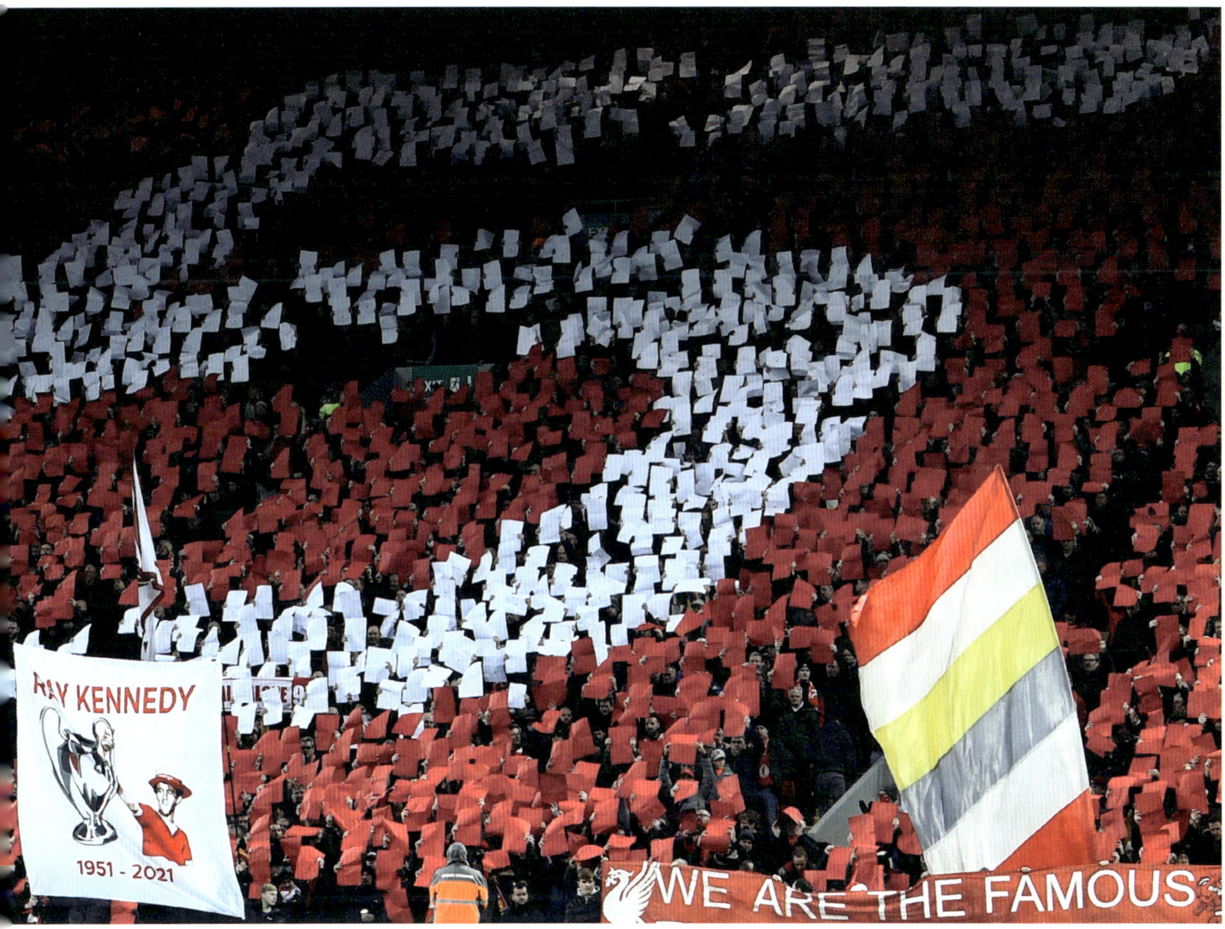
RAY KENNEDY
1951 - 2021
WE ARE THE FAMOUS

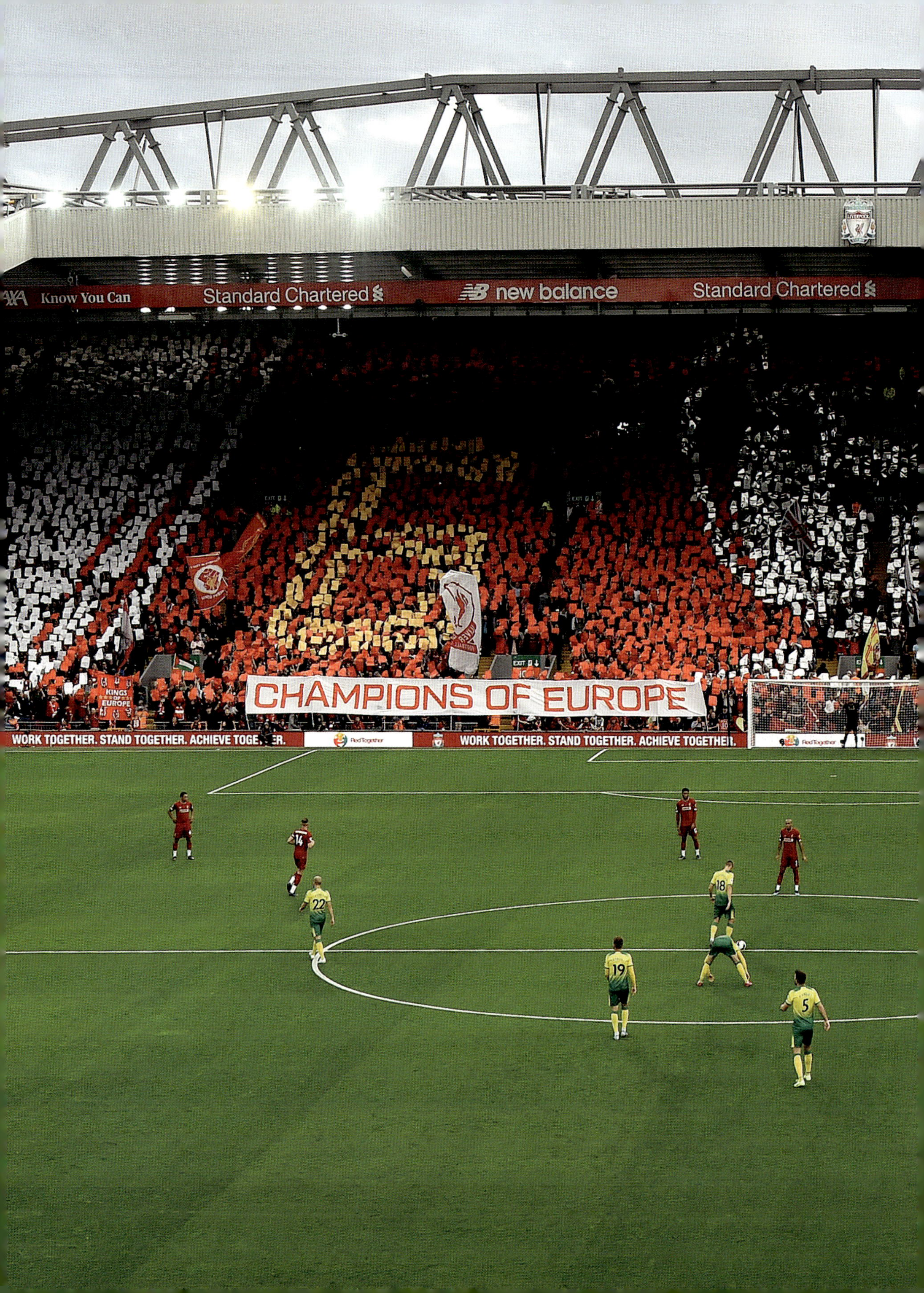

Know You Can
Standard Chartered
new balance
Standard Chartered
CHAMPIONS OF EUROPE
WORK TOGETHER. STAND TOGETHER. ACHIEVE TOGETHER.

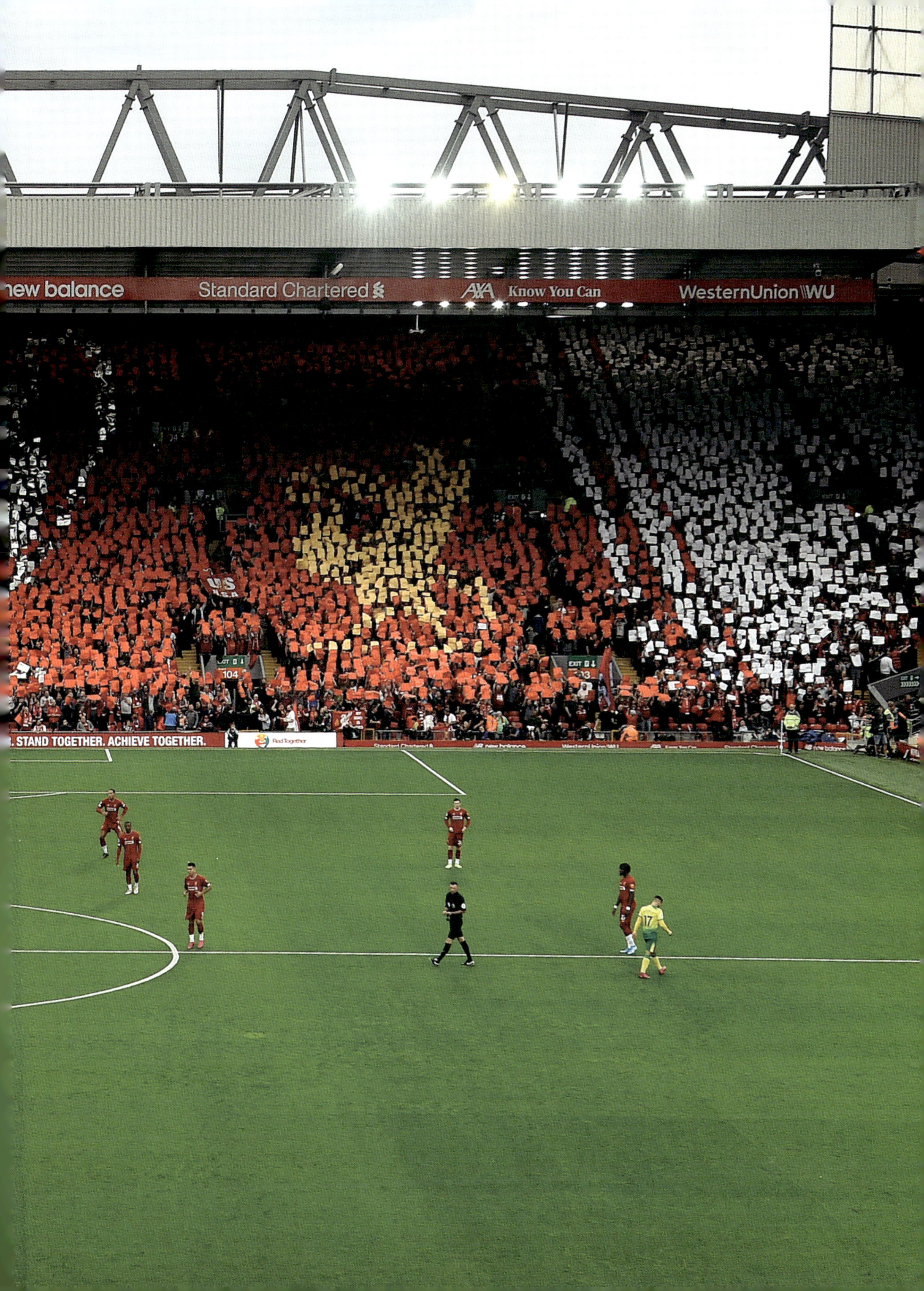
new balance
Standard Chartered
AXA Know You Can
WesternUnion WU
STAND TOGETHER. ACHIEVE TOGETHER.

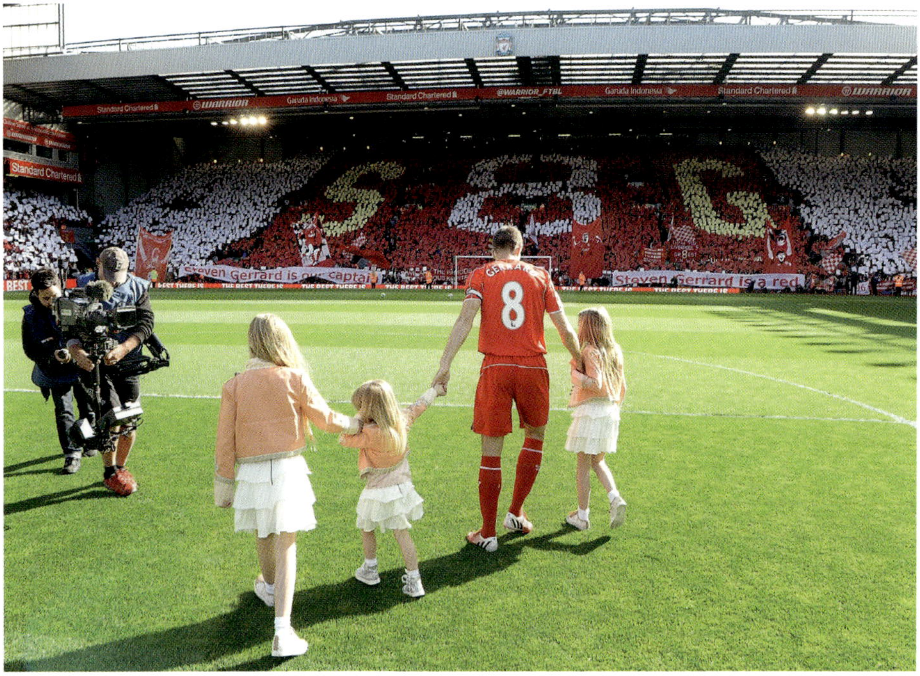

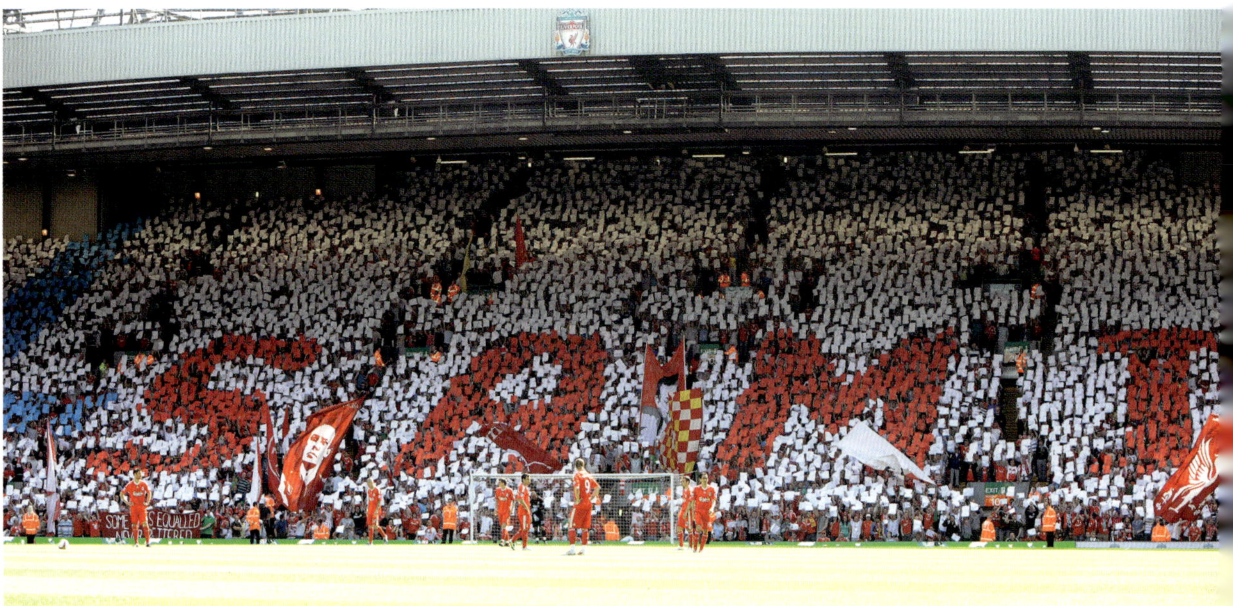

Back in May 2015 departing skipper and all-time great Steven Gerrard was presented with a mosaic in his own honour, and two years previously it was retiring centre-half and fellow local hero Jamie Carragher – both in the final home games of the season in question. Another central defender, Sami Hyypia, was reduced to tears by his send-off with a colourful Kop mosaic in 2009.

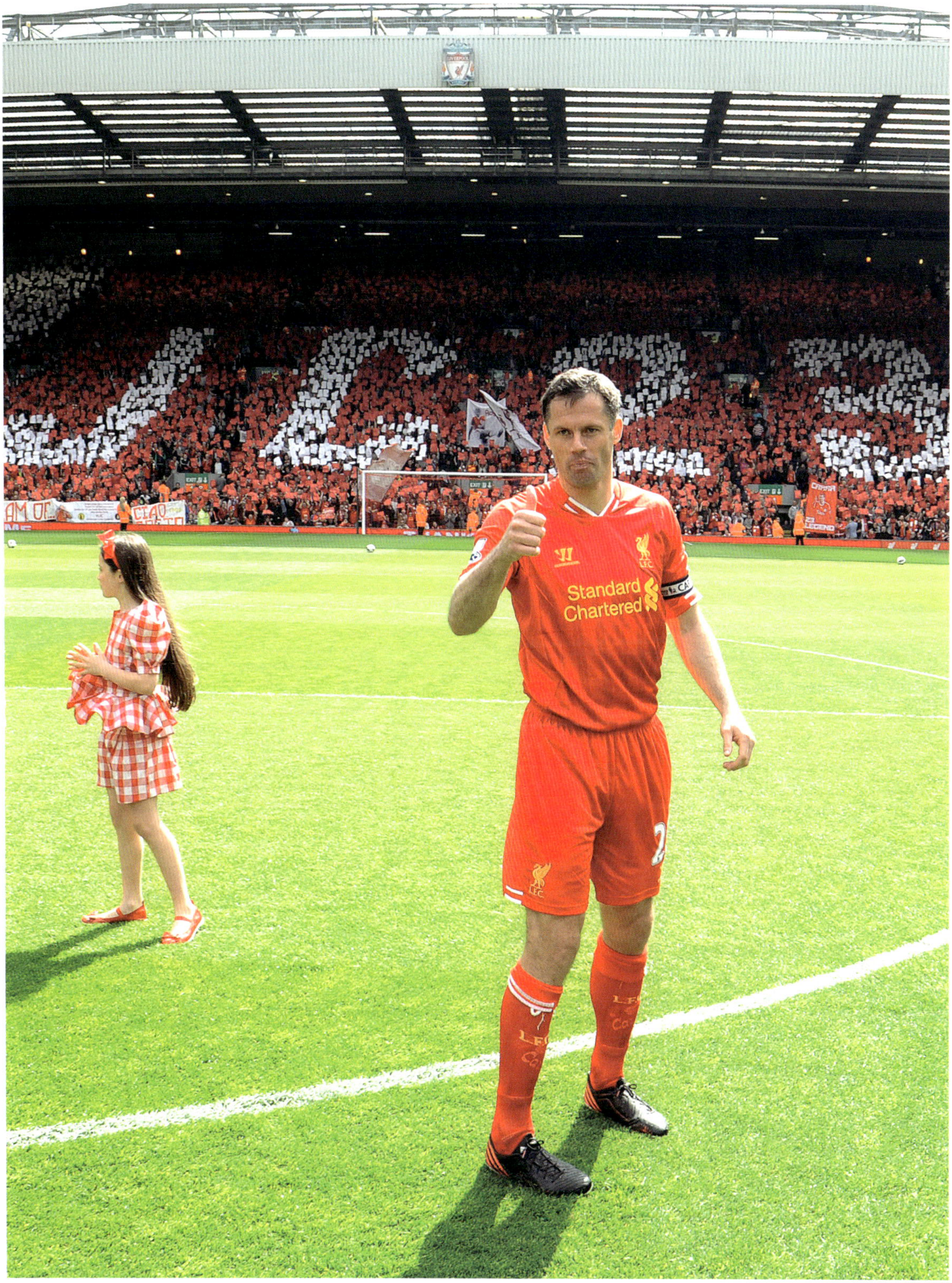
Standard Chartered

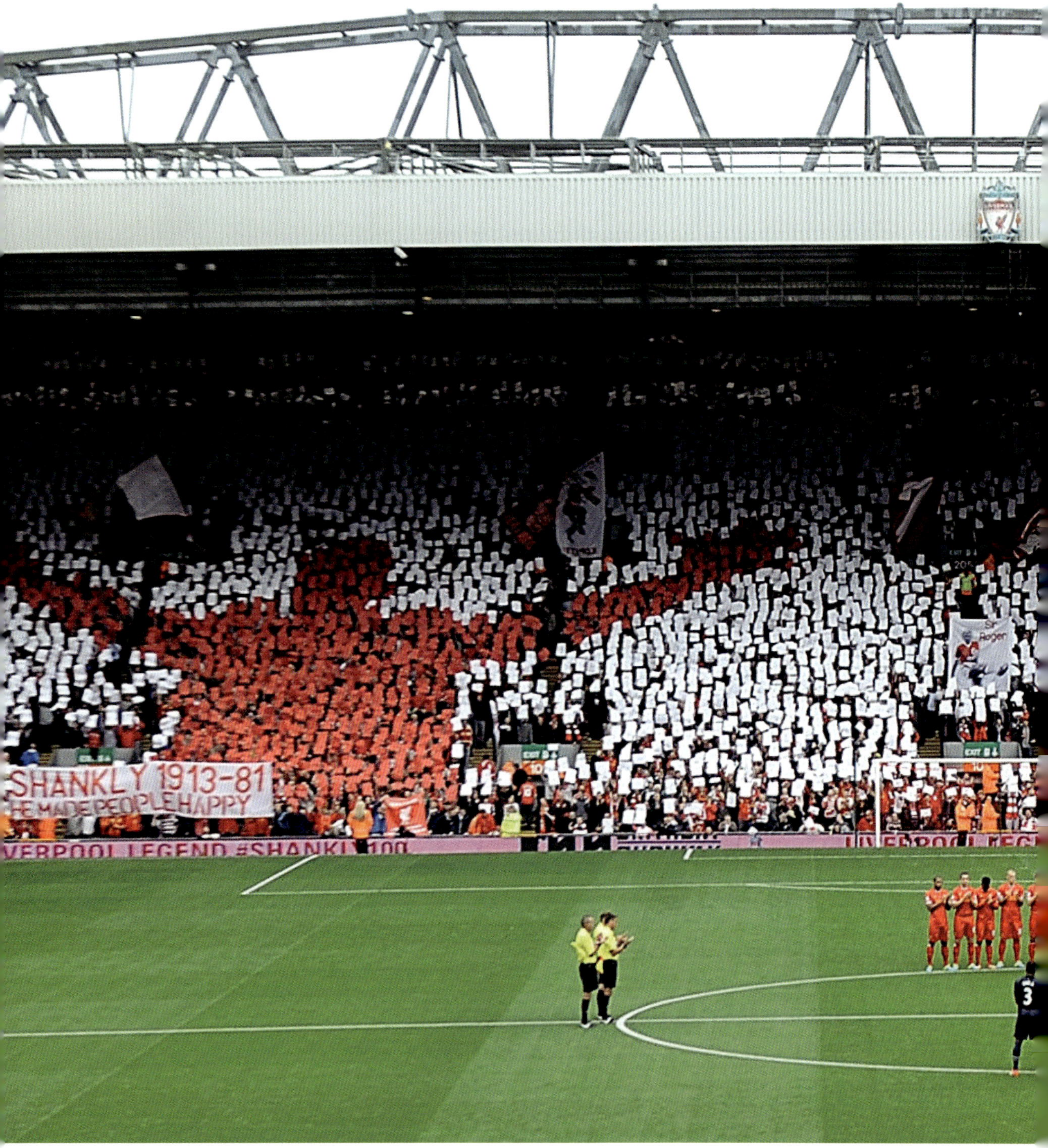
SHANKLY 1913-81
HE MADE PEOPLE HAPPY

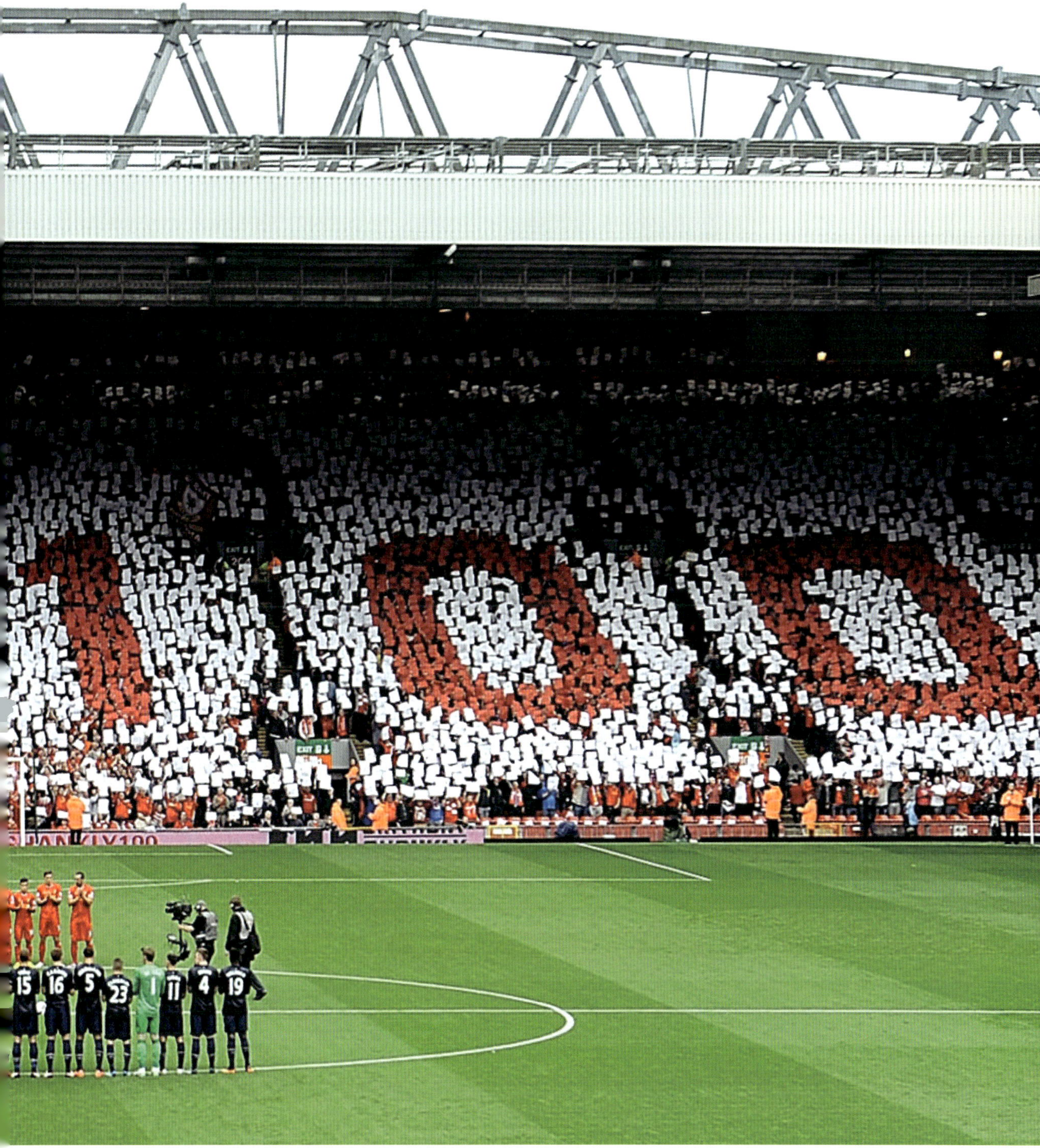

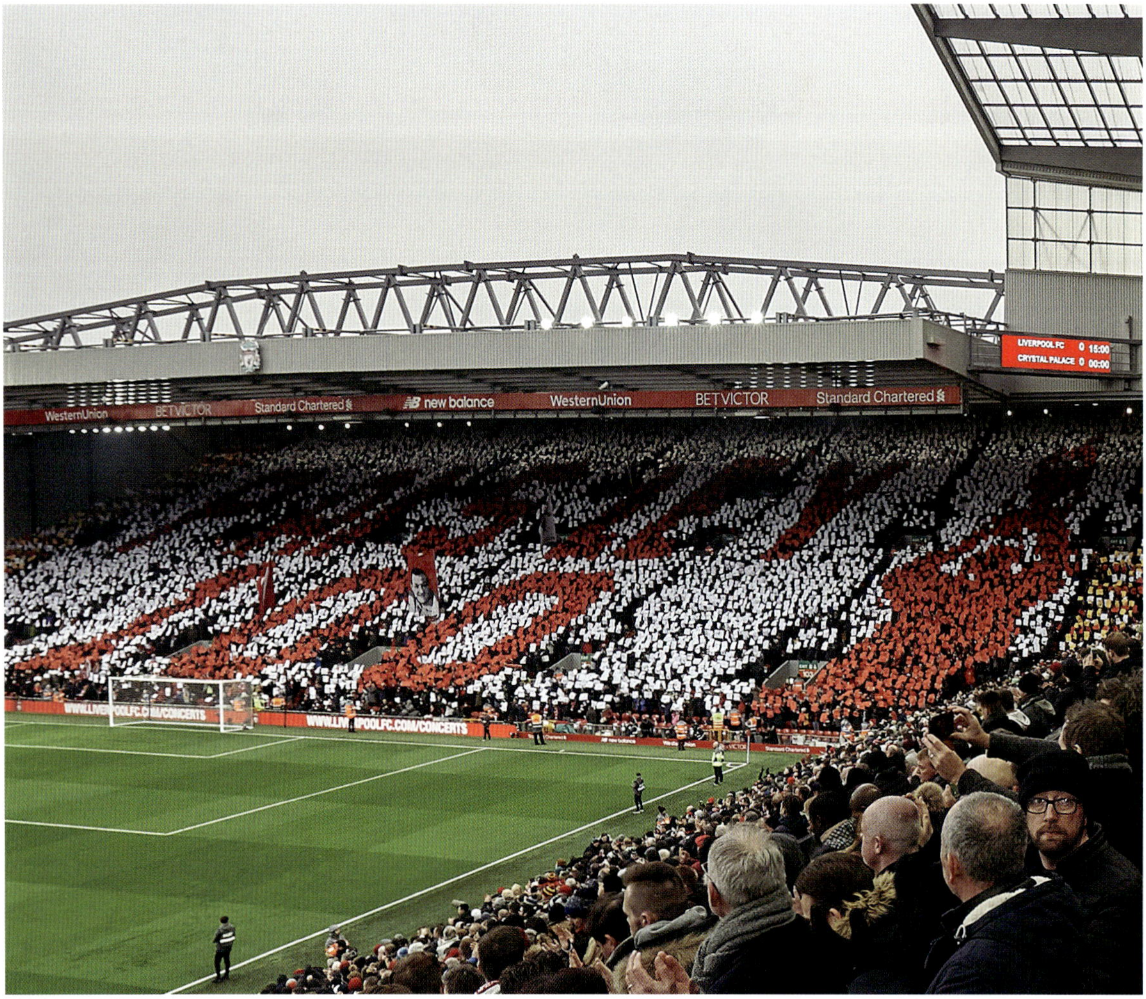
WesternUnion
BETVICTOR
Standard Chartered
new balance
LIVERPOOL FC 0 15:00
CRYSTAL PALACE 0 00:00
WWW.LIVERPOOLFC.COM/CONCERTS

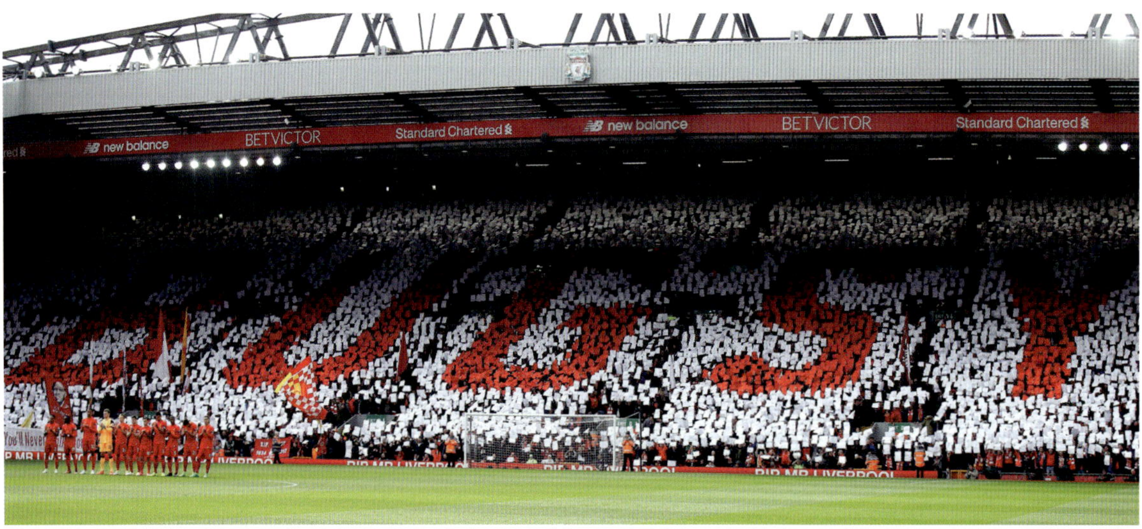
new balance
BETVICTOR
Standard Chartered

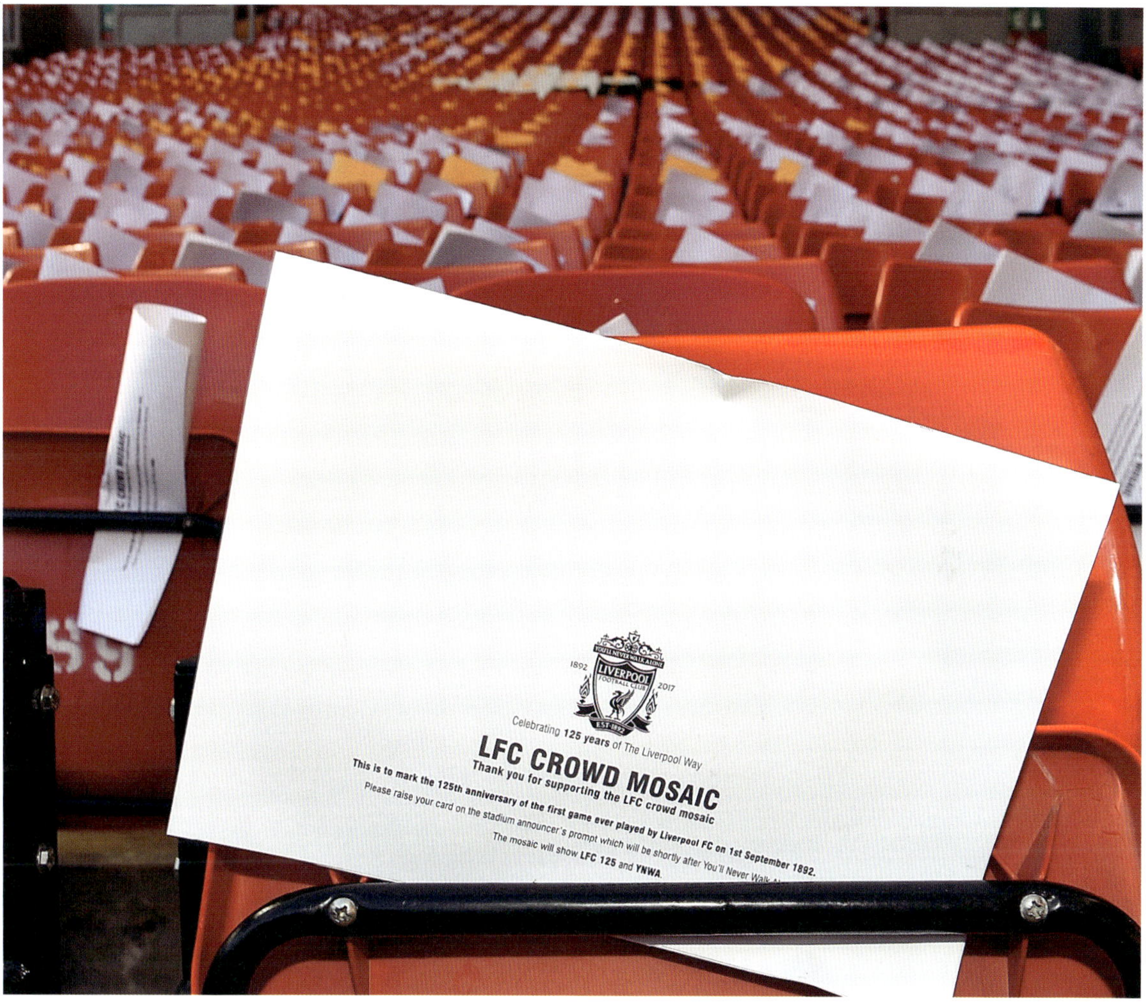

The great Bill Shankly was honoured both in 2009 on the 50th anniversary of his arrival at Anfield and in 2013 on the centenary of his birth. So too were Bob Paisley upon his 100th birthday in 2019 and Ronnie 'Bugsy' Moran, another great club servant, when he passed away in 2017. And earlier in the millennium there were three mosaics for ex-manager Gerard Houllier.

There have been celebrations, too, to mark the return to Champions League participation in season 2014/15 and Liverpool FC's sixth European Cup success in 2018/19.

Designer Andy told *The Guide Liverpool* website that the mosaic phenomenon originated from "a meeting with club officials in the mid-1990s about how to get a good atmosphere back into the Kop after the stadium became an all-seater. Genoa had done a mosaic when we played them [in the 1991/92 UEFA Cup] and I thought I could do that. I had my own printing business at the time and I offered to do it – we just had to overcome the logistics of attaching sheets of card to the seats [in the stand] and praying the fans would lift them up!"

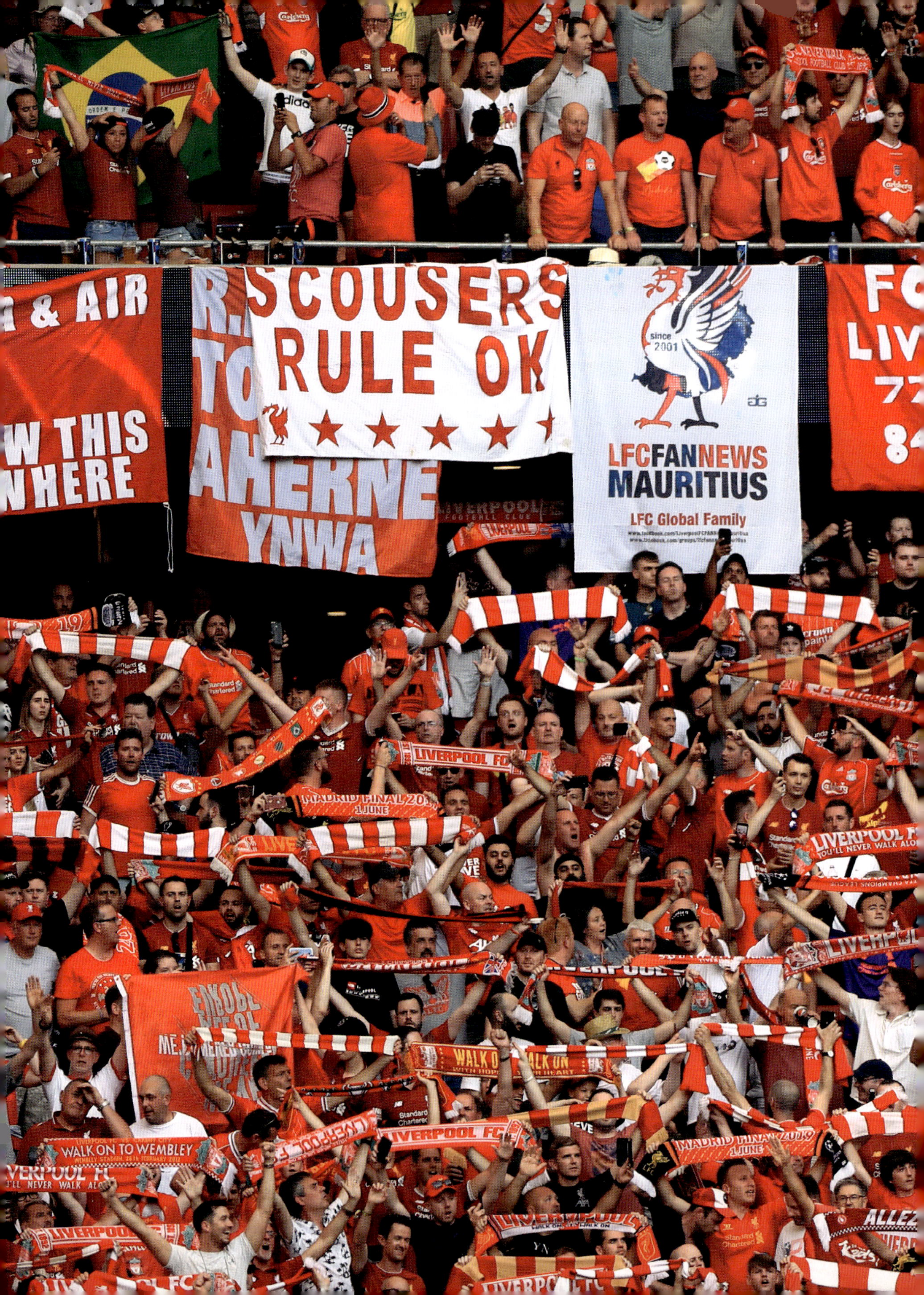
SCOUSERS
RULE OK
since 2001
LFCFANNEWS
MAURITIUS
LFC Global Family
YNWA
MADRID FINAL 2019
1 JUNE
LIVERPOOL FC
WALK ON TO WEMBLEY
ALLEZ

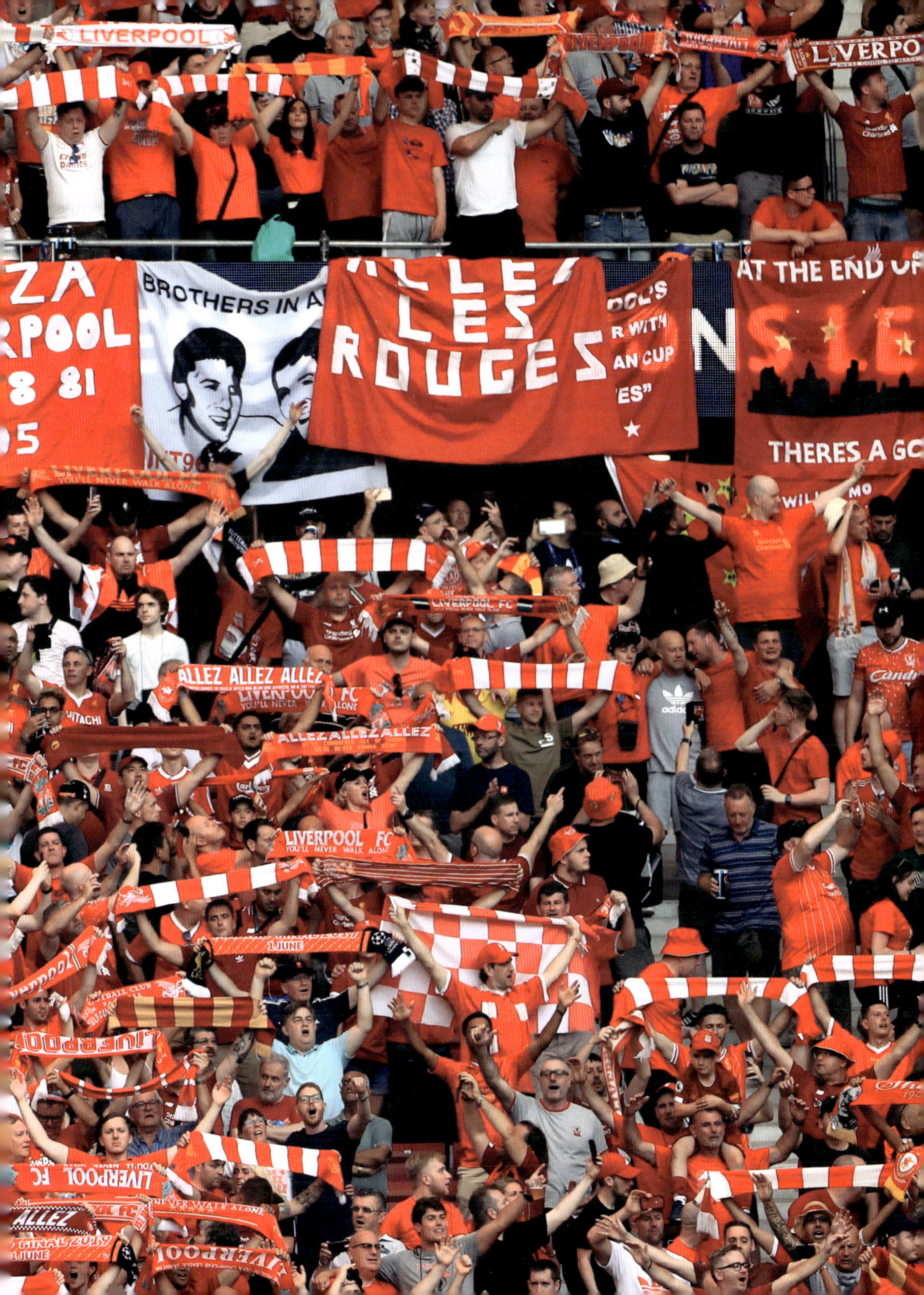
LIVERPOOL
ZA
RPOOL
8 81
5
BROTHERS IN A
LES
ROUGES
AT THE END OF
THERES A GO
ALLEZ ALLEZ ALLEZ
LIVERPOOL FC
ALLEZ ALLEZ ALLEZ
LIVERPOOL FC
YOU'LL NEVER WALK ALONE
1 JUNE
LIVERPOOL FC
ALLEZ
1 JUNE
LIVERPOOL

Kop on tour

Cup finals are an LFC speciality and bring out the very best in the travelling Reds

We are loyal supporters, and we come from Liverpool... Win or lose, one thing you can guarantee about a major final featuring Liverpool is an epic sea of flags and banners in the Red end of the ground. And it's always overwhelmingly red – with concessions only to white and occasional yellow – thanks to an unwritten rule among supporters about what it means to be part of this fabulous LFC family.

Season 2021/22 saw three trips to Wembley, long dubbed 'Anfield South', as Jürgen Klopp's side claimed first the Carabao Cup then (via a semi-final victory over Manchester City under the arch) the FA Cup, both after a penalty shootout against Chelsea and both serenaded by a Spion Kop transported *en masse* to the capital with all those familiar flags and banners from Anfield and then some. Liver Birds and legends, modern-day heroes, witty one-liners and motivational words writ large and draped all over the national stadium's tiers.

After all those miserable months of behind-closed-doors football it felt like a huge, collective, colour-saturated cry of joy. One banner proclaimed simply, just like the Jürgen song, 'I FEEL FINE'.

It's been the same in Europe of course. Klopp's first two such finals ended in defeat: to Sevilla in the 2016 Europa League in Basel, then to Real Madrid in the 2018 Champions League in Kyiv. It hurt, but the Reds were back competing for continental silverware and the party had well-and-truly started and one of the hundreds of banners on display in the Ukrainian capital summed it up: "If LFC were playing on the moon, we'd find a way to get there."

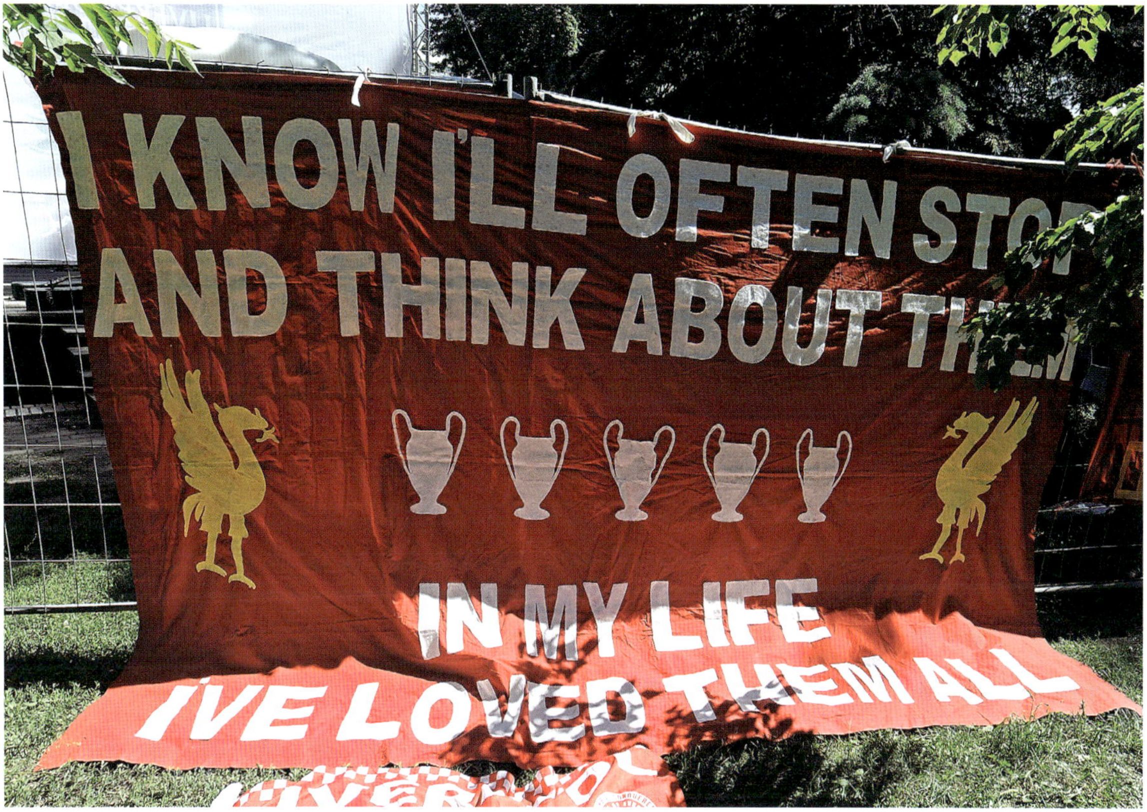
I KNOW I'LL OFTEN STO
AND THINK ABOUT TH
IN MY LIFE
IVE LOVED THEM ALL

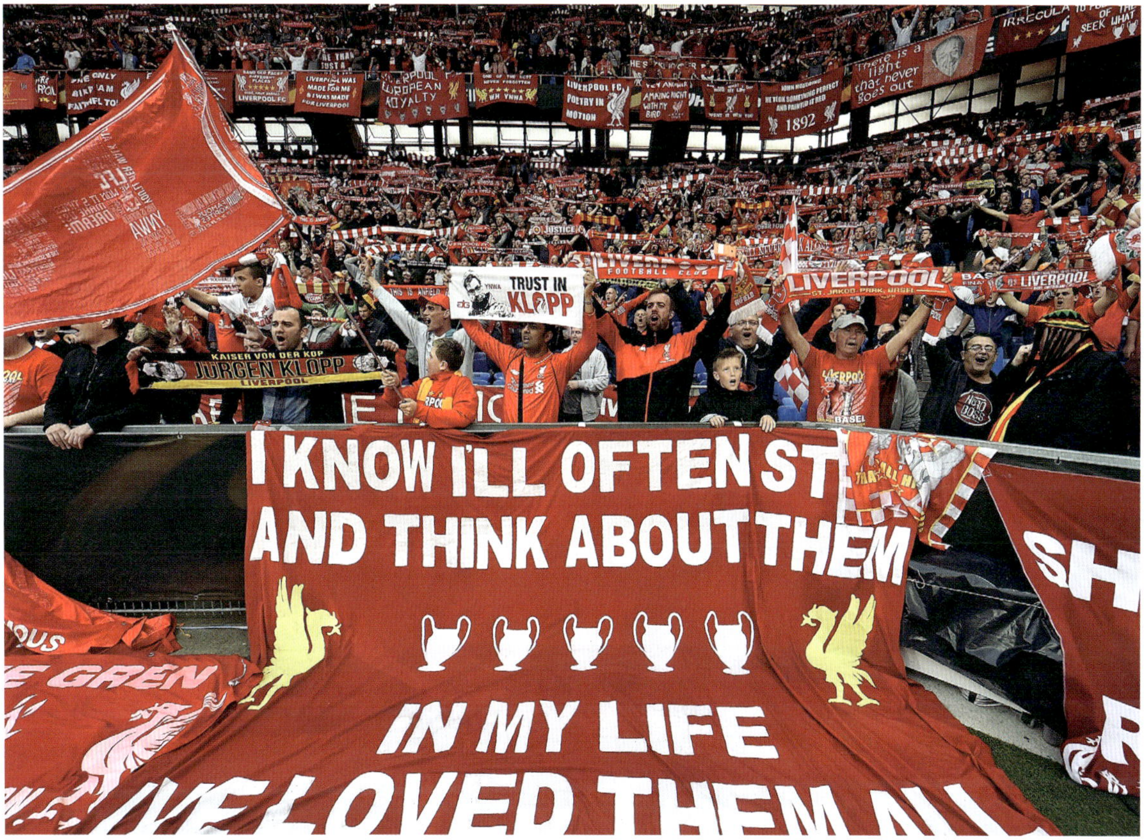
TRUST IN
KLOPP
KAISER VON DER KOP
JÜRGEN KLOPP
LIVERPOOL
I KNOW I'LL OFTEN ST
AND THINK ABOUT THEM
IN MY LIFE

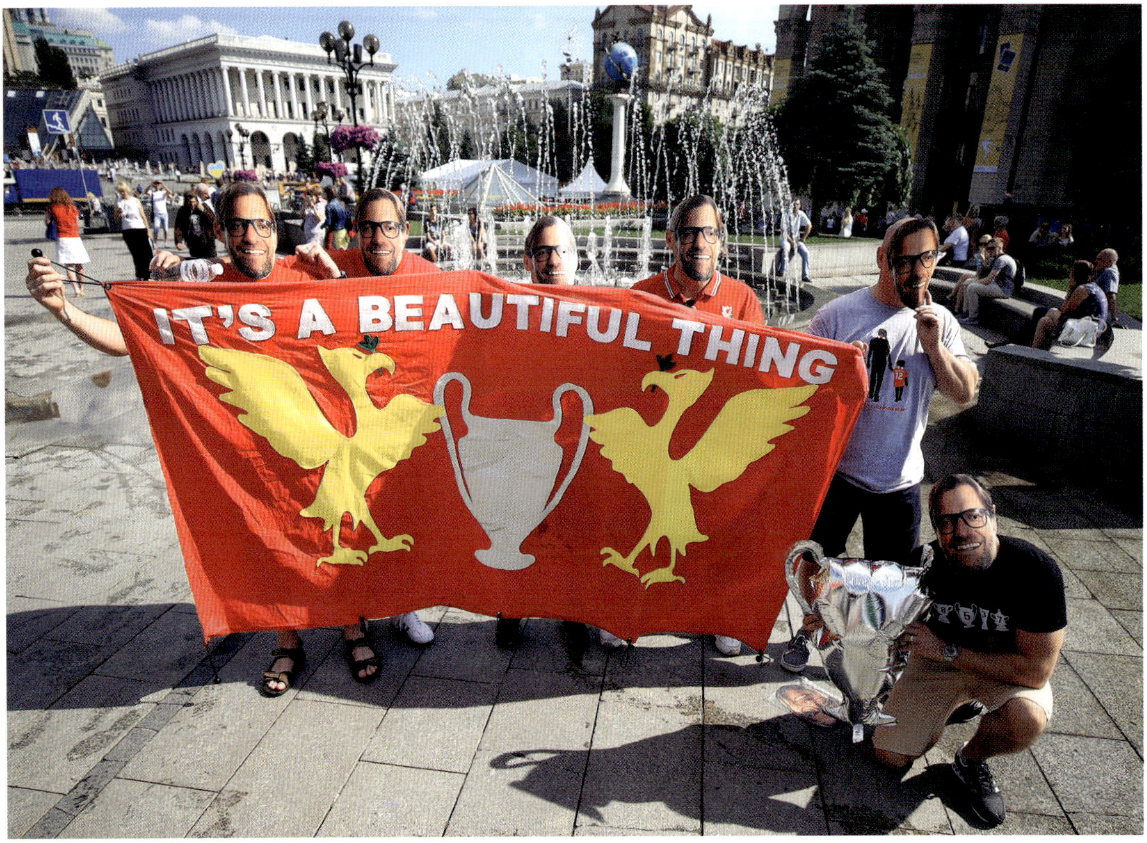
IT'S A BEAUTIFUL THING

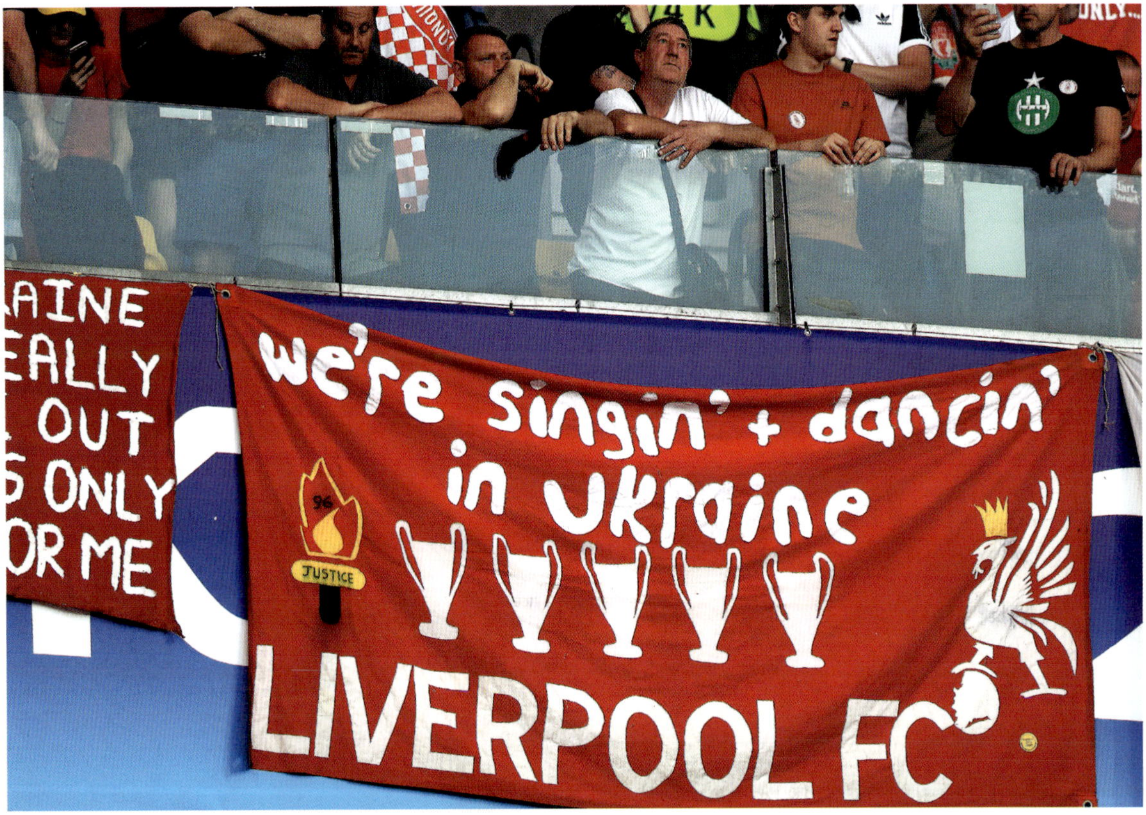
AINE
EALLY
OUT
S ONLY
OR ME
we're singin' + dancin'
in Ukraine
96
JUSTICE
LIVERPOOL FC

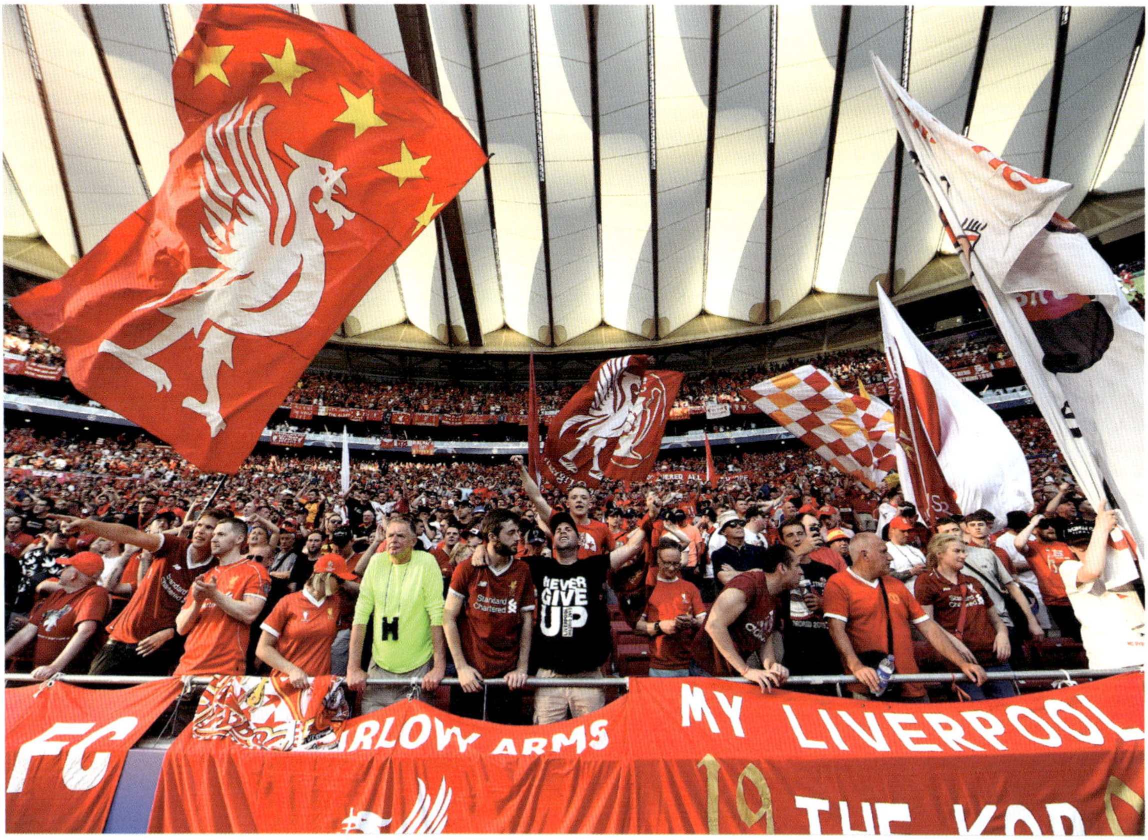
MY LIVERPOOL
FC
NEVER GIVE UP

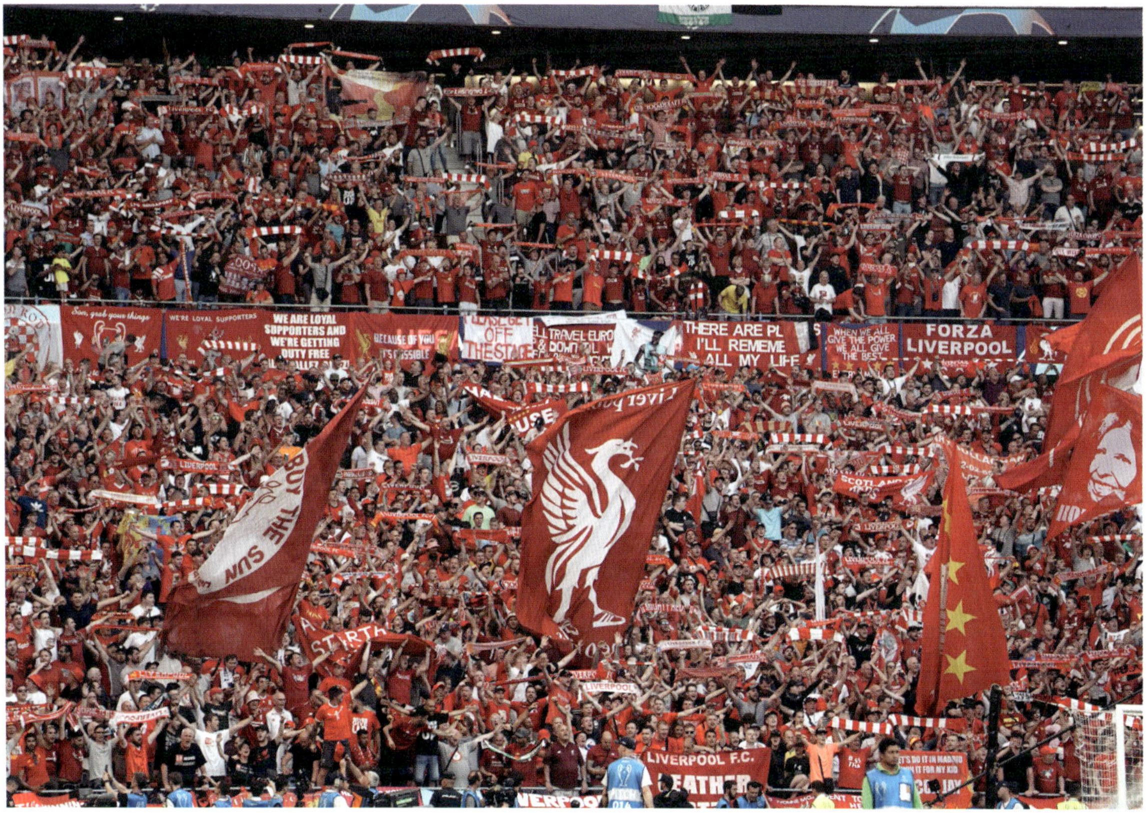
FORZA LIVERPOOL
WE ARE LOYAL SUPPORTERS AND WE'RE GETTING DUTY FREE
LIVERPOOL F.C.

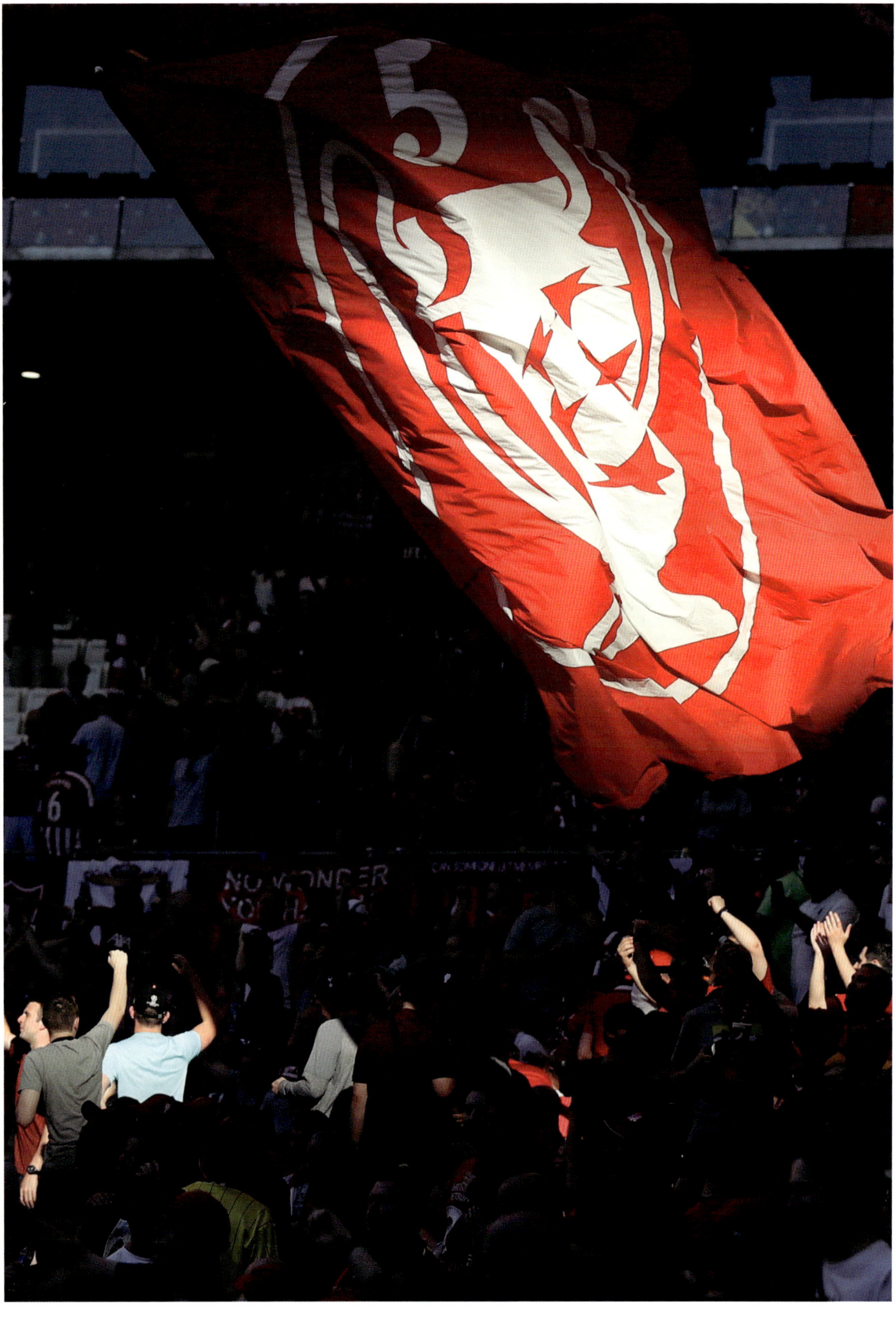

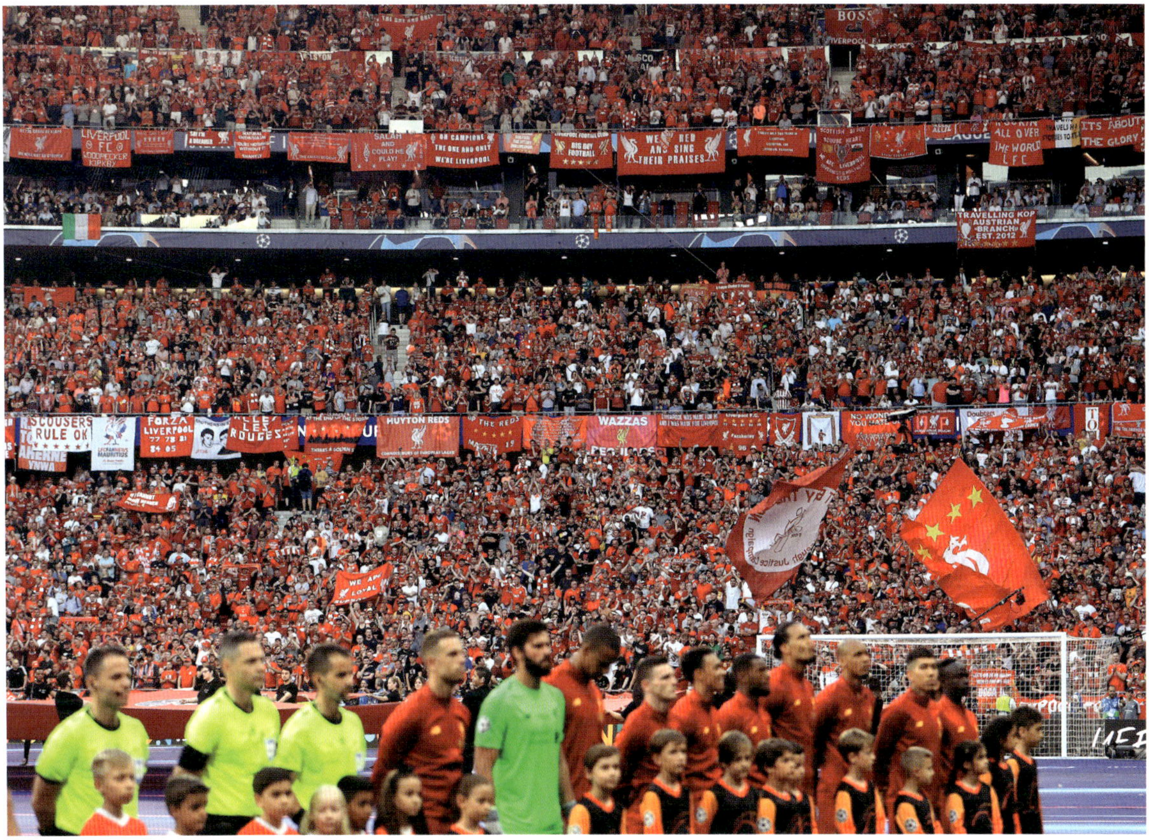
TRAVELLING KOP
AUSTRIAN
BRANCH
EST. 2012
SCOUSERS
RULE OK
HUYTON REDS
WAZZAS
WE ARE LOYAL

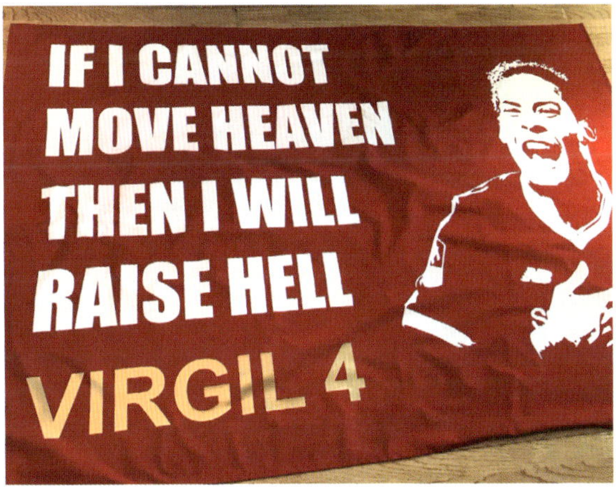
IF I CANNOT
MOVE HEAVEN
THEN I WILL
RAISE HELL
VIRGIL 4

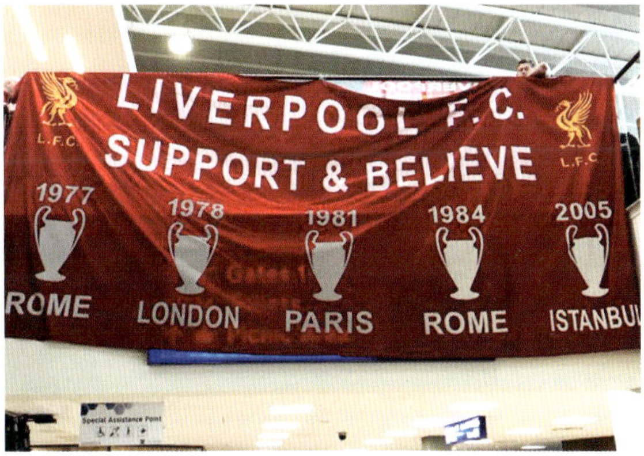
LIVERPOOL F.C.
SUPPORT & BELIEVE
1977
ROME
1978
LONDON
1981
PARIS
1984
ROME
2005
ISTANBU

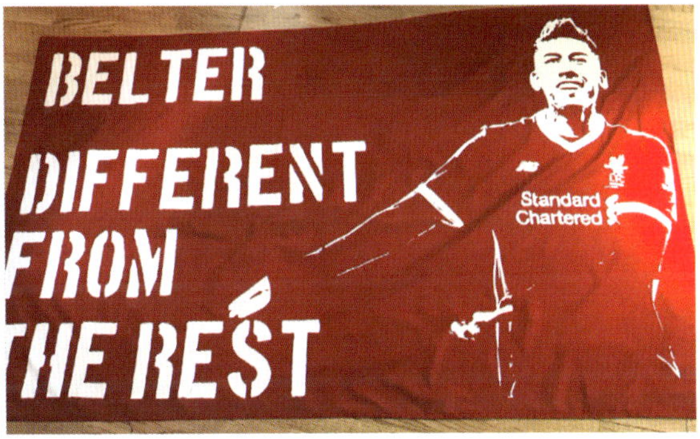
BELTER
DIFFERENT
FROM
THE REST
Standard Chartered

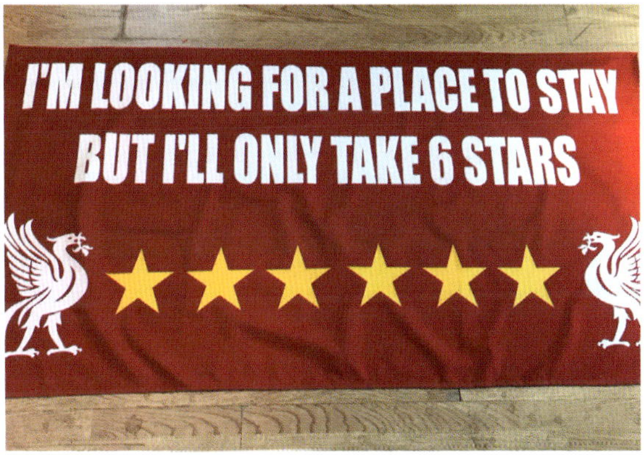
I'M LOOKING FOR A PLACE TO STAY
BUT I'LL ONLY TAKE 6 STARS

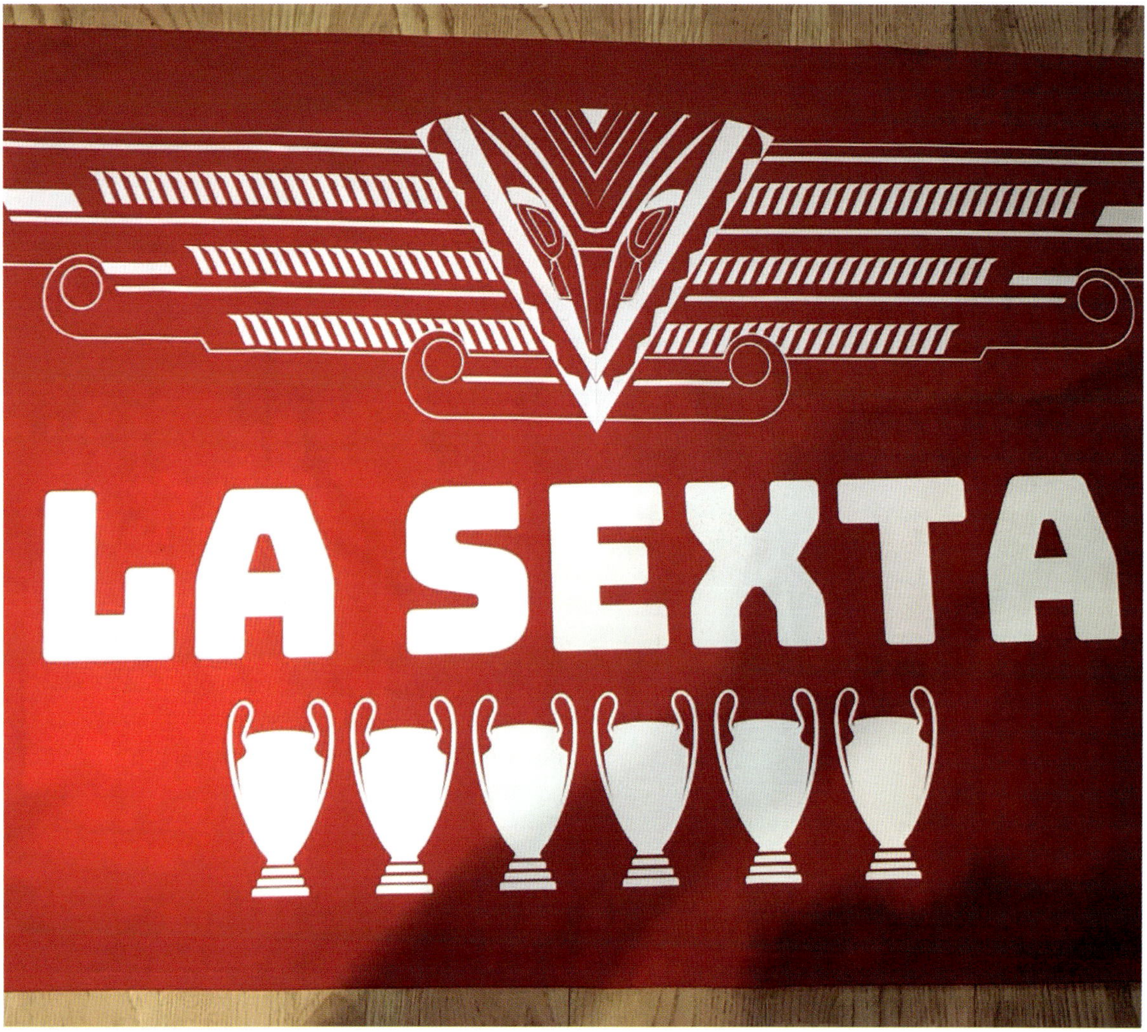

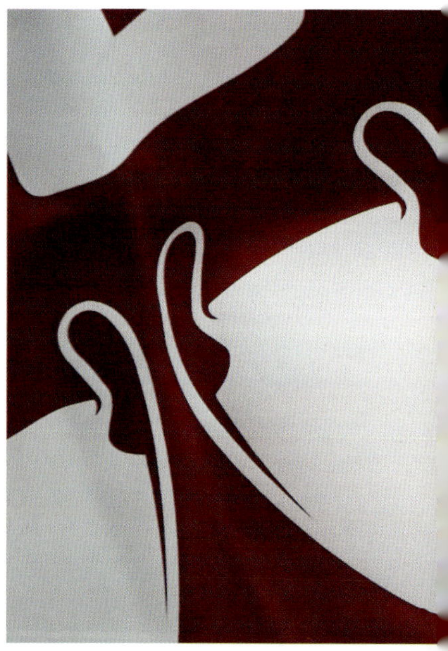

Spain is easy-peasy by comparison but even so Liverpool fans staked out Madrid as their own days before the Champions League final against Tottenham Hotspur in 2019. Seventy-five thousand was the modest estimate with many enjoying the pre-match fun in LFC's designated fan-park but resigned (without tickets) to watching the action in bars and restaurants around the city.

Inside the Wanda Metropolitano some familiar big flags made it feel like home – the Liver Bird in trainers, Ol' Big Ears with five stars on it, the dancing Kopite from the bygone *Football Echo*, Hillsborough campaigner Anne Williams always remembered – and that was the whole idea.

Tony Barrett, the club's head of supporter liaison, would later tweet: "One of the reasons why the Liverpool end looked so spectacular was @SpionKop1906 decided to bring the Kop to Madrid. The effort that they put in to make this happen was well above the call of duty."

Not present in the ground but surely there in spirit was the daddy of them all: the giant Joey Jones banner from 1977, back when it all began. One of its creators, supporter Phil Downey, would pass away a week later.

Then there were all those brand new flags and banners created especially for the final. The LFC matchday programme subsequently ran a feature about a local business called Fitwell TimE Design, which already supplied the club's

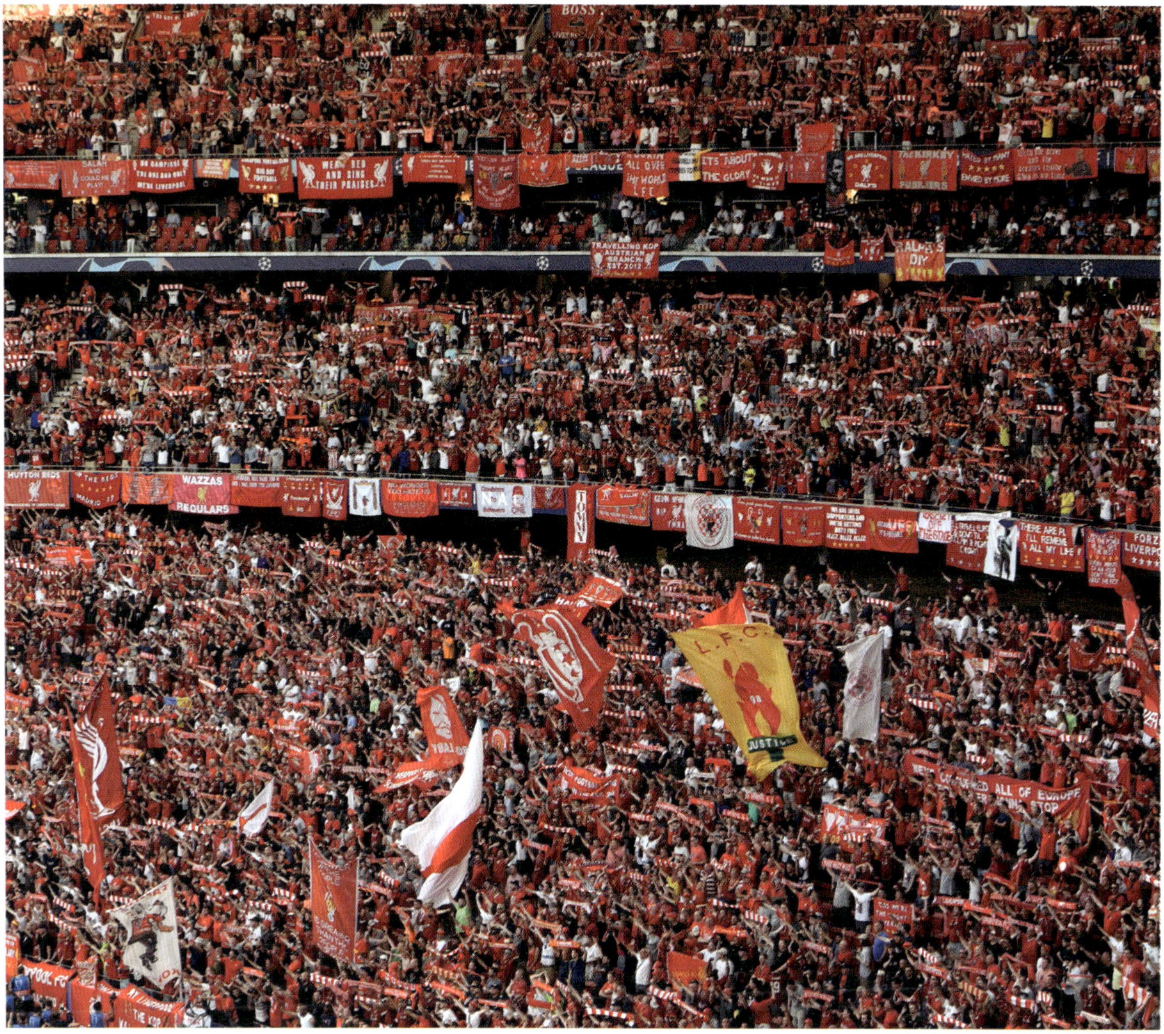

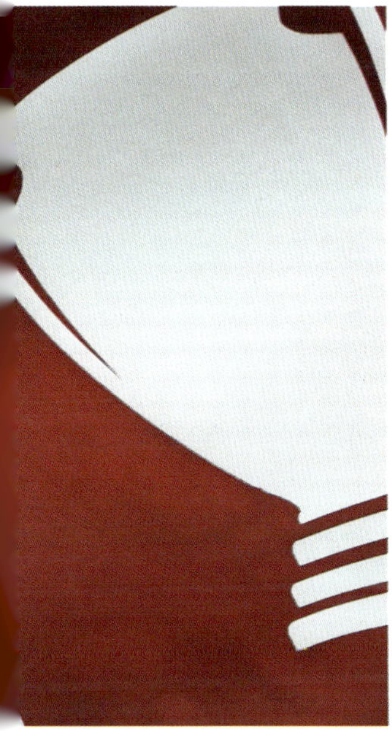

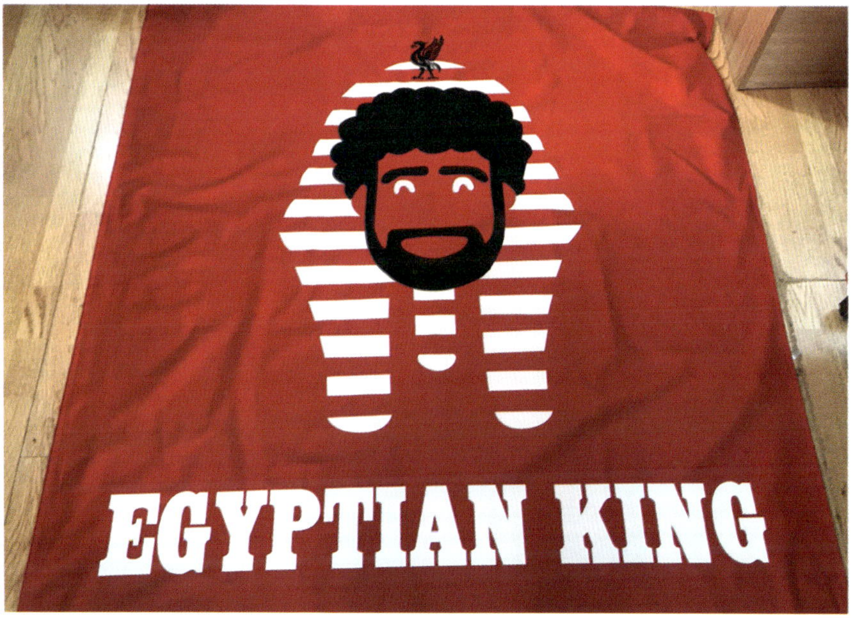
EGYPTIAN KING

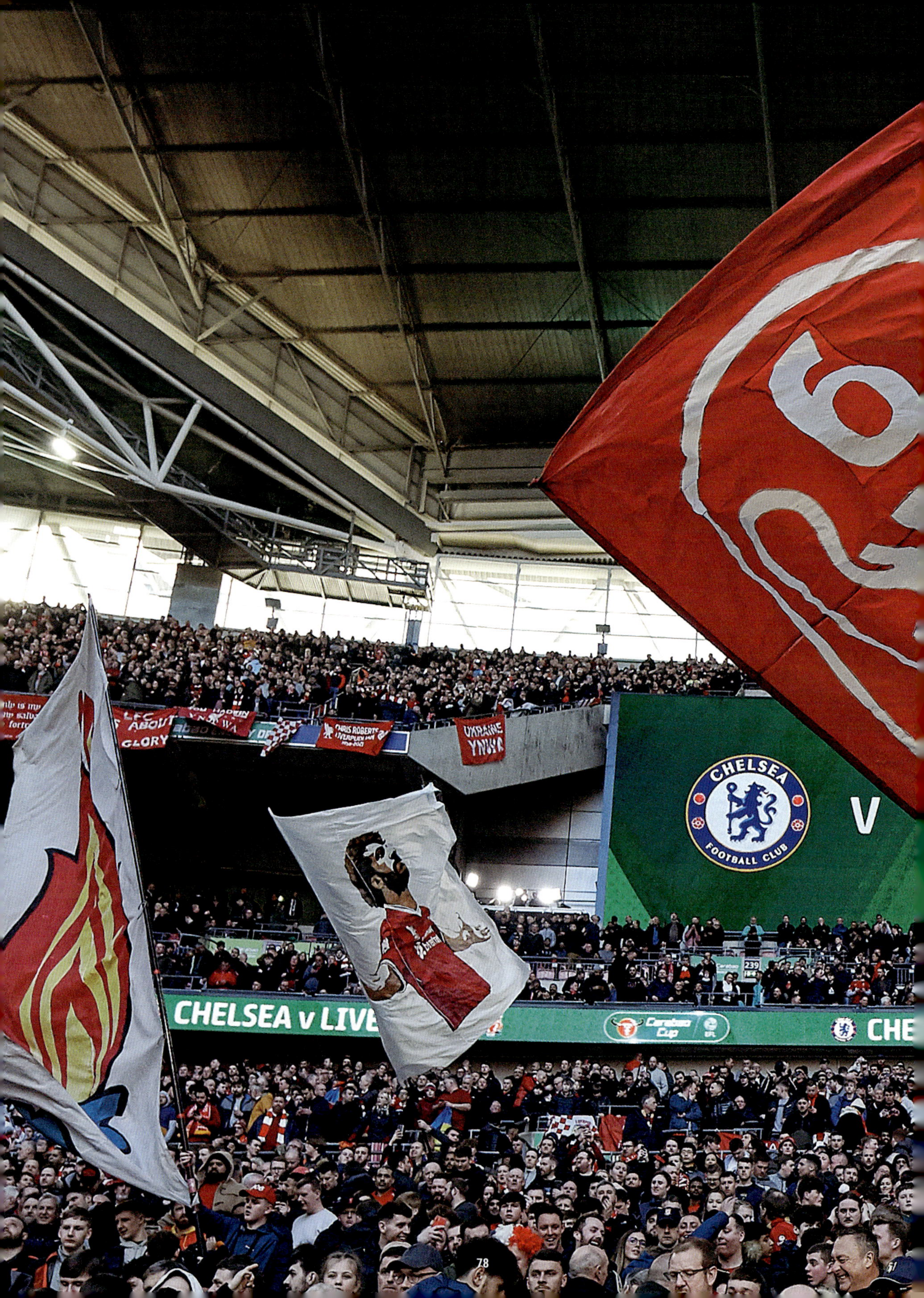
CHELSEA FOOTBALL CLUB
V
CHELSEA v LIVE
Carabao Cup
CHE
UKRAINE
GLORY

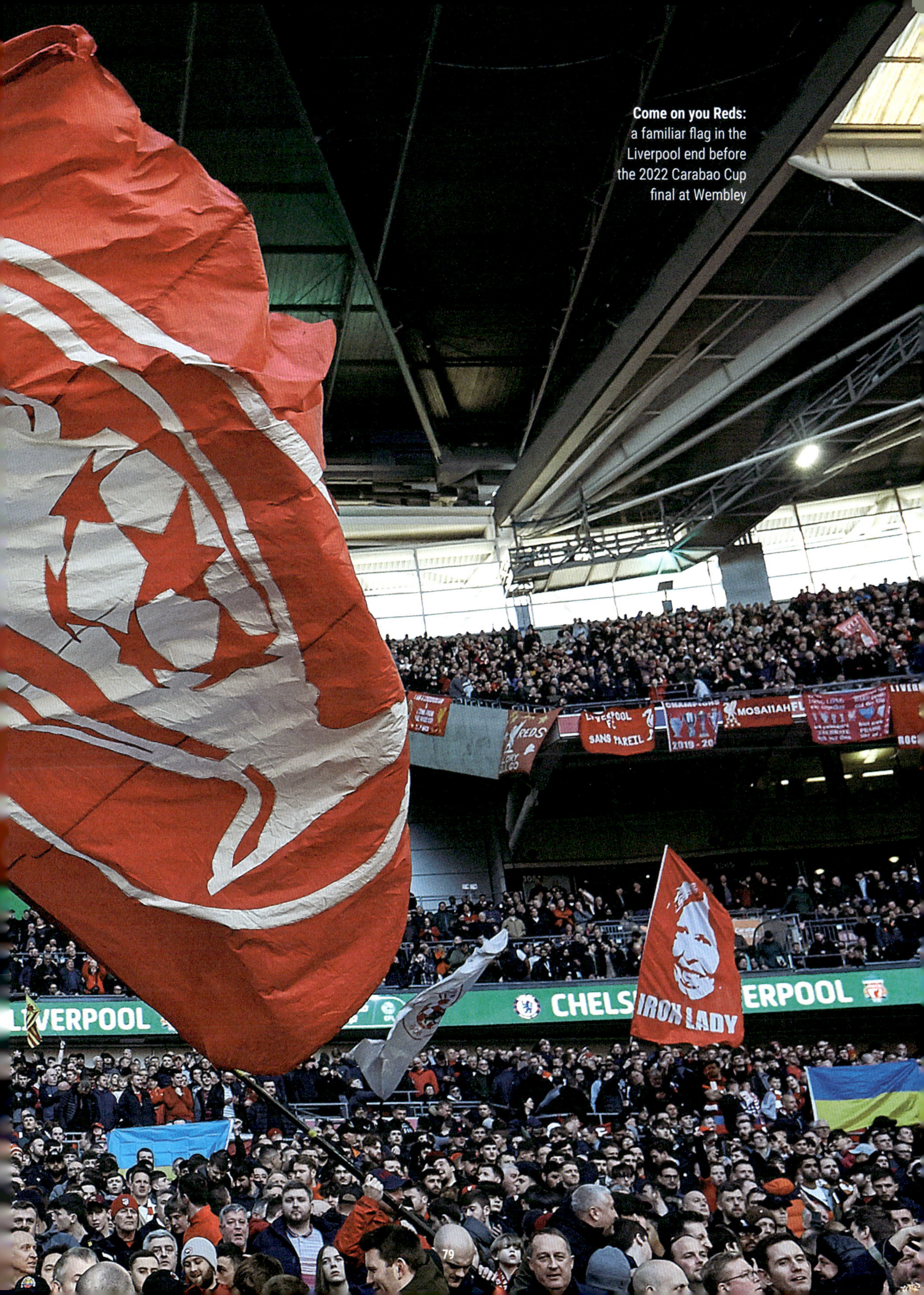

Come on you Reds: a familiar flag in the Liverpool end before the 2022 Carabao Cup final at Wembley

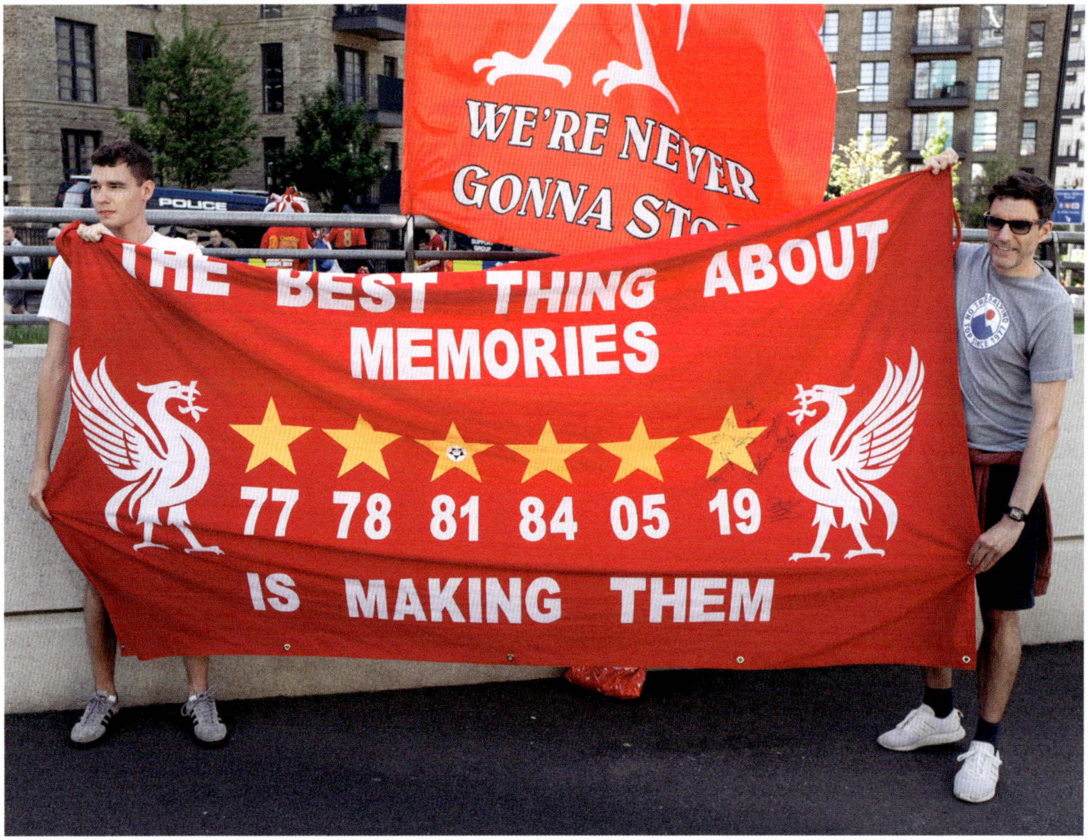
WE'RE NEVER
GONNA STO
POLICE
BEST THING ABOUT
MEMORIES
77 78 81 84 05 19
IS MAKING THEM

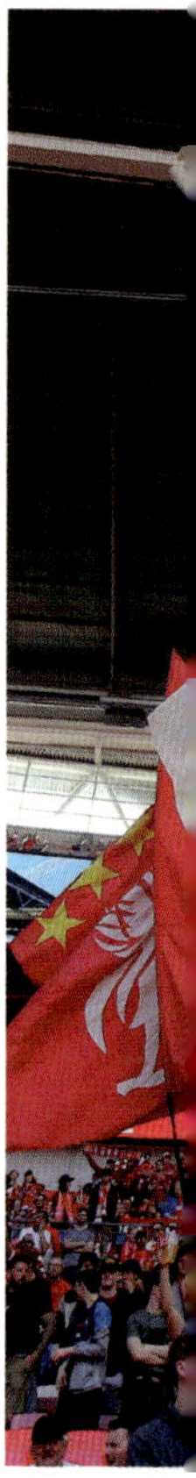

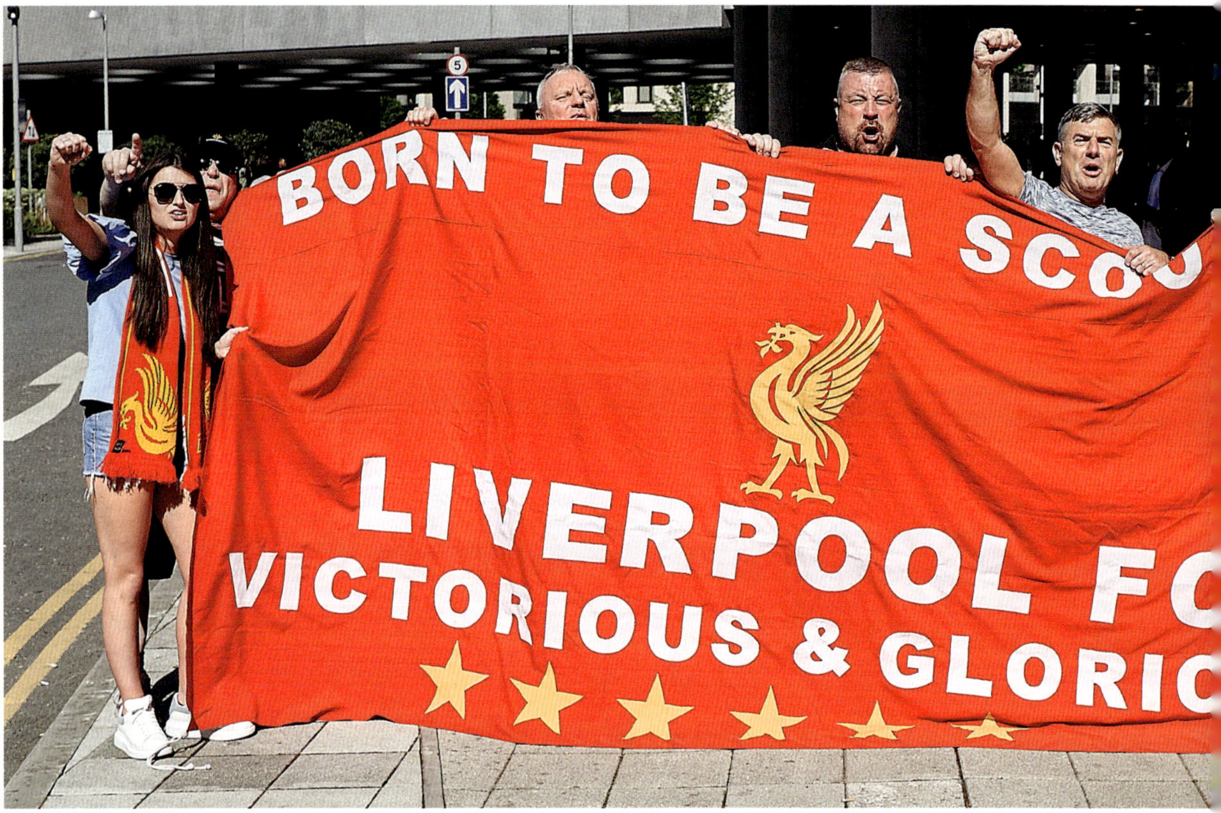
BORN TO BE A SCO
LIVERPOOL F
VICTORIOUS & GLORI

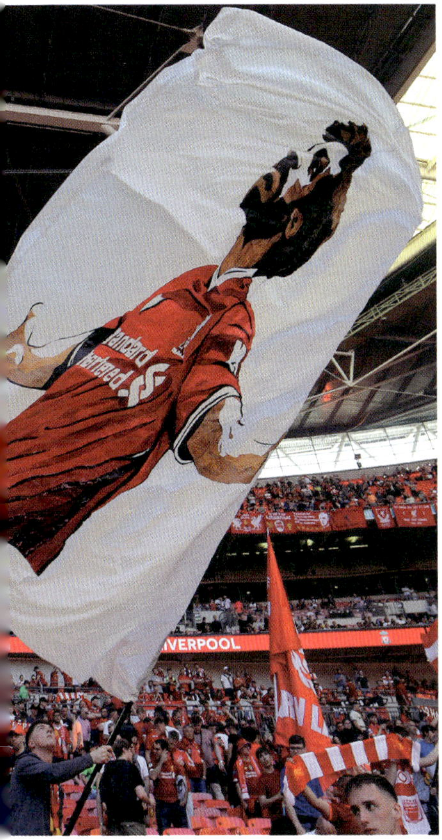

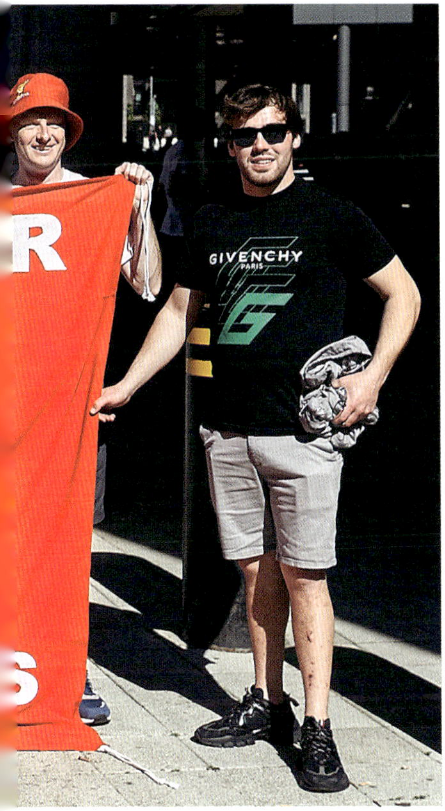

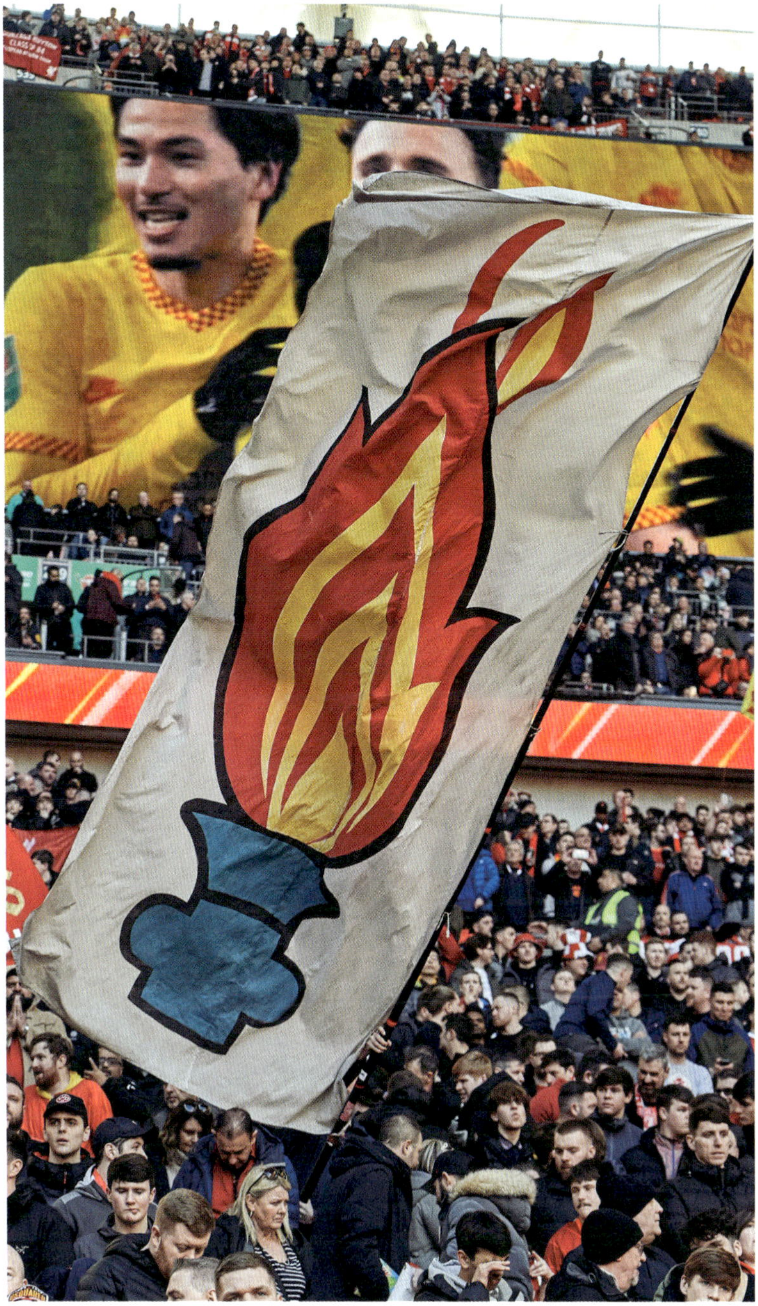

official pennants and was inundated with orders from supporters no sooner had the semi-final against Barcelona been decided so breathtakingly.

Peter MacFarlane, the company's head of marketing, called it "a manic time – we were all coming in early and staying late and I was also running our Twitter page with enquiries through the night.

"We were making them right up to the day of the final as even people who weren't lucky enough to be going to Madrid wanted to be part of it. It was funny to see so many of our flags hanging from houses and buildings on the way to work. It shows how much of an effect something like this can have – it was a great occasion for the city."

Our
Liverp

ANFIELD AND THE AXA

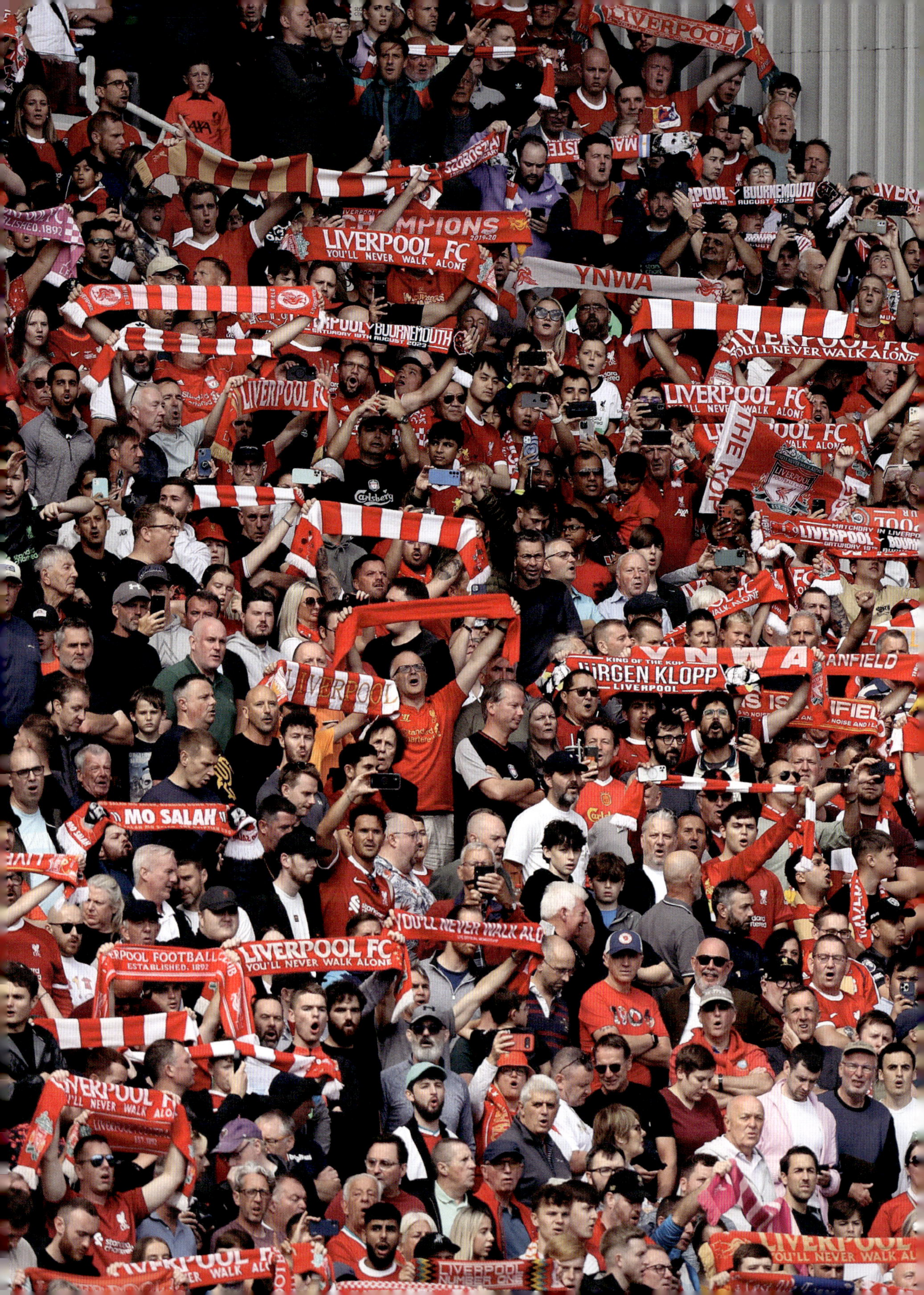
LIVERPOOL
CHAMPIONS
LIVERPOOL FC
YOU'LL NEVER WALK ALONE
YNWA
BOURNEMOUTH
LIVERPOOL FC
JÜRGEN KLOPP
MO SALAH
ANFIELD
LIVERPOOL FC
YOU'LL NEVER WALK ALONE
ESTABLISHED 1892
LIVERPOOL
NUMBER ONE

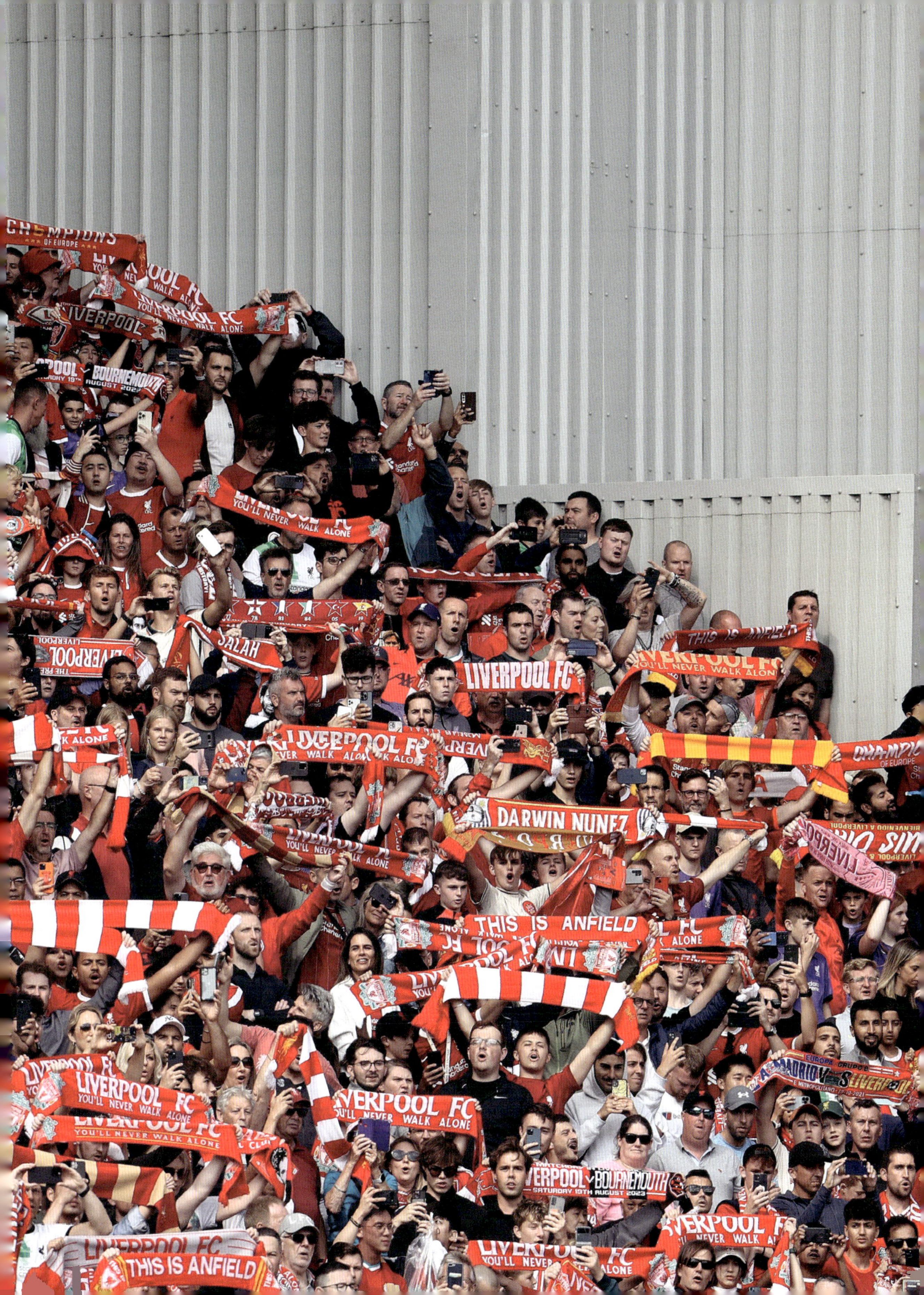
CHAMPIONS
OF EUROPE
LIVERPOOL FC
YOU'LL NEVER WALK ALONE
BOURNEMOUTH
SALAH
THIS IS ANFIELD
DARWIN NUNEZ
SATURDAY 19TH AUGUST 2023

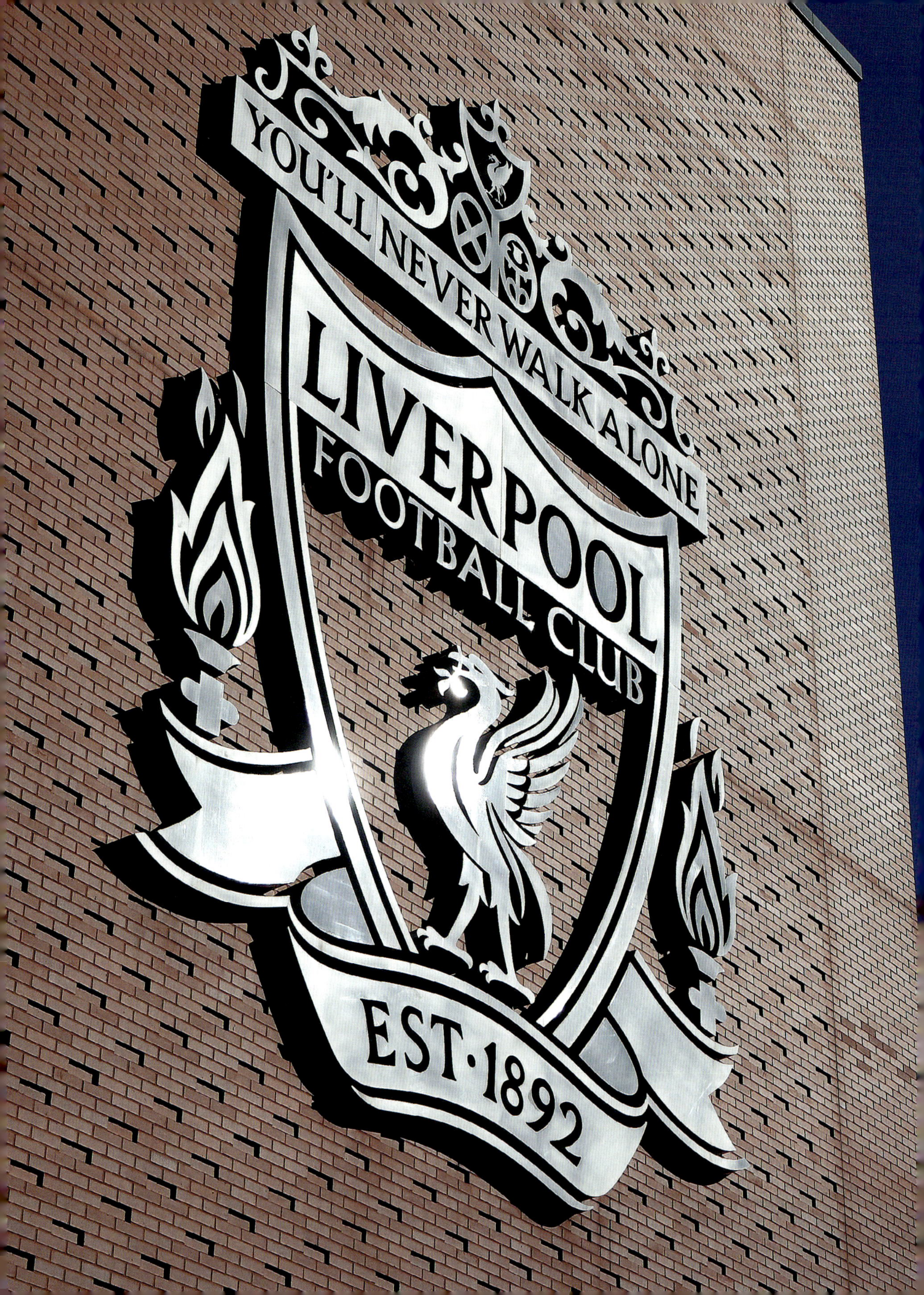
YOU'LL NEVER WALK ALONE
LIVERPOOL
FOOTBALL CLUB
EST·1892

This is Anfield

The home of LFC is also a place where the art is

Anfield's aesthetic is a combination of the stadium's architectural heritage, the club's modern identity reflecting its traditions and values – 'The Liverpool Way' – and that elusive quality called a sense of place. Above all, this is home for Reds supporters from everywhere with a welcoming and inviting spirit.

History resonates through Anfield and over the years the venue's four-stand configuration has been maintained and that unique aura and atmosphere reinforced, while the stadium's redevelopment has gone hand-in-hand with regeneration in the local community.

Around the ground today are statues and ceremonial gates for two legendary Liverpool FC managers and a bust of the club's founder, memorials for the Hillsborough and Heysel disasters respectively, plus other artistic installations.

But arguably the first things which fans notice on the walk-up to the stadium from most directions are the impressive club crests on the outside of the expanded Main Stand and Anfield Road Stand. These are LFC's coat of arms, so to speak – the flag it flies in the city and across the world.

The Main Stand's two large, metallic-grey crests – each around 30ft high and 20ft wide – were installed in July 2016, a few weeks before the entire redeveloped stand was officially opened. They contrast neatly with the greens of a ground-level column of oak trees and the reds of a grove of acer trees nearby.

In June 2023 a new gleaming crest was added to the expanded Anfield Road Stand, close to the Shankly Gates and Sir Kenny Dalglish Stand. Due to its measurements and weight, it took three days to carefully install in pieces – if laid flat on the ground it would cover one of the pitch's 18-yard boxes.

Impressive stuff, and that's not all as you're about to discover...

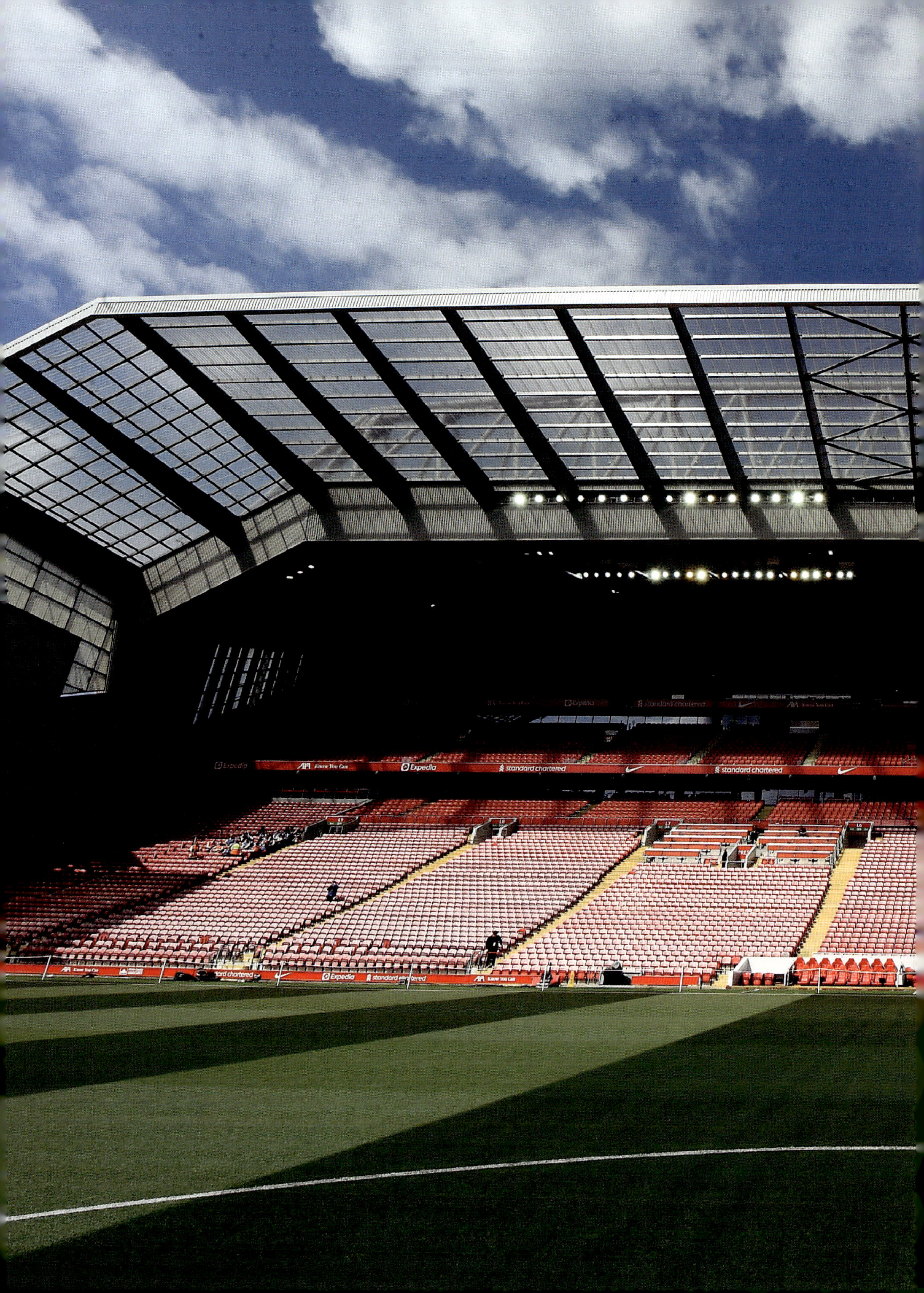
Expedia
standard chartered

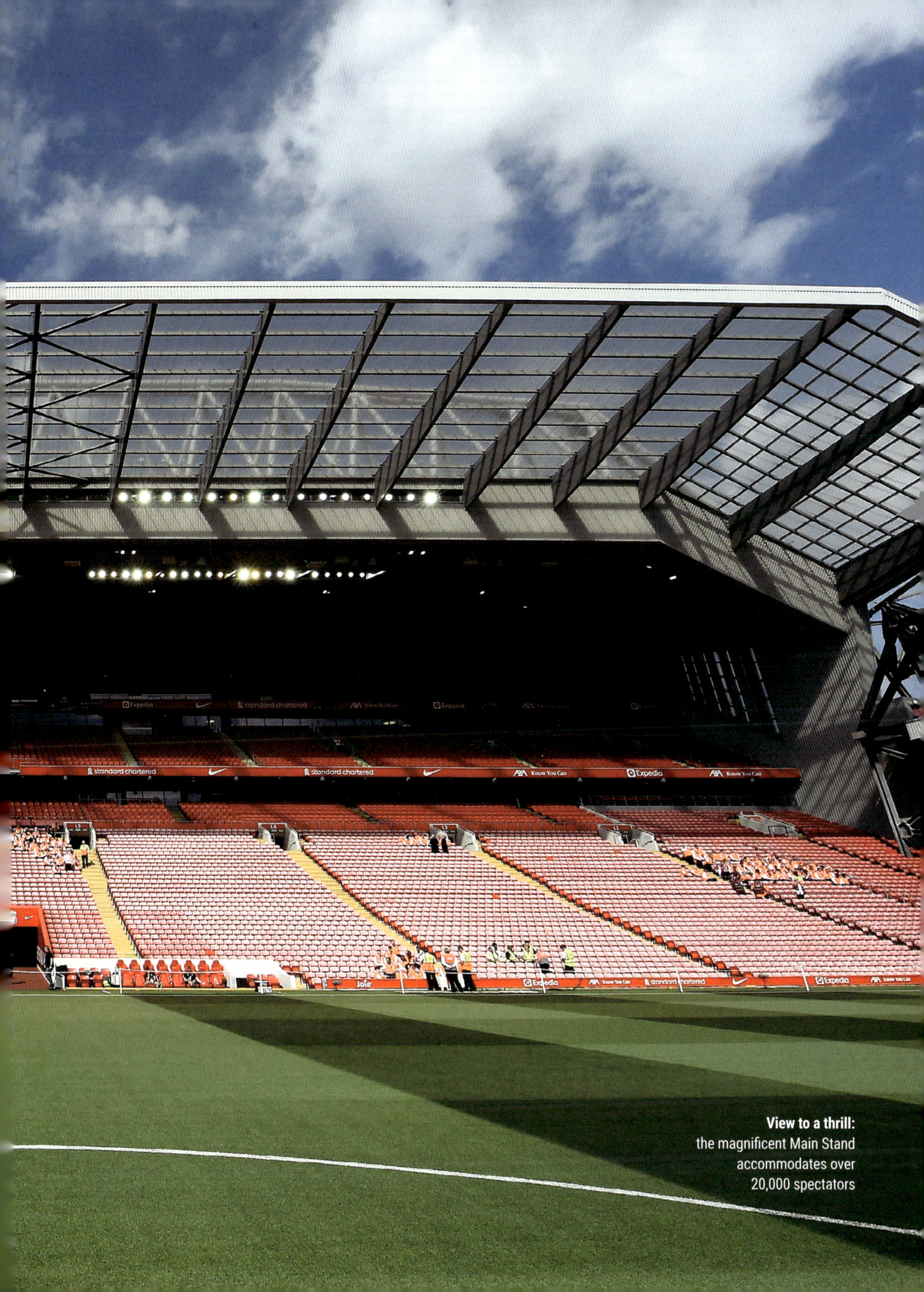

View to a thrill: the magnificent Main Stand accommodates over 20,000 spectators

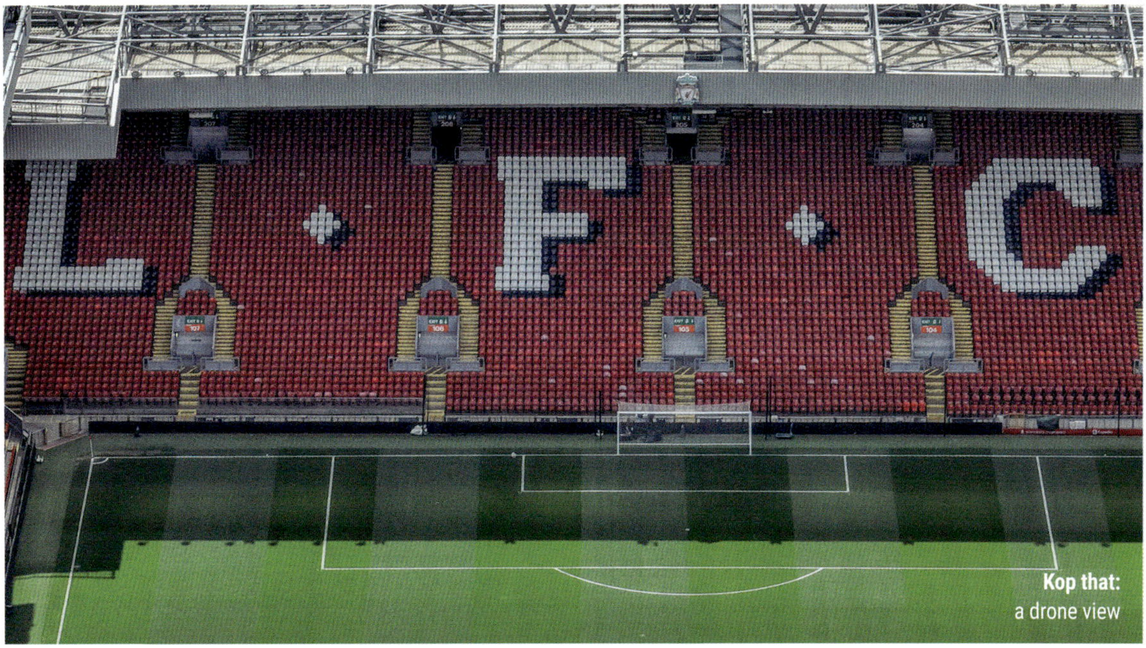

Kop that: a drone view

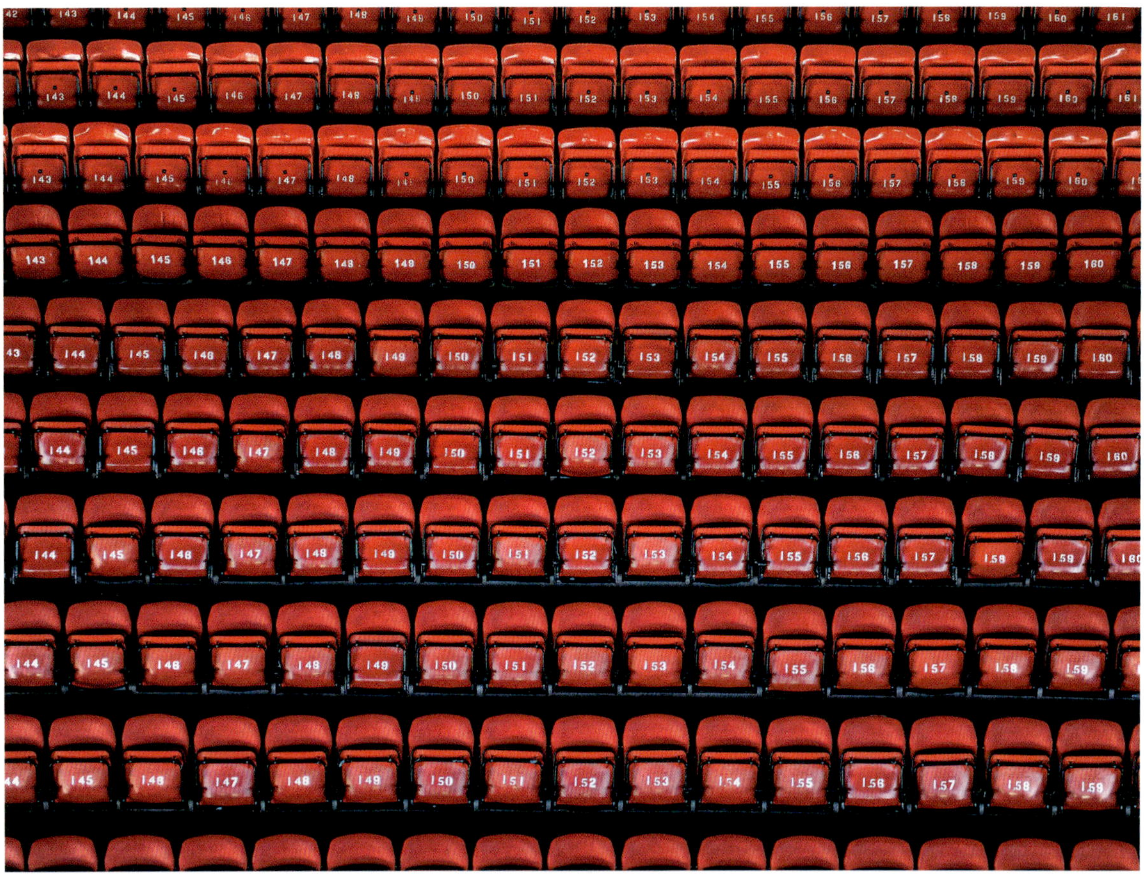

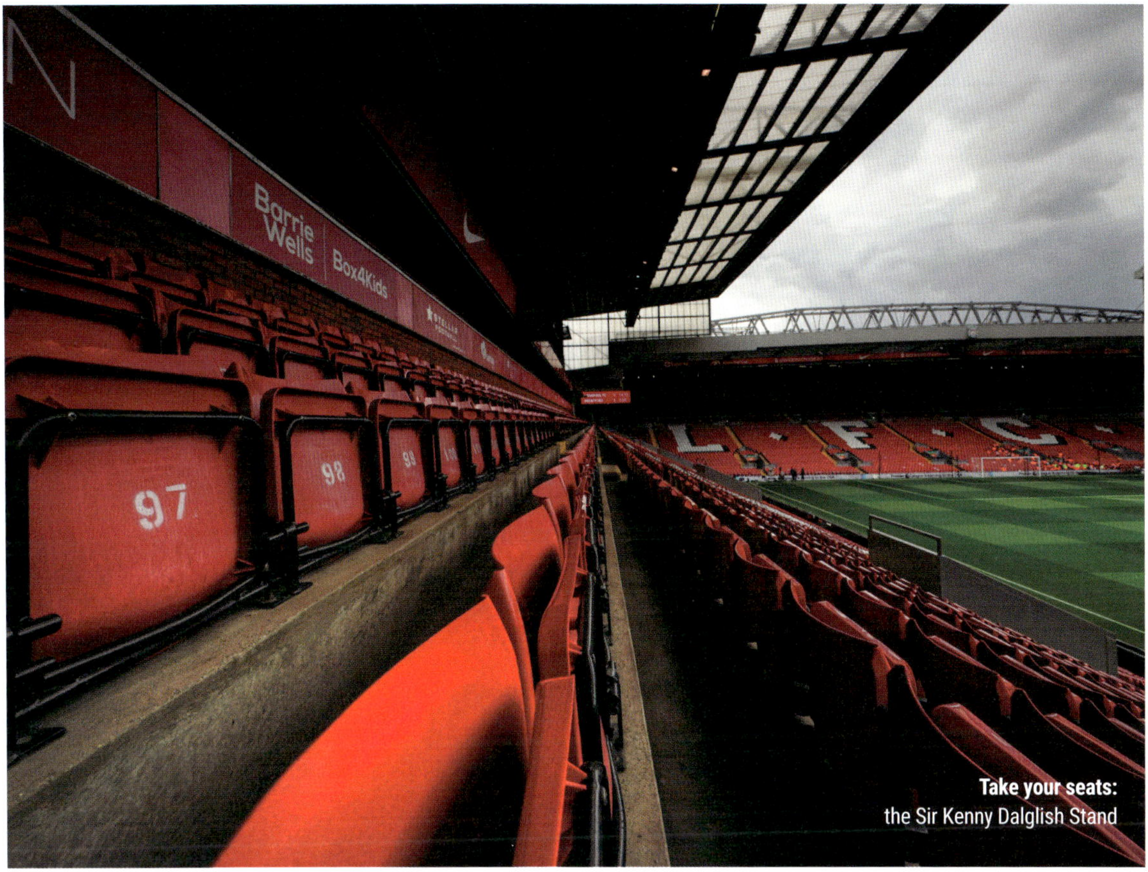

Take your seats:
the Sir Kenny Dalglish Stand

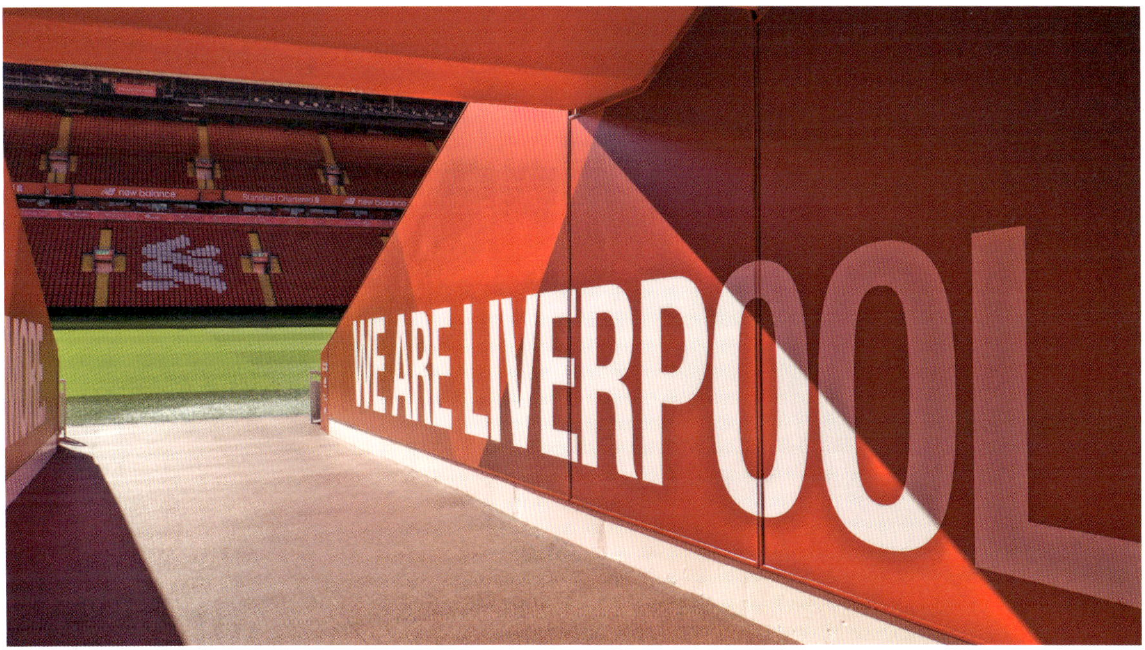

You'll Never Walk Alone

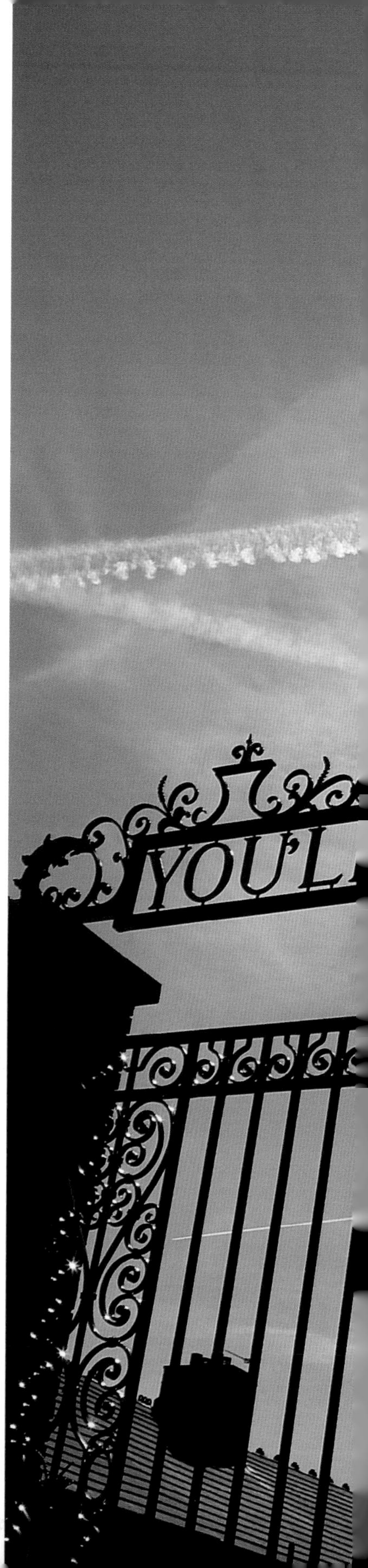

The most photographed gates in football, surely, can be found at the southeastern corner of the Sir Kenny Dalglish Stand and Anfield Road (they were formerly at the northeastern end of the stadium).

The Shankly Gates were officially opened in August 1982 by Bill's widow Nessie accompanied by their grandchildren plus Liverpool FC chairman John Smith, manager Bob Paisley and skipper Graeme Souness.

"Mrs Shankly was keen for a memorial which showed Bill's affiliation with the supporters," club secretary Peter Robinson told a subsequent matchday programme. "It is not thought a similar honour exists in football. A comparison would be the Grace Gates at Lord's in honour of WG Grace."

There in spirit that day was Ken Hall, the man who'd designed and built the gates – which weigh more than three tons – from his foundry in Somerset.

Ken, a lifelong Liverpool fan, kept his original blueprint for the design as well as some old snaps of the gates being offloaded by crane from the lorry which had transported them 200 miles north to Anfield. From commission to completion, between the end of one football season and start of another, the job had taken ten hectic summer weeks.

"I was 25 at the time and I'd been a Liverpool fan for years, since the Keegan and Toshack era of the early 1970s," he later recalled. "It was my father who originally saw the advert in the paper for a Shankly memorial. We rang up and eventually got through to Peter Robinson who gave us the number of the architects [Mather & Nutter].

"They gave us the brief and our design was one of ten which were submitted. The story goes that they were all laid out on a table in front of the selection committee which included Mrs Shankly, who chose ours. There was nothing to touch it, she said. I remember when we got the phone call my dad said I went as white as a sheet – we were in shock!"

On 13 August 1982 the *Somerset Standard* newspaper reported how County Forge had 'gained the contract in the face of tough opposition from all over the country' and approached a master blacksmith, Chris Brooks from Melksham in neighbouring Wiltshire, to assist with the most technical and elaborate elements of the job.

The paper remarked upon the 'astounding' detail of the ironwork whose most ornate part, the overthrow, sits atop and apart from the 14ft x 16ft gates and always gleams in the sunshine. Above the legend 'YOU'LL NEVER WALK ALONE'

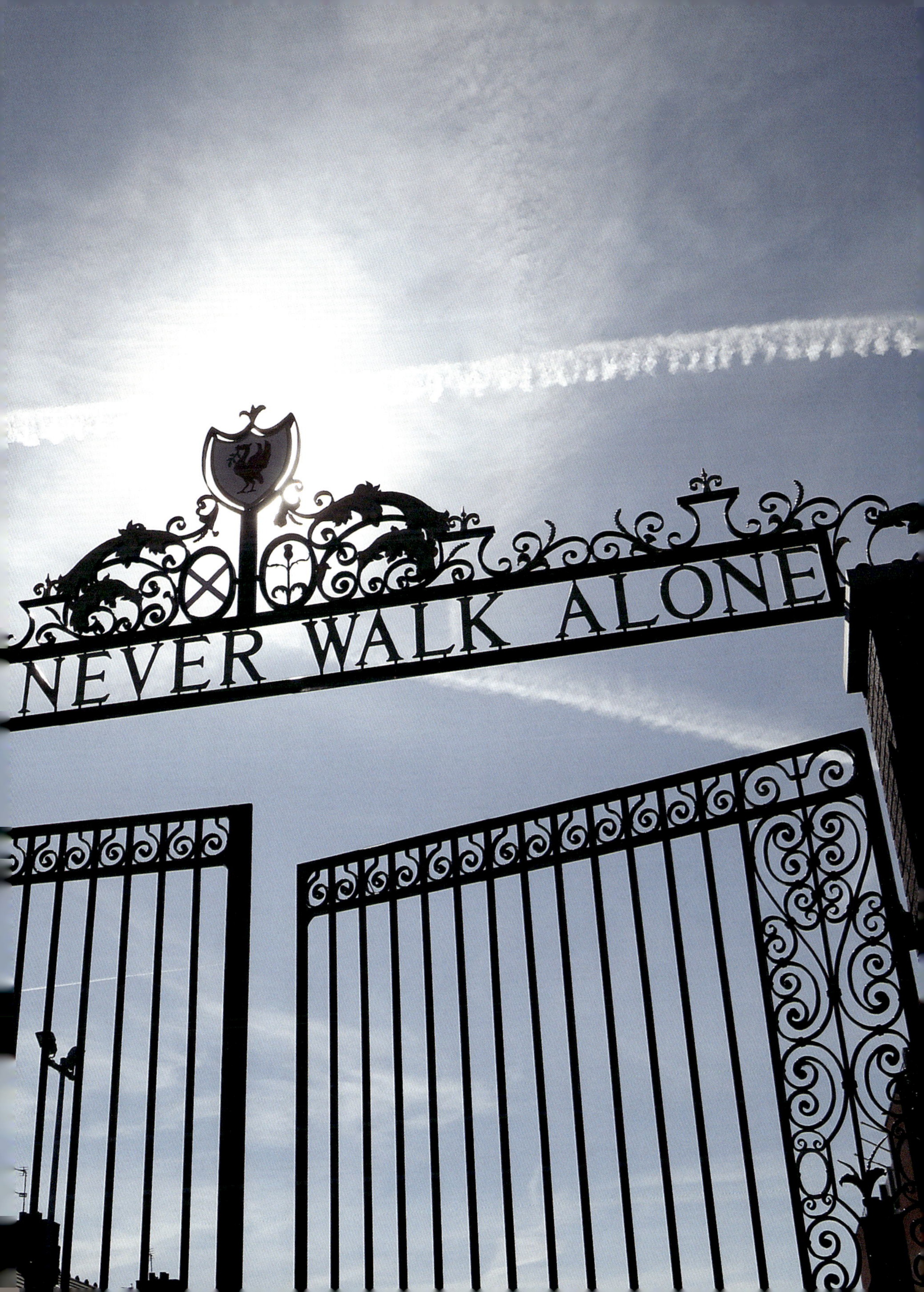
NEVER WALK ALONE

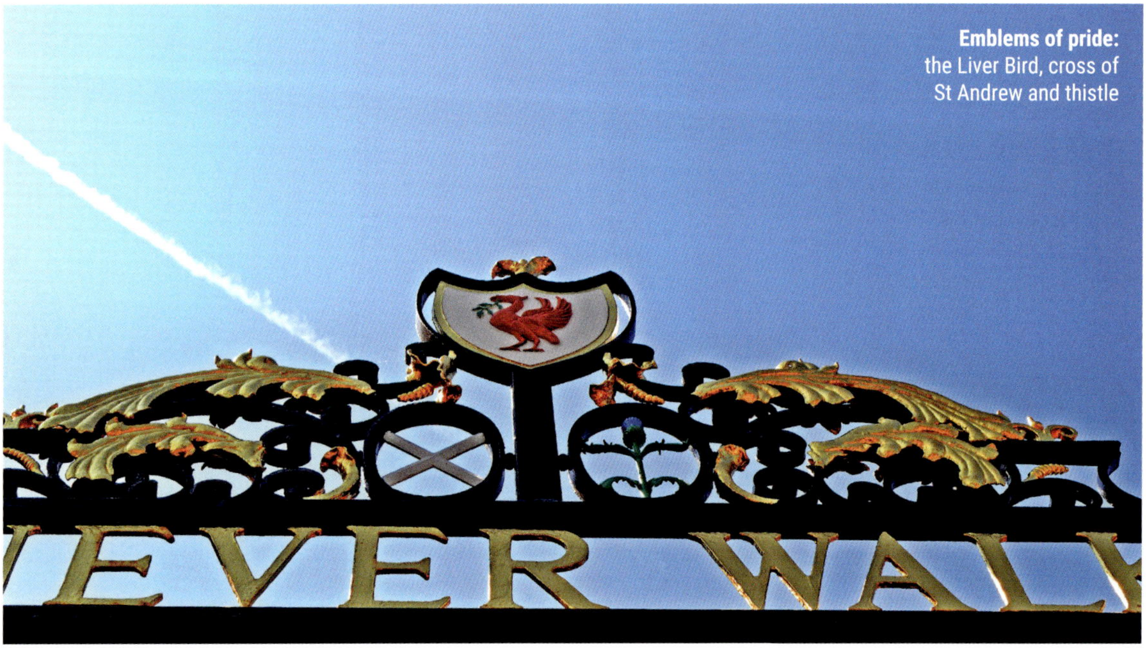

Emblems of pride: the Liver Bird, cross of St Andrew and thistle

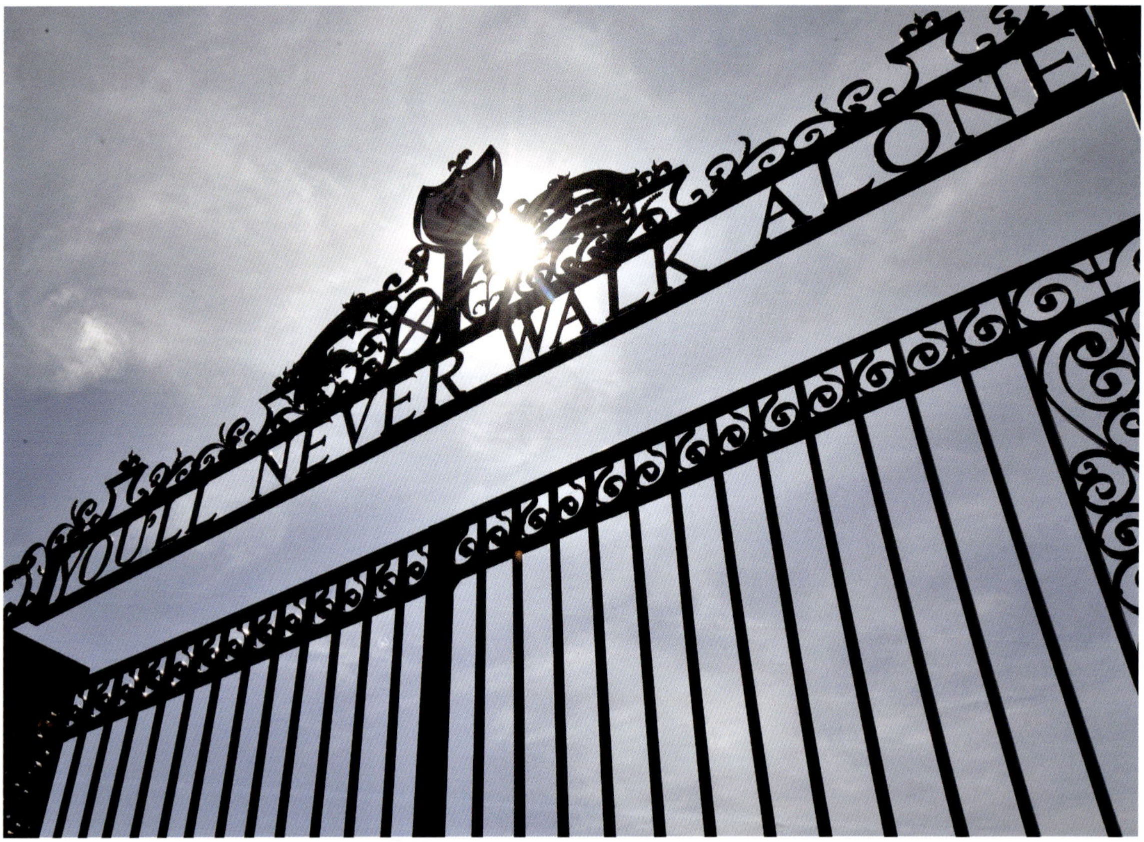

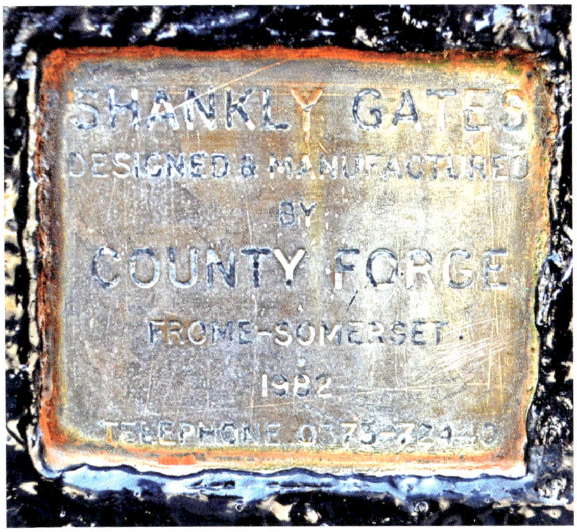

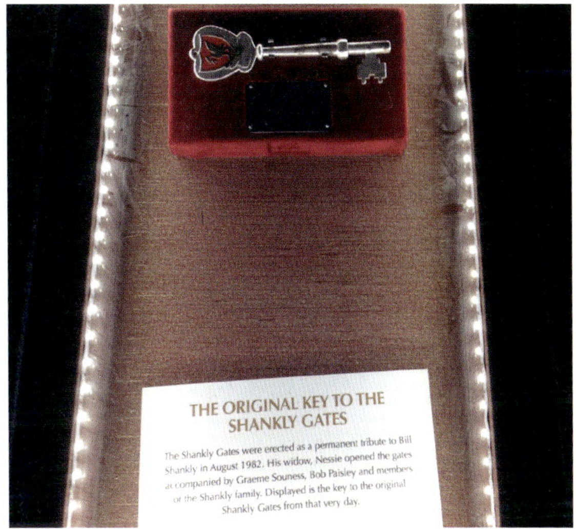

and embellished with swirling gold acanthus leaves is to all intents and purposes the Shankly heraldic device: the white cross of St Andrew and a green-stalked thistle with a bluish-purple flowerhead, together denoting Bill's Scottish roots, and a crest bearing a blood-red Liver Bird to symbolise his sustained passion.

"Originally the club were only thinking about a set of gates but we came up with the idea of the overthrow and they liked it," said Ken.

"We both had apprentices so there were four of us working on it in the end. Chris did the leafwork on the overthrow and I forged the gates, which we had to make one at a time, laid flat on top of each other like a big table because my workshop was quite small."

The overthrow was coated with primer but not painted until the entire structure was loaded by crane onto the lorry which took it to Anfield before the start of the 1982/83 season. Less than 12 months after Bill's death aged 67, Nessie unlocked the gates. The key she used is now on display in The Shankly Hotel in Liverpool city-centre (pictured above right).

Today you can still make out, at waist-height next to the central deadlock, a small brass panel engraved with the words 'SHANKLY GATES DESIGNED & MANUFACTURED BY COUNTY FORGE 1982' and followed by an old telephone number with an obsolete area code.

"Enthusiasm got us through it," admitted Ken. "We were shattered at the end but always confident about completing the gates on time. The only worry was about getting them to fit. We were nervous but the installation was perfect – just 3mm out on one of the hinges.

"I've only been back to Anfield twice since. The last time, we were in a taxi heading for the ground and when we told the driver he wouldn't charge us for the fare. I've still got an enamel brooch of a Liver Bird that was given to me by another chap who came down [to the forge] when we were still making the gates, just to be photographed next to them. He told me his grandfather had given it to him. I'd love to return it to him some day."

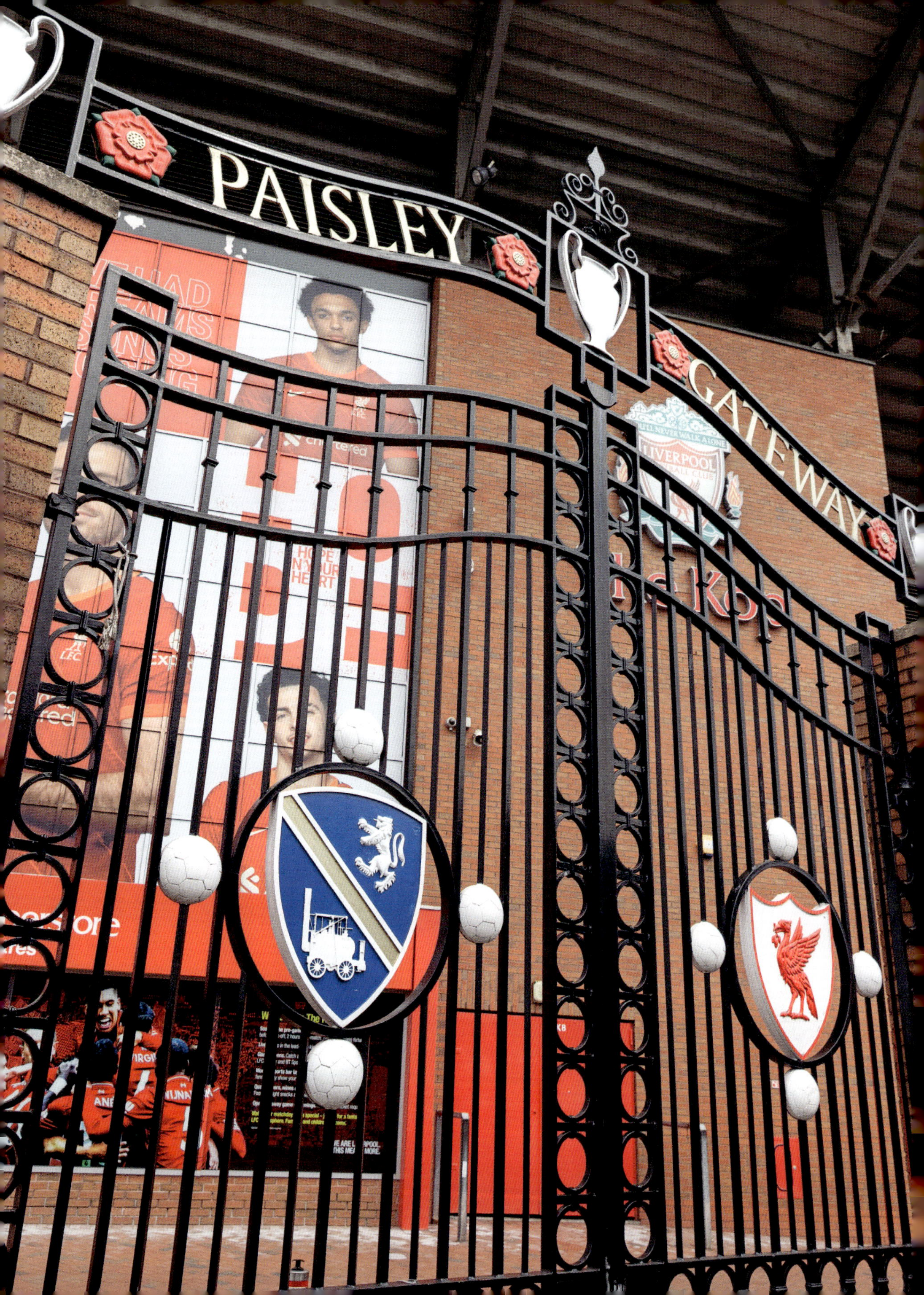
PAISLEY
GATEWAY

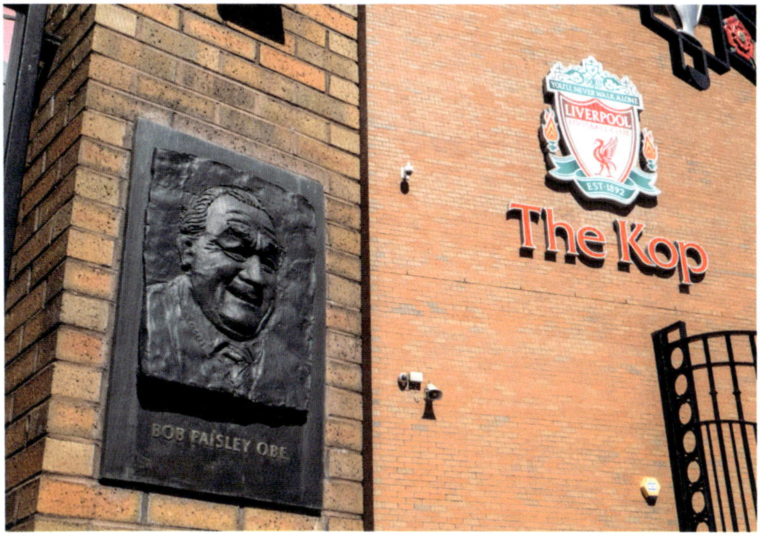

Paisley's pride

The Bob Paisley Gateway and the Shankly Gates make up a pair of grand entrances to the stadium that mark the achievements of two of Liverpool FC's greatest managers. Standing on Walton Breck Road, the former was completed in April 1999 and now leads fans neatly to Paisley Square, the new space named after the most successful English football manager of all-time.

Bob was the first man to guide the same club to three European Cups (1977 in the final in Rome, 1978 in London, and 1981 in Paris) and accordingly three such trophies feature in the decorative ironwork of the gates, either side of which are bronze plaques on brick pillars depicting the great man himself sculpted in relief and a roll-call of his honours.

Present at the unveiling were Bob's widow Jessie, who had taken an instrumental role in the design of the gates, their sons Robert and Graham and their daughter Christine as well as Paisley's brother Hughie and his wife Mary.

Upon being presented with a ceremonial key, Jessie said: "If this was an Oscar ceremony I would be expected to fling my arms around, burst into tears and say Bob didn't deserve it. But although the tears aren't far away, I'm not going to say that. If you ask me if Bob deserved it, I say yes, 100 per cent."

Standing four-and-a-half metres in height and weighing over two tons (the foundations beneath them had to be specially strengthened to hold them in place), the gates also feature a Liver Bird and the crest of Bob's birthplace, Hetton-le-Hole – complete with a steam-engine acknowledging the area's pioneering role in the coming of the railways – plus eight white footballs.

'He made the people happy'

There was only ever one candidate for Anfield's first statue: Bill Shankly. Arms aloft and scarf around neck, the modern-day founding father of Liverpool Football Club was cast in bronze and unveiled outside the Spion Kop in December 1997, fifteen years after the Shankly Gates were erected.

It stands on a plinth of Scottish granite in deference to Bill's mining background with the simple message 'He made the people happy'.

Among those present for the official ceremony were his widow Nessie and Jessie Paisley, widow of Bob Paisley, along with members of Shankly's first great team in the 1960s: Roger Hunt, Tommy Lawrence, Chris Lawler, Peter Thompson, Ron Yeats (the former captain who cut the ribbon at the unveiling), Willie Stevenson, Ian Callaghan and Gerry Byrne.

Commissioned and donated by Carlsberg to mark its association with Liverpool Football Club, the statue was sculpted by local artist Tom Murphy. "I wanted to make it look like a living thing," he said. "The pose I chose is one people will immediately recognise: arms straight out and triumphant, saluting victory before his adoring fans."

Tom's impressive CV also includes statues of Everton legend Dixie Dean, former Tranmere Rovers manager Johnny King, the Hillsborough Monument near the city's St John's Gardens, the Moores brothers (Sir John and Cecil of football pools fame) on Church Street, John Lennon at Liverpool Airport, and Ken Dodd and Bessie Braddock in Lime Street Station.

He's also an honorary fellow of Liverpool John Moores University and in 2016 was awarded an honorary doctorate from the University of Liverpool. The following year, Liverpool City Council recognised him as a 'Citizen of Honour'.

More recently the statue was adorned with its very own cape as part of the *Statues Redressed* documentary on Sky Arts in August 2021. Fashion designer and Reds fan Nadia Atique created the piece with the words 'Shankly Our Hero' on the back. Previously Nadia had created a collection inspired by the colours and styles of the club kit, which was written about in Vogue.

Bill's statue remains a favourite place to meet before and after the match at Anfield and for many it was the first place of pilgrimage when the Reds clinched the Premier League title in June 2020.

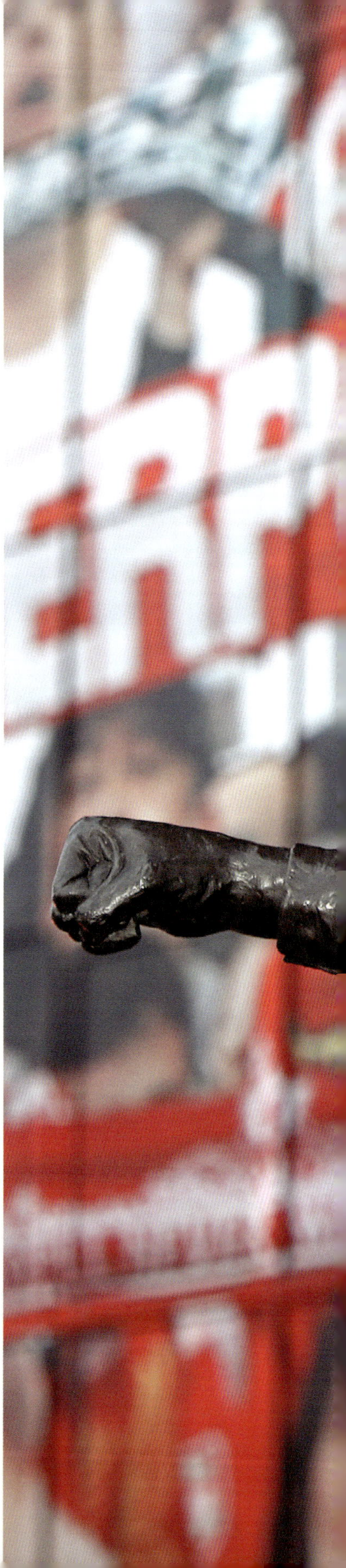

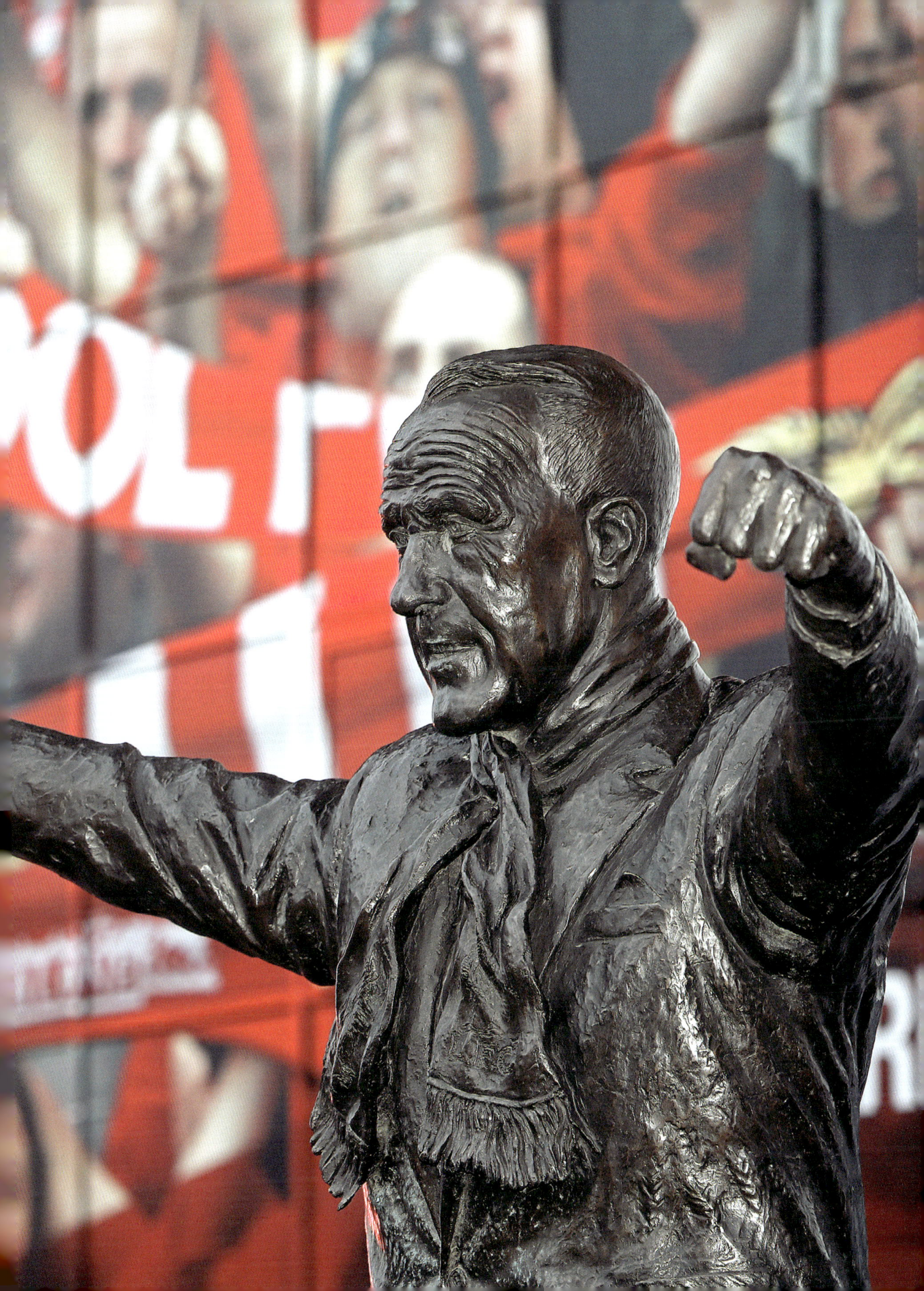

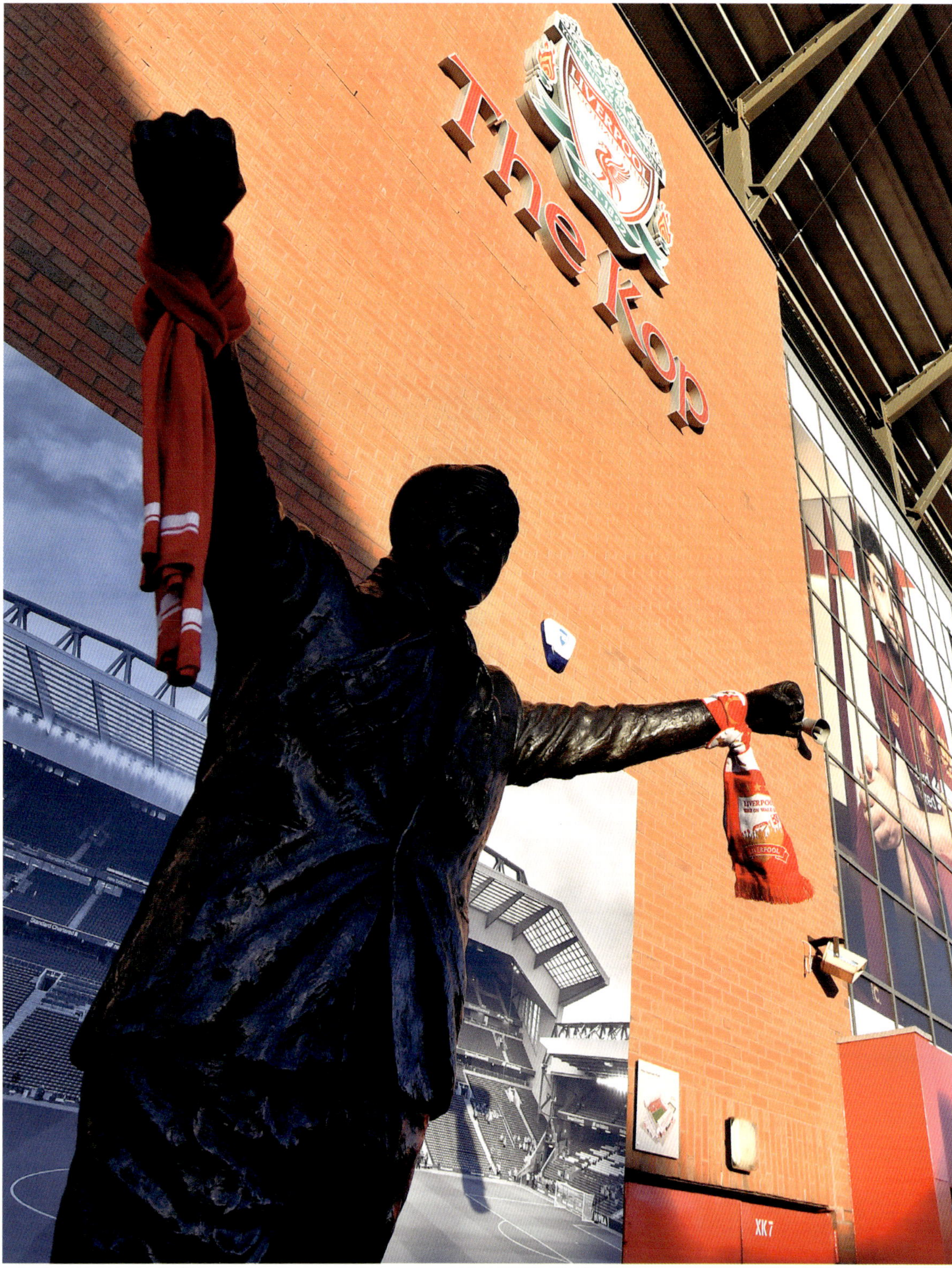
The Kop
LIVERPOOL
XK7

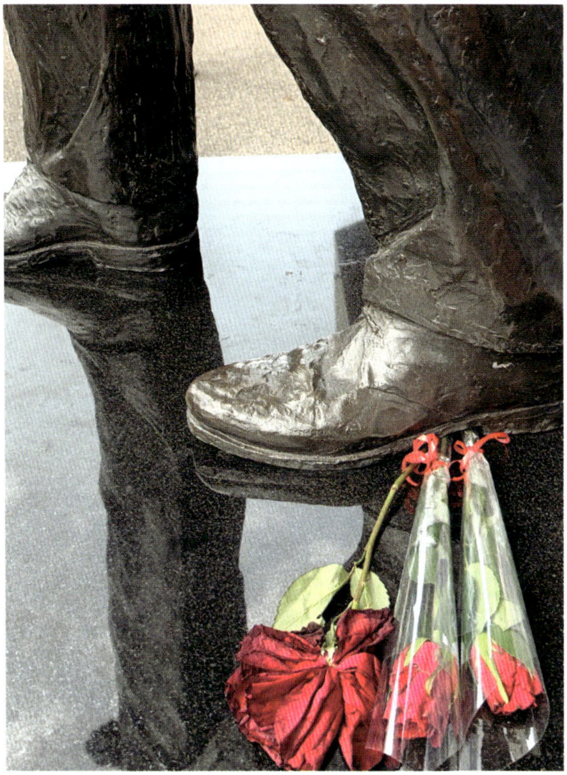

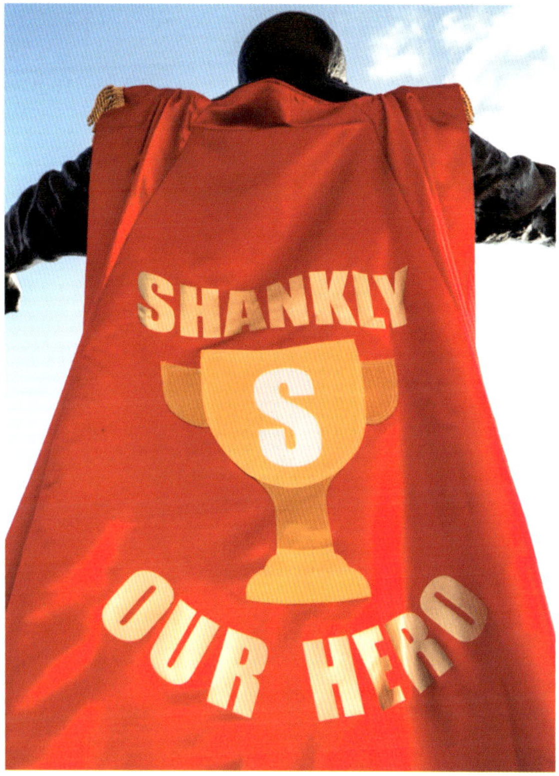

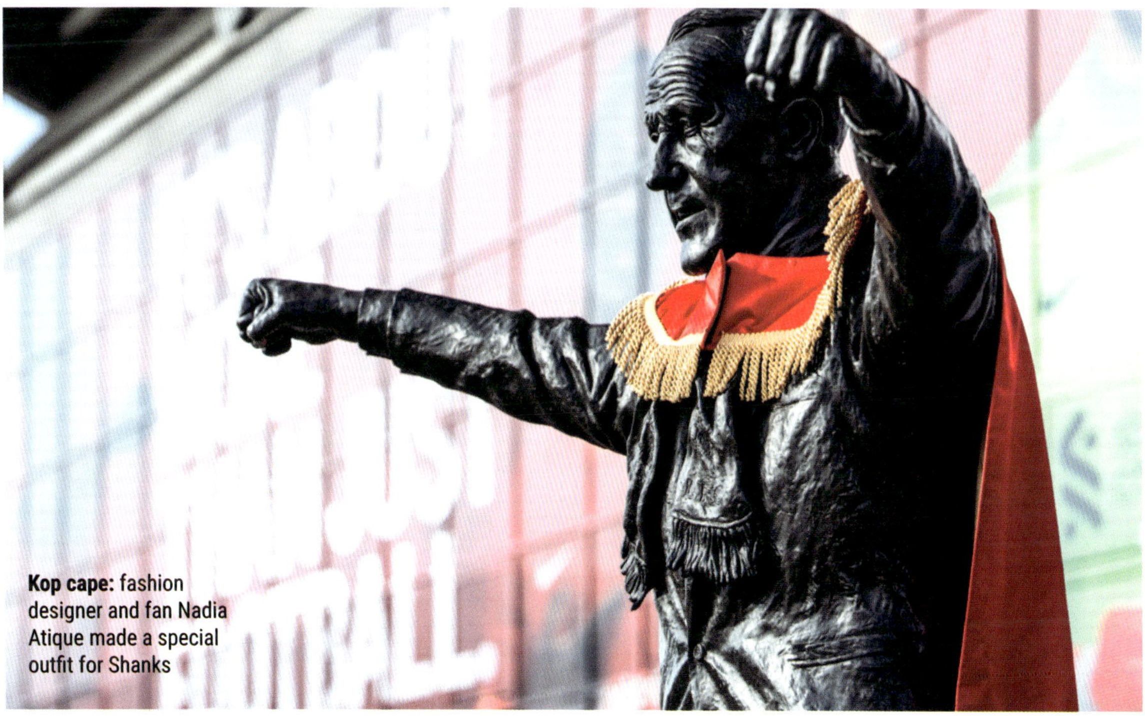

Kop cape: fashion designer and fan Nadia Atique made a special outfit for Shanks

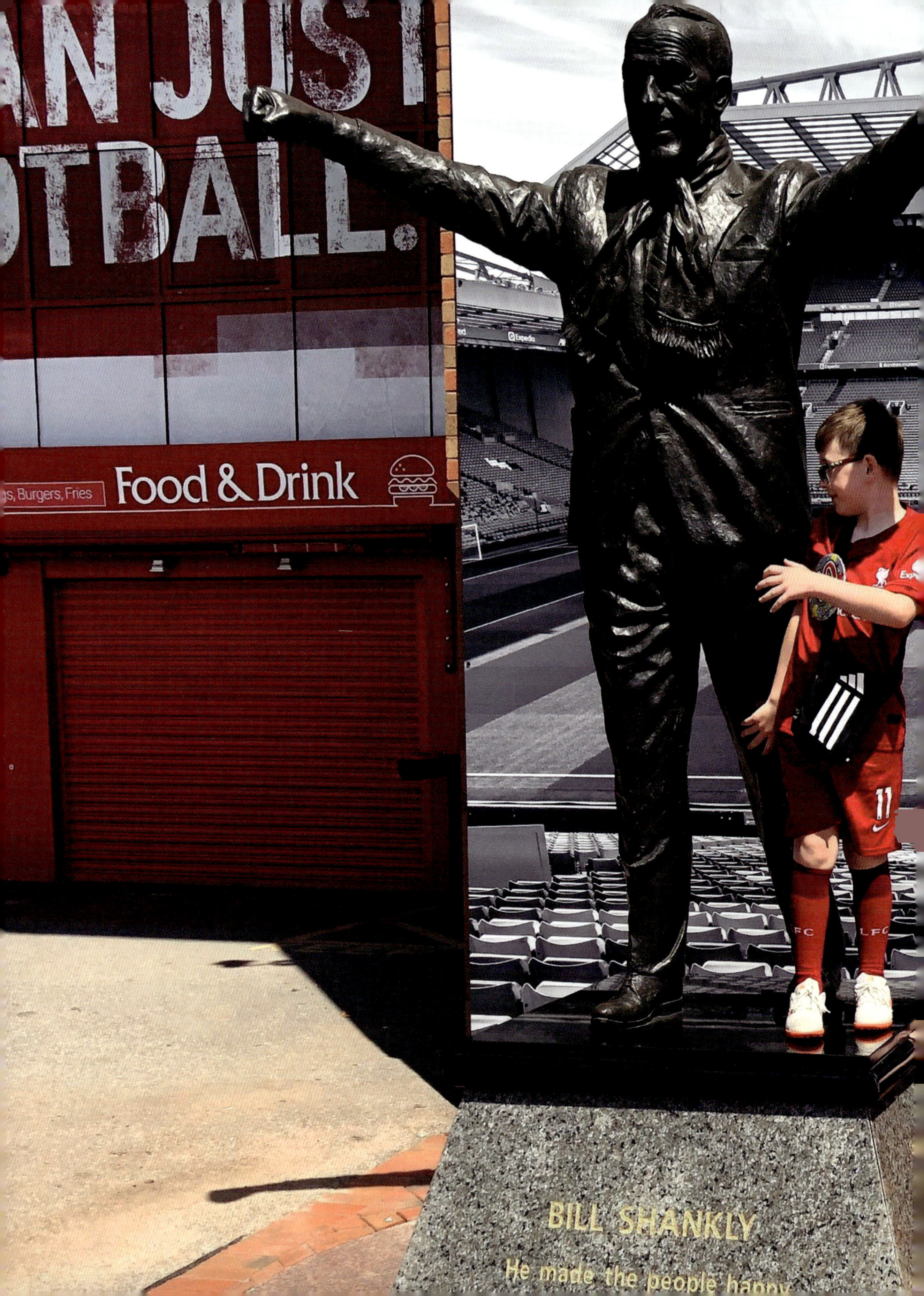

AN JUST
TBALL.
s, Burgers, Fries
Food & Drink
BILL SHANKLY
He made the people happy

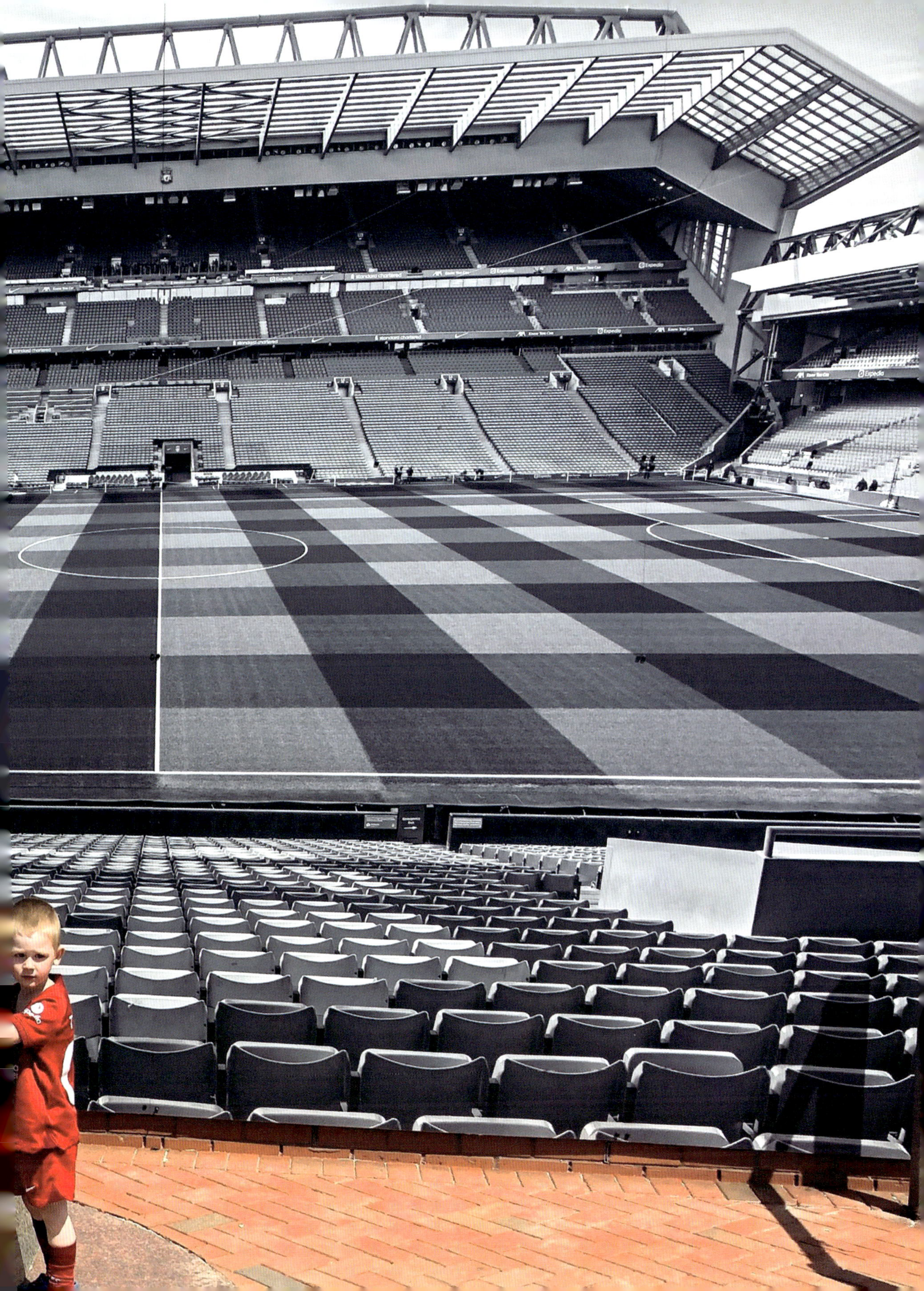

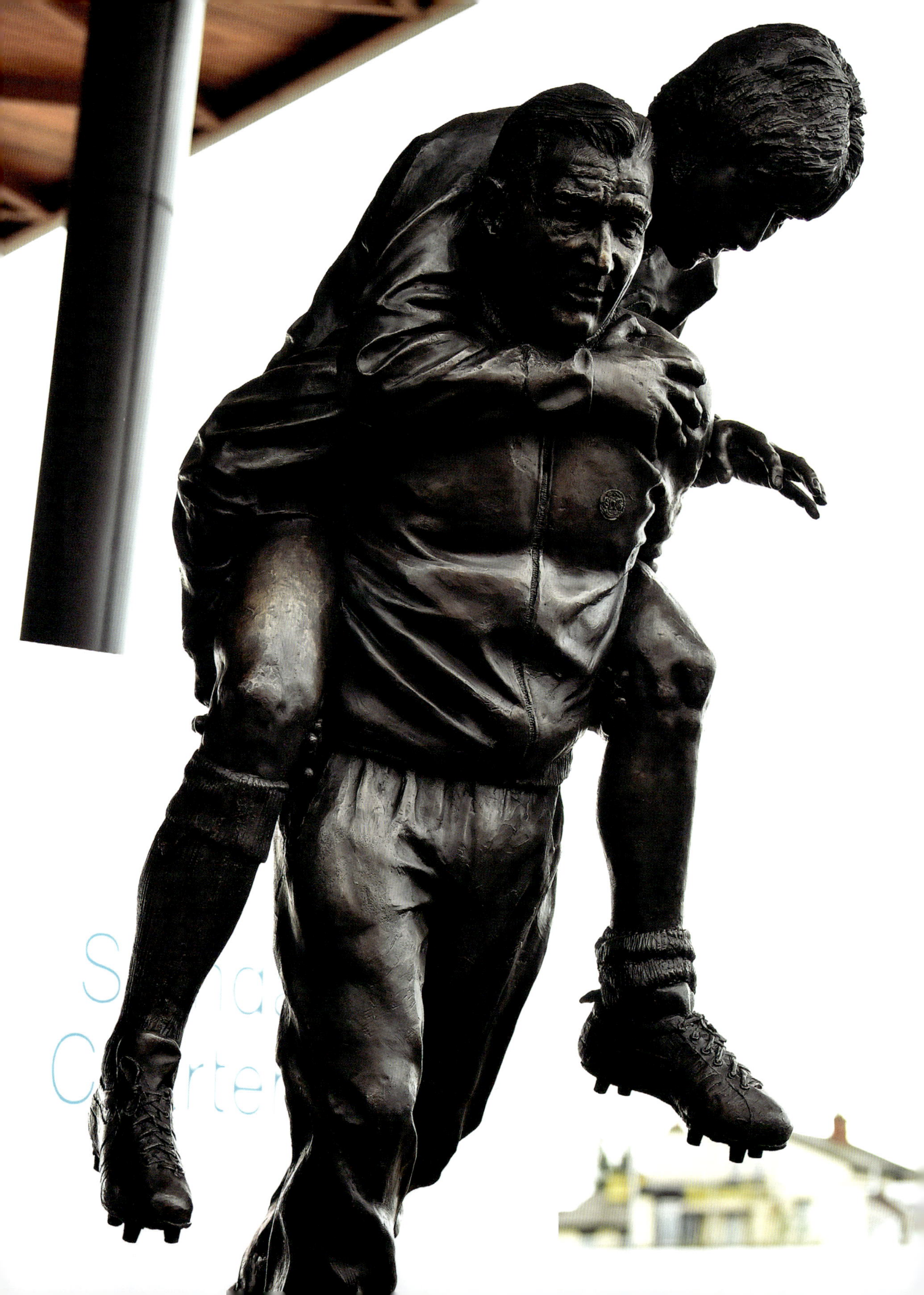

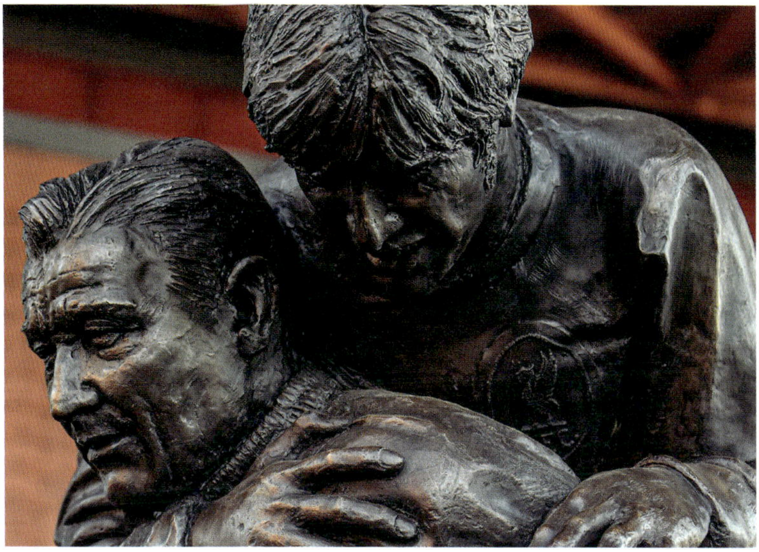

Bob in bronze

For years a statue for Bob Paisley had felt long overdue by general consent, despite the presence of the Paisley Gateway on Walton Breck Road with its bronze plaque showing a sculpture of the great man in relief.

No one, though, could really have foreseen something as brilliantly original as what ultimately appeared on Paisley Square (naturally), having been unveiled in late January 2020 by members of Bob's family and relatives of the late, great Emlyn Hughes, ahead of Liverpool's Premier League home game against Southampton.

Standing 8ft tall and designed to sit at the right height to enable supporters to take selfies alongside, it was the realisation in bronze of a real, dramatic moment from LFC history captured by a photographer over half-a-century ago. The outcome of the game in question is incidental: Liverpool 1 Tottenham Hotspur 1, on Monday 29 April 1968; centre-forward Tony Hateley on target for the hosts and Jimmy Greaves scoring for the visitors, as manager Bill Shankly embarked upon building his second great team in red.

Bob Paisley, then aged 49, was Shankly's first-team coach. He'd already been with Liverpool FC for almost 30 years. Emlyn, the injured player on Paisley's shoulders, blood streaming from a gash in his knee, was a 20-year old left-half. Twelve months a Liverpool player, and a future European Cup-lifting captain, he epitomised the next generation's raw gladiatorial ethic.

The moment has echoes of a wounded soldier being rescued from the frontline by a brave comrade. But Bob, strong, selfless and ever the pragmatist, would say he was just doing his job: get the casualty off the pitch quickly and safely, get him treated, get the team going again.

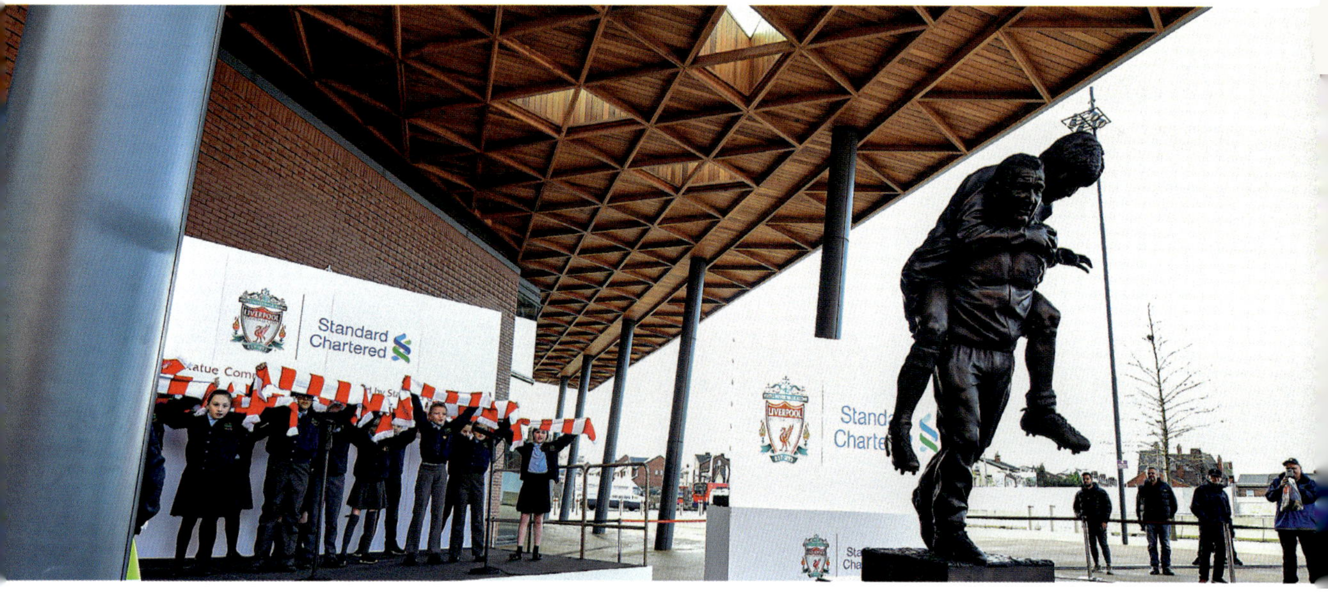

The previous January, in 2019, the 100th anniversary of Paisley's birth had been marked on the front cover of LFC's official matchday programme (for the visit of Crystal Palace) with a vintage photo of Bob the player, taking a throw-in with one of those hefty old 'case-balls'.

Subsequent commemorations of his life and legacy included main club sponsor Standard Chartered producing a film series in which current and former Reds stars presented a gift to a computer-generated Paisley whose voice had been recreated using smart technology. The 2019/20 kit also paid homage to Liverpool FC's most successful manager and ultimate one-club man, with his signature featuring on the inside-neck of every jersey. Indeed it was Standard Chartered which had commissioned the statue to mark its own ten-year relationship with the Reds.

Sculptor Andy Edwards, who previously worked upon the Beatles statue at Liverpool's Pier Head, called it "an amazing image that takes football statuary to a different level." He'd read up on the subject to refresh his memory of Paisley and Hughes "and the characters they were. I started thinking about the enormity of this job, how significant it is and what it represents, and I felt a lot of pride as I put the first clay on. The anniversary is an historic occasion, there are people who don't know that much about Bob Paisley, so there's a huge responsibility to not only get the detail authentic but to get the spirit and the feel because you're telling a story – it's kind of like 3D journalism."

Working alongside Andy was the foundry's managing-director Chris Butler, who explained how the creative process was a combination of individual talent and state-of-the-art technology: "I hadn't seen this picture before and what's great is that it shows a different side of football. These days if something like this happened during a match there would be hundreds of pictures of it, you could go online and find every angle you could possibly want. But as far as we know this is the only photograph of that moment.

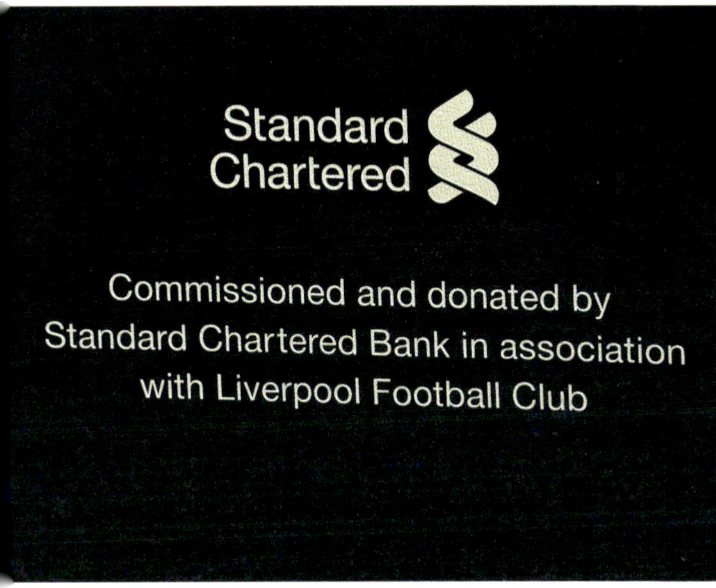

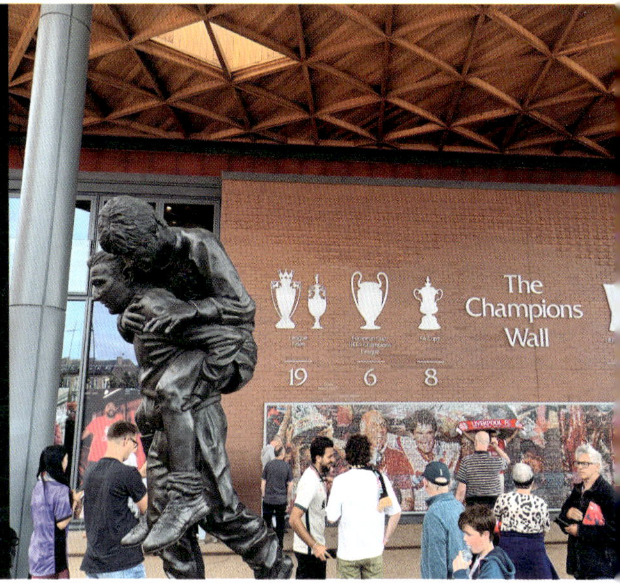

"Andy originally made a one-fifth scale 'maquette' from that one photo, which is quite a skill in itself. We mapped out the model five times bigger and once we had the accurate internal structure, as well as the creases and folds of the clothing, we could cover the frame with clay and Andy could come and start work. We made a silicon-rubber and fibreglass mould over the whole surface then divided it into sections to be cast in their individual pieces. Of course that means there are seams, and our work then is to make it look like you don't know how it's been made."

Chris and the team most certainly succeeded. Another former skipper, Phil Thompson, who played under Bob Paisley and alongside Emlyn, vouched for that: "The likeness is astonishing – everybody who comes to Anfield will be thrilled to see it. I joined Liverpool in 1969, so this moment is from the year before, and it epitomises everything about the club in that era. Nowadays you see medics, stretchers, everything, but this was Bob as the humble 'sponge man', as they used to call them, because he was the physio as well as a coach. He did all of these roles."

Inscribed on the base of the statue is a famous Paisley quote: "This club has been my life. I'd go out and sweep the street and be proud to do it for Liverpool FC, if they asked me to." The same words appeared on the cover of the Liverpool v Southampton matchday programme on Saturday 1 February 2020, along with the original photo of Paisley and Hughes.

At the time of the unveiling, Liverpool were reigning European champions, newly-crowned Club World Cup winners, and 19 points clear at the top of the Premier League. By the end of the week they'd beaten Southampton 4-0 and now held the biggest lead by any team at the end of a matchday in English top-flight history, having earned 100 points from the last 102 available to them, winning 33 of their last 34 matches.

Bob Paisley would have been very, very proud.

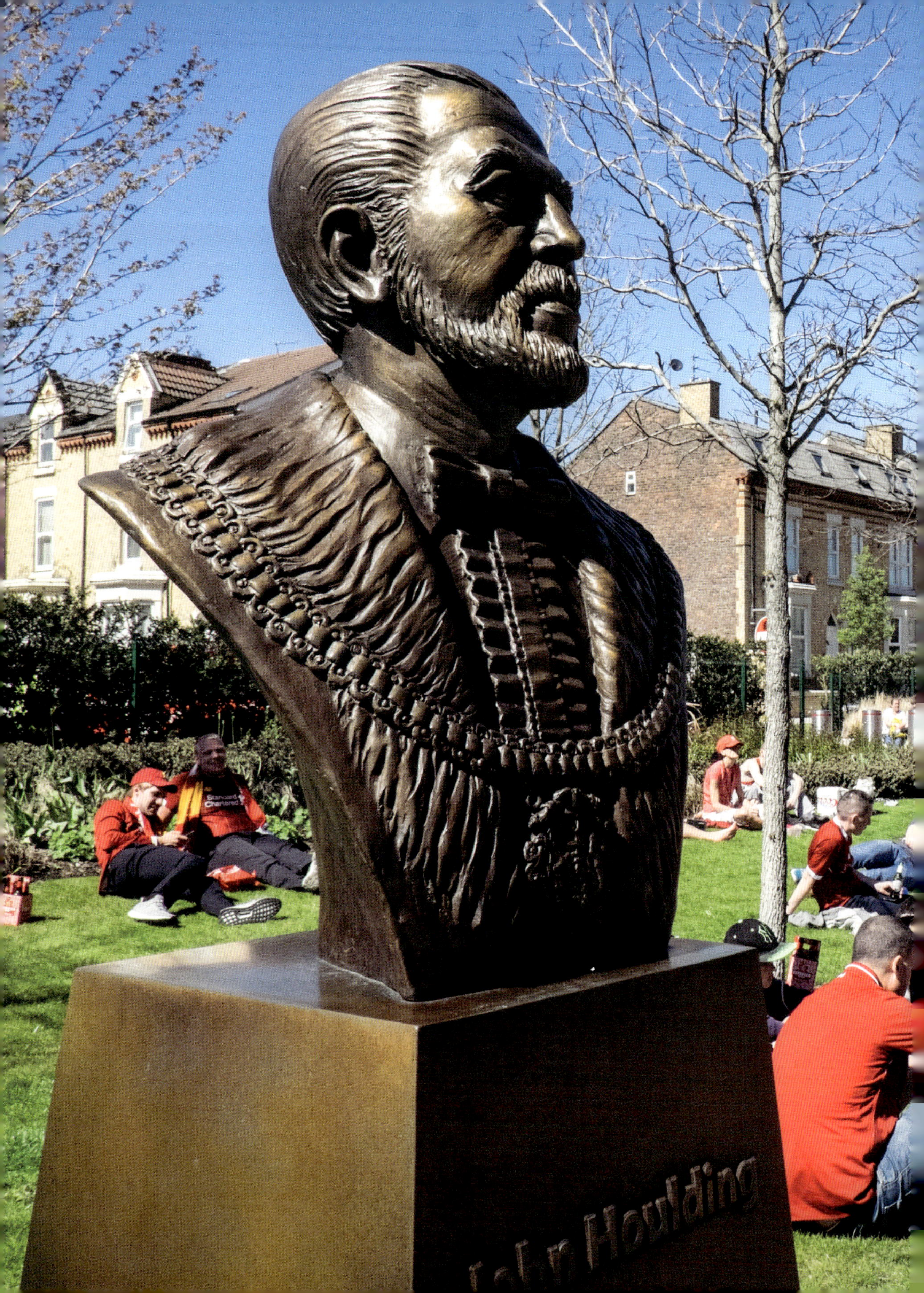
Houlding

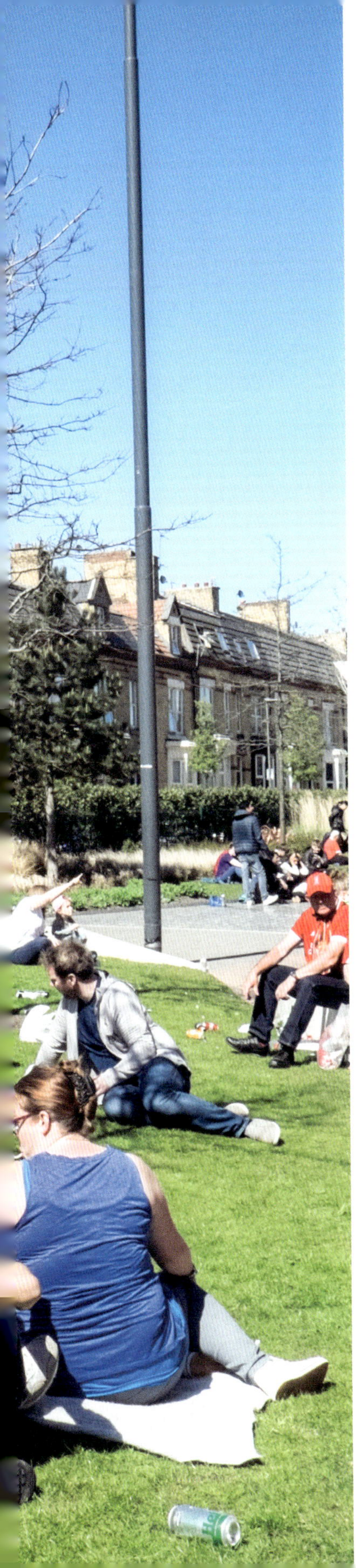

Dear John

December 2018 saw the official unveiling of a bronze bust of John Houlding – 'Founder of Liverpool Football Club' – on what is now 97 Avenue, near to the Anfield Forever stones. The bust and its base stand just under seven feet tall and were created by Tom Murphy, the local sculptor behind the Shankly statue, as part of the club's 125th anniversary celebrations.

There was no 97 Avenue all those years ago, of course. No Paisley Square nor massive Main Stand. In late 1892, according to an Ordnance Survey map of the time, there was practically nothing on that side of the playing field formerly belonging to Everton FC, not until you got to Lothair Road and the ladder of terrace streets running northwest between Rockfield Road and Anfield Road.

That's how it was in John Houlding's day. And in 2018, amid the landscaped public domain outside the modern stadium, this is where the monument to Houlding, portrayed in his mayoral finery, was erected.

"We didn't have any symbol at Anfield that was a representation of our founder that our supporters could see and touch and reflect upon," said then Reds chief-executive Peter Moore. "One hundred and twenty-five years is a long time and it was all started by this man – without him, football on Merseyside certainly wouldn't be what it is today. I hope our supporters take the time to go and visit as he looks proudly upon our Main Stand."

As every Reds (and Blues) fan knows, Houlding officially formed Liverpool Football Club on 3 June 1892 following a dispute with Everton who played at Anfield, the ground he owned. The Toffees left and Houlding recruited players for a new team to play here – and LFC was born. He was subsequently appointed Lord Mayor of Liverpool in 1897.

"There are very few pictures of him in existence so I did a lot of research around the style of dress that would have been worn at the time," revealed sculptor Murphy. "I was also lucky enough to be able to visit the Town Hall to understand the detail of the mayoral chain which can be seen around his neck [featuring the city of Liverpool's coat of arms]. He was a really interesting person to work on and completely different from the Shankly statue."

Still standing at the opposite corner of the present stadium is the house in which Houlding once lived – a red-and-cream-bricked mansion at no73 Anfield Road and otherwise known as Stanley House. He'd progressed from working as a drayman delivering beer at Clarkson's Brewery in Soho Street, in the city's Islington district, to owning his own brewery in Everton's Tynemouth Street.

'Houlding's Sparkling Ales' were the tipple of choice in late Victorian Liverpool, and using profits from the brewery he set up home at Stanley House with his wife Jane and children Alice and William. With a garden and steepled tower overlooking (the then six-year-old) Stanley Park, it gave him the perfect base from which to keep an eye on the city's footballing affairs.

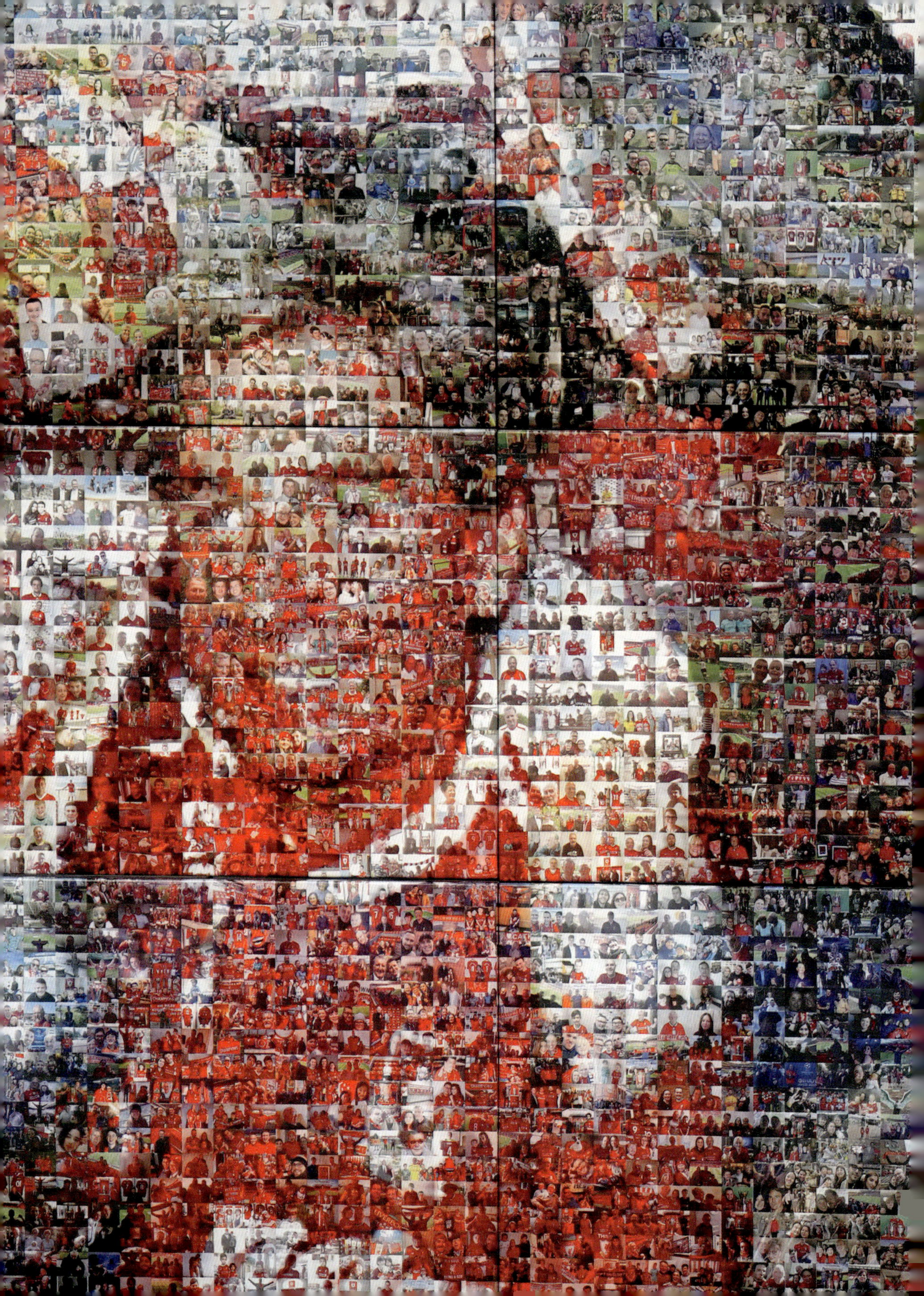

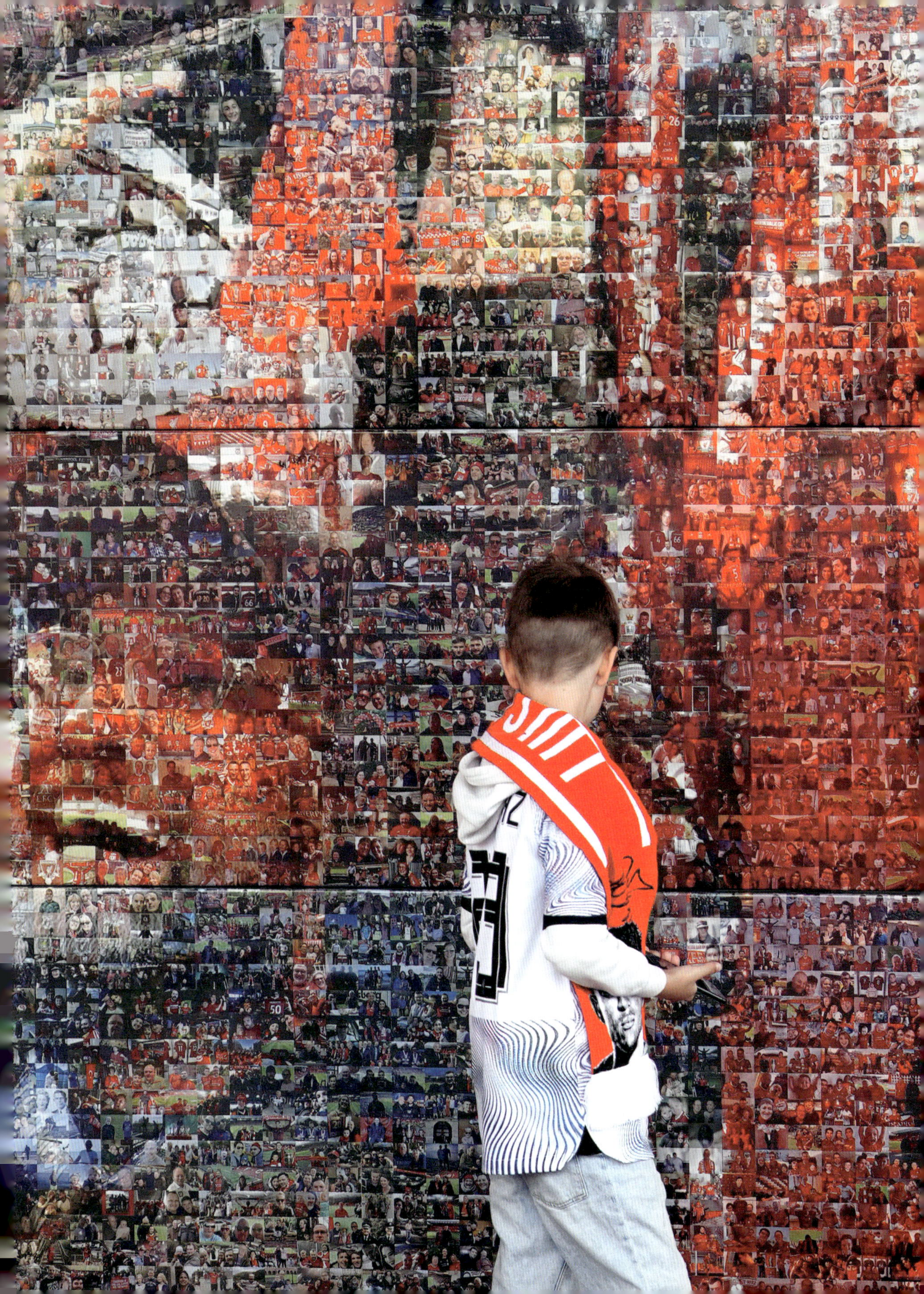

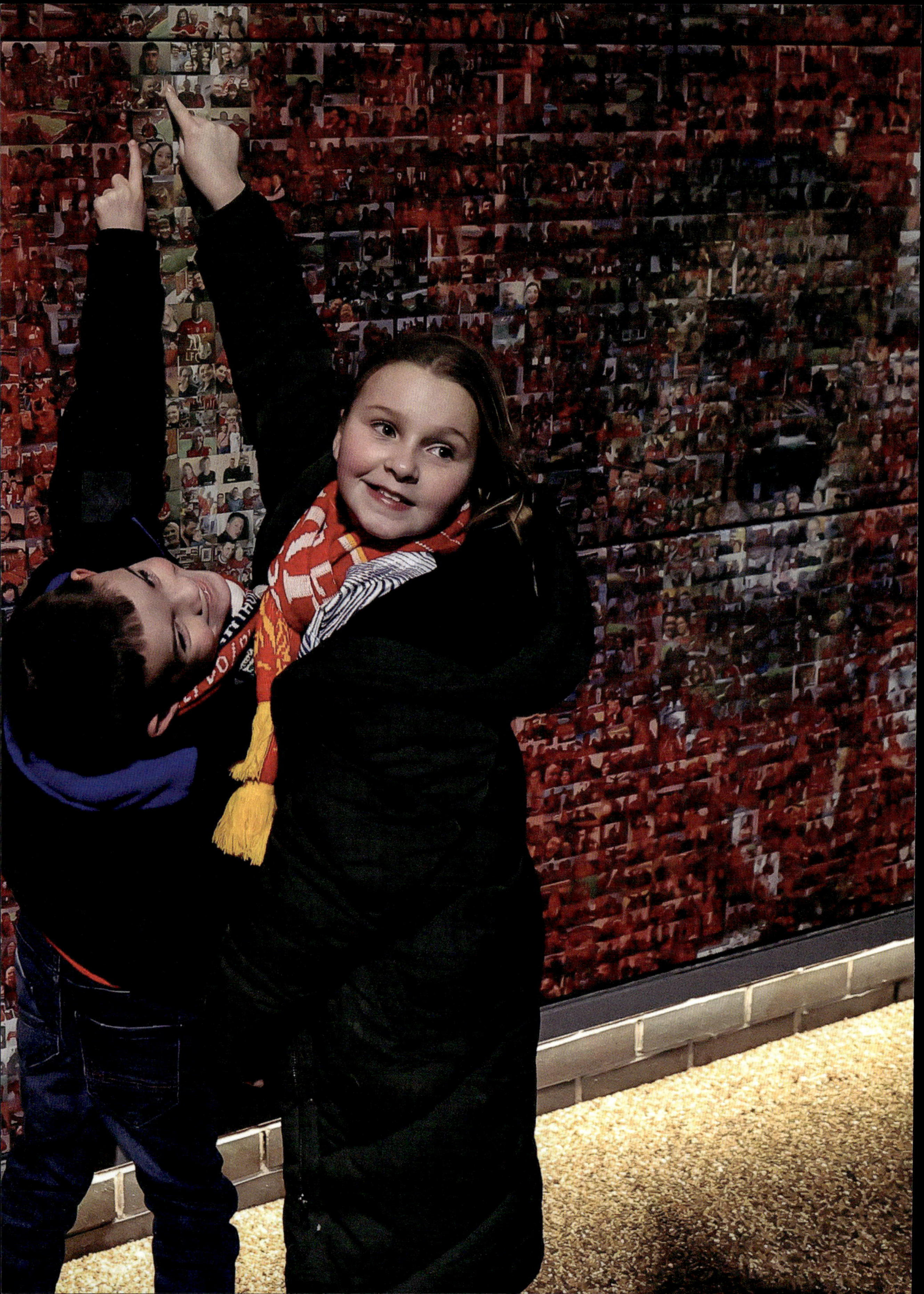

Twelve thousand champions

From left to right, it's big Sami Hyypia with the UEFA Cup in 2001, then the one and only Kenny Dalglish with Ronnie Moran and Roy Evans and the old League Championship trophy in 1990, followed by Jürgen Klopp with the Champions League trophy in 2019, Jordan Henderson with the Premier League trophy in 2020, and previous captain Steven Gerrard with the European Cup in 2005.

They're all there on a long-format artwork below an LFC roll-of-honour on what's called The Champions Wall, between the official club store at Anfield and the Bob Paisley statue, where fans like to gather for selfies before the match.

Look a little closer, though, and you'll see that there's much more to this installation than first meets the eye. It's actually a photo-mosaic composed of 12,000 personal snaps submitted by Reds supporters on a first-come, first-served basis over season 2020/21 then uploaded and assembled into the finished piece. Special software was used to analyse the photos and allocate each one to the best available colour-matched spot.

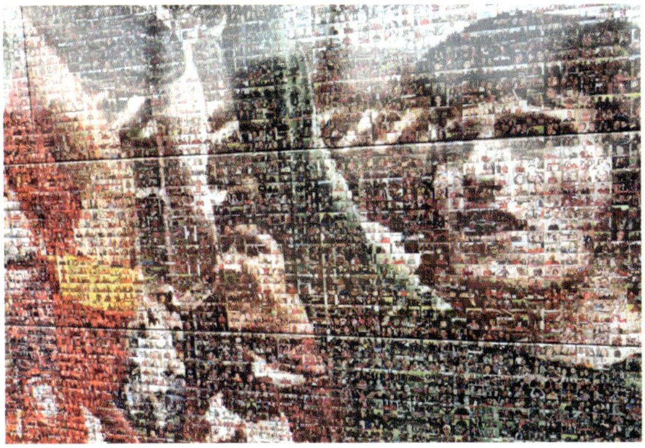

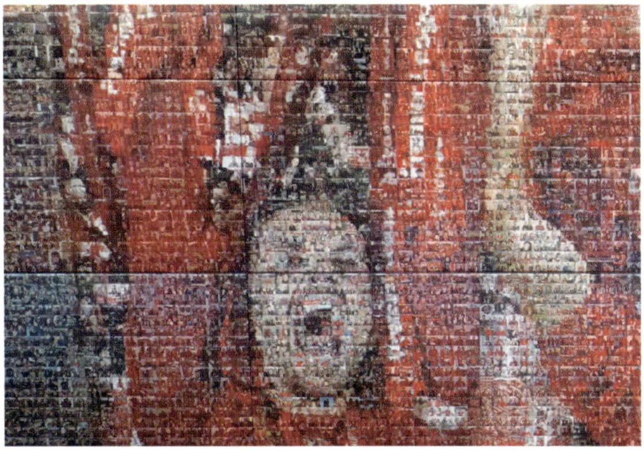

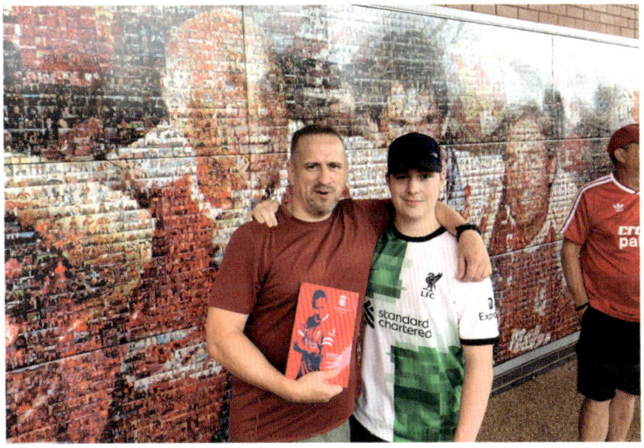

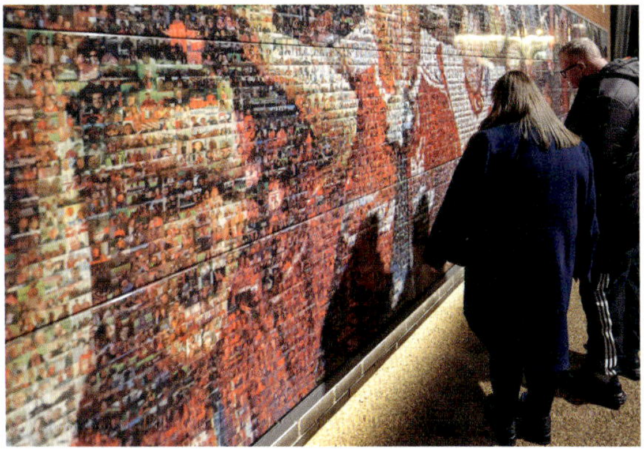

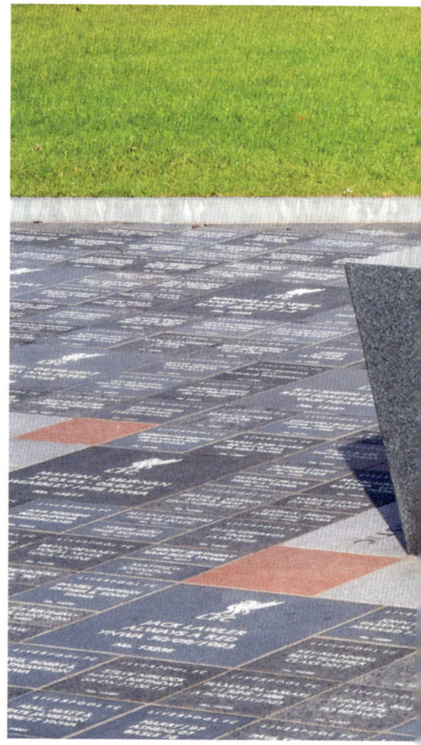

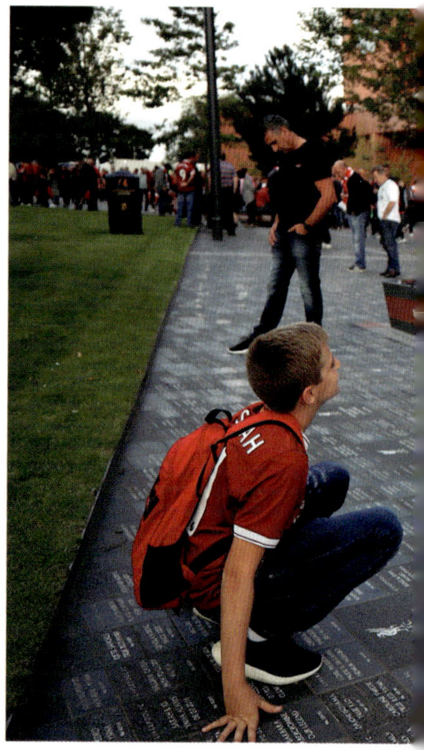

On the bench

Seven 'Men who built Anfield' are immortalised along 97 Avenue outside the Main Stand in a series of dark granite benches engraved in red and white. They are: Elisha Scott, Billy Liddell, Bill Shankly, Bob Paisley, Kenny Dalglish, John Barnes and Steven Gerrard.

Each bench is engraved with the legend's name and stats plus an evocative quotation, a brief biography and a match which mattered. In the case of Steven Gerrard: "Ooooohhhh you beauty! What a hit! What a hit!" followed by '86:00' (the Sky TV commentator's reaction and the time of his crucial goal against Olympiacos in the 2004/05 Champions League group stage). Then: 'This game, more than any other, showed Liverpool FC's inspirational captain Steven Gerrard at his very best as he rescued the team from Champions League elimination and paved the way for the glory of Istanbul'.

Shankly and Paisley, of course, have their own statues while Dalglish and Barnes, like the former captain, are the subjects of street murals near the stadium.

One of the football's finest-ever goalkeepers, Elisha Scott was brought over from Belfast in 1912 for an LFC career which would span 22 years and 468 appearances and include two consecutive top-flight titles (1922 and 1923), and he was reportedly the subject of the first-ever player chant at Anfield.

In 2013, a century after his debut, he was honoured with a special hour-long documentary on LFCTV.

'King' Billy Liddell made his debut for the Reds in January 1946. The Scottish winger would go on to find the net more than 200 times for Liverpool over 14 years, and remains fourth in the all-time LFC scorers list behind Ian Rush, Roger Hunt and Gordon Hodgson. "He was everything everyone said he was," recalled Ian Callaghan, who replaced Liddell in the team in the early 1960s.

"So strong on the ball it wasn't true, with a hammer of a shot in both feet. His name is like a neon sign on Merseyside."

All around the seven benches in this specially-landscaped area are hundreds of personalised stones in three different sizes engraved with the names of fans and collectively known as 'Anfield Forever'.

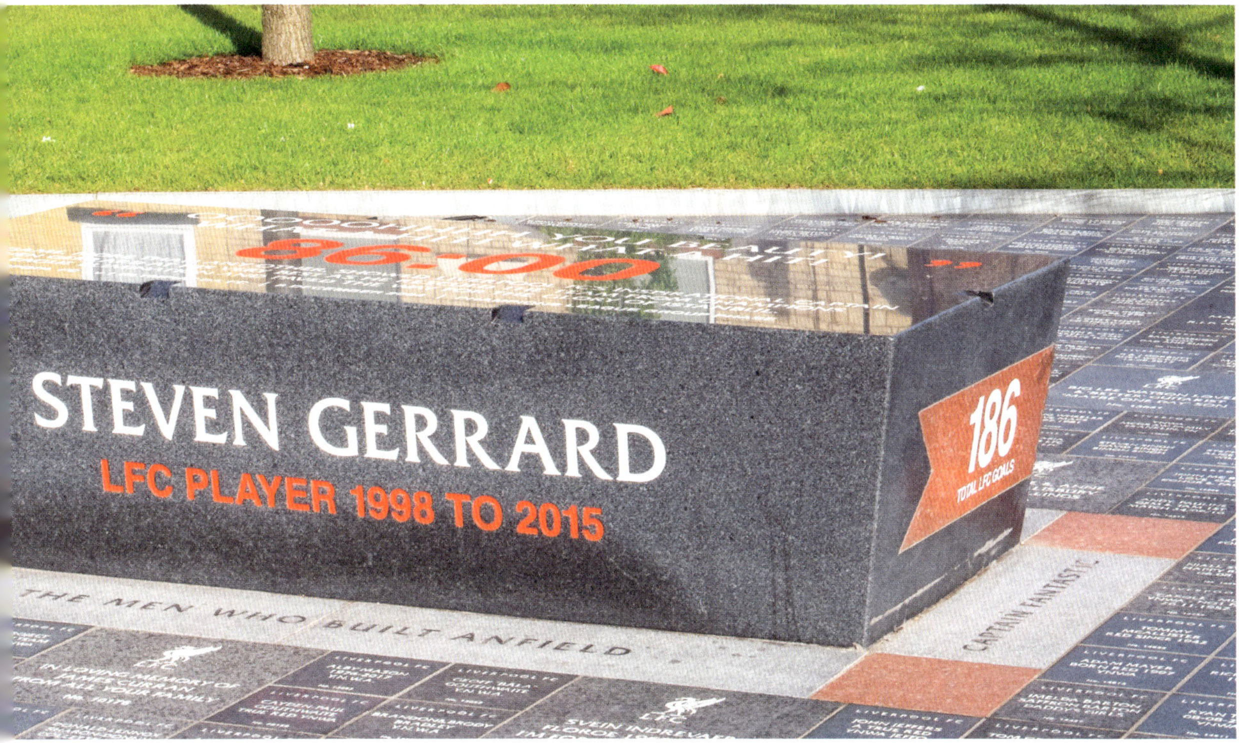
STEVEN GERRARD
LFC PLAYER 1998 TO 2015
186
TOTAL LFC GOALS
THE MEN WHO BUILT ANFIELD
CAPTAIN FANTASTIC

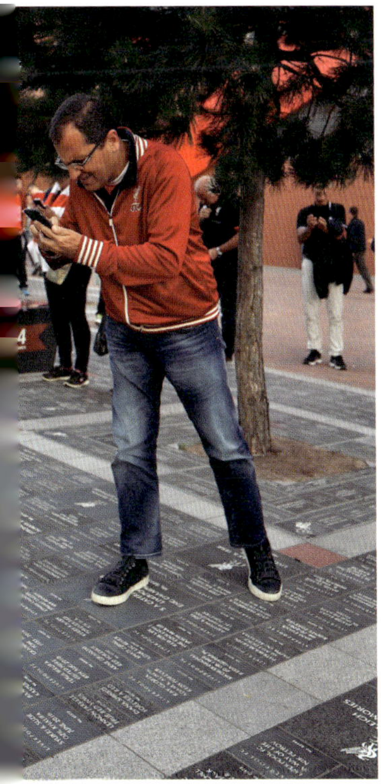

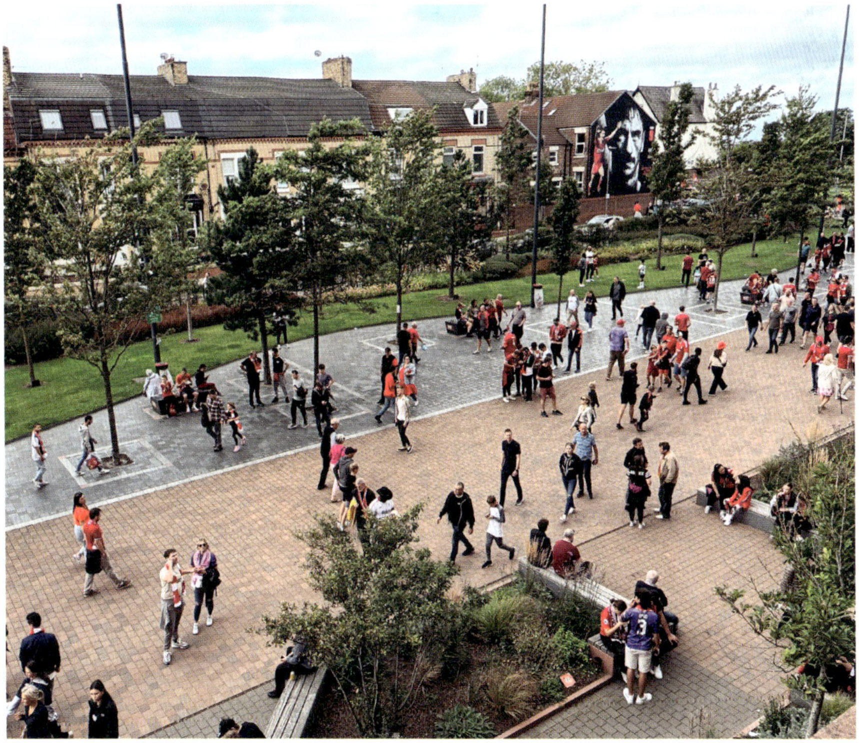

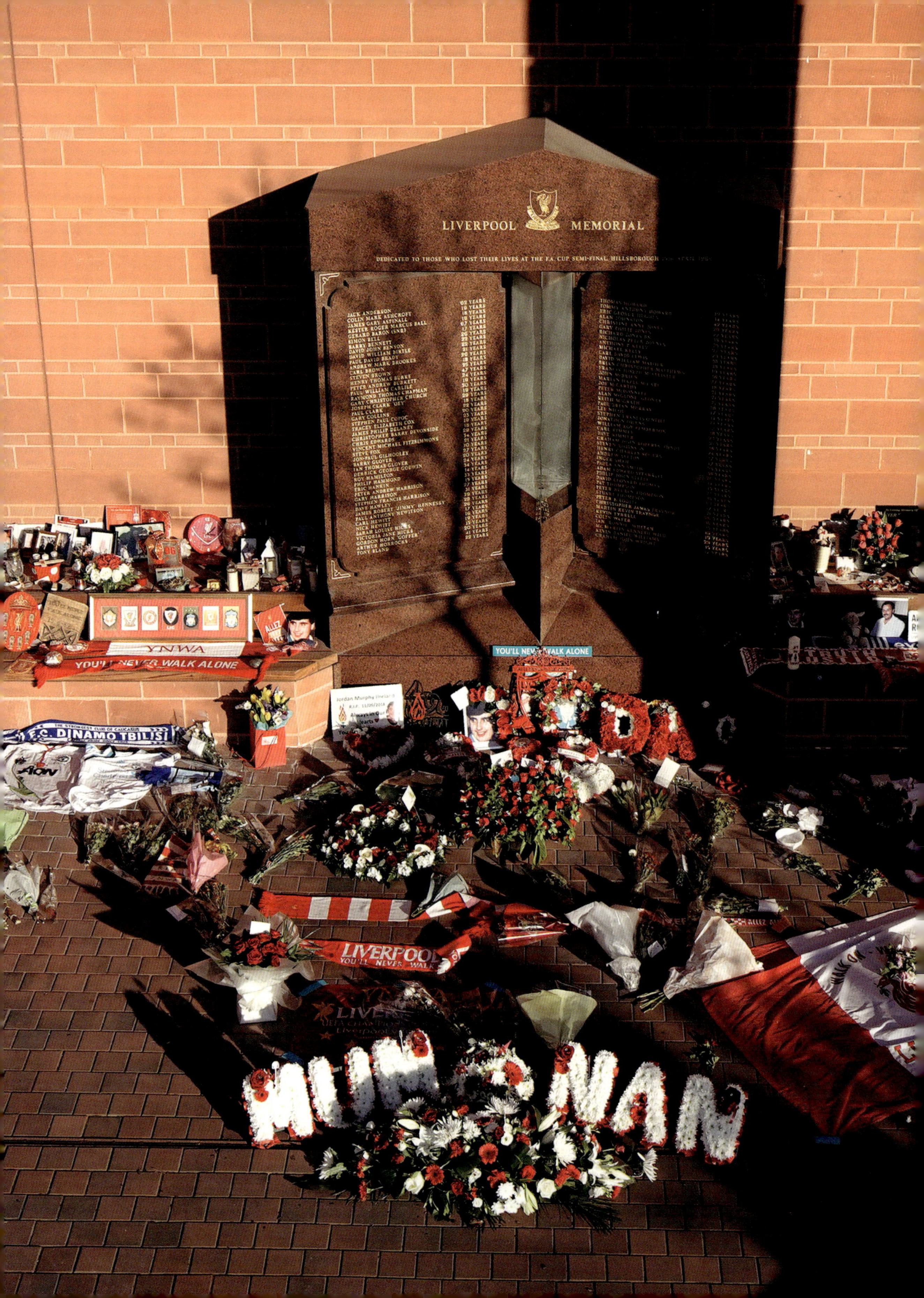
LIVERPOOL MEMORIAL
YNWA
YOU'LL NEVER WALK ALONE
YOU'LL NEVER WALK ALONE
F.C. DINAMO TBILISI
LIVERPOOL

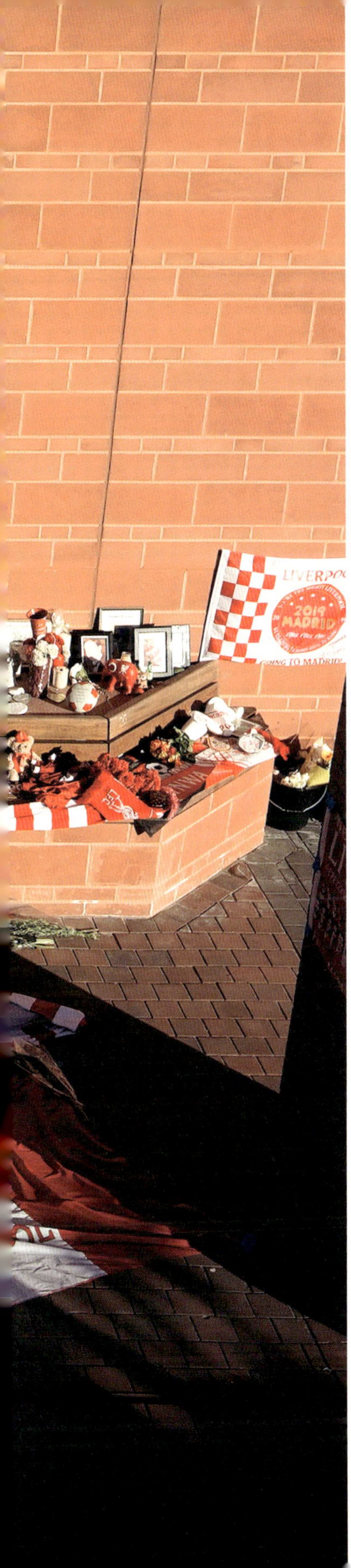

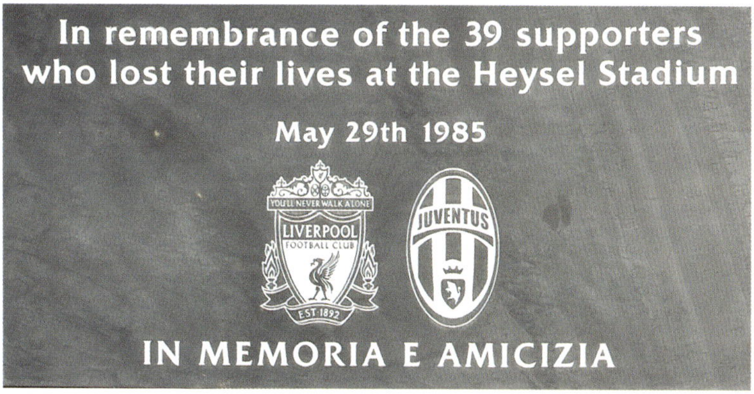

Never forget

Ninety-seven names and ages etched in 24-carat gold leaf on two adjacent slabs of polished Balmoral granite either side of an eternal flame. Above them, the Liverpool Football Club crest at the time of the Hillsborough disaster on Saturday 15 April 1989.

The 'LIVERPOOL MEMORIAL', as it is inscribed, is located in a cloister on 97 Avenue, having been relocated from Anfield Road during the Main Stand expansion. It's a place of pilgrimage for supporters of every football club, providing moments of poignancy and reflection on matchdays.

January 2022 saw the name of Andrew Stanley Devine added to those of the original 96 fans who were unlawfully killed. Lifelong supporter Andrew had passed away in July 2021 at the age of 55 as a result of the life-changing injuries he sustained.

On the opposite side of the stadium, outside the Sir Kenny Dalglish Stand, is the Heysel Memorial installed in 2010 as a permanent tribute to the 39 people who died at the 1985 European Cup final in Brussels. Underneath the club crests of Juventus FC and Liverpool FC it reads: IN MEMORIA E AMICIZIA ('In Memory And Friendship').

The memorial plaque was unveiled at Anfield by former Reds full-back Phil Neal and ex-Juventus player Sergio Brio. Every year floral tributes are placed beside it by club officials, and flags across all LFC sites are flown at half-mast.

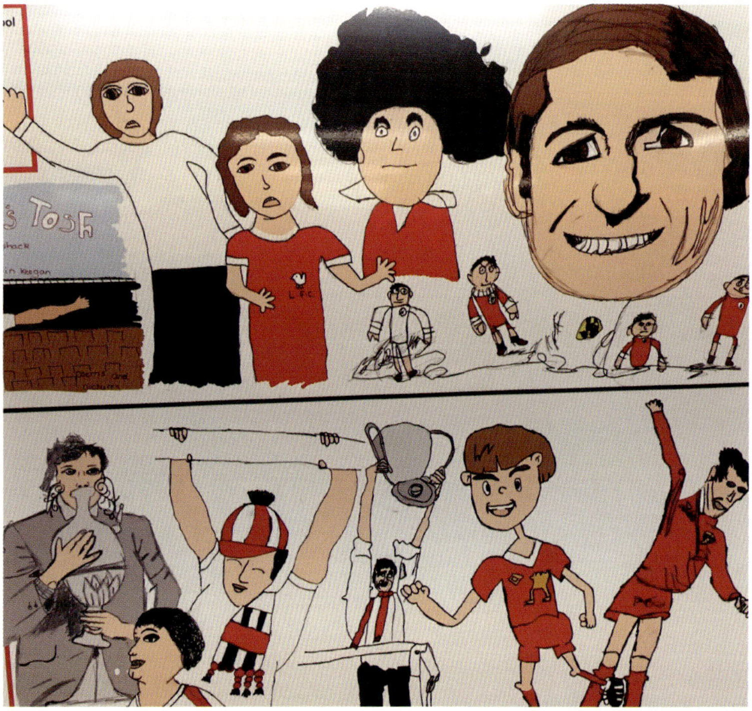

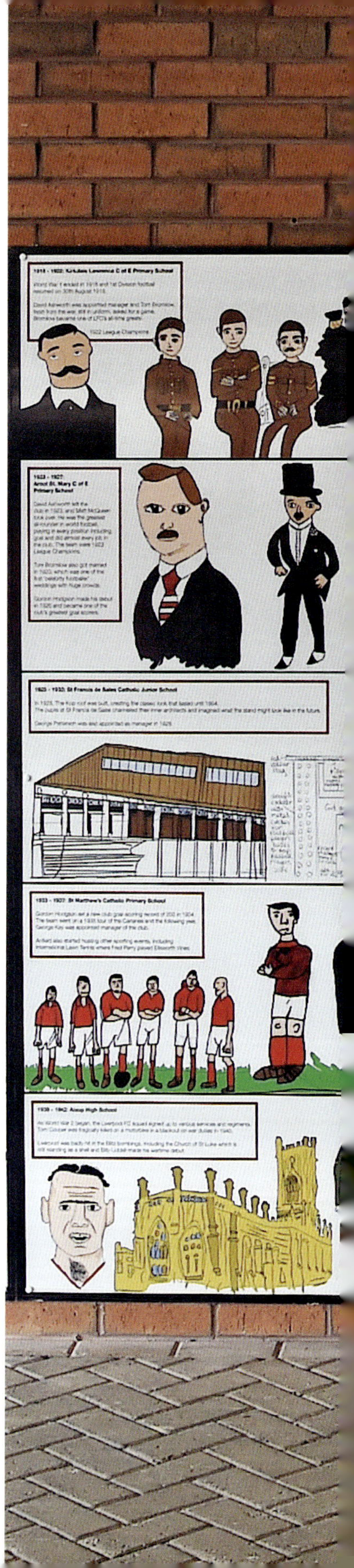

Class act

In the summer of 2018 a new mural with a difference was unveiled at Anfield commemorating the club's 125th anniversary. Permanently installed onto the Sir Kenny Dalglish Stand, it was created by hundreds of children from 25 schools neighbouring the stadium, all of them working closely with the club's Red Neighbours programme.

Liverpool FC commissioned local artist David Andrews to collaborate with the schools to create the canvas timeline artwork. He called it "an honour to know that the mural will be displayed at Anfield for all to see, for many years to come. The schoolchildren were brilliant, as were their illustrations – they should be extremely proud of what they've achieved."

David hosted workshops at each of the 25 schools, during which LFC's museum curator Stephen Done taught the youngsters about the history of the club. They allocated each school a specific five-year period from the 125-year history on which they should focus their piece of artwork.

One design from each school was chosen to be incorporated into the timeline, ensuring that the full 125 years were represented.

When assembling the full-sized mural, David scanned a selection of the most poignant drawings and added colour digitally to ensure that it had a uniform style throughout and appeared in comic-book style.

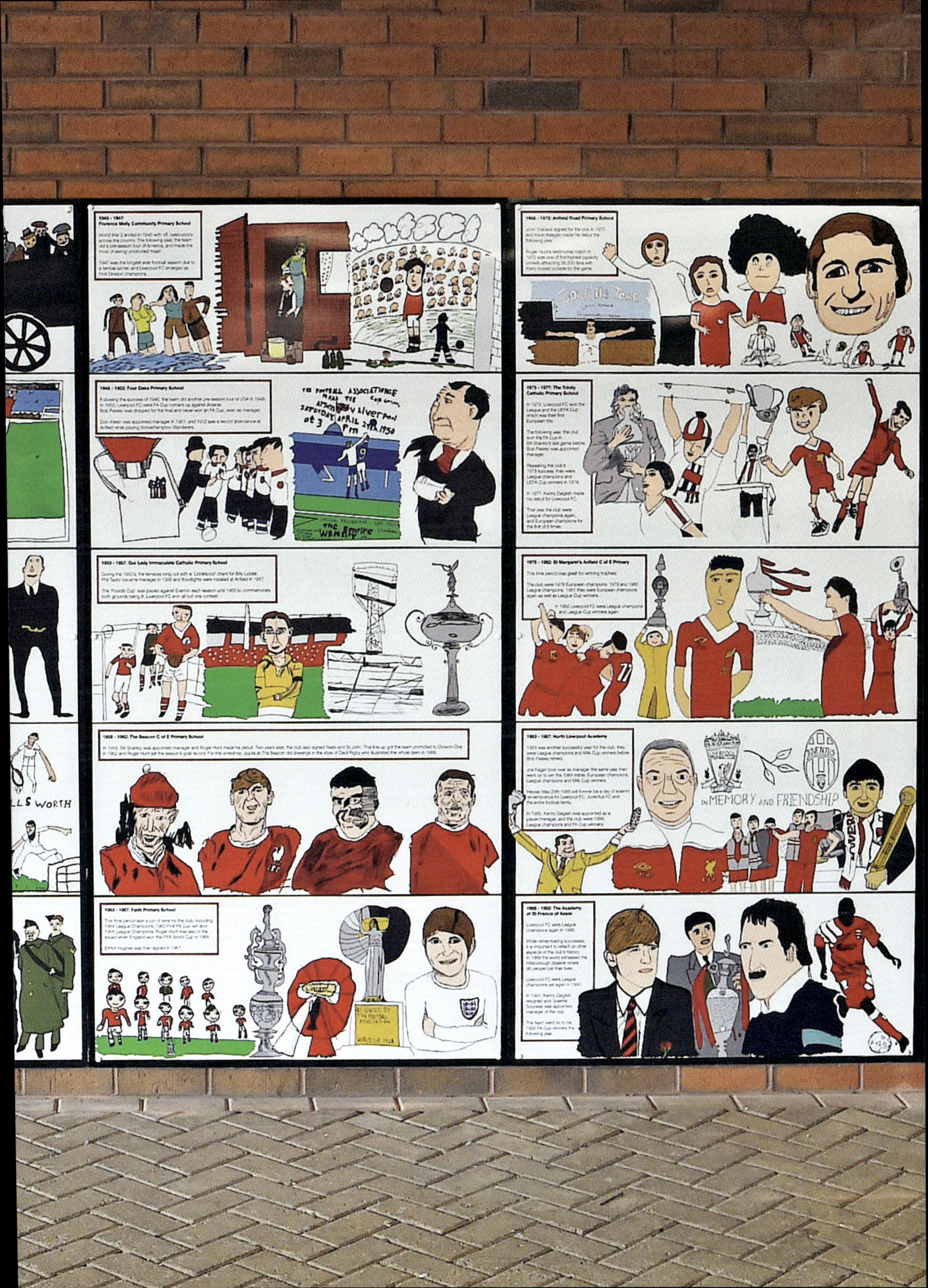
IN MEMORY AND FRIENDSHIP

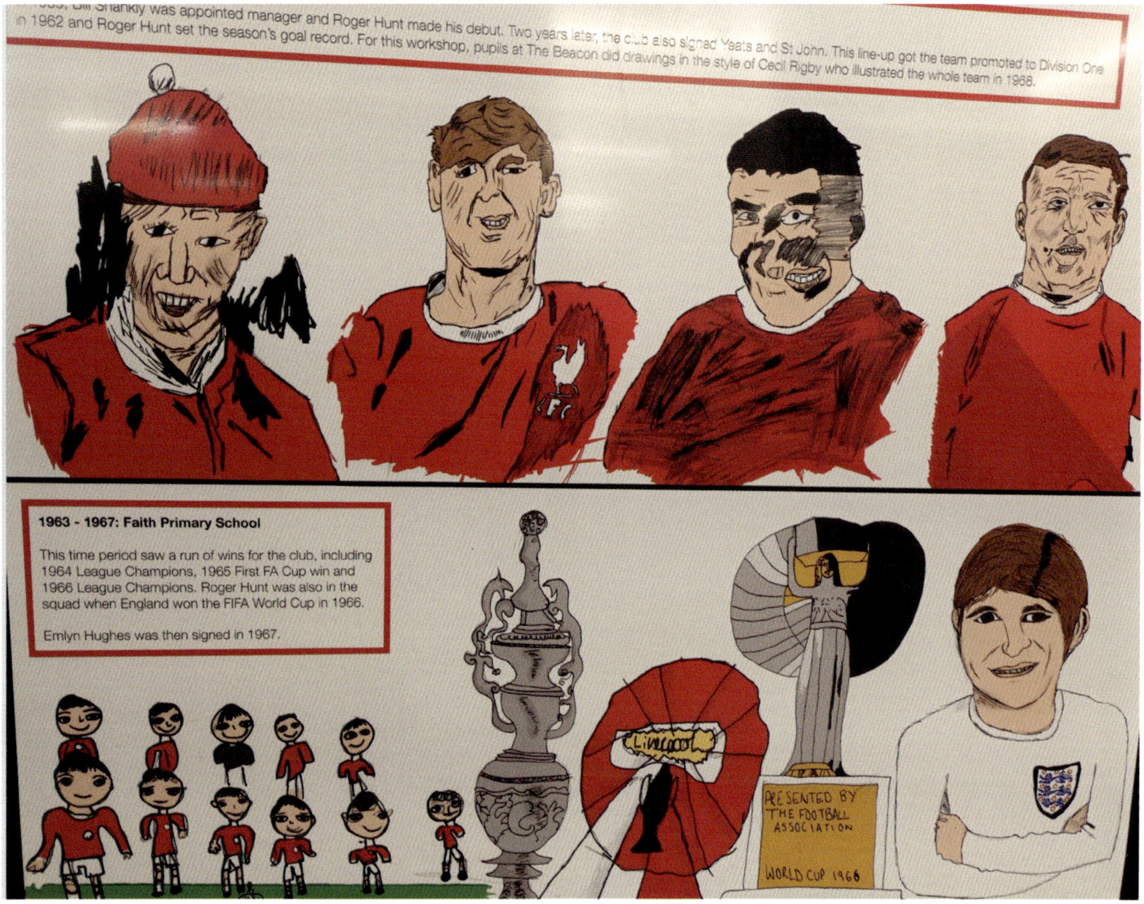
Bill Shankly was appointed manager and Roger Hunt made his debut. Two years later, the club also signed Yeats and St John. This line-up got the team promoted to Division One in 1962 and Roger Hunt set the season's goal record. For this workshop, pupils at The Beacon did drawings in the style of Cecil Rigby who illustrated the whole team in 1968.
1963 - 1967: Faith Primary School
This time period saw a run of wins for the club, including 1964 League Champions, 1965 First FA Cup win and 1966 League Champions. Roger Hunt was also in the squad when England won the FIFA World Cup in 1966.
Emlyn Hughes was then signed in 1967.
PRESENTED BY THE FOOTBALL ASSOCIATION
WORLD CUP 1966

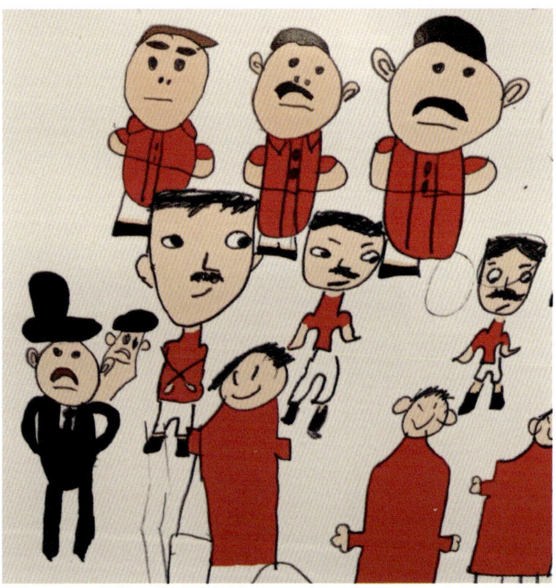

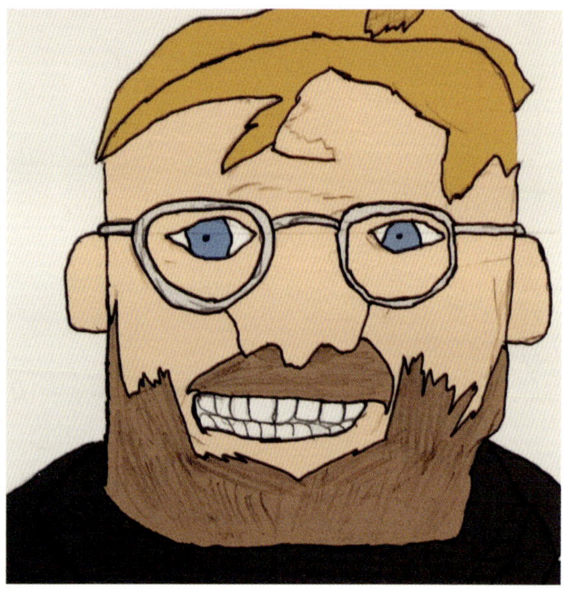

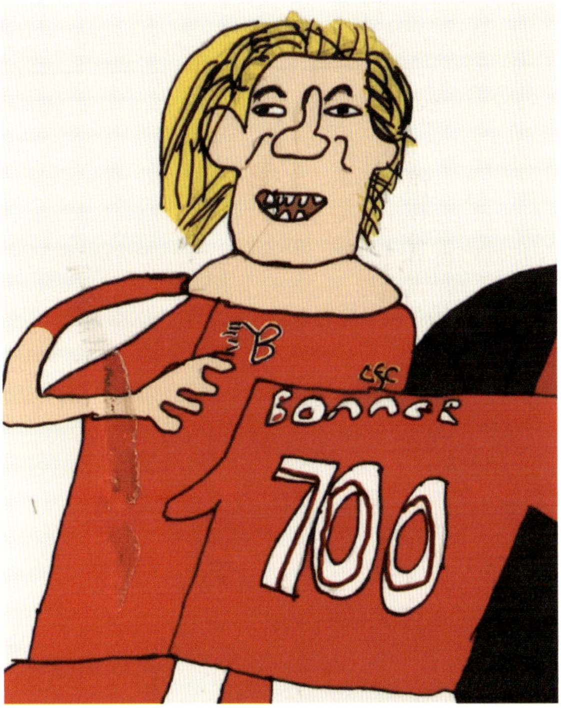
LFC
BONNER
700

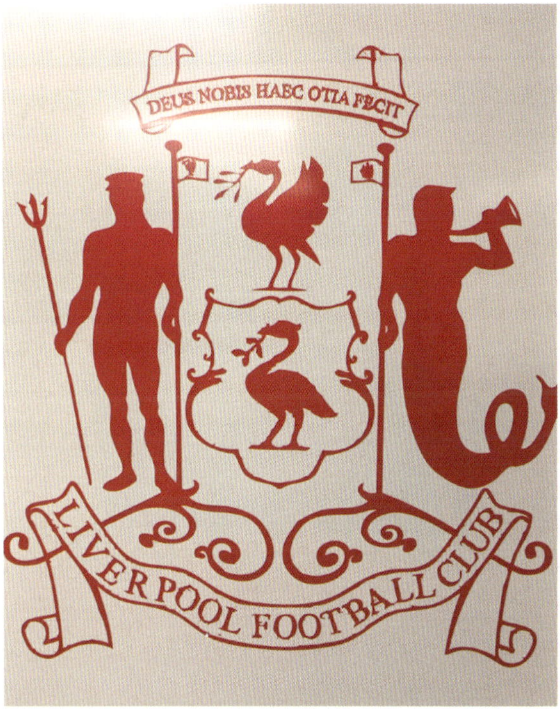
DEUS NOBIS HAEC OTIA FECIT
LIVERPOOL FOOTBALL CLUB

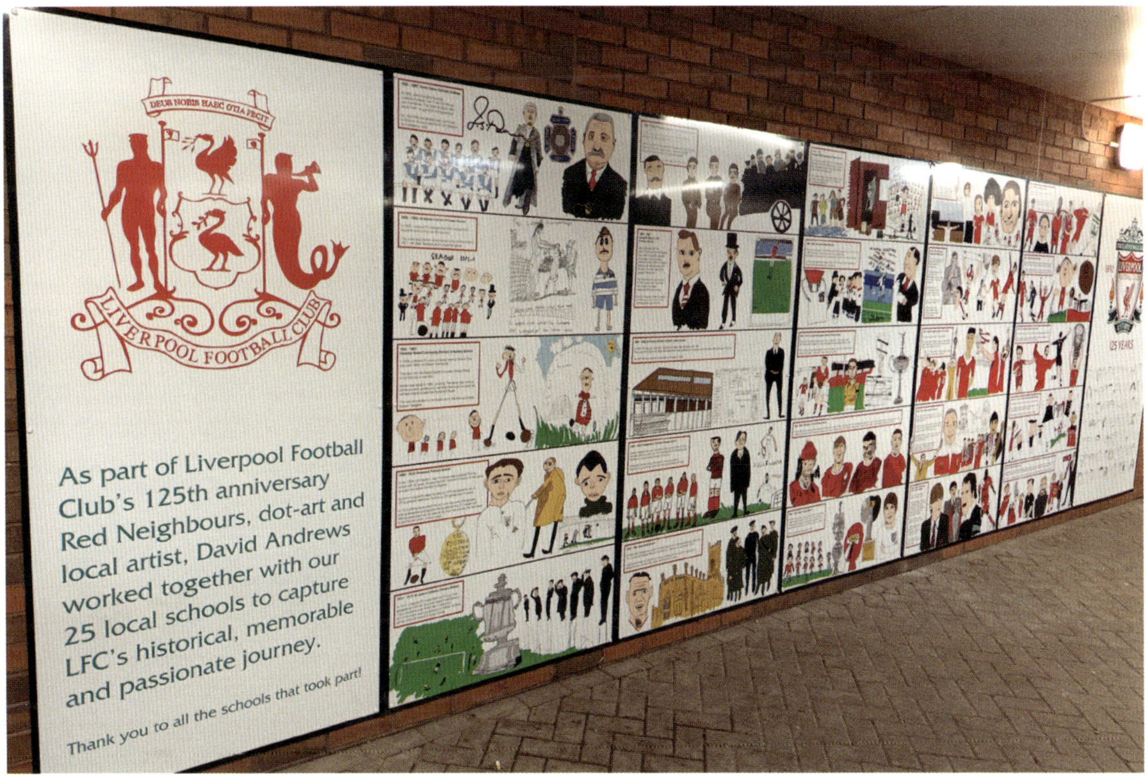
DEUS NOBIS HAEC OTIA FECIT
LIVERPOOL FOOTBALL CLUB
As part of Liverpool Football Club's 125th anniversary Red Neighbours, dot-art and local artist, David Andrews worked together with our 25 local schools to capture LFC's historical, memorable and passionate journey.
Thank you to all the schools that took part!
125 YEARS

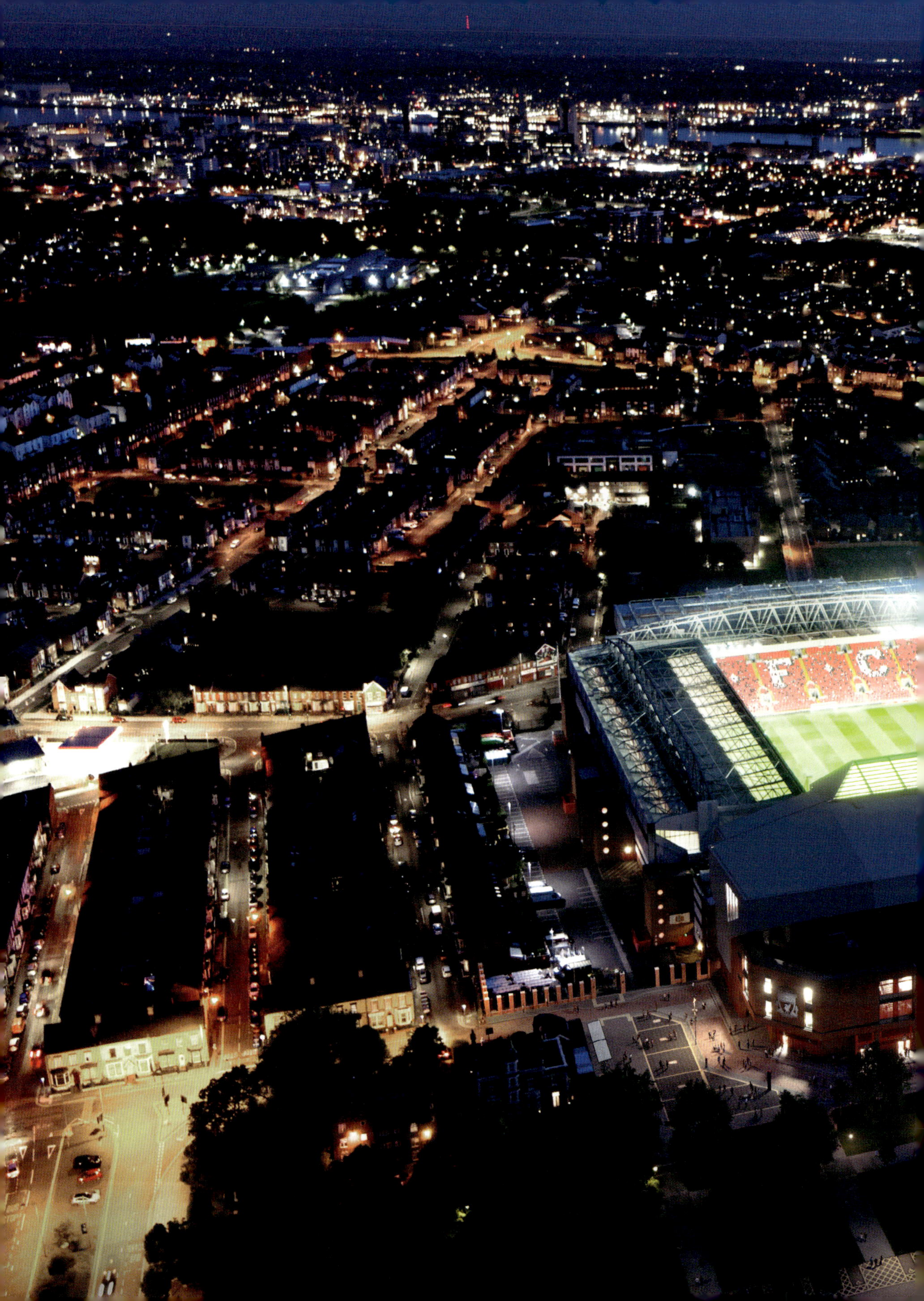

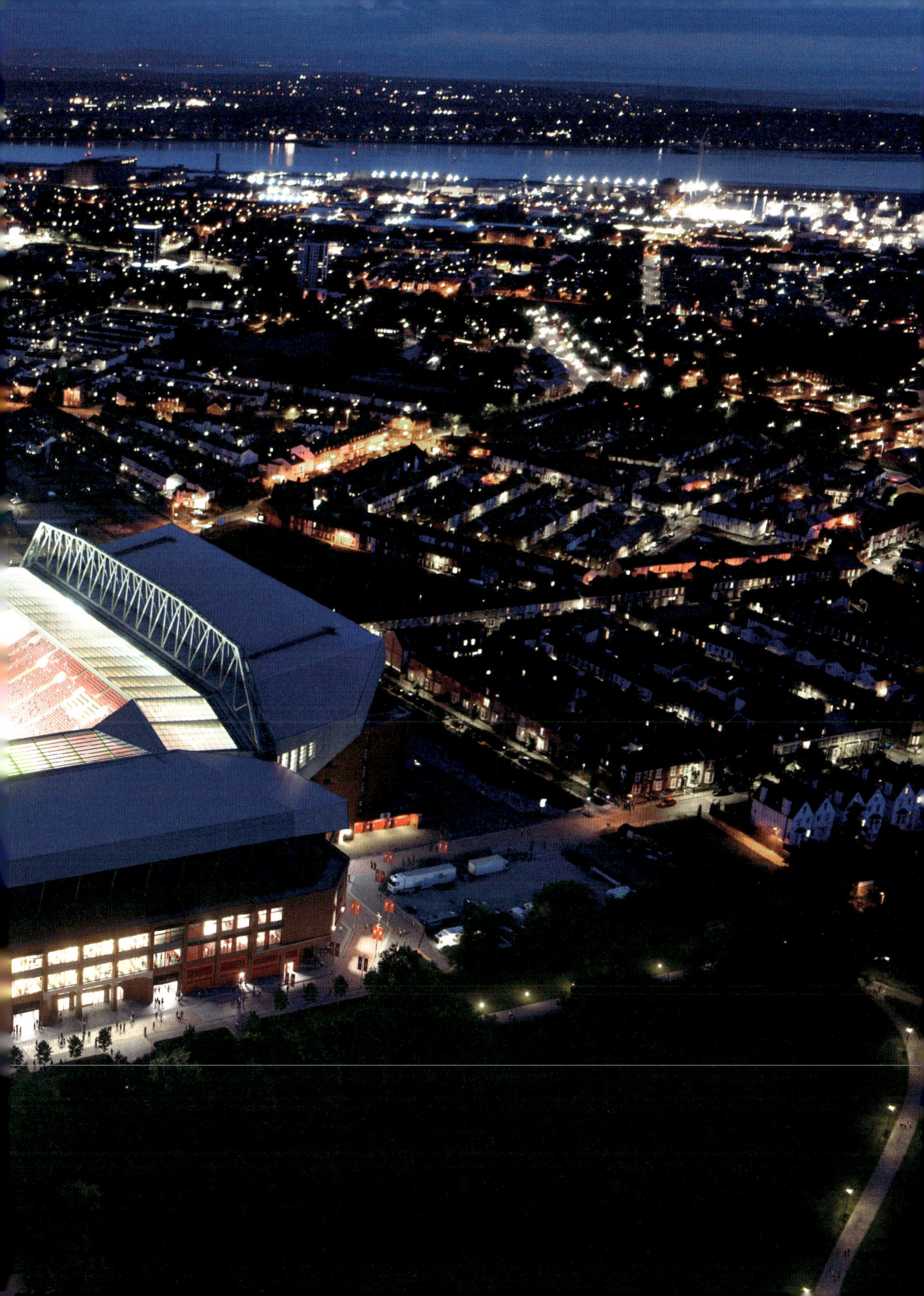

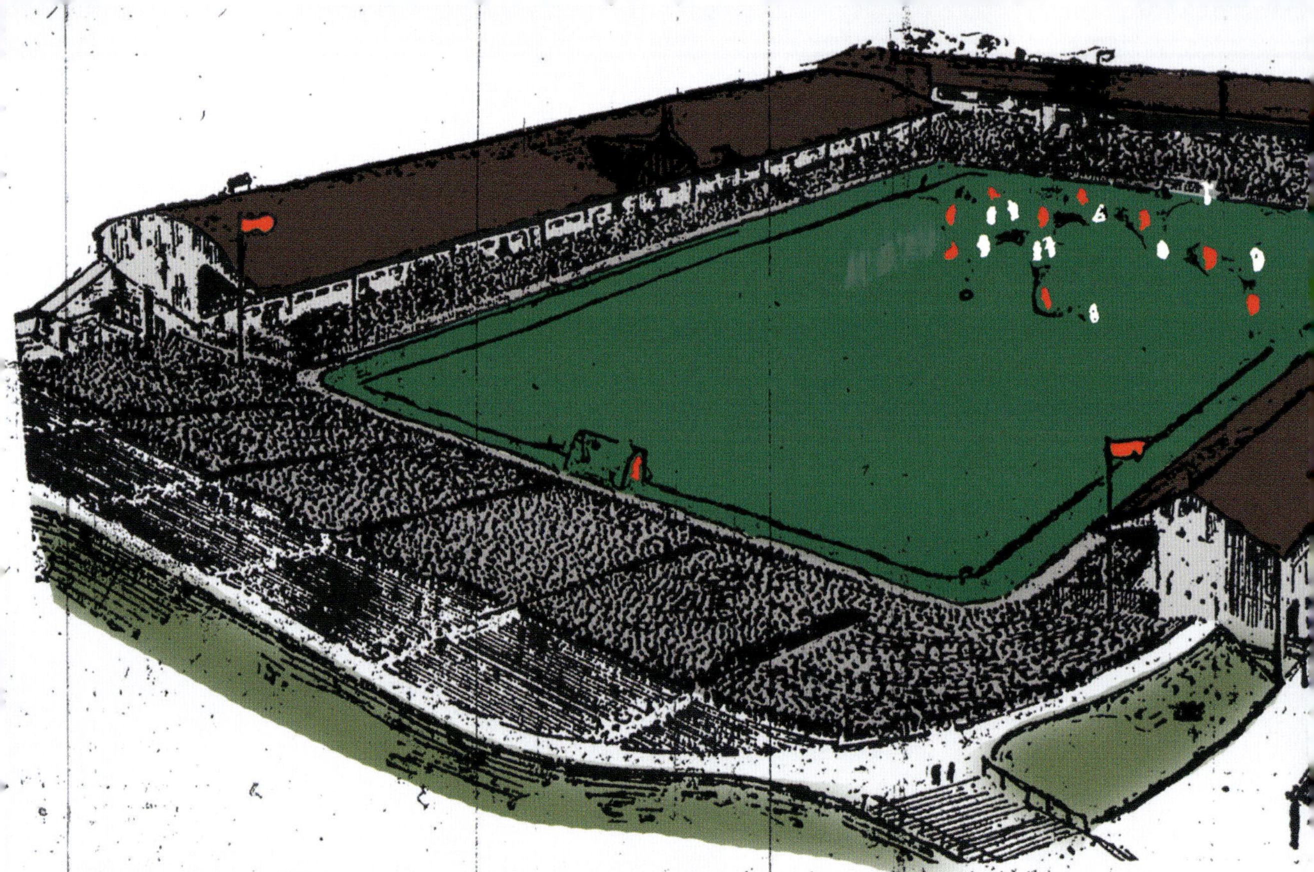

BIRD'S-EYE VIEW OF THE NEW LIVERPOOL FOOTBALL GROUND AS IT WILL APPEAR WHEN

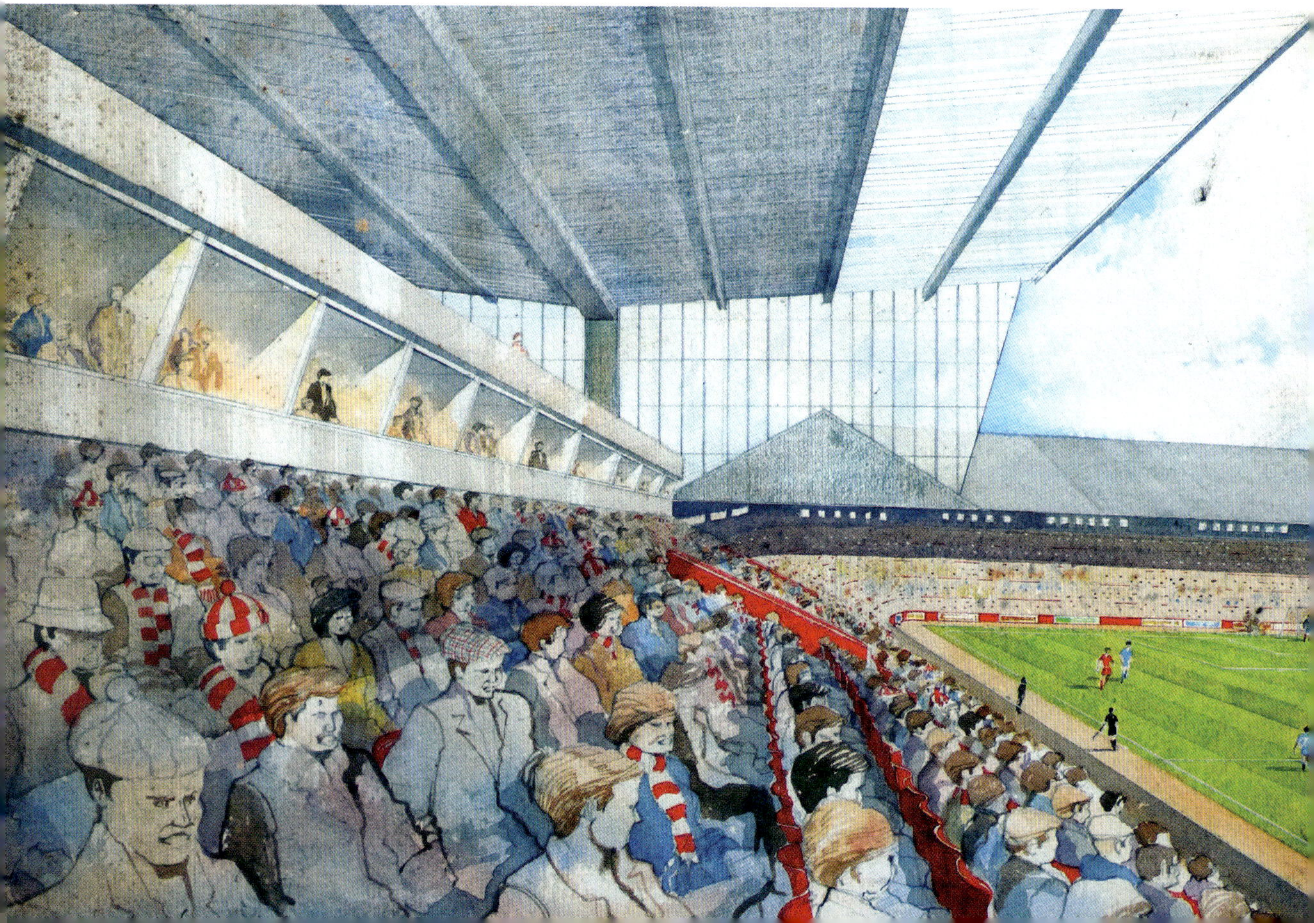

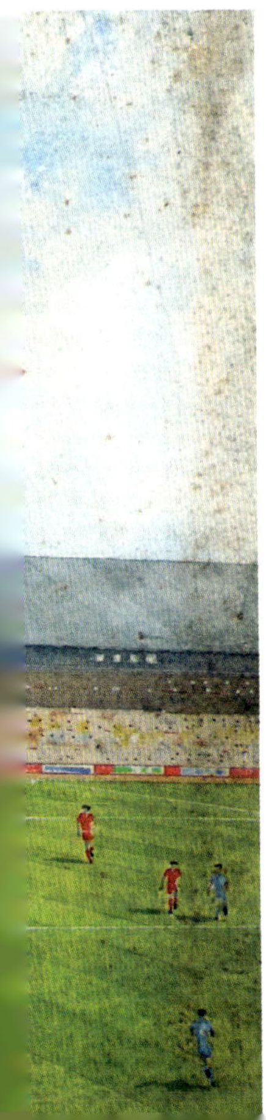

First impressions

With two major redevelopment projects taking place at Anfield in recent years – the expansions of the Main Stand then the Anfield Road Stand – fans have become used to seeing the future revealed by computer-generated imagery or CGI as it's more commonly known, with the real thing looking uncannily like its digital depiction in due course. These can include not just panoramic views of the stand in question but also its interior and the immediate neighbourhood.

Once upon a time, though, these visualisations literally were artist's impressions rendered in ink or paint. When the football season kicked off in August 1906 it's a fair guess that Liverpool fans were as excited about returning to Anfield as they'd be in 2023. Back then it wasn't an extended Anfield Road Stand they were raving about – it was an all-new Spion Kop, constructed after the team's second top-flight title win.

Except it wasn't officially called the Kop, at least not for another few years. It was known as the Oakfield Road Embankment. Two local newspapers, *The Liverpool Echo* and *The Liverpool Weekly Mercury*, ran with "a bird's-eye view of the new Liverpool football ground, as it will appear when completed" [colourised here on the left by today's matchday programme design team] and this is how the *Echo* reported upon the vast terrace's arrival...

The Anfield Review 'Pic' of the Week

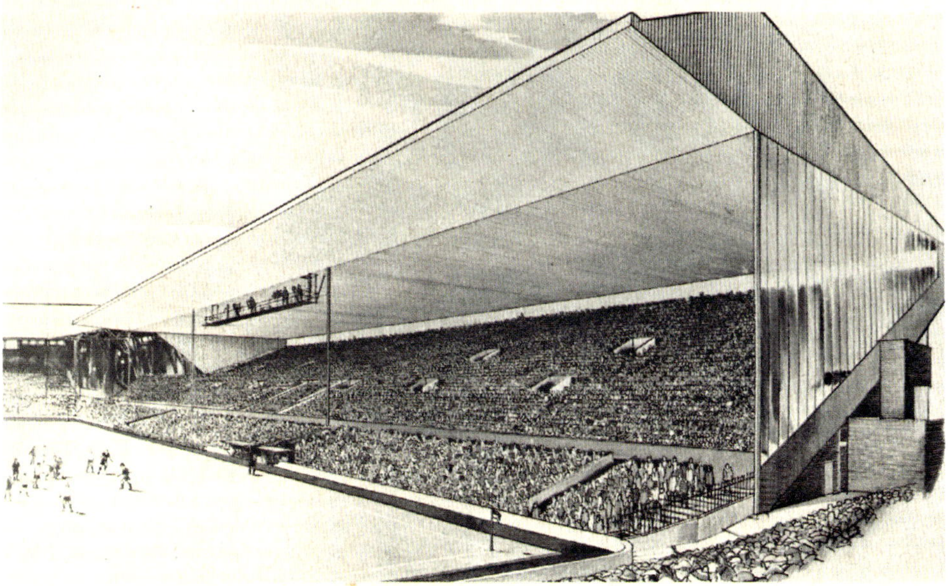

An artist's impression of our new main stand (see page 4).

"From the sketch here (for which we are indebted to Mr Archibald Leitch, the engineer who has laid out the ground) it will be seen that the aspect of the old football enclosure at Anfield has been entirely changed. The ground has been completely walled-in with fancy brick setting, with large exit gates on the four sides, as well as numerous entrances. Therefore there will be no difficulty in either entering or leaving the enclosure.

"The directors' aim has been to provide as compact and comfortable a ground as possible, in which every person, no matter what portion he may visit, will have a full view of the game. The playing pitch has been raised about five feet, with a paddock all round. Roofed-in stand accommodation will be plentiful, and at one end, as seen in the sketch, will be an elevated terrace consisting of 132 tiers of steps, which will afford space for something like 20,000 spectators.

"The entire scheme is modelled on a new departure from what football grounds are generally supposed to be, and when completed will provide ample space for about 60,000 visitors. The stands, of which two only are erected at present, are built on massive brick foundations, and are as safe as skill and good workmanship can make them, and ample provision for the comfort of players in the way of bath and recreation rooms has been attended to."

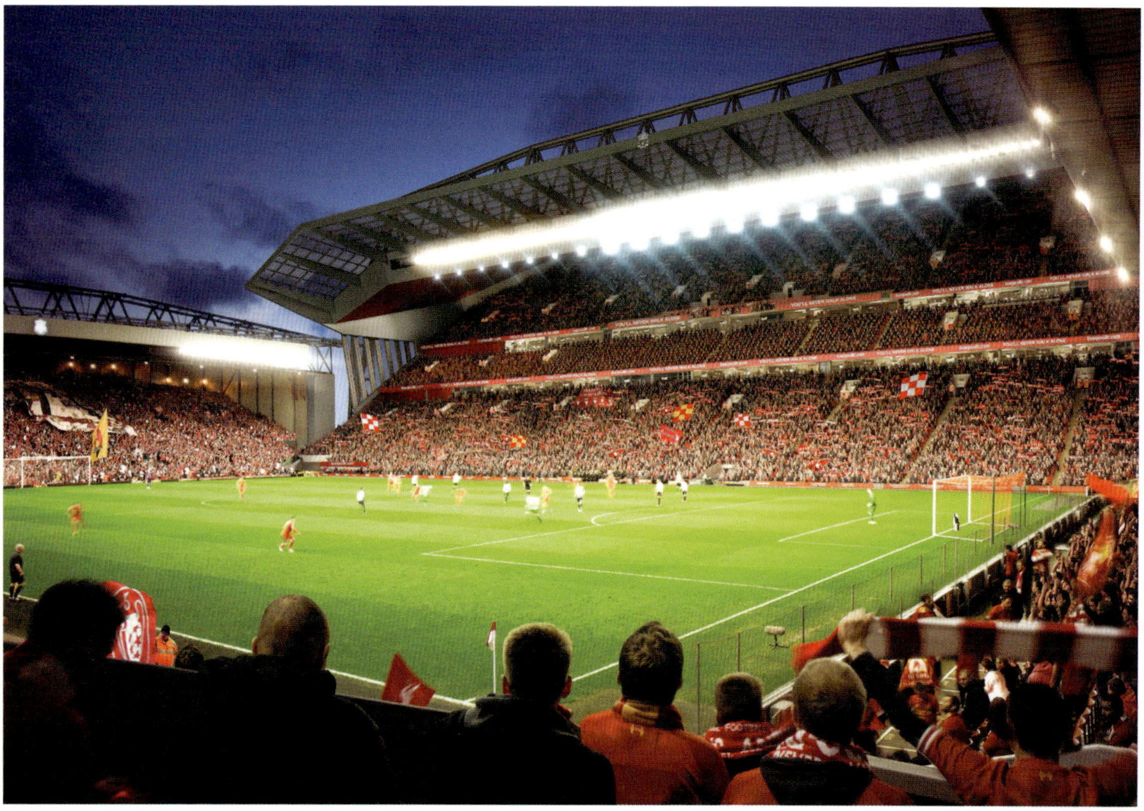

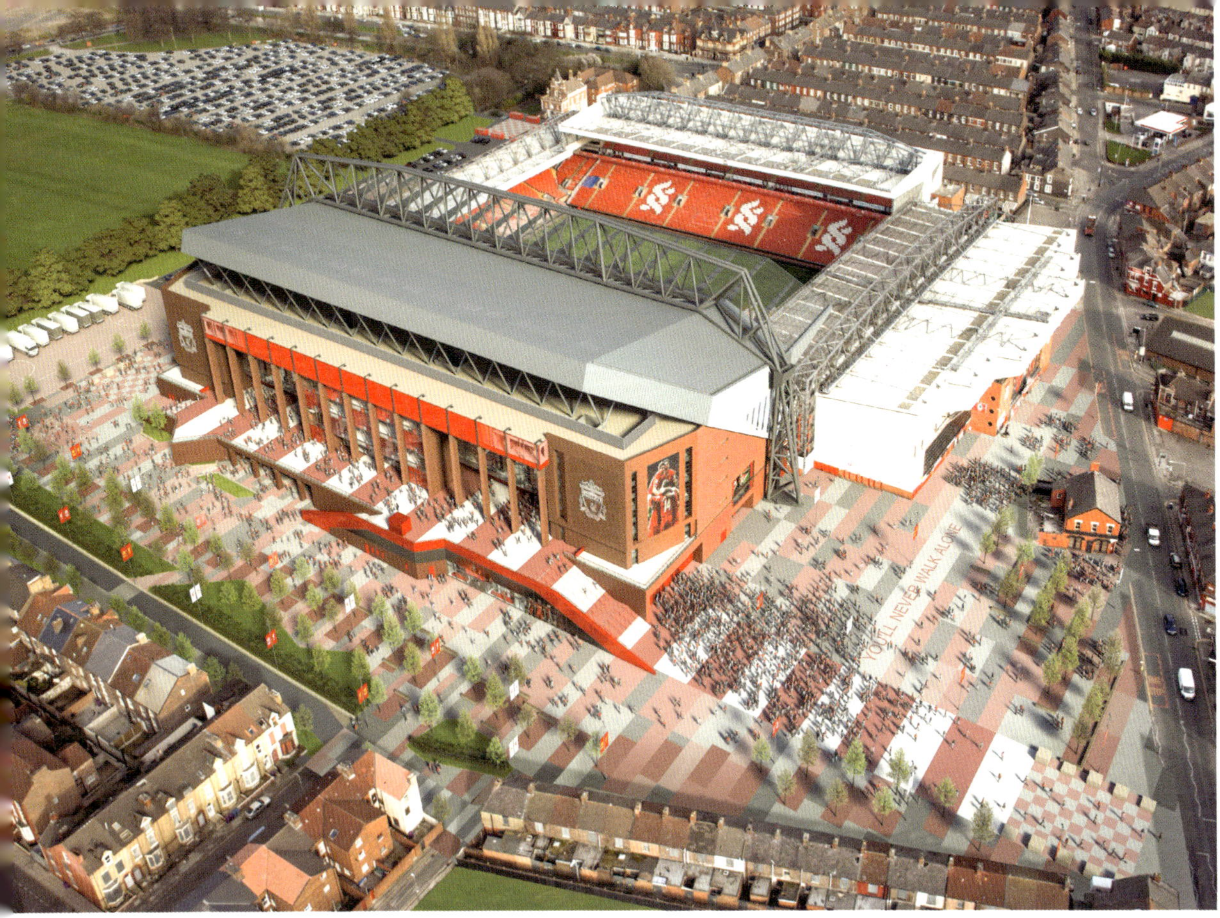
YOU'LL NEVER WALK ALONE

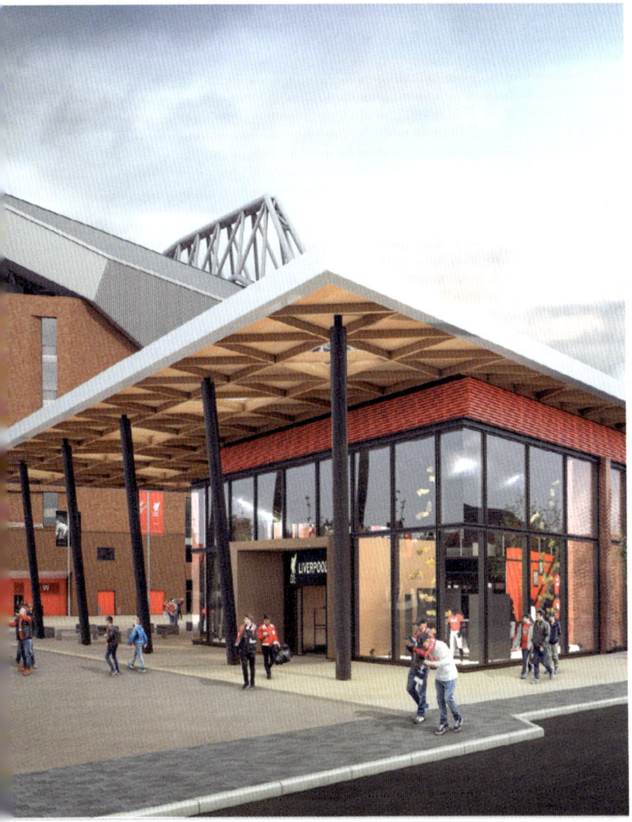
LIVERPOOL

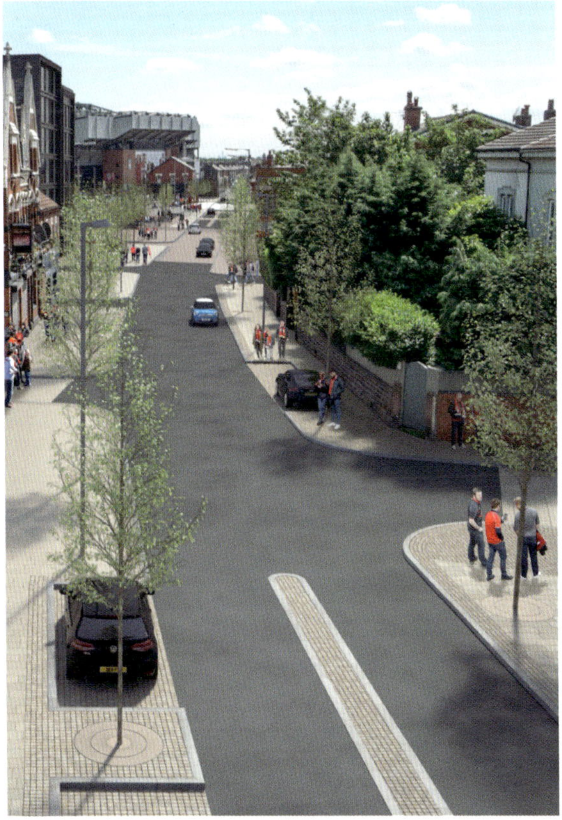

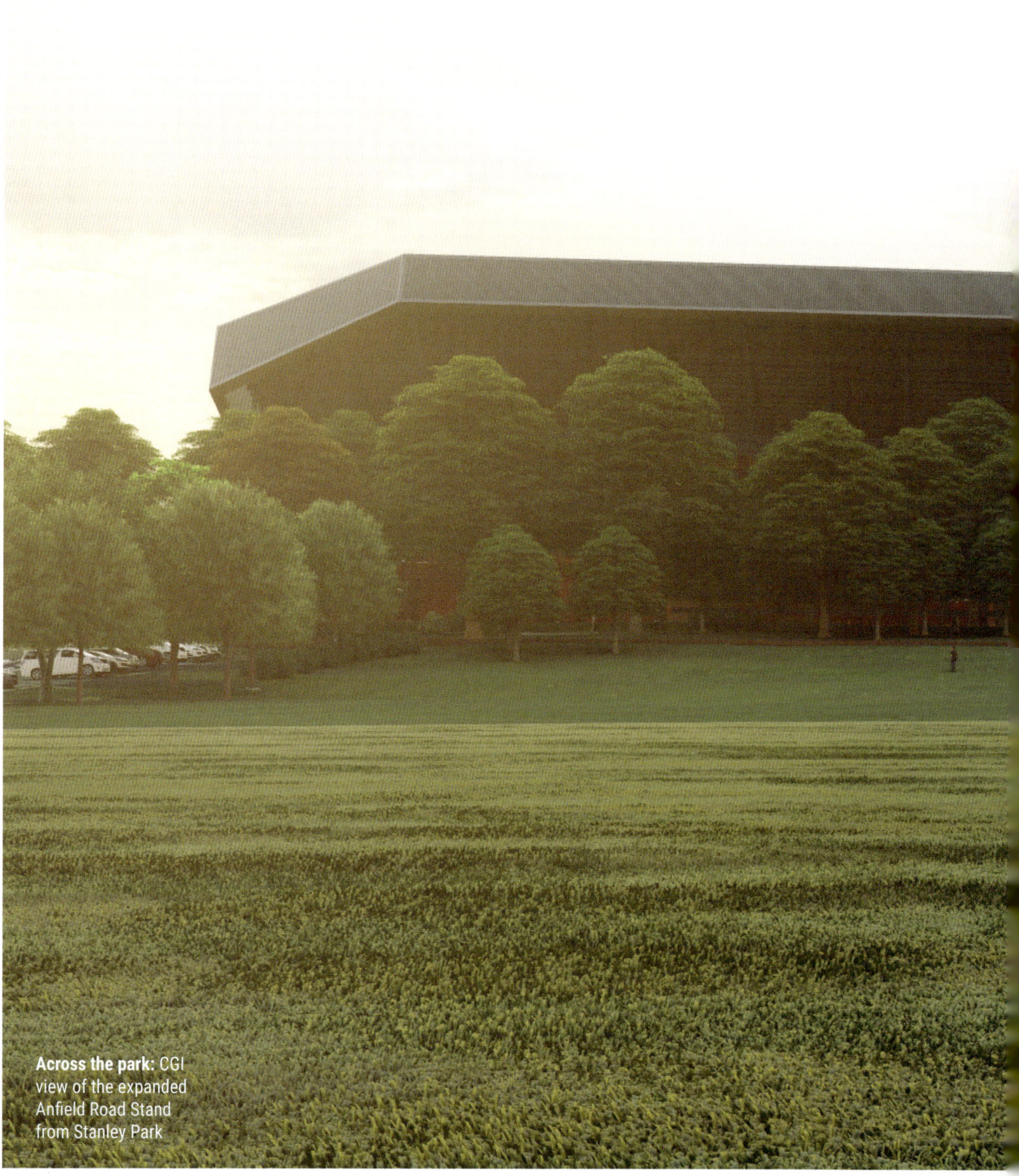

Across the park: CGI view of the expanded Anfield Road Stand from Stanley Park

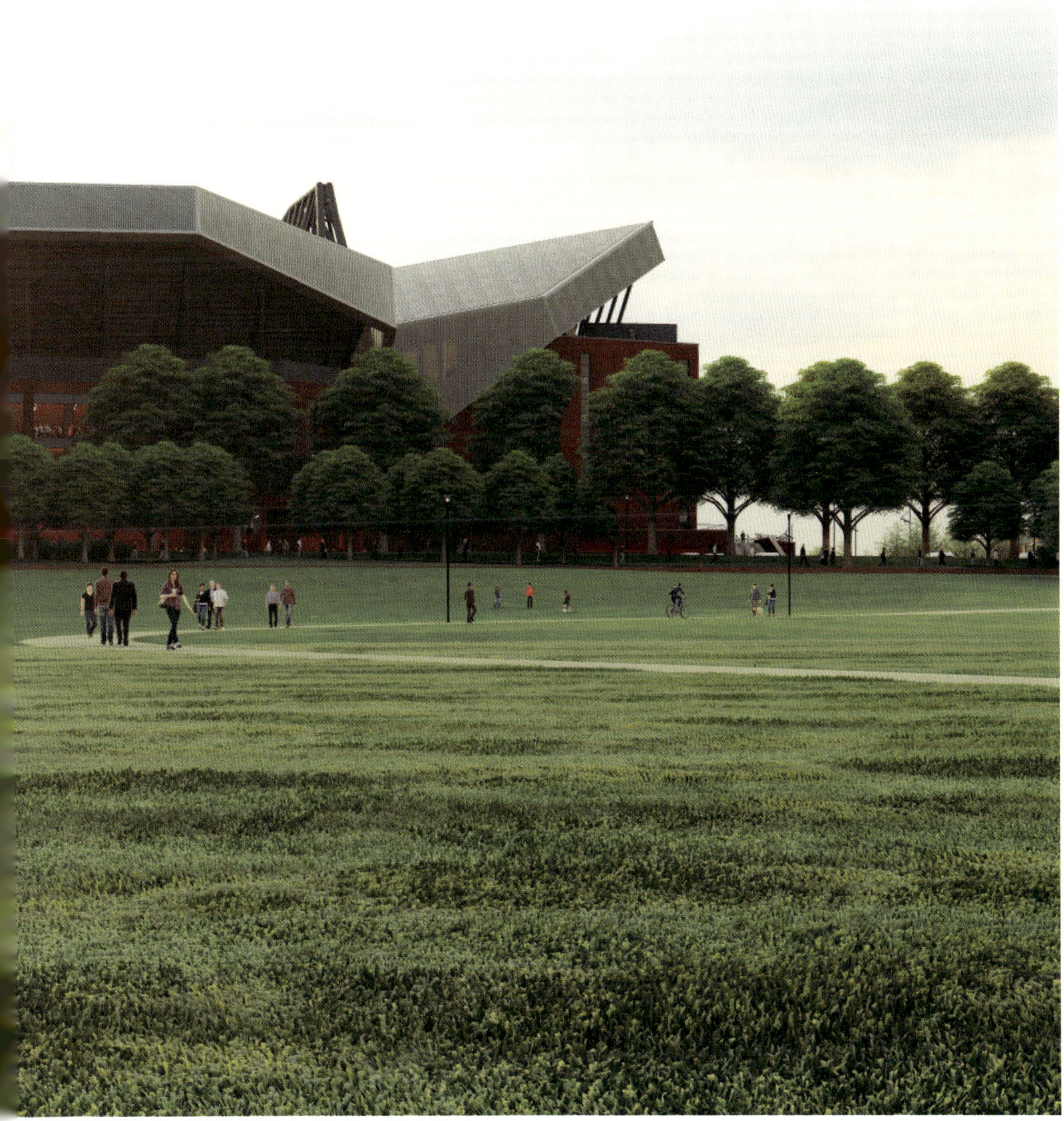

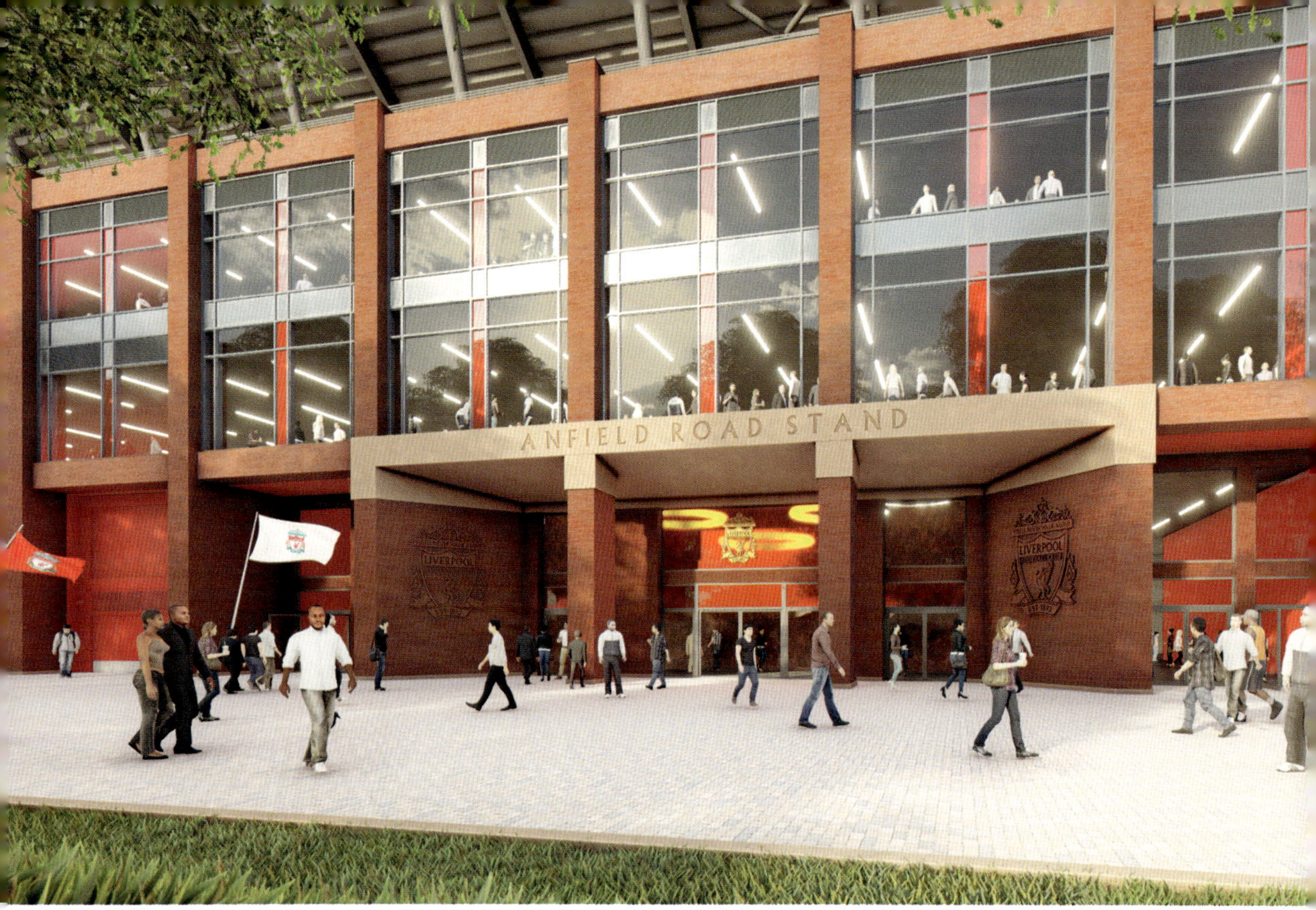
ANFIELD ROAD STAND
LIVERPOOL
LIVERPOOL
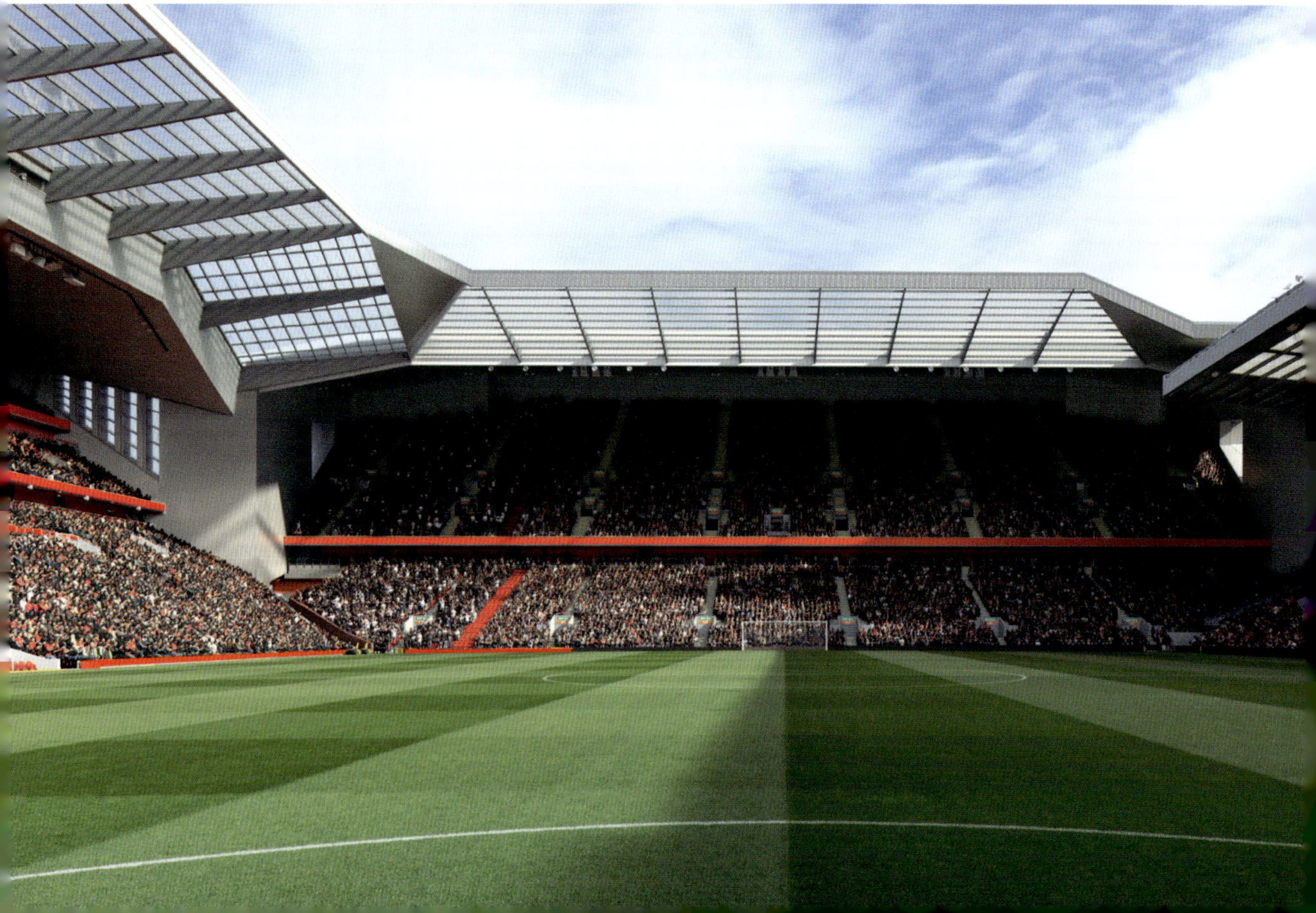

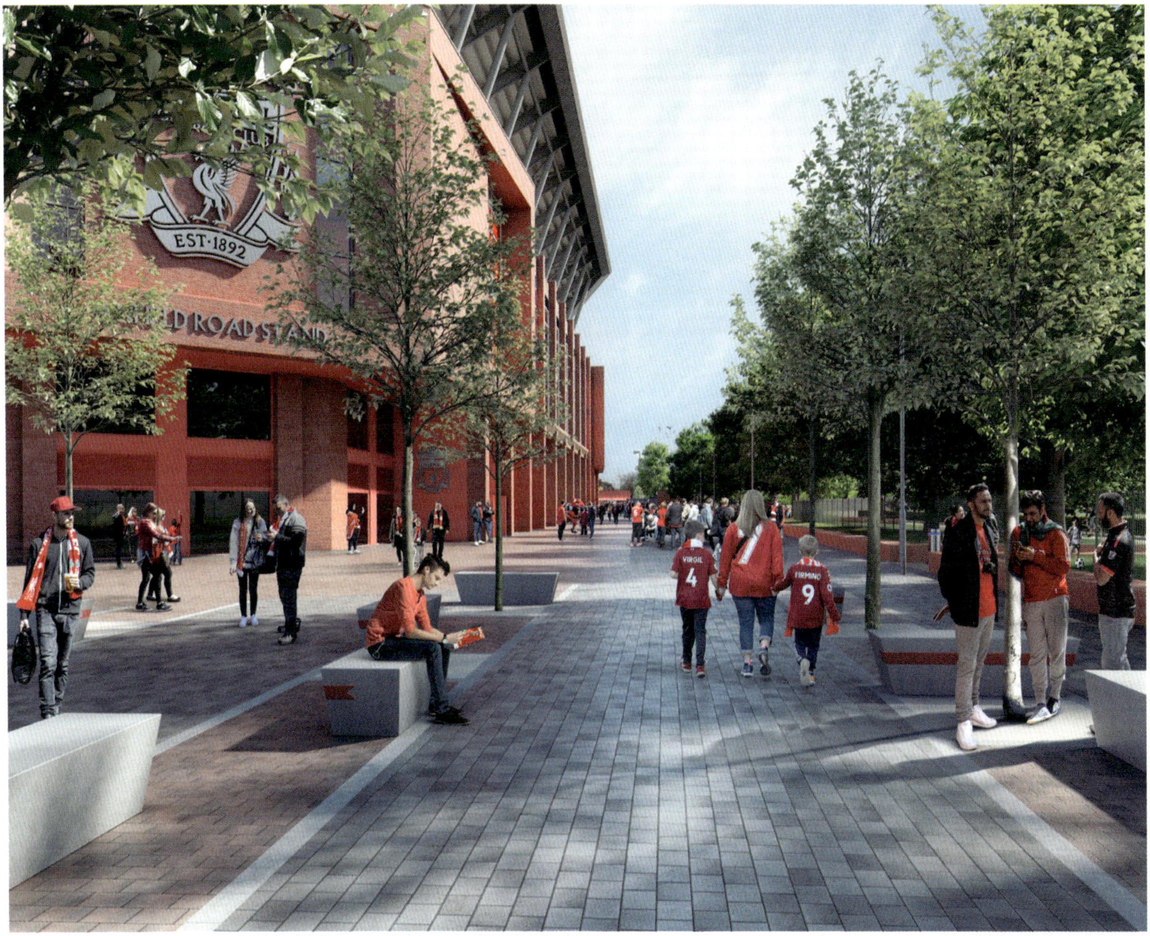

Sixty-four years later, in February 1970, the matchday programme carried a pen-and-ink portrayal of Anfield's new Main Stand – then also known as the Lake Street Stand – which would be increased in height and covered by a modern roof. With it came new dressing-rooms, a new players lounge, and a new restaurant. It was officially opened in March 1973.

In 1990 it was the turn of what would soon become the Centenary Stand, rendered in watercolours, as football entered a new era. The publication of the Taylor Report called for safety improvements at stadiums across the country and the Kemlyn Road Stand – as it was known at the time – underwent a major overhaul in time for the club's 100th anniversary. As well as the addition of a second tier, there was a new cantilever roof, executive boxes and function rooms.

Which brings us to the modern era and dynamic digital depictions of the extended Main Stand and Anfield Road Stand, officially opened in the autumns of 2016 and 2023 respectively. These images have whetted the appetite of Reds supporters and neutral observers alike with their perspectives from street and drone levels and high above.

Inside the stands

Nothing inside Anfield Stadium is there just for show – its comfortable and friendly spaces are there to welcome fans and visitors alike with a touch of something special, and its stories are a celebration of past, present and future.

Artwork flourishes throughout the interiors of the most recently expanded stands, the Anfield Road Stand and Main Stand, alongside a 'DNA' of design, colour palette and typography which weaves through the stadium like a red thread.

The magnificent double-tier Anfield Road Stand was set for competition in late 2023, the second part of the masterplan vision for Anfield increasing the stadium's overall matchday capacity to around 61,000.

With it has come a focus on curating and celebrating what makes Anfield so special, with interior visual treatments and themes inspired by the unique spirit and personality of one of world football's most famous grounds – and of course the part which the 'Annie Road' has played in its history.

It's the fourth major capital-build project undertaken by Liverpool FC in recent years, following the expanded Main Stand in 2016, the Anfield Megastore in 2017 and the AXA Training Centre in 2020. A fifth project came with the re-purchase of Melwood to become the new state-of-the-art training centre for Liverpool FC Women.

Accommodating 20,500 spectators amid Anfield's impressive capacity, the Main Stand is one of the largest all-seater single stands in European football. It comprises three tiers plus two interior concourses designed to celebrate fans and their passion for the club and provide space for them to gather and enjoy modern facilities.

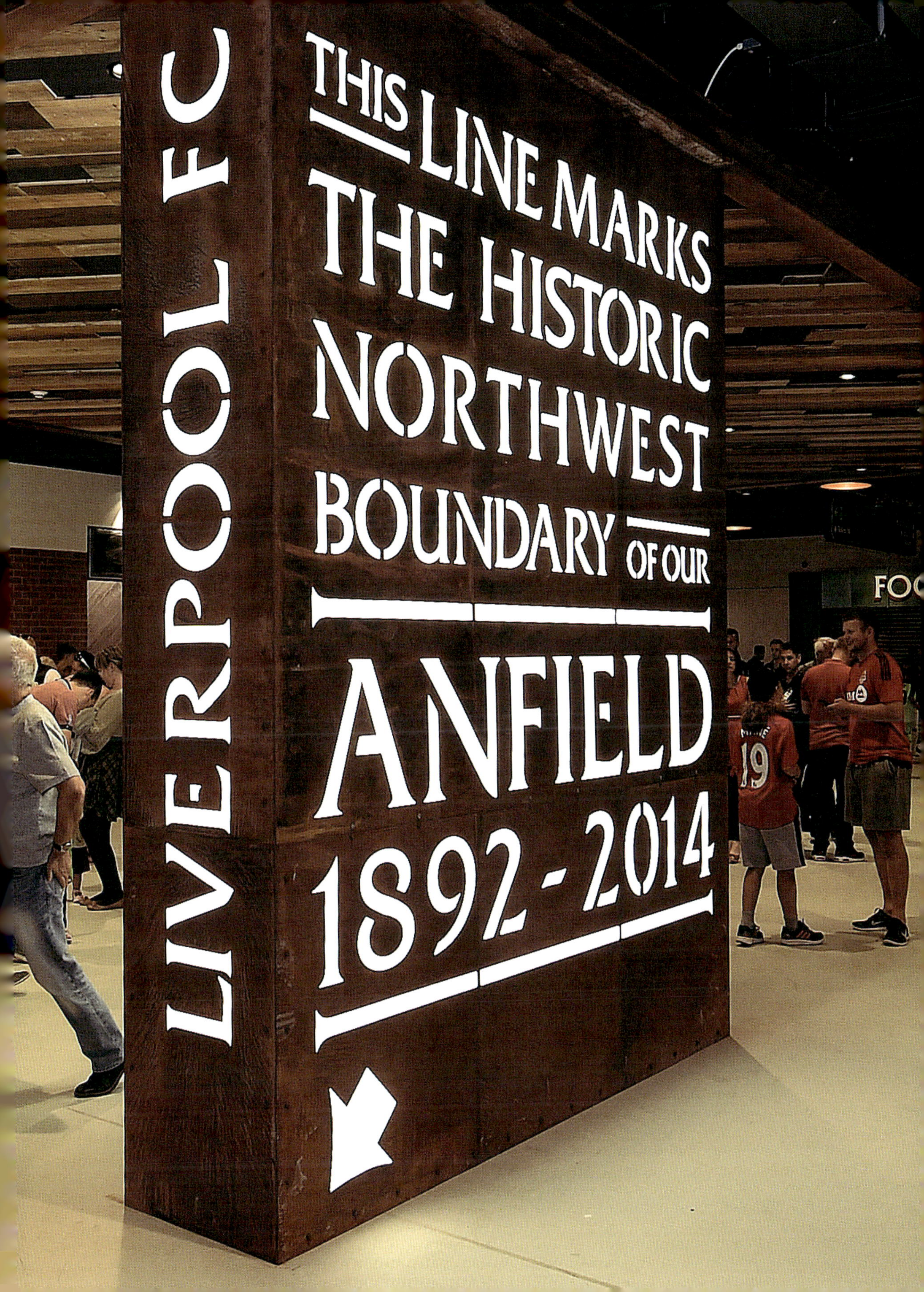
LIVERPOOL FC
THIS LINE MARKS
THE HISTORIC
NORTHWEST
BOUNDARY OF OUR
ANFIELD
1892 - 2014

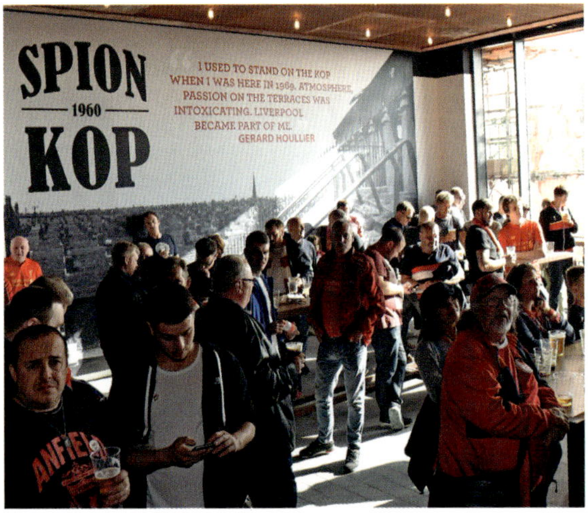
SPION
1960
KOP
I USED TO STAND ON THE KOP WHEN I WAS HERE IN 1969. ATMOSPHERE, PASSION ON THE TERRACES WAS INTOXICATING. LIVERPOOL BECAME PART OF ME.
GERARD HOULLIER

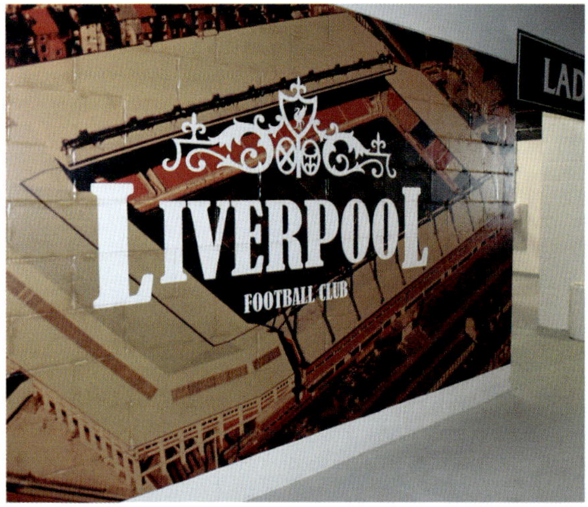
LIVERPOOL
FOOTBALL CLUB

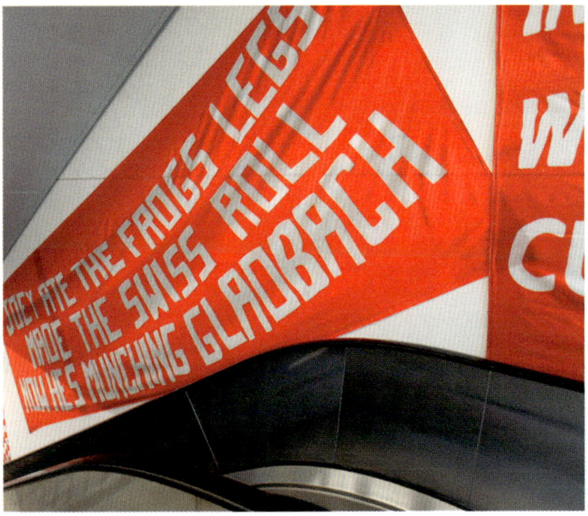
JOEY ATE THE FROGS LEGS
MADE THE SWISS ROLL
NOW HE'S MUNCHING GLADBACH

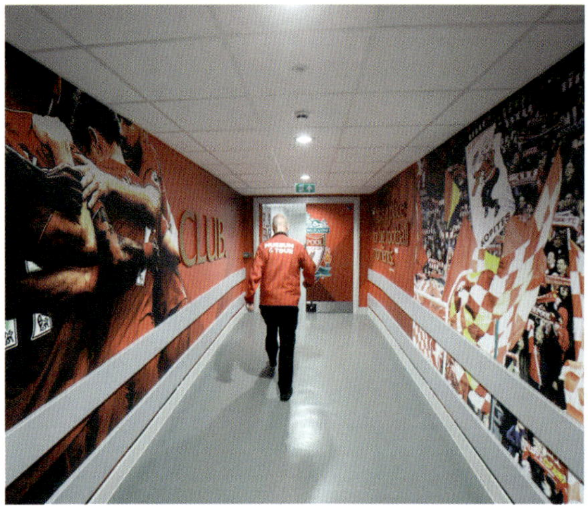

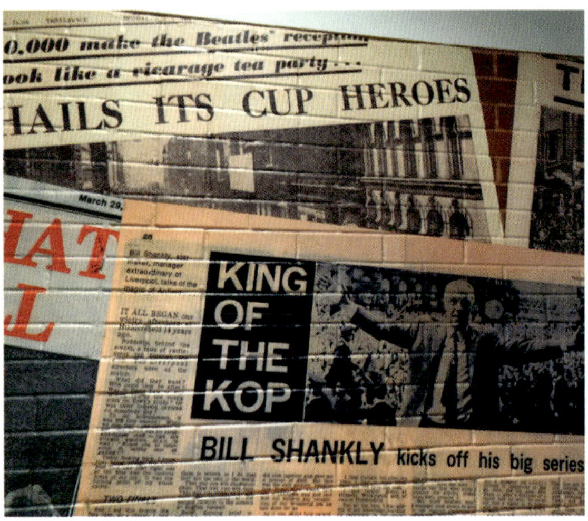
HAILS ITS CUP HEROES
KING OF THE KOP
BILL SHANKLY kicks off his big series

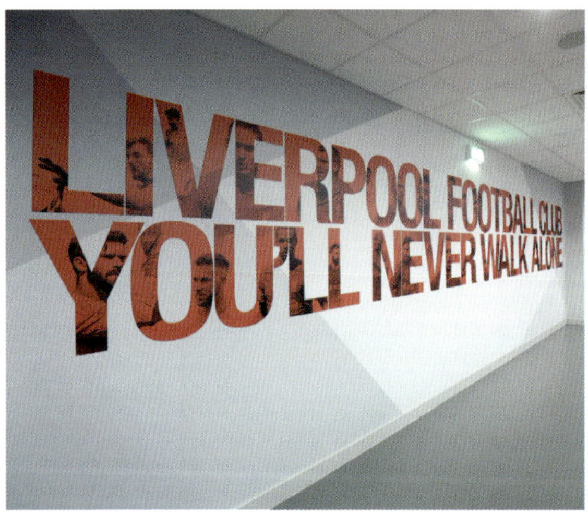
LIVERPOOL FOOTBALL CLUB
YOU'LL NEVER WALK ALONE

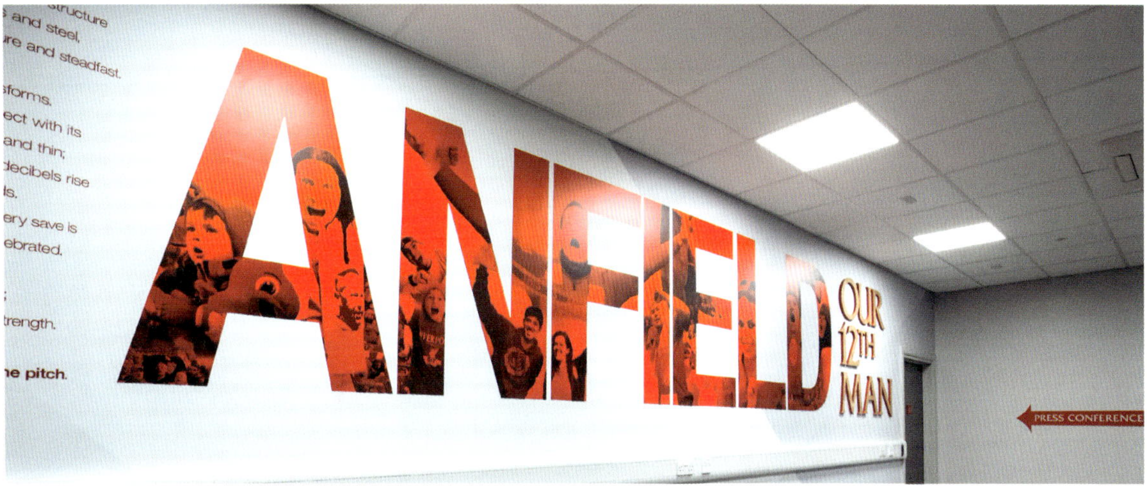

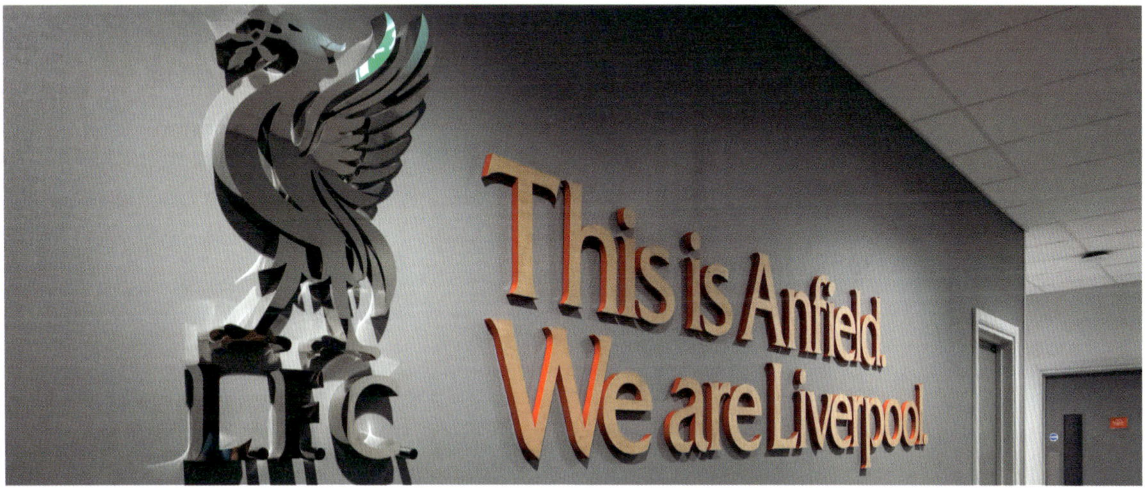

The concourse artwork takes inspiration from scarves and flags with colours and materials inspired by Anfield's architecture and the city of Liverpool's maritime heritage – indeed there are spectacular, sweeping views down to the River Mersey from the windows of the upper levels of the stand.

On the walls are back-pages reproduced from newspapers, celebrating some of Liverpool FC's finest hours, and graphics reflecting club history with lettering used in the style of past matchday programmes.

At ground-level in and around the dressing-rooms and players' tunnel are stirring motivational messages plus of course the world-famous 'This is Anfield' sign.

On the opposite side of the stadium, the Sir Kenny Dalglish Stand features cutouts of legendary players on the back of seats within the concourses, 'Anfield Moments' celebrating great games and goals and the heroes behind them with excerpts of famous commentary, and a Captains Hall of Fame.

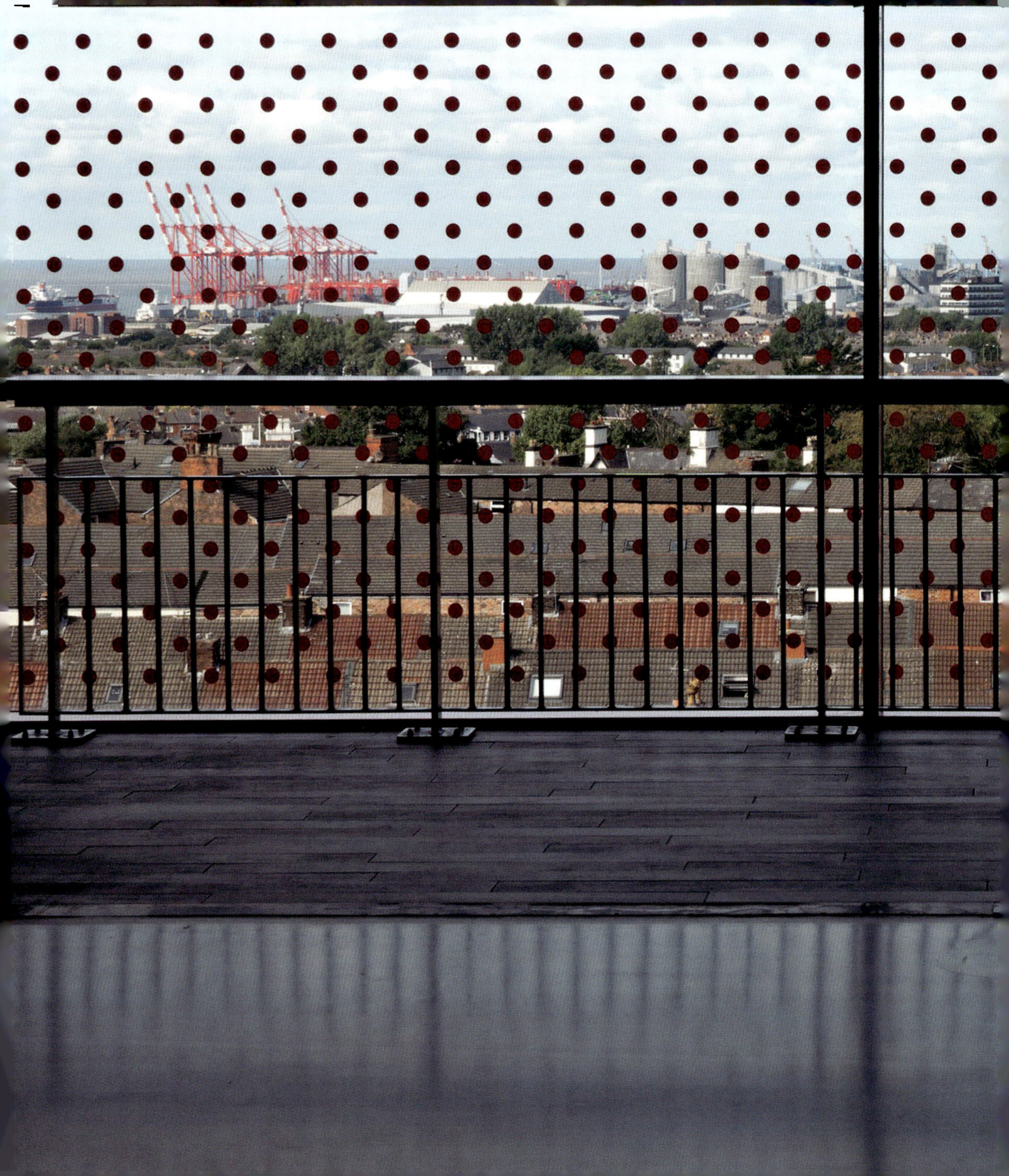

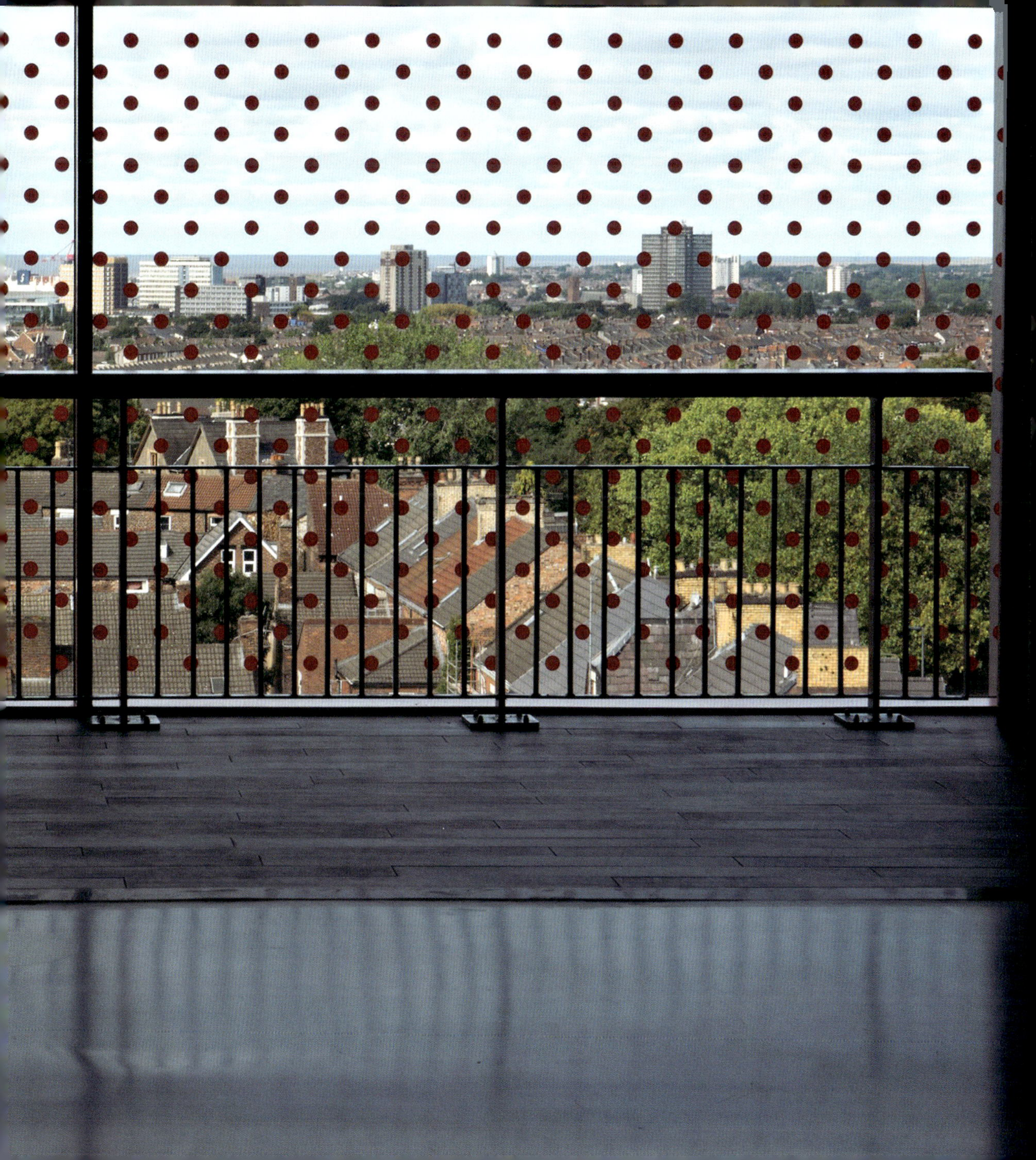

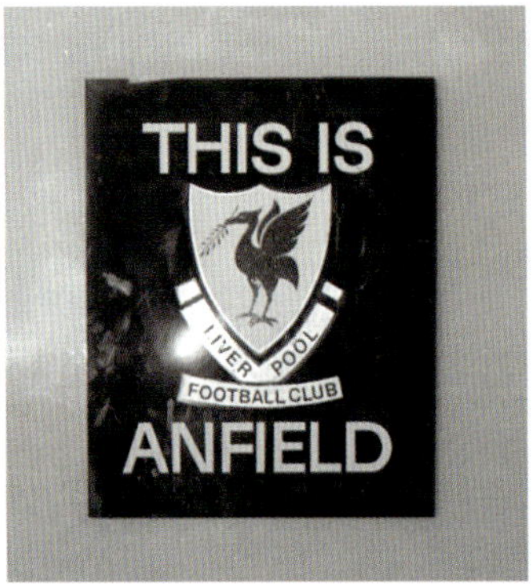

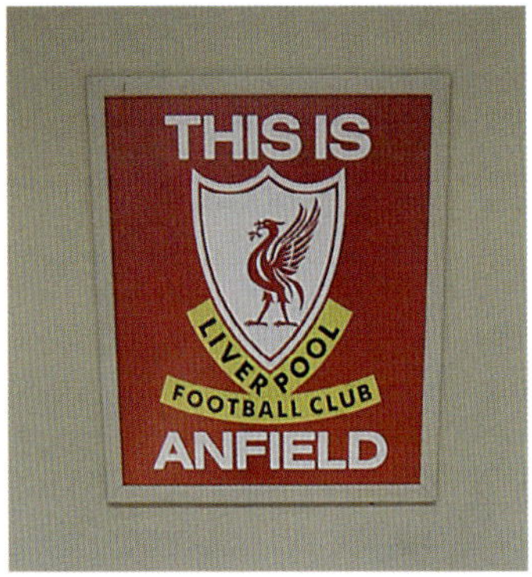

Three little words

A bird, a badge, a simple fact in red-and-white...who needs huge murals when you can get the message across so succinctly yet powerfully in the minutes before a match commences?

It's arguably the most famous sign in football and it's been back in place for the last decade (aside from a temporary absence during the Main Stand expansion work) over the entrance to the pitch in the players' tunnel at Anfield.

The original (above left) was made in the mid-1970s by maintenance foreman Bert Johnson at the request of manager Bill Shankly who believed it would serve the dual purpose of intimidating the opposition while inspiring those in red. Bill's logic behind those three words was simple: "It is there to remind our lads who they're playing for and to remind the opposition who they're playing against."

Home players soon got into the habit of touching the sign for good luck, Kenny Dalglish revealing that he used two hands instead of one because it "made me feel six feet tall."

The current version appeared throughout the 1980s and until the design was updated in the late 90s (above right). Brendan Rodgers reinstated the more popular sign as one of his first acts as Liverpool boss in 2012. "The nostalgia around this football club is immense," he explained. "I just felt that this was a sign and a symbol of what Liverpool was for many years."

LFC museum curator Stephen Done added: "This sign has seen the greatest glory years of our club. It has been the talisman for some of our greatest players. It is arguably the single most important thing at Anfield. It still resonates, it still makes us emotional and means so much to so many."

Subsequent manager Jürgen Klopp remarked in 2016: "I don't really know exactly how it works but I think you need to win something before [you get to touch it], I'm not sure. I didn't ask until now, but it's a sign of respect that we don't do it. Maybe these players one day will be allowed to do it."

A wealth of major trophies later, they certainly have earned that right.

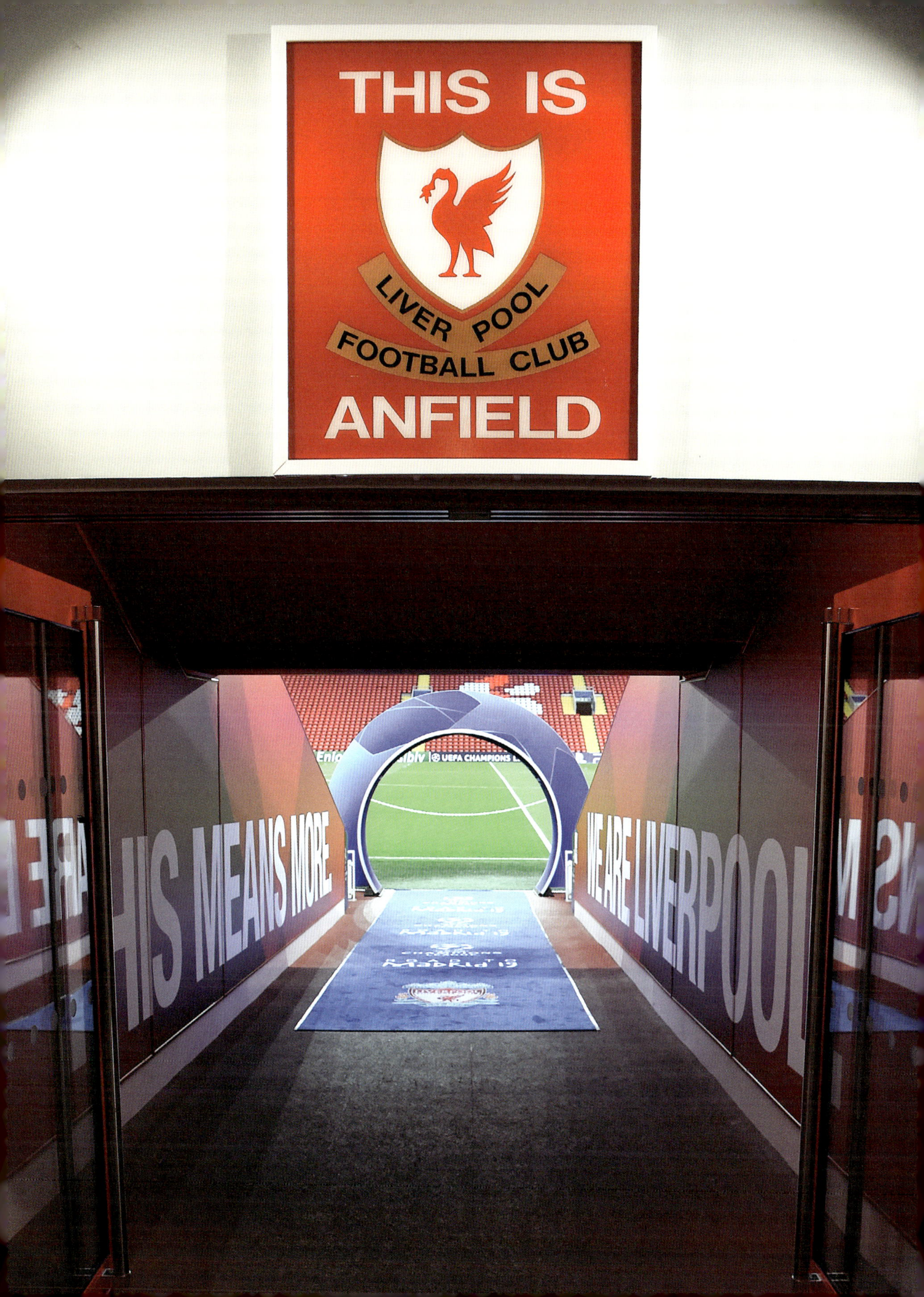
THIS IS
LIVER POOL
FOOTBALL CLUB
ANFIELD
THIS MEANS MORE
WE ARE LIVERPOOL

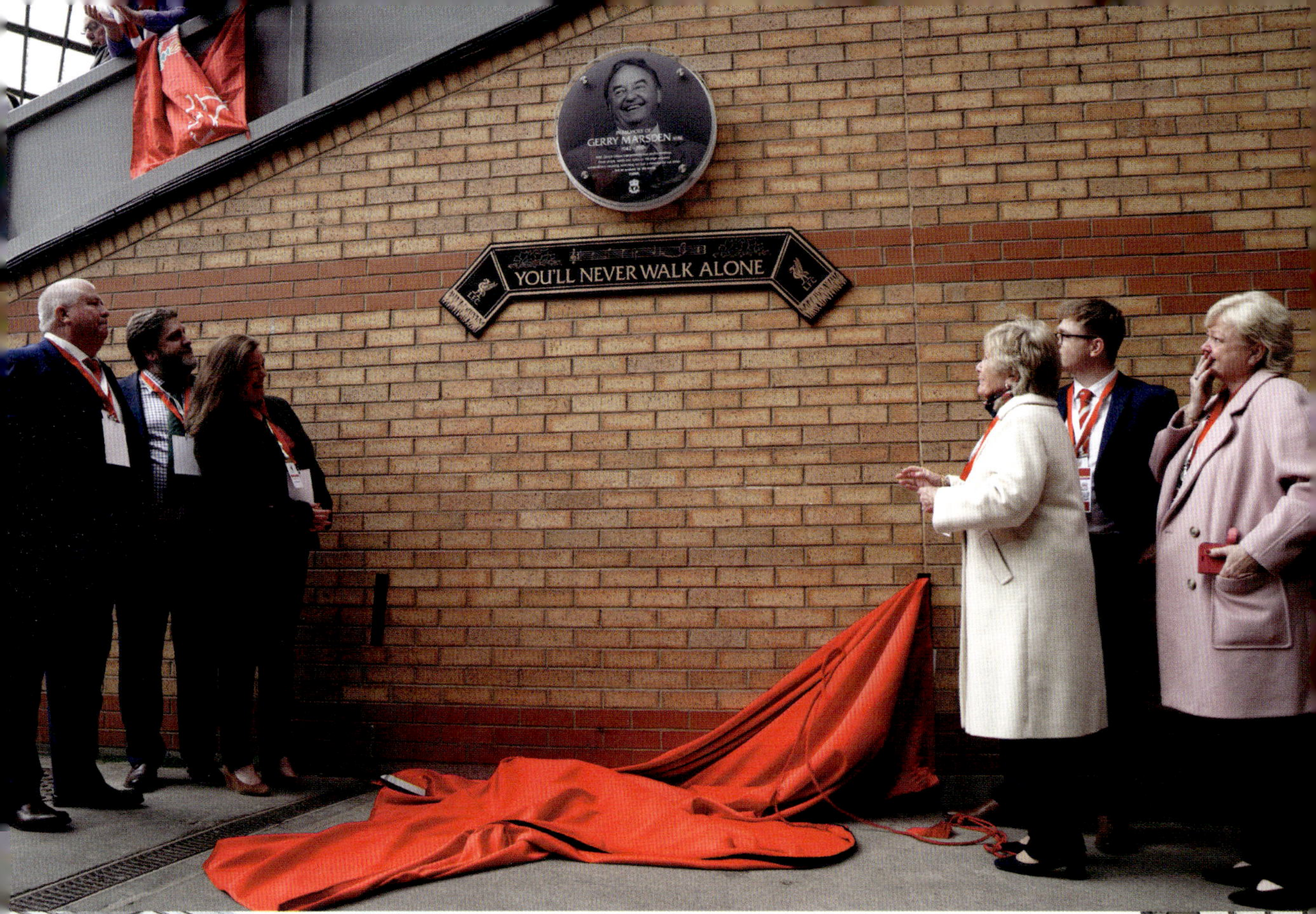
GERRY MARSDEN
YOU'LL NEVER WALK ALONE

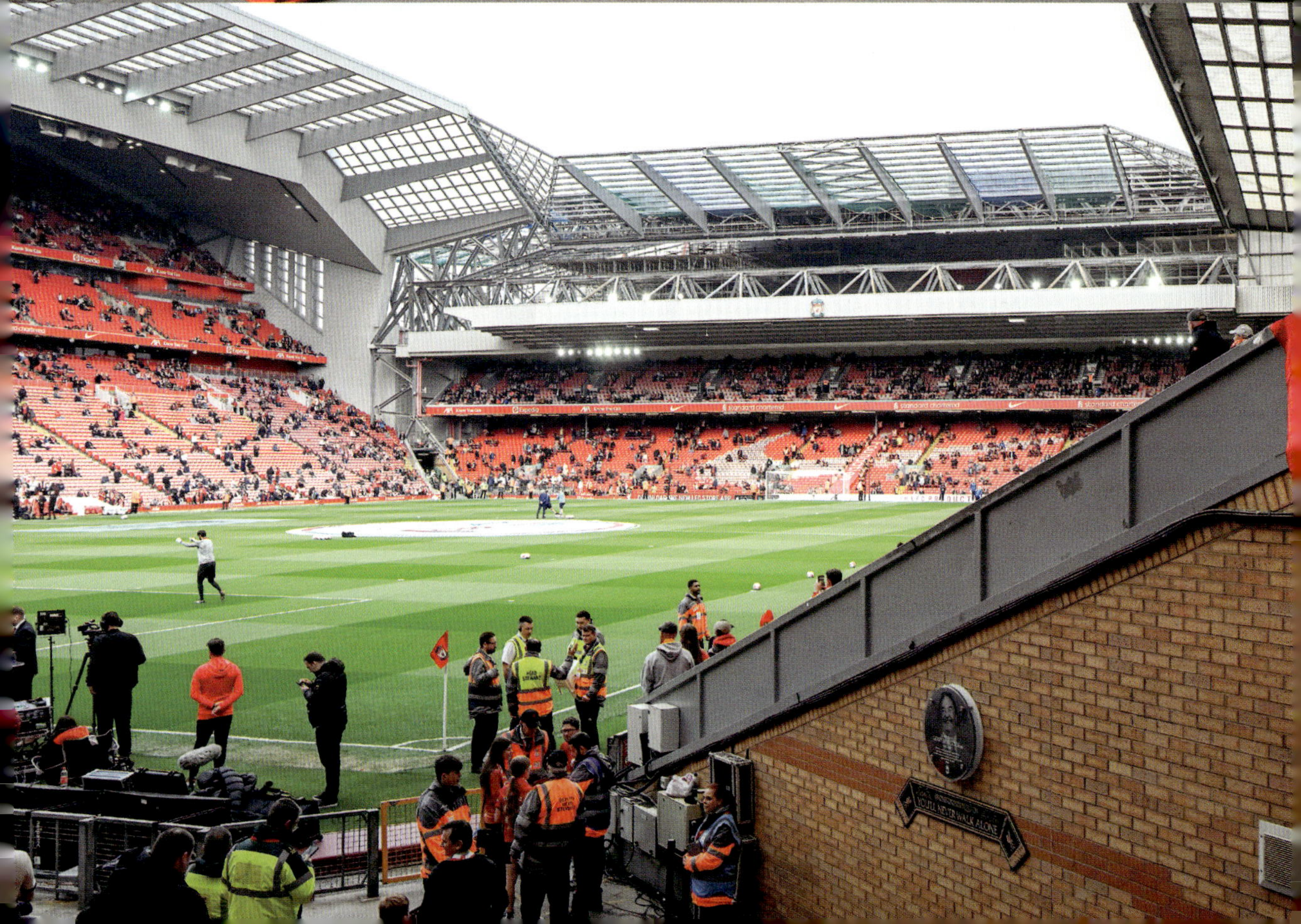
YOU'LL NEVER WALK ALONE

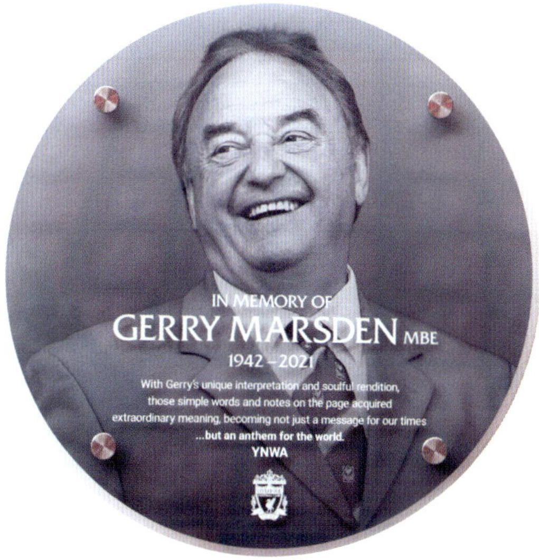

Our Gerry

While the permanent memorials for Bill Shankly, Bob Paisley and John Houlding can be found outside the stadium, it's fitting that a special tribute for the late, great Gerry Marsden is found inside Anfield's beating heart. Officially unveiled in April 2022 by his wife Pauline ahead of a Merseyside derby, it's situated between the Spion Kop and the Sir Kenny Dalglish Stand and features a bronze scarf with the words 'YOU'LL NEVER WALK ALONE' and a photo of Gerry wearing a Liverpool FC tie gifted to him by Bill Shankly.

Gerry, who with his band The Pacemakers gave the club its heart-and-soul anthem 58 years ago, passed away in January 2021. His voice and particularly that song is not just part of the fabric of Anfield – it *is* Anfield. Matchdays would not be the same without it.

Marsden was born-and-raised in Liverpool 8, never forgot his roots and regularly appeared at Anfield down the years, sometimes on the pitch leading the crowd in singing YNWA for testimonials and concerts. He was made an MBE in 2003 for his music and his services to charity, and was awarded the Freedom of Liverpool in 2009.

The song itself was adopted by the Kop in the early 'Swinging Sixties' when the fans on the terrace were also belting out hits by The Beatles and Cilla Black. The team's kit had changed to all-red, and heroes like manager Shankly and players Roger Hunt, Ian St John and Ron Yeats were idolised.

On 2 November 1963 the single went to the top of the 'Hit Parade' and stayed there for four weeks. When a DJ called Stewart Bateman first played *YNWA* inside the ground he "could not believe the reaction from the crowd" who sang along. When the single eventually dropped from the charts, he kept playing it at Anfield before kick-off by popular demand – and it seemed to inspire Shankly's Reds to the 1963/64 title. The rest is history.

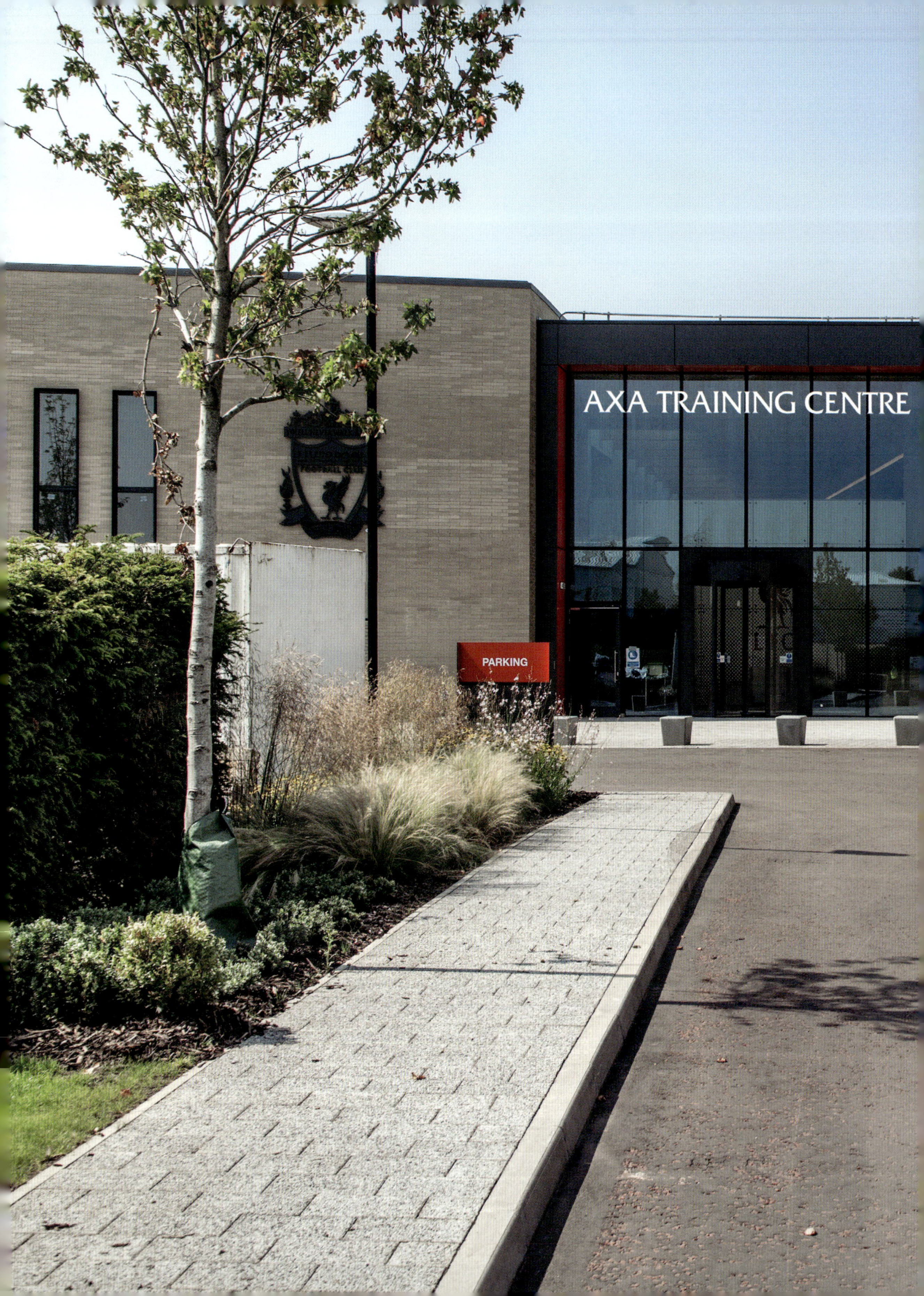
AXA TRAINING CENTRE
PARKING

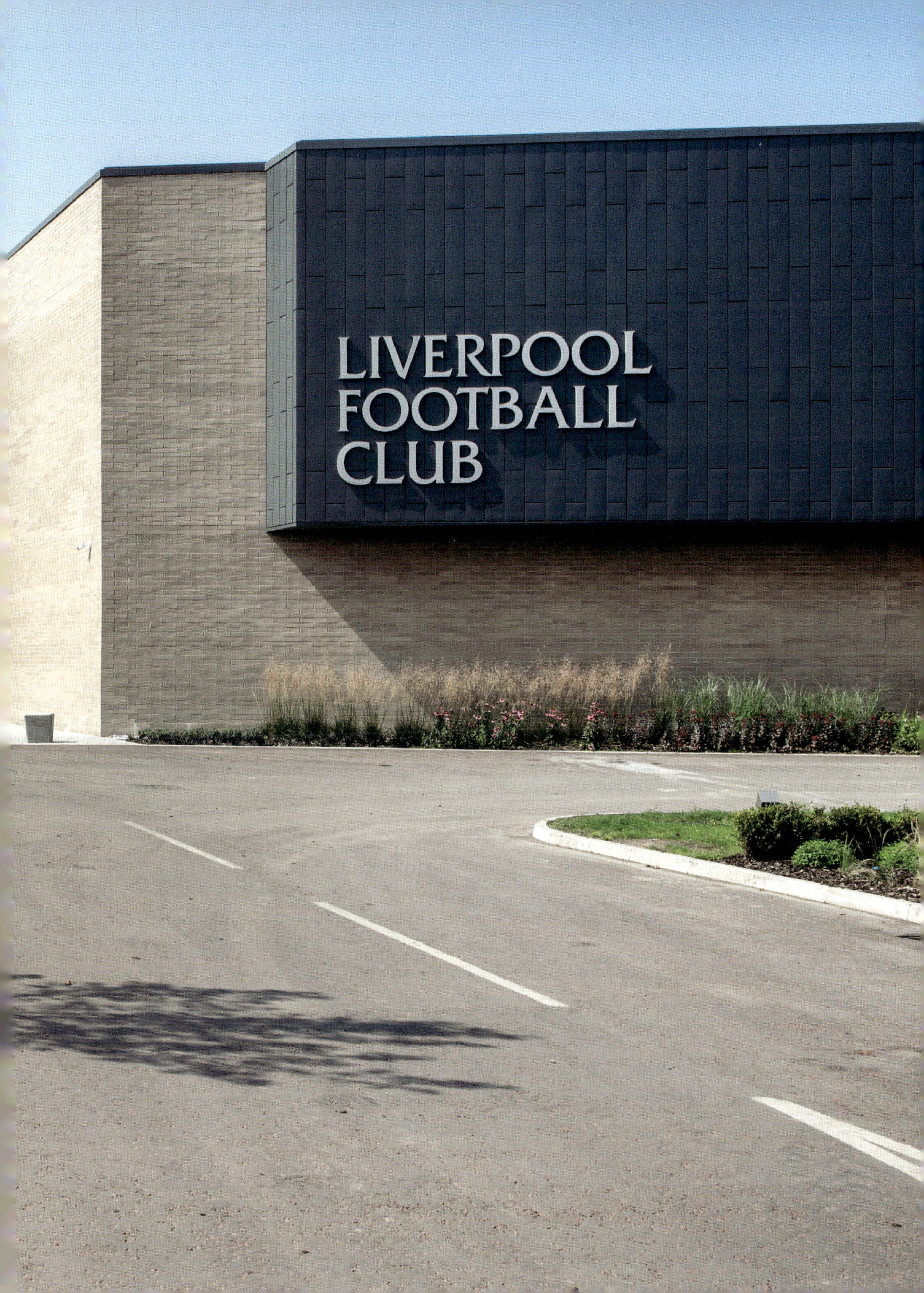
LIVERPOOL
FOOTBALL
CLUB

Art at The AXA

Officially opened in November 2020 and marking a new chapter in the club's history, the AXA Training Centre was always going to boast the finest facilities for Liverpool FC's combined first-team and youth-football operations. But just as important was how it looked and felt – and art and design played a big part.

The Reds moved to the 9,200 sq metre complex in Kirkby after bidding a fond farewell to Melwood which had been their famous training ground for 70 years and would later become a new home for LFC women's teams.

The AXA, as it's known (the club and its official principal partner expanded their partnership to include the naming rights for the site), boasts three full-size pitches – made to mirror Anfield's hallowed turf as closely as possible – complete with under-soil heating and floodlighting. There's a decidedly eco-friendly aspect too with the pitches consisting of natural-grass seed supported by organic products, a borehole extracting groundwater to irrigate the playing surfaces and tend to the landscaping on-site, and a biological vehicle-wash system to service maintenance equipment.

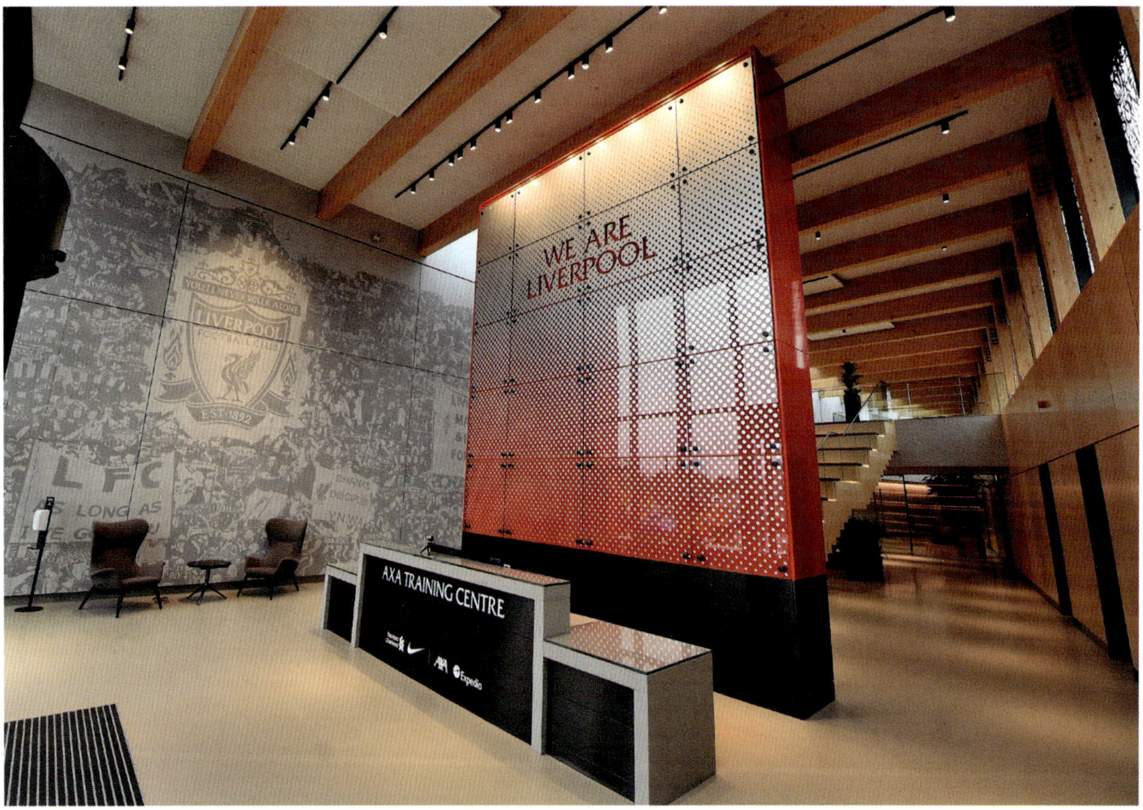

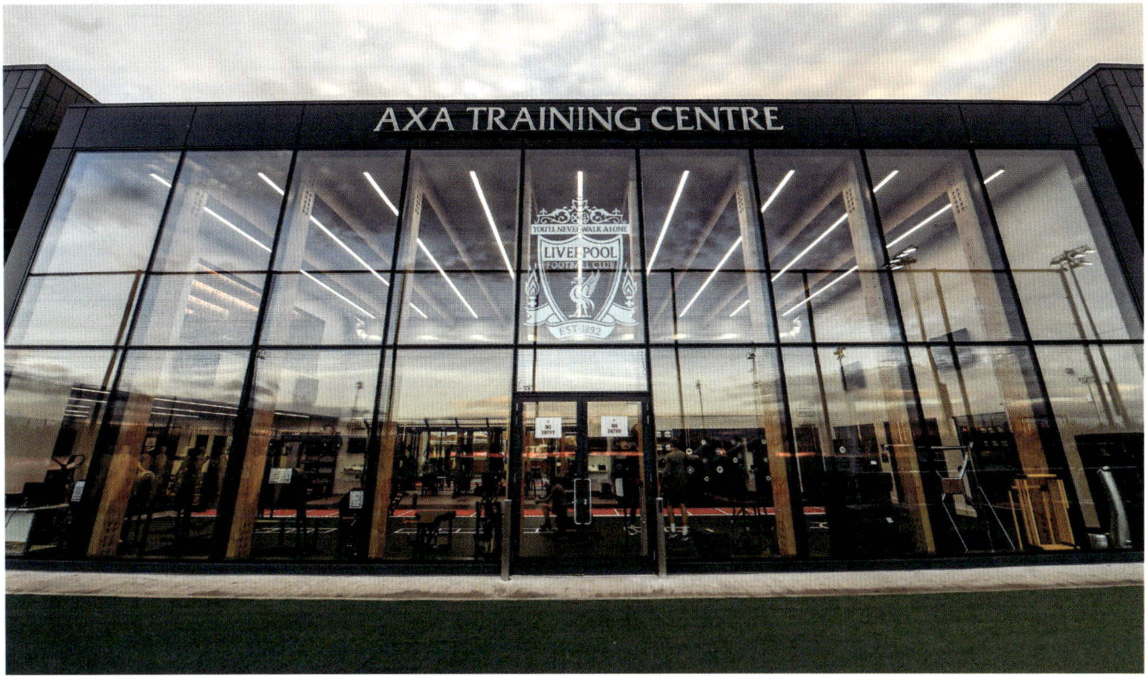
AXA TRAINING CENTRE
YOU'LL NEVER WALK ALONE
LIVERPOOL
FOOTBALL CLUB
EST 1892

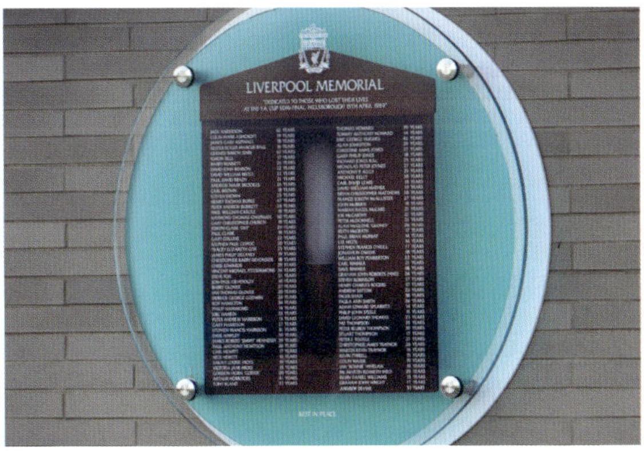
LIVERPOOL MEMORIAL

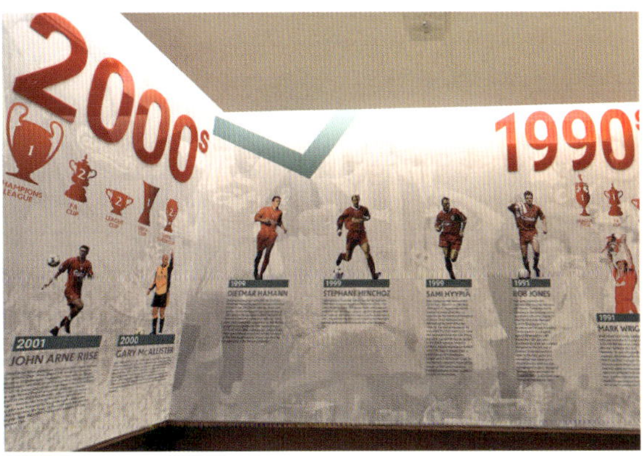
2000s
1990
2001
JOHN ARNE RIISE
2000
1999
DIETMAR HAMANN
1999
1999
SAMI HYYPIA
1995
1991

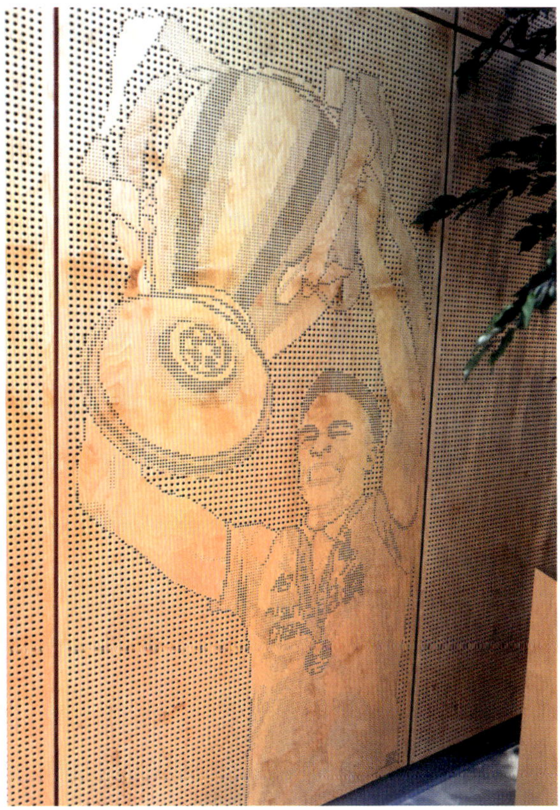

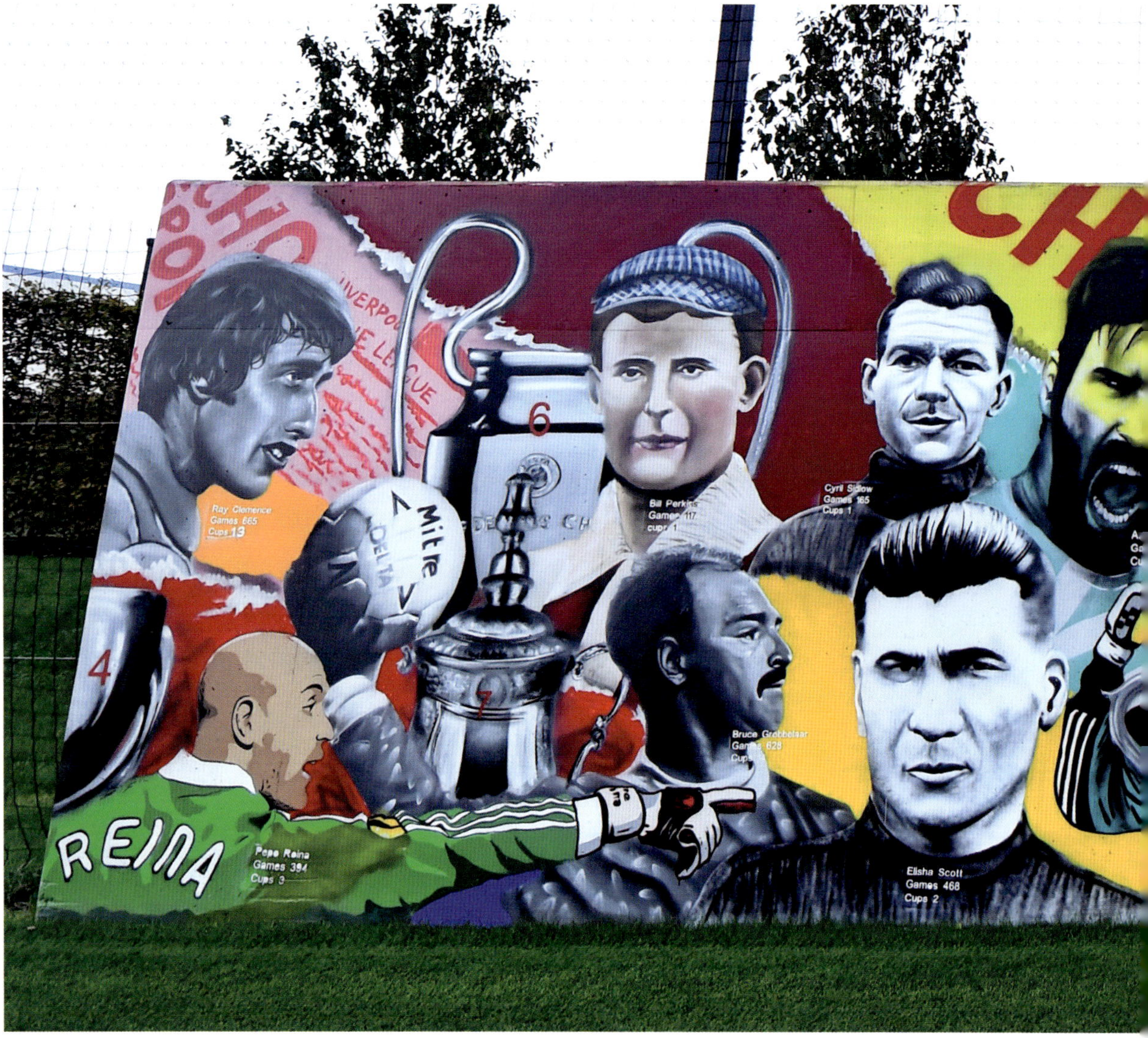

There are also goalkeeping and warm-up areas and indoor facilities including two gyms, a full-size sports hall, pool, hydrotherapy complex and specialist sports rehabilitation suites, plus dedicated TV studios, press-conference facilities and office accommodation and a Hillsborough memorial before which the first-team squad gather at every anniversary of the tragedy.

The Centre's grand opening was commemorated by the installation of a steel time-capsule which includes, among various memorabilia, video messages from Jürgen Klopp and legendary players.

Klopp has described it as "pretty much perfect, a wonderful building with everything you need now and for the future." He also recalled "a lot of steps, meetings with architects, designers, everybody!"

Those architects were KSS, working alongside civil-engineering contractors McLaughlin & Harvey and club personnel to incorporate imagery acknowledging and celebrating Liverpool FC's greatest moments. In terms of design, a strong reference-point was the academy of Austrian club Red Bull Salzburg which is admired for its abundant natural light, spacious corridors, open offices and innovative use of glass, wood and concrete.

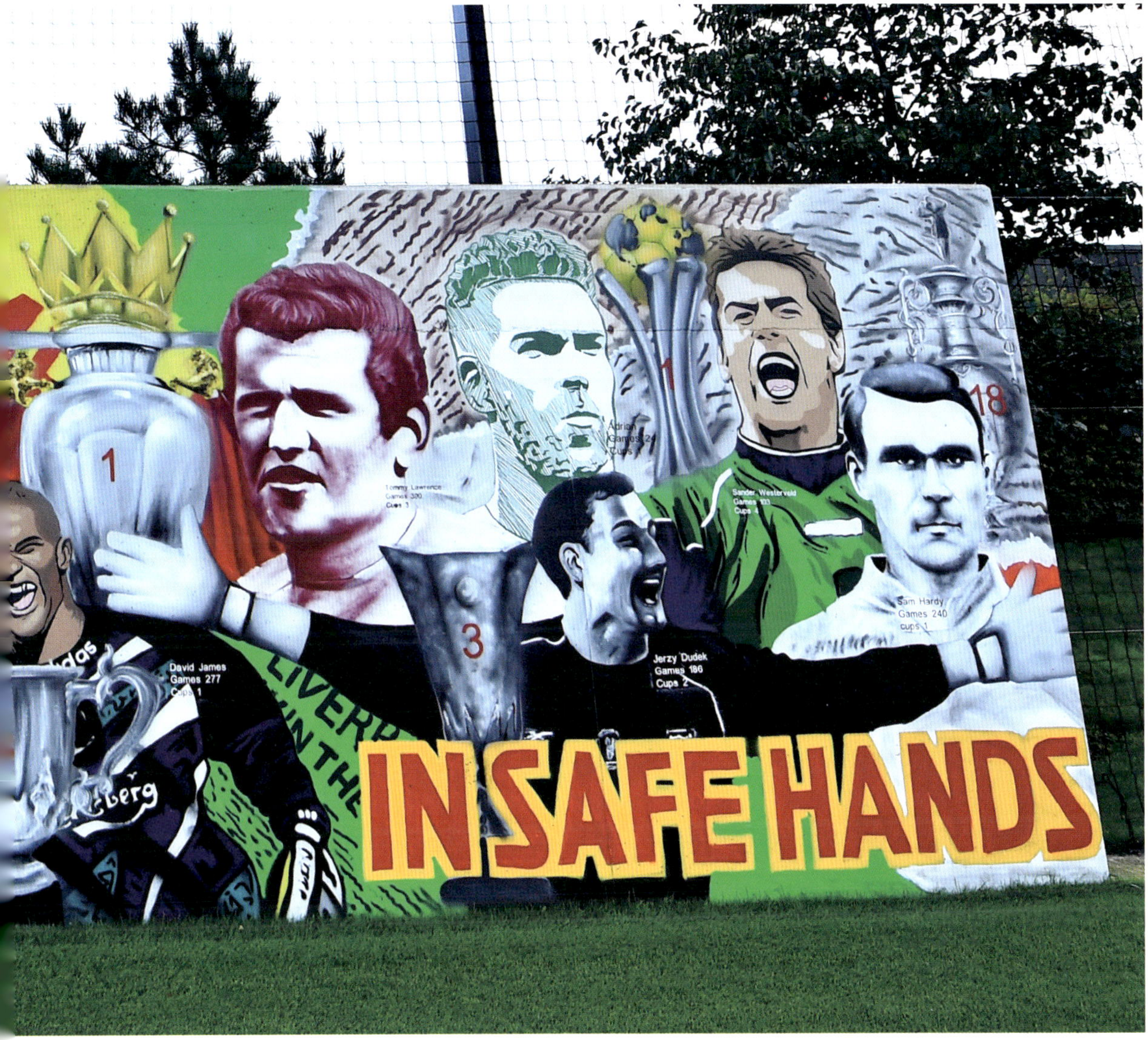
IN SAFE HANDS
David James
Games 277
Jerzy Dudek
Games 186
Sam Hardy
Games 240

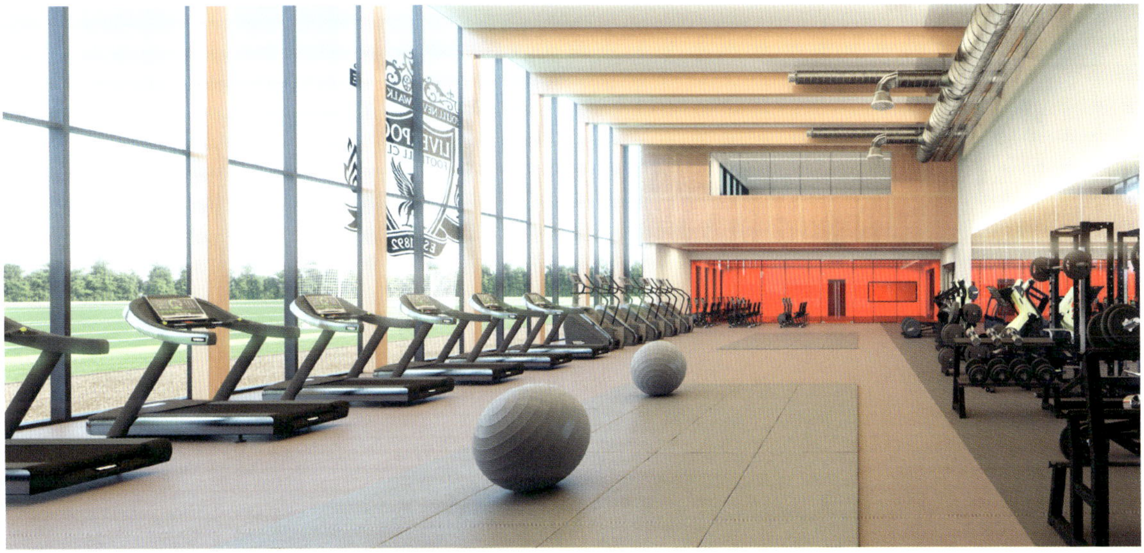

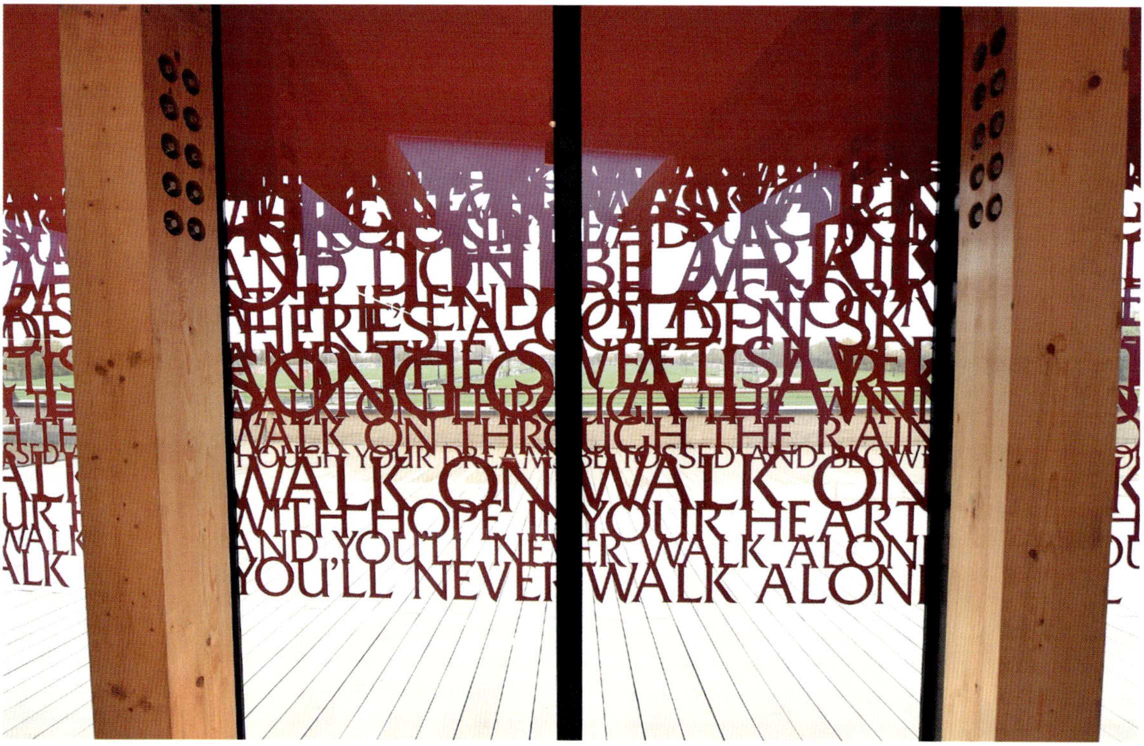
WALK ON WALK ON
WITH HOPE IN YOUR HEART
YOU'LL NEVER WALK ALON

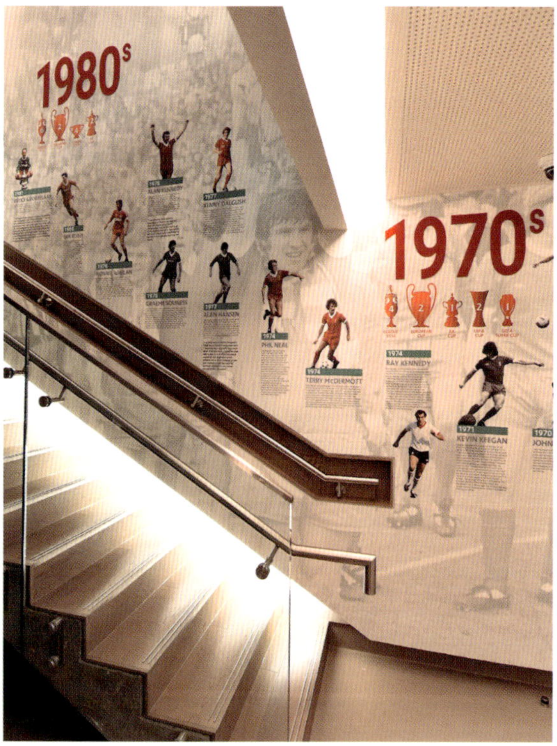
1980s
1970s
KENNY DALGLISH
PHIL NEAL
TERRY McDERMOTT
RAY KENNEDY
KEVIN KEEGAN

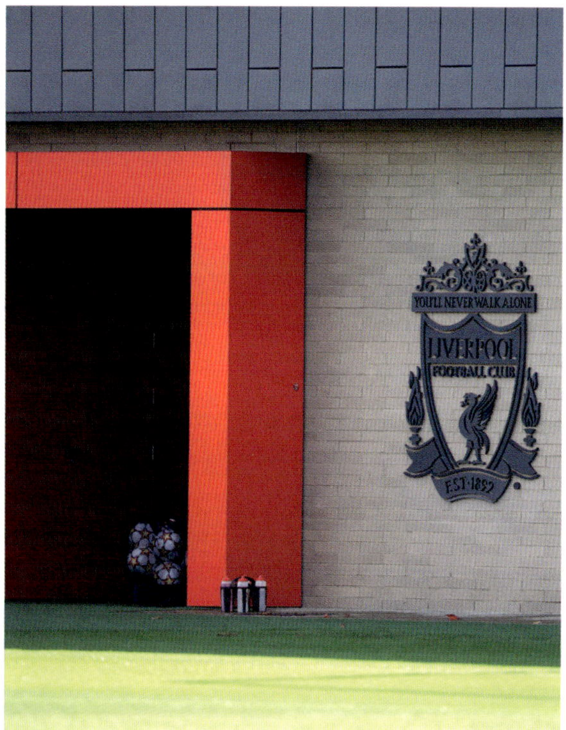
YOU'LL NEVER WALK ALONE
LIVERPOOL
FOOTBALL CLUB
EST 1892

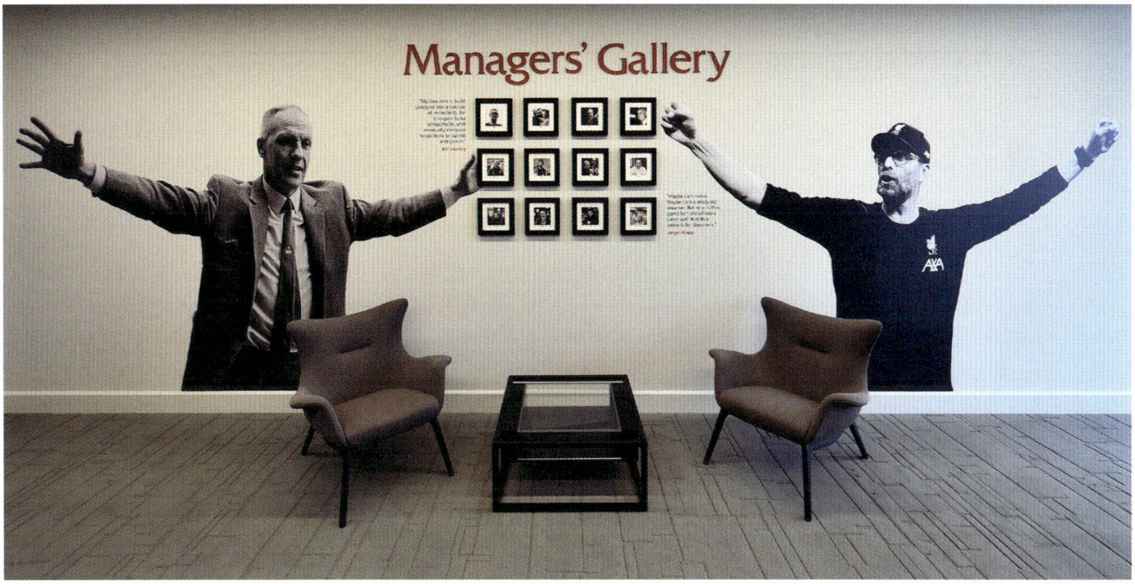

However, explains KSS associate director Debbie Power, "to ensure the facility is uniquely Liverpool FC, the club's core values have been embedded within the architecture, interior and graphic design of the building to create a cohesive and holistic approach. Each wing has key references to fans, trophies, players, and song lyrics, integrated in varying ways, but all designed together as part of the user experience journey.

"Everything about the design was developed specifically for LFC – and it feels that, when you are there, it could be no other club's place of work."

A year after the launch, in November 2021, a colourful outdoor mural was unveiled at the AXA celebrating some of Liverpool FC's most legendary goalkeepers.

Commissioned by first-team goalkeeping coach John Achterberg and created by local artist John Culshaw, whose other murals decorate the streets around Anfield, the artwork provides inspiration to the club's modern-day goalies as they undergo their daily drills.

Achterberg told the club website: "We'd had something at Melwood which was a painting of the Kop, and then I saw the murals around town so I thought it'd be good to do something with the goalie area [at the AXA] because it was originally just concrete.

"So I had the idea to put all the legendary goalkeepers on there. We got a list of all the keepers who won a trophy playing as the no1 for the club. We've put the stats on there of how many games they played and how many trophies they won for us. There are 13 goalies going right back to the start of the club's history up until now.

"For everyone who comes out to train here, it's a little bit of motivation seeing all the top goalies that have been here – and if they want to get there themselves, they have to produce. It is to show how hard you have to work to get to that position at the club."

Hall
Le

MURALS AND STREET ART

Streets ahead

For Liverpool supporters all over the world, Anfield means home – and that means pictures on the walls. These days it's not just a place of pilgrimage on matchdays but an all-year-round destination with its own outdoor gallery commissioned by local businesses and fan groups and created by local artists.

In the past a crudely-daubed 'LFC RULES OK' was about the nearest we came to 'street-art'. These days, though, devotional graffiti has been replaced by spectacular murals in the streets around the stadium.

Utilising techniques such as spray-painting and stencilling, and originating from the late 1970s graffiti scene in New York (one of its pioneers, Keith Haring, was recently the subject of a retrospective at Tate Liverpool), street-art has been described as a city's outdoor museum. Banksy is the most famous current exponent.

National Geographic magazine comments: "While it is easy, upon coming across a beautiful work of art on a city's wall, to simply snap a photo, upload it to Instagram and move on, the best street-art merits spending a few moments to think about what it wants to say."

Back in Liverpool in the summer of 2017, artist Paul Curtis created a striking image of Liver Bird wings in Jamaica Street, in the city's cutting-edge Baltic Triangle neighbourhood. People flocked to be photographed 'wearing' the wings and it quickly became one of the most Instagrammable places in town.

In December 2018 it was joined by a mural of Jürgen Klopp in nearby Jordan Street, the work of graffiti-artist Akse over the course of one weekend. Then in the summer of 2019, when the Reds won their sixth European Cup, a bar in Concert Square commemorated the triumph with a mural of Mohamed Salah, Virgil van Dijk and skipper Jordan Henderson lifting the Champions League trophy in Madrid, while the following year on nearby FACT Square, club sponsor Nivea Men unveiled a 'hyper-real' mural to celebrate Liverpool FC's Premier League title triumph.

Since then, Paul Curtis, Akse and fellow artist John Culshaw, to name but three – along with the prolific collective MurWalls – have been enlisted to create more and more works of art celebrating famous players from all eras, bringing further vibrancy to Anfield's matchday neighbourhood which has changed dramatically over the last few years.

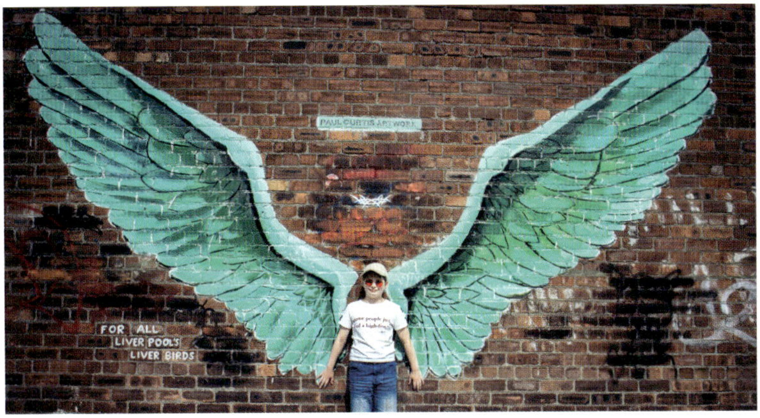

Paul spoke about the street-art explosion in a piece with the LFC matchday programme in late 2020. "A first-ever London Mural Festival has taken place and BBC Breakfast got in touch with me to talk about my own work here in Liverpool," he revealed. "I've also had personal seals of approval from people like Jordan Henderson and Jamie Carragher [the latter appearing on Paul's mural for Hotel Anfield on Anfield Road, alongside Steven Gerrard and the Champions League trophy in 2005]. Of course these are great times to be a Liverpool fan but we should always remember that none of this current success would've been possible without the foundations built by the legends of the past.

"I used to be a geologist in the oil industry, with an MSc in Petroleum Science, so you could say that I've swapped oil for oils! I love working large-scale and transforming a blank wall into something vibrant and alive, and to date I've created over 150 public pieces.

"It began with 'Wings' in the Baltic Triangle, which was make-or-break for me really. It allows anyone to transform themselves into a Liver Bird and the idea was to make people smile and have a laugh. It's since become one of the most geo-tagged destinations in the country. Back then there wasn't that much street-art in Liverpool but it's clearly a trend now."

John Culshaw, the man behind the murals of Mo Salah on Anfield Road, Alisson on Walton Breck Road, and Steven Gerrard, Luis Diaz and Kenny Dalglish on the walls of the famous Sandon Hotel in Anfield, told the LFC website: "People don't necessarily realise that they actually enjoy art [because] they don't go to museums and art galleries. But with street-art, they don't realise that they're going to see it until they do – and then they realise that they enjoyed it.

"When I'm in Anfield, I just knock on houses and ask if they'd be interested in having something on the wall, and most people say 'yeah'. Everybody in that whole Anfield area loves football and, like I say, they may not realise that they love art too, but they do."

Will the trend continue? There's no reason why not, according to one university arts professor who recently told the BBC: "The fans who go and support their team in all weathers are reclaiming the street with these murals. There's something about the craft of painting, seeing these huge murals being put up, that stops people in their tracks."

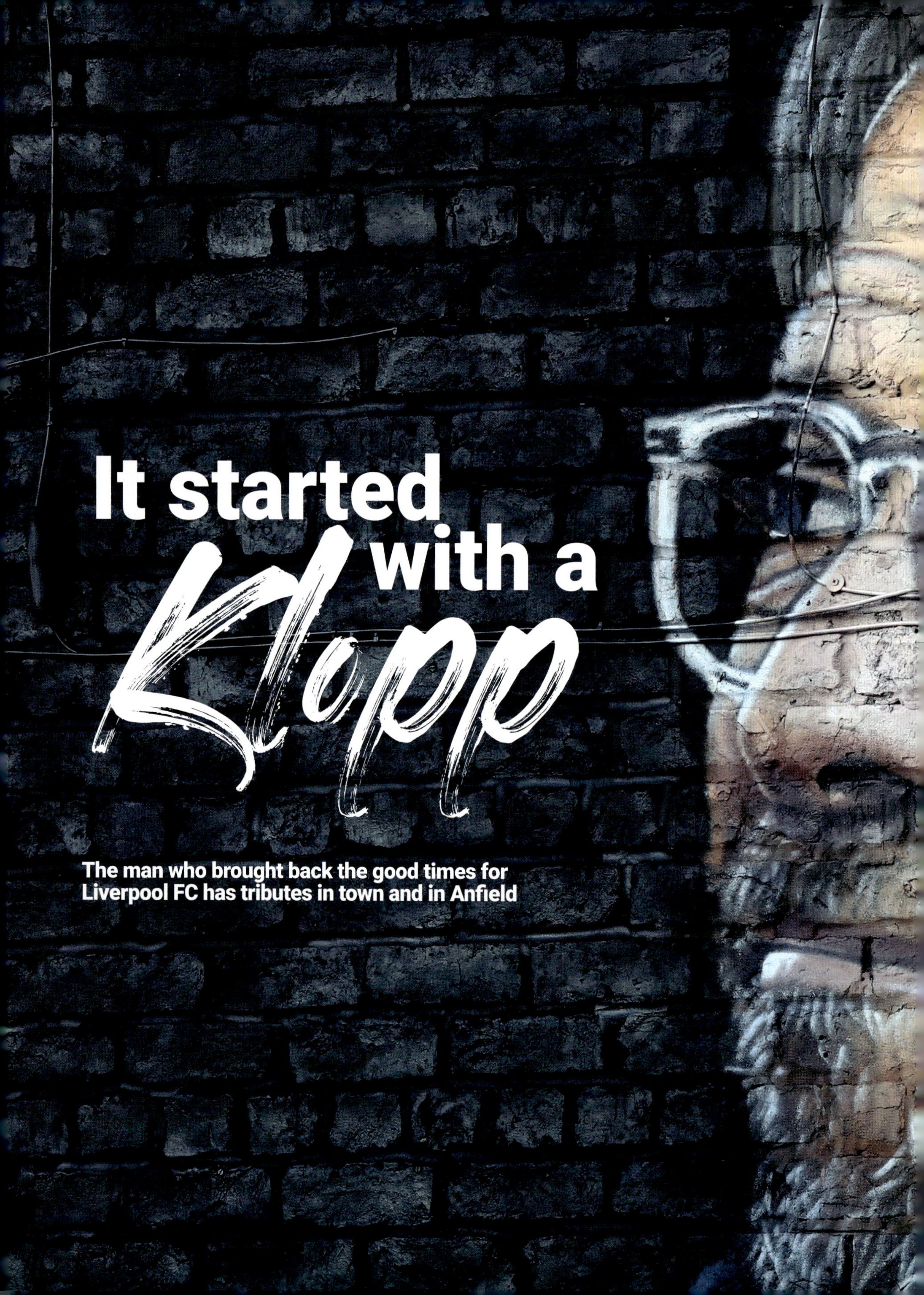

It started with a Klopp

The man who brought back the good times for Liverpool FC has tributes in town and in Anfield

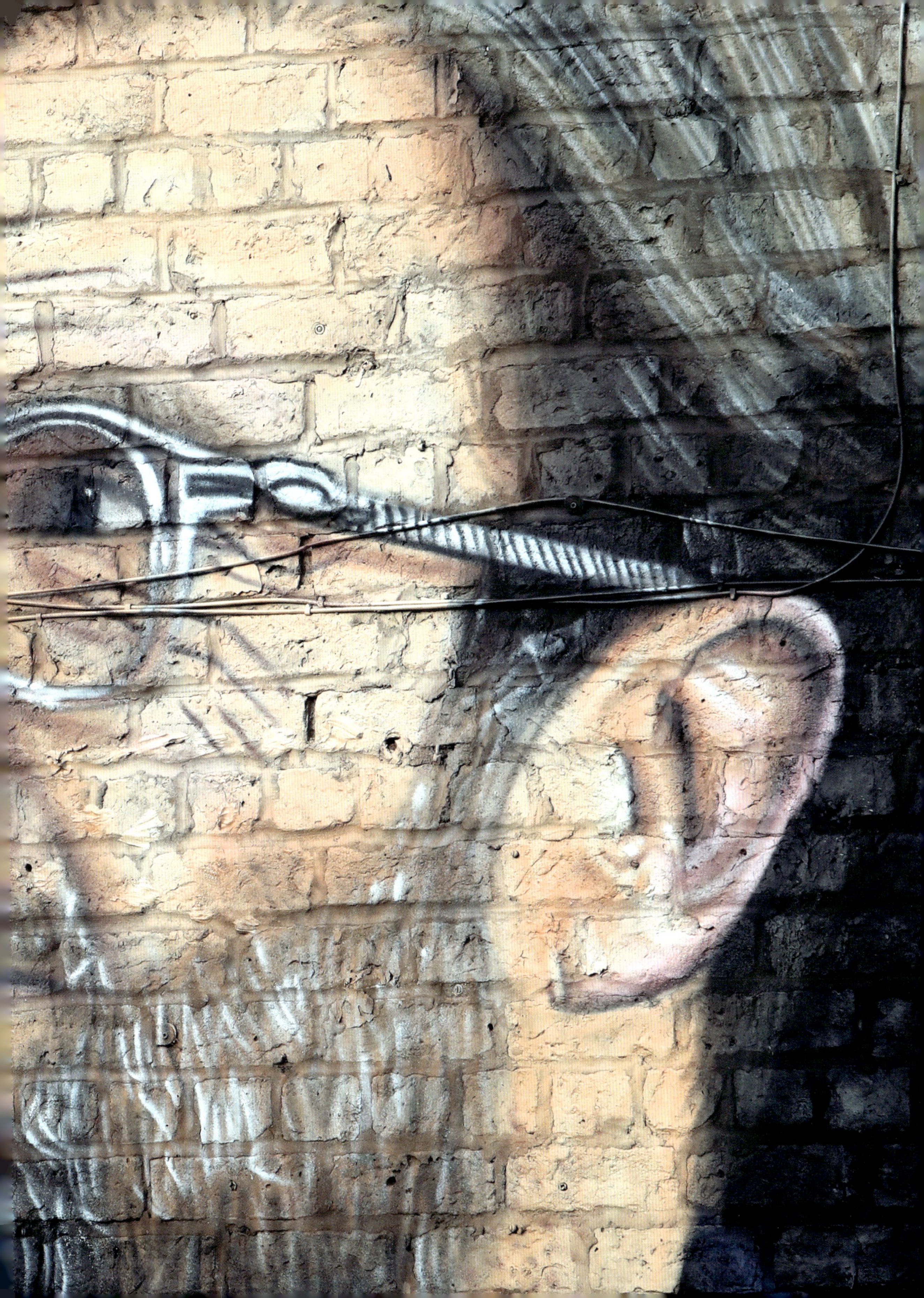

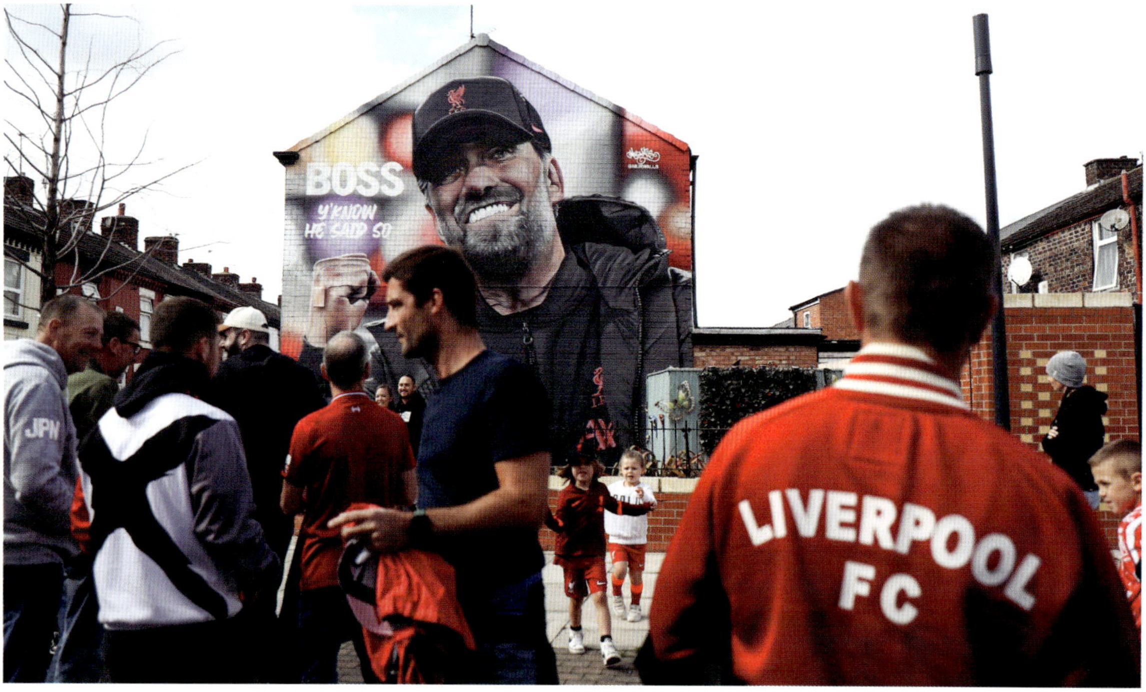

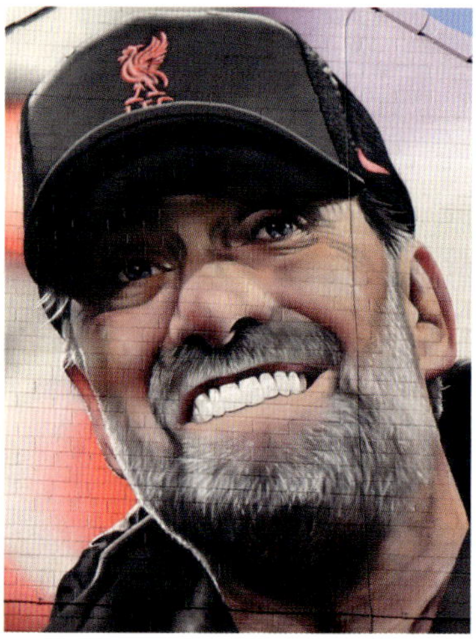

Liverpool were winning 4-0 away to Bournemouth in the Premier League when something positively seminal happened back in the city's Baltic neighbourhood. It was December 2018 and while Mohamed Salah was firing the Reds to the top of the table with a hat-trick down on the South Coast, graffiti artist Akse was putting Jürgen Klopp for posterity upon a wall on Jordan Street over the course of the same weekend.

Akse's previous subjects had included Muhammad Ali, David Bowie and Stephen Hawking. The Baltic meanwhile was a vibrant area already famous for its street-art as well as its football screenings, making it the ideal location for the mural. Klopp himself, instantly recognisable with that infectious smile and once described by the club's former chief-executive Peter Moore as "one of the more holistic human beings you will ever meet," was the perfect subject.

The following August another depiction of the Reds boss appeared on the wall of an Anfield bar, Klopp's Boot Room on Houlding Street. It was created by street-artist John Culshaw who described the commission as "a pleasure to work on because I am a huge LFC fan. I would say he is our best manager since Bill Shankly and this mural is a personal tribute to him from me.

"It was at the beginning of the season where we won the league," he told the club's website. "Everyone just had this feeling that we were going to do it that year, so I thought: I want to go and paint Jürgen Klopp somewhere. I got in touch with a few mates who are in Liverpool fan-groups and said, 'Can anyone get me a wall?' One got back to me saying his friend had a little matchday hotel called Klopp's Boot Room, right opposite The Sandon, and they said I could use it.

"They thought I was going to do a little something, but when I got there I said to him, 'Do you mind if I board your windows up?' And he went, 'Why – how big is it going to be?' I said, 'As big as I can, basically!' So I boarded the windows up and stuck a massive Klopp piece on the side, and it came out well."

Three years later in September 2022 a third Jürgen tribute appeared, close to the stadium and covering a whole end-terrace in Randolph Street. The work of another street-artist, Hugh Whitaker, and a collaboration between MurWalls and

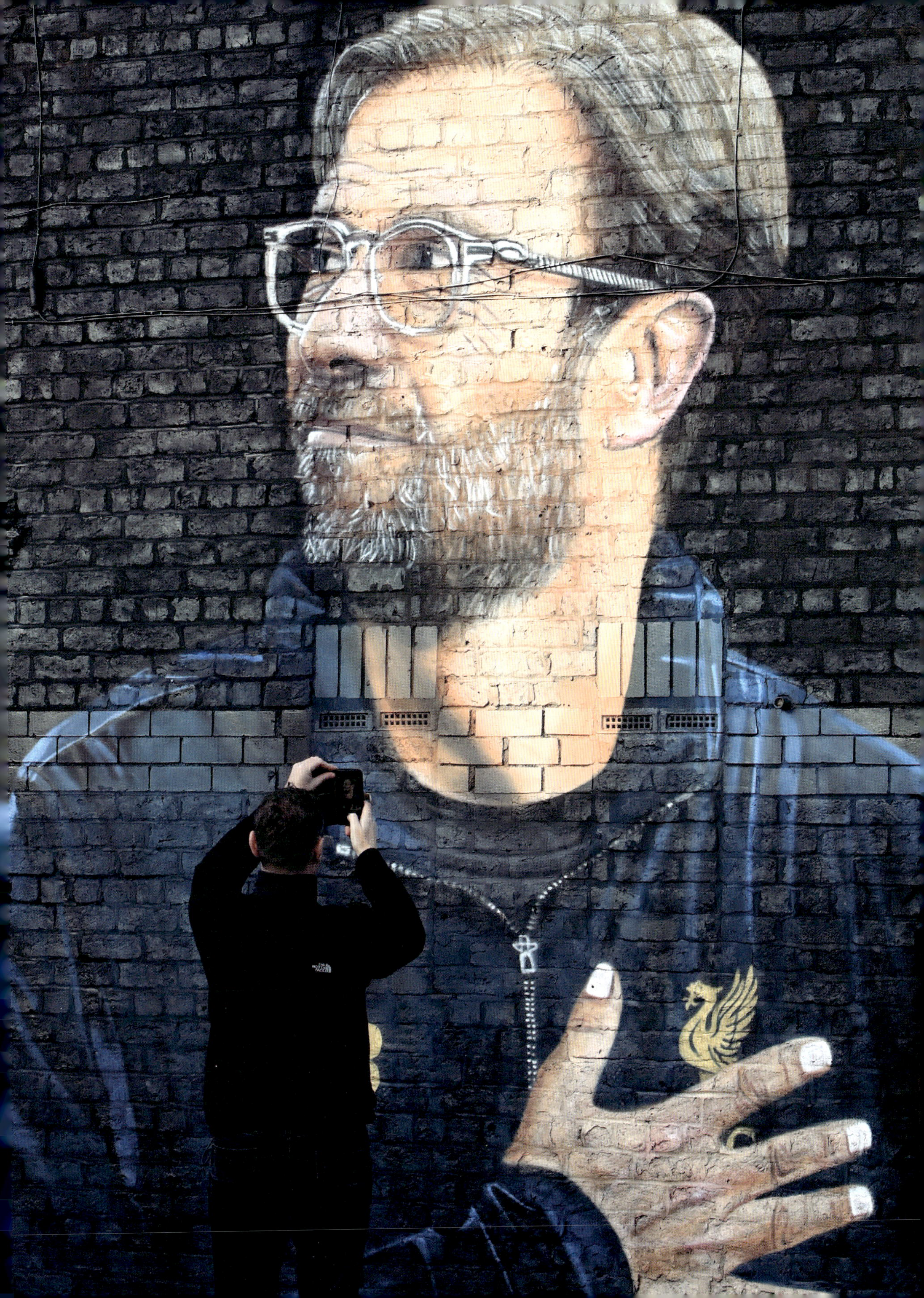

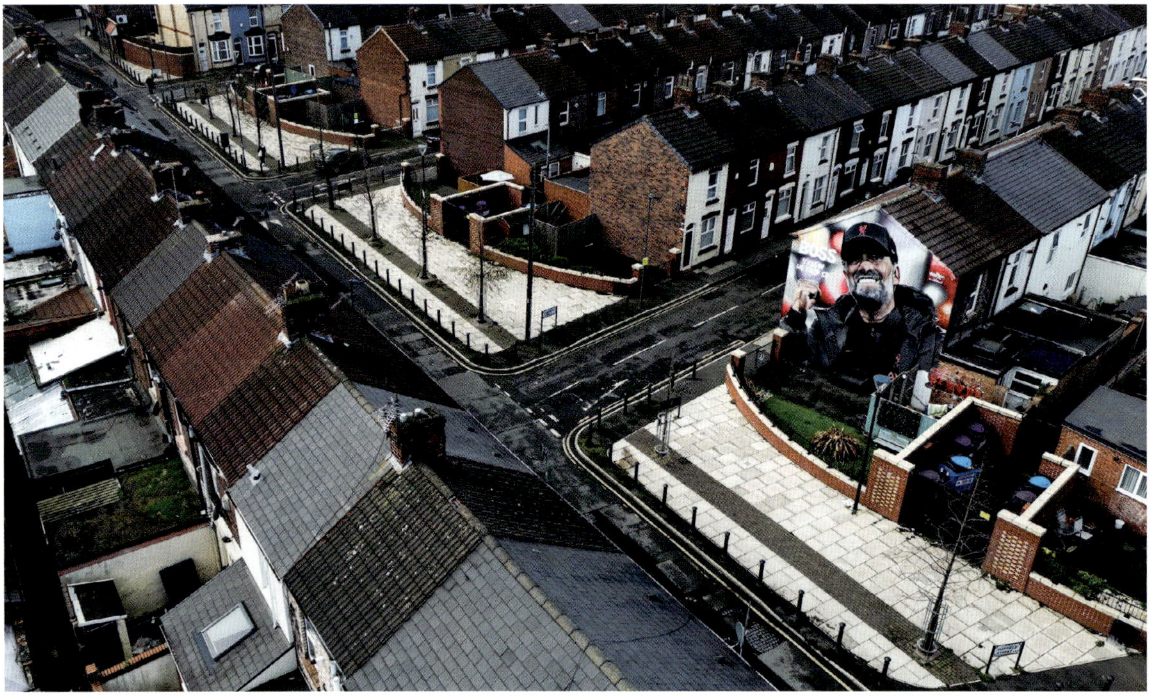

BOSS Night, it took four days to create and featured a line from the *I Feel Fine* song reworked by the Kop in honour of the manager.

Daniel Nicolson, on behalf of BOSS Night, told the club's website: "It's been fantastic to see the streets around the ground decorated over the past couple of years with murals, but we felt there was one person absent: Jürgen. While there is a superb Klopp painting in the Baltic, the man who has brought us so much joy over the past seven years was missing from L4.

"All of us at BOSS feel a connection on and off the pitch to Jürgen. He's been to our events, he speaks highly of [musician] Jamie Webster, we know he enjoys watching all the videos from gigs. And, of course, for the wider fanbase as a whole he is revered. So we wanted to show appreciation to him on behalf of all Reds around the world.

"The support for it has been unbelievable. Chatting to the locals, I know how much this means to them – the football club is a big part of the community. What Jürgen has done for them, it's a very proud moment for me to do this."

Two months later, Klopp was officially awarded the Freedom of the City of Liverpool at a ceremony held in the Town Hall, in acknowledgement of his achievements since arriving at LFC in 2015. In that time he'd overseen seven trophy successes, including of course the Champions League in 2019 and the Premier League in 2020 to end the club's three-decade wait to win the top-flight title again.

But, as Daniel Nicolson and Peter Moore both touched upon, there is more to Jürgen Klopp than winning silverware, not least the way he has orchestrated a communion with loud, colourful, youthful LFC fan culture. "It's not 'glory hunting', it's 'journey hunting'," he once wrote in his matchday programme column.

Don't mention that *I Feel Fine* tune, though. "I still struggle that it's for me. I am every day in front of a camera so I'm obviously not shy...but I am not the main man. The players play, and [even though] you sing all the time my name, I don't play. But I love the song, I'm very, very, very thankful for the idea."

Not nearly as much as the rest of us, boss.

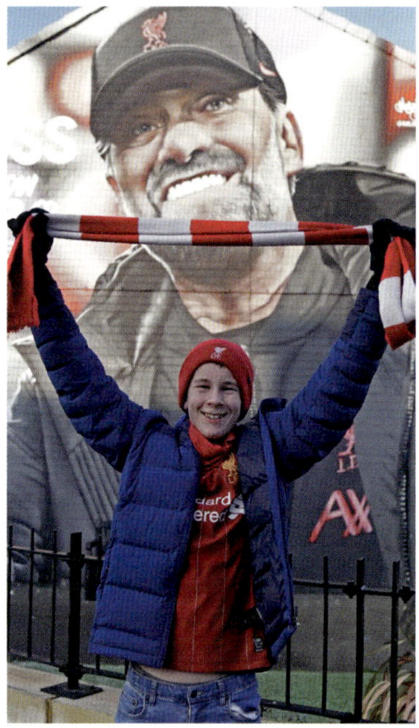

Top and above: the Randolph Street tribute to Jürgen at Anfield
Right: John Culshaw's Klopp mural outside a bar near the stadium

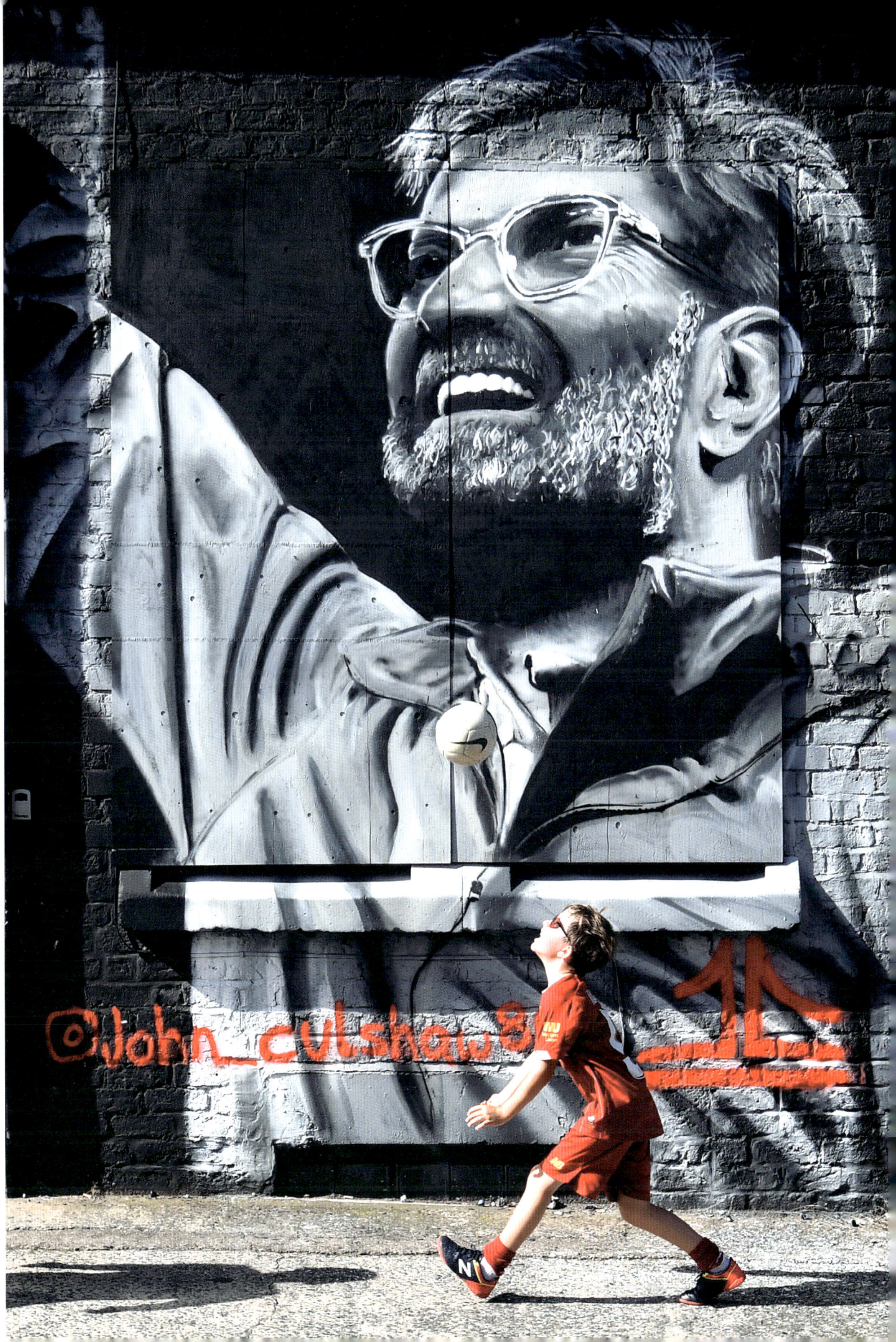
@John_culshaw8

More more Mo

The Egyptian King welcomes fans on the northwest walk-up to Anfield

In March 2022, following the famous murals of then captain Jordan Henderson and right-back Trent Alexander-Arnold around the streets of Anfield, it felt high time for some local street-art celebrating the winger who's broken record after goalscoring record in LFC colours over recent years.

The result was a stunning mural on Anfield Road opposite the King Harry pub, created by local artist John Culshaw and commissioned by Peter Schriewersmann, proprietor of Hotel Anfield, along with other owners of businesses at that end of the famous thoroughfare.

It features two iconic celebrations from the Egyptian ace's LFC career to date, and Mo was selected by fans to be the subject following a poll held by supporters group Spion Kop 1906.

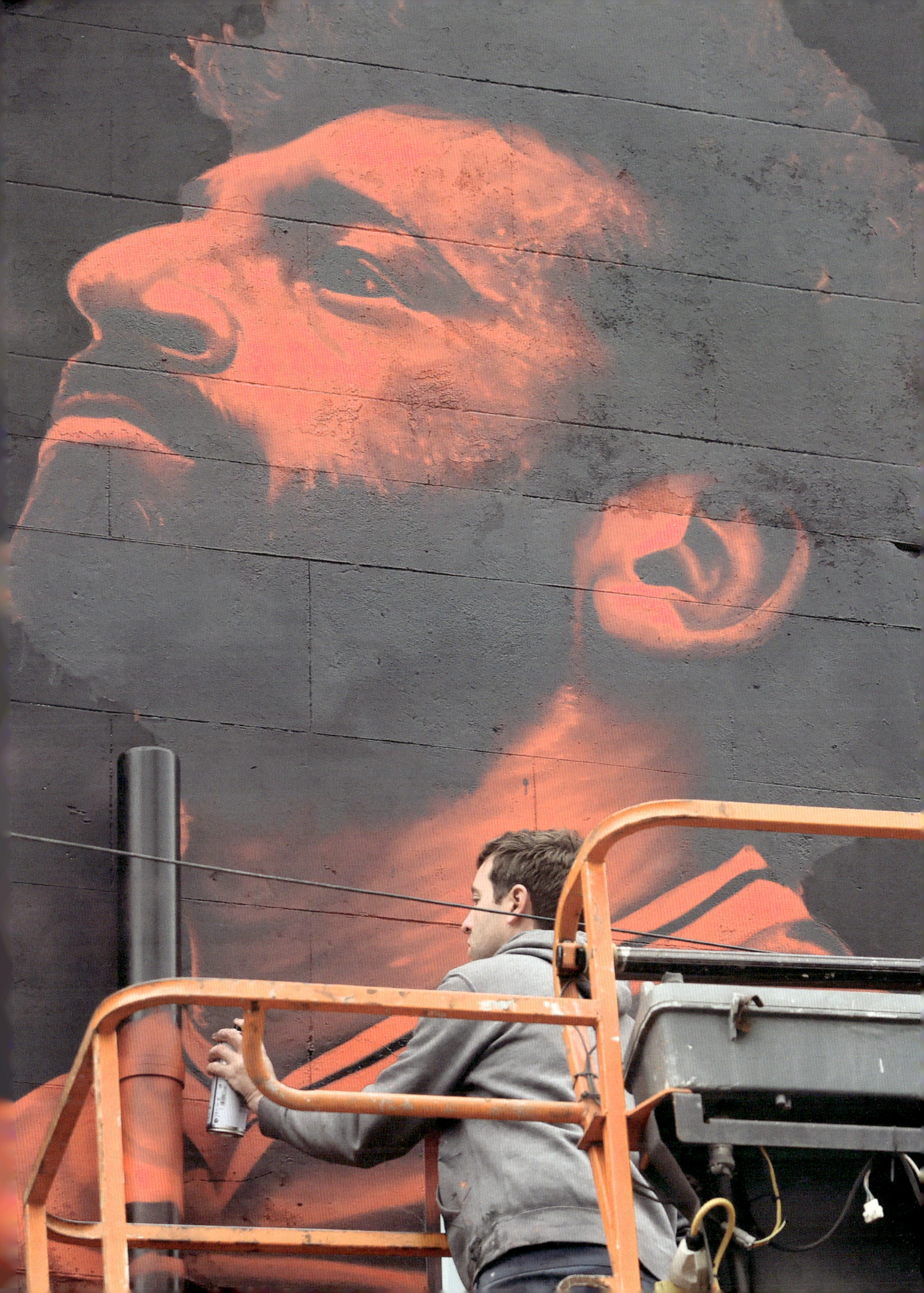

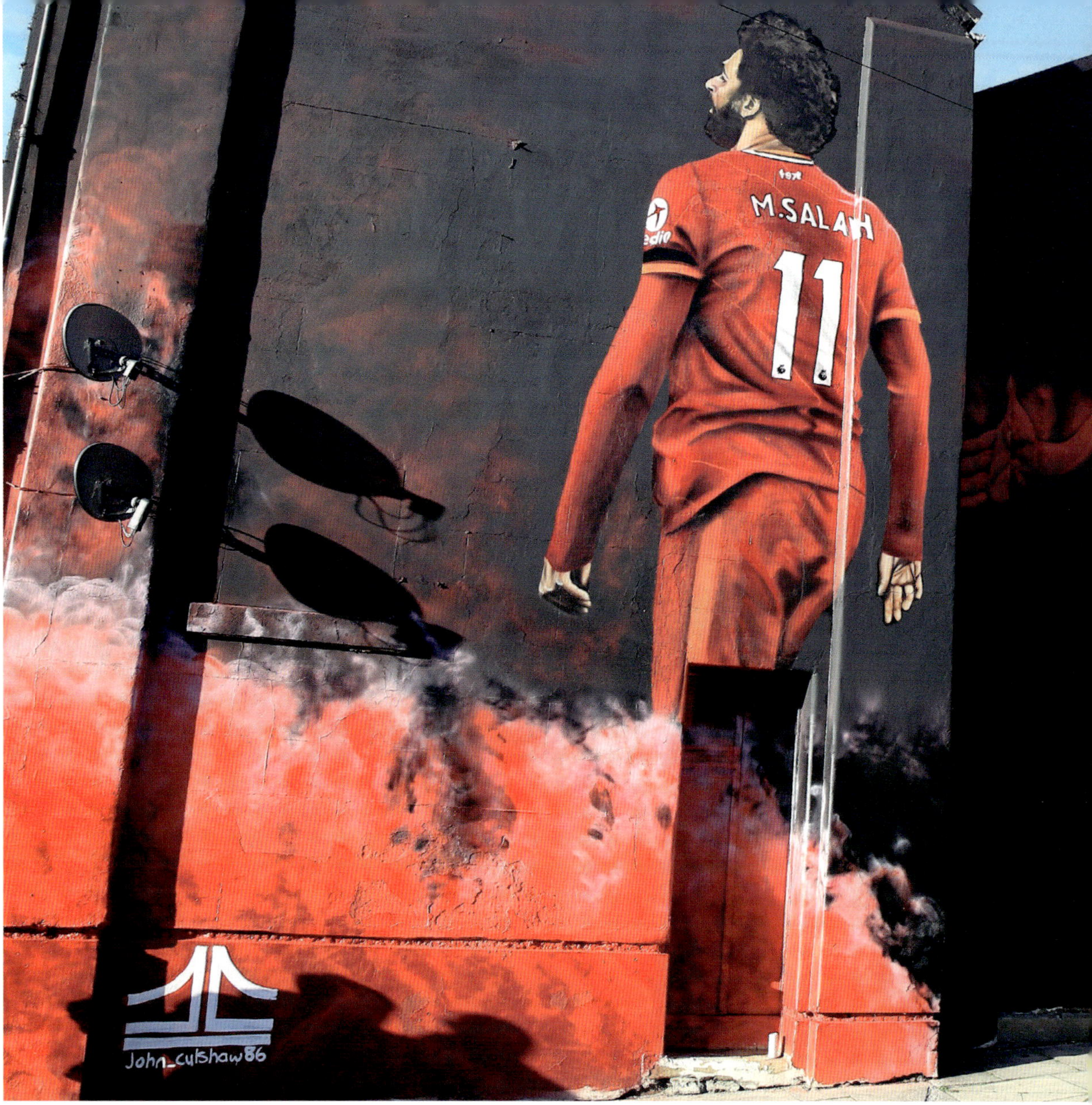
M.SALAH
11
John_culshaw86

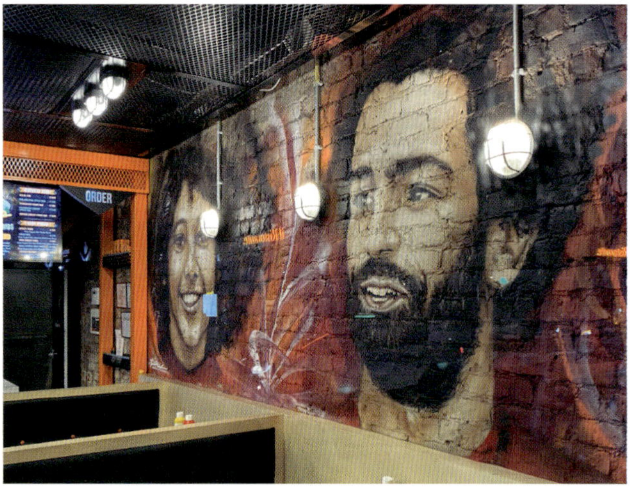
ORDER

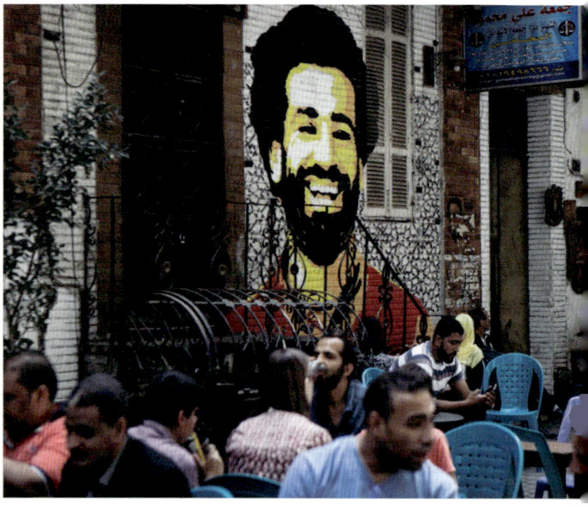

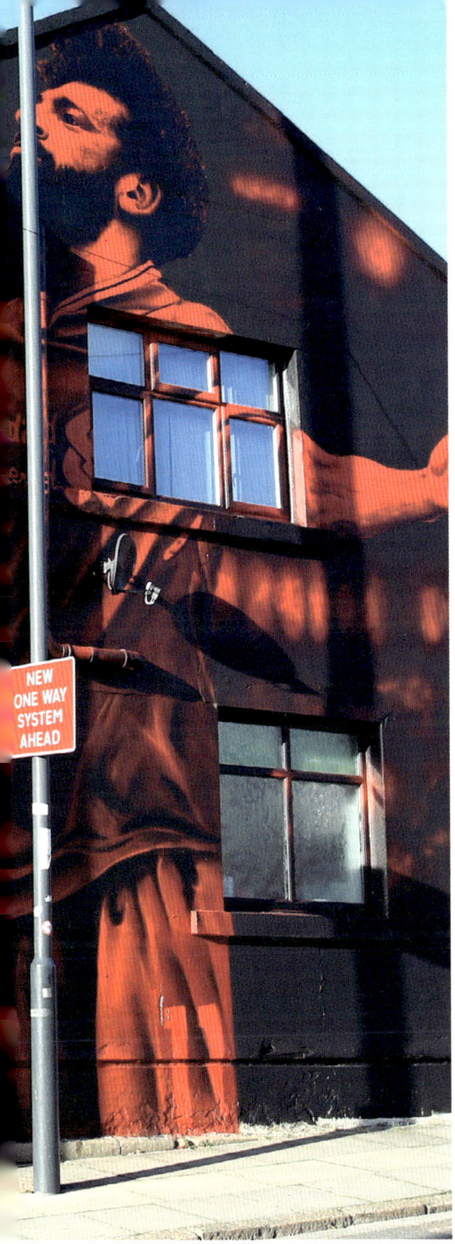

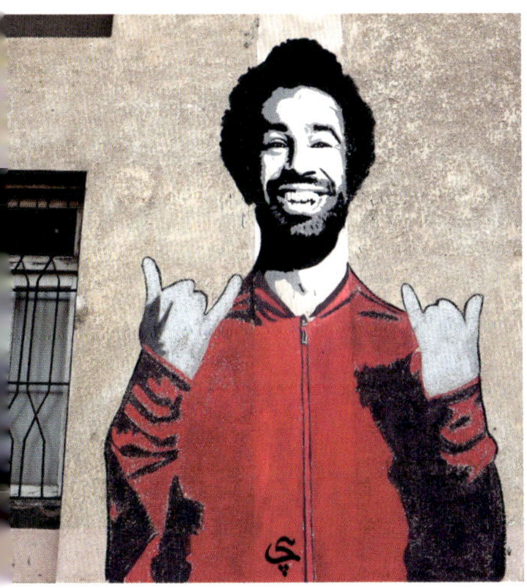

Double vision: two sides to Mo on Anfield Road
Bottom left: Salah on the wall of a South Liverpool cafe and in two locations back home in Egypt

Salah of course is a global superstar and a national hero in his home country of Egypt. Four years previously, in May 2018 and towards the end of Mo's record-breaking debut season with the Reds, his image appeared on the wall of a cafe in downtown Cairo – the artwork forming part of a project honouring the country's most iconic figures.

The cafe-owner revealed: "It's become very popular. Everyone takes pictures of it – foreigners, Egyptians. So many people come to see it that I've even had to turn people away. I tell them Salah is asleep, he's having a rest!"

There's another Mo mural in his hometown of Nagrig in the Nile delta, where residents talk of how he's poured money into local projects from schools to mosques to a dialysis machine at a hospital.

Over in New York City, for a while a huge artwork adorned the side of a brick building in Times Square, depicting Salah's head and shoulders with colourful patterns – along with miniature versions of him playing – in his hair and beard.

American artist Brandan 'Bmike' Odums created it for the sports website Bleacher Report, as part of a celebration of World Cup stars, and on a flying visit to the city Mo tweeted a selfie with it behind him. No surprise it went viral.

By then he'd become the inspiration for city-centre street-art back home. There was an 'Ode to Mo' near Church Street in Liverpool's shopping district, made by poet Musa Okwonga and local street-artist and Reds fan Guy McKinley, to coincide with the 2018 Champions League final.

Ode to Mo: a tribute in Liverpool's city-centre
Opposite page: the Salah mural in New York City

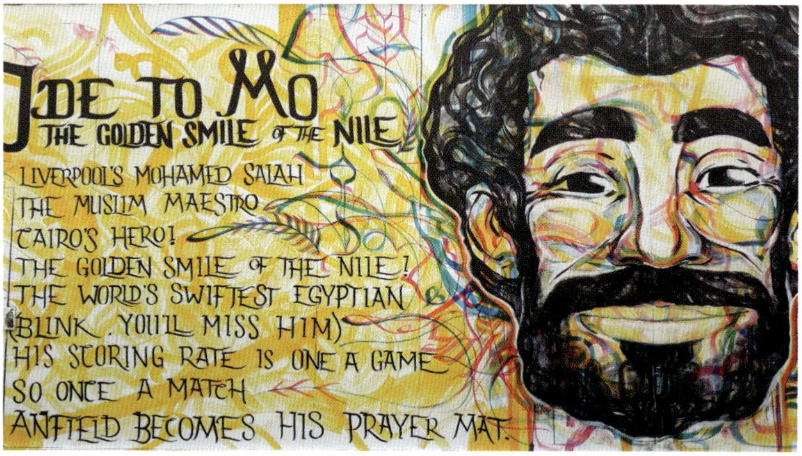

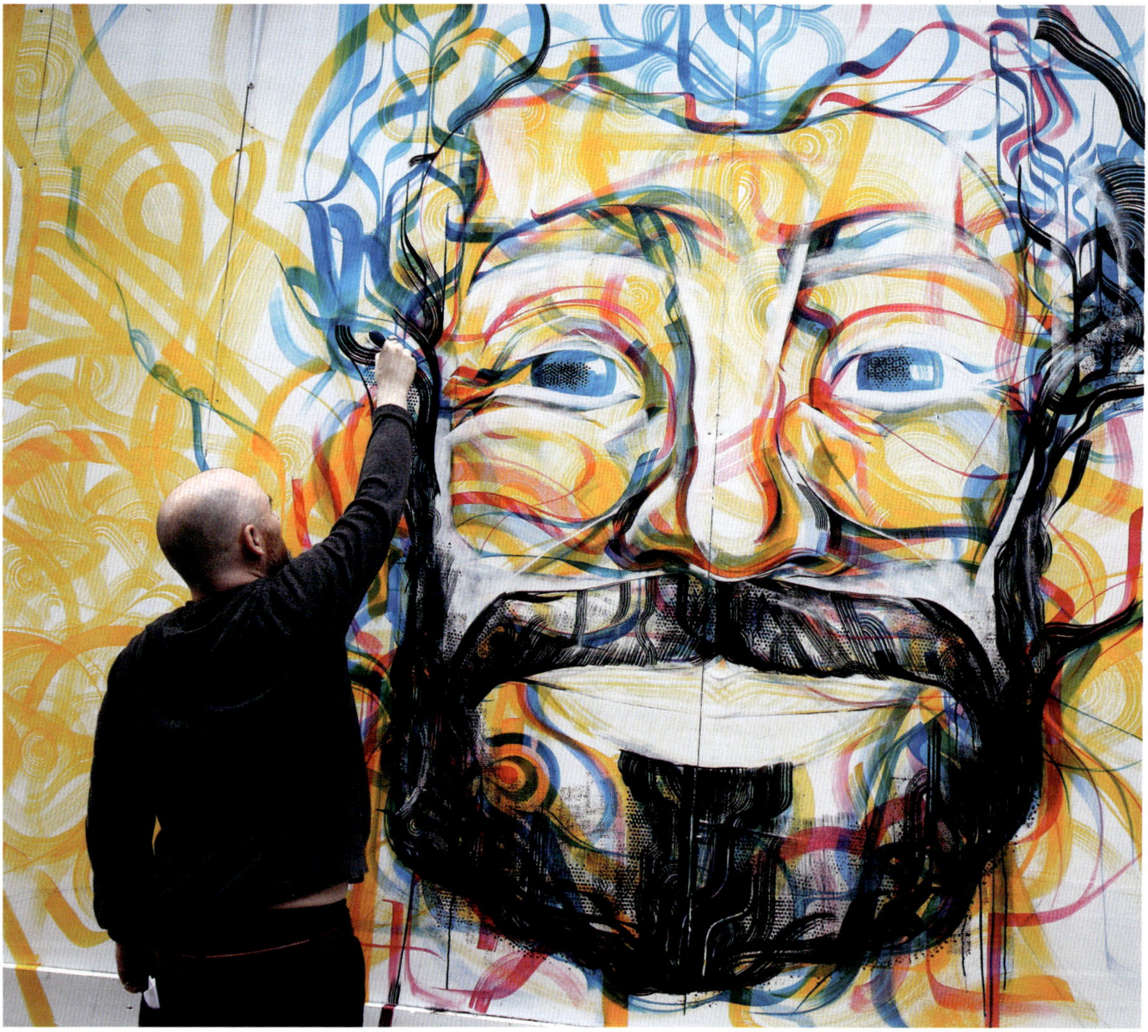

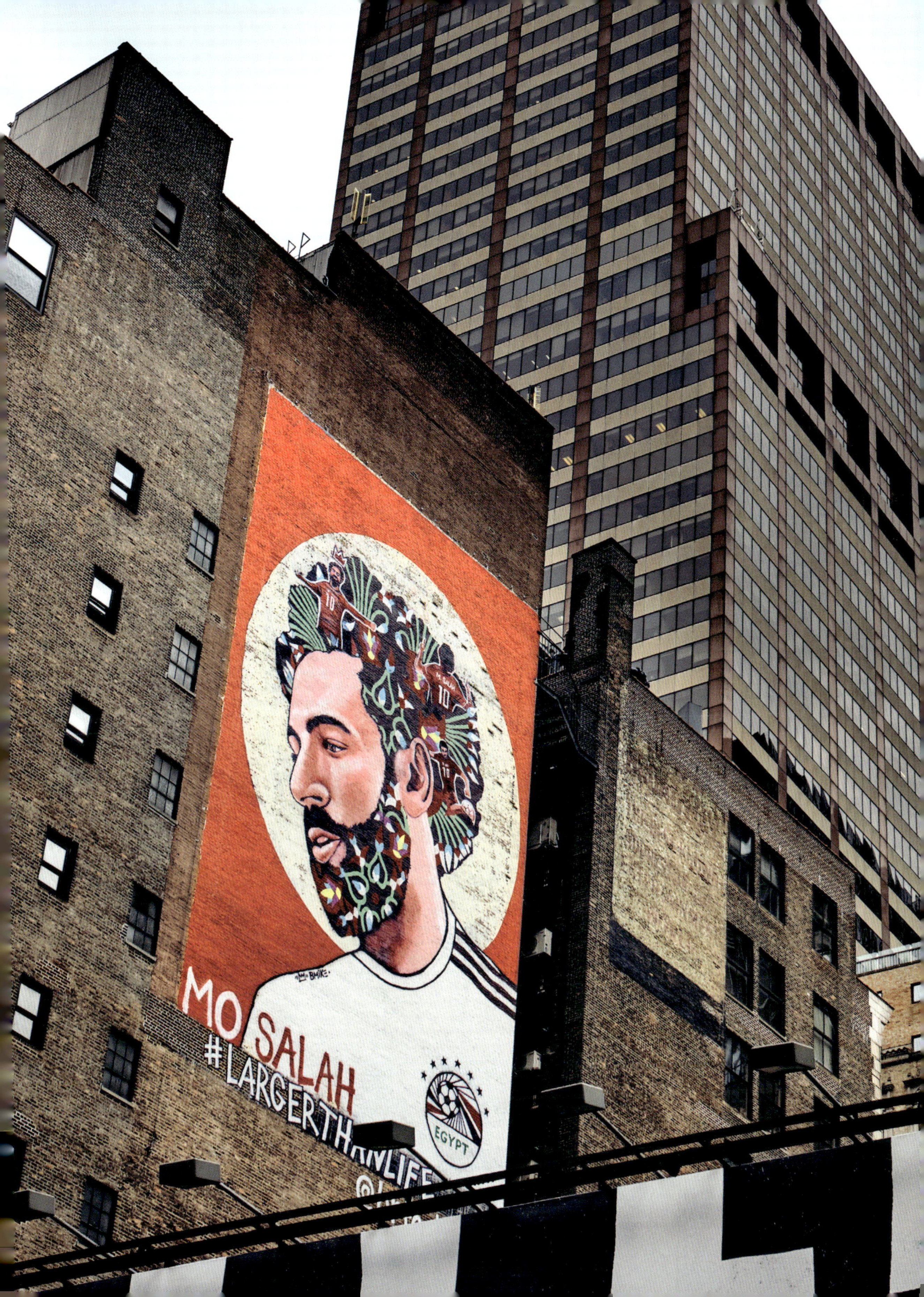
MO SALAH
#LARGERTHANLIFE
EGYPT

Heaven sent

Goodbye Bobby – this way we'll never forget what you did for the mighty Reds

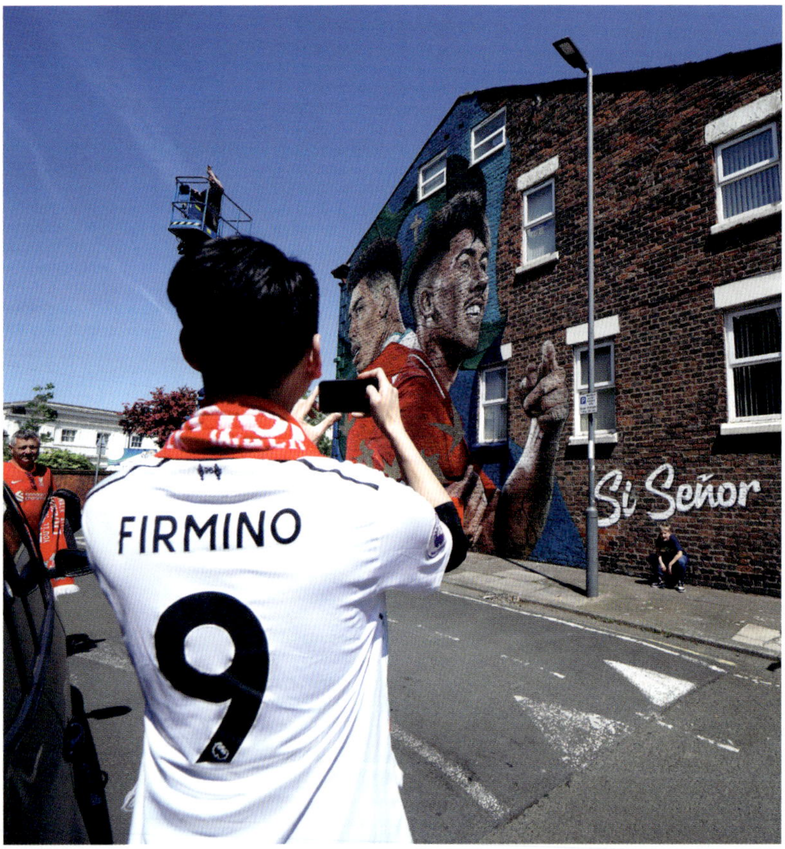

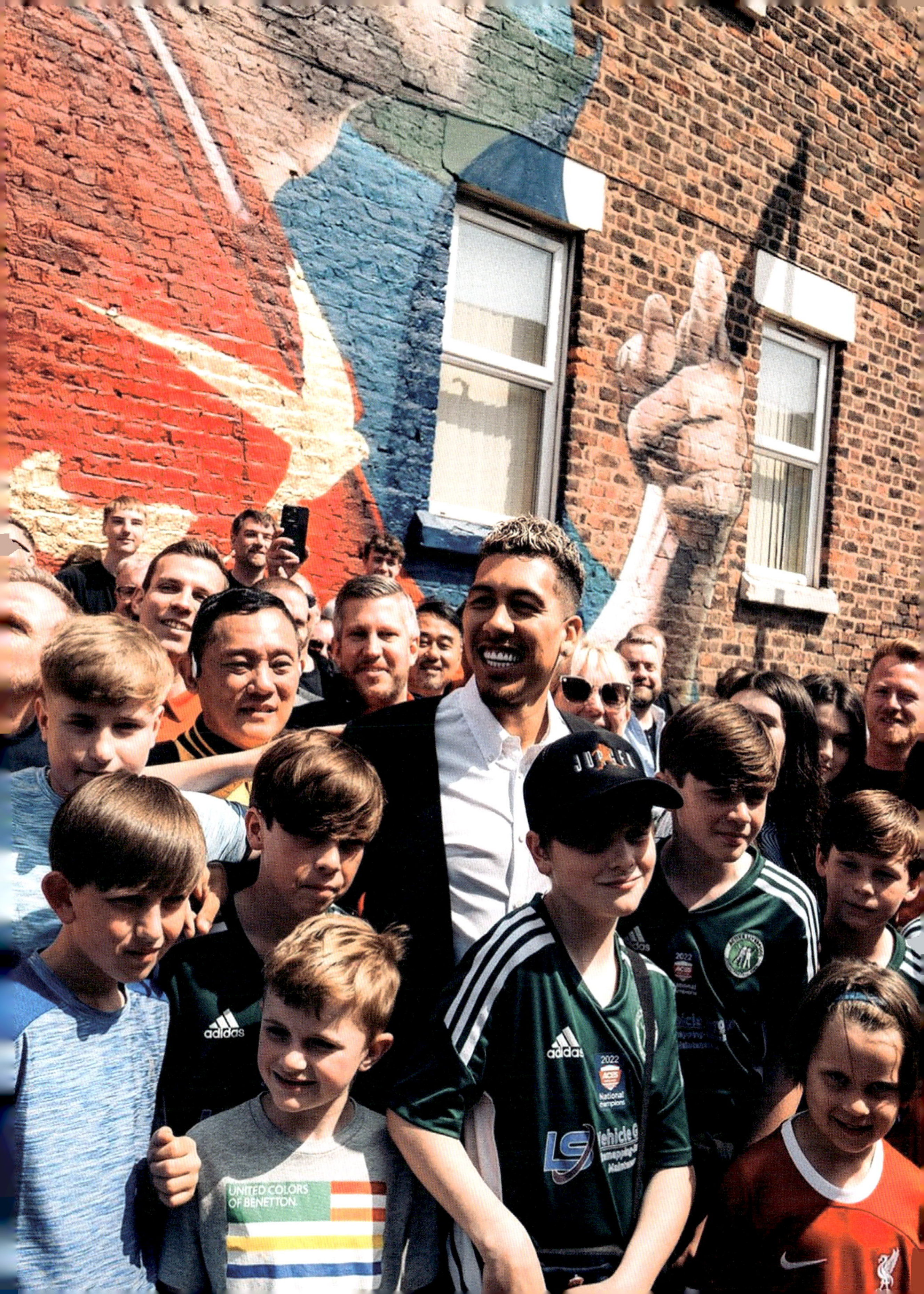
adidas
2022
National champions
UNITED COLORS
OF BENETTON

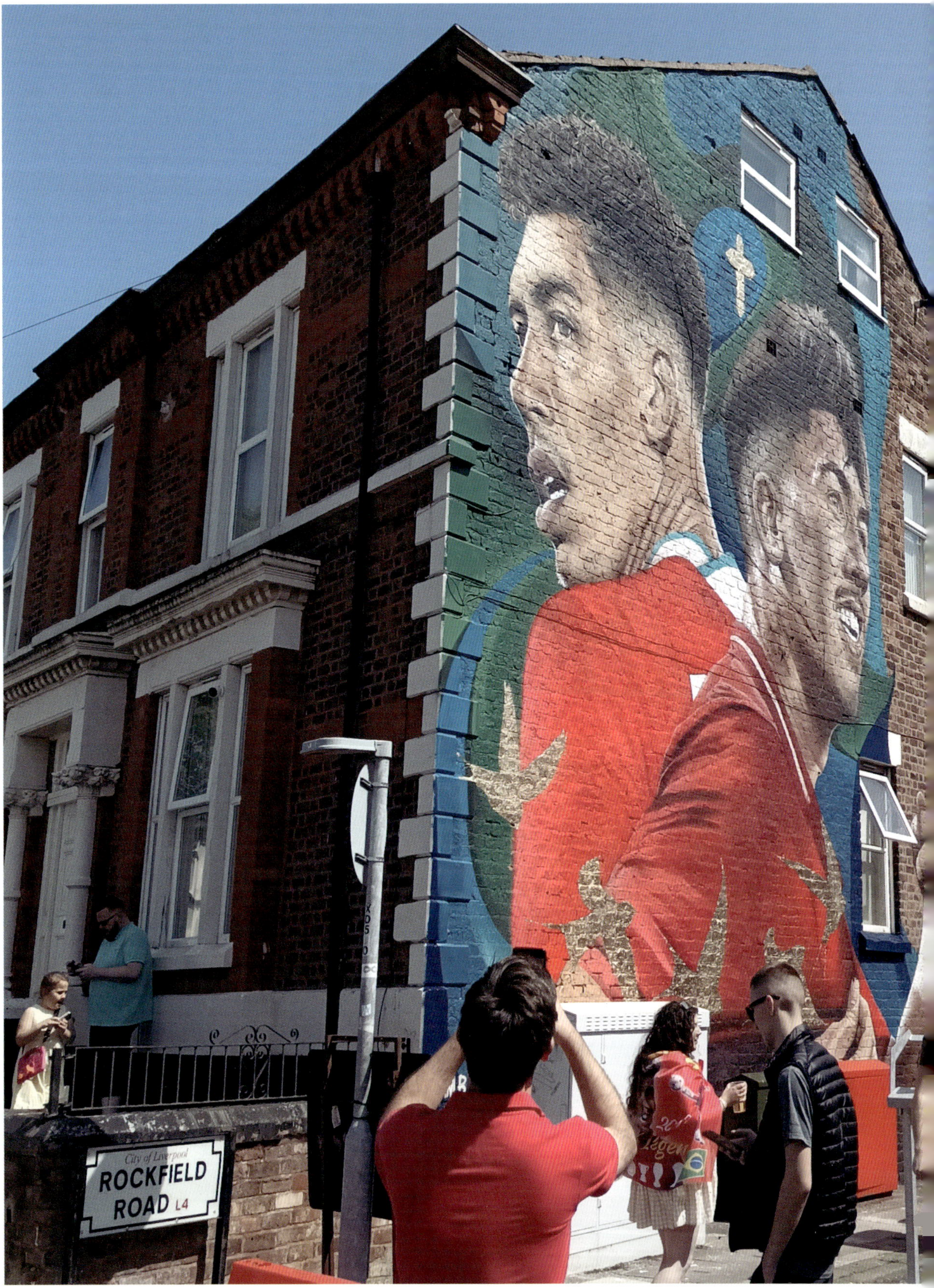
City of Liverpool
ROCKFIELD
ROAD L4

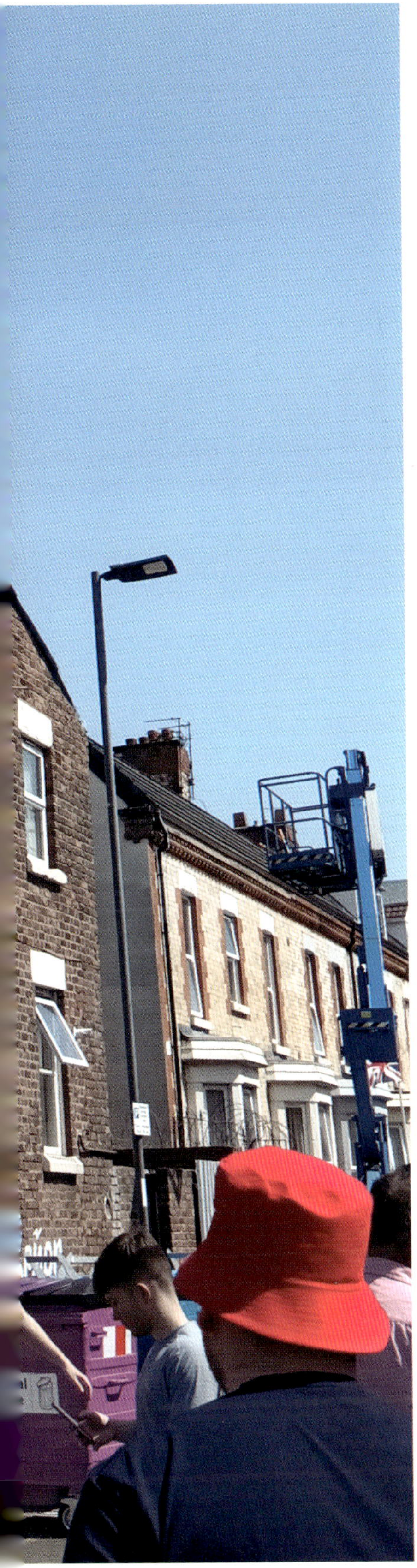

At the end of season 2022/23 the one and only Roberto Firmino bade farewell to his beloved Liverpool FC – the club he always felt he was destined to join – and there was no way that Reds fans would let it pass without honouring him with a mural.

Accordingly a new piece of street-art was unveiled on the corner of Rockfield Road and Anfield Road ahead of the final home of the campaign – and the morning after his goal rescued a point for the Reds against Aston Villa, who else but Bobby checked out the stunning tribute in person. The mural features two images of the Brazilian from his LFC career, along with the words 'Si Senor' in reference to his Kop song, and it's the work of the MurWalls collaborative.

With his no-look goals, fabulous assists, high-kicking celebrations and an ability to start the heralded high-press, Firmino soon became a favourite after signing from Hoffenheim in the summer of 2015, aged 23. He became the sixth Brazilian to play for the Reds and the first to regularly occupy a forward position once Jürgen Klopp was appointed as manager. "When I knew I was coming here, I knew I had a good player," said the boss.

"He is a very important player, a connecting player, a finisher, a fighter, a defender, the first defender – that is important. He's a good listener and a good trainer. He likes to learn, so that is excellent – a nice package."

Bobby netted his first Reds goal under Klopp in an impressive 4-1 win at Manchester City in November 2015. By the time he left in the summer of 2023, he'd got 111 goals and supplied 72 assists in 362 appearances. In the Premier League those totals are 82 and 50 respectively in 256 games – goalscoring contributions of better than one every other game.

Among the many trophies he won with Liverpool was the FIFA Club World Cup in December 2020 when he scored the winners in both the semi-final against Monterrey and the final against Flamengo.

Back home in 2022/23 he scored twice and provided a hat-trick of assists in the record-equalling 9-0 home win over Bournemouth. Then having announced that he'd be leaving the club, he came on and scored – naturally – in the record-setting 7-0 victory over Manchester United. "I loved the reception he got," said Klopp post-match. "He told me [his decision] and then the only other thing he said is, 'Now I want to bring this wonderful story to a positive end.'

"Whenever he will come back, everybody knows that the ['Si Senor'] song will still be for a long, long time in everybody's ears."

At the end of the season Firmino spoke exclusively with official club channel LFCTV, describing his "very difficult decision [to leave]. We love being here [and] I'm grateful for everything we achieved here, the beautiful history we made, fulfilling God's will at this great club. [But] I know that the Lord has new plans for my life and I'm prepared for the new cycle ahead of me.

"I'll always miss them [the fans] dearly. They've supported me a lot over the last eight years. I thank God for every one of them, they sang my name and got behind me during all these years together. I thank God for their love for me, the affection they have for me, from the bottom of my heart.

"They are unique, real and passionate."

Here's to Phil and Cally

Together their LFC playing careers spanned over a quarter-of-a-century and they've got the honours – and now the street-art – to show for it

Anfield's Randolph Street is the location of a 2023 mural celebrating two of Liverpool FC's greatest-ever servants, with over 1,500 appearances between them plus countless winner's medals, including domestic leagues and cups and the most prestigious trophies in Europe.

In recent years former winger-turned-midfielder Ian Callaghan and full-back Phil Neal have regularly welcomed Reds fans as part of the club's matchday hospitality, regaling them with wonderful tales from their playing era.

One such group of supporters, who attend the Main Stand's Beautiful Game suite, decided to honour the duo by commissioning MurWalls to create a new piece on one of the 'walk-ups' to the ground. When they revealed their tribute to Callaghan and Neal and presented them with framed pictures at the Liverpool v Arsenal game in April 2023, the two legends were visibly moved. Ian and Phil later visited the mural in person and personally signed it, with the unveiling supported by Forever Reds, Liverpool FC's official former players association.

Cally was the only player to experience Liverpool's journey from the old Second Division to the summit of European football. He was also part of England's 1966 World Cup-winning squad, the first Liverpool player to claim the Football Writers' Association Footballer of the Year award (in 1974), and he was later recognised with an MBE for his services to the game.

Bill Shankly once said of him: "He is a model professional, and a model human being. If there were eleven Callaghans at Anfield there would never be any need to put up a team-sheet. He typifies everything that is good in football, and he has never changed. You could stake your life on Ian."

Callaghan made his senior debut on Saturday 16 April 1960 when the Reds were in the old Second Division and Bristol Rovers were the opposition at Anfield. Recently he recalled that day with LFCTV: "I lived in Toxteth and I went to the bus-stop about one o'clock to get here for two o'clock, to make my debut at three. At the bus-stop the queue was long but the conductor recognised me and said, 'We better let him go to the front of the queue – he's making his debut today'. Anyway I had a good debut, we won [4-0], and I got the number 26 bus going home."

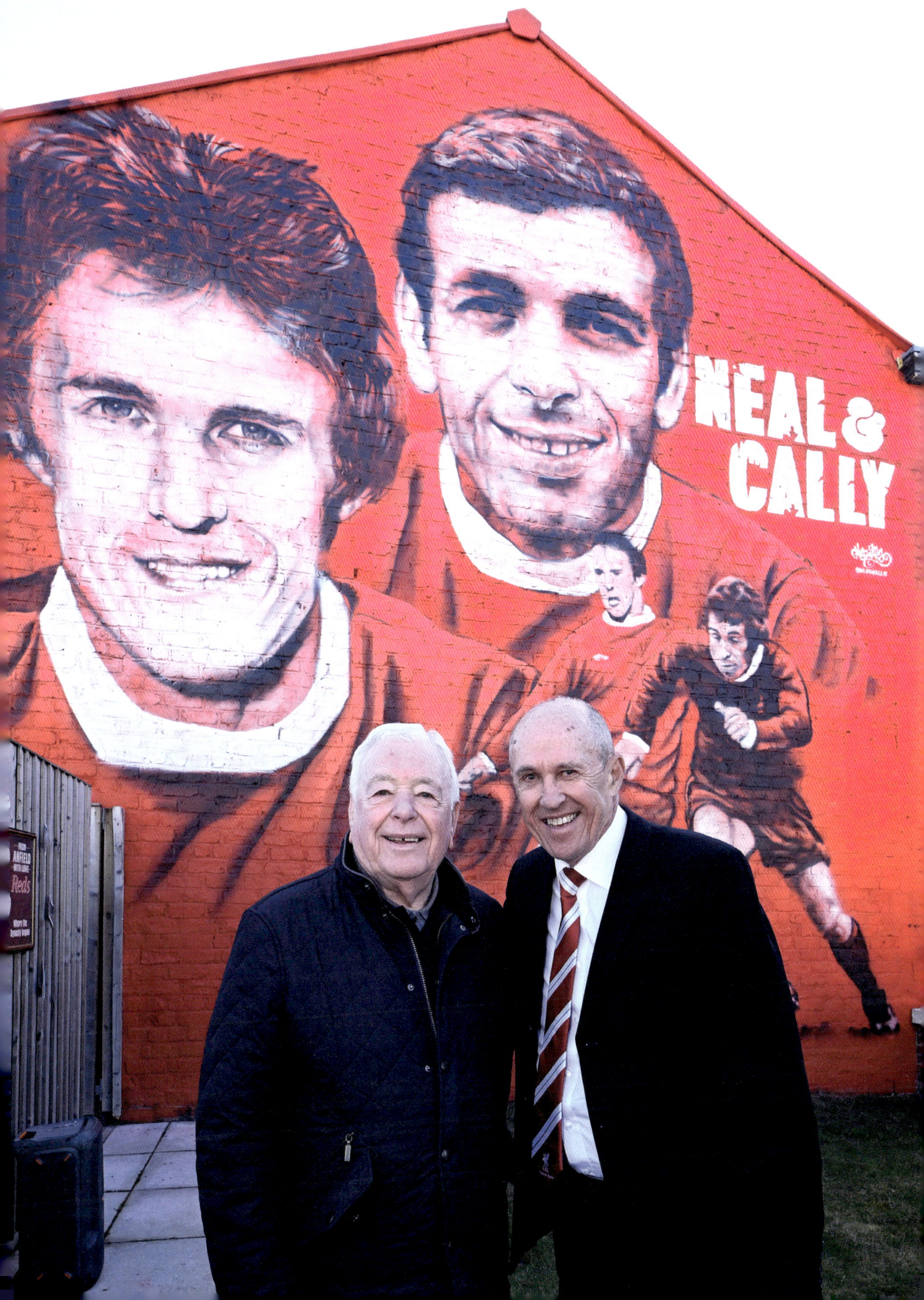
NEAL &
CALLY

Boys in red: Liverpool supporters of all ages were out in force to see Ian and Phil visit the new mural in person

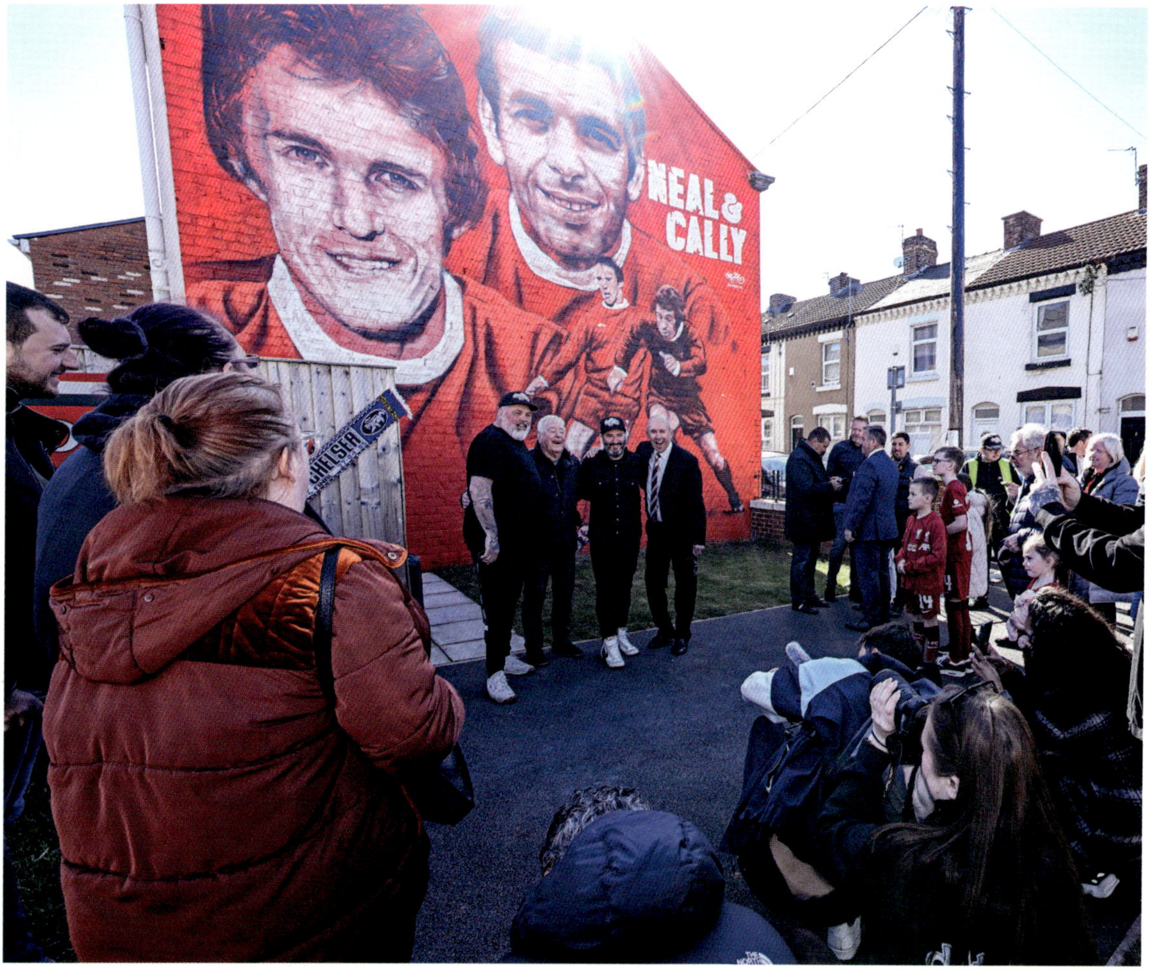

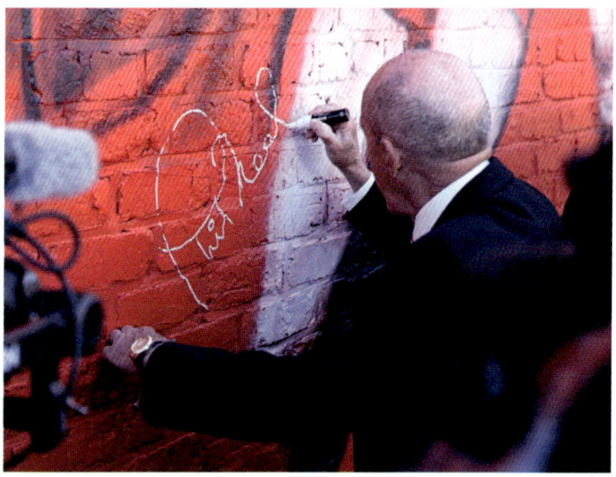

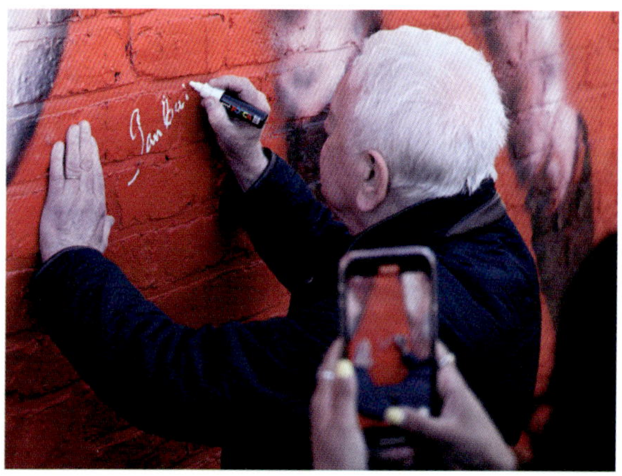

Over the next 18 years Ian would appear in a club-record 857 matches for Liverpool; the next-closest to that total are Jamie Carragher on 737 games and Steven Gerrard with 710. He scored 68 goals and famously he was booked only once, and never sent off. He was part of the Shankly side which swept to promotion in 1961/62 just as Beatlemania began to shake the world.

With the Reds he then won the top-flight title in 1964, 1966, 1973, 1976 and 1977; the FA Cup in 1965 and 1974; the European Cup in 1977 and 1978; and the UEFA Cup in 1973 and 1976.

In April 2022 he celebrated his 80th birthday and at half-time during the home match with Manchester United the club presented him with a framed print of Anfield's 'Champions Wall' along with a signed shirt featuring 'Callaghan 80' on the back.

Earlier the owners of Hotel TIA on Anfield Road had given him a special cake. Author and Reds fan Ragnhild Lund Ansnes, along with another Liverpool legend, David Fairclough, interviewed him for her LFC Talk podcast and the first thing he told her was: "I've been blessed." At the end of the podcast he reflected: "I still get recognised and I think it's lovely. People come up to you and talk football or say thank-you for what you did for the club. It's very special, it really is.

"As I've mentioned before, the first thing my dad said when I was playing in the first team was, 'Ian, don't you forget – always give people time'.

"It's been a massive part of my life – it's been my life. Fans don't let you forget. It doesn't matter how long ago you played, they still remember you."

Those sentiments would certainly be echoed by Phil Neal, who to this day remains the club's most decorated player with eight top-flight titles and four European Cups won during his eleven years at Liverpool. He was Bob Paisley's first managerial acquisition and made a record 365 consecutive league appearances between December 1974 and September 1983.

His debut came away to Everton, no less, with Phil only being told on the morning of the match. He'd recall: "There wasn't much time for nerves and, obviously, that had been the idea all along: to make me think I'd little chance of playing so I didn't become too tense and freeze on the field. Bob Paisley was a clever man in every shape and form.

"I must admit it came as a bit of a shock to be thrown in at the deep-end, but everything went fine. Ian Callaghan was brilliant on the day. 'I'll be around always for a pass even if it's tight', he said. It was great, really. I remember towards the end of the second half I had a shot that just whistled over and I thought: I can handle this."

All told, Phil won eight league titles, four European Cups (the only LFC player to play in all of the first four winning finals, scoring in two), four League Cups and one UEFA Cup, with his 650 appearances bettered by only six others. He also skippered the Reds and won 50 caps for England.

No one had scored as many spot kicks for the club (38) when he surpassed the great Billy Liddell's total of 34 until Jan Molby hit 42, and more recently Steven Gerrard converted 47.

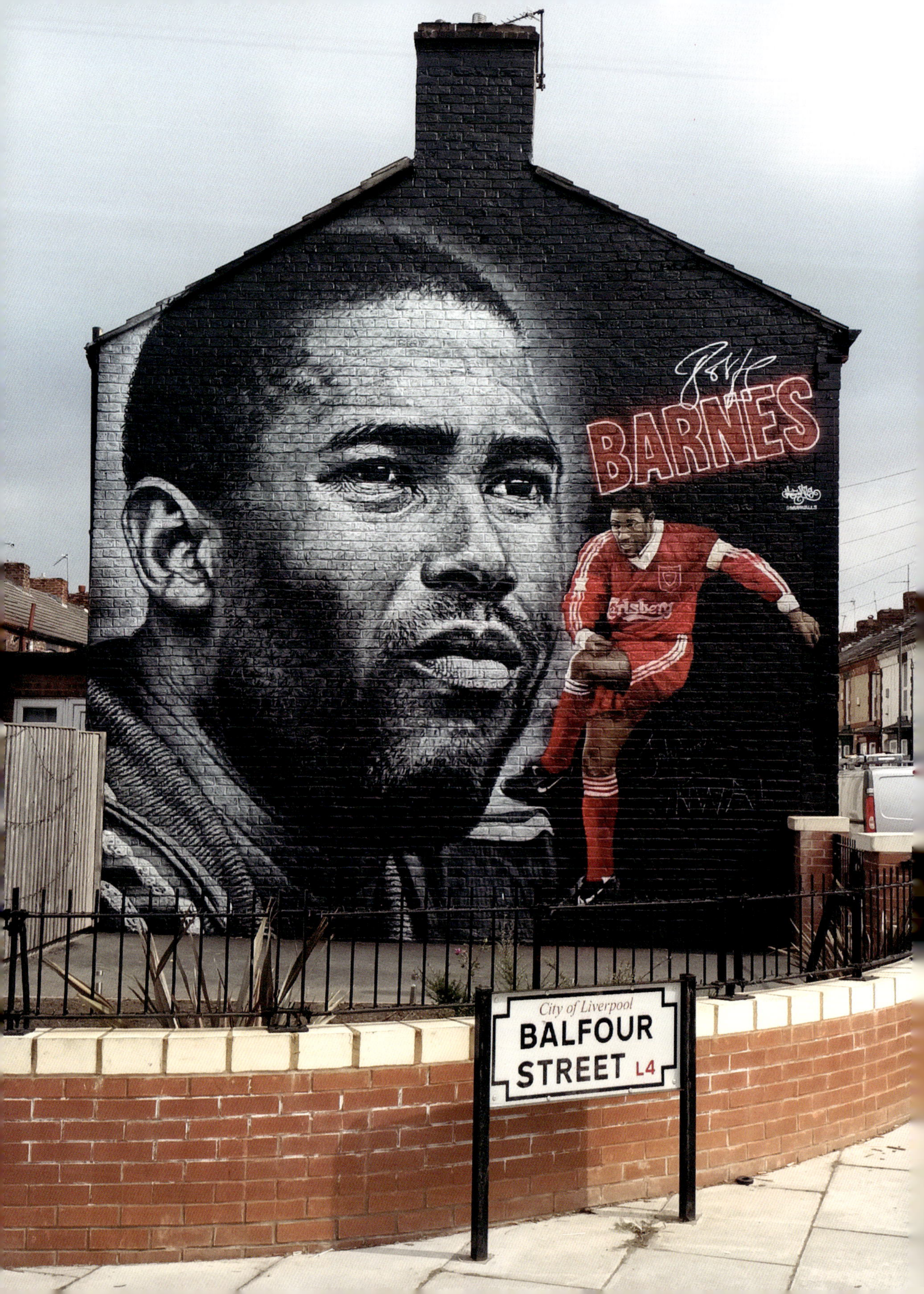
BARNES
Carlsberg
City of Liverpool
BALFOUR
STREET L4

Catch me if you can cos I'm the England man

And he's a Liverpool legend, too – honoured for his sensational service

Around the same time in April 2023 that the Ian Callaghan and Phil Neal mural appeared on Randolph Street in Anfield, another LFC work of art was going up on nearby Balfour Street.

Both streets are rungs along the terraced-house ladder of Blessington Road which runs from Walton Breck Road to Anfield Road, and whose end-houses lend themselves so perfectly to the creation of murals.

Another MurWalls commission, this one was dedicated to John Barnes, one of the most gifted footballers ever to wear the red jersey.

Jamaican-born John was the first piece in player-manager Kenny Dalglish's exciting new Liverpool jigsaw for season 1987/88. He joined from Watford for a fee of £900,000 and spent the next few seasons tearing teams apart and delighting audiences with his grace, pace and skills – first on the wing and then in a more central midfield position.

He scored 108 goals in 407 appearances, won top-flight titles with the Reds in 1988 and 1990, and amassed 79 international caps for England despite a few injuries later in his career.

Upon first seeing the mural, he commented: "I'd been walking around, looking at pictures of Rushie and all the other boys, and I thought to myself: I would love to have one of them. It's one of the best things that has ever happened to me and it is appropriate, the location, because this is part of the community, this is where it should be. I'm delighted."

As a player Barnes was unquestionably one of LFC's finest, and today he's an articulate and captivating social commentator on a broad range of issues. And when he talks about the Reds, people always listen.

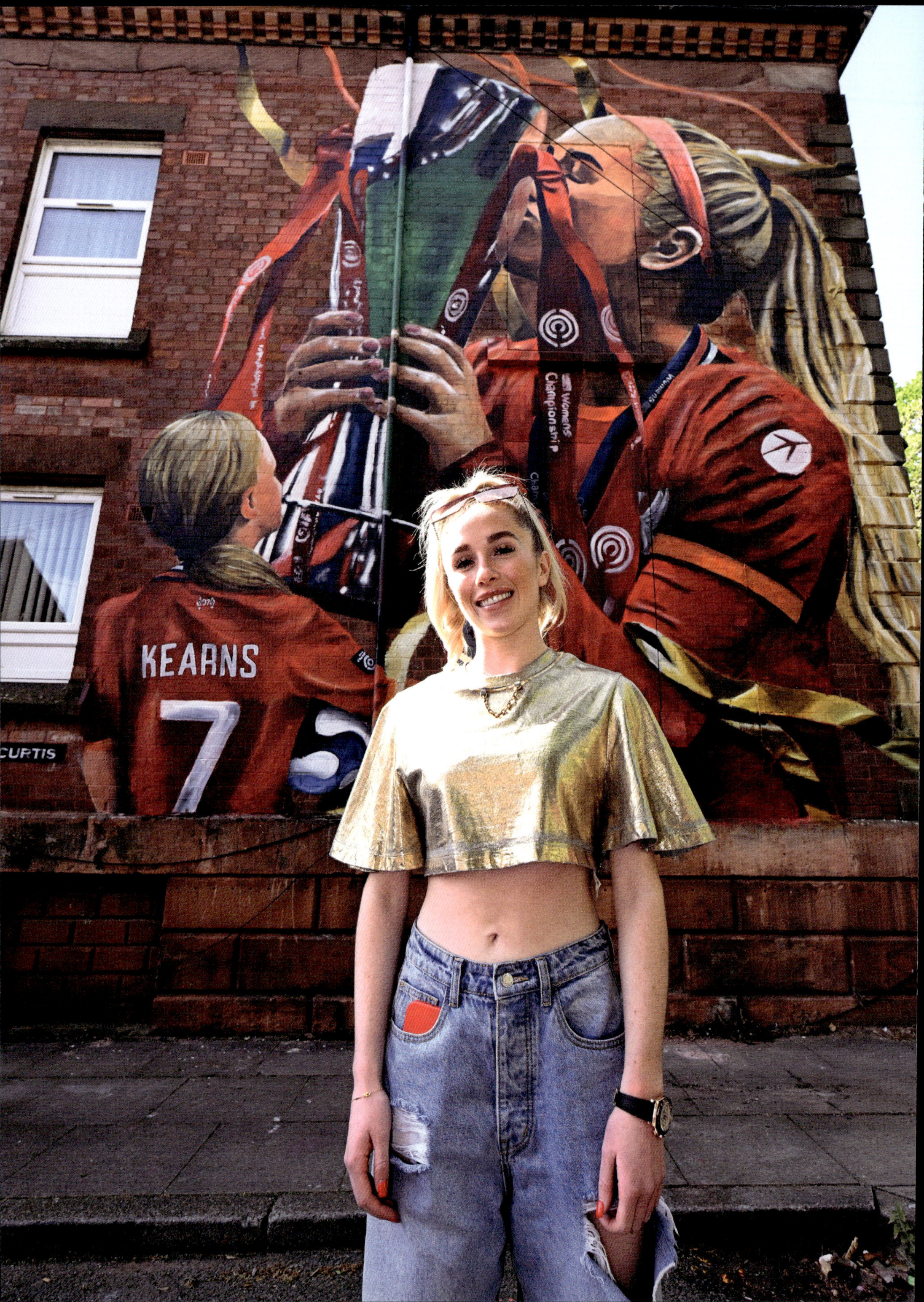
KEARNS
7
CURTIS

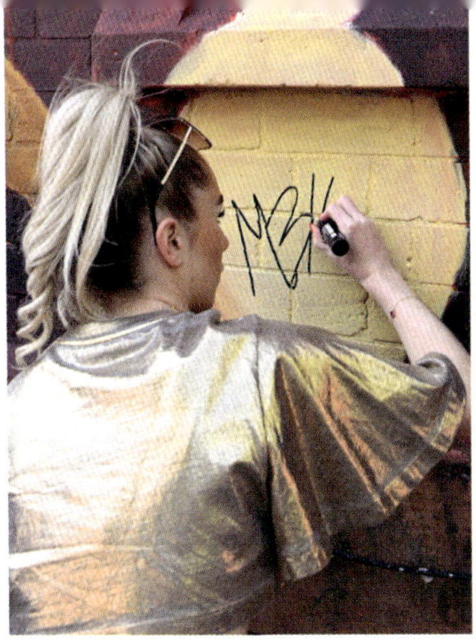

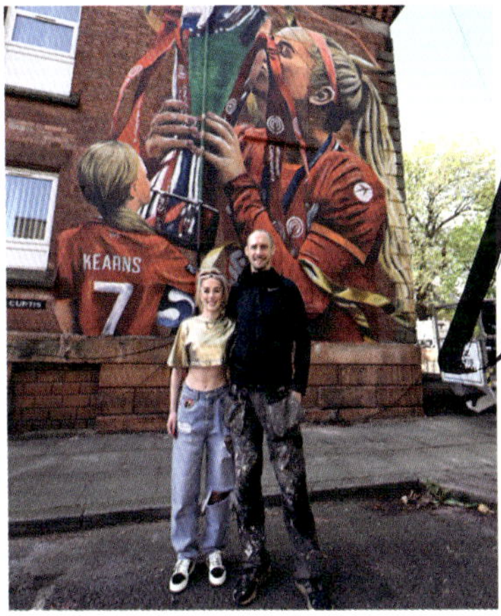

Missy Bo's mural

The unveiling of the local girl's likeness was a celebration for one and all

History was made on 16 May 2023 when a player from Liverpool FC Women was depicted in street-art for the first time. Scouse midfielder Missy Bo Kearns admitted she was speechless at the reveal on Anfield's Tancred Road which shows her younger self looking up at the future no7 lifting the FA Women's Championship trophy.

Commissioned by the Liverpool FC Women Supporters Club, it's the work of Paul Curtis, already well-known for other LFC-related work around L4 including the tributes to Kenny Dalglish, Anne Williams, Alan Hansen and Jordan Henderson. "I understand it's the first women's football mural in Merseyside," he said. "It's made up of several photos from that day but when I saw the ticker-tape and the ribbons, I thought that was a nice touch, so I added a lot more to kind of give it some movement.

"It should have taken about three days but we had to do some boarding-up of the old windows and that was a job in itself! That took a day-and-a-half to get done so it took the best part of five days in the end."

The location was extra-special for the player whose dad used to live in a flat directly opposite. "It's just a mad scenario and my dad is really proud," revealed Missy Bo. "He was crying when he first saw it and you just couldn't write it, could you?

"The hours of work that have been put into it have paid off because it's unbelievable. It's special for me but without the team and what we achieved in winning the Championship and getting back into the WSL, I don't think it would have been possible for one of the women's players to be pictured like this around Anfield. Hopefully it inspires young girls to want to play football one day."

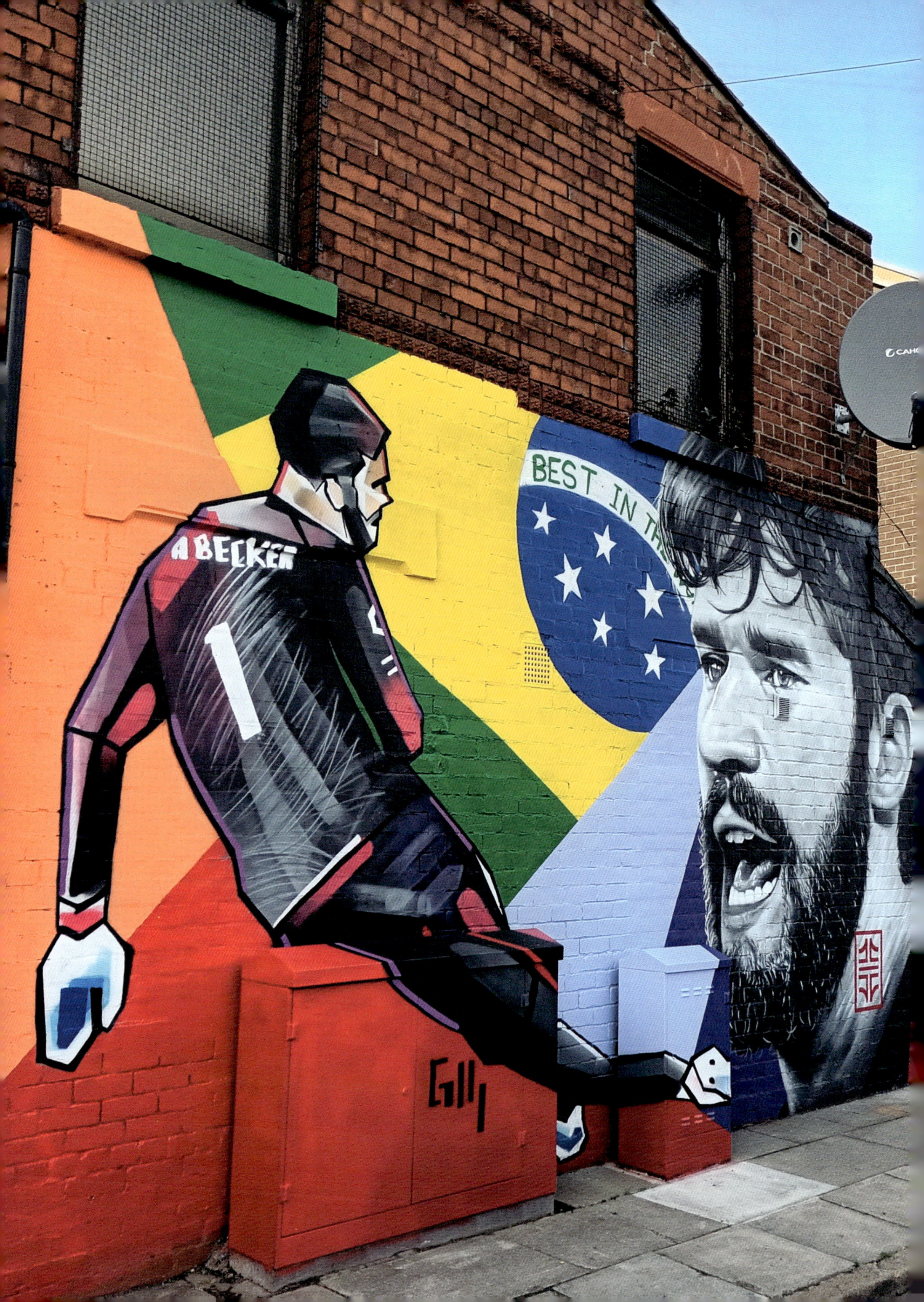
A BECKER
1
BEST IN

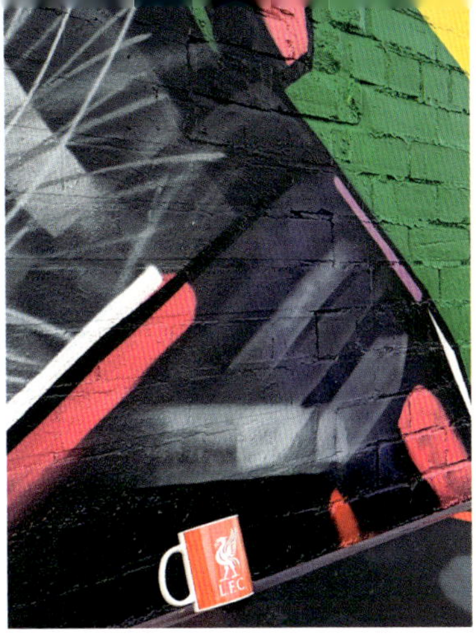

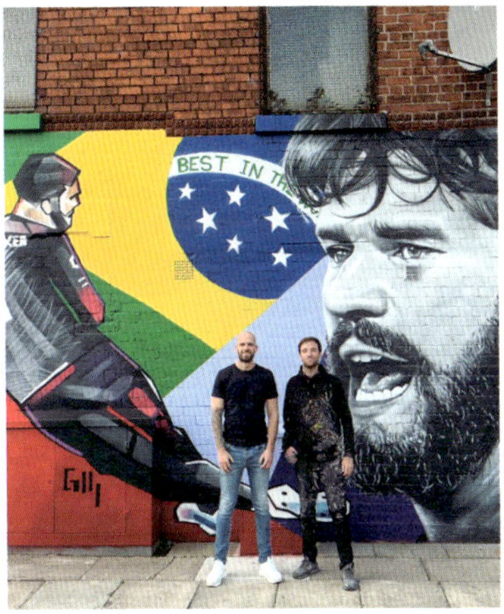

October 2023 saw the Brazilian keeper captured in two stunning styles

Alisson! Alisson!

One of the most recent LFC murals to be unveiled, just under eight weeks into the 2023/24 season, was a doubly-dynamic tribute to goalkeeper Alisson Becker, featuring the distinctive styles of local artists John Culshaw and 'Cally'.

John (right in the inset photo) created the monochrome portrait of Alisson on the right-hand side of the artwork then upscaled Cally's digital rendition of the Brazilian's famous late headed goal for the Reds at West Bromwich Albion in May 2021. Between each image is the Brazilian national flag.

The mural can be found on the side of a bookmakers on Pulford Street, just off Walton Breck Road and near The Twelfth Man public house. It took John four days to complete, accounting for weather conditions, after Alisson came out top in a fan poll to decide which modern Liverpool player should be depicted.

The Brazilian, recently turned 31, joined the club in 2018 from AS Roma and in autumn 2023 was approaching both the 200-appearance mark in the Premier League and his 250th time between the LFC posts in all competitions.

As well as his goal at WBA, he's also provided three Premier League assists – all for Mo Salah. And as well as his winner's medals for the 2019 UEFA Champions League and FIFA Club World Cup, 2020 Premier League and 2022 League Cup and FA Cup, he's also been named as UEFA's goalkeeper of the year and the Best FIFA Football Awards goalkeeper of the year, both for 2019.

Manager Jürgen Klopp has called him "unbelievably important. Ali is not only the goalkeeper – he is an outfield player as well and that helps of course."

The man himself says: "I always like to play, to be involved in possession. Of course you see goalkeepers playing more with their feet from the back these days, not only kicking long balls. That affects our position as keepers a little bit, but I don't think it has changed too much – we've just improved things because of the necessity of what football is asking for.

"Football today is asking for a team who builds up. The goalkeeper needs to play, to be good with his feet, but the main part is always making saves and doing what a goalkeeper does – leading the team, claiming crosses."

"I was once that kid"

The Trent Alexander-Arnold mural near the stadium was the first of its kind in the Anfield neighbourhood and it remains a favourite for Liverpool supporters

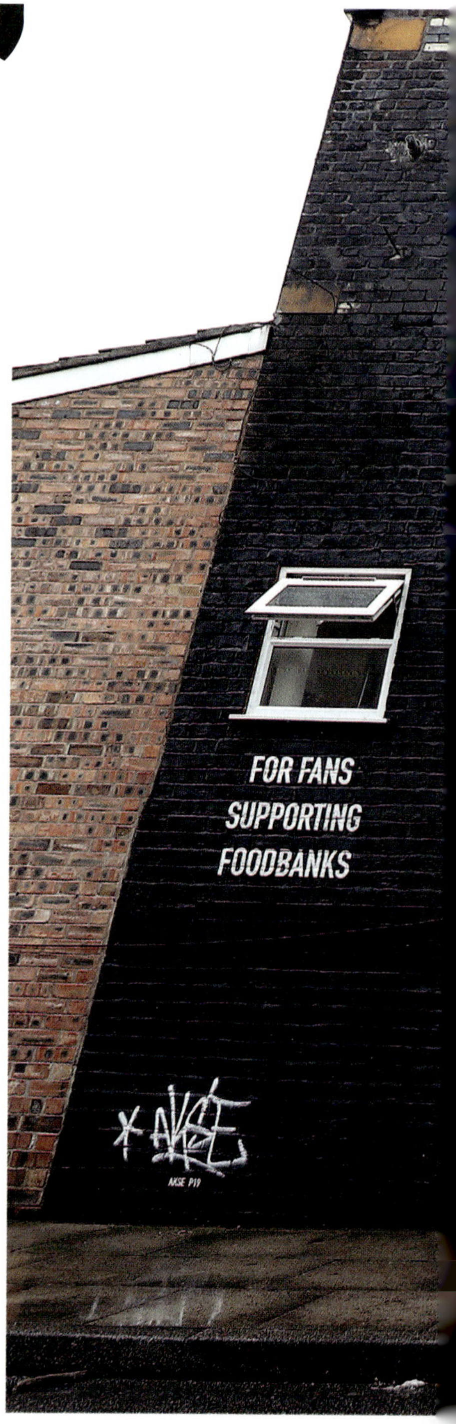

The Scouse lad, the skipper, and the Shankly boys. That's the order in which three large-scale murals appeared on Sybil Road, just around the corner from Anfield's Main Stand, starting in 2020 and since joined by the sticker-card homage to Jan Molby.

Indeed the Trent Alexander-Arnold artwork, to coin a phrase, provided the assist for the profusion of LFC murals now around the stadium. It was unveiled the day before the 2020/21 season's opening Premier League match against Norwich City and visited by the man himself.

On 1 June 2019, on the night that he helped his boyhood heroes to clinch a sixth European Cup, right-back Trent was asked what it meant to join the Liverpool greats who'd lifted the trophy before him. "It's hard to think of myself as a legend," he said. "I'm just a normal lad from Liverpool, whose dream has just come true."

That quote formed the basis of the artwork, created by street-artist Akse in association with The Anfield Wrap podcast team. It also highlighted the work of Fans Supporting Foodbanks, an organisation of whom Trent is a great supporter and whose co-founder Ian Byrne said: "As someone who lives in the next street, it's brought something unique to Anfield.

"Well done to all involved as we are very proud of this 'boss' piece of art and of Trent, a great role-model to the kids in our community."

Trent added: "It's not just the picture – it's important that it has that message there. It shows the fans that it's only a few metres down the road, so it will just raise a bit more awareness for it and they can give back whenever they can.

"The main message that kids should be picking up from me and my story is that anything is possible, anything can happen. I was once that kid in a Gerrard or Carragher shirt. They were the players that made me feel as though anything could happen."

A spokesman for The Anfield Wrap said: "We're really proud of the mural. We've worked so hard on it and we hope people enjoy celebrating the local lad living all of our dreams with us."

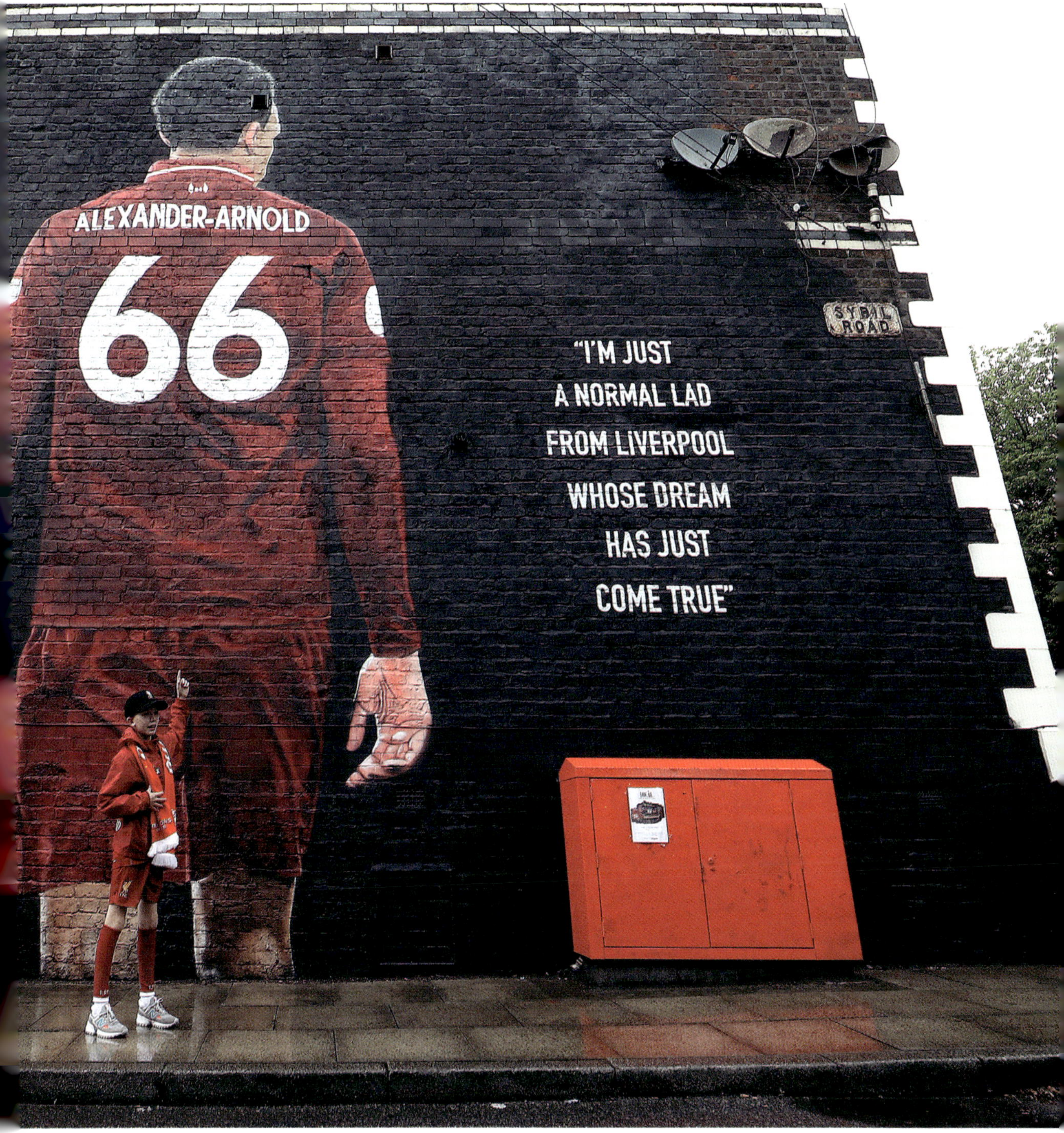
ALEXANDER-ARNOLD
66
SYBIL ROAD
"I'M JUST
A NORMAL LAD
FROM LIVERPOOL
WHOSE DREAM
HAS JUST
COME TRUE"

The captain's Art

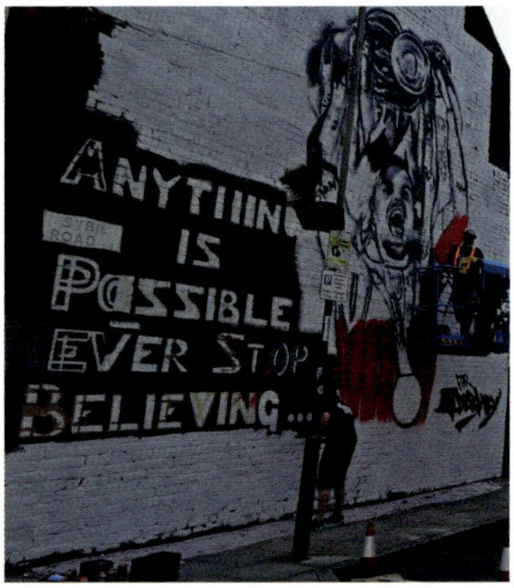

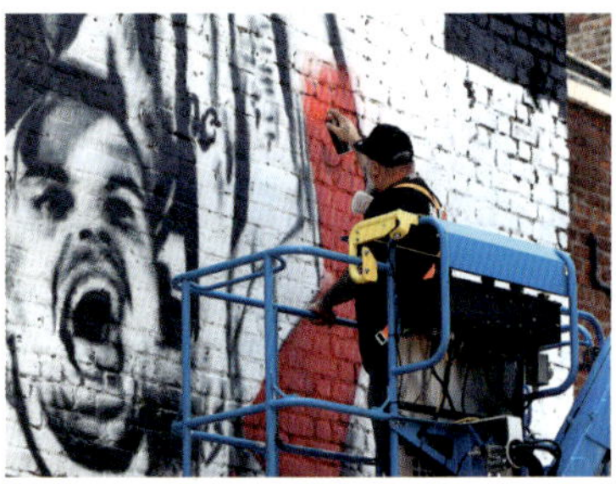

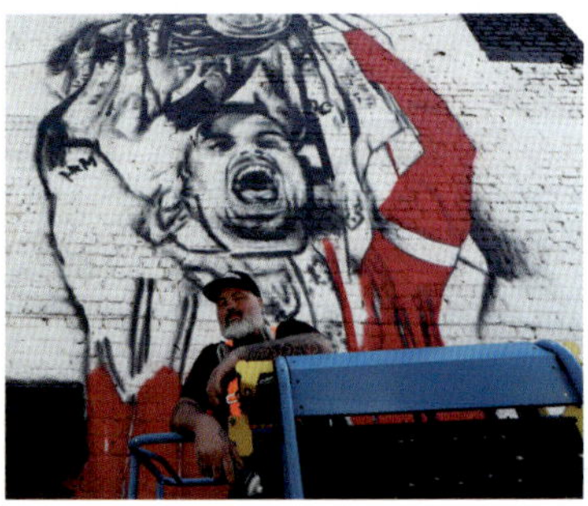

The former skipper may no longer be with LFC but his mural remains as testament to his achievements

One thing you probably already knew about Jordan Henderson, and another you might not. The first: his captain's column, thoughtful and savvy, was one of the highlights of each Liverpool FC matchday programme.

The second: like the manager Jürgen Klopp, he preferred not to have his picture splashed over his page or across the programme's front cover. It was never about him – it was about the team, the club, the fans. Just as it was for the man he succeeded as skipper, Steven Gerrard.

Imagine then how humbled he was to see his own image, holding aloft the Premier League trophy, on the wall opposite the Trent mural on Sybil Road – an artwork created by MurWalls and commissioned by Redmen TV in support of Alder Hey Children's Hospital, to celebrate LFC's 2020 title success.

Jordan was there in person to show his appreciation when it was unveiled at the end of the unprecedented 2019/20 season. Three days earlier he'd written in his matchday programme notes for the final home fixture of the campaign, against Chelsea: "I've been asked many times since we were confirmed as champions to sum up how I feel and I'm not too proud to admit I don't think I've produced a good answer yet.

"I think now I can find the right word: gratitude. There are so many different people responsible when a team is successful and as players we are privileged to attract the most attention, the most praise and the biggest rewards. But behind the team there are so many different individuals and groups who make a side successful."

Every team, though, needs a leader, and Hendo was arguably Liverpool's greatest-ever captain. By season 2022/23 he was also the longest-serving senior player at the club, having been signed by Kenny Dalglish back in the summer of 2011. Manager Jürgen Klopp once said: "If I had to write a book about him it would be 500 pages. Steven Gerrard [as skipper]. In the mind of the people it was like: if it's not Stevie, then it's not good enough. And Jordan has dealt with that outstandingly well, so he can be really proud."

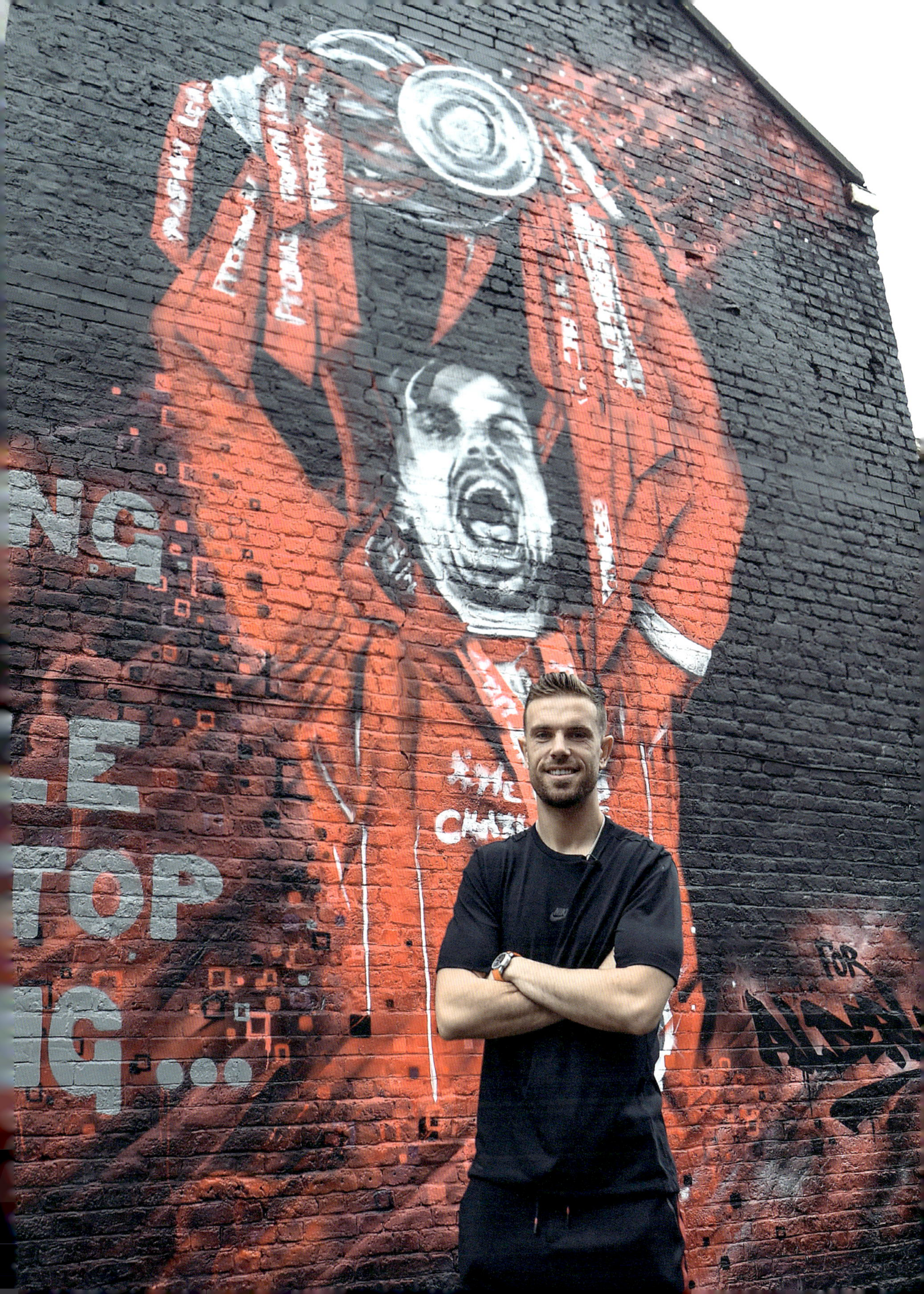

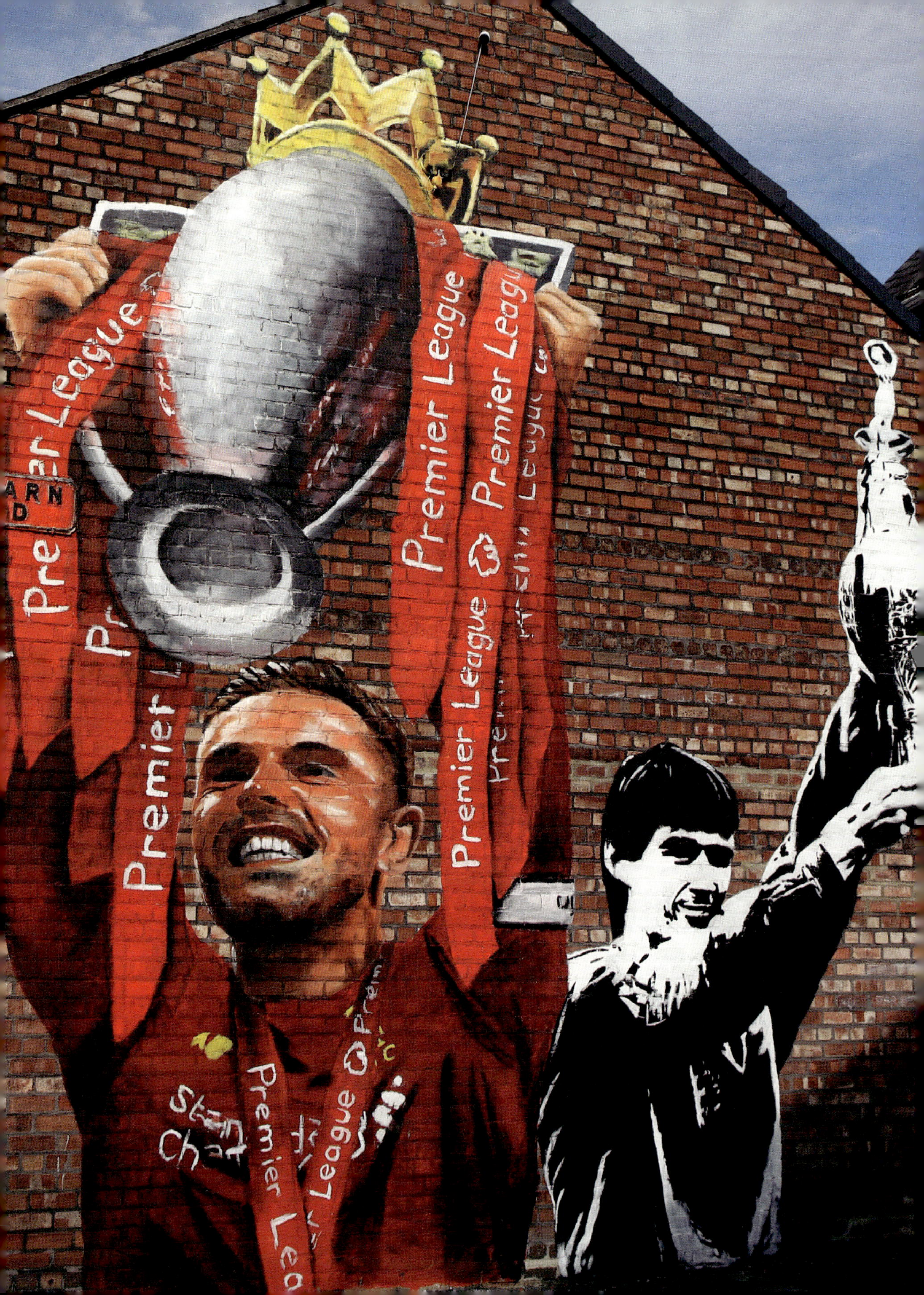
Premier League
Premier League
Premier League
Premier League
Premier League
Premier League
Premier League

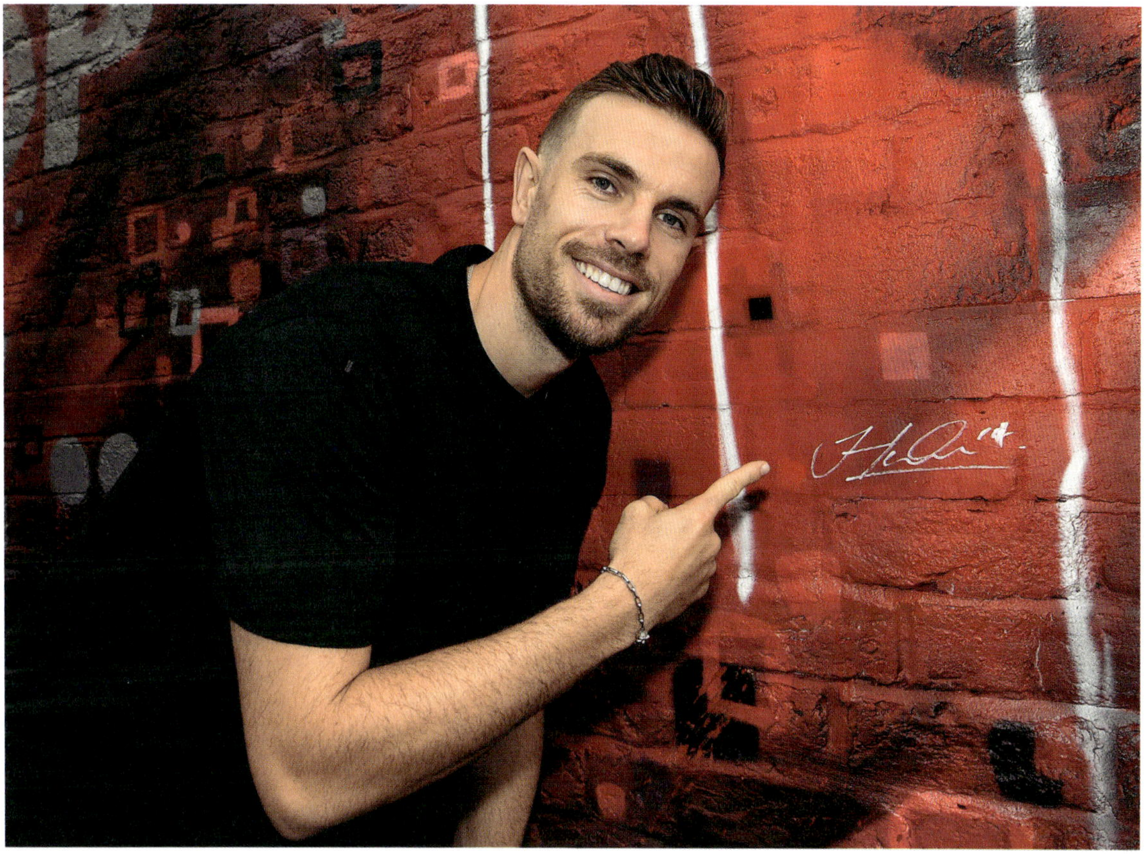

Henderson was once asked what the best thing was about being a captain. "Lifting the trophies! That's a nice thing, but for me I would say it is seeing my team-mates doing well, flourishing and winning awards. My responsibility is for the team."

As well as all those tap-dancing, circle-shimmying trophy-lifts, he now has an MBE – received in June 2021 for his work and contribution throughout the coronavirus pandemic. The previous year he became Liverpool's first title-winning skipper since Alan Hansen to be named as the Football Writers' Association Footballer of the Year.

Fittingly, both players are honoured by another mural on the gable-end of a house on Old Barn Road in Anfield, displaying the Premier League and old First Division trophies respectively. Artist Paul Curtis explained it was "to mark the end of that 30-year wait. Henderson looks towards the stadium and contrasts nicely with Hansen in black-and-white. I hope it helps to brighten up the area even more, and I'm happy and relieved to say that Jordan messaged me on Instagram to say he liked it."

FWA chair Carrie Brown described Henderson as "the ultimate professional and now a bona fide Liverpool legend. The voting criteria for the Footballer of the Year award is one who leads by precept and example and in this country's darkest moment, Jordan, unprompted, personally rallied club captains to establish #PlayersTogether.

"Millions of pounds have been raised for the NHS and #PlayersTogether is now an established collective power-base for players to engage in campaigns, none more so evident in the ongoing and powerful anti-racism #BlackLivesMatter campaign. He is a truly worthy winner of our award."

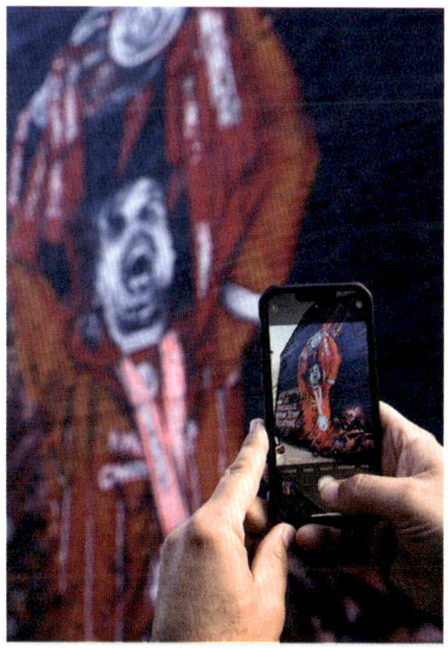

Top: Jordan visited the artwork, loved it and left his signature
Opposite: the Hendo and Hansen mural on Anfield's Old Barn Road

Spirit of Shanks

He's there, within earshot of his beloved Spion Kop, captured on a special day and always waiting for the roar when the relentless Reds find the back of the net

"The main thing, and our bread and butter, is this... I'm glad we're in Europe, it's been a great thing for Liverpool, a great thing for the country. But this is our bread and butter – and this is the one that we want all the time."

Bill Shankly's words, of course, in a TV interview at Anfield in 1973, spoken as he pointed to his left at the old league championship trophy, the camera panning up from its base, past red ribbons to the gleaming silver figure at the top.

The title – LFC's eighth at the time – had been clinched earlier that same year, on Saturday 28 April 1973, after a goalless draw at home to Leicester City, and the scenes at the end would live long in the memory of those who were there, as the players paraded the trophy and Shanks saluted the Kop.

John Culshaw's mural at the back of The Park pub on Walton Breck Road, right opposite the stadium, brilliantly captures that moment, albeit with Bill holding a red scarf aloft emblazoned with the pub's name. It was created in 2019 to celebrate the 60th year since the great Scot's appointment at Anfield.

Back to 1973 and those scenes at Anfield, described by *The Liverpool Echo*, thus: "For colour, Liverpool's vivid red of course, fervour, song and sound, this was the day of days... Mr Shankly's appearance increased the bedlam to deafening volume as the swaying Kop stretched their scarves end to end, moving rhythmically to present a vast, almost dazzling sea of colour."

Oh to have been a Liverpool FC fan back then, and even earlier in the 1960s. Several decades have now passed since Shankly captivated the Kop but his spirit continues to touch every aspect of the club. During his 15-year reign he transformed LFC from second-tier also-rans to a footballing powerhouse, taking over a team that had lain dormant in the Second Division and turning them into top-flight champions within five years. He led the Reds to another title in 1966, a first FA Cup triumph in 1965 and a second nine years later, plus the League and UEFA Cup double in 1973. Arguably the most-quoted manager of all time, his quick wit added to the legend while his infectious enthusiasm unified the fans like never before. Hardened Kopites openly wept when he sensationally announced his resignation, but the great man will never be forgotten.

John Culshaw painted another Shankly, posing with the FA Cup in 1974, alongside a double-winning Kenny Dalglish from 1986, on a wall of the nearby Sandon Hotel.

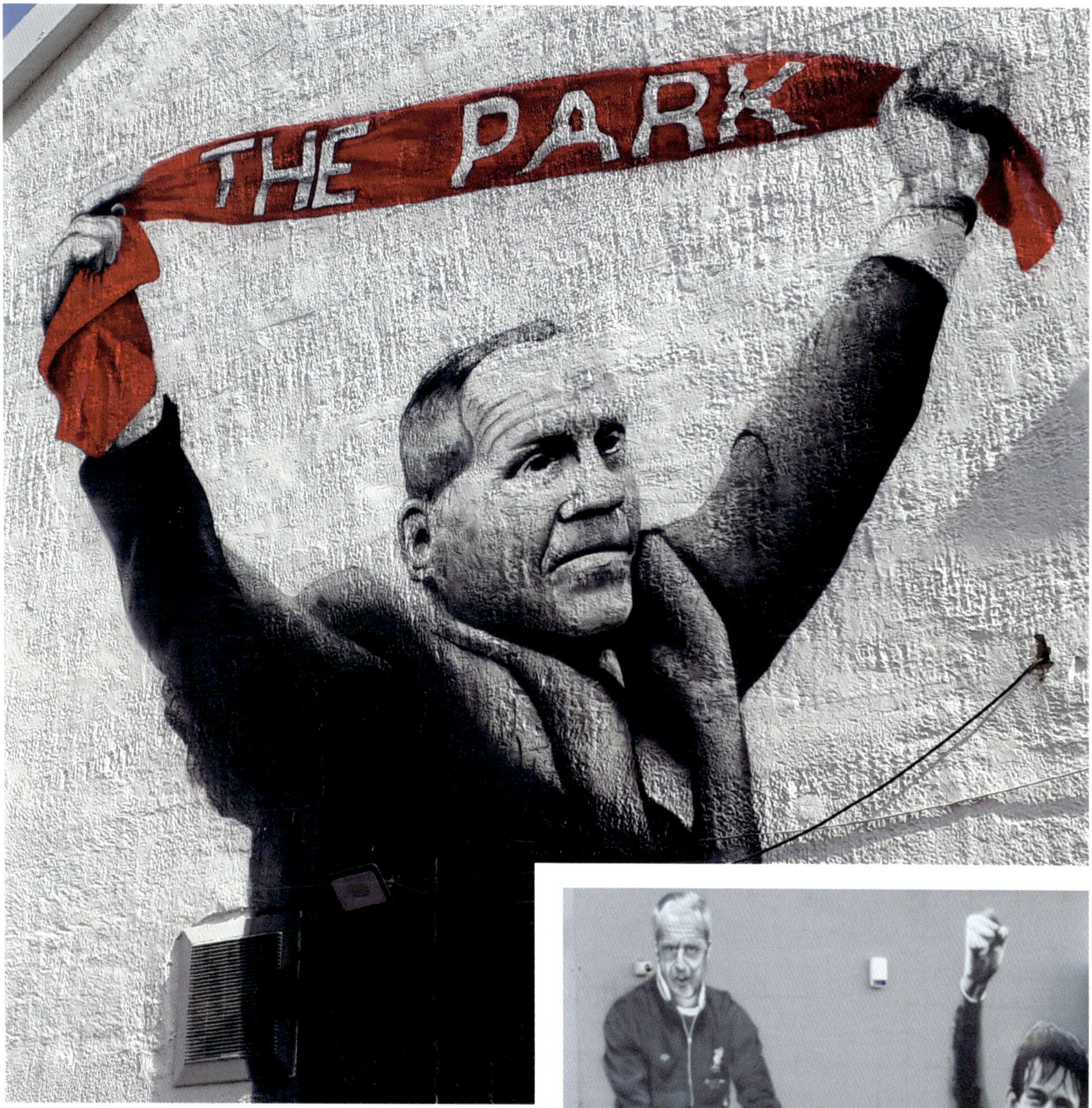
THE PARK

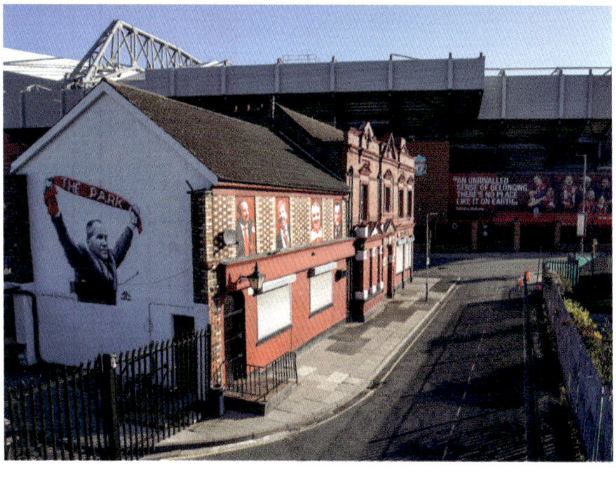
THE PARK

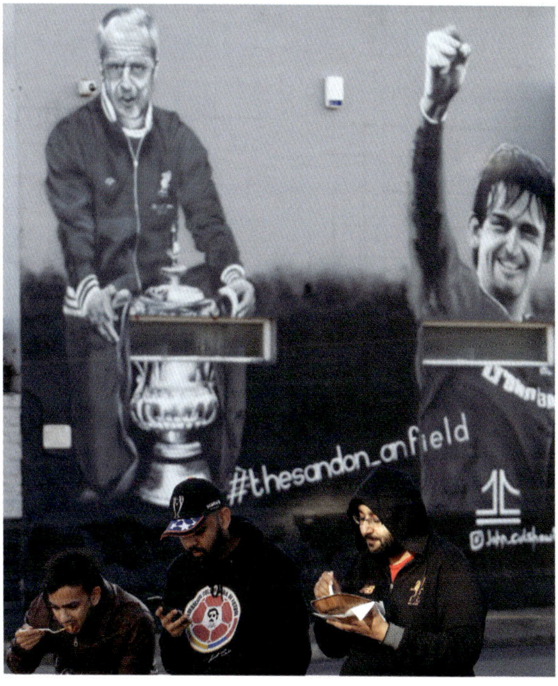
#thesandon_anfield

The Saint and Sir Roger

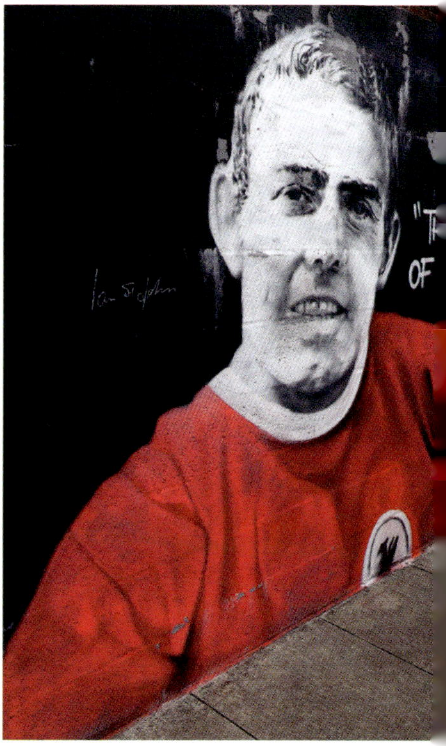

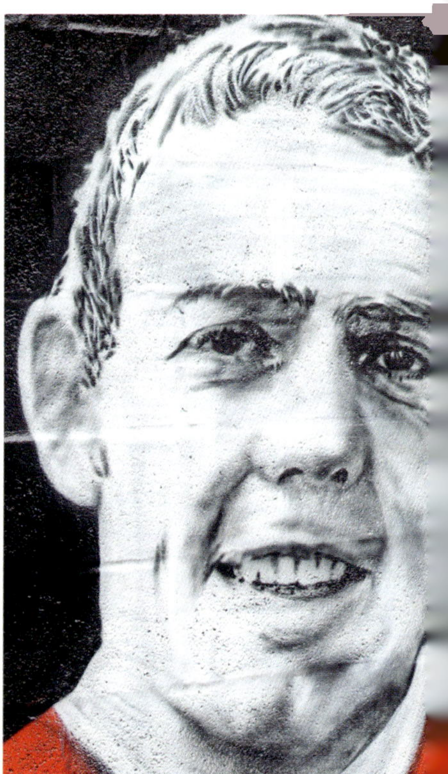

The very mention of their names can still bring a tear to a seasoned Kopite's eye – and they're together forever within shooting distance of the stadium

The double head-and-shoulders mural in honour of 1965 FA Cup final goalscorers Ian St John and Roger Hunt – created by MurWalls like the adjacent Jordan Henderson artwork – completes the street-art trinity on Anfield's Sybil Road and was the most recent addition. The Saint signed it in November 2020 and the subsequent passing of both legends has made the mural even more evocative.

Over six decades have passed since Hunt, the modest Lancastrian with the unerring eye for goal, was signed by then manager Phil Taylor for Liverpool Football Club – three years before St John, the livewire Scot, was lured south of the border by Bill Shankly to join him in the red jersey.

Both men scored at Wembley as Liverpool finally won that first, elusive FA Cup in the days when, by some stroke of cosmic serendipity, the city of Liverpool had become the centre of the universe to a soundtrack of Beatlemania and the Spion Kop, Ee-aye-addio and *She Loves You*.

The duo shared a Reds dressing-room for pretty much all of the Swinging Sixties, eight years from the summer of 1961 to the winter of 1969 when Hunt bade farewell to Anfield, St John departing 18 months later.

If Roger was worshipped by Kopites as the sharpshooter of Shankly's barnstorming team, he was also as much a heart-throb as local crooner Billy Fury with whom he shared the same bequiffed hairstyle. Not that he ever let it go to his head: two hundred and eighty-six goals in 492 appearances, and hardly a hair out of place all along.

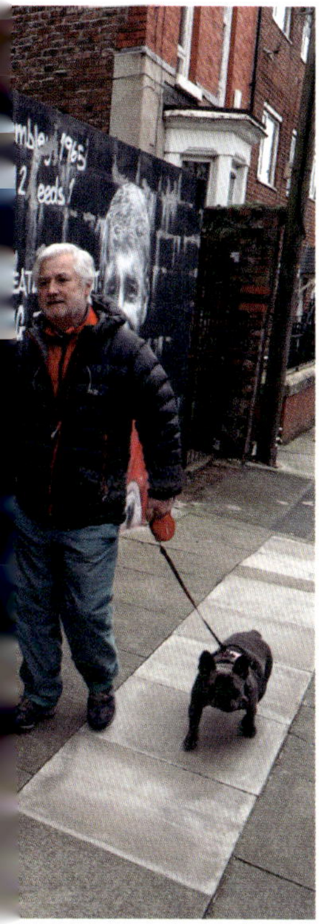

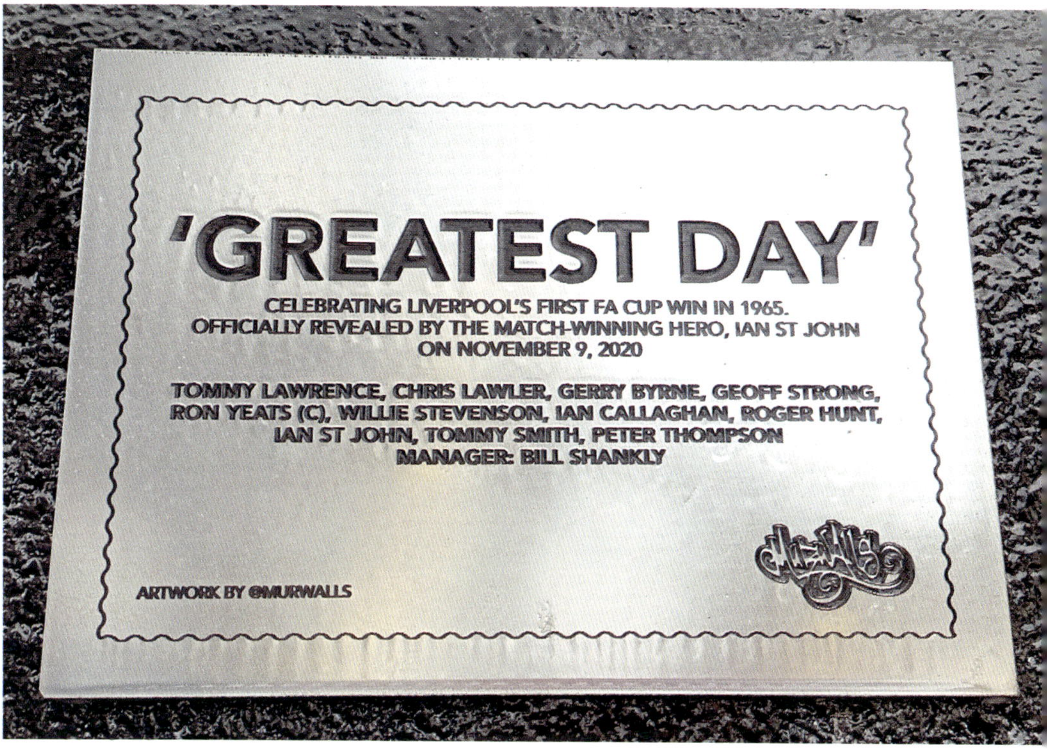
'GREATEST DAY'
CELEBRATING LIVERPOOL'S FIRST FA CUP WIN IN 1965.
OFFICIALLY REVEALED BY THE MATCH-WINNING HERO, IAN ST JOHN
ON NOVEMBER 9, 2020
TOMMY LAWRENCE, CHRIS LAWLER, GERRY BYRNE, GEOFF STRONG,
RON YEATS (C), WILLIE STEVENSON, IAN CALLAGHAN, ROGER HUNT,
IAN ST JOHN, TOMMY SMITH, PETER THOMPSON
MANAGER: BILL SHANKLY
ARTWORK BY @MURWALLS

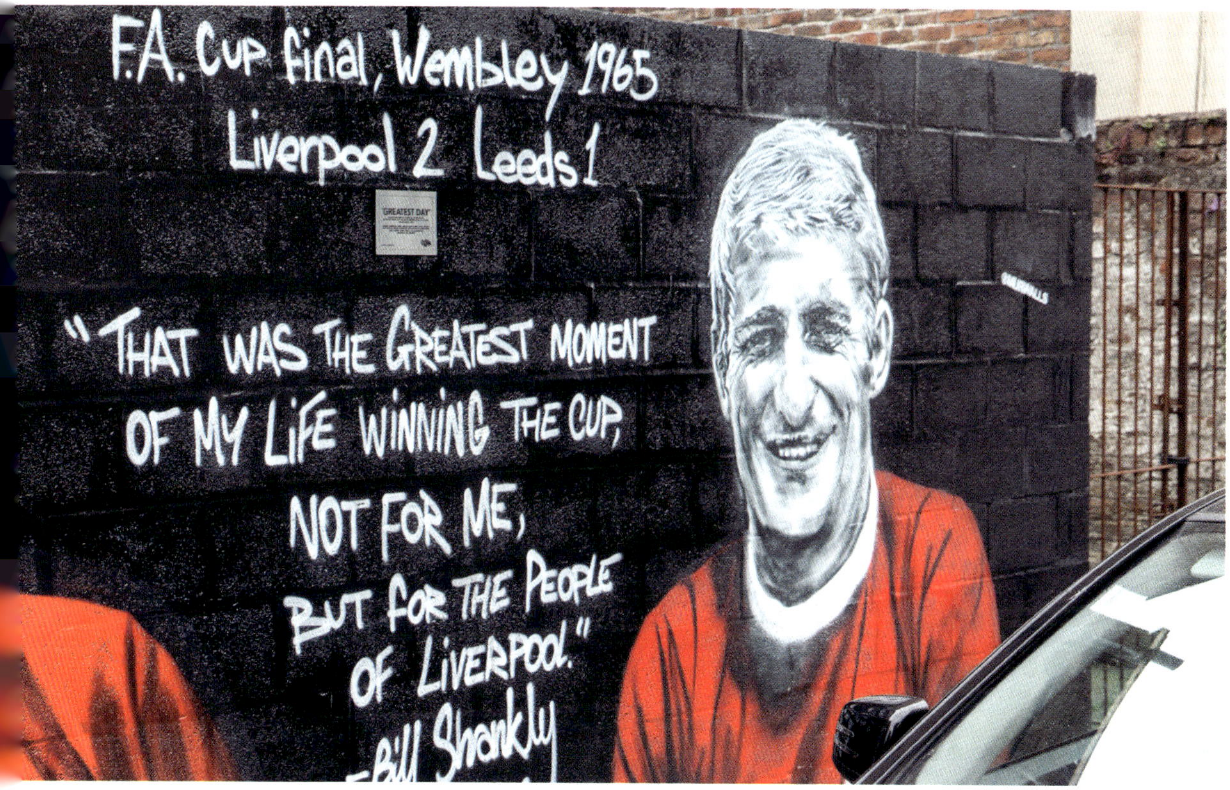
F.A. Cup final, Wembley 1965
Liverpool 2 Leeds 1
"THAT WAS THE GREATEST MOMENT OF MY LIFE WINNING THE CUP, NOT FOR ME, BUT FOR THE PEOPLE OF LIVERPOOL."
– Bill Shankly

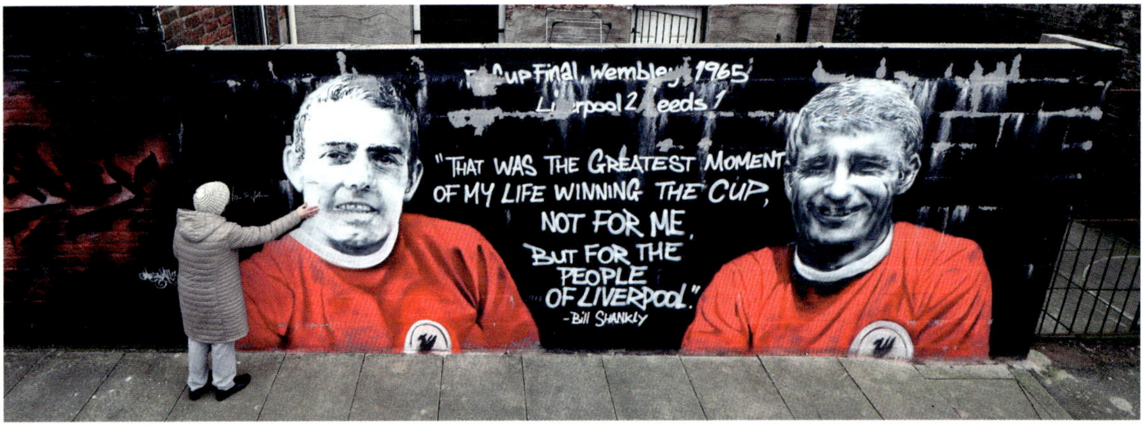
Cup Final, Wembley 1965
"THAT WAS THE GREATEST MOMENT
OF MY LIFE WINNING THE CUP,
NOT FOR ME,
BUT FOR THE
PEOPLE
OF LIVERPOOL."
-Bill SHANKLY

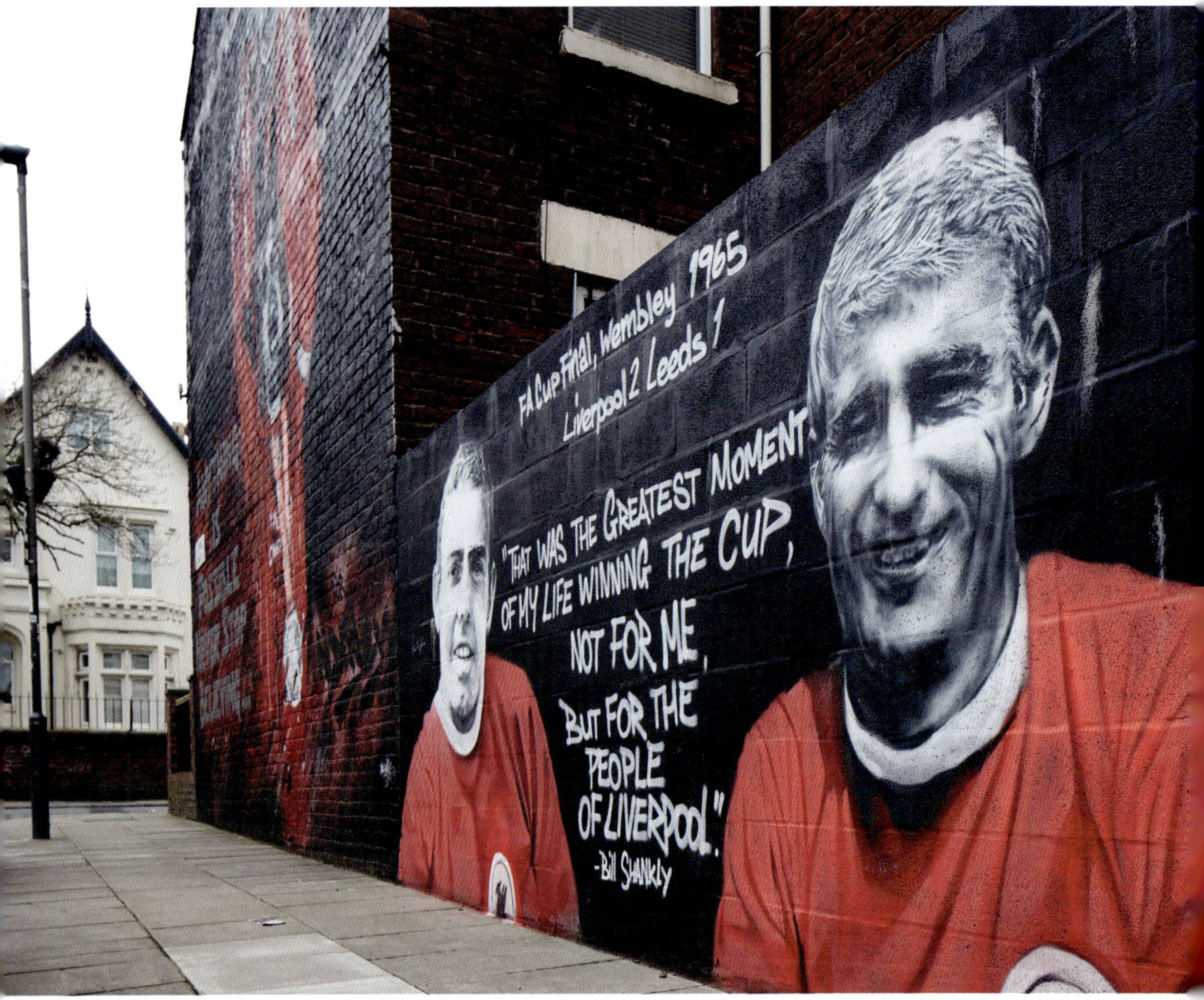
FA Cup Final, Wembley 1965
Liverpool 2 Leeds 1
"THAT WAS THE GREATEST MOMENT
OF MY LIFE WINNING THE CUP,
NOT FOR ME,
BUT FOR THE
PEOPLE
OF LIVERPOOL."
-Bill SHANKLY

He was LFC's top-scorer for an incredible eight consecutive seasons (1961/62 through to 1968/69) and registered 12 hat-tricks along the way. Ian Rush eventually overtook him for goals scored in all competitions, but Roger's total of 245 in the League is unlikely ever to be beaten.

In the club's first tilt at the European Cup in 1964/65 he scored in every round up to and including the semi-final with Inter Milan, and he was part of England's legendary World Cup-winning team – Hunt's medal from 1966 is also in The Liverpool FC Story museum at Anfield.

The Saint got his share of European goals, too – ten in 32 appearances – but he will always be remembered for his Wembley winner in that historic FA Cup final against Leeds United in May 1965. The opening 90 minutes had failed to produce a goal, so extra-time was played in the final for the first time since 1947.

Three minutes into it, Liverpool half-back Willie Stevenson picked out full-back Gerry Byrne whose cut-back was headed home by Hunt. Leeds levelled before the change-around through Billy Bremner's fine strike. On 111 minutes, however, came the moment that would confer hero status upon St John as he met winger Ian Callaghan's cross to win the match with a diving header.

In 2014 when many of the Sixties side gathered at Anfield to celebrate the 50th anniversary of the 1963/64 title win, the Saint talked about his partnership upfront with 'Sir' Roger, as the Kop called him.

"Our styles of play just married. Mine was dropping off a bit. People talk about the game today as if it'd only just been invented, but Alfredo Di Stefano was dropping deep 50 years ago [for Real Madrid]. If I was being marked by a defender the boss would say to me, 'Take him for a walk, son', and it suited Roger. He never told Roger to track back. 'You stay up there, son', he'd say."

In turn Hunt had written in his 1969 autobiography: "Not surprisingly Ian was immediately popular with our fans. I have played alongside him for hundreds of hours, in all sorts of conditions, and he is one of the finest forwards in the game. At first he was mainly a striker, but as our tactics changed he has become a link-man – and he can do both wonderfully well."

Seasoned Kopites remains forever grateful that both players graced the hallowed Anfield turf in the same era.

Dynamic duo: the men who won the FA Cup for Liverpool for the very first time

One for the album

Big Jan Molby on an even bigger sticker... The street-art tribute to Liverpool's Danish midfield maestro from the 1980s and 90s is just a little bit different

Snow was falling in March 2023 when Jan Molby was immortalised on Sybil Road in a piece of sticker-style street-art created by MurWalls – a striking contrast to the more traditional murals of Trent Alexander-Arnold next door and those of Ian St John, Roger Hunt and Jordan Henderson across the way.

'What would Jan Molby do?' It's a line from the repertoire of Troy Hawke, otherwise known as character comedian Milo McCabe (who studied at the University of Liverpool) and described by one critic as "an erudite homeschooled 1930s throwback...the Errol Flynn of the high street."

Big Jan, who won two top-flight titles and two FA Cups with the Reds, shared a hug with Tricky Troy in the sleet before the latter described him as "the Scousest Danish person I've ever come across in my entire existence.

"Why not Jan Molby? He is the most selfless player who's ever existed in any sphere of footballing genre you can think of. He never left the centre circle and existed to make others look good. He was the obvious choice."

The former midfielder told the fan website This Is Anfield: "I like it. Murals have become very popular around the Anfield stadium. I come here on most matchdays and I see the interest that there is. You know, people go around looking for them, wanting to take pictures."

But again, for those who never saw him in his playing pomp – what would Jan Molby do? "Turn a game with one pass," was team-mate Mark Lawrenson's verdict. "He could disappear for long periods and then pop up with a moment of inspiration.

"With a player like Ian Rush in the side you only needed one chance to score a goal, and more often than not Molby was our man to unlock a defence – he was an inspired signing for Liverpool."

Today the Dane is widely-regarded as the first of Liverpool's successful overseas outfield imports of the modern era. As well as effortlessly acquiring a Liverpudlian accent – "I used to get changed next to Sammy Lee and everything he said I'd pick up" – he netted 61 goals and provided 42 assists in his 292 appearances for the Reds between 1984 and 1995.

Forty-two of those goals came from the penalty-spot with only Steven Gerrard having scored more often from 12 yards during his Liverpool career. His 42 successes came from 45 attempts, an incredible success rate of over 93 per cent.

Today he's a popular after-dinner speaker, regaling fans with tales from the old days with that warm, familiar voice.

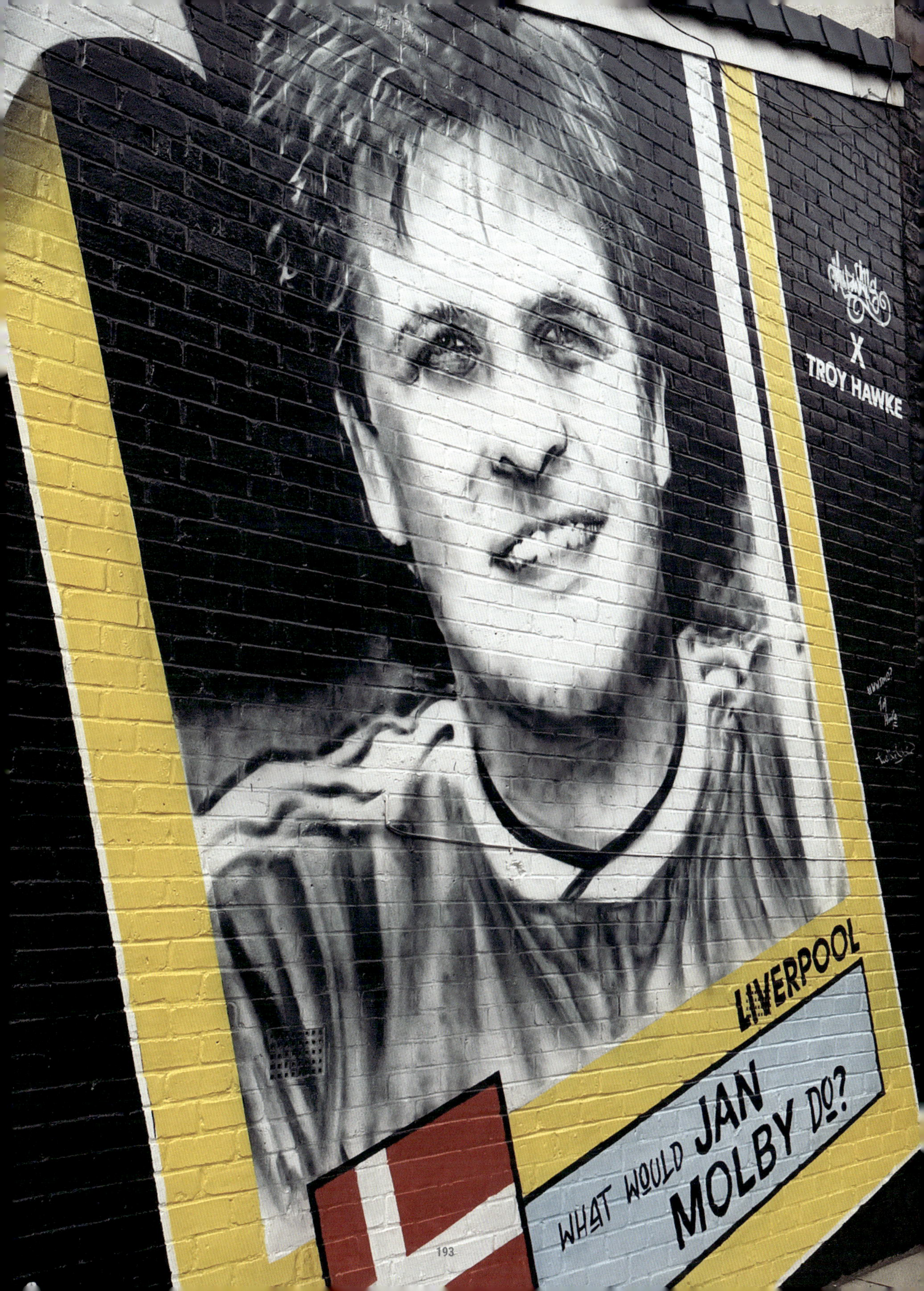
X
TROY HAWKE
LIVERPOOL
WHAT WOULD JAN MOLBY DO?

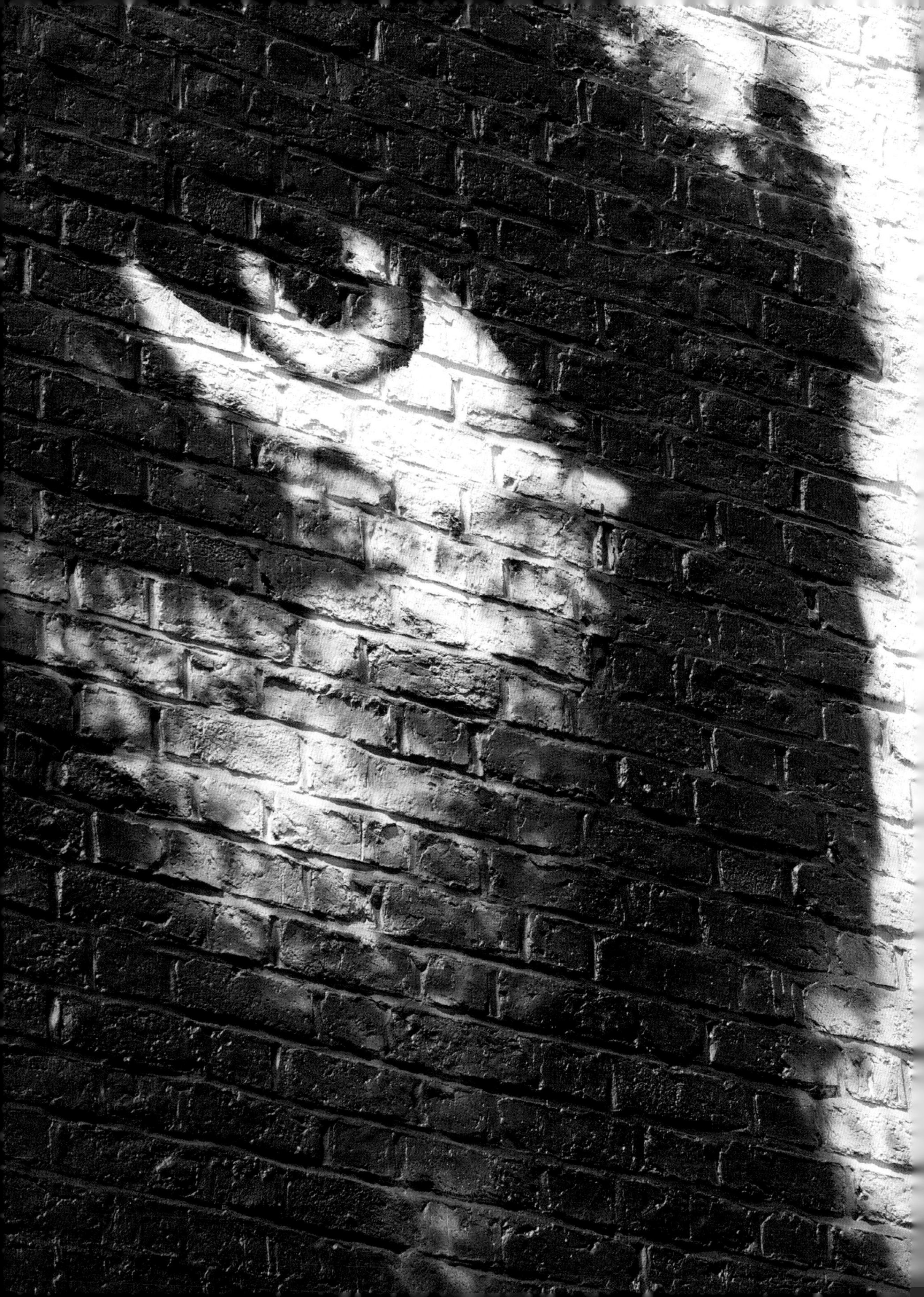

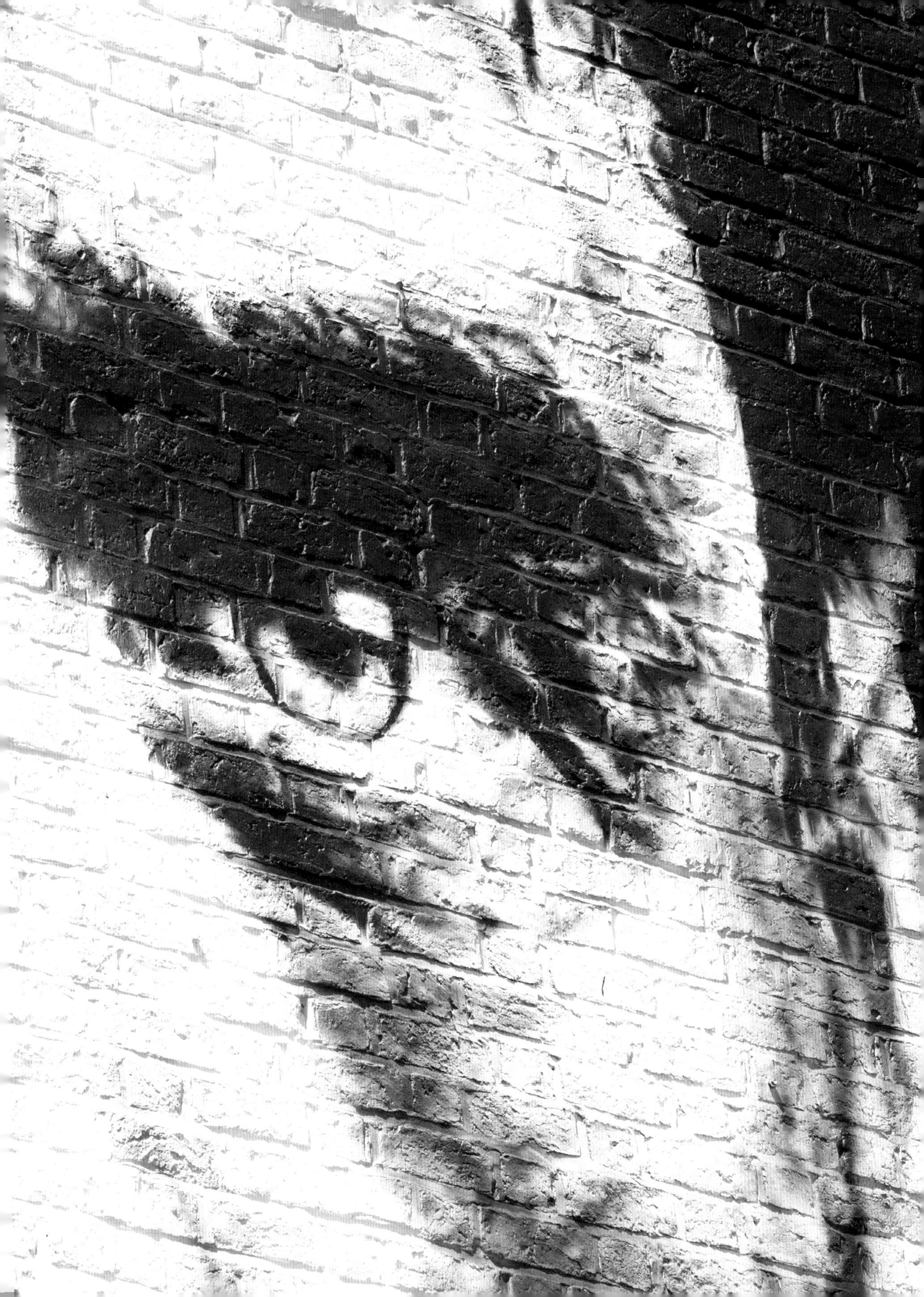

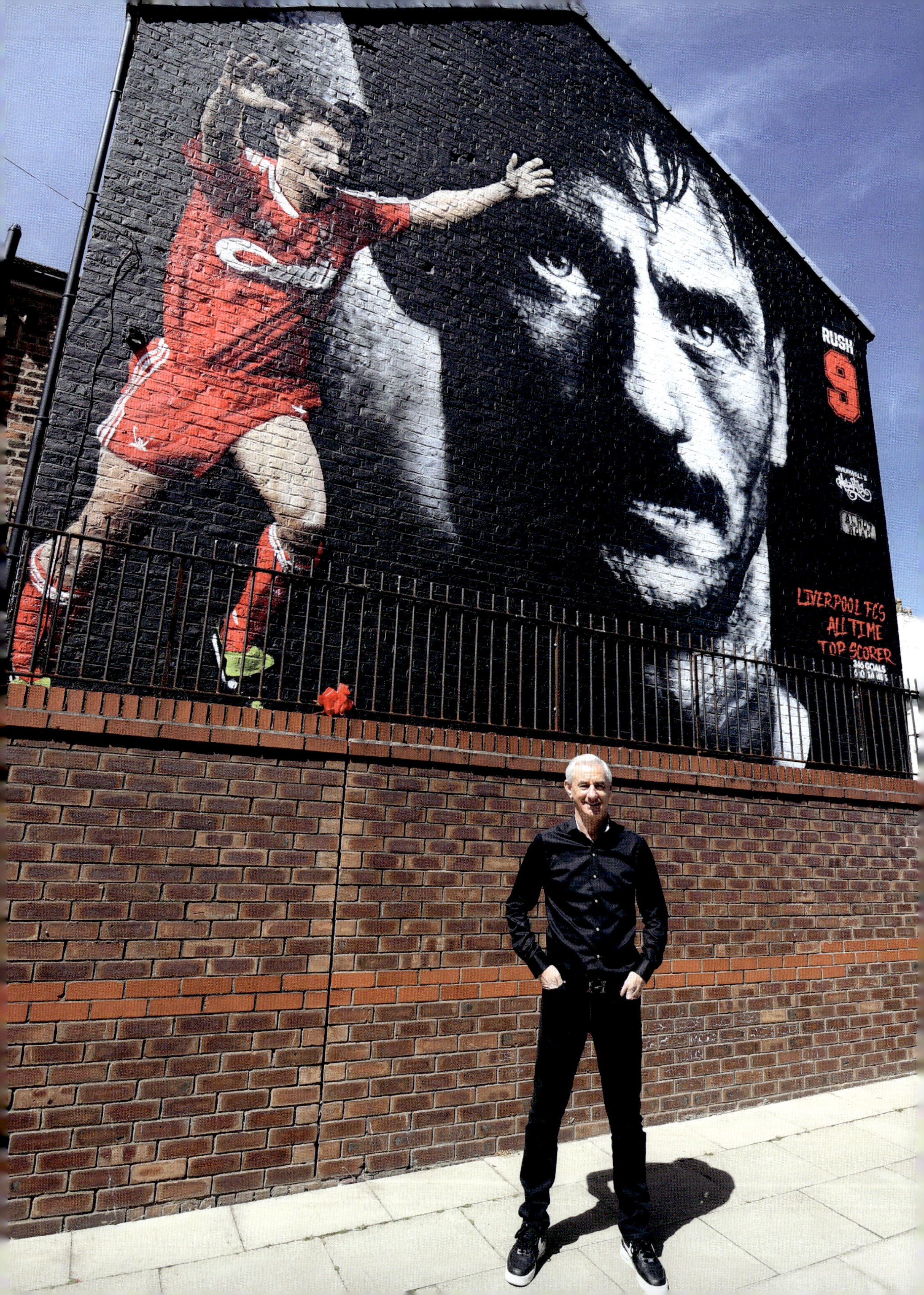
RUSH
9
LIVERPOOL FCS
ALL TIME
TOP SCORER
346 GOALS

All you need is Rush

A prolific, record-setting goalscorer and the first line of LFC's defence

It's not much more than an ace goalscorer's lethal finish from the exterior of the Main Stand to terraced Alroy Road, home to Anfield's Ian Rush mural which was unveiled in May 2022.

With its juxtaposition of classic arms-aloft celebration in all-red late 80s kit next to brooding black-and-white portrait, the 'striking' work – created by street-art collective MurWalls – is a fitting tribute to Liverpool FC's greatest-ever marksman.

Rush checked out the mural for himself soon after its appearance and declared it "amazing – it's a great honour for me to have my face on the wall, so close to Anfield. It's most probably to scare the opposition!"

Ian's 15 seasons at Liverpool, with a brief spell in Italy with Juventus in-between, yielded medals, awards and goalscoring records galore, and he remains the net-busting benchmark. He scored 346 goals for the Reds in 660 appearances between 1980 and 1996, won five top-flight titles, a European Cup, three FA Cups and five League Cups.

One of the most recent tributes came from modern goal-machine Mo Salah, who said: "Ian is a great guy, we have a good relationship. We talk from time to time but I don't understand all of what he says because of his accent!

"Of course he is the number one top scorer for the club in history. I don't know how many games he was playing a season, but he scored too many goals! His finishing was unbelievable."

Rush is still actively involved with LFC, regularly co-managing the Legends teams, and he's also been a UEFA ambassador for big European finals.

Kenny Dalglish, in his 1996 autobiography, described Rush as "easily the best partner I've ever had – we could have been made for each other. He could run and I could pass. Rushie said that he made runs knowing the ball would come to him. That was true but only because his runs were so clever.

"We had another role, too, which people don't often give Liverpool strikers credit for. Bob Paisley told us that we were his first line of defence when any Liverpool attack broke down – and Rushie was one of the best strikers at closing defenders down."

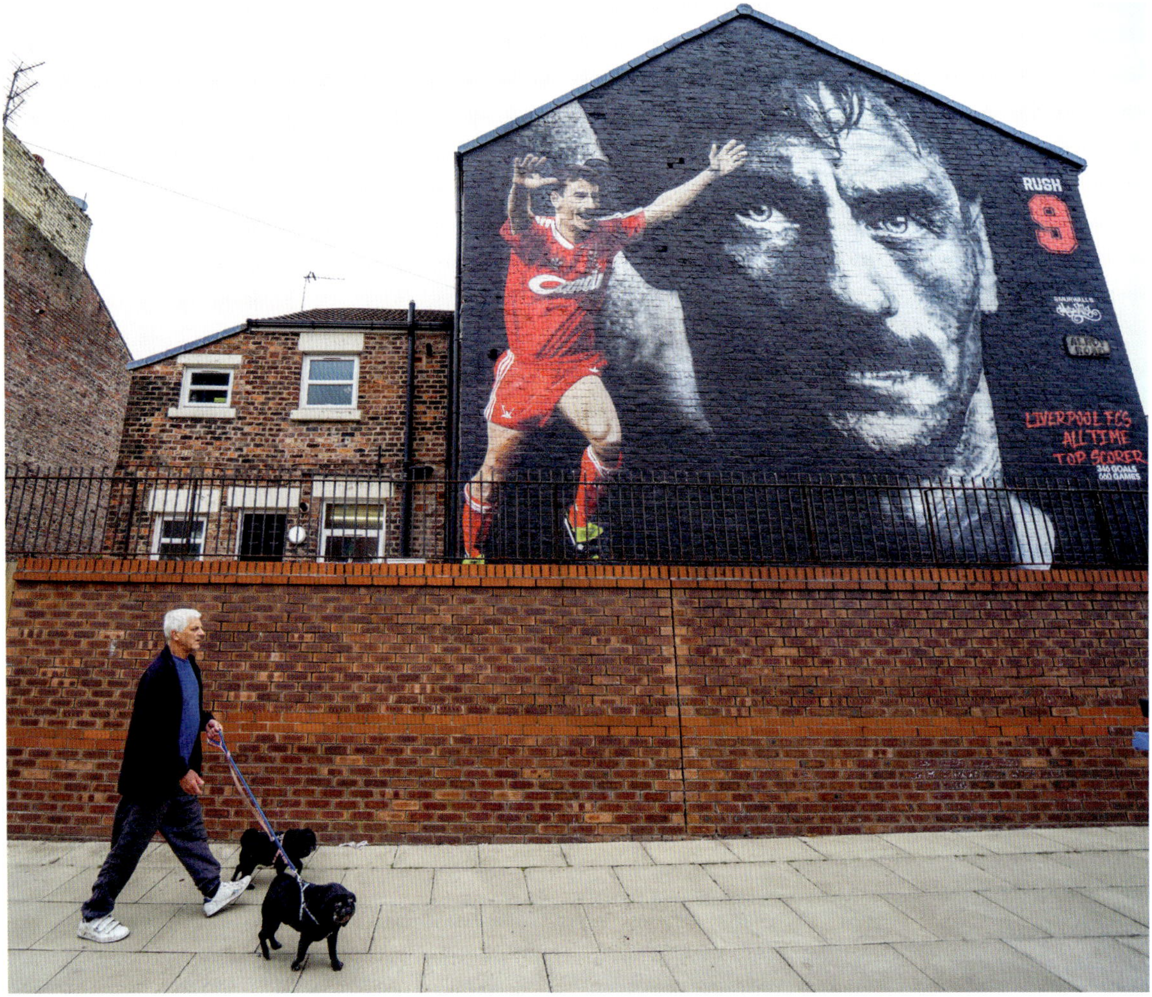

Walk on: if this blue-topped chap walking his dogs is an Evertonian, no wonder he won't look left!
Opposite: view of the mural from the Main Stand podium on matchday

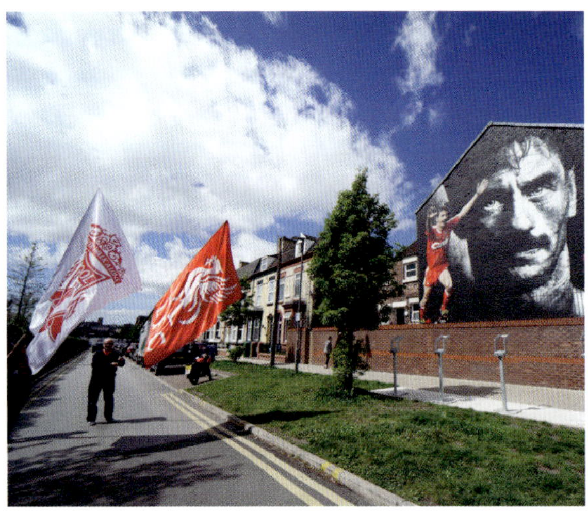

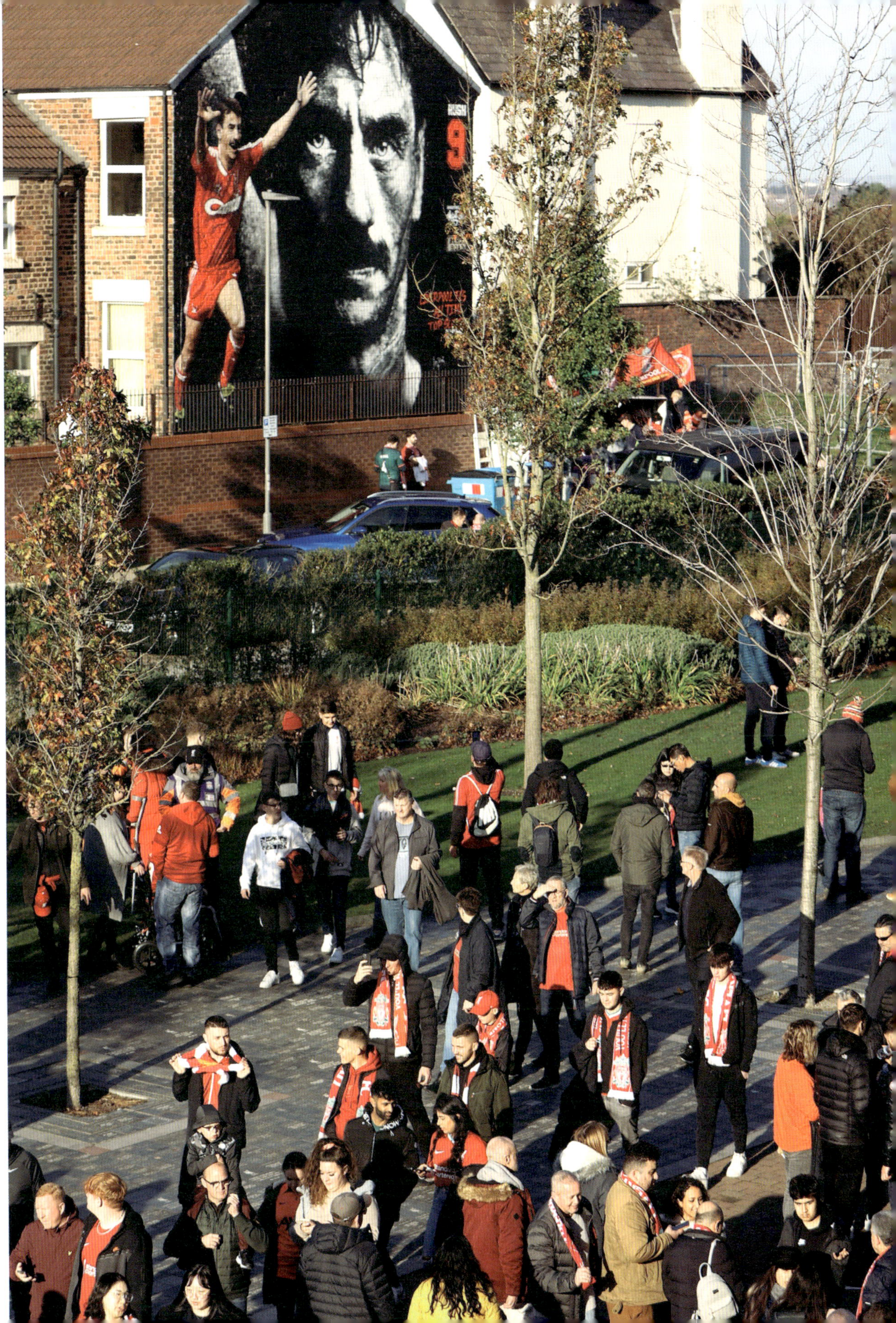

All around the fields of

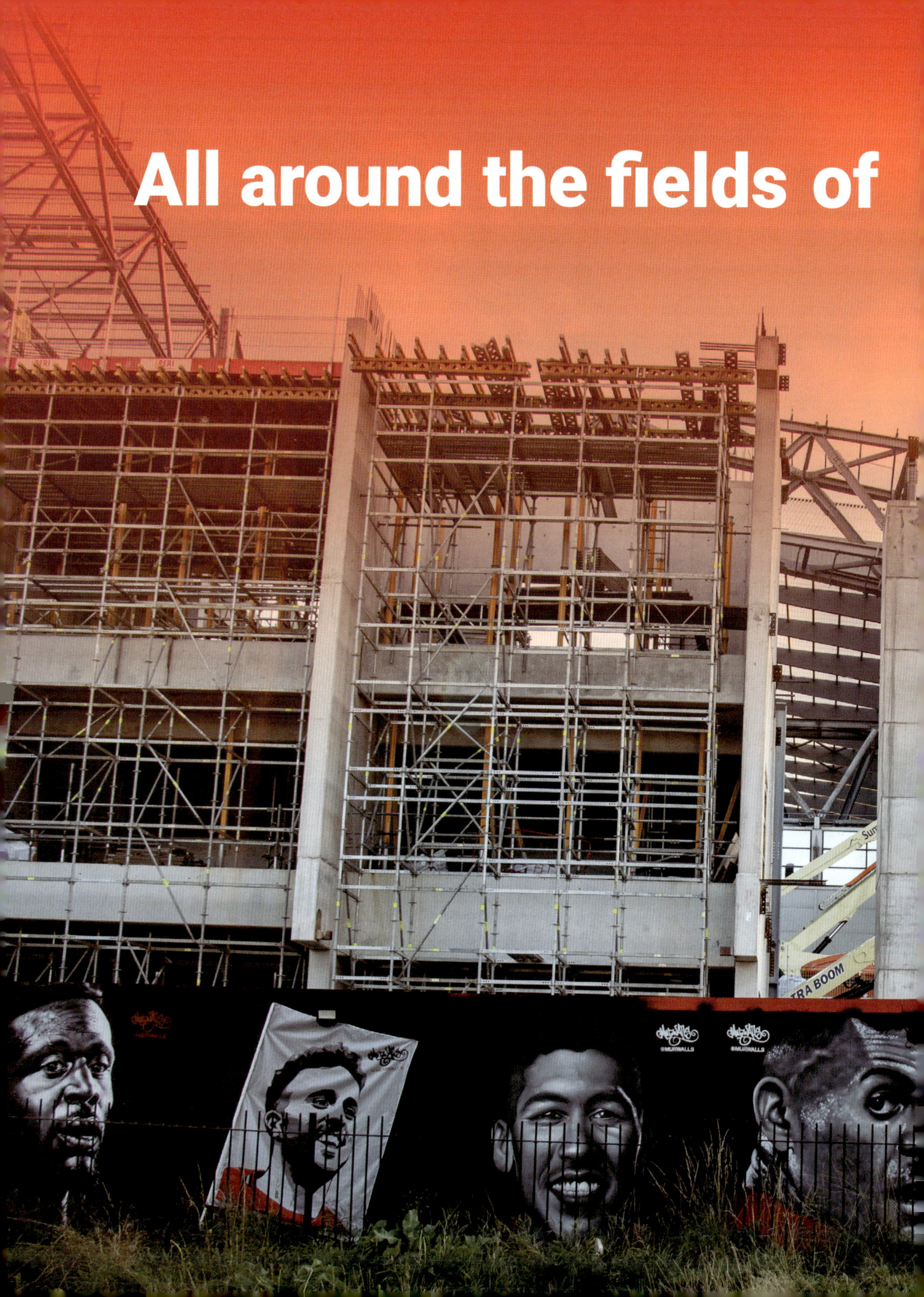

Anfield Road

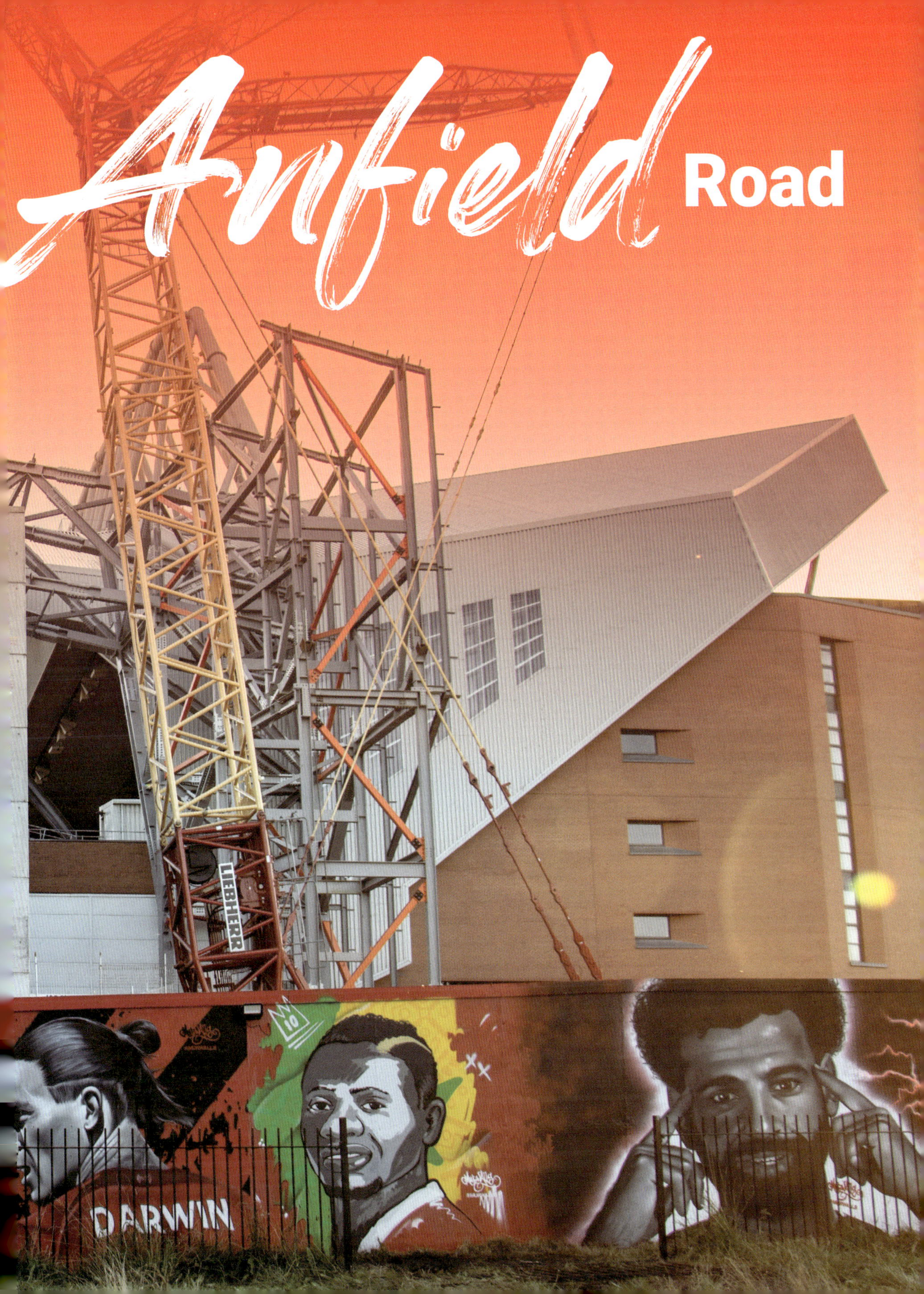

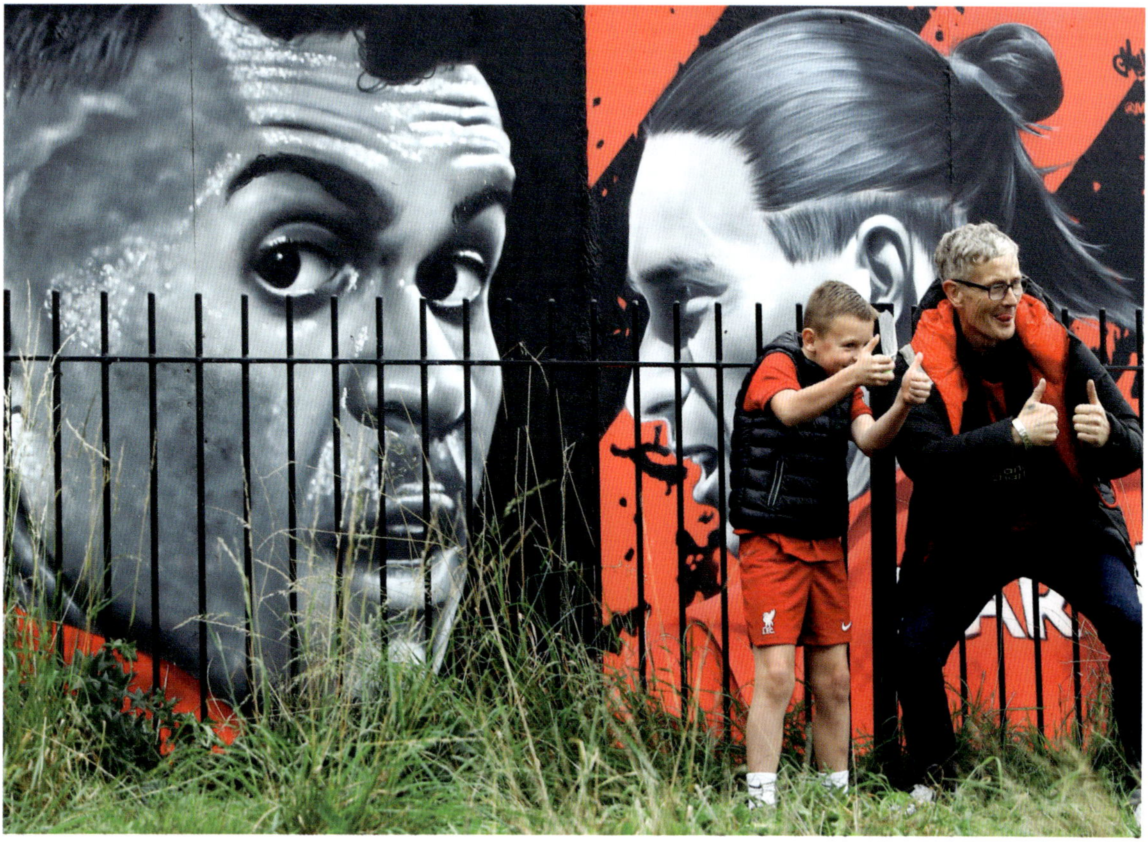

For a few months during the Anfield Road Stand expansion matchgoers were in for a striking treat

On the fourth weekend of September 2022 there may have been no home game for Liverpool's senior side but Anfield was buzzing. First there was LFC Foundation's 'Legends of the North' charity match between the Reds and their counterparts from Manchester United. Then came the women's Merseyside derby.

To top it off – bringing even more vibrancy to the matchday neighbourhood – a new gallery of sensational street-art was revealed outside the stadium.

But first, a triv question for you: how many out-and-out strikers have scored a goal in open-play for Liverpool in a Champions League final? Three by our reckoning: Kenny Dalglish against FC Bruges at Wembley in 1978, Dirk Kuyt versus AC Milan at the Athens Olympic Stadium in 2007, and Divock Origi versus Tottenham Hotspur at Madrid's Wanda Metropolitano in 2019.

They were among the 14 celebrated Reds forwards past and present depicted on a long-format gallery running along the hoardings of the Anfield Road Stand expansion site. As well as Sir Kenny, Dirk and Divock, it featured Roberto Firmino, Mohamed Salah, Diogo Jota, Luis Diaz, Darwin Nunez, Sadio Mane, Ian Rush, John Aldridge, Luis Suarez, Fernando Torres and Robbie Fowler.

The mural was created by a team of 16 artists from MurWalls whose CEO Marc Silver said: "We wanted to create some artwork for the community while the building work is in progress, and together with LFC we came up with the concept to celebrate the club's attacking legends. Each one is a different style for each individual portrait."

It took around seven hours to finish and upon the completion of the Anfield Road development, the artwork was set to be cut into 14 individual pieces and auctioned off, with all proceeds donated to LFC Foundation and its good causes.

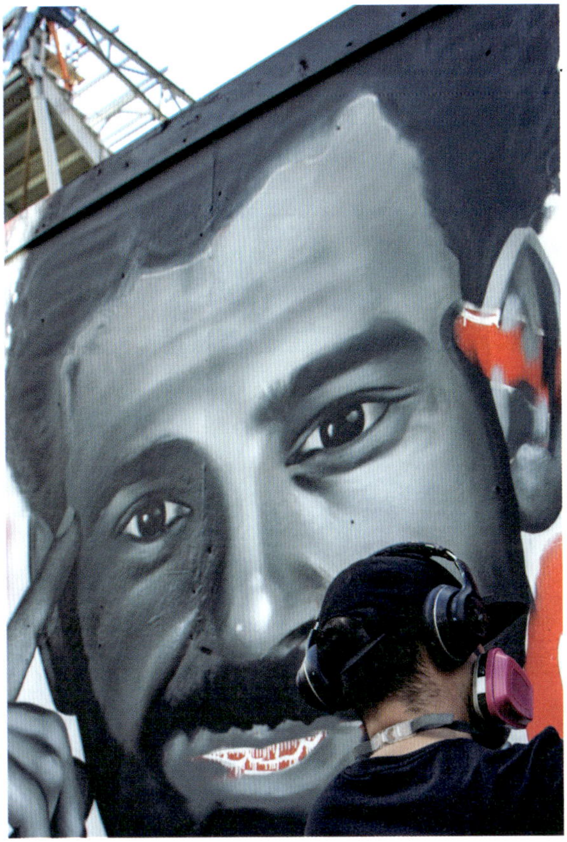
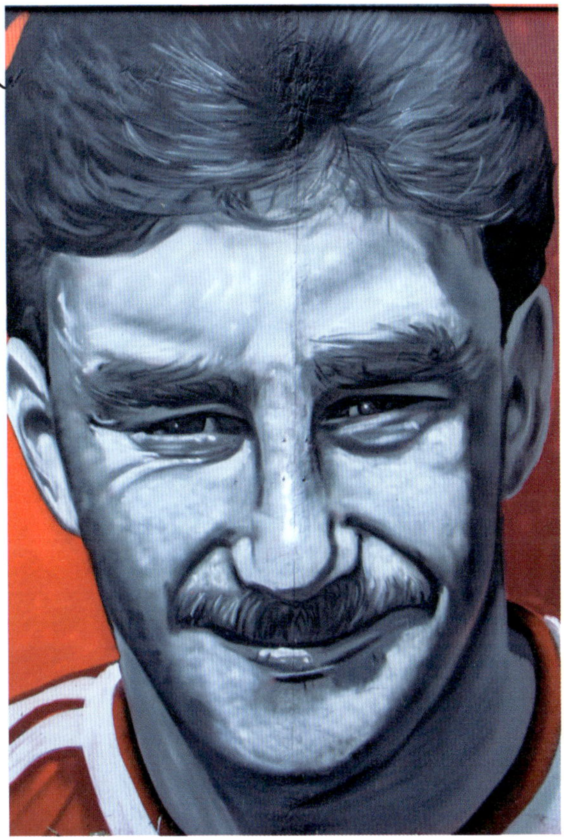
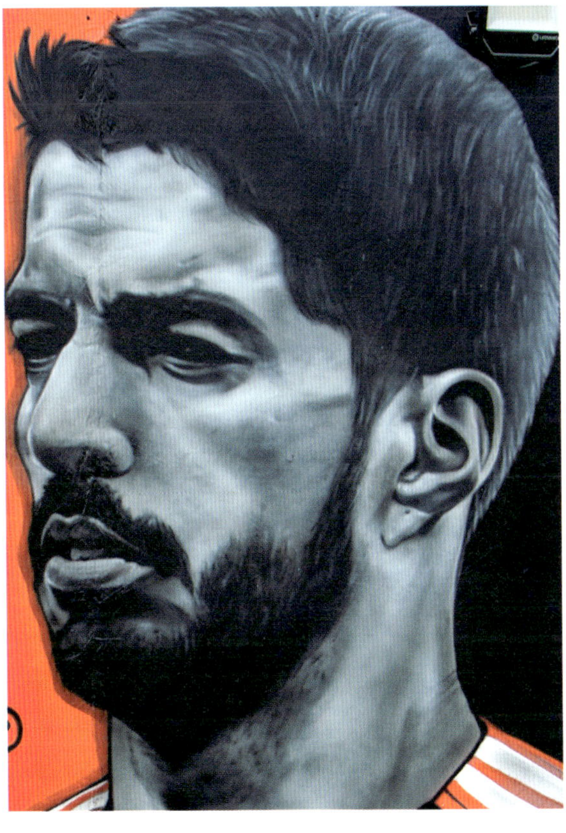
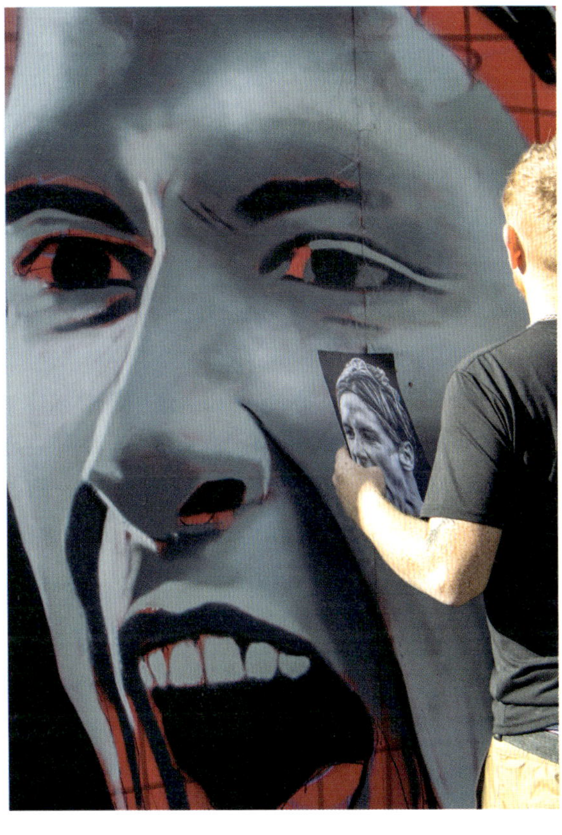

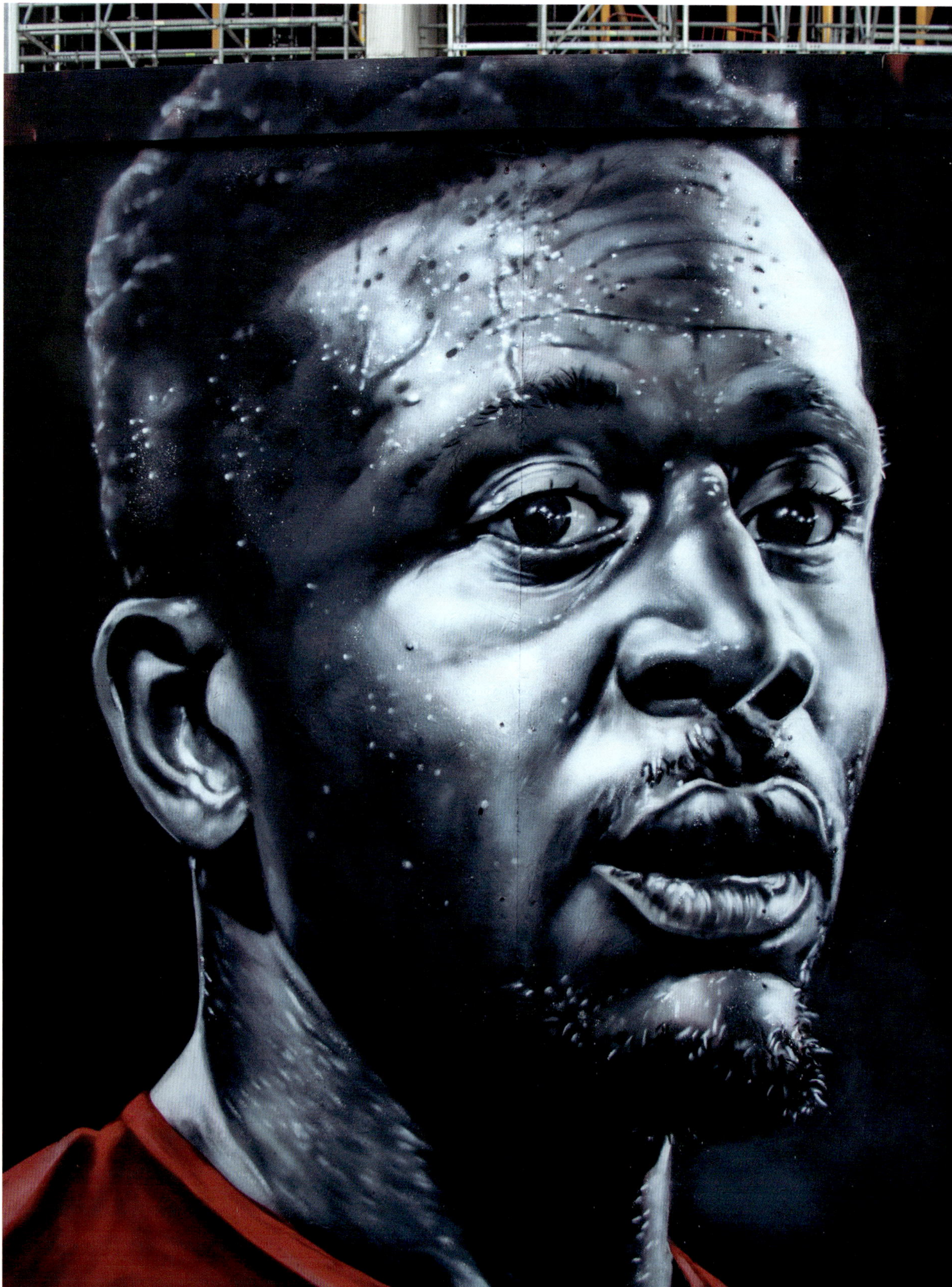

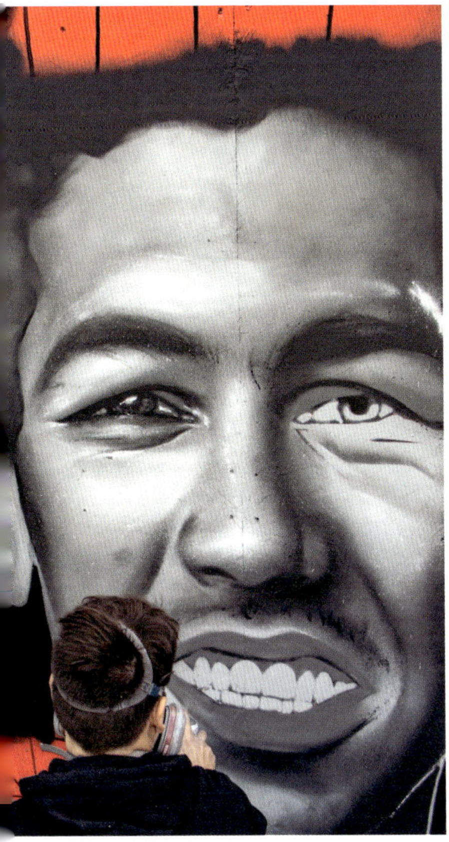

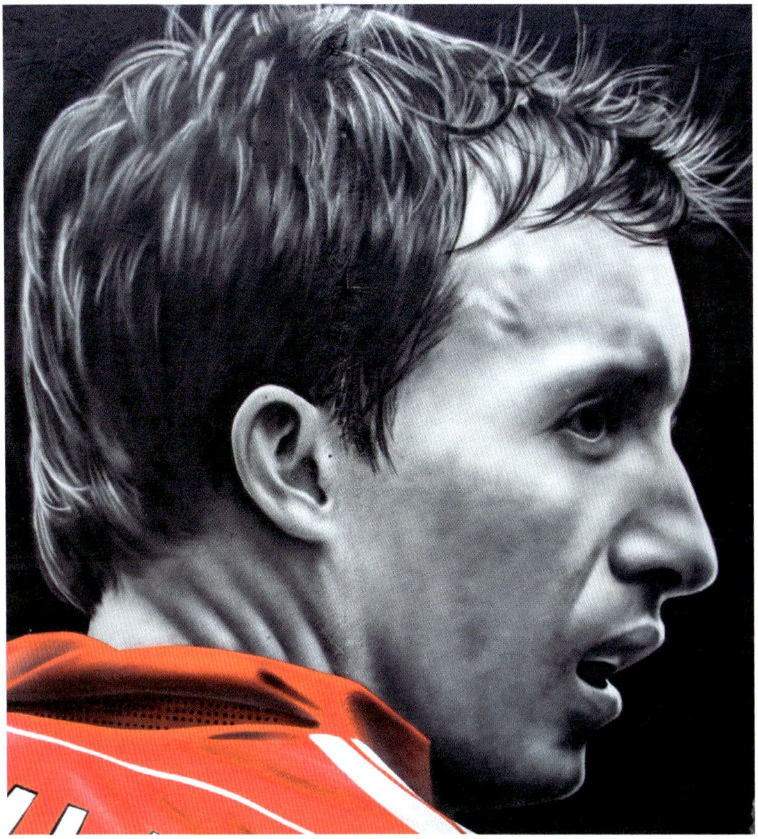

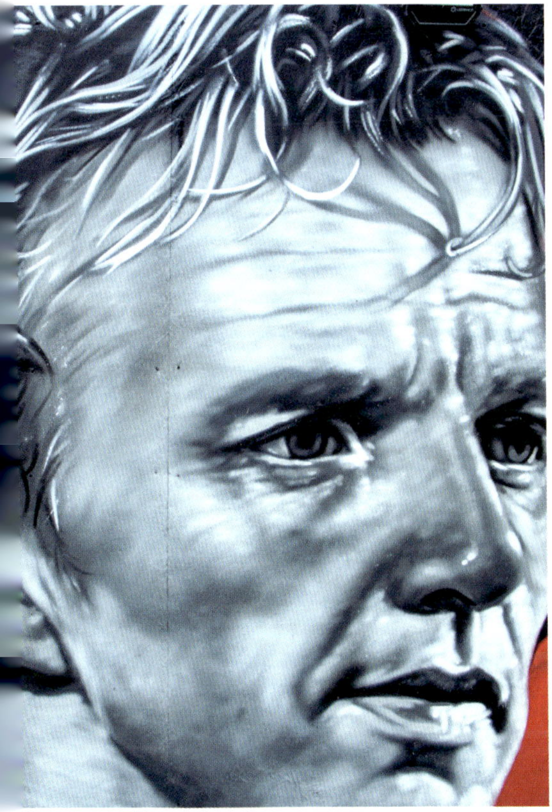

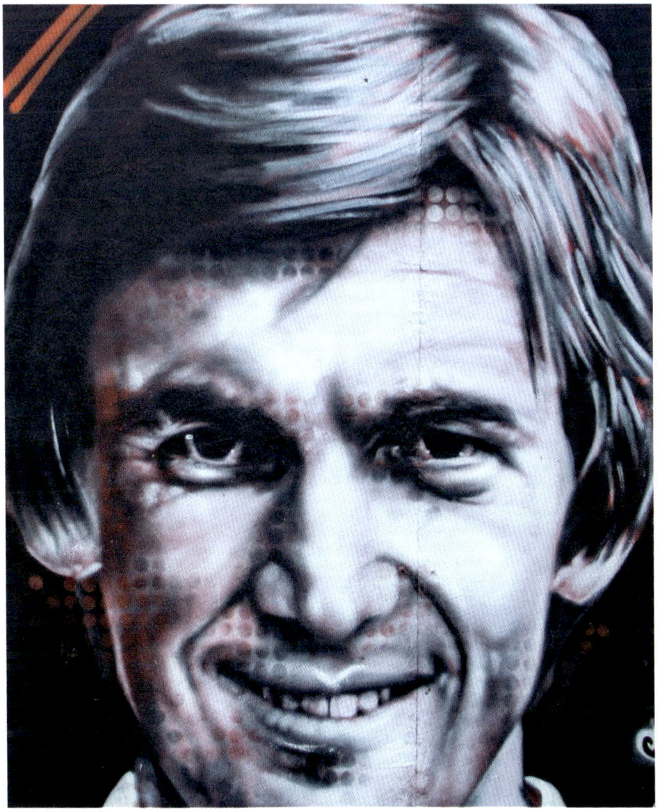

Liverpool's number one

That green jersey and the red shorts, those years of sterling service and the countless saves which helped the Reds to reach the dizziest of heights

Ray Clemence became the first former Liverpool FC player to be commemorated in Anfield street-art when his image in that classic green goalkeeper's jersey appeared on the side of a house in Wylva Road in October 2020, accompanied by a quote from Bill Shankly: "Ray had everything, he's quick, he doesn't wanna be beaten. He's just a great goalkeeper."

A MurWalls creation, it was officially unveiled by his daughter Sarah and four grandchildren, Harry, Lilly, Freddie and Claudia in October 2020 a month before he passed away. Sarah tweeted: "So, so proud to help unveil this amazing mural of my dad @RayClem1 next to Anfield today. Although his health wouldn't let him attend he is beaming with pride #ynwa #LFC."

Rated by many as the greatest keeper to represent the Reds, he was athletic, agile, brave and reliable across his 13 years and 665 appearances – a formidable last line of defence as Liverpool dominated the 1970s. Ray was in the team which won three European Cups, five top-flight titles, two UEFA Cups, a UEFA Super Cup, an FA Cup and a League Cup.

In the summer of 1967 he'd been signed by Shanks from Scunthorpe United for £18,000. After serving his apprenticeship in the Central League (contested by reserve-teams) he replaced Tommy Lawrence in the Reds goal on a permanent basis during the 1969/70 campaign, and in the eleven subsequent seasons he missed just six league matches.

Reflecting on his LFC career, Clem once said: "I loved every minute of it. I loved the affiliation with the fans. I gave them everything I had. Hopefully it was enough to please them."

It most certainly was.

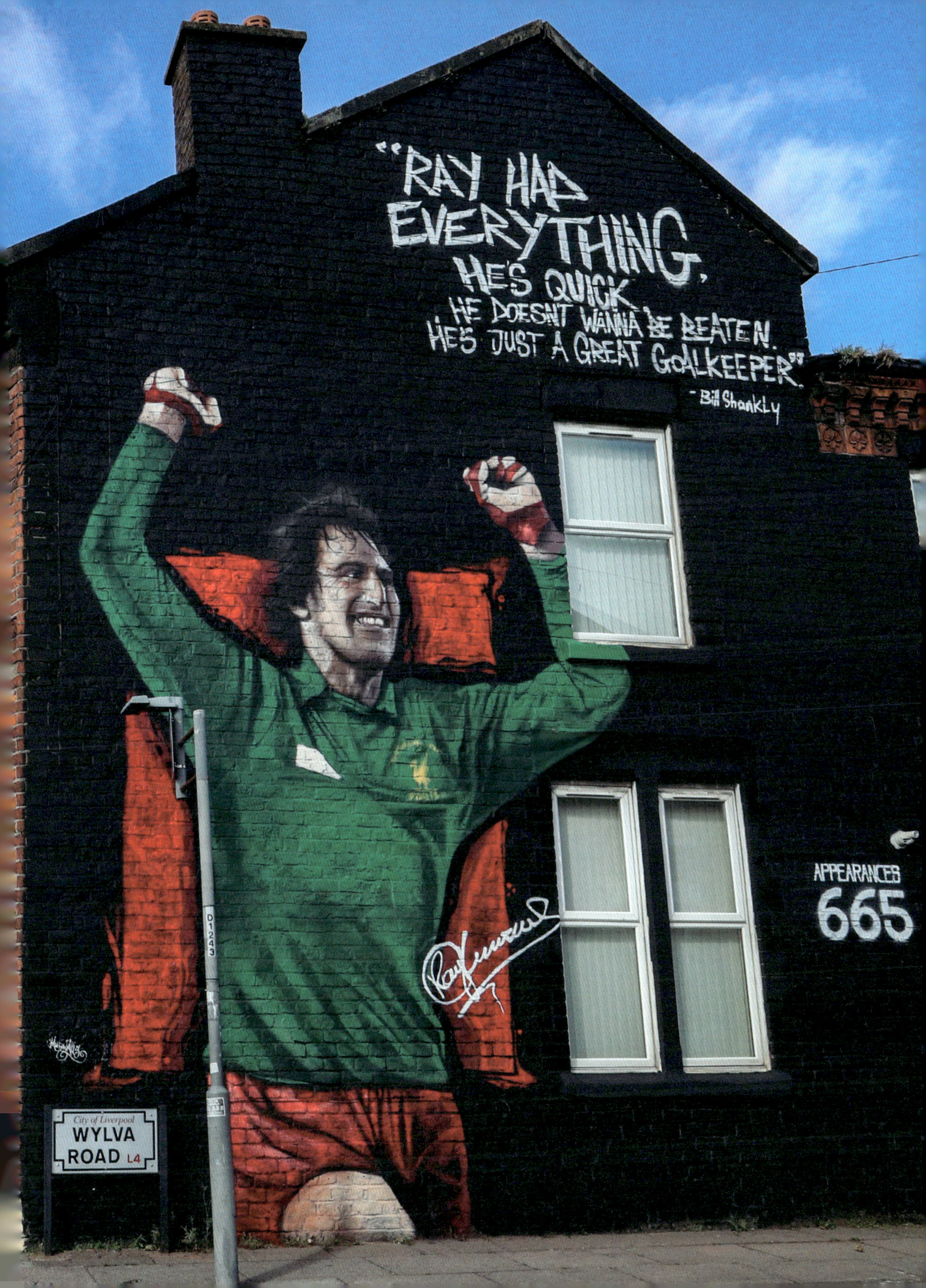
"RAY HAD EVERYTHING.
HE'S QUICK
HE DOESNT WANNA BE BEATEN.
HE'S JUST A GREAT GOALKEEPER"
- Bill Shankly
APPEARANCES
665
City of Liverpool
WYLVA
ROAD L4

To Anne with love

The Hillsborough campaigner has a special place in the hearts of everyone connected to Liverpool Football Club and her mural is a fitting honour

August 2021 saw the arrival of a mural unlike any other in Anfield: a tribute to Hillsborough campaigner Anne Williams on the corner of Anfield Road and Sunbury Road, a short walk from the stadium. Anne passed away in April 2013 and the piece by artist Paul Curtis – depicting Anne and an eternal flame for her son Kevin – was commissioned by Rupen Ganatra, a friend of the family and owner of the building in question.

Paul told the club website: "Rupen wanted something on the side of the building but didn't want a footballer, he wanted it to stand out and be a little different. He couldn't decide then he came back to me after about a year and said, 'Okay, I know what to do now'.

"He's friends with Anne's daughter, Sara, and he thought it would be nice to recognise her. With the footballer ones, they get a lot of recognition anyway, and Rupen thought it was important to recognise someone who's not a megastar, who's one of the people, but who did a lot of good and is important to Liverpool fans.

"It also coincides with an ITV drama about Anne that's coming out, and the actress Maxine Peake – who's playing Anne – came down and got photos with the mural. So it's good timing, and I think the mural is going to be used on the programme, maybe on the credits. I met Sara as well and she loved it. She was in tears but in a good way."

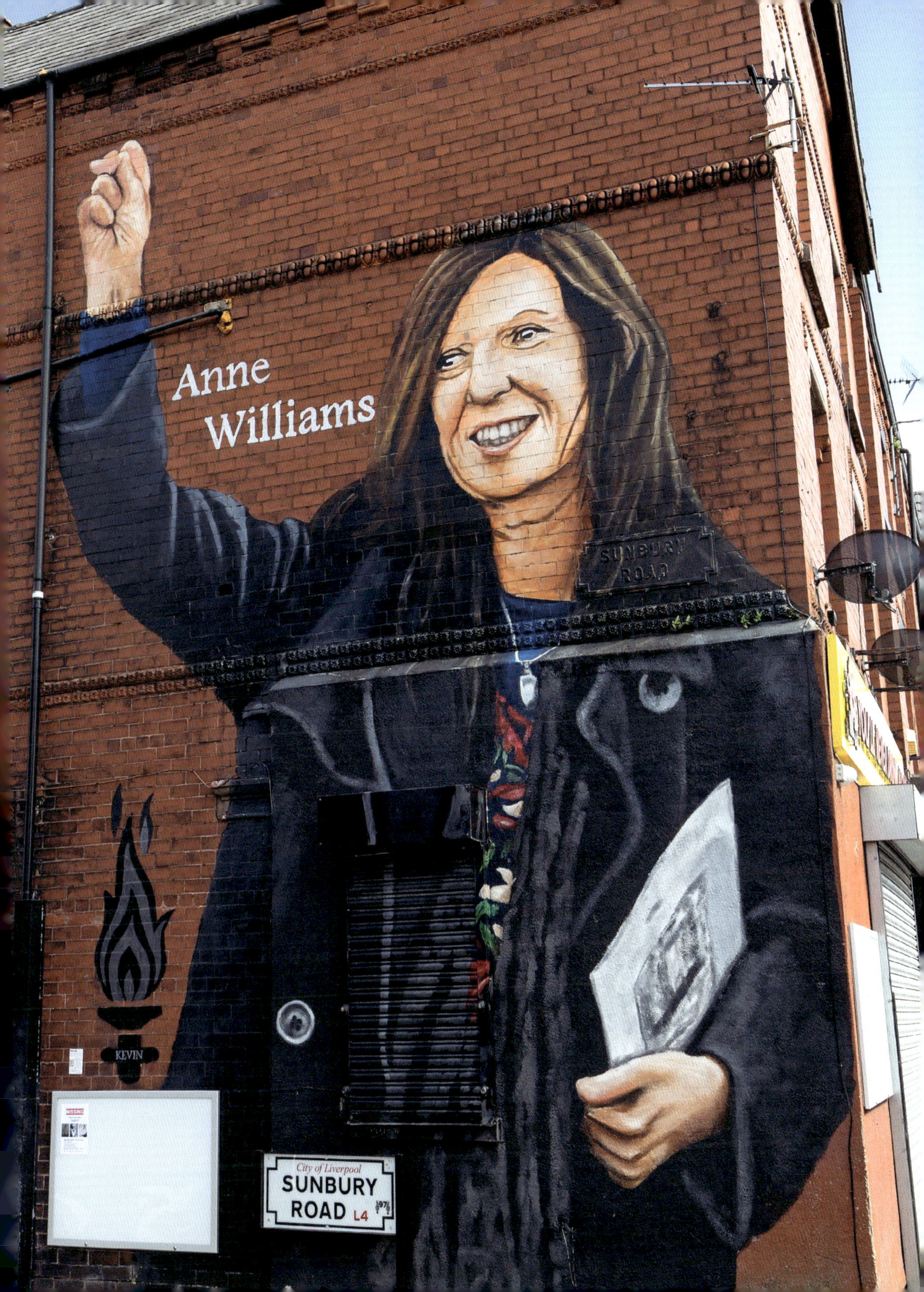
Anne
Williams
SUNBURY
ROAD
KEVIN
City of Liverpool
SUNBURY
ROAD L4

The famous *Five*

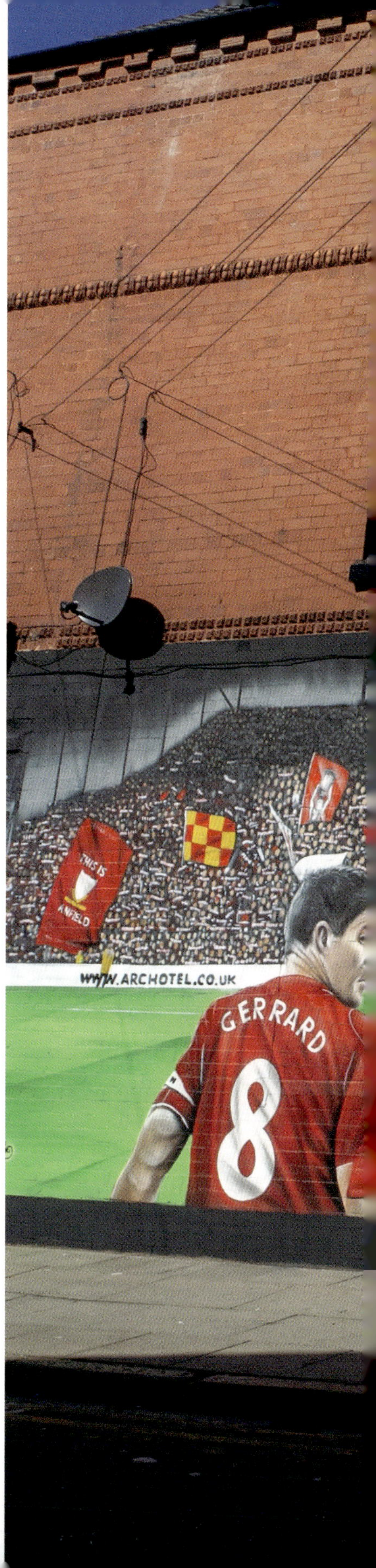

Two defenders, one midfielder and two strikers, and all of them legends of Liverpool Football Club

Stevie G, Carra, God, Virgil and King Kenny. That's quite a line-up on the wall of The Arc Hotel on the corner of Anfield Road and Hornsey Road, five minutes or so from the stadium. Between them, the five legends have racked up over 2,500 appearances for Liverpool over several decades and won every trophy around.

Covering the facade of the entire lower floor of the building, the mural was created by MurWalls in the summer of 2020 as the Reds celebrated that first Premier League title.

As the five legends in their classic kits face their adoring crowd, there are some fascinating details to be picked out – among them flags for the 96 originally lost at Hillsborough and individual fans, Kenny's number seven and the former goalkeeping great Elisha Scott.

Inside the family-run Arc Hotel are replica trophies, signed shirts and plenty of other memorabilia as well as a bar, lounge and large plasma screen.

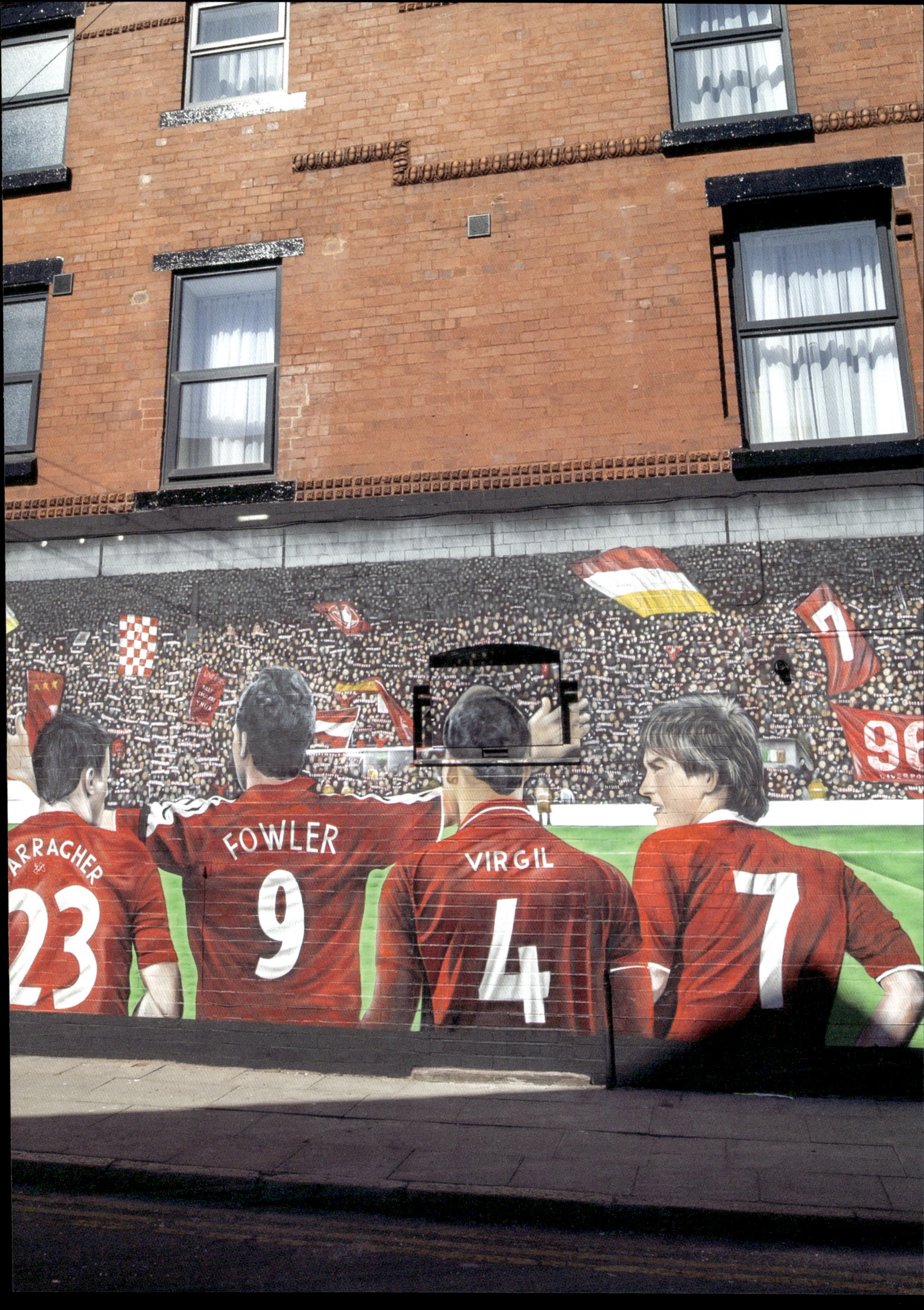
ARRAGHER
23
FOWLER
9
VIRGIL
4
7

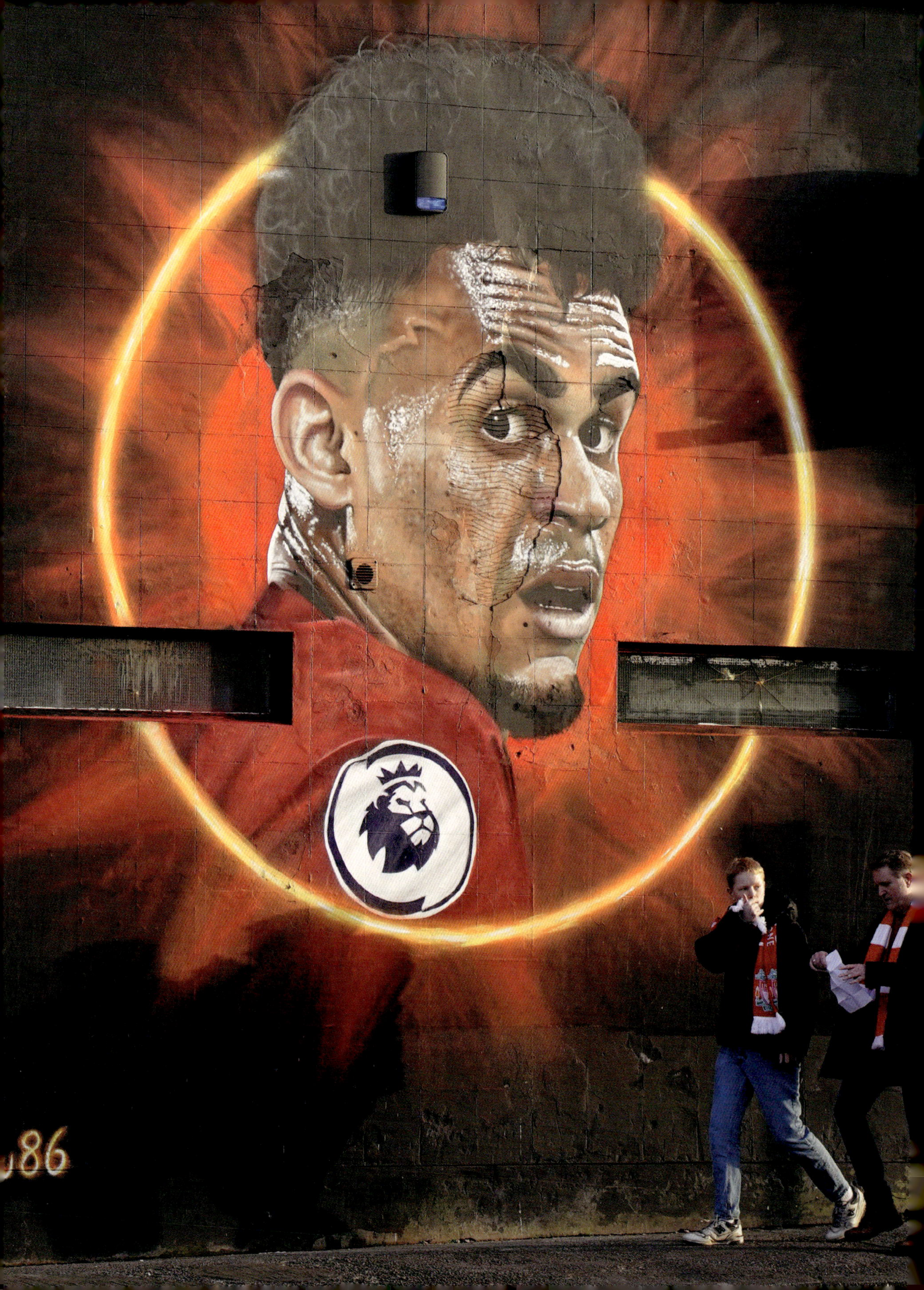

Diaz of glory

It's the Colombian ace's head and shoulders captured on the side of a famous venue close to the ground

While season 2022/23 was a bit of a hit-and-miss affair for the players on the pitch – by Liverpool's mighty standards at least – it was another colourful campaign on the streets around the stadium, with Reds star Luis Diaz one of the newest additions in the outdoor gallery of Anfield murals.

The Colombian attacker's image appeared on a wall of The Sandon Hotel in January, planned as one of three new depictions of modern favourites by artist John Culshaw who revealed: "I [originally] chose him because he'd been a fantastic new signing and even though he got a major injury I thought I'd just go with it because he's definitely who most fans would have chosen."

The job took just three days and John told *The Guide Liverpool* website that the red-and-gold colour-scheme deliberately matches that of his nearby mural of Steven Gerrard. "I do a lot of portraits but people usually want them in black-and-white, so I thought I needed to push myself into more colour and see how I do. This one's turned out really nice and I've already had a couple of Colombia news channels in touch about it."

Diaz joined the Reds from FC Porto in late January 2022 and dazzled immediately. Within 14 weeks he'd appeared three times at Wembley – in the Carabao Cup final and the FA Cup semi-finals and final, tasting victory on each occasion.

Although he made it all look easy, he admitted: "It's been a bit difficult at times, getting used to a new lifestyle, culture and food as well as a new language. [But] sharing a dressing-room with this group of great athletes as well as this manager...well, it's an absolute pleasure.

"I've been told to just keep doing what I've been used to – play my football with joy and happiness while obviously taking the tactical instructions into my game."

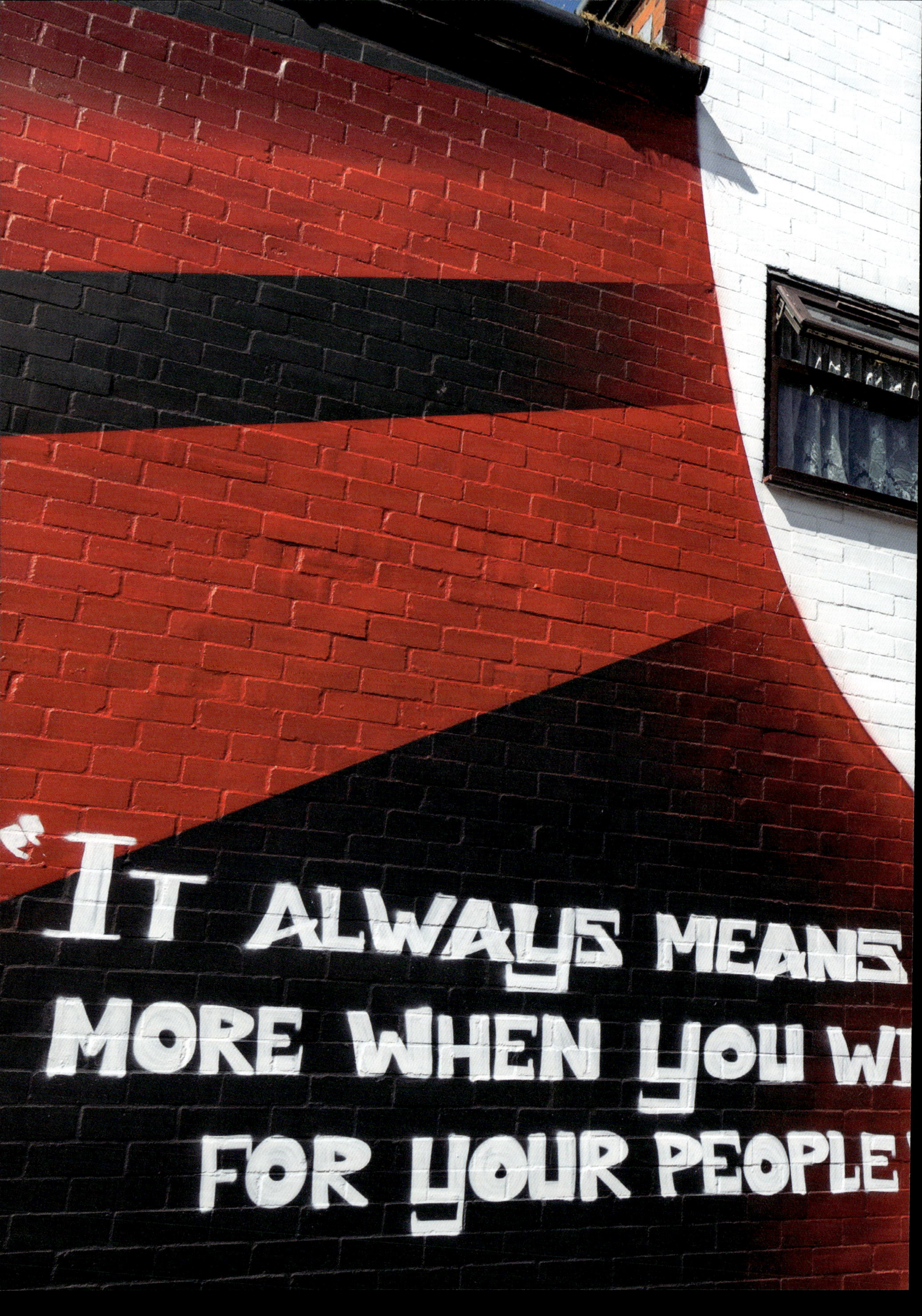
"IT ALWAYS MEANS
MORE WHEN YOU WI
FOR YOUR PEOPLE

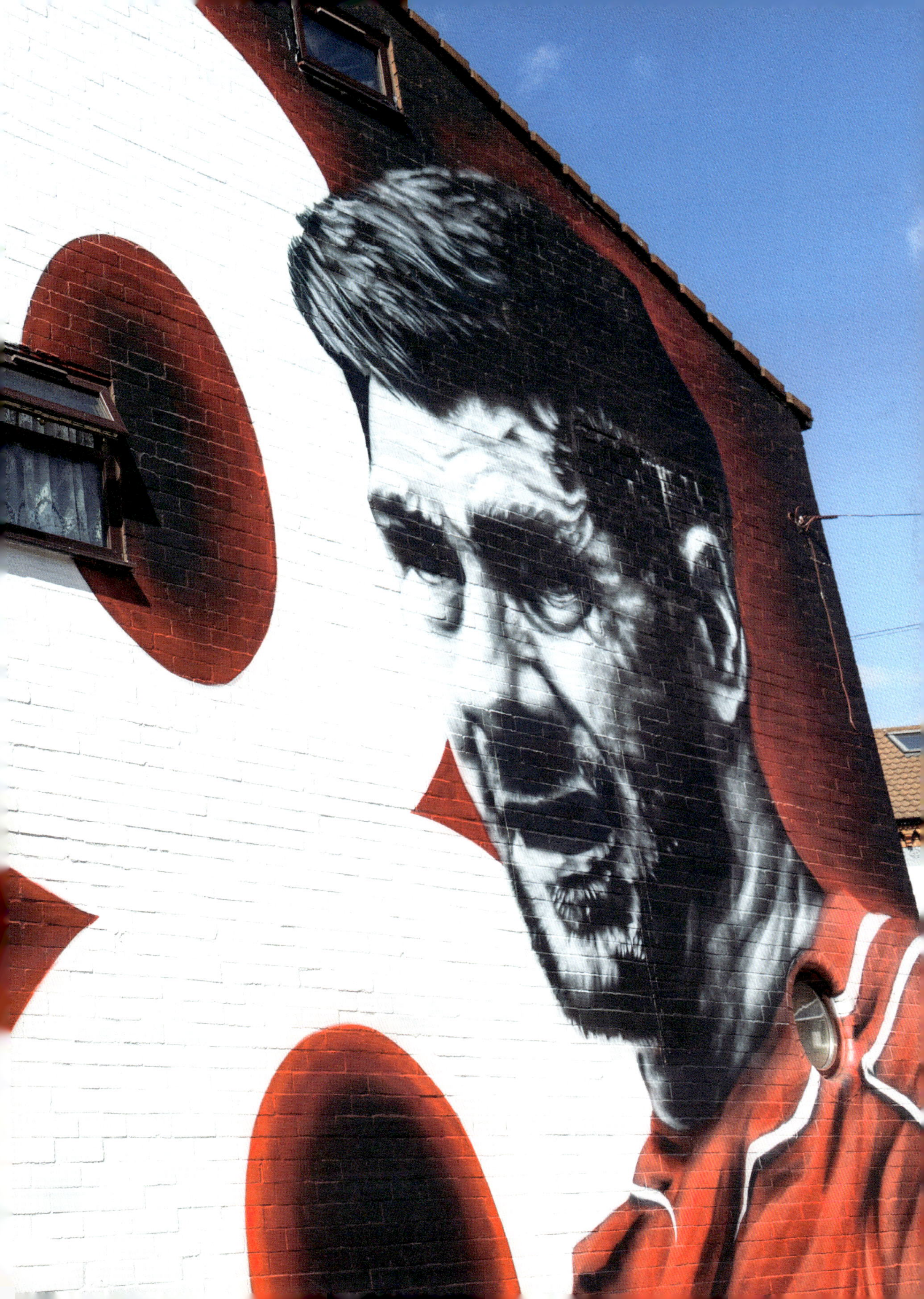

'The best there is, the best there was, the best there ever will be'

No half-measures for two portraits of Steven Gerrard which command attention

So said the banner on the Kop in 2014/15 – Steven Gerrard's last season as a Liverpool player – and it summed up the feelings of every single Reds supporter. So if you're going to create a very public mural of one of Liverpool's greatest-ever players – who's surely in the top three alongside Kenny Dalglish and Billy Liddell – it better be better than good, and those on the outside of the historic Sandon Hotel on Hawkesworth Street and a corner-house on Dinorwic Road most certainly are.

First came The Sandon's breathtaking artwork, courtesy of John Culshaw, in September 2021. In an interview with the club's website he claimed it was "my best one to date, especially with the size of it. And it's been the best-received project by miles. Ste Gerrard messaged me, which was just amazing."

Local lad and lifelong fan John also produced the nearby Jürgen Klopp and Bill Shankly murals outside, respectively, Klopp's Boot Room on Houlding Street and The Park public house on Walton Breck Road, plus tributes to Shankly, Kenny Dalglish and Luis Diaz on different facades of The Sandon, and the colourful goalkeeping artwork at Liverpool FC's AXA Training Centre.

Commissioned by social sports app Sportening, The Sandon's Gerrard mural is street-art at its most spectacular, able to stop people in their tracks with its portrayal of Steven celebrating his goal against Everton at Anfield in January 2014 – the 4-0 win was Liverpool's biggest against the neighbours since Ian Rush famously scored four in a 5-0 away win in 1982.

Culshaw explained: "There's a lot of murals out there with dark backgrounds but I'd been messing about with light effects in my painting and wanted to get some in there. I messed about with fire and light, and those beams of light really came across the best, so I thought: I'm gonna have a go at that. I was made-up with the finished product."

So was venue owner Kate Stewart: "The Sandon will always be the birthplace of LFC and it's absolutely fitting to have a true Scouse and LFC legend such as Stevie G with us."

A month later, a second sensational Gerrard mural was unveiled, this one on Anfield's Dinorwic Street. The work of artists from MurWalls, it was the former skipper in more studied mode next to a large number 8 – his shirt number of course – with the quote 'IT ALWAYS MEANS MORE WHEN YOU WIN FOR YOUR PEOPLE' eventually added to the finished piece.

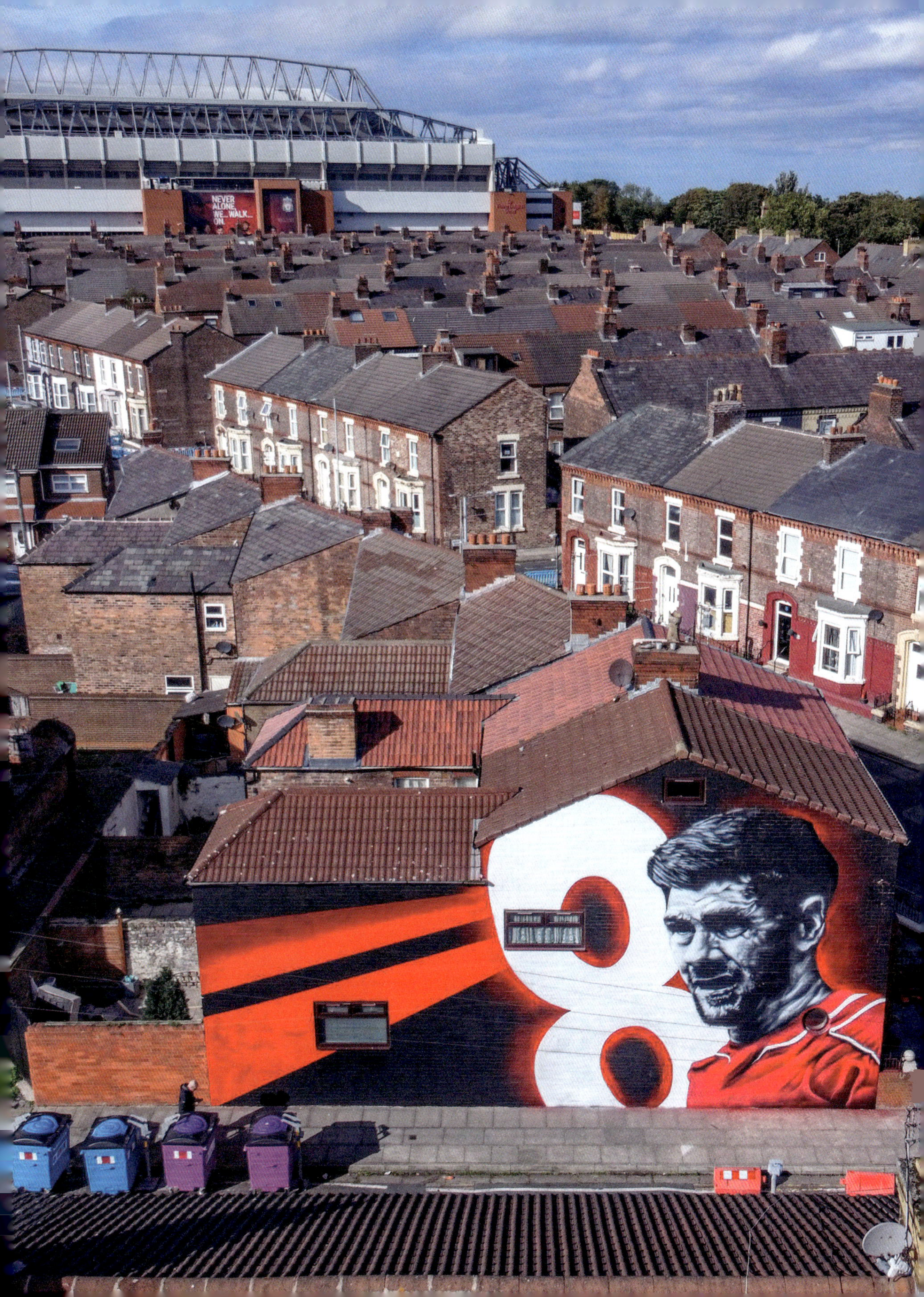
NEVER ALONE, WE... WALK... ON.

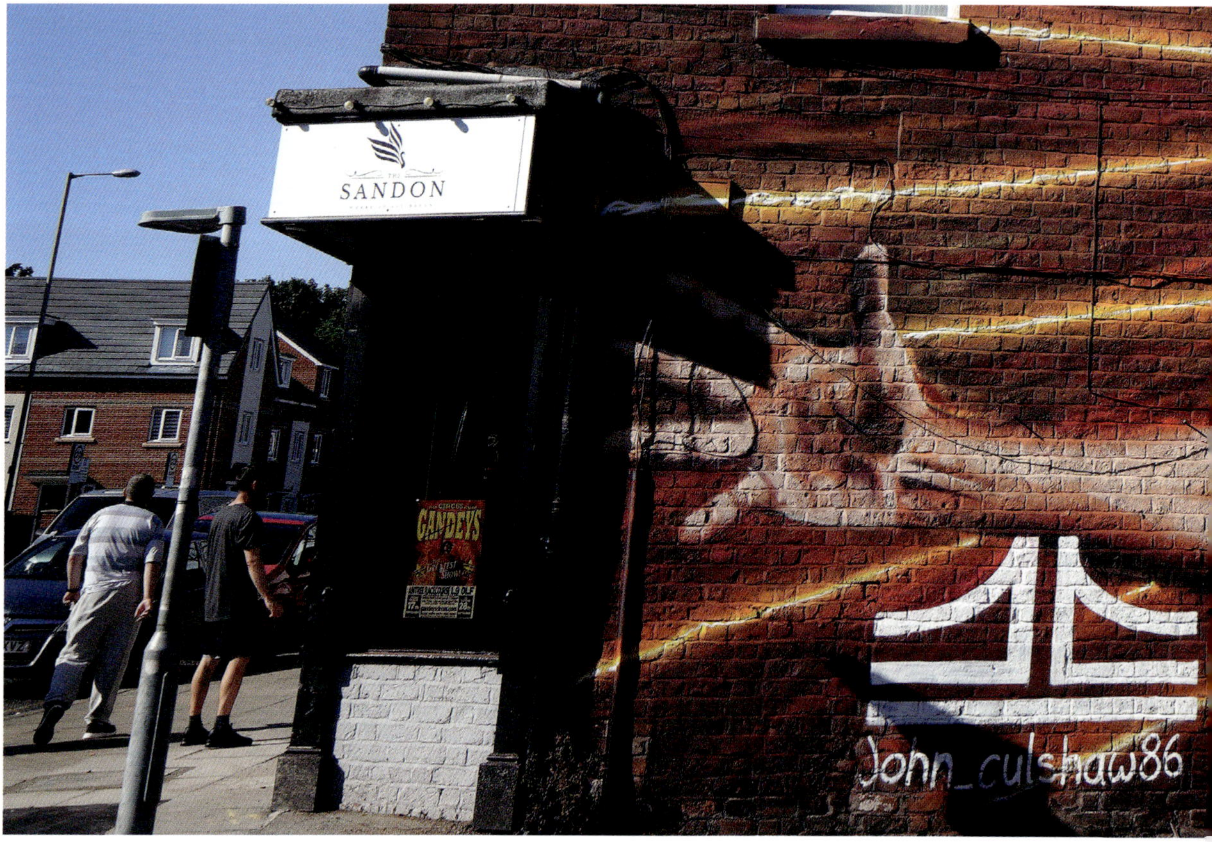

Steven expressed similar sentiments in his final matchday programme notes, for the Premier League game against Crystal Palace at Anfield on 16 May 2015.

"Inevitably there will be comparisons between myself and other players from the past now," he wrote. "I think those debates always occur when someone is about to leave a club. None of that talk matters to me. I just want to be remembered as a local lad who did everything he could to represent the fans on the pitch. That was always my priority – to give them the wins and the success they want.

"Making the supporters happy is an incredible feeling for me because I am one of them and always will be – the only difference is I've been lucky enough to live the dream and play for the club. While doing so I've cherished the superb backing we receive. It has often made the difference between us winning and losing, with Istanbul being the biggest example of that.

"So from the bottom of my heart I would like to say a huge thanks to every supporter. No matter where we've played, whether it's here at Anfield or thousands of miles away, they have always been there for us."

For the record, Gerrard made 710 appearances for Liverpool between 1998 and 2015 – 472 as captain – and scored 186 goals from midfield, putting him sixth in the all-time table of LFC scorers (behind only Ian Rush, Roger Hunt, Gordon Hodgson, Billy Liddell and more recently Mo Salah).

Of those goals, 120 were scored in the Premier League and 30 in the Champions League. He also scored in an FA Cup final, a League Cup final, a Champions League final and a UEFA Cup final.

Steven also scored 21 goals in 114 games for his country – he's third on the all-time England men's appearances list.

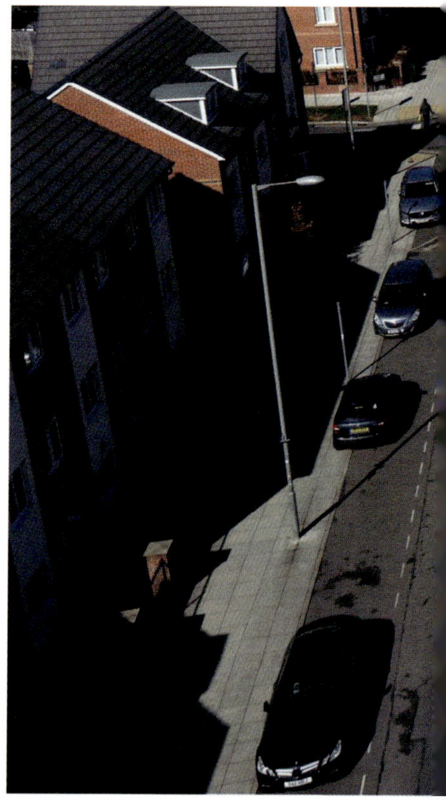

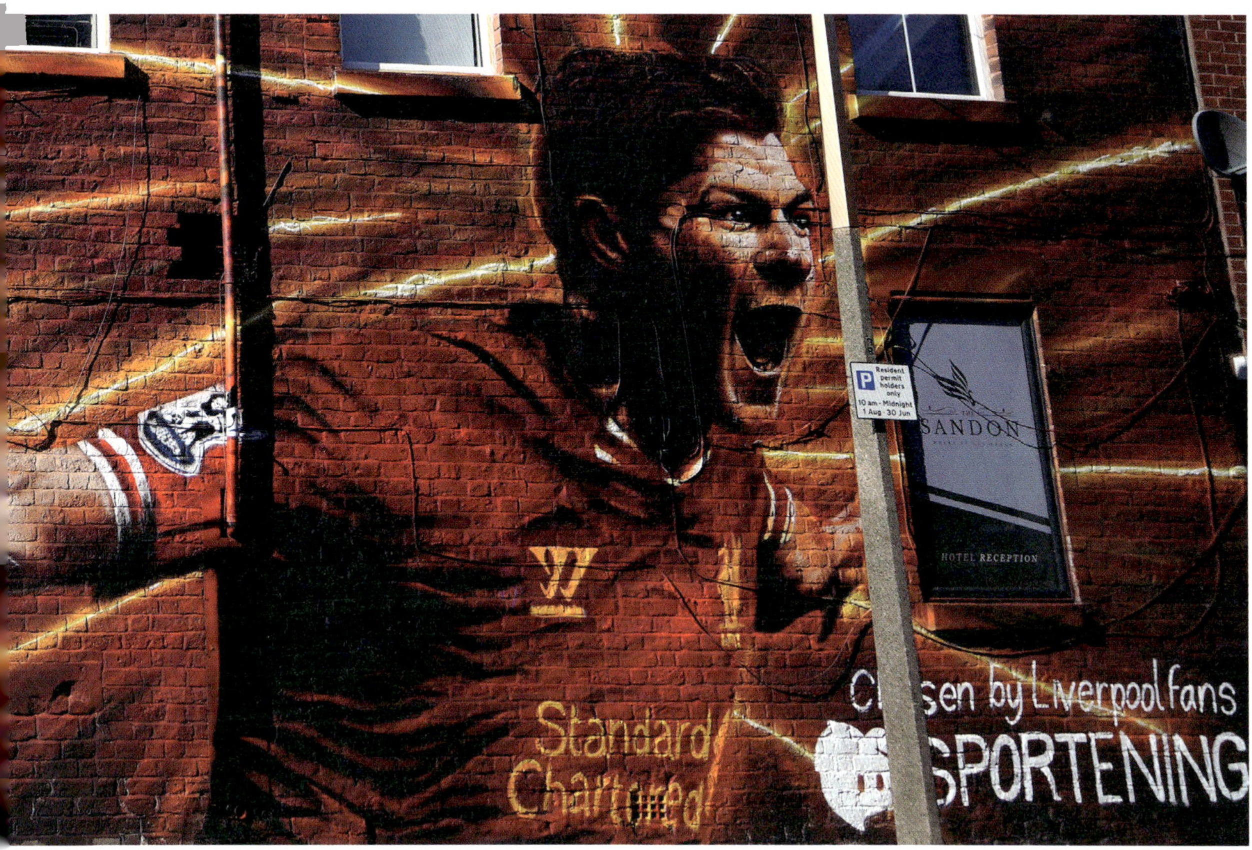
Standard
Chartered
sen by Liverpoolfans
SPORTENING
SANDON
HOTEL RECEPTION

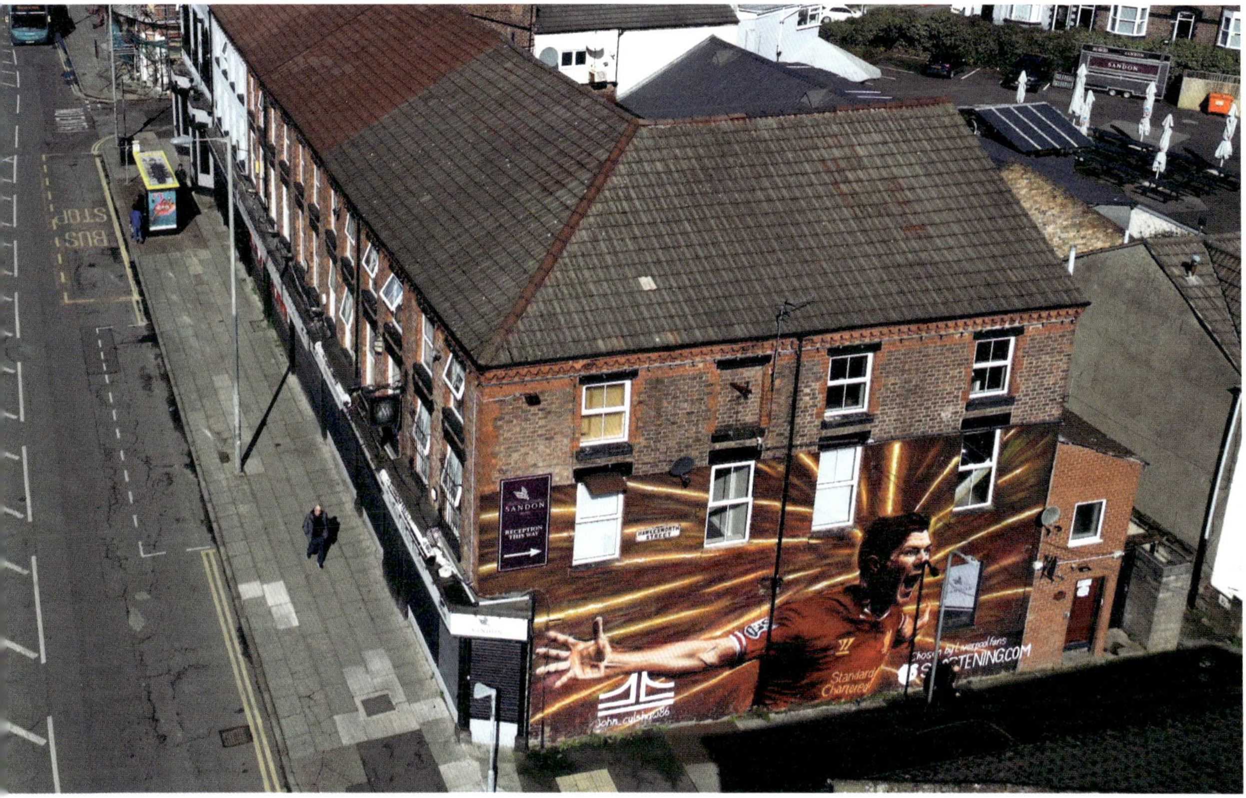

Class of 81

Alan Kennedy's winner in the 1981 European Cup final is part of LFC folklore – and the man himself couldn't wait to get his hands back on 'Old Big Ears'

An enduring photograph from an unforgettable night: Alan Kennedy cuddling the big, beautiful European Cup after his late winner against Real Madrid in the Paris final of 1981. Four decades on, it's been immortalised on the side of a terraced house on Anfield's Dinorwic Street, with the former left-back giving his approval in person (photographed here by Courtney Neary).

And what a feat not just to capture the likeness of the player in that classic early 80s 'V'-neck kit but also the gleaming splendour of the famous trophy itself. MurWalls were the collective behind both this and the Steven Gerrard artwork on the same street.

The weather played nice in Paris in 2022, as it did for Madrid 2019 and Kyiv 2018, but in Paris 1981 it was another story. It came down in stair-rods on the day of the final, but no downpour was ever going to dampen Liverpudlian spirits all those years ago – not least when Alan Kennedy's shot rippled the raindrops off the back of the Real Madrid net.

It's hard to convey just how unlikely a scorer, let alone match-winner, the likeable Geordie left-back was. His nickname was Barney Rubble, after the *Flintstones* cartoon character, for his barraging runs down the flank. What he may have lacked in ability – compared to some of his team-mates anyway – he more than made up for in energy and desire. And with nine minutes remaining at a soggy Parc de Princes in the French capital, it was Kennedy who broke the deadlock with a piece of explosive improvisation, racing onto a throw-in from his namesake Ray on the left-flank and crashing a shot past Real keeper Agustin.

In a recent interview with UEFA.com he recalled: "I never knew I'd be the first full-back to score a goal in a European Cup final. My job, as Bob Paisley described it, was: 'There to support, there to start moves, there to be at the end of moves, and let other players score the goals and take all the credit'.

"But I certainly changed that in 1981 against Real Madrid. The game itself wasn't great. It was on a poor pitch. We had one or two injury problems. I had a broken wrist I was playing with and, in the end, we absolutely knew that one goal was going to separate the two teams.

"They did have a couple of chances, we had several, and I just thought to myself: it's time we showed what Liverpool is all about. I made the run forward not expecting the ball to be coming to me. I chested it down and one of their players tried to take me out but missed. I'm not saying I was going to hit the target, but my mind was made-up: I was going for a goal.

"The goalkeeper left the near-post open and the ball flew into the back of the net. I didn't think it would be me scoring that goal. We had Kenny Dalglish, David Johnson and the likes of Terry McDermott and Ray Kennedy, who were more qualified to score goals than I was. But I think, in some ways, when I got in those positions, I just went for it. You know, it didn't matter who scored the goal. We all said that – it didn't matter as long as we won the game."

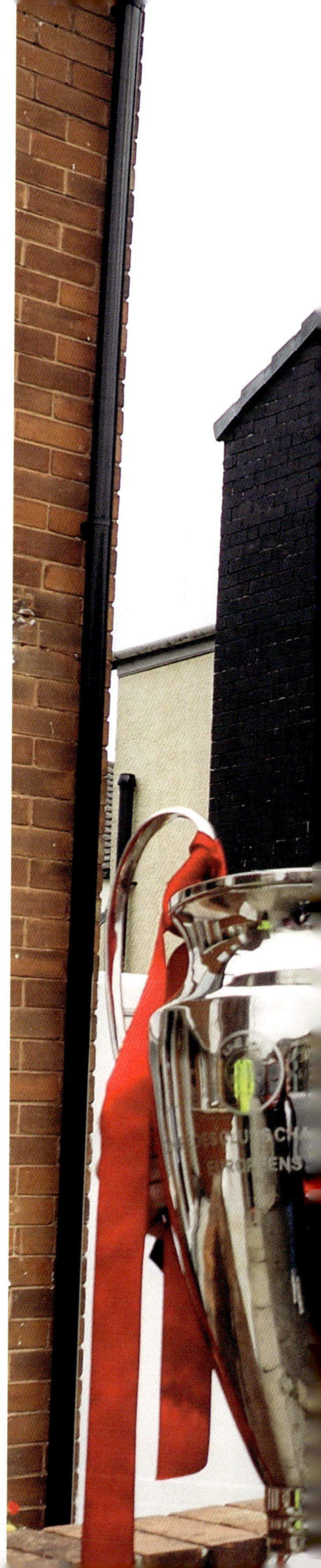

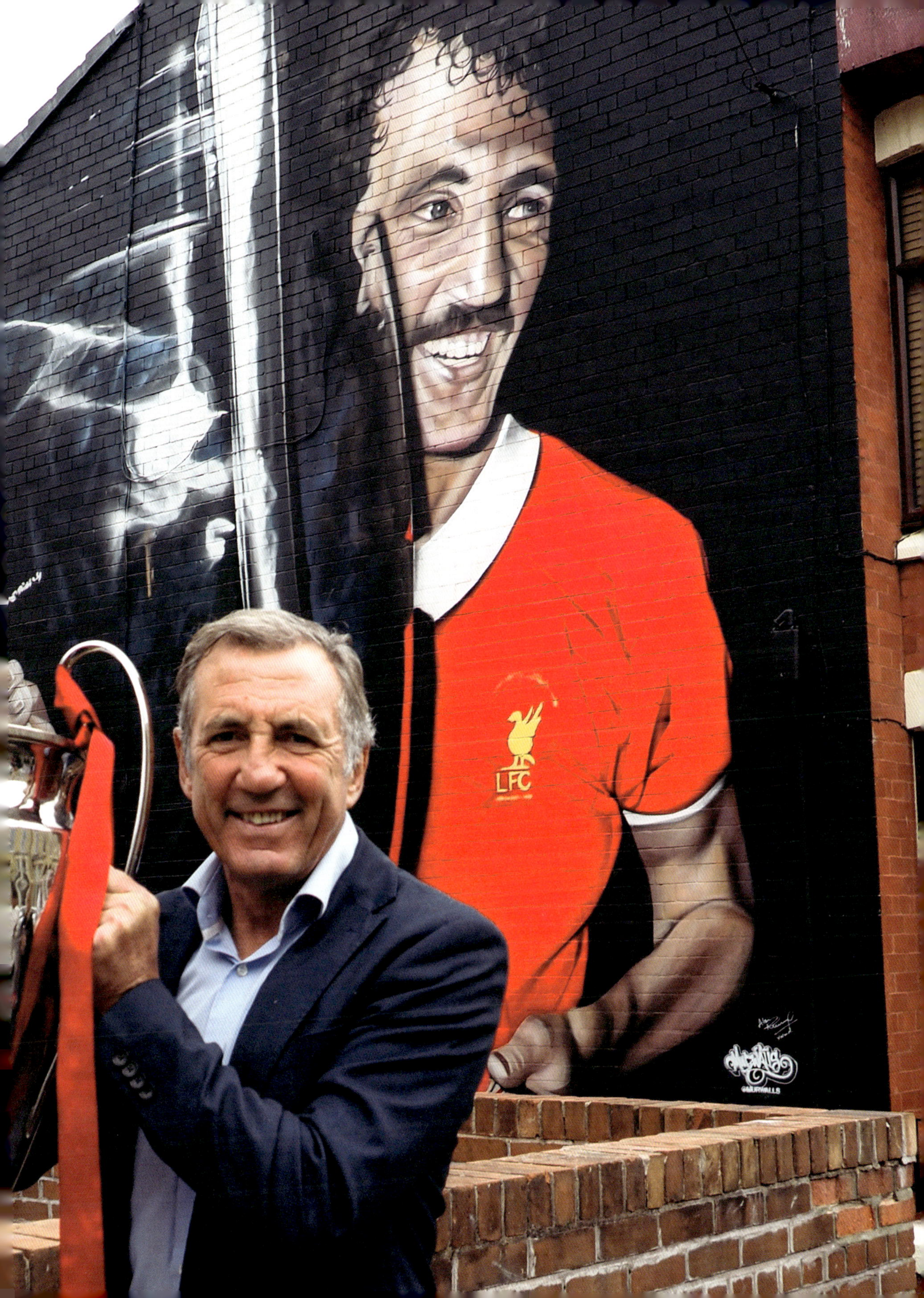
LFC

King Kenny

We'd walk a million miles for one of his goals but fortunately his mural is a lot closer-at-hand

It took a little while – until January 2022 to be exact – but it was worth the wait when Reds legend Kenny Dalglish was recognised with his own towering mural, located on the Kop End Bar on Oakfield Road near the stadium, courtesy of artist Paul Curtis. There he is in his playing pomp in the classic 'V'-neck, pinstripe Reds kit of the early 1980s, skilfully rendered between two pairs of windows.

Kenny's association with Liverpool FC began in the summer of 1977 when he arrived from Celtic and took possession of the no7 shirt. The Spion Kop was smitten by the style and the smile and today's YouTube clips hardly do him justice. He was strong, skilful and so, so canny in possession – shielding the ball from aggressors, turning on a sixpence, playing in team-mates to score – and manager Bob Paisley was delighted. "I just hoped that after the trials and tribulations of my early years in management, someone up high would smile on me and guide my hand," he said in later years. "My plea was answered when we got Kenny Dalglish. What a player, what a great professional."

In his first season, 1977/78, he scored 31 goals in all competitions, including the winner in the European Cup final against FC Bruges at Wembley. The next two seasons saw Kenny help the Reds to back-to-back league titles and win the League Cup, and in 1981 he tasted European Cup glory for a second time as Liverpool beat Real Madrid in the Paris final.

By 1981/82 his link-up with spring-heeled young Welsh marksman Ian Rush was taking the football world by storm. The duo shared 30 league goals and 52 in all competitions as Liverpool regained their top-flight title. The following campaign was arguably Dalglish's best in a Liverpool shirt. He and Rush again shared more than 50 goals, with the Scot netting 20 of them as the Reds retained the championship, and he was voted player of the year by his peers in the Professional Footballers Association.

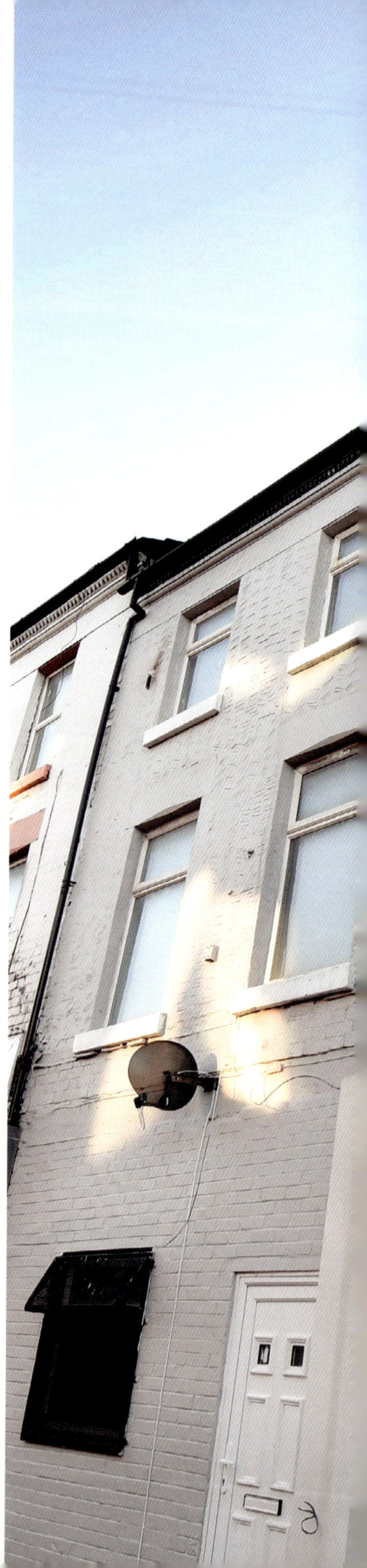

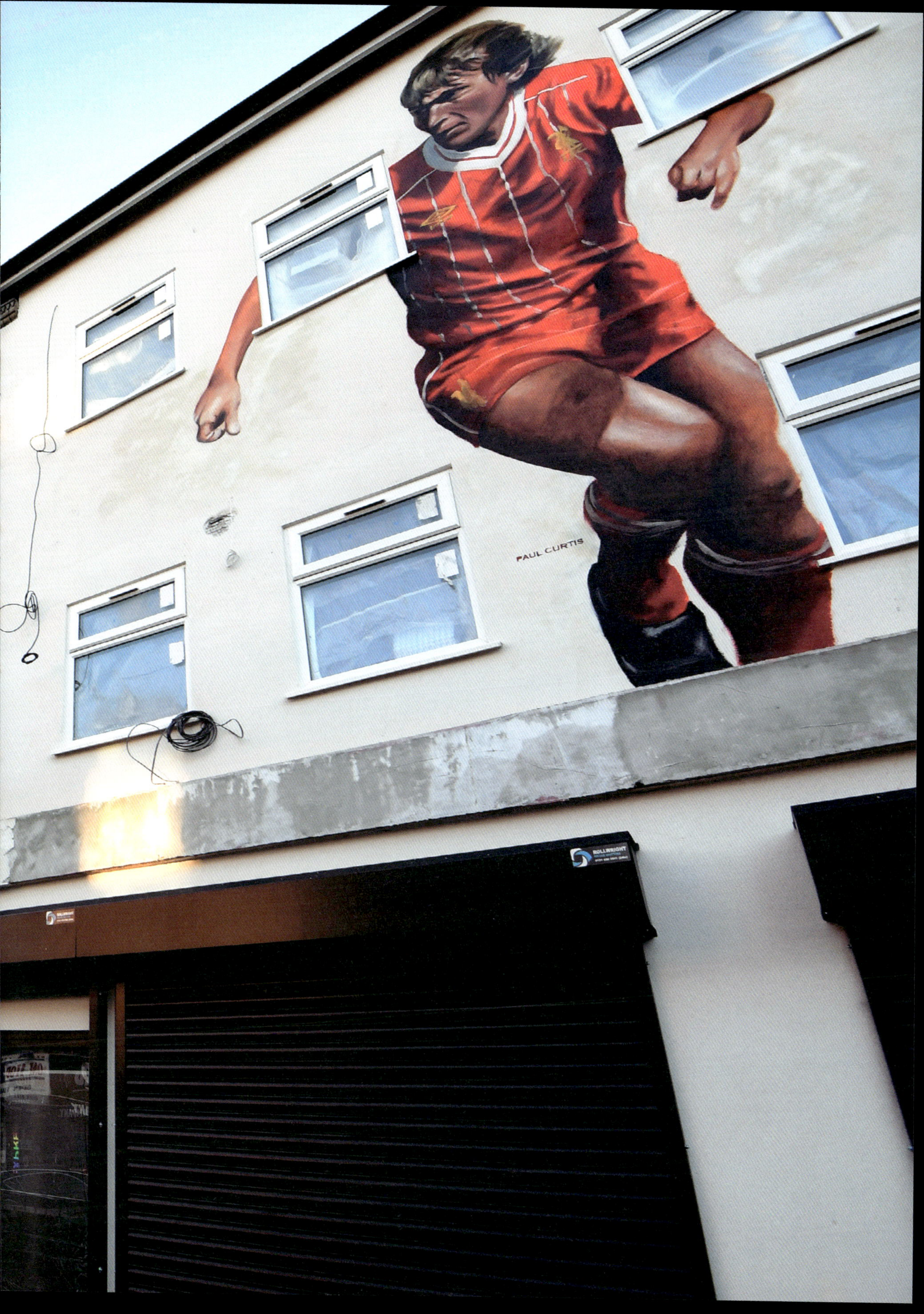
PAUL CURTIS

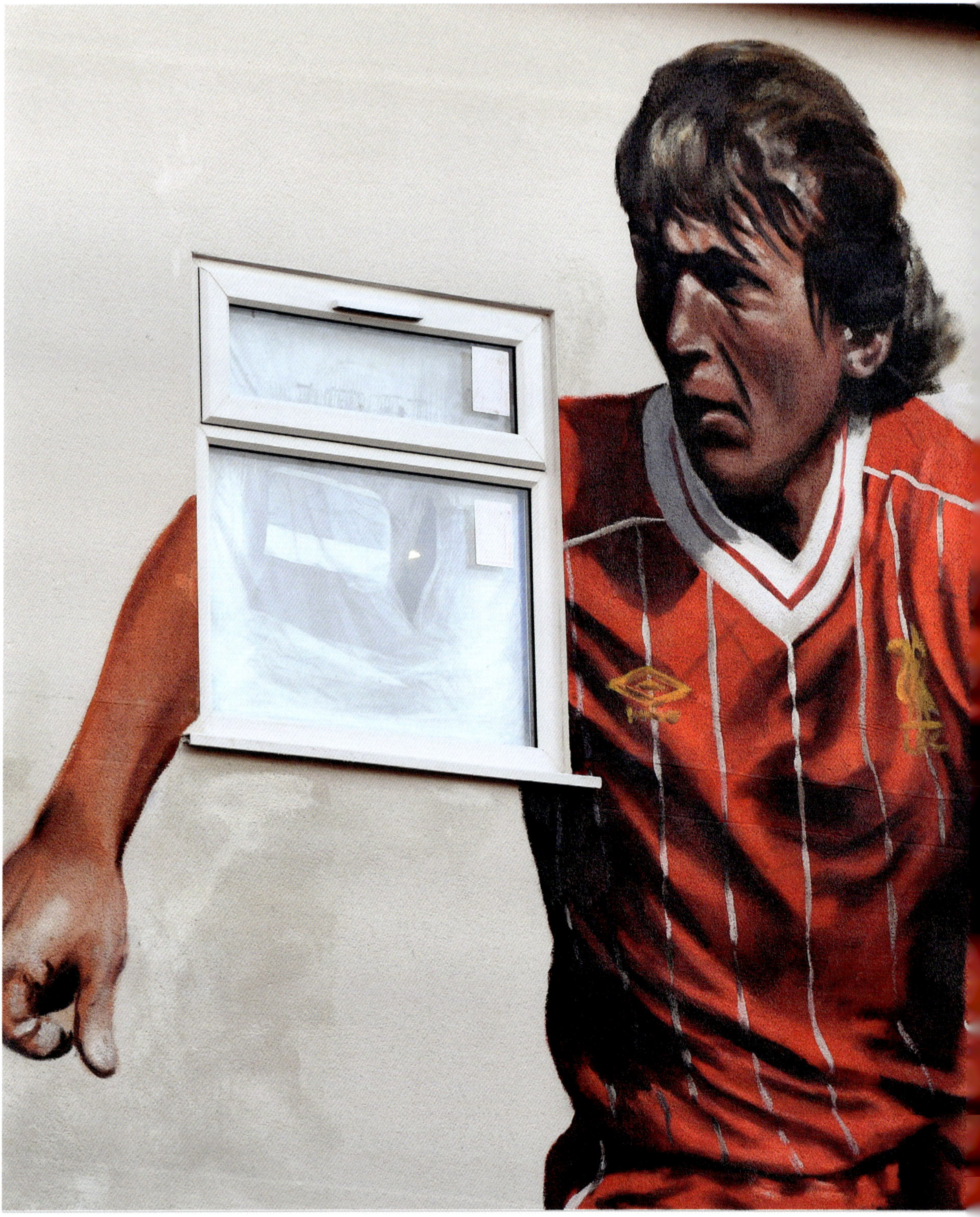

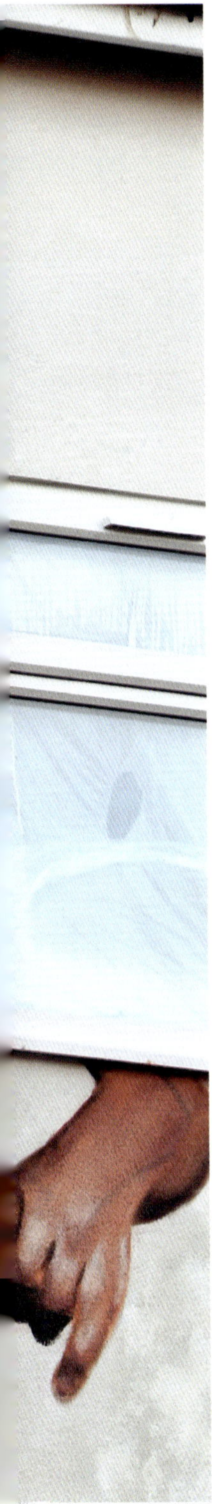

Season 1983/84 saw Liverpool claim a treble of league, League Cup and, for the third time in Kenny's Liverpool career, the European Cup, under a new manager Joe Fagan. The 1984/85 campaign, during which he turned 34 years of age, was to be his last as a member of the 'rank-and-file' in the Anfield dressing-room before a new role as player-manager beckoned. Kenny's remarkable contribution was further recognised when he was awarded an MBE in the 1984 New Year's Honours list for his services to football.

In his dual-role Dalglish landed the club's first league-and-FA Cup double in 1986, then built one of Liverpool's finest-ever teams around new signings John Barnes, Peter Beardsley and John Aldridge in 1987/88.

Then came Hillsborough. At the age of 38, Dalglish led Liverpool FC through the aftermath of the disaster with he and wife Marina attending as many funerals as they could, as did the players.

The team bounced back in 1989/90 by winning an 18th title, but the impact of Hillsborough took its toll and he officially retired from playing in 1990 then shocked the football world by resigning as manager the next year. He returned to the game as boss of ambitious Blackburn Rovers, guiding them first to promotion and eventually the Premier League title in 1995.

Dalglish returned to his beloved LFC in the summer of 2009 with a senior role at the Academy while also becoming the club's new ambassador. Less than two years later he was appointed manager for a second time to replace Roy Hodgson, calling it a "no-brainer. Just to be back among the people at Anfield meant a huge amount to me and my family."

He steered the side to an eighth League Cup success and an FA Cup final in 2011/12 before Brendan Rodgers succeeded him. In the autumn of 2013 he became a non-executive director, and four years later Anfield's Centenary Stand – opposite the newly-expanded Main Stand – was renamed in recognition of his unique contribution to the club.

In 2016 he and the Hillsborough families received the Freedom of the City at Liverpool Town Hall. Three years later, King Kenny was knighted at Buckingham Palace for services to football, charity and the city of Liverpool. The stand signage at Anfield was recalibrated accordingly, but the Kop was the spiritual setting in July 2020 when Dalglish presented Jordan Henderson with the Premier League trophy.

And could he play: Kenny in his pomp was truly world-class as every Kopite who was there will vouch for

Super Carra

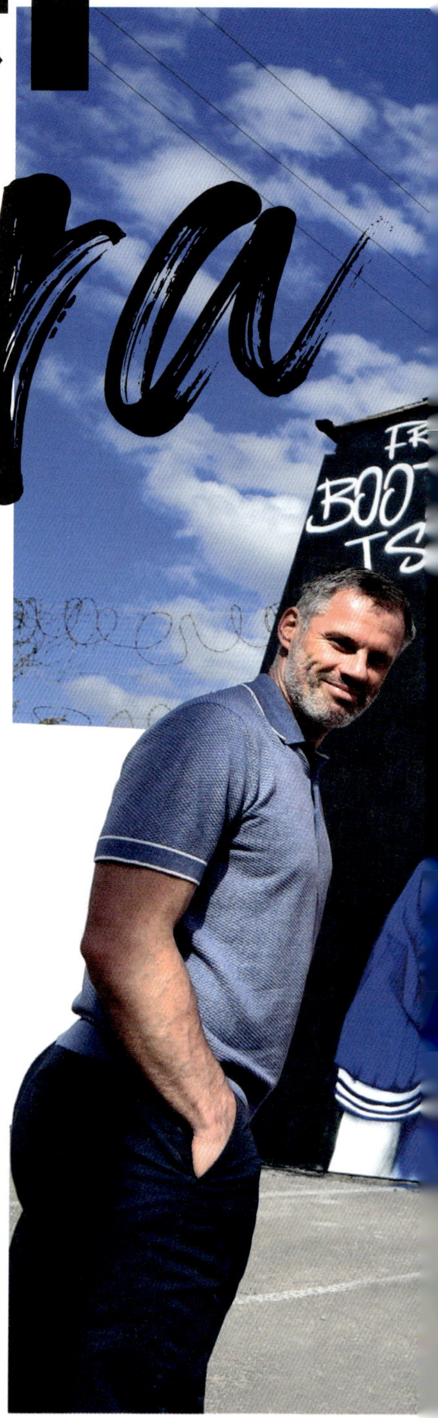

The heart-and-soul former defender has never forgotten his roots and always wanted to give something back to the place where he grew up

For around 18 unprecedented months from early 2020 to mid-2021, times were harder than ever for everyone, and Liverpool Football Club and specifically its charities LFC Foundation and Red Neighbours worked flat-out to support the most vulnerable in its local community.

One ex-player also played his part in his home neighbourhood of Bootle, and in June 2021 a huge mural was unveiled on Marsh Lane to commemorate the work of Jamie Carragher's own 23 Foundation, which has raised over £3 million for various causes across Merseyside and the wider world over a decade.

Created by MurWalls, it depicts him both as a young Everton fan and as a Reds defender raising the Champions League aloft in 2005. It also pays tribute to the 96 fans originally lost at Hillsborough with the iconic image of two young mascots taken at a Goodison derby back in 2012.

The former centre-back, who played 737 times for Liverpool, signed the mural to put the finishing touch to a piece that took around 30 hours to complete.

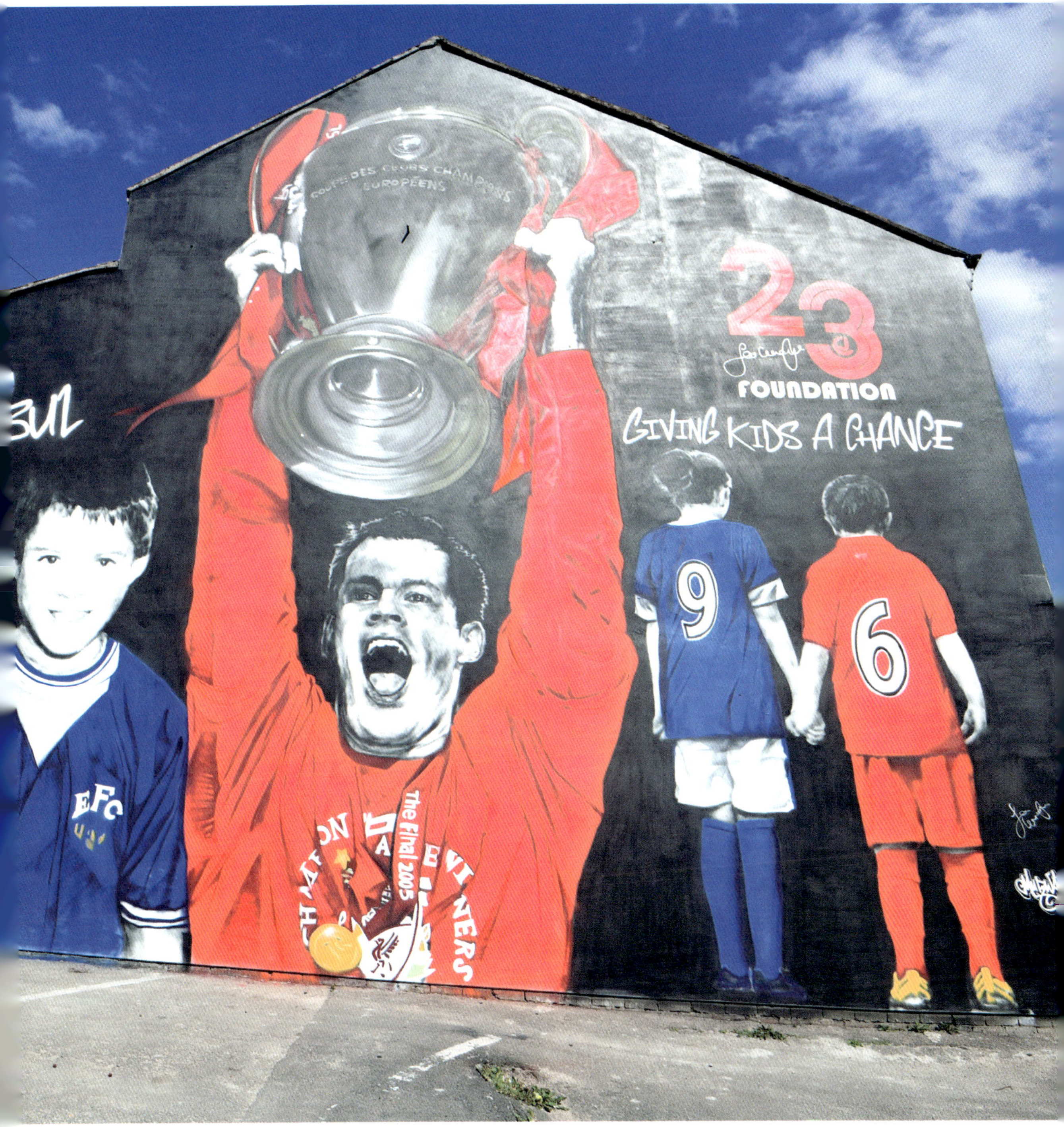
COUPE DES CLUBS CHAMPIONS EUROPÉENS
23
FOUNDATION
GIVING KIDS A CHANCE
9
6
EFC
The Final 2005

Carra in red and blue: the mural is an eye-catching addition to the neighbourhood where the former central defender grew up

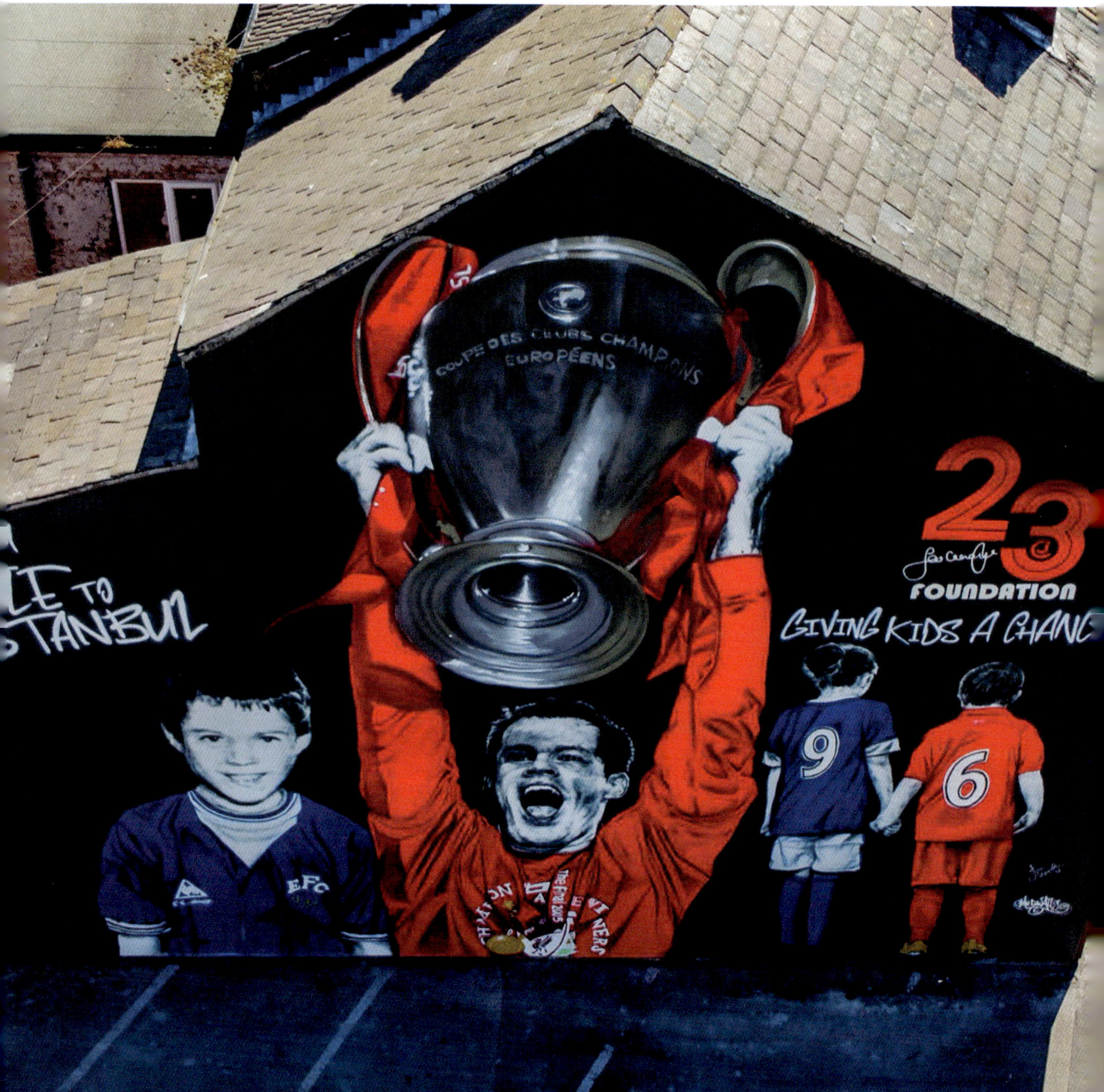

Carra called it "big and bold" and "a big thank-you to the 23 Foundation for all of the work they have done, specifically throughout the pandemic. It's a team effort, there are a lot of people involved and you couldn't run a charity or a foundation with just one person.

"It's been tough for people around here. Bootle is a really tough upbringing for anyone. I wouldn't change it for the world – I was exactly the same and I love it to bits – but it's not easy for families and kids especially.

"It's great to see all the kids out here in their kits this afternoon and we try and help them as much as we possibly can, certainly around here and in other parts of Merseyside. But if we can do something in Bootle that's what we like to do.

"I am very lucky and this is a very proud day for me and my family."

During the pandemic the 23 Foundation provided over 10,000 meals for families and supported local schools with tablets and equipment to help with learning. It's also supplied defibrillators and a new 4G pitch for the community.

More recently Jamie took a tour of Bootle with comedian and Reds fan John Bishop, in a show presented by club partners Quorn ahead of the Anfield derby of February 2023. The pair met people who work at local foodbanks before visiting the mural.

"When you've got a mural on a wall, that must give you a sense of belonging and pride?" asked Bishop.

"It does and it was nice that it was different, not just a Liverpool thing – it had to reflect where I was as a kid," replied Carra. "I don't think it would have lasted two minutes if it was just a Liverpool one!"

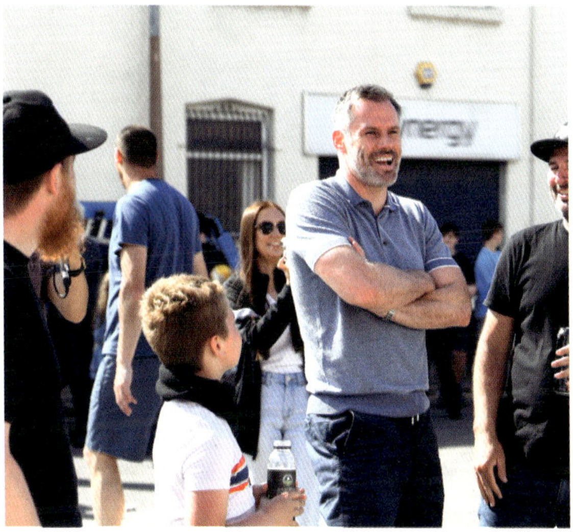

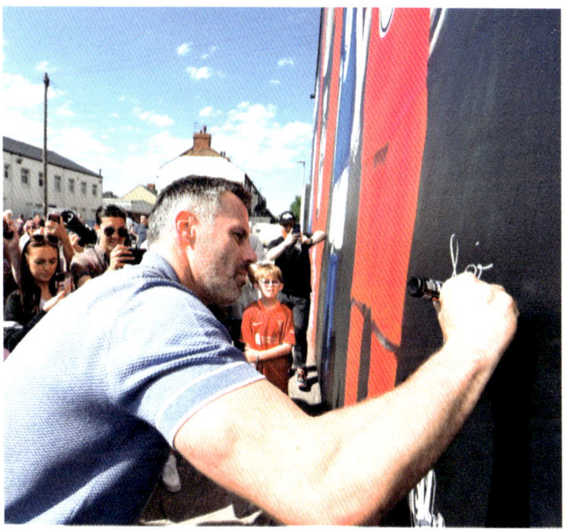

Never

Wa

lk Alone

AN LFC ART MISCELLANY

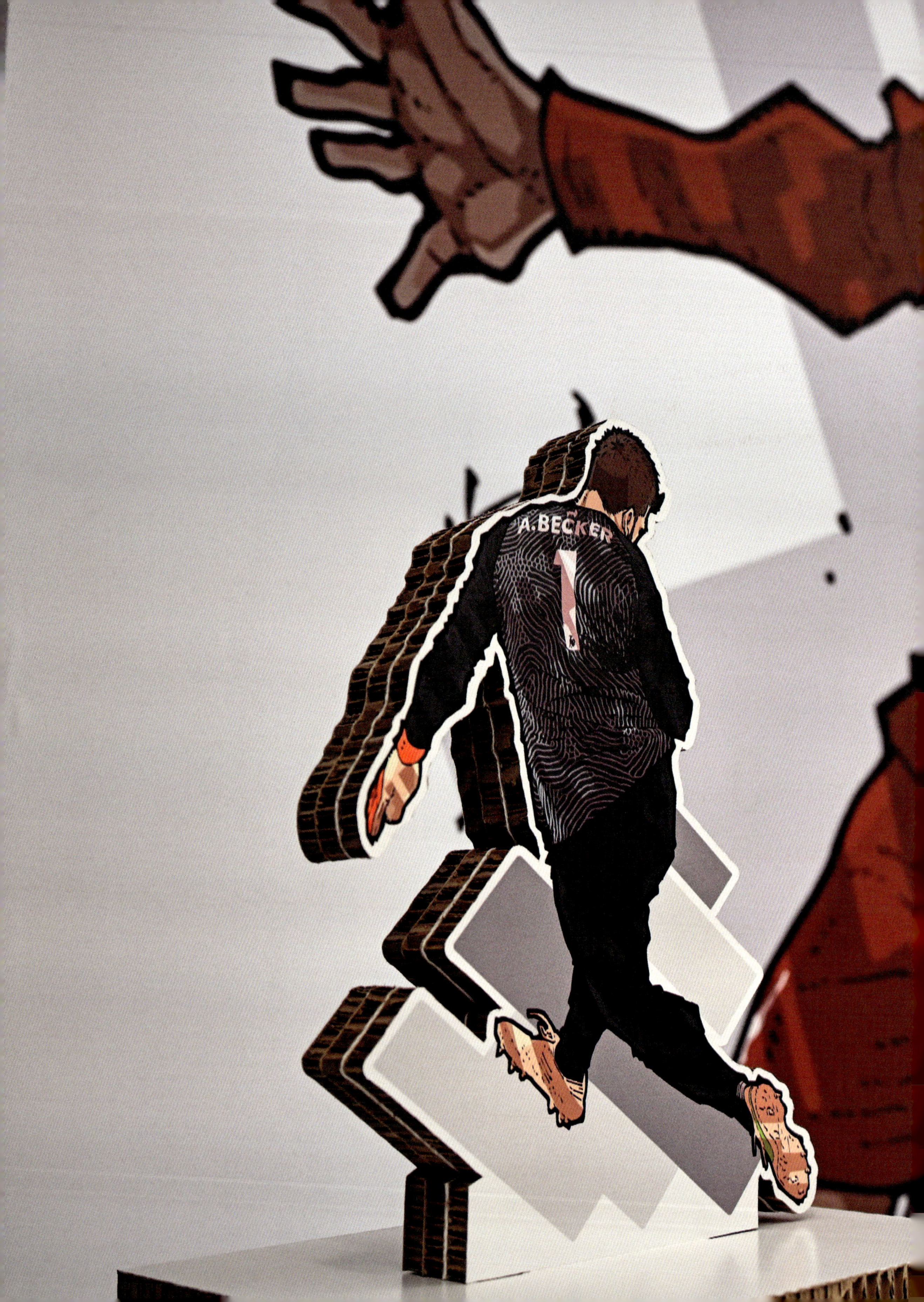
A.BECKER
1

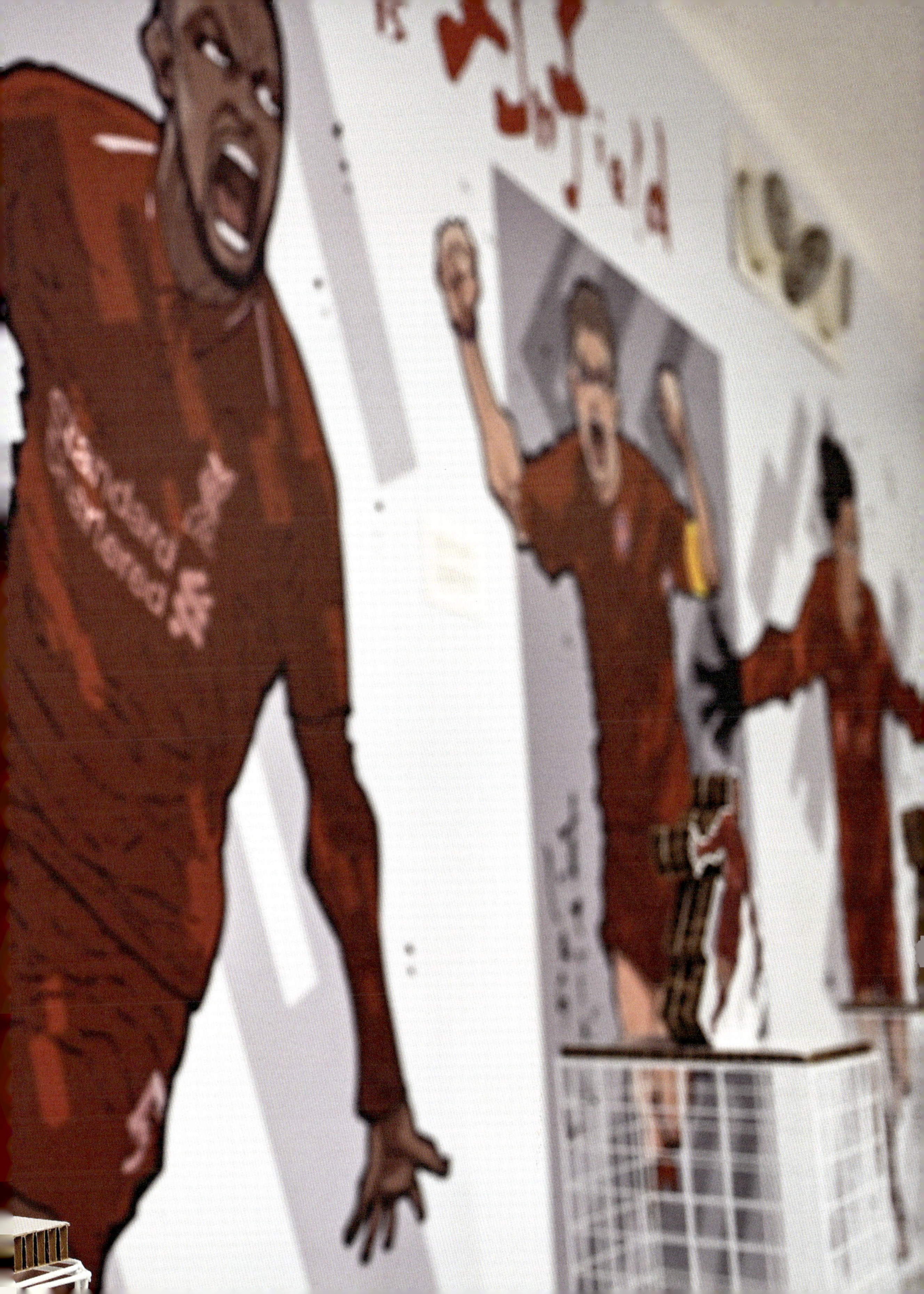

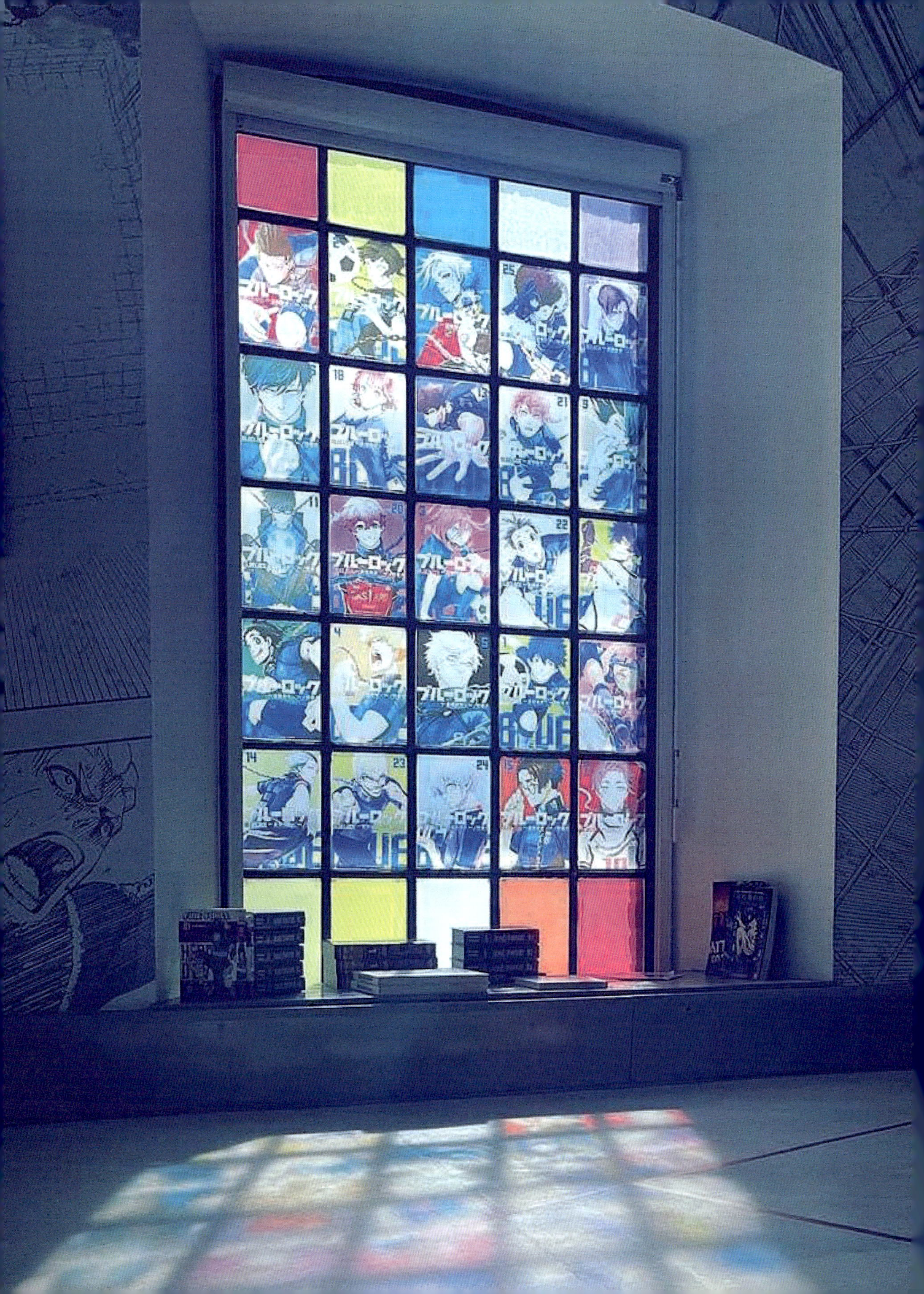

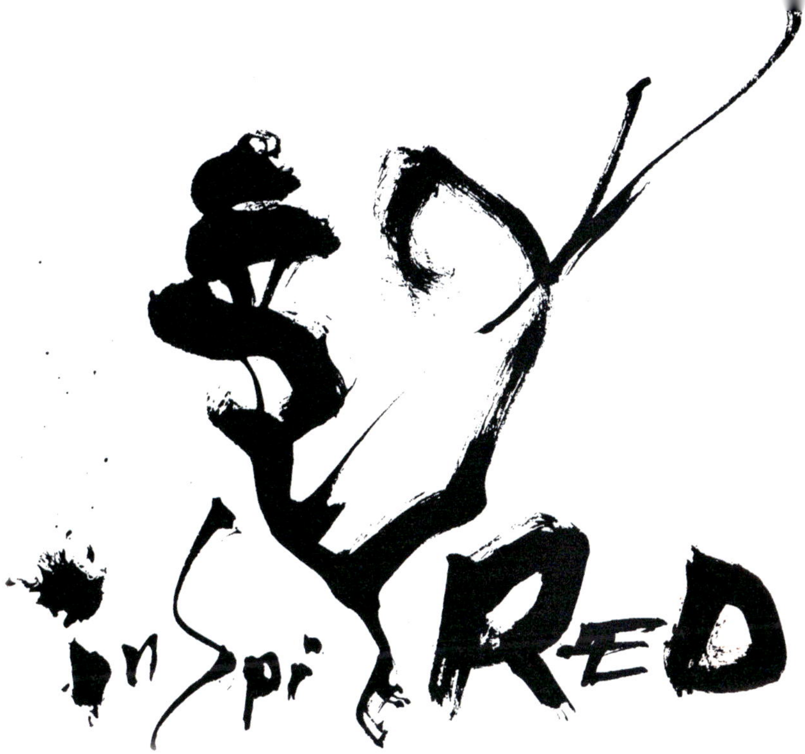

Made in Japan

A club and city transformed by the world's greatest comic-book artists

LFC manga – it had to happen some time! A selection of just such artwork took pride of place at the city's Tate Liverpool galleries in July 2023 for local schoolchildren and the public to view and enjoy.

The InspiRED art display, which brought together the club's official charity LFC Foundation and its publishing partner Kodansha, focused on the theme of 'Inspire Impossible Stories' – echoing Kodansha's belief that stories can change people's lives and introduce new worlds.

The display featured a collection of pieces from cityscapes and iconic buildings to Jürgen Klopp and his players, designed by an array of talented Japanese artists. Artwork designed by local youngsters participating in the exhibition was also on display.

Alongside the pieces, which were created and compiled throughout Liverpool FC's three-year partnership with Kodansha, children from five local schools and young people from LFC Foundation's mental health and employability programmes took part in a range of fun and interactive workshops.

Kodansha is Japan's largest publisher and produces not just manga but novels, magazines and children's books. It works collaboratively with LFC Foundation to support children's literacy and inspire creativity to show that with determination anyone can achieve the impossible.

This includes donating art-and-craft material and delivering creative drawing workshops in local schools, as well as launching the LFC Foundation Creative Works programme which inspires young people from challenging backgrounds to achieve careers in the creative industry.

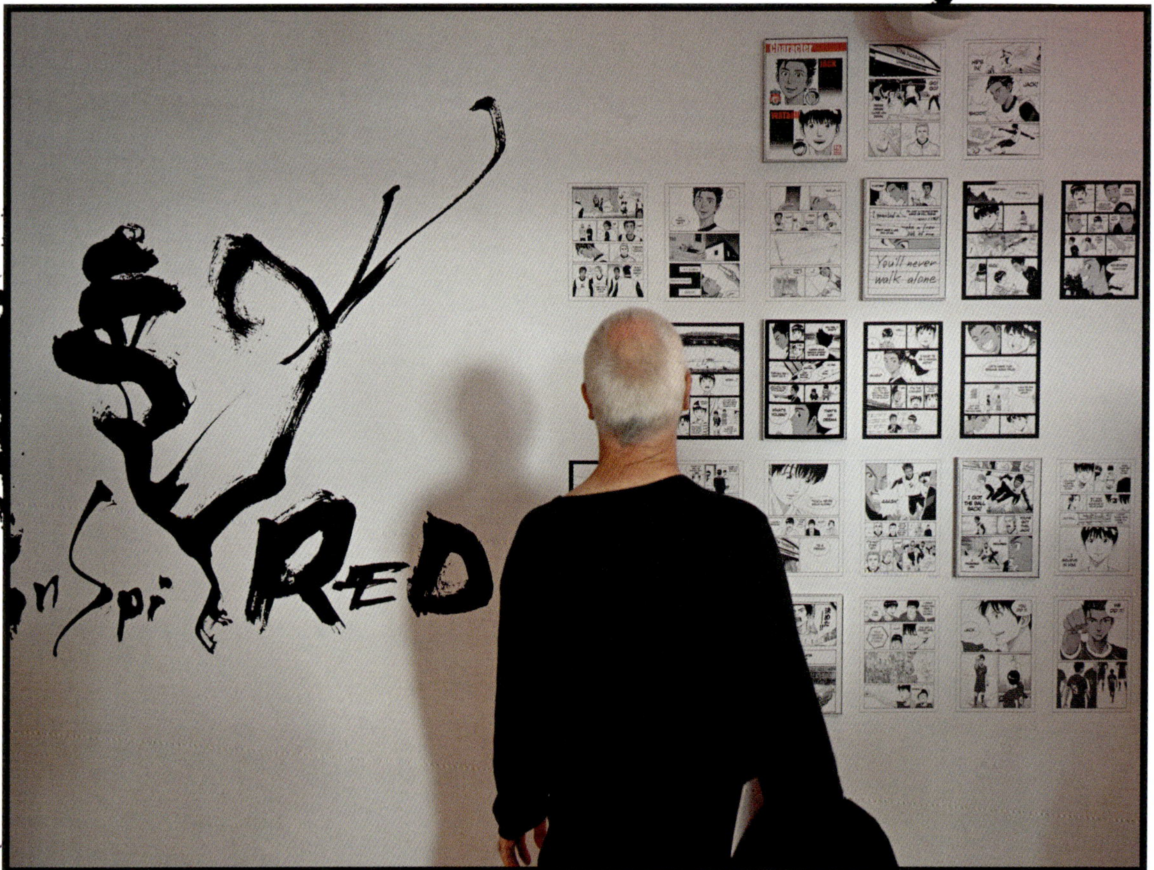
You'll never walk alone

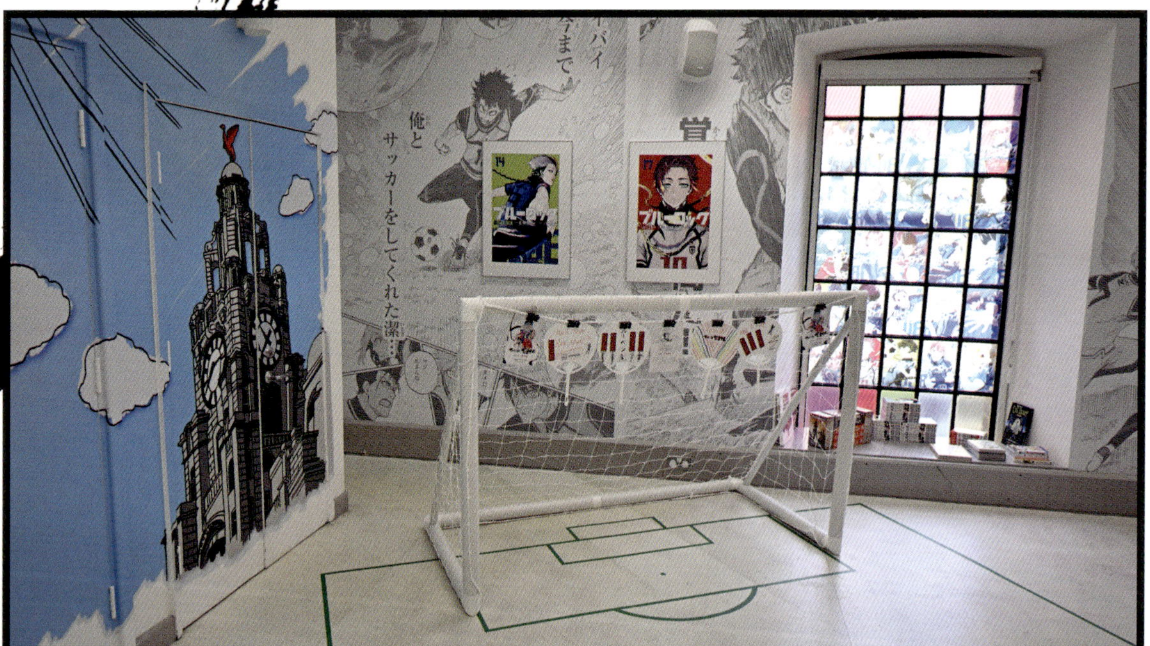
俺と
サッカーをしてくれた潔…

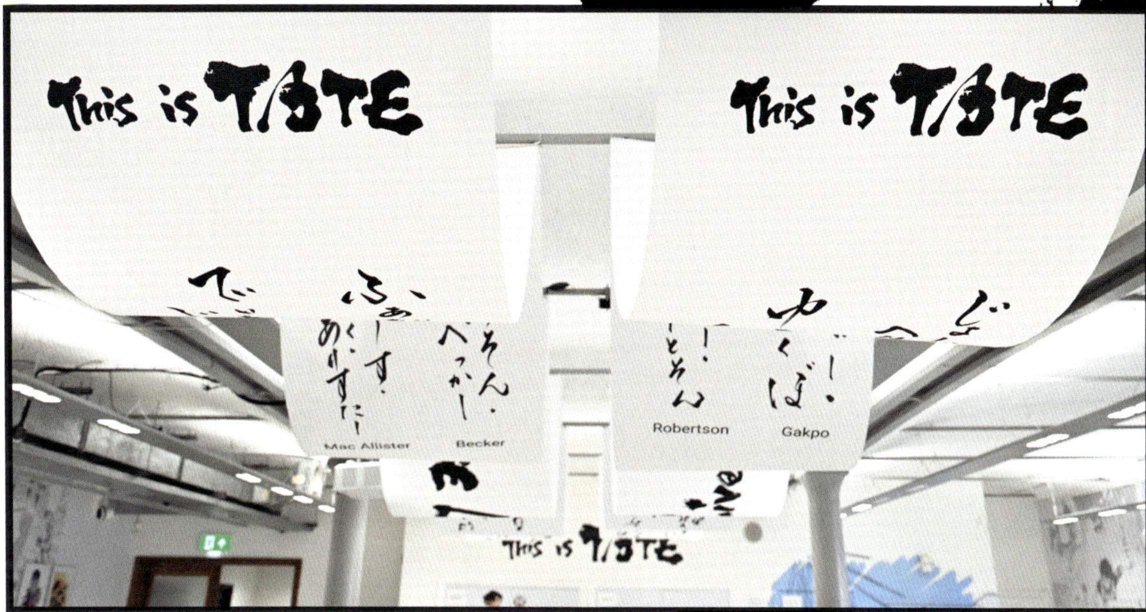
This is TATE
This is TATE
Mac Allister
Becker
Robertson
Gakpo
This is TATE

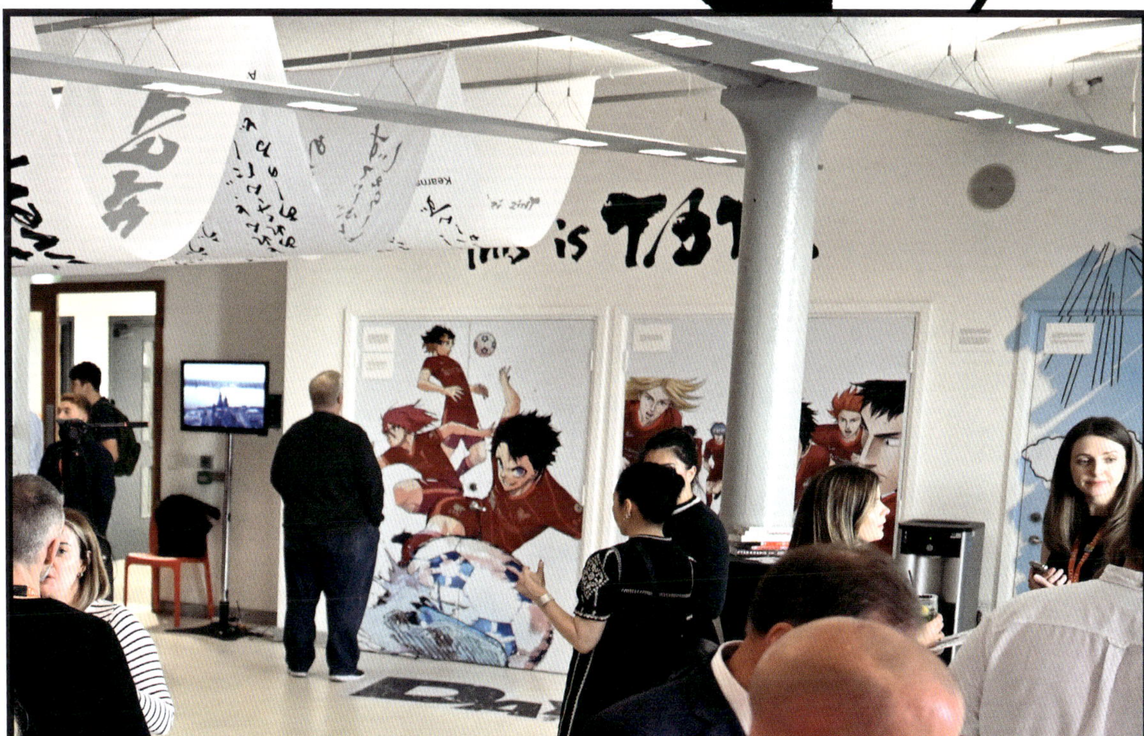
This is TATE

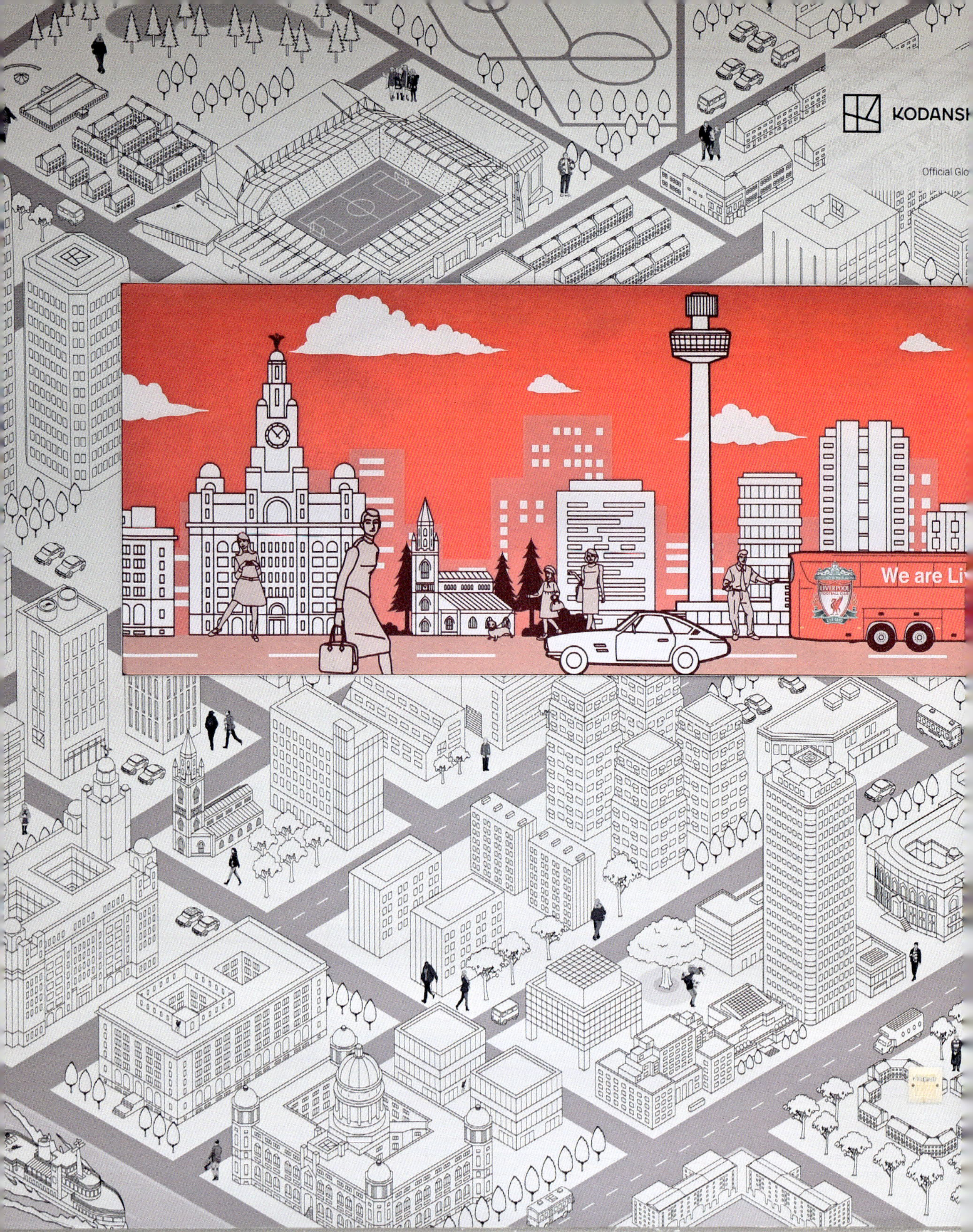
KODANSH
Official Glo
We are Li
LIVERPOOL

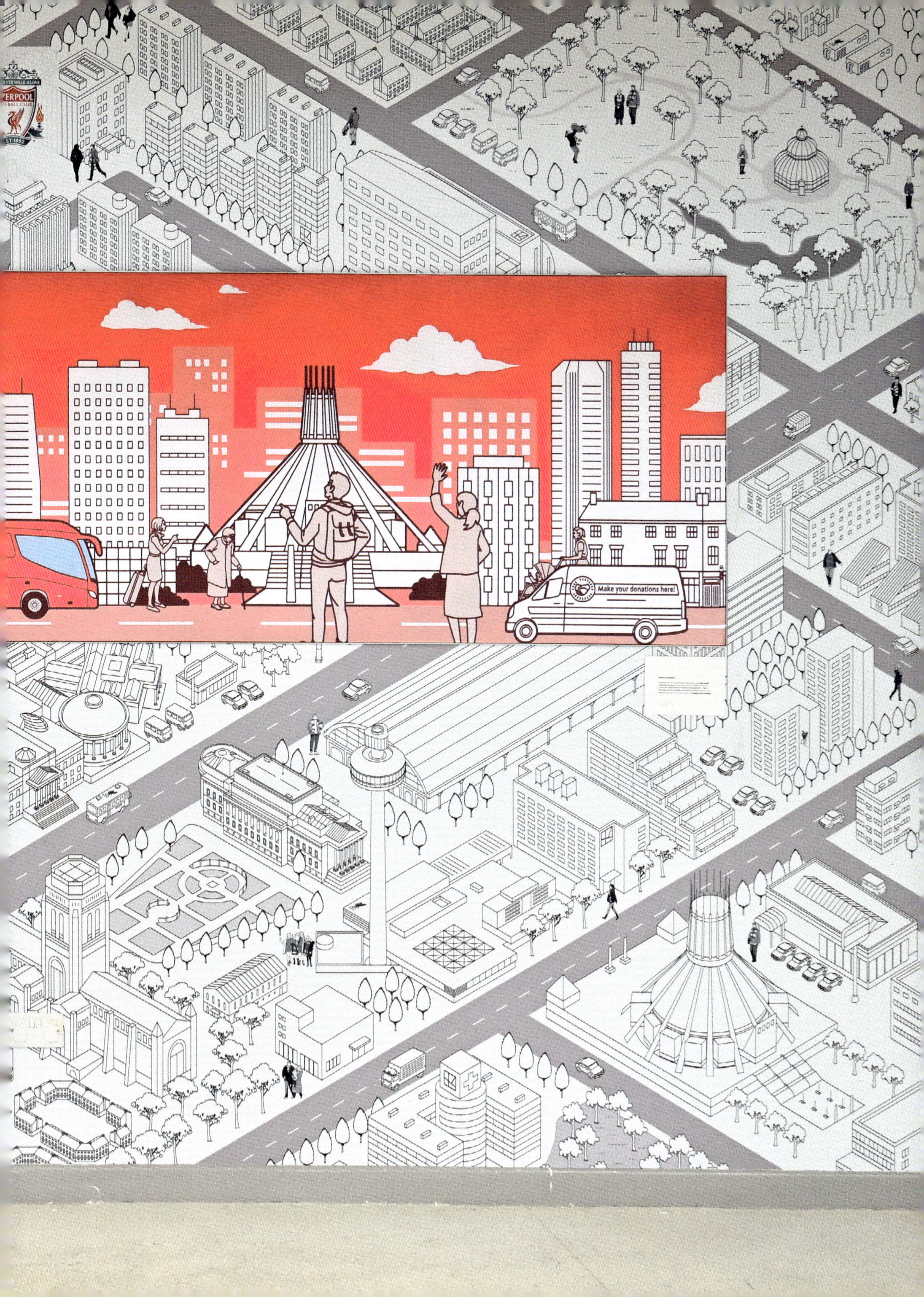
Make your donations here!

"A magical room"

Of all the celebrations to mark Liverpool Football Club's 125th anniversary in season 2016/17, one in particular stood out: the commissioning of a unique artwork which distils the past, present and future of LFC: the Dream Scene.

International sports artist Jamie Cooper created the stunning, three-metre oil-on-canvas which brings together 19 of Liverpool FC's greatest servants and one lucky young competition winner in one magical moment in time. It also offers keen-eyed fans a number of subtle nods to other key figures and events in the club's story.

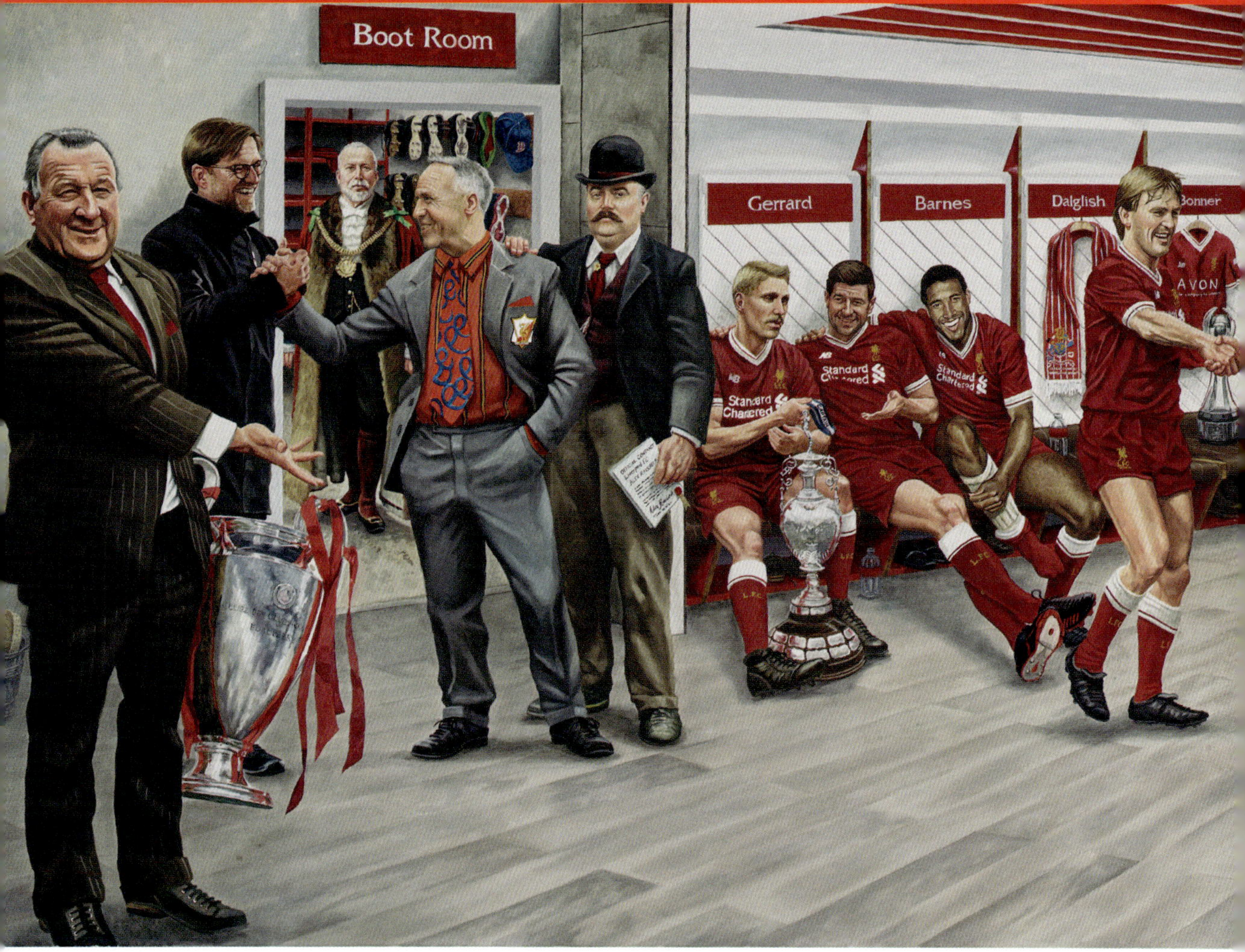

Jamie, an ex-professional footballer from Australia, called it "a great honour to have been entrusted with this challenge and responsibility, one I take very seriously. A club like Liverpool has meaning beyond the football field. It's a family that extends beyond those white lines."

Since retiring from the playing game he spent two decades honing this skill – "creating images for sporting clubs in the US, Australia and now Europe, where players from several generations are brought together into a 'Dream Scene'.

He continued: "I painstakingly piece together hundreds of images from different times to create a believable scene where these legends live and breathe together. They interact in a moment that is surely every fan's dream-come-true."

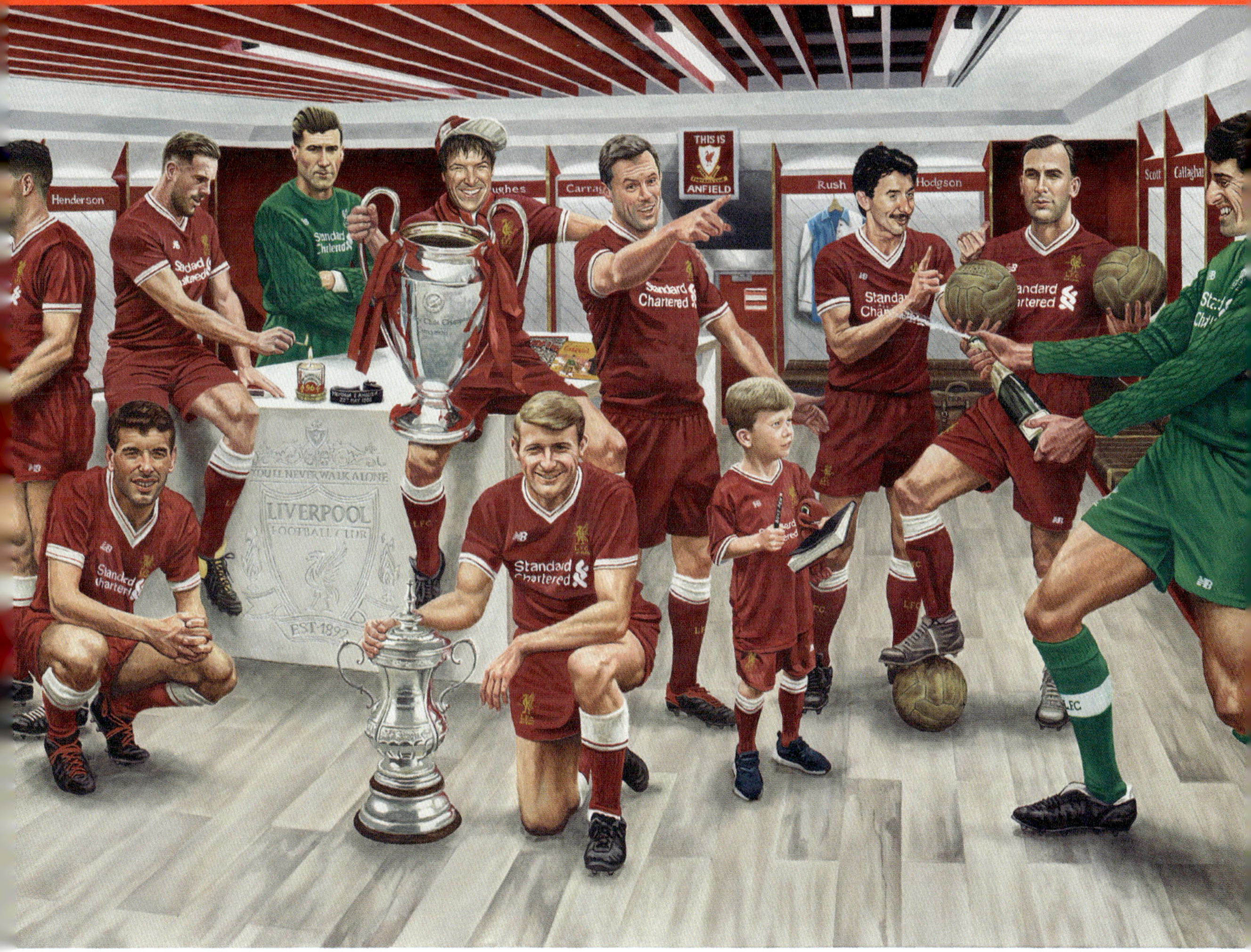

Jamie's challenge is "to tell a story, to imagine what these characters would have said to each other; what tales they would've told and what personalities would've been drawn together in this impossible gathering.

"As fans, wouldn't we love to walk among them, to mingle with them as they celebrate playing the greatest game of all?"

The Dream Scene unveiling took place in November 2017 at the club store at Anfield – where the work remains on display today (with a half-size version in the Main Stand Boardroom) – and was attended by Reds legends John Barnes, Ian Callaghan and Roger Hunt as well as representatives of the Shankly, Paisley and Raisbeck families.

Special guests, invited through the Red Neighbours programme, included 95-year-old 'Pure LFC' kit-launch star Charlie Gallagher and members of local charity the League of Welldoers. Young fan Joseph Thurston, who won a competition to appear in the Dream Scene, helped reveal the image.

A few days later, the Dream Scene was on the front cover of a special gatefold edition of the matchday programme, for Liverpool's home fixture against Southampton in the Premier League.

Jamie told the assembled guests at the launch: "Come with me and imagine, if you will, to a very special gathering inside the dressing-room in the new Main Stand. Founding father John Houlding has called together some of the greatest personalities from across our 125-year history.

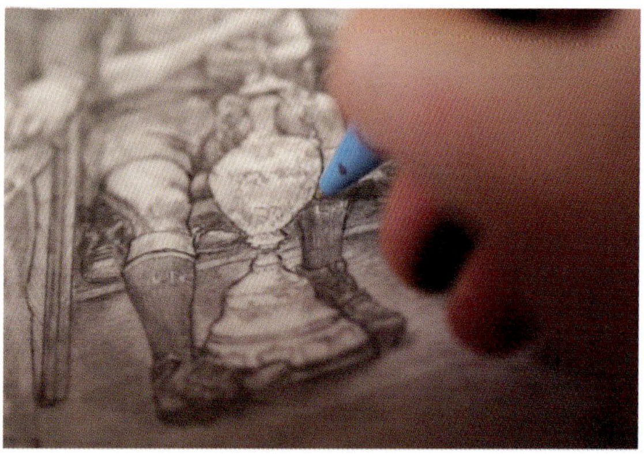

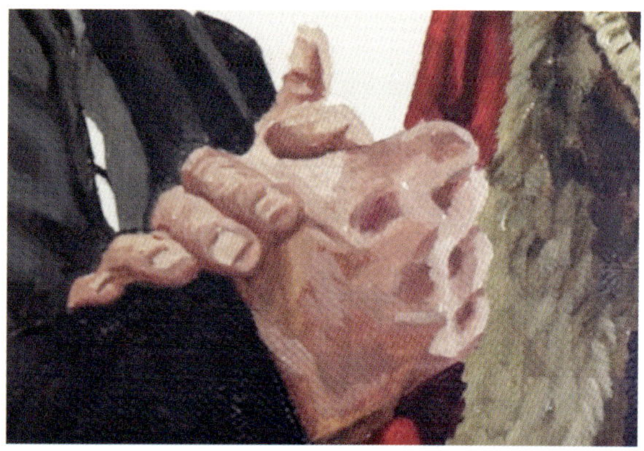

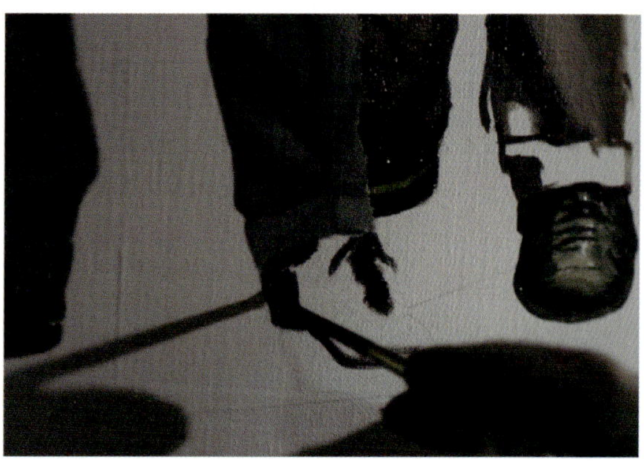

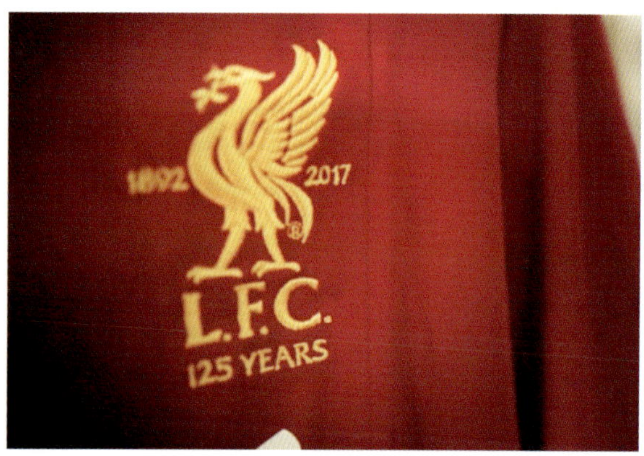

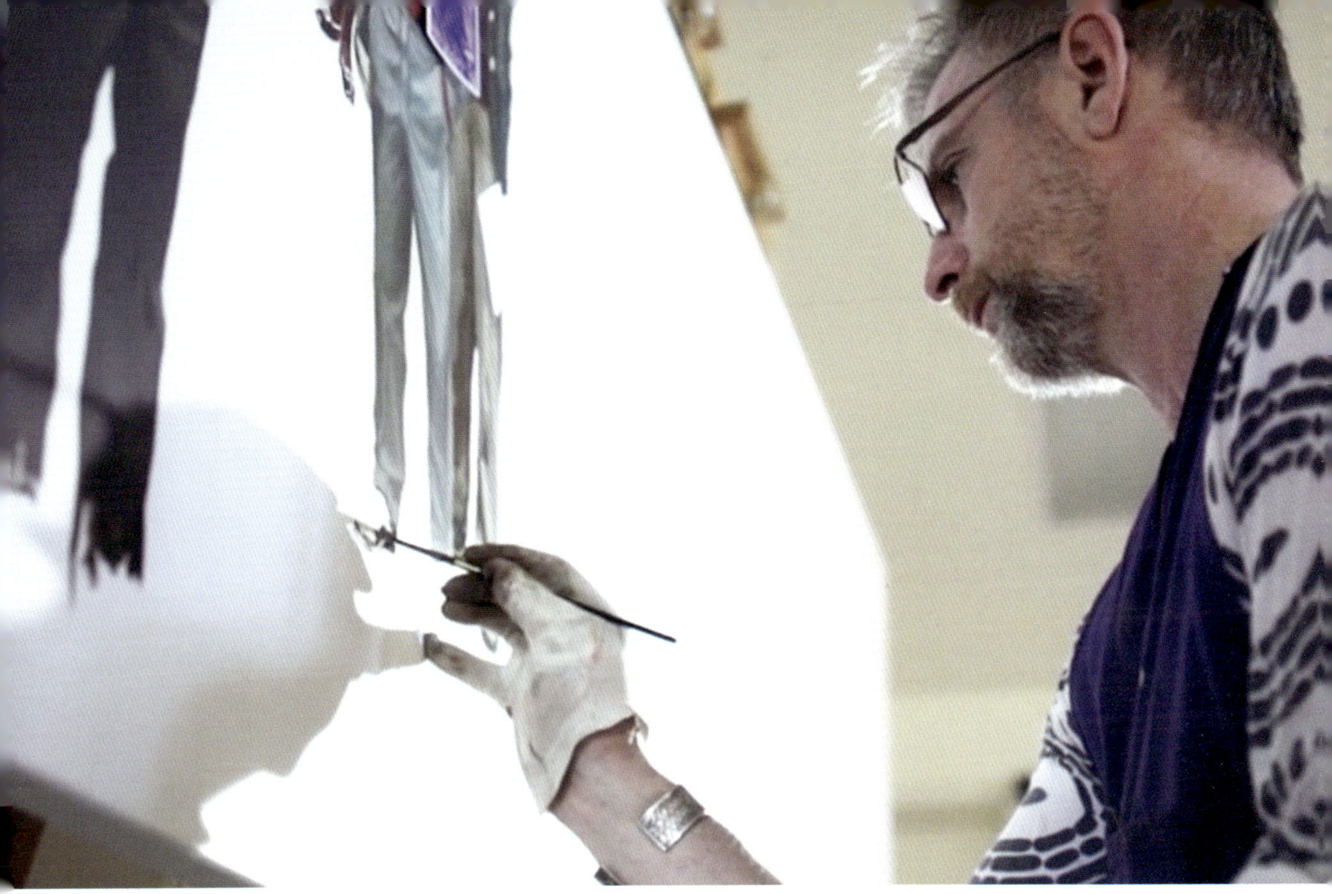

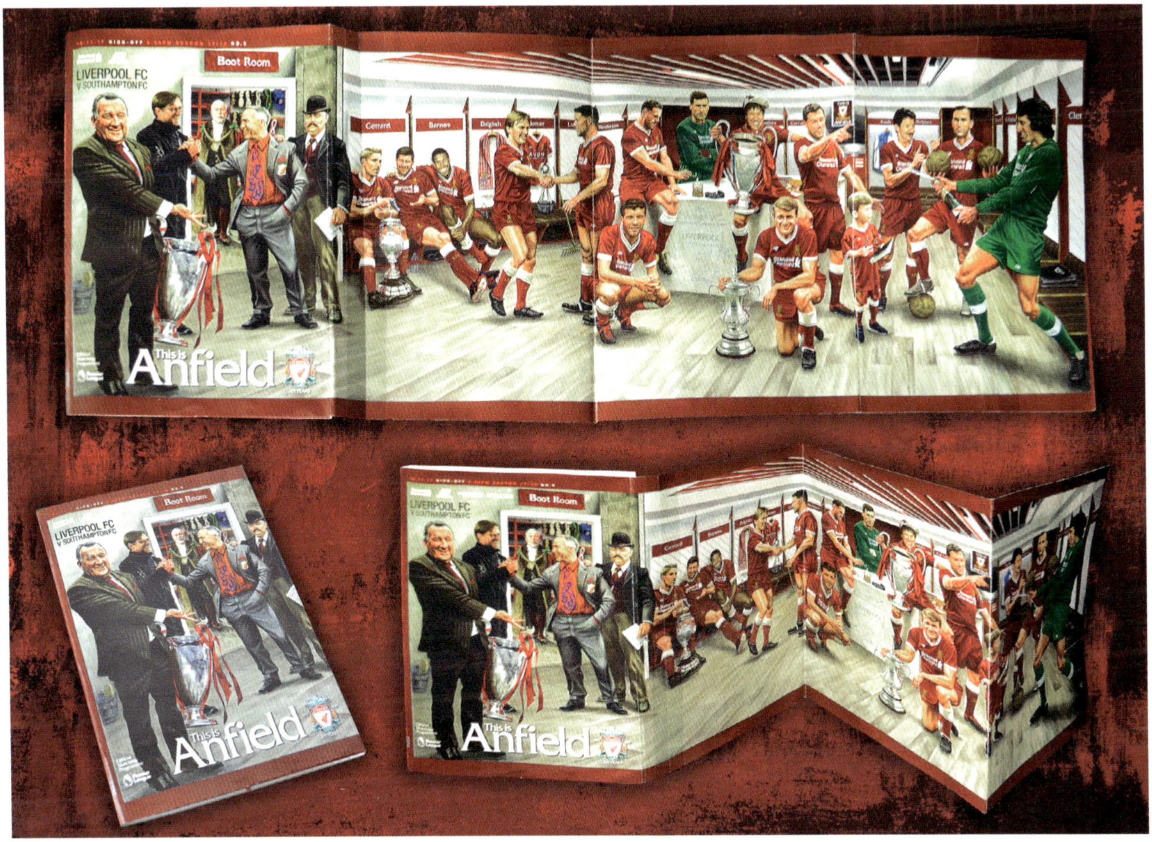
Boot Room
LIVERPOOL FC
V SOUTHAMPTON FC
Gerrard
Barnes
Dalglish
This is
Anfield

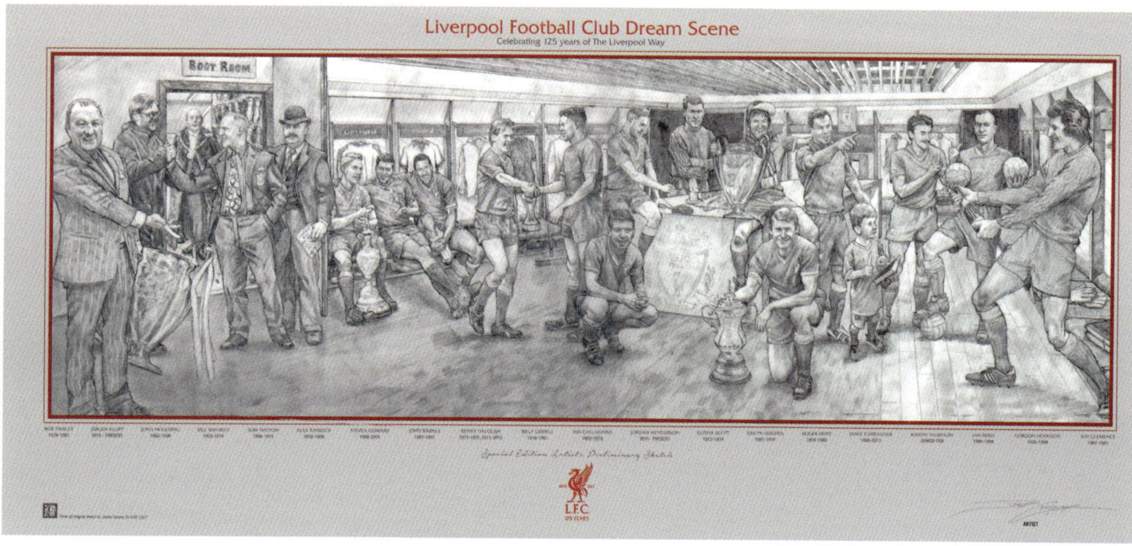
Liverpool Football Club Dream Scene
Celebrating 125 years of The Liverpool Way
Boot Room
LFC
125 YEARS

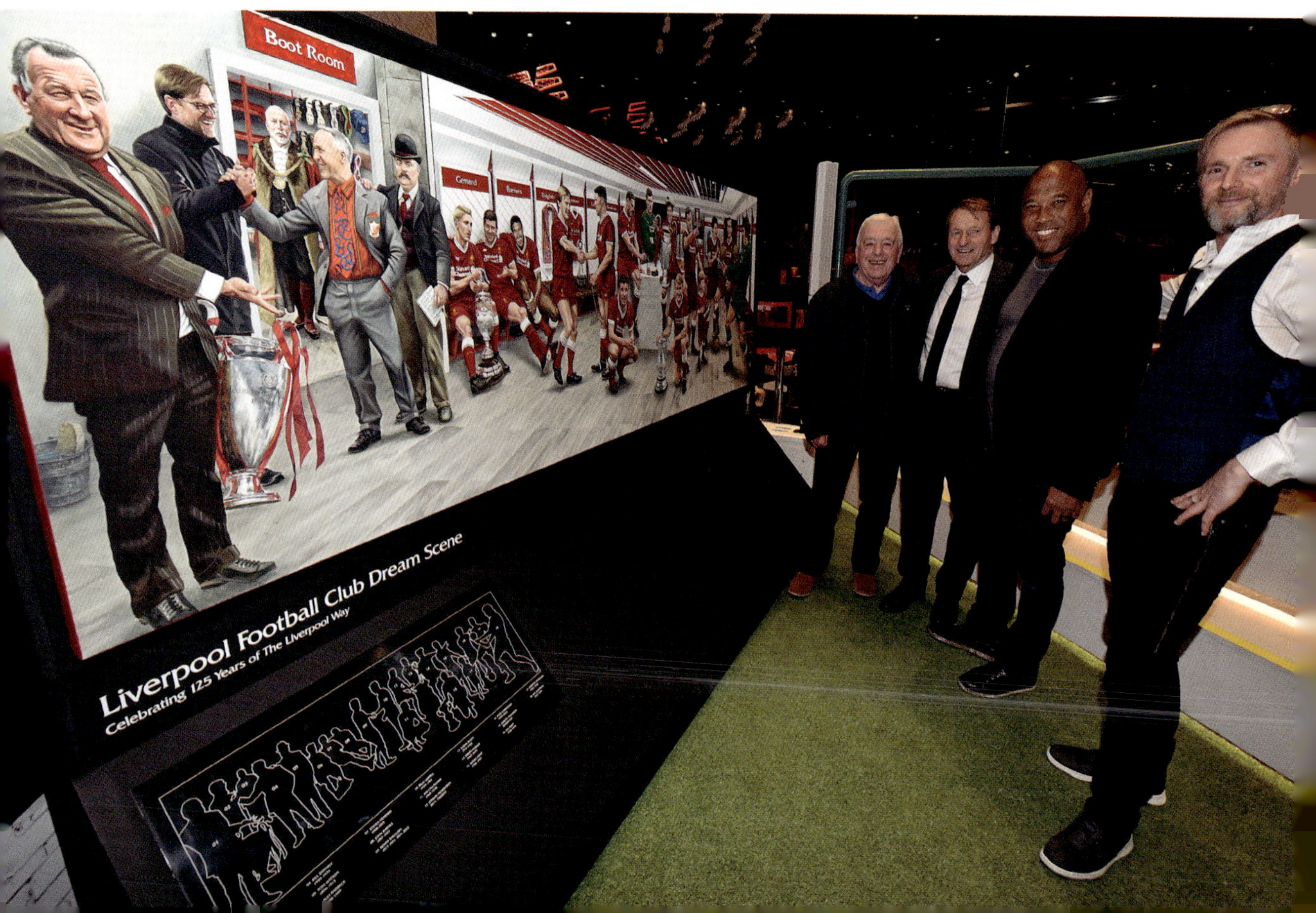
Boot Room
Gerrard
Liverpool Football Club Dream Scene
Celebrating 125 Years of The Liverpool Way

"We can see the changing personal appearance of the players over time: in hairstyles, the boots worn and even how they wear the 125th anniversary kit as they gather in the Reds' inner sanctum. Some have also brought along objects deep with meaning. This is now a magical room adorned with trophies and cultural references from the club's proud history.

"Imagine LFC legends from across the ages, plus the current manager and captain, sharing their memories as the veil is pulled back on the greatest scene a Kopite could hope for."

These are the legends who appear: Bob Paisley (at LFC from 1939 to 1983), Jürgen Klopp (2015-present), John Houlding (1892-96), Bill Shankly (1959-1974), Tom Watson (1896-1915), Alex Raisbeck (1898-1909), Steven Gerrard (1998-2015), John Barnes (1987-97), Kenny Dalglish (1977-91; 2011-12), Billy Liddell (1939-61), Jordan Henderson (2011-23), Elisha Scott (1912-34), Ian Callaghan (1960-78), Roger Hunt (1958-69), Emlyn Hughes (1967-79), Jamie Carragher (1996-2013), Joseph Thurston – mascot competition winner, Ian Rush (1980-87 and 1988-96), Gordon Hodgson (1925-36), and Ray Clemence (1967-81).

Also featured: Gemma Bonner's Liverpool Ladies 2017/18 shirt; the original blue-and-white Liverpool FC shirt; a Hillsborough candle and Heysel armband; an international supporters scarf; Kop Choir and Carousel records; Geoff Twentyman's scouting book; Ronnie Moran's bucket and sponge; a Boston Red Sox cap; groundsman Arthur Riley's commemorative 'golden rake'; and club secretary Peter Robinson's briefcase.

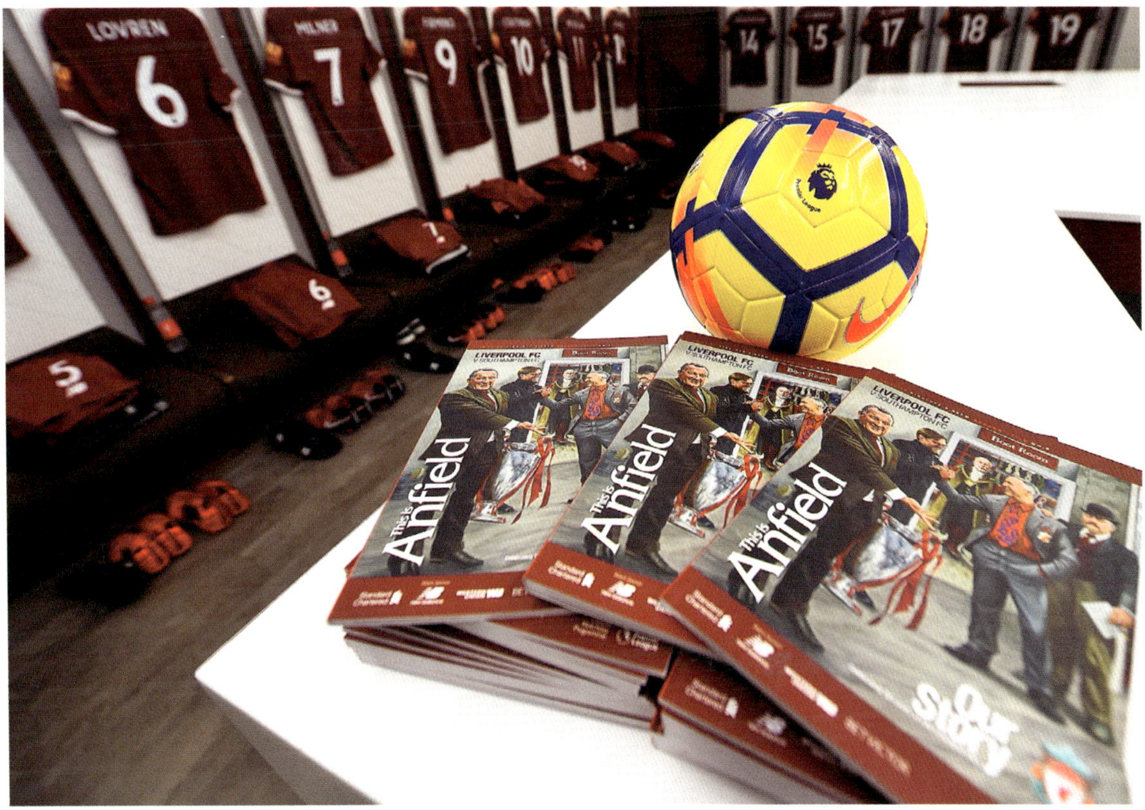

When it all began

Liverpool FC's first-ever match took place on Thursday 1 September 1892 – and 125 years later it was celebrated with a brilliant animated film running for one minute and 45 seconds and showcased on LFCTV.

The 1892 fixture was a friendly at Anfield, commencing at 5.30pm, against Rotherham Town, champions of the Midlands League. The home team, all Scotsmen, were wearing blue-and-white halved shirts, long blue shorts and blue socks – the same strip left behind by former tenants and reigning champions Everton.

Andrew Hannah, formerly Everton's captain, was the skipper. They won the toss, they had the wind at their backs, and club founder John Houlding ceremonially started the game himself.

No sooner had 'King John' done his turn in the centre-circle than Liverpool were one-up, the honour of scoring the first goal falling to John Miller. Two more goals followed in quick succession from Andrew Kelvin, breaking through the opposition backline, and Joe McQue, from a free-kick. By half-time it was 5-0, Tom Wyllie converting Kelvin's cross before Wyllie sent in a shot which beat Town keeper Arthur Wharton, the country's first black professional footballer.

With the wind now favouring them Rotherham made more of a fist of it after the interval and threatened home goalie Sydney Ross. But in the closing stages Liverpool scored two more – Miller, unmarked in the box, then Wyllie with an instinctive finish, and McQue smashing in off the crossbar – before the visitors netted a late consolation. Final score: seven-one to the 'Team of Macs'.

The following day's *Liverpool Mercury* felt "the eleven played well together and are sure to improve with more practice. Ross, in goal, had little to do, but in the few cases in which he had to handle, he showed great coolness and courage."

"The backs played well," it continued, "thoroughly understanding each other and showing great resource when pressed. The trio of halves could hardly be improved on, [Jim] McBride in particular playing a brilliant game. Forward the combination is sure to improve in time, but [Jock] Smith showed a slight tendency to keep the ball too long, much to the detriment of his comrades."

In two days' time Liverpool would play their first competitive match, at home

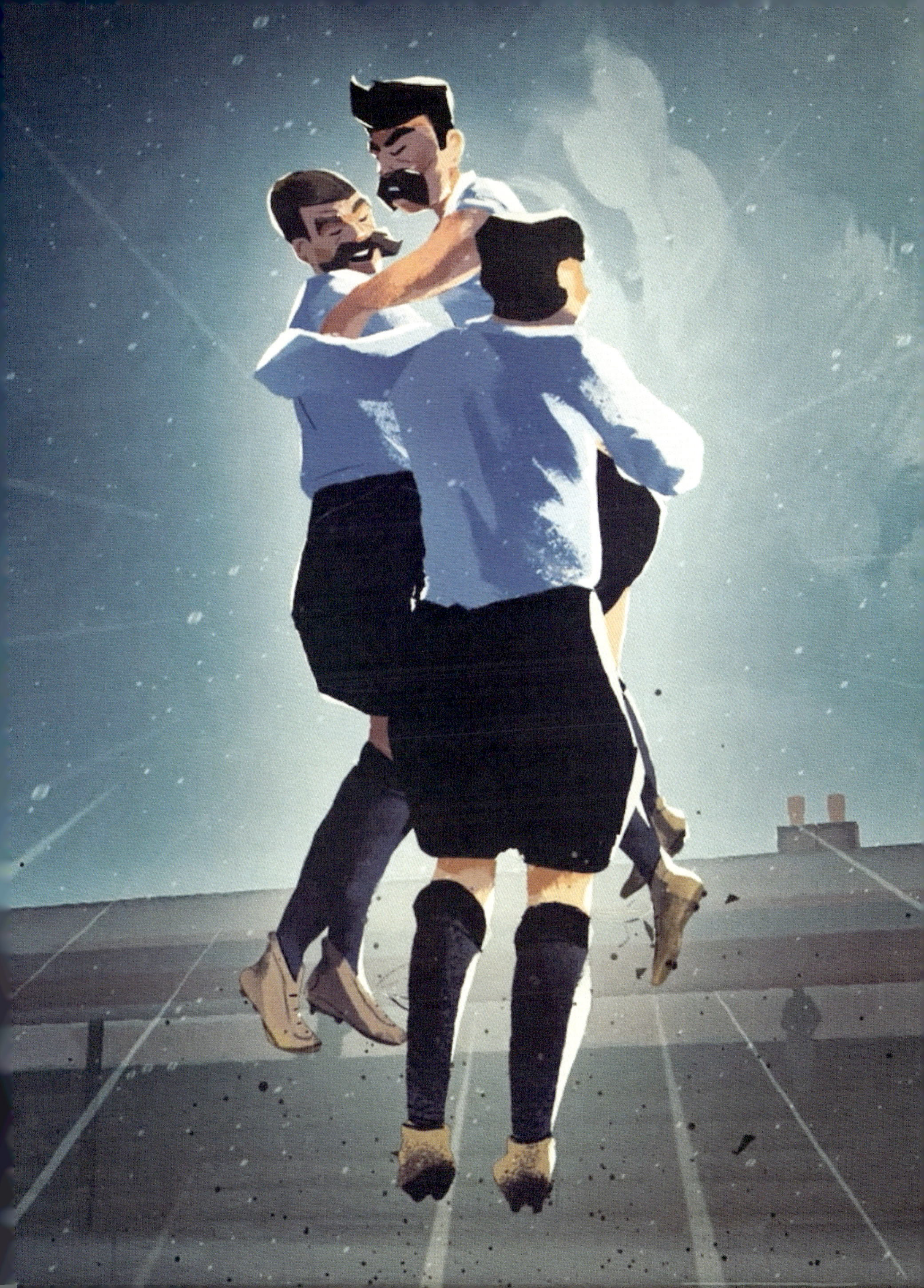

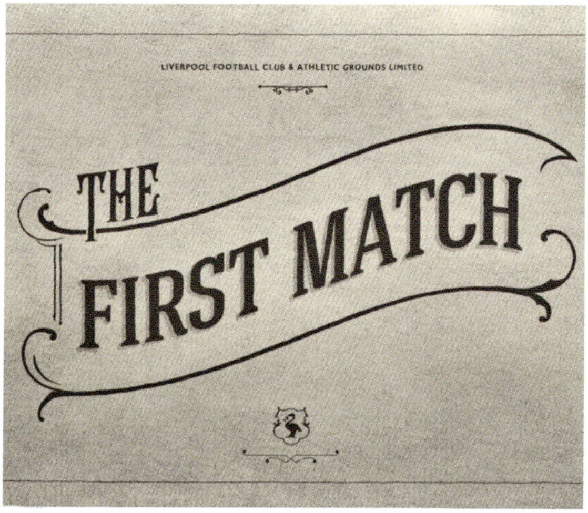
LIVERPOOL FOOTBALL CLUB & ATHLETIC GROUNDS LIMITED
THE FIRST MATCH

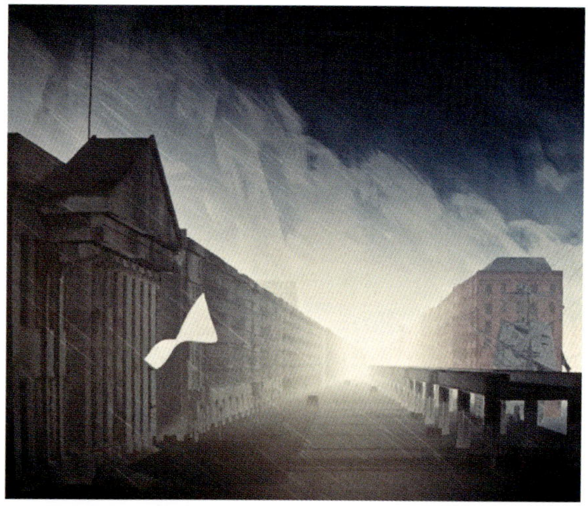

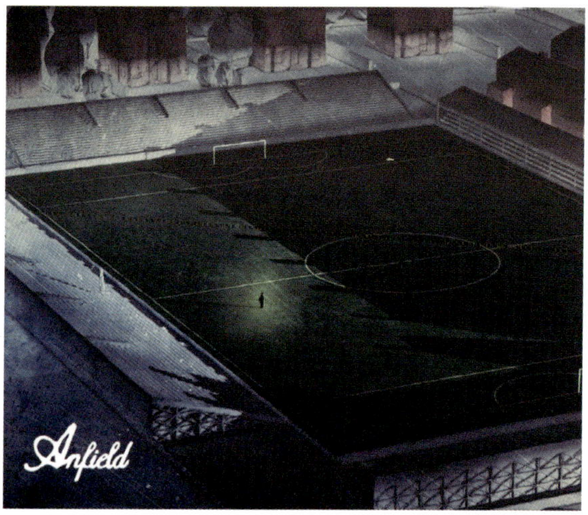
Anfield

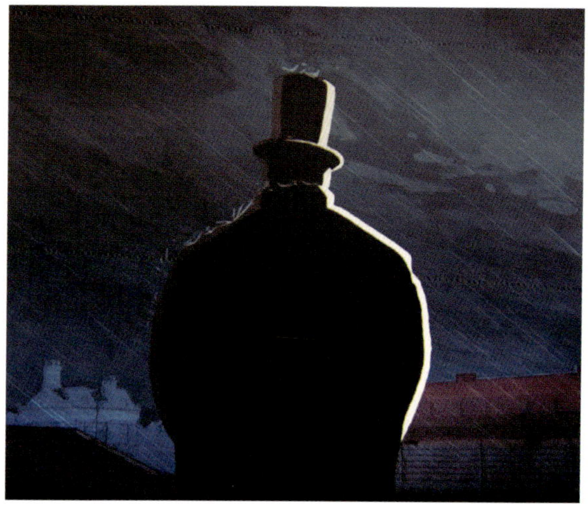

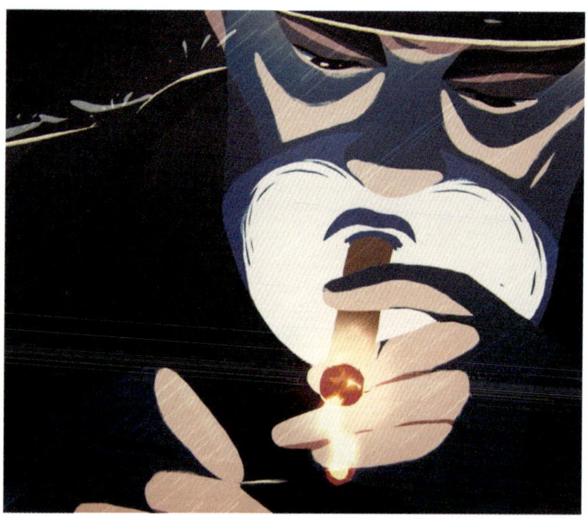

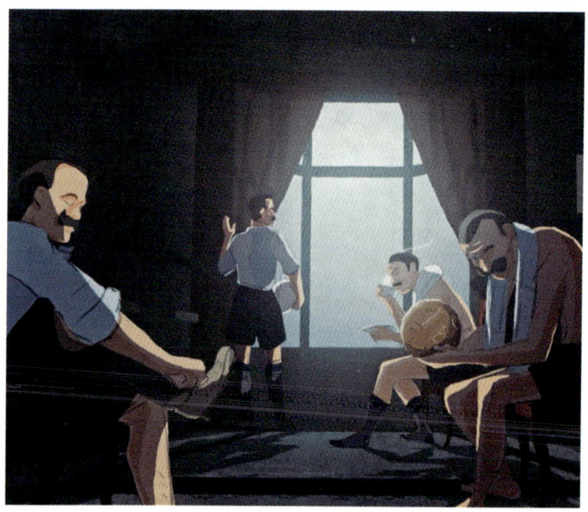

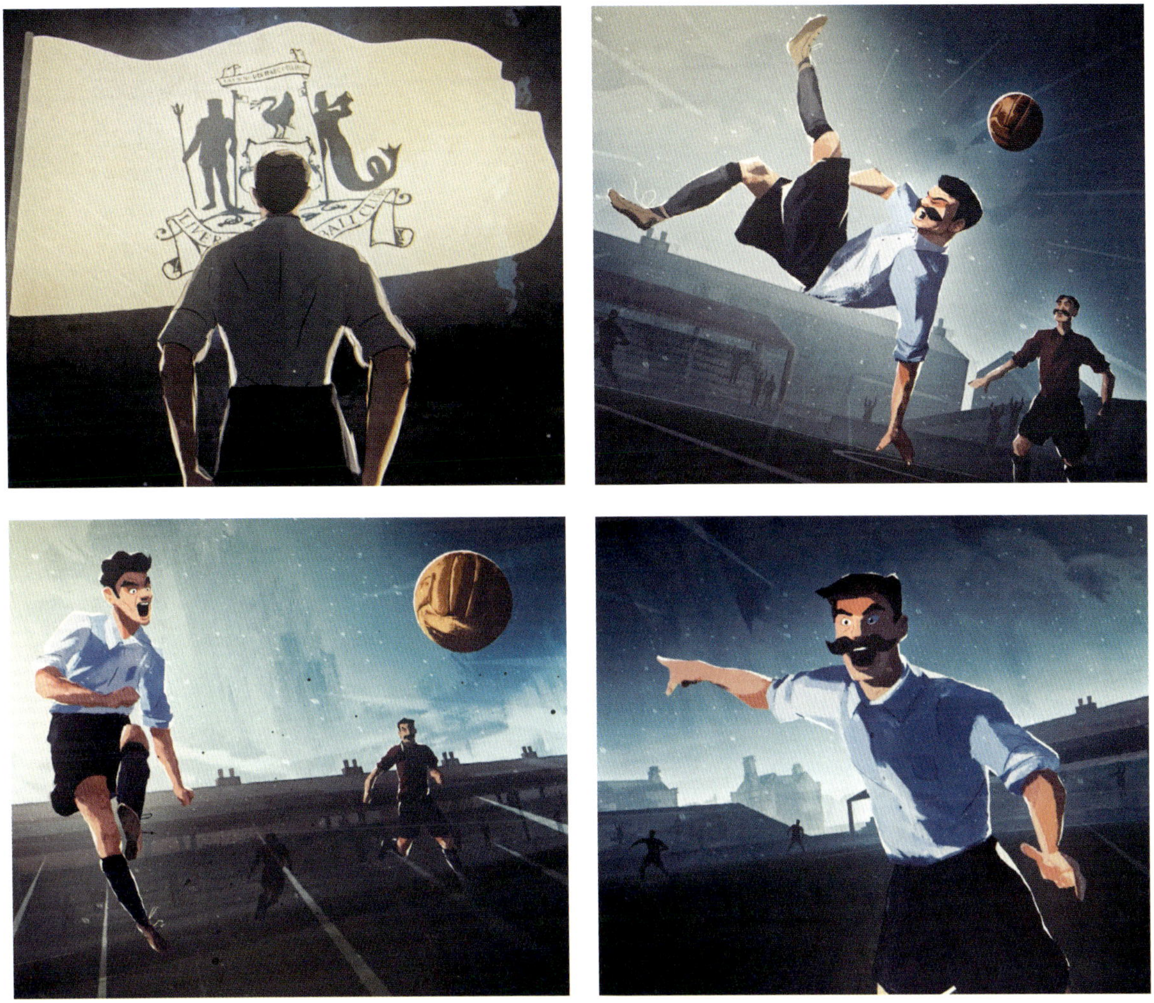

to Higher Walton in the Lancashire League, and they'd win eight-nil. A few weeks later, the new team in town were starting to cause a stir. "They have in their ranks some of the cleverest exponents of the Association code who will quite uphold the best traditions of the Anfield enclosure," noted *The Liverpool Review of Politics, Society, Literature and Art.*

"That the public are cottoning on to the prowess of Liverpool is shown in the fact that the gates at the matches are steadily increasing. The first fixture attracted a few hundred; last Saturday quite 6,000 people were present. Of course the Everton team were away and that may have had a beneficial influence for the Liverpudlians. But the fact remains that the team is growing in public favour."

Around the same time a flag was hoisted above Houlding's ground. It bore, as the *Field Sport* journal put it, "the liver, [which] proudly waves over the field of battle and seems to beam on its patrons with a hopeful smile."

The story of Liverpool Football Club had only just begun.

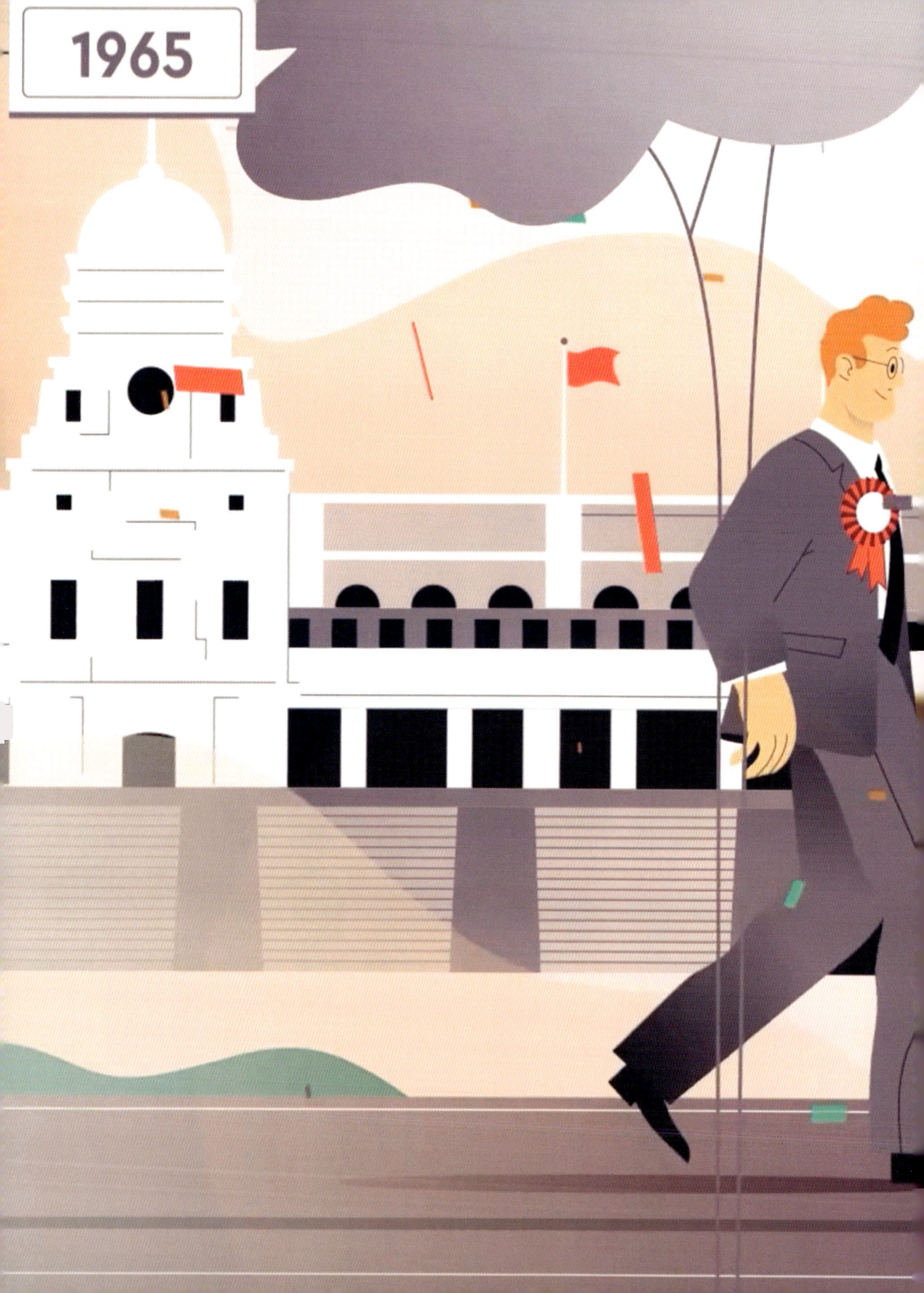
1965

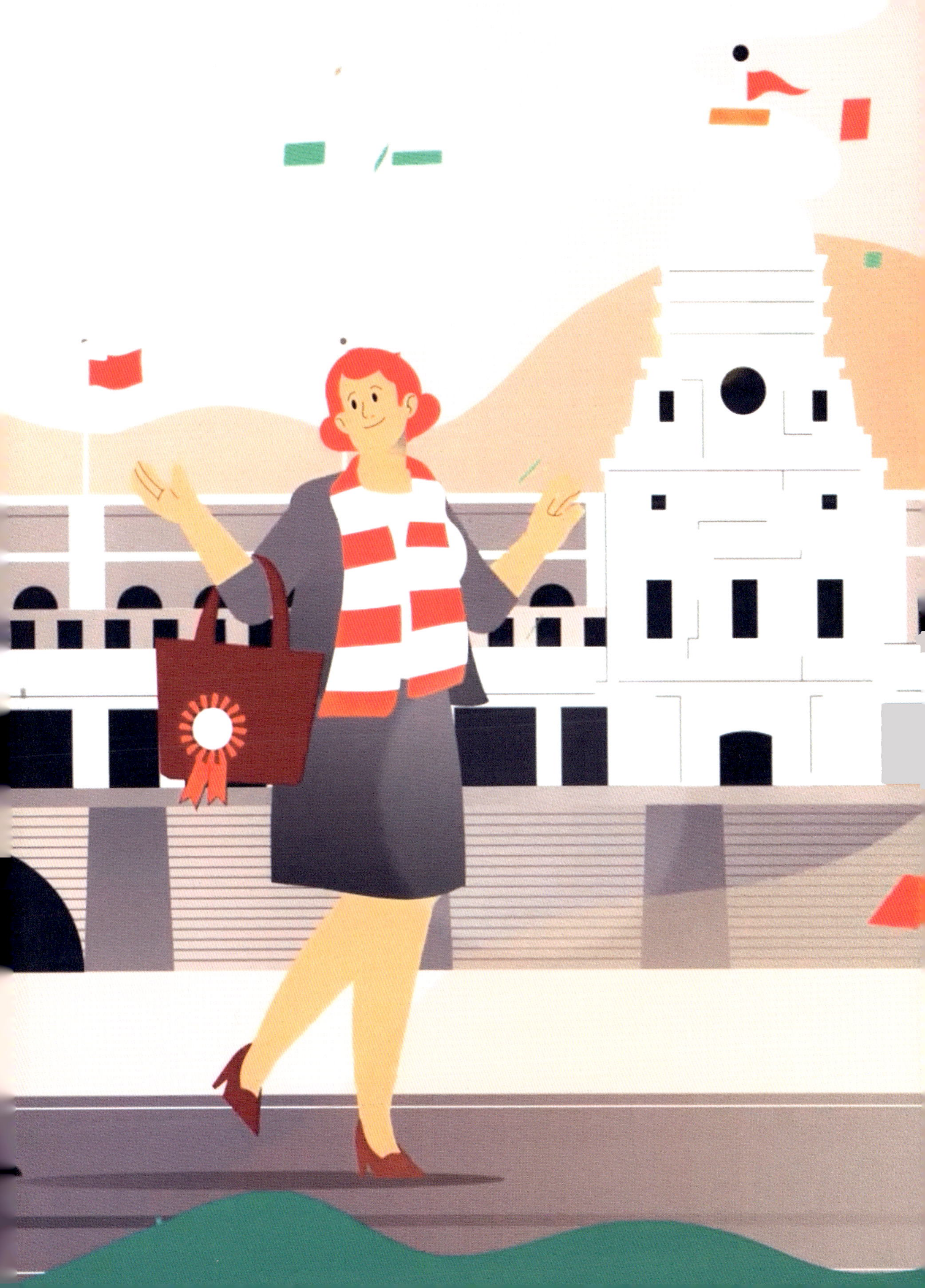

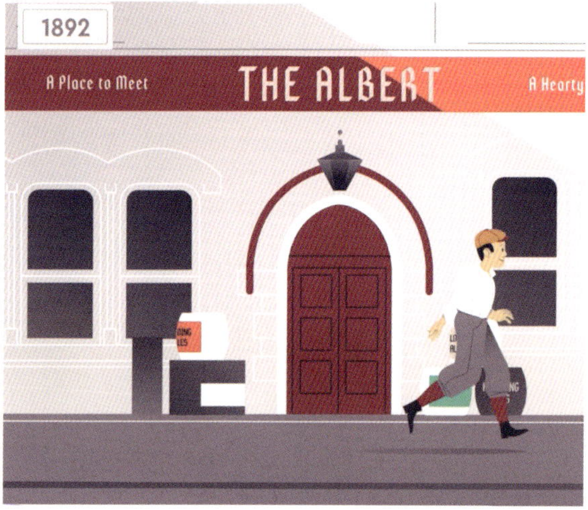
1892
A Place to Meet
THE ALBERT
A Hearty

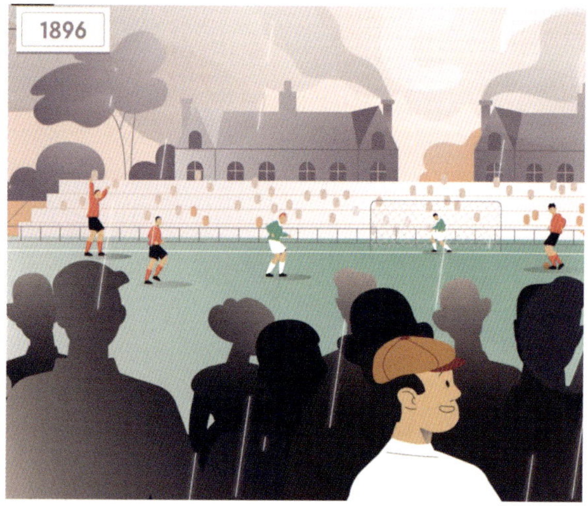
1896

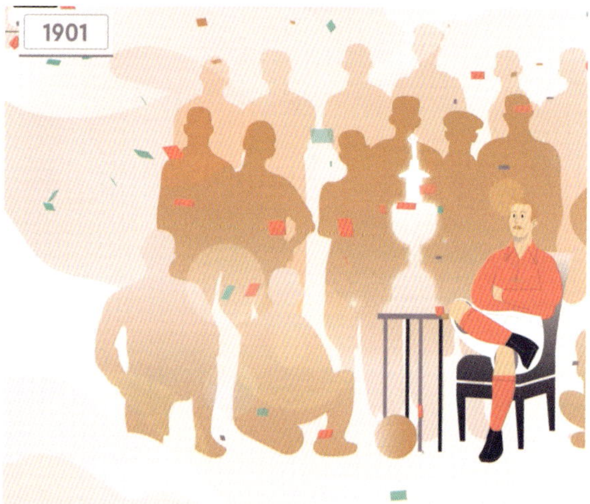
1901

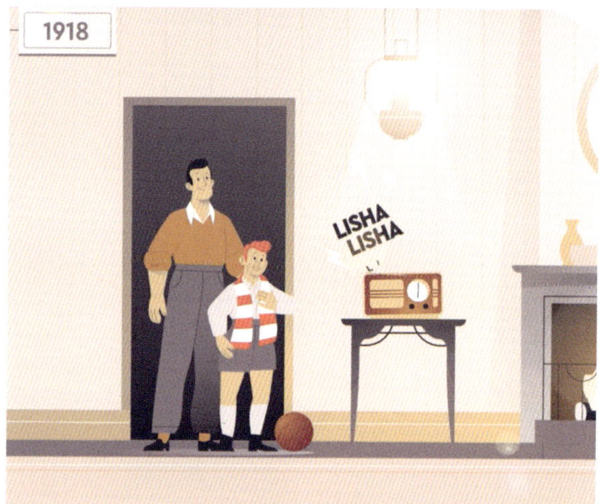
1918
LISHA
LISHA

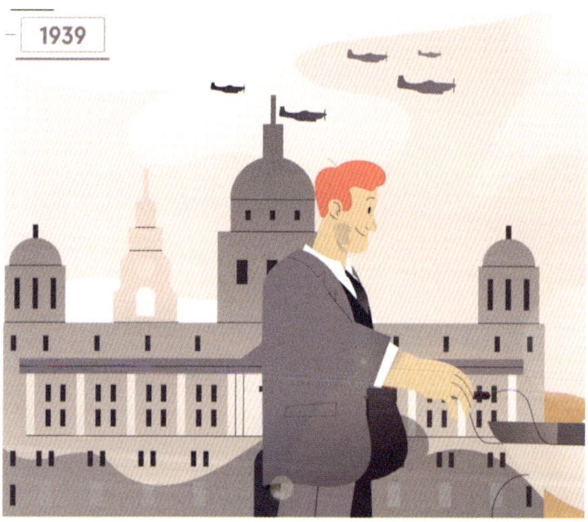
1939

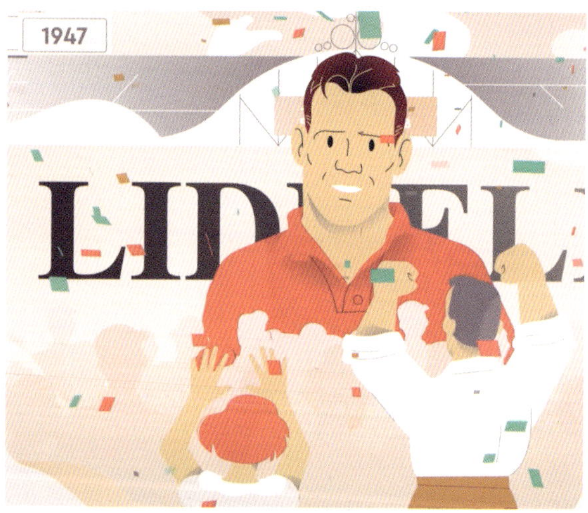
1947

Scouser Tommy

Another fabulous animation was created in 2022 to celebrate the club's 130th anniversary and it was narrated by a young Reds fan like this...

"A hundred-and-thirty years ago my great-great-great-grandad Tommy was there at Liverpool's first-ever game. We won 7-1 – not a bad start, eh?

"He was 17 when we won our first-ever league title. Alex Raisbeck was the captain, Tom Watson was the boss, and everyone's muzzies were off the charts! Liverpool won the league again in 1906 – that's when they built the Spion Kop. See that little fella there? That's my great-grandad Joe. He didn't half miss his dad when the War broke out.

"We were so good in the early Twenties – champions twice. When they stuck a roof on the Kop it stopped Tommy and Joe from getting drenched, but the trophies dried up.

'They say my great-grandma Lily was delivered by a Liver Bird, but when her dad Joe went off to war he never came back and they never got to go to the match together. So Grandad took her to the footie after the war. Guess who won the league the first season back? They had Stubbins and Balmer and the legendary Billy Liddell.

"My great-grandma Lily was mad on the Reds even though they were no good in the 1950s – she was crying when they went down. But get on this: she met my great-grandad Ted at an away game in the old Second Division.

"That's when Shanks came along – the great man with big ideas and a big booming voice, and the same year my grandad John was born.

"The Beatles were Scousers, they conquered the world and the people on the Kop sang their songs in suits and ties. But there was one Merseybeat tune which went more than the rest. Special, isn't it? And the players were special too: the Saint, Sir Roger, Big Ronnie, and the great Ian Callaghan.

"My great-nan and great-grandad went to Wembley in '65 to see us win the FA Cup for the first time. It took so long, people said we were cursed and that the Liver Birds would fly away if we did it.

"Shanks leaving was a bombshell, but Bob Paisley made us even better. And in Rome it was tears of joy as Emlyn lifted 'Ol' Big Ears' aloft. We had Hansen, Souness and Dalglish and we conquered all of Europe.

"Rome again. My grandad John went with his mates – they had trendy haircuts and the best clobber you could get your hands on. And in the lion's den Joe Fagan won us number four. My mum came along that same year and the Reds kept on winning and winning.

"But while there was unbelievable success, there was unbearable tragedy too – and those who were affected will always be in our hearts.

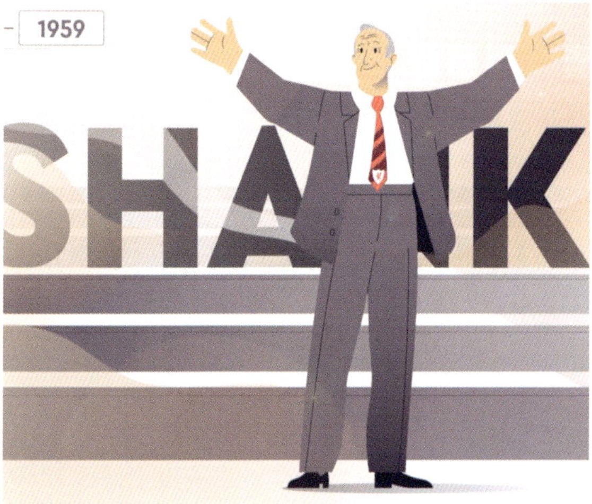
1959

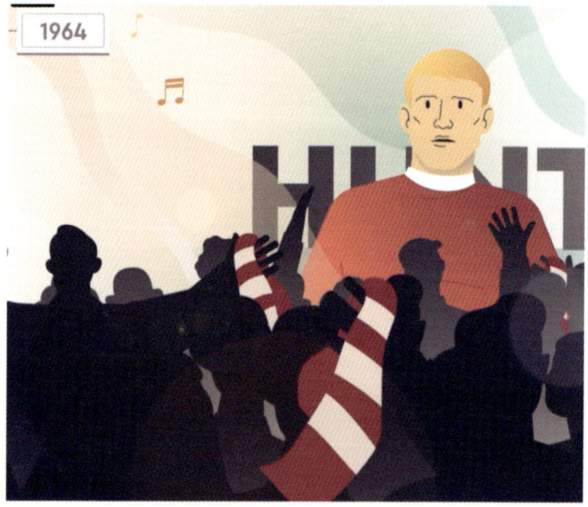
1964

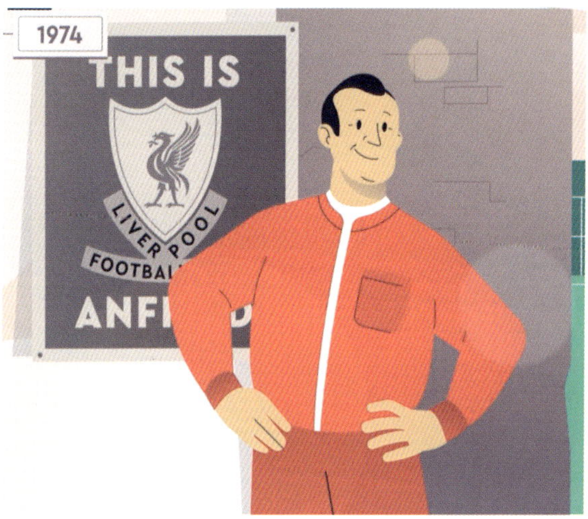
1974
THIS IS
LIVERPOOL

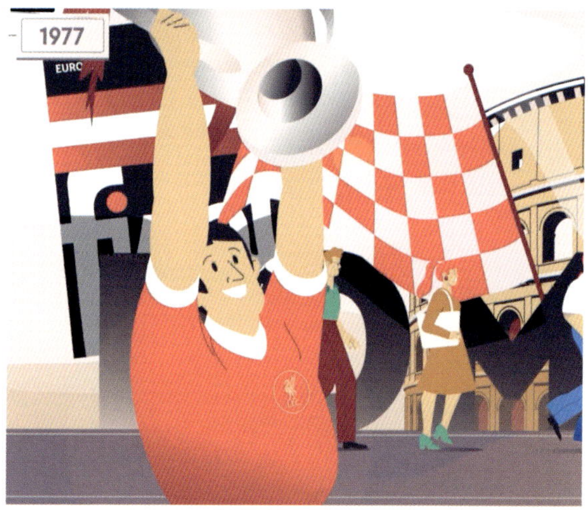
1977

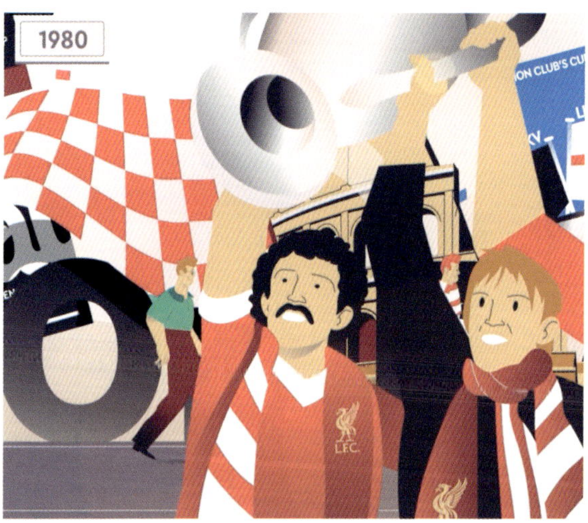
1980
L.F.C.

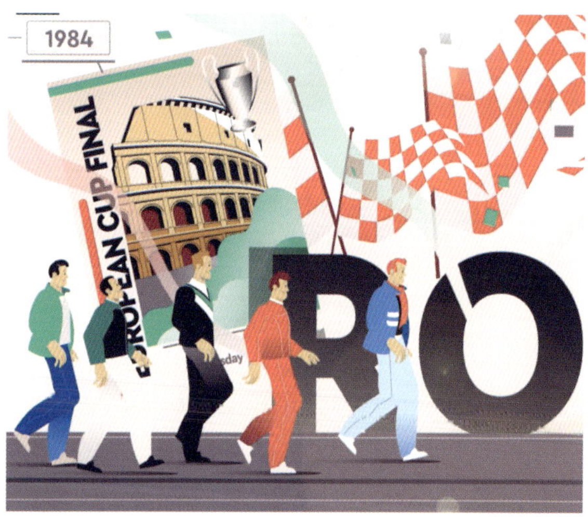
1984
CUP FINAL

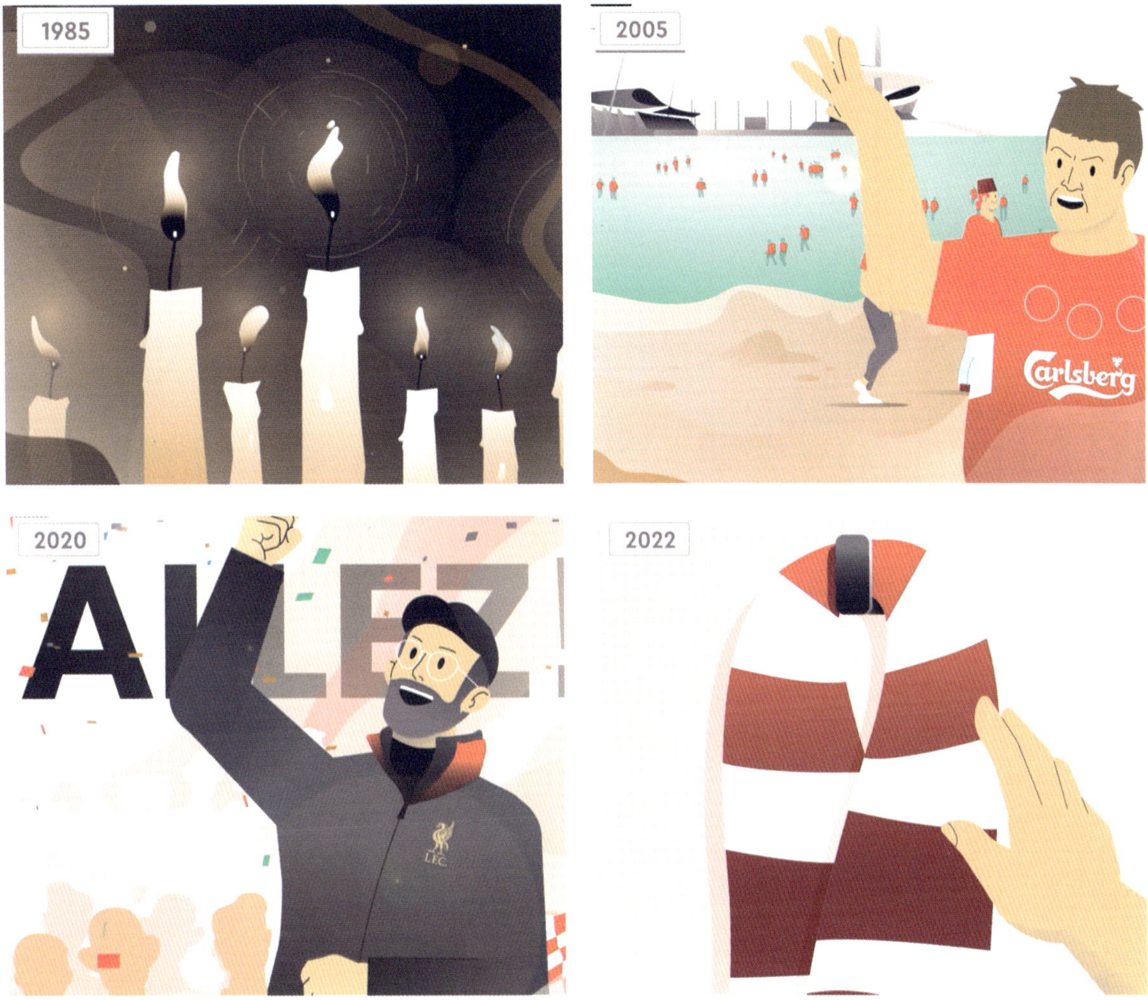

"Number 18 arrived in 1990 and the whole family was at Anfield to see it. Kenny's Reds paraded the goods and they all went to the pub! Little did they know it would be the last one for a while.

"The Nineties was a decade of ups and downs, but at the turn of the millennium my mum had something to smile about. And then, on that crazy night in Istanbul, it looked like we had nothing left, but Stevie Gerrard lit the fire and Carra refused to give in and we came back from the dead.

"And this fella, that's me. I think my mum thought I was a good-luck charm because the year I came along we were so close but we didn't quite do it, and it hurt like mad.

"Jürgen Norbert Klopp. He took us from doubters to believers. He made us Europe's kings and champions once again.

"Not bad for 130 years, eh? I'm just glad my great-great-great-grandad Tommy was a Red."

The Humble Genius

January 2019 saw a series of commemorations for the 100th anniversary of Bob Paisley's birthday, with a special edition of the matchday programme for the fixture against Crystal Palace, a mosaic on the Spion Kop before kick-off plus a minute's applause for the great man along with former Liverpool winger Peter Thompson, who'd passed away on 31 December 2018.

Inside the programme acclaimed local author and broadcaster John Keith, who knew Bob well, wrote: "His knowledge of football was incredible, I've never met anyone like him in that regard.

"He could watch a game and give his analysis of it and your head would be spinning. How did he see that? As [former midfielder] Ian Callaghan once said, Bill Shankly was the motivator but Bob was the knowledge.

"I always say Liverpool couldn't be where they are now without Bill starting it, but they couldn't be where they are without Bob carrying it on. I would put them on a par but you have to say that Bob was the most successful manager pro-rata for trophies per season that English football has ever seen.

"Nineteen in nine seasons including three European Cups and six championships is phenomenal. Even when you say it, it sounds unbelievable."

Another evocative tribute was produced by LFCTV in collaboration with Liverpool-based design studio Uniform. Entitled *The Humble Genius*, it was a 100-second animation of Paisley's life story narrated by the man himself and there to view on the club's official website – an absolute treat.

Later that year the wonders of technology brought Liverpool FC's past and present together to further commemorate 100 years since Bob's birth.

Main LFC sponsor Standard Chartered, working closely with the Paisley family, produced a five-part video series in which modern-day Reds respectfully join forces with a computer-generated Bob as part of their 'Project Stand Red' campaign.

Using smart technology, including Voice Modulation, Artificial Imagery (AI) and Computer Generated Imagery (CGI), the films were released from November 2019 into January 2020.

Legends Ian Rush, Roy Evans, Phil Neal, Bruce Grobbelaar and Terry McDermott starred alongside Joe Gomez, James Milner and Jordan Henderson.

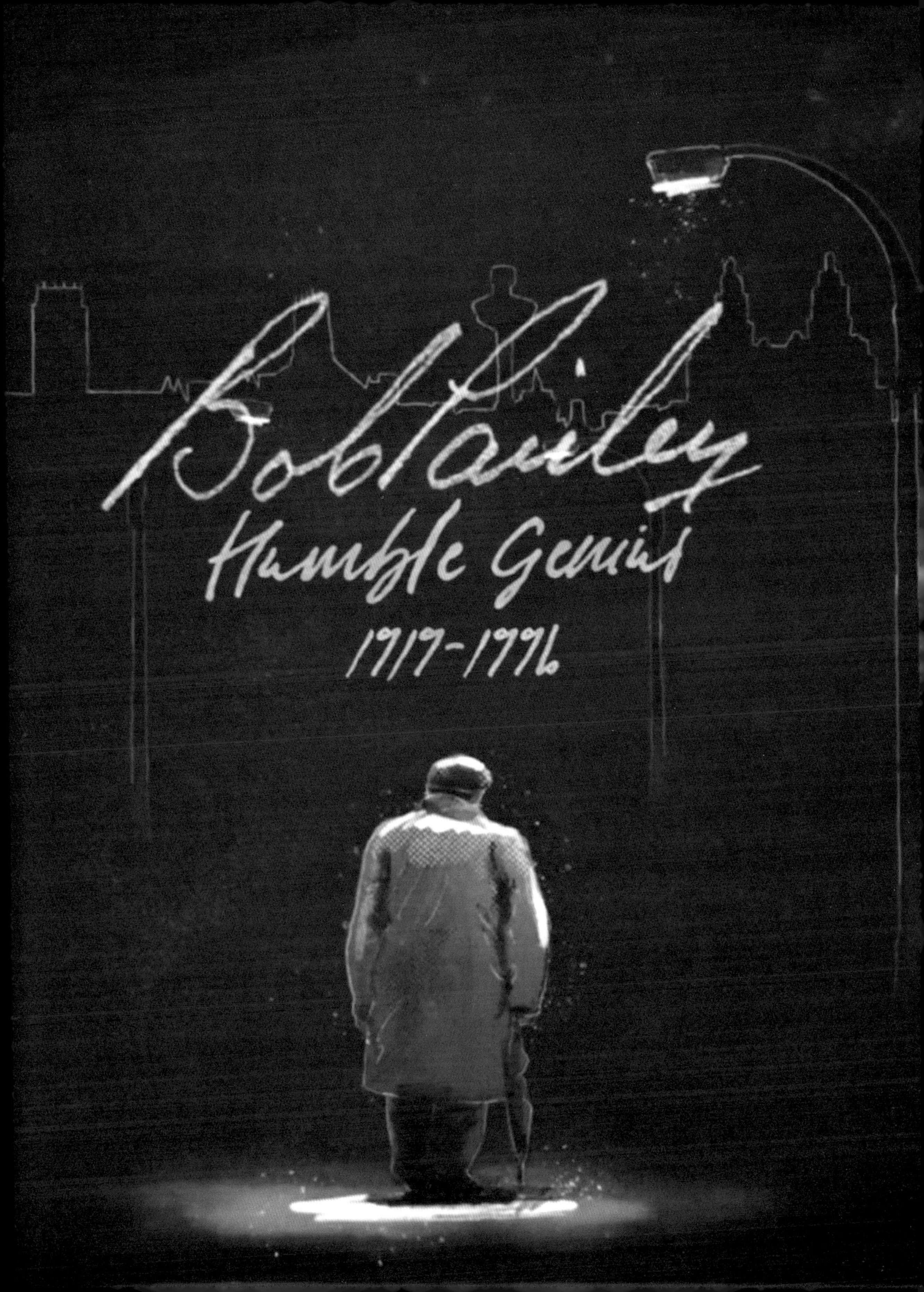
Bob Paisley
Humble Genius
1919-1996

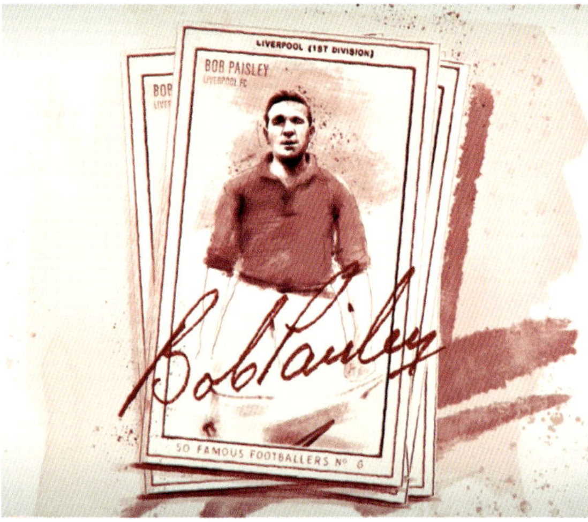
LIVERPOOL (1ST DIVISION)
BOB PAISLEY
Bob Paisley

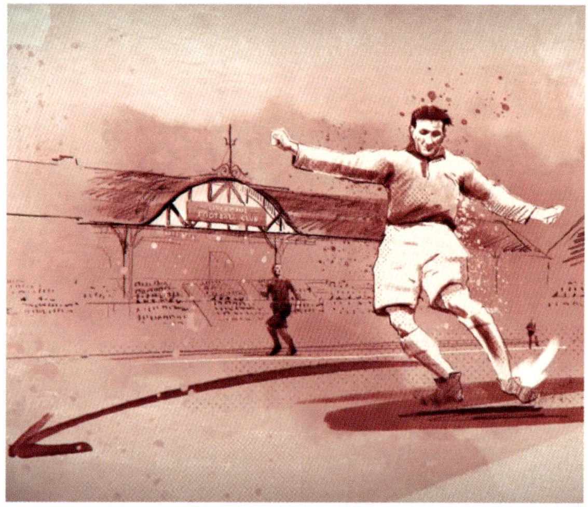

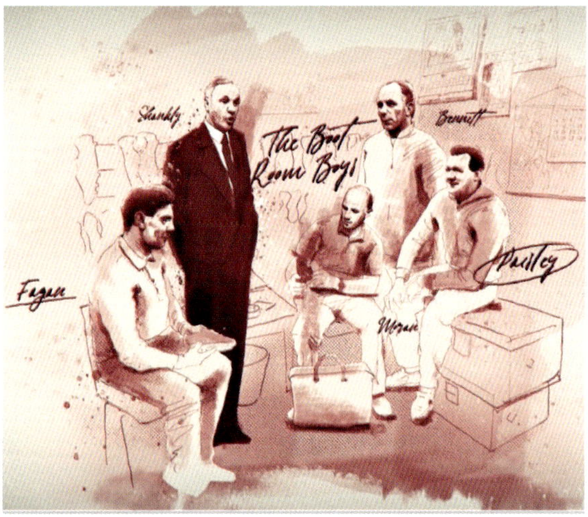
Shankly
The Boot Room Boys
Bennett
Fagan
Paisley
Moran

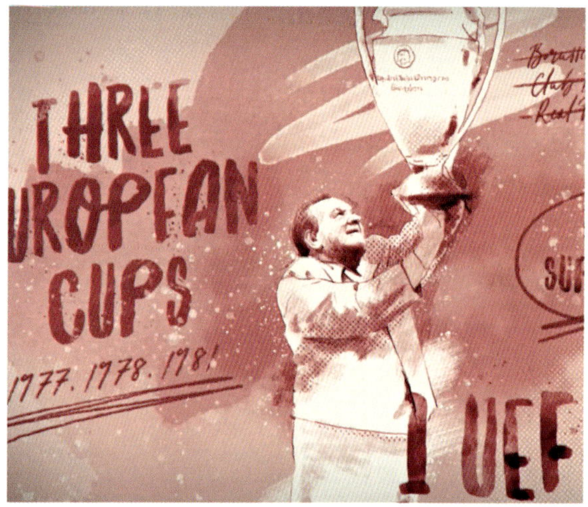
THREE
CUPS

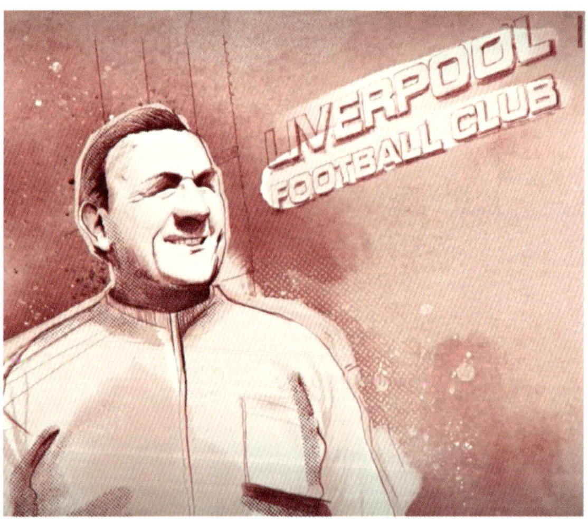
LIVERPOOL
FOOTBALL CLUB

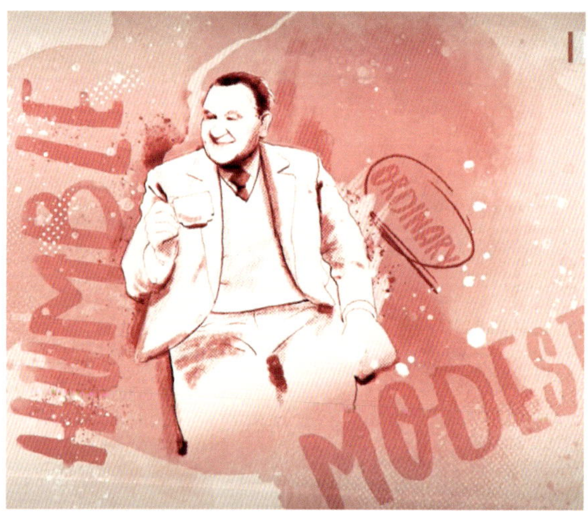
HUMBLE
ORDINARY

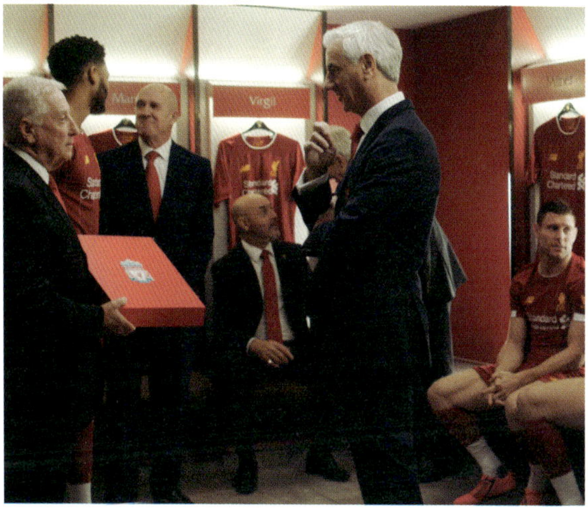

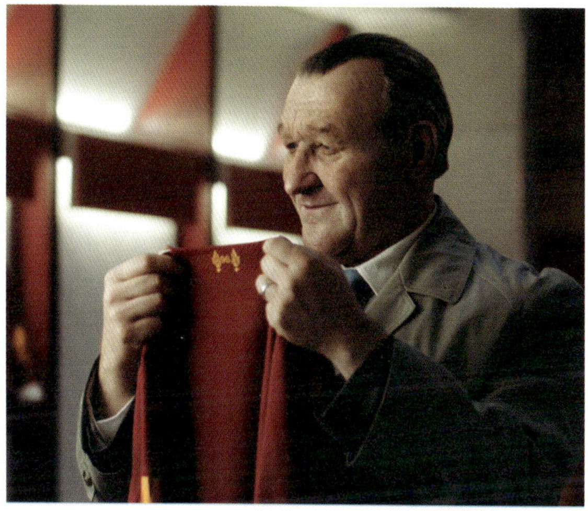

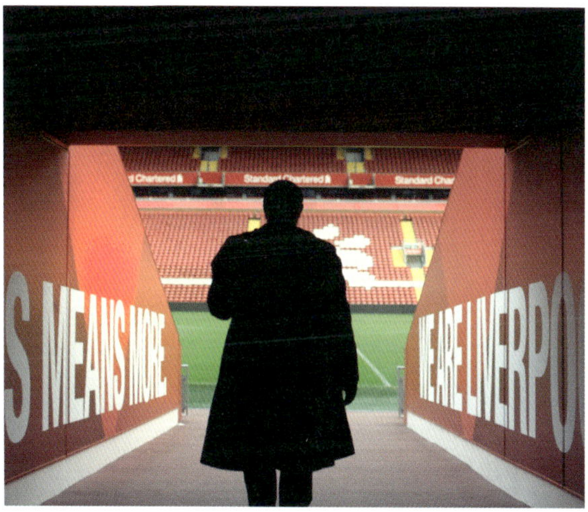

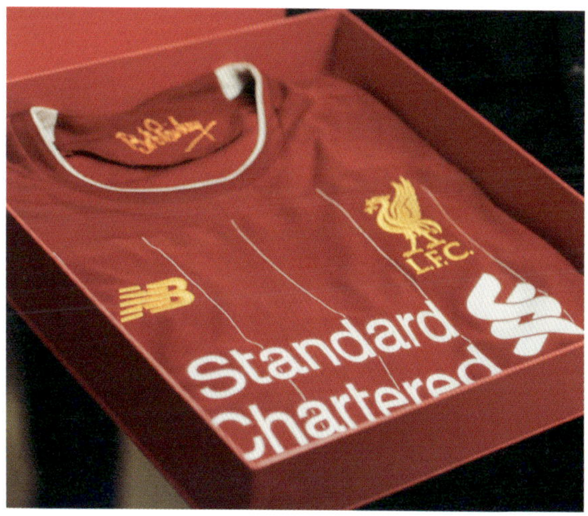

Not just Paisley's likeness was featured – audio clips were analysed to recreate his voice, too, seeing the CGI Bob interact with Rush and even Jürgen Klopp as he received a gift from current Reds and Anfield greats who played under him.

"Bob, you gave me my first Liverpool shirt, and it changed my career," said Rush. "It's a privilege to give this shirt in your honour."

Upon seeing the footage, Bob's son Graham called the technology "amazing – I thought it was a picture." Paisley's granddaughter Rachael added: "My little boy never got to meet Grandad but [with these films] there will be some sense of him knowing him."

The video also showed the computer-generated Bob walking out at a modern-day Anfield, while Liverpool FC's 2019/20 kits paid homage with the famous pinstripes of the early 1980s worn during Paisley's reign and his signature featuring on the inside-neck of every jersey.

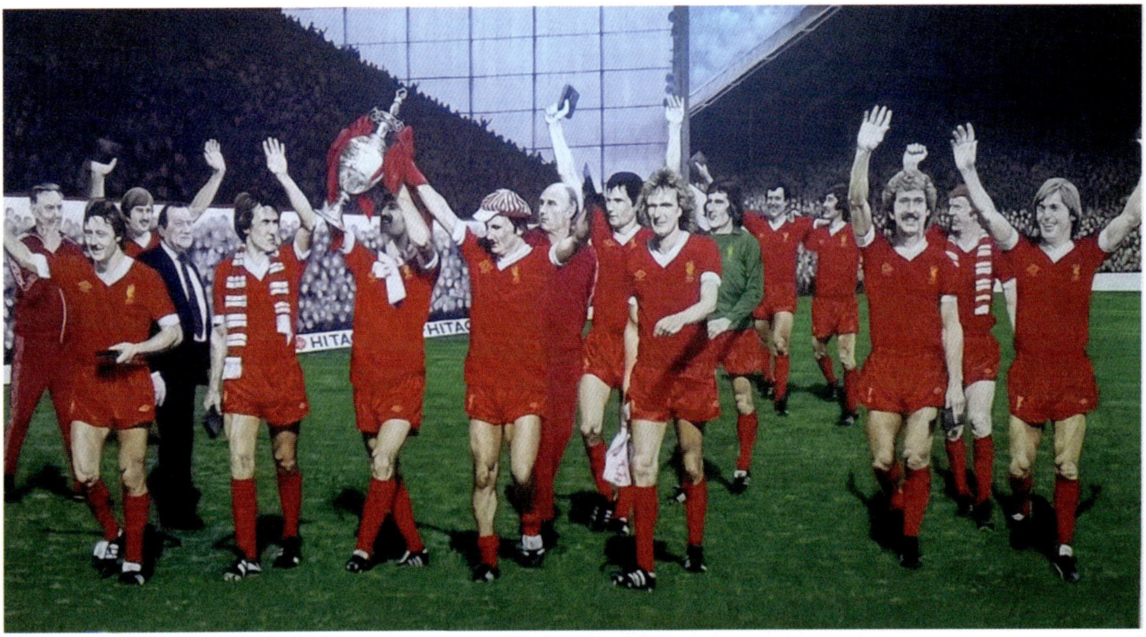

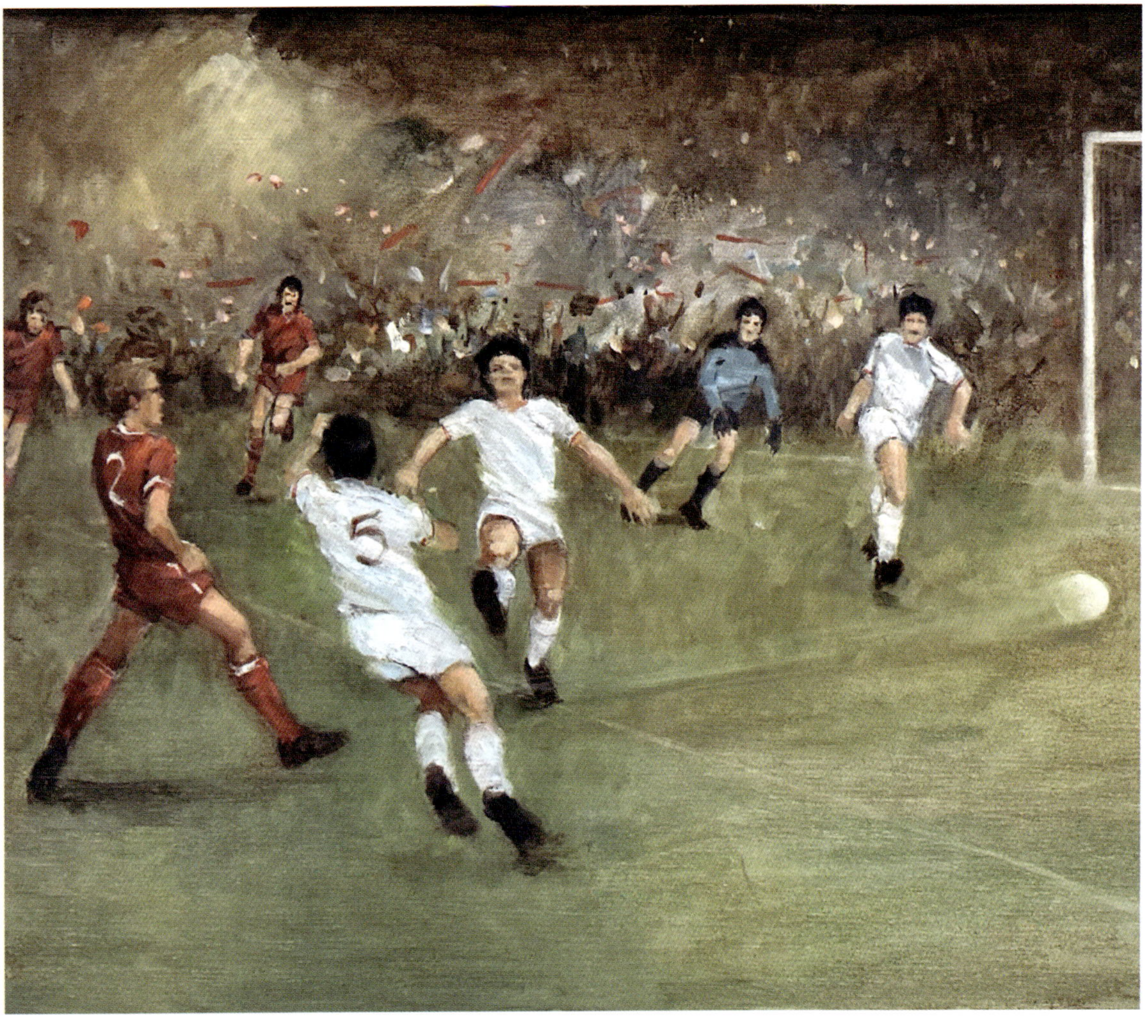

Anfield gallery

The Liverpool FC Story Museum is the club's official museum at Anfield – home to silverware, memorabilia and much more – and can be experienced as part of the popular Stadium Tour. It holds a collection of fascinating artworks, some of which are on display in the Main Stand Boardroom.

There are several pastel and oil-on-canvas portraits of managers, players and other club luminaries by local artist George Thompson – all of them originally commissioned by LFC directors and for many years hung in the club's old trophy room. Shown overleaf are Bob Paisley (painted in 1983) and goalkeepers from different eras, Bruce Grobbelaar and Elisha Scott (both painted in 1988).

Thompson also produced two match-action paintings depicting Phil Neal's goal for Liverpool against AS Roma in the 1984 European Cup final (opposite below) and Italy playing Russia at Anfield in a European Championship group game at Anfield in June 1996.

The oldest portrait on display in the Boardroom shows club founder John Houlding upon becoming Lord Mayor of Liverpool in 1898, painted by George Hall Neale and hanging in a gilt frame (also overleaf).

Reds fans of the Paisley era may fondly remember an oil painting of the team on a lap-of-honour after clinching yet another top-flight title (opposite top). It's entitled 'We are the Champions' and a matchday programme from October 1980 reported: 'You could be looking at a big-screen parade of honour by the Liverpool players after their League championship success last season...and in a way, you are. But this is no picture transmitted via television; it's a lifelike oil painting by artist Roger Harvey which now adorns the Anfield trophy room.

"It was commissioned by Hitachi to commemorate a successful first year of sponsorship involvement with Liverpool. And, as you can see, the detail in the picture – 5ft 6in by 3ft 6in – is remarkable. Not surprising, for it took about four months to complete."

More poignant is the 1989 oil painting 'Flowers for Liverpool' by Adrian Henri (next page), an artist and poet who was part of the so-called 'Mersey Sound' of the Sixties. He painted this canvas in response to the outpouring of grief following the Hillsborough Disaster when Anfield's Kop end was covered in floral tributes, and it was loaned to LFC by his partner Catherine Marcangeli.

Hugely evocative is 'Kop Entrance' by David Barrow (also next page), an oil-on-canvas depicting the exterior of the old standing terrace just before it was rebuilt as an all-seater stand in 1994. It shows queues beginning to build outside the turnstiles by 'Flagpole Corner' on Walton Breck Road as cars and taxis pass on a rainy early evening.

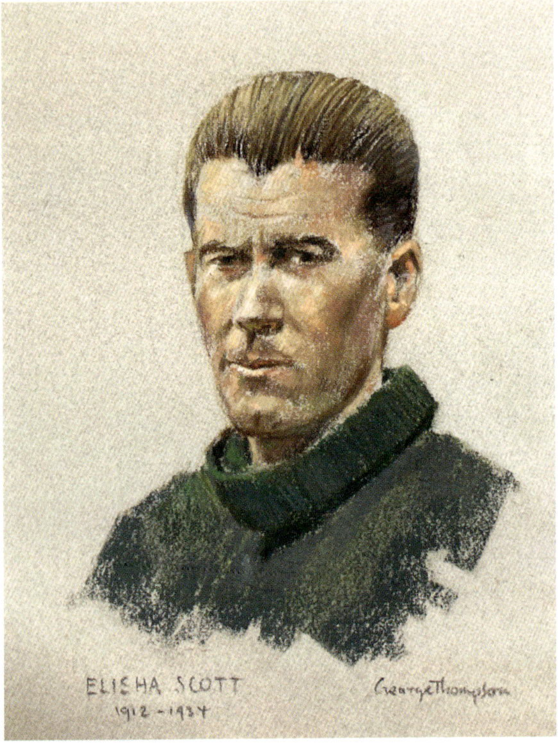
ELISHA SCOTT
1912 - 1934
George Thompson

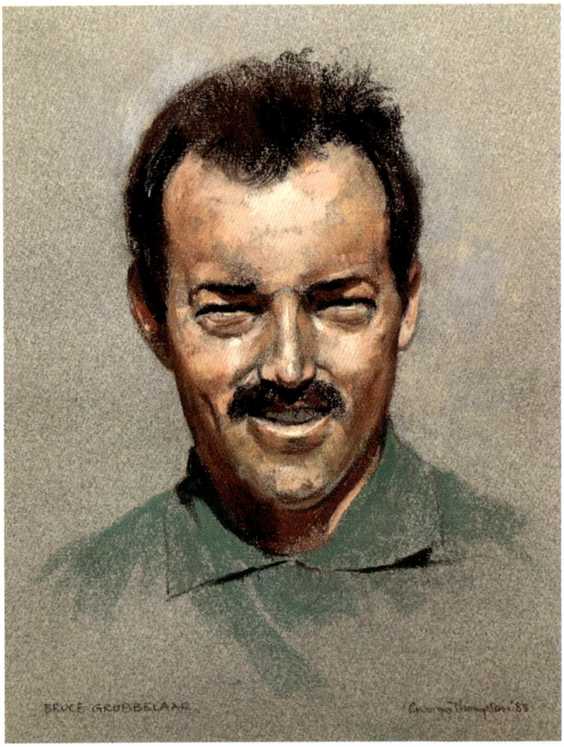
BRUCE GROBBELAAR

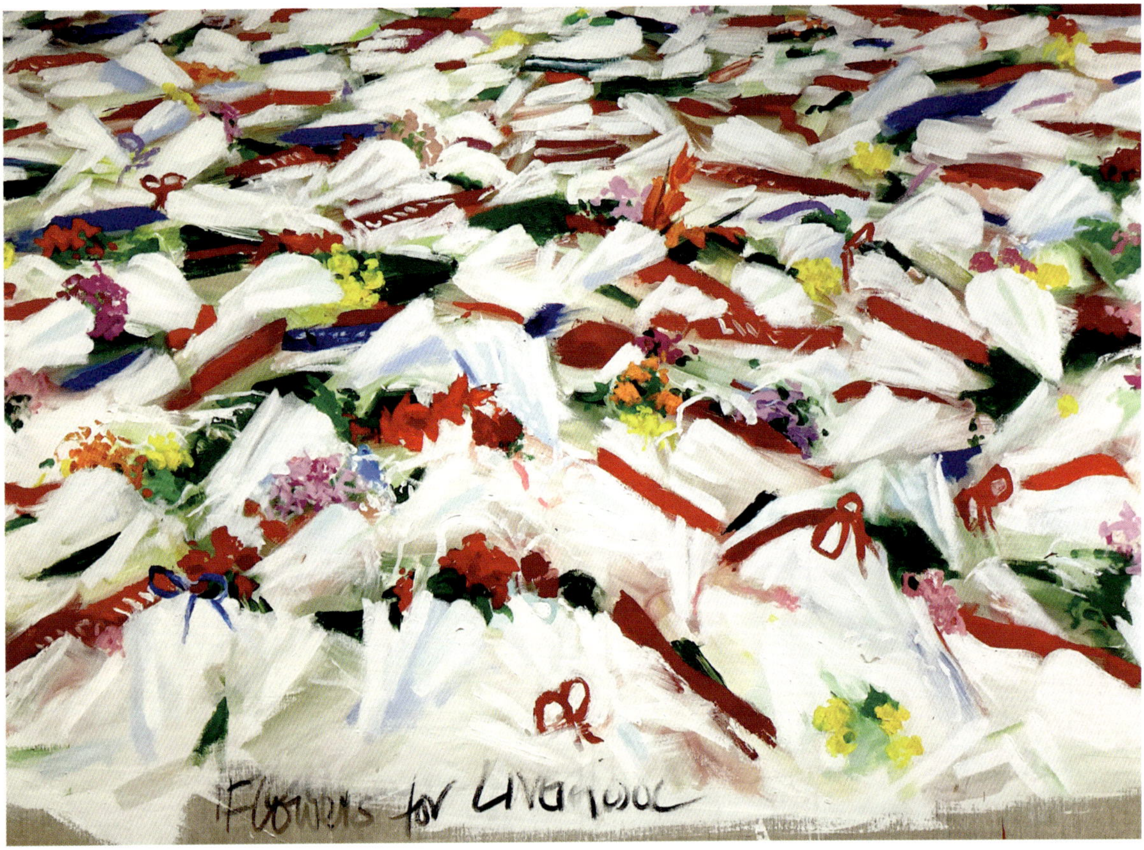
Flowers for Liverpool

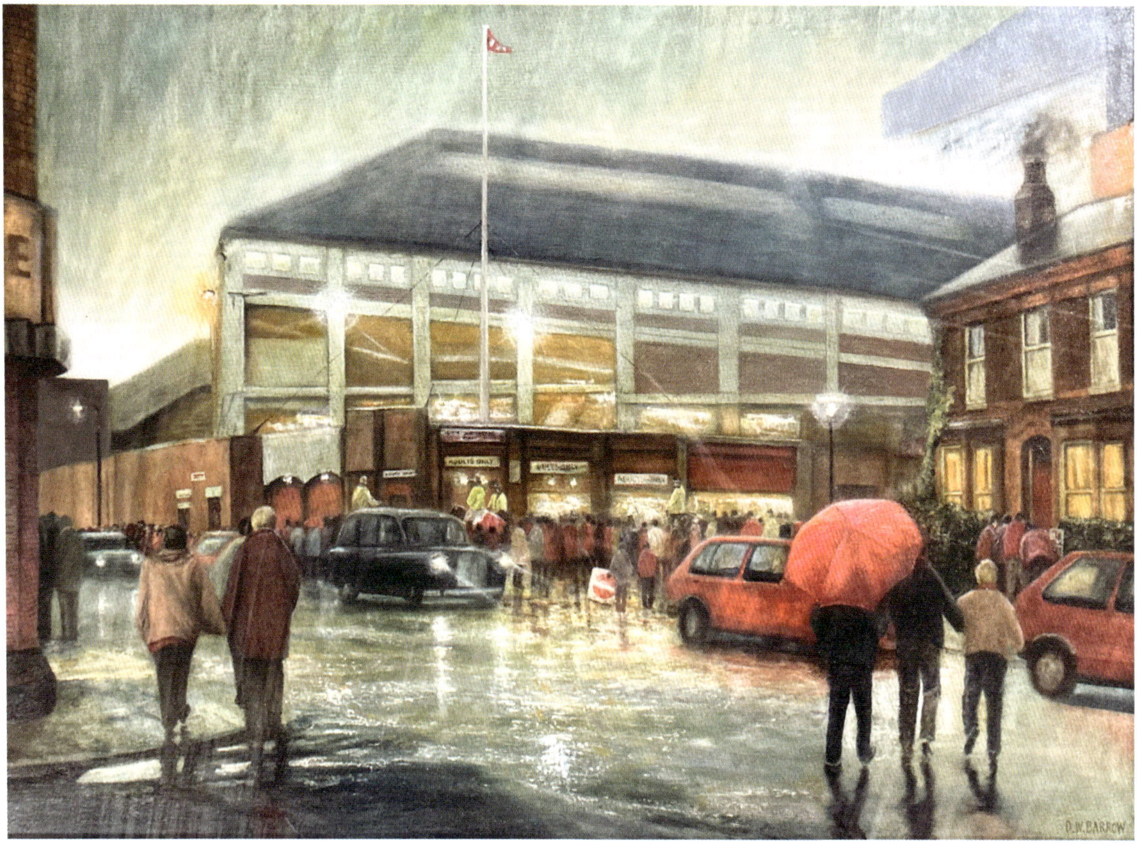
D.W. BARROW

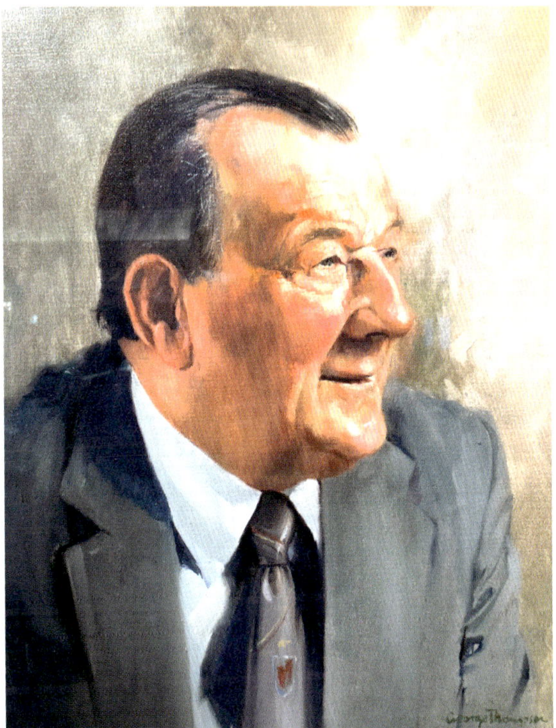

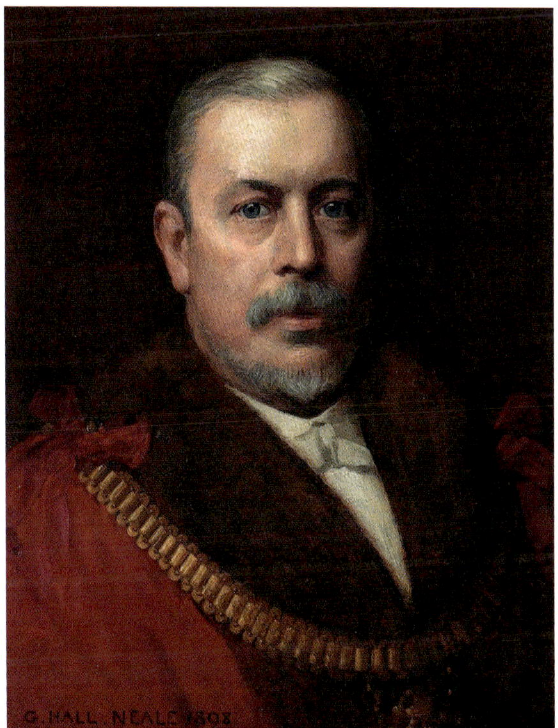
G. HALL NEALE 1898

The Liver Bird

It's not a legendary player or manager but it's one of the star attractions in the Main Stand Boardroom: a beautiful and historic water-colour painting of a cormorant, from which the Liver Bird of Liverpool Football Club traces its origins.

On the city of Liverpool's heraldic coat of arms ratified in 1797 – alongside Neptune, the god of the sea – it's officially a cormorant, 'the wings elevated, in the beak a branch of seaweed called Laver; the motto *Deus Nobis Haec Otia Fecit*, which comes from a poem by the Roman writer Virgil and means 'These gifts God has bestowed upon us'. The Liver Bird made its first bow upon the club crest in 1901, nine years after the dispute between LFC founder John Houlding and the ground's original occupants, Everton FC.

Today our fabulous feathered friend is on the scarves, replica shirts, hats and flags of LFC supporters and of course the chests of all those great players who have run out onto the hallowed turf since the 1950s – when the Liver Bird first appeared on the kit. As early as 1901, though, it was inscribed upon medals awarded for Liverpool FC's first league title triumph, and it was also stitched gloriously upon the club's official 'Championship flag' for 1921/22.

The print behind glass in the Main Stand Boardroom depicts a double-crested cormorant, and it's the work of American artist John James Audubon who disembarked with a dream at Liverpool on 21 July 1826.

Born in Haiti in 1785, the son of a French sea captain and a Creole mother, he was raised in France then spirited to North America to escape the Napoleonic draft. At the age of 41 he sailed to England to find subscribers for a grand project: a large-scale book of life-size, action-packed paintings of every bird species native to (what would become) the United States.

The Rathbone family took him under their wing, so to speak, at their Greenbank residence in south Liverpool and introduced him to wider society whom he entranced with 'Red Indian' war cries, owl hoots and tales from the frontier.

A dozen years passed while Audubon voyaged to and fro across the Atlantic and explored the American interior for bird species – the whole of the eastern seaboard from Maine to Florida, and the Ohio and Mississippi river systems from Kentucky to Louisiana, and west to Texas which was then a separate Republic – before 200 sets of the work were finally published in London with craftsmen etching his striking watercolours onto copper plates then hand-colouring the prints.

Today it's the world's most valuable natural history book and, as one rare-book dealer in London has described it, "the greatest book on American heritage – there is no competition." Only 120 complete copies are known to exist, of which the majority are held by museums and libraries with a few in private collections.

There are digitised versions of the double elephant folio set (i.e. all four books) online, but nothing beats seeing *The Birds of America* for real and appreciating its profound beauty and universal value. Each volume measures 4ft across when fully opened and weighs almost four stone – and there's a copy on display in Liverpool's Central Library.

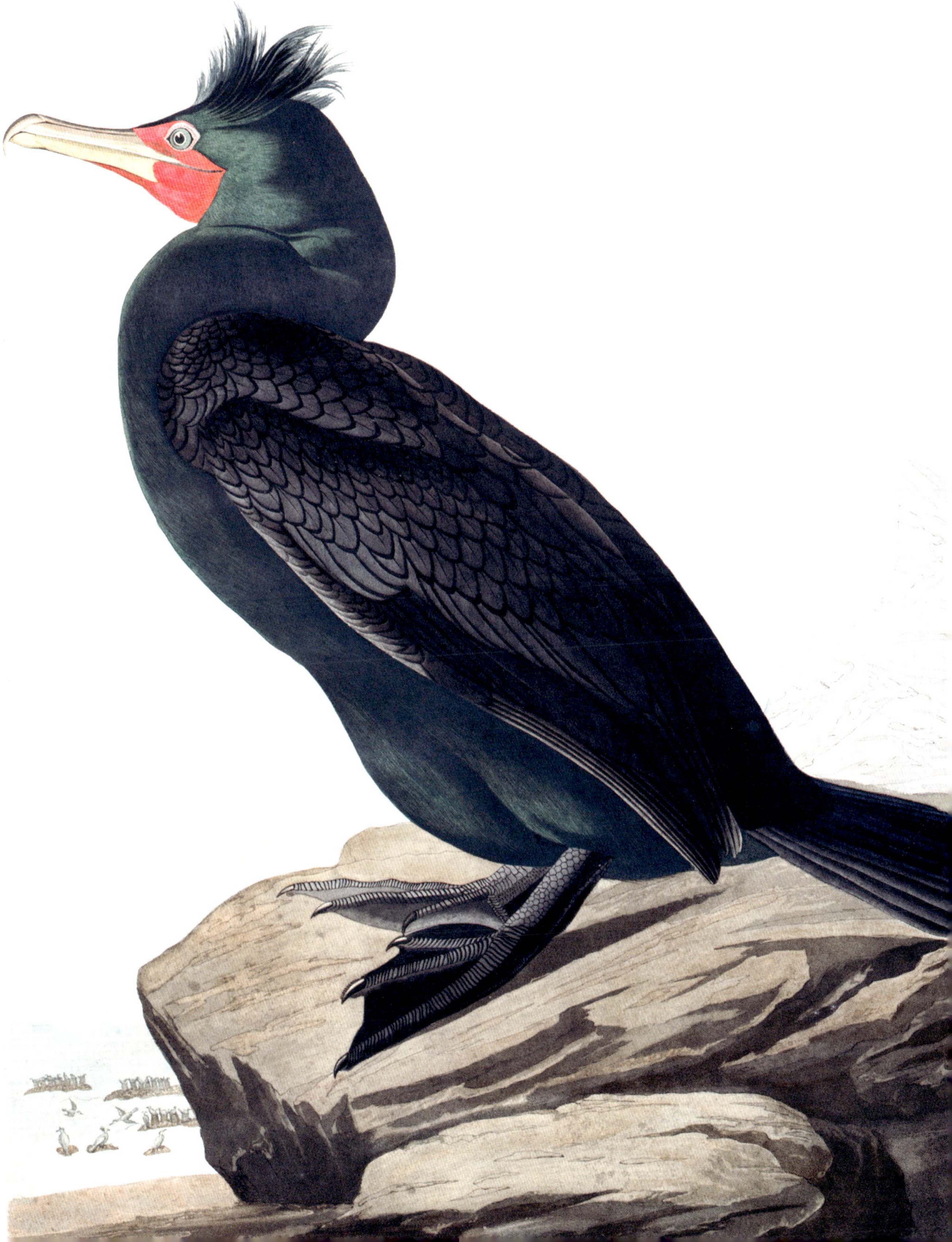

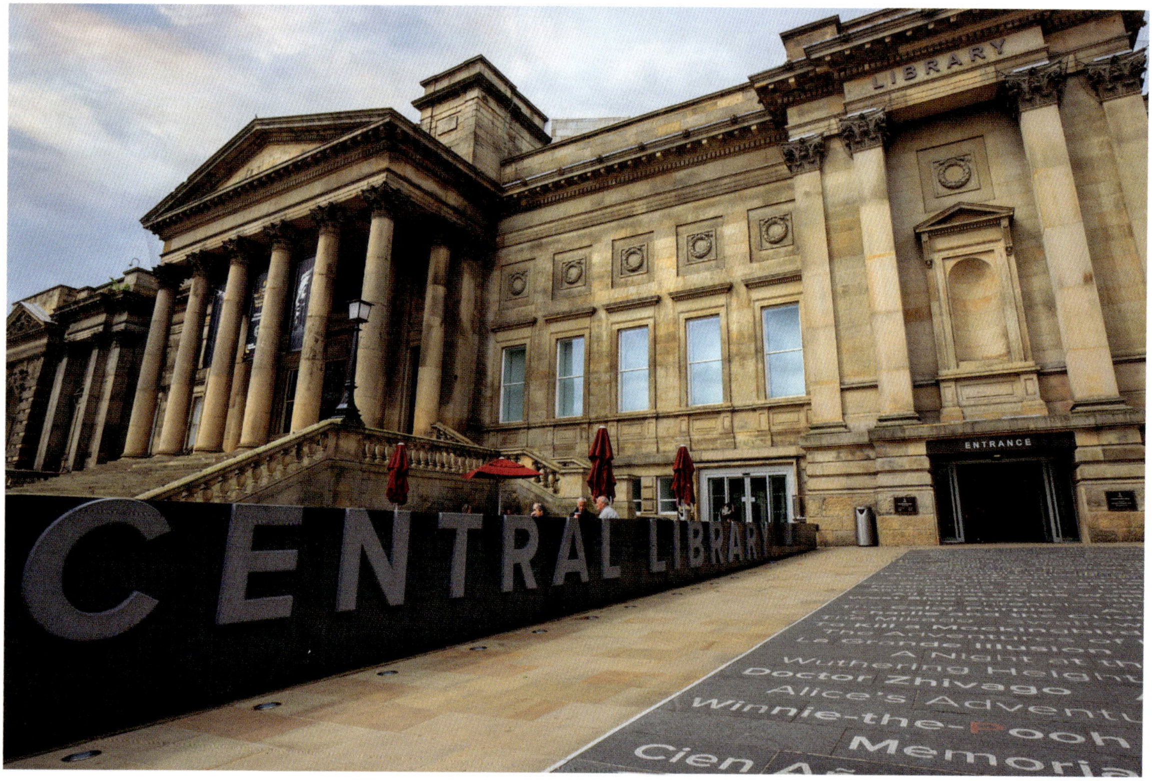
LIBRARY
ENTRANCE
CENTRAL LIBRARY
La Grande Illusion
Doctor Zhivago
Winnie-the-Pooh

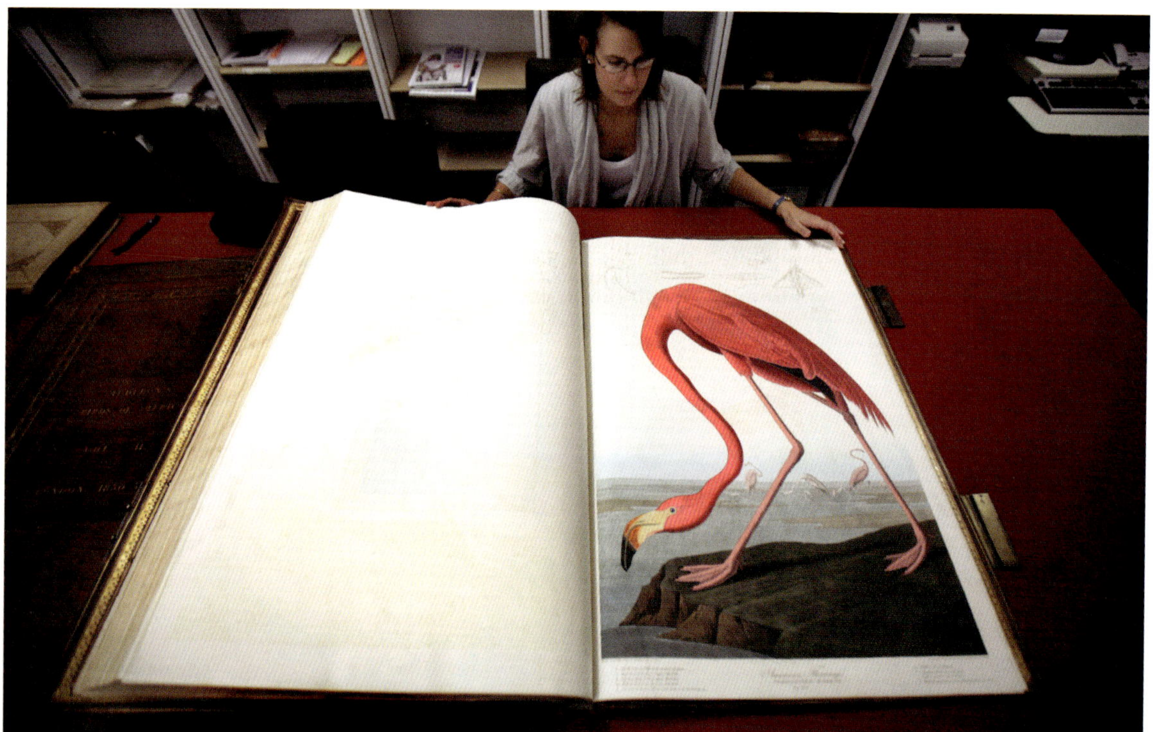

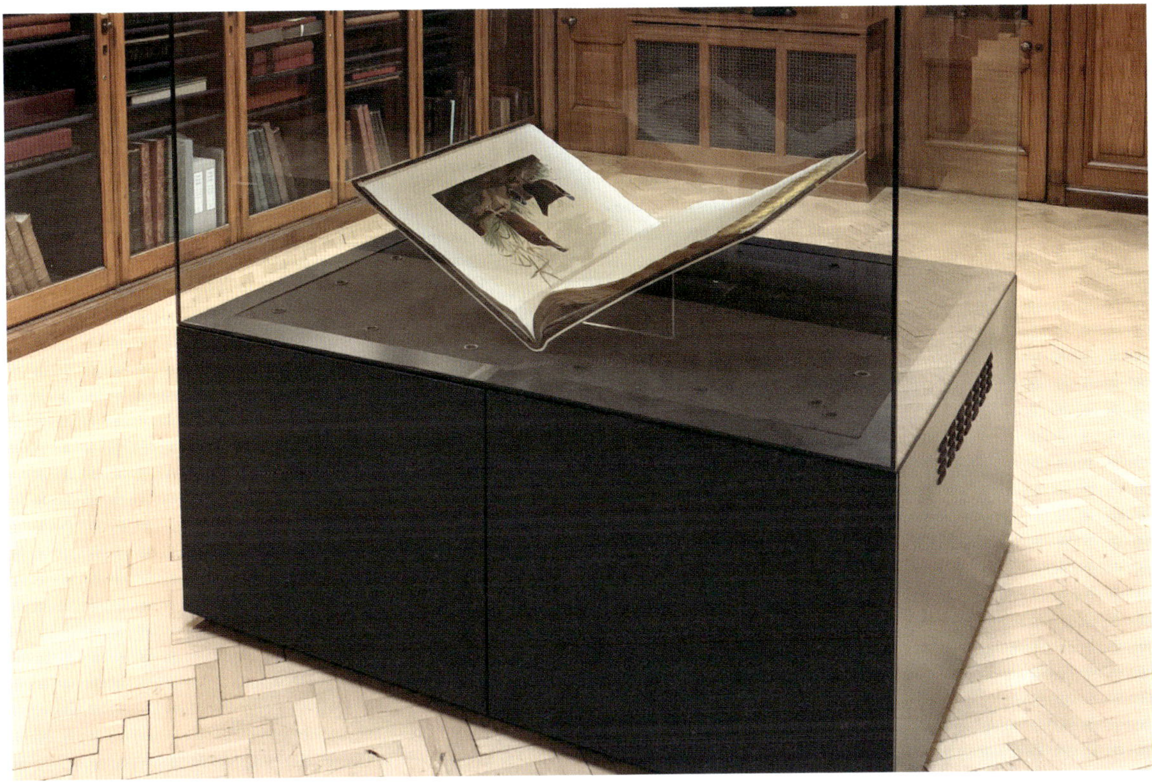

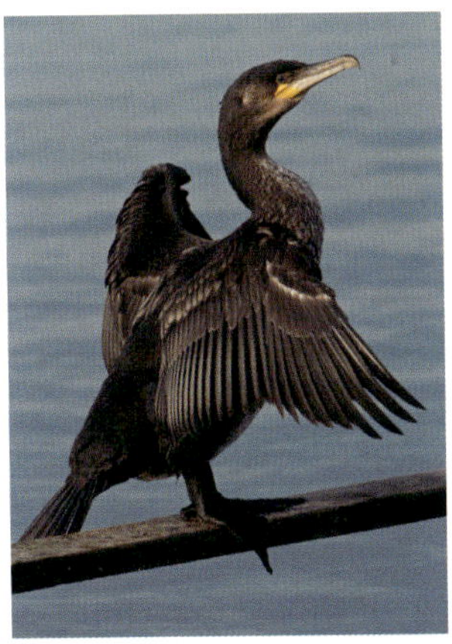

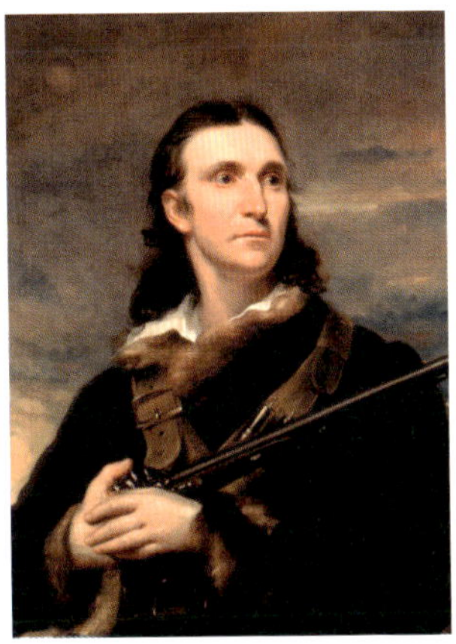

Opposite: The entrance to Liverpool's Central Library where a copy of the book is held, and an idea of its size
This page: The book on display, a 'real' cormorant on the Mersey, and the American artist John James Audubon

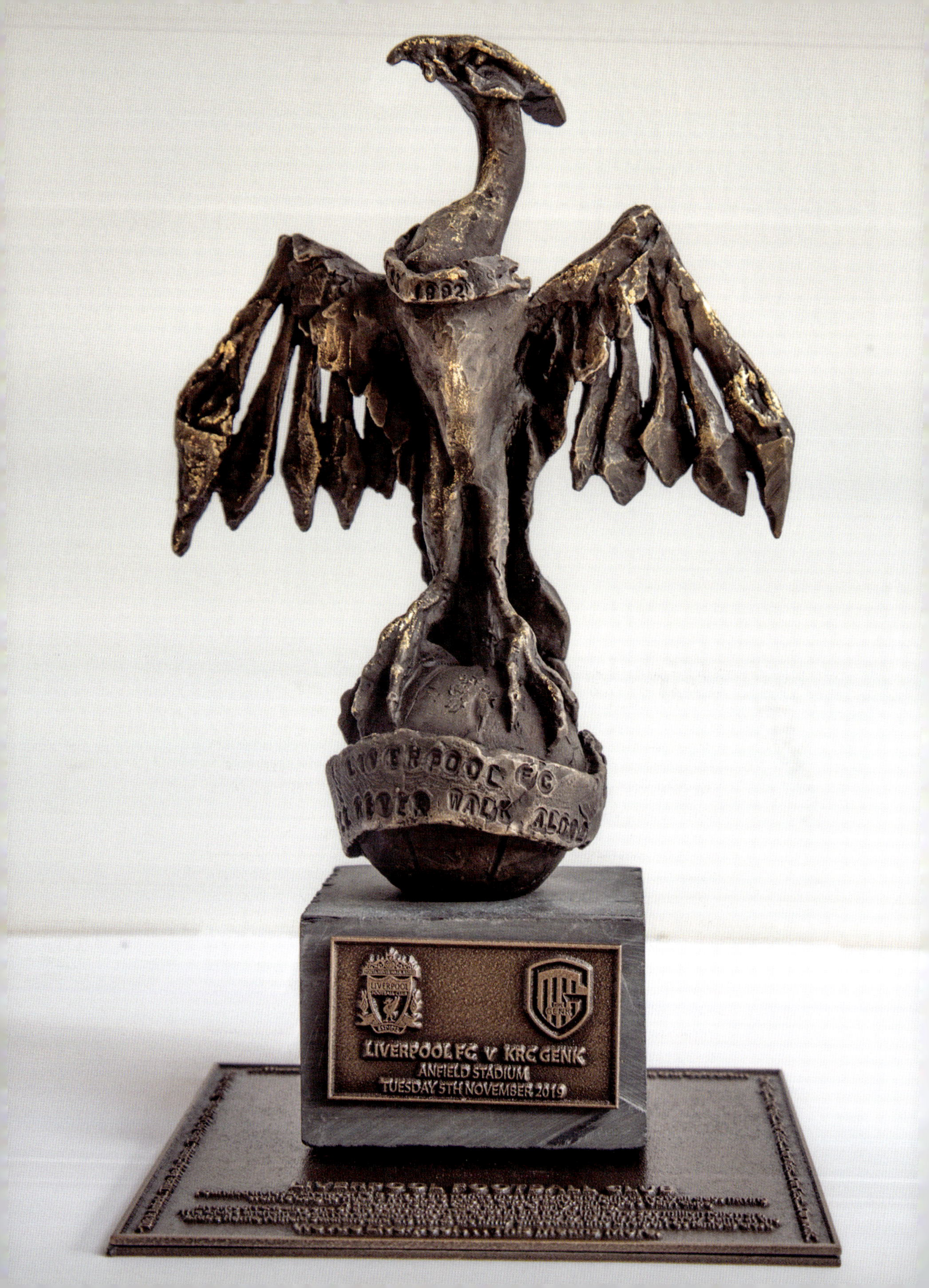

1892
LIVERPOOL FC
LIVERPOOL FC v KRC GENK
ANFIELD STADIUM
TUESDAY 5TH NOVEMBER 2019

Wings of desire

In recent seasons of European competition, clubs from the Continent have been leaving Anfield with a splendid memento of their encounter with Liverpool FC: a Liver Bird sculpted in bronze, wings spread, perched upon a globe around which is furled a banner proclaiming 'You'll Never Walk Alone'.

It's the work of artist Emma Rodgers who creates commemorative gifts for the club's opponents in Europe as well as awards for charities and individuals, Steven Gerrard and Pele among them, from her foundry in Liverpool city-centre.

In June 2019 one of these majestic bronze Liver Birds was presented to Tottenham Hotspur along with an inscribed plaque at the Champions League final in Madrid. Then chief-executive Peter Moore later tweeted: "Thank you @emmarodgersart for the application of your unique talent in support of our club and city. Your Liver Bird sits proudly in the boardrooms of numerous great clubs that have been part of our European adventures in recent years."

The city's mythical symbol has been something of a theme in Emma's work. Her 30ft high Meccano Liver Bird presided over the site of the old Frank Hornby toy factories on Edge Lane which were redeveloped into a shopping park, while a magnificent beaten-copper version – originally created for the 2014 International Business Festival held in Liverpool – roosts proudly in the Cunard Building on the waterfront.

She's also sculpted human figures (she collaborated with a fellow artist on the Cilla Black statue on Mathew Street) as well as everything from birds, bees and bulls to horses, wolves and rabbits.

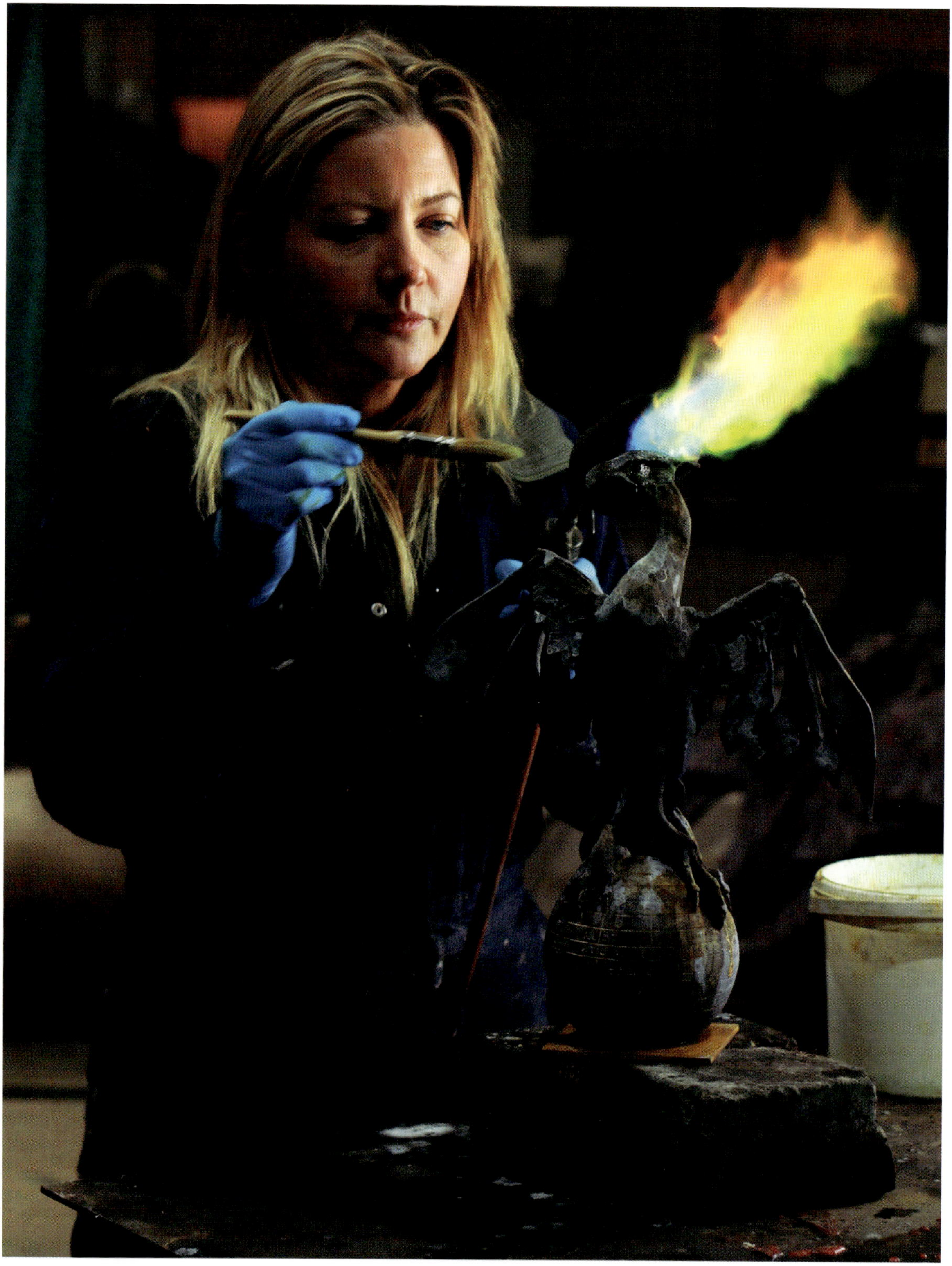

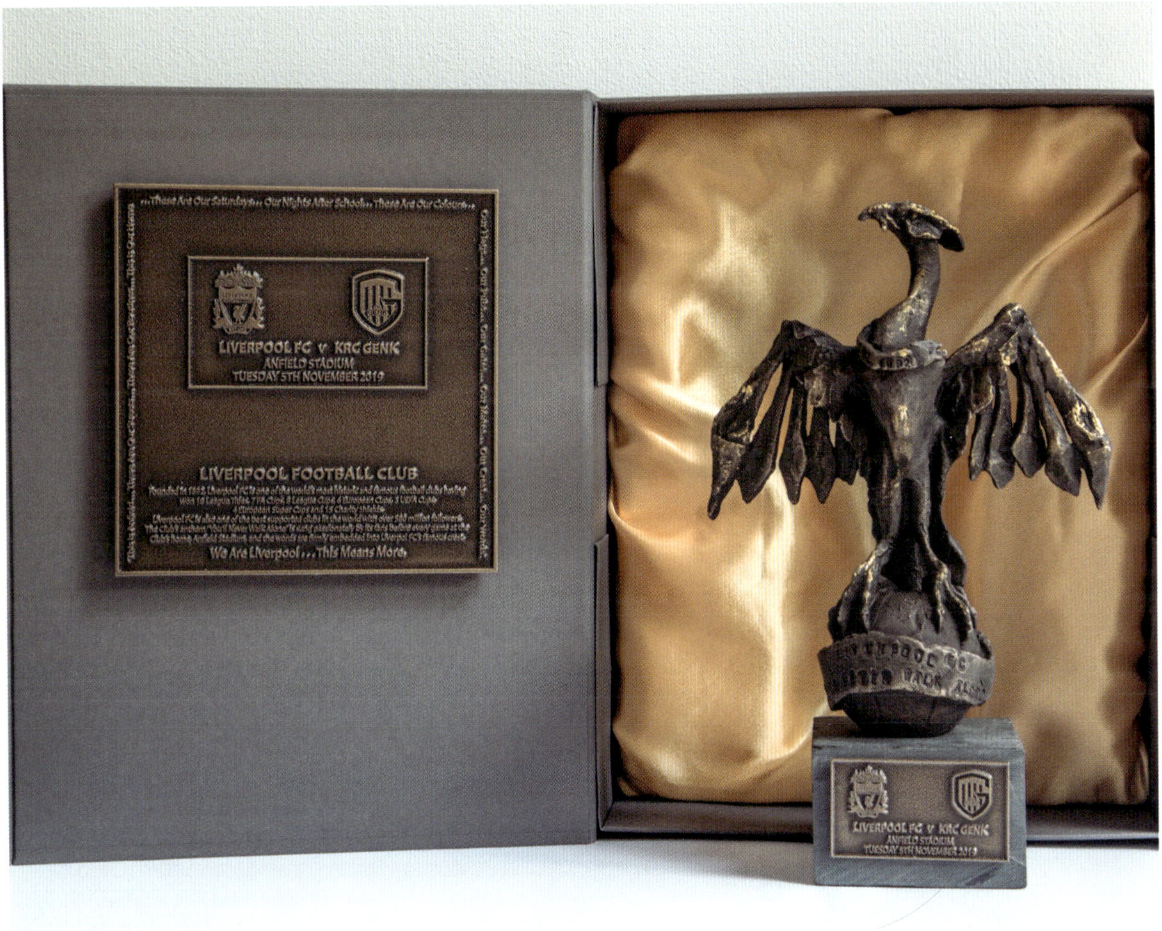

An honorary fellow at Liverpool John Moores University and ambassador for Clatterbridge Cancer Centre, she's been hailed by one arts critic as "among the foremost ceramic sculptors working anywhere in the world, she really inhabits the spirit of her creatures… Her creative process involves not only great technical skill and acute observation but powerful intuition and imagination – this is what makes her work so fresh and alive."

Typically Emma begins with sketches to capture "the spirit of the beast" then transfers it to clay, tearing and gouging the body to show muscle and bone structure then constructing outwards before firing continuously to over 1,100 degrees.

When sculpting in bronze she tries to replicate these techniques, patinating each piece with the same brush-marks she'd use with glaze and often "stretching the imagination" by casting clock-parts and weaving fabric onto the figures.

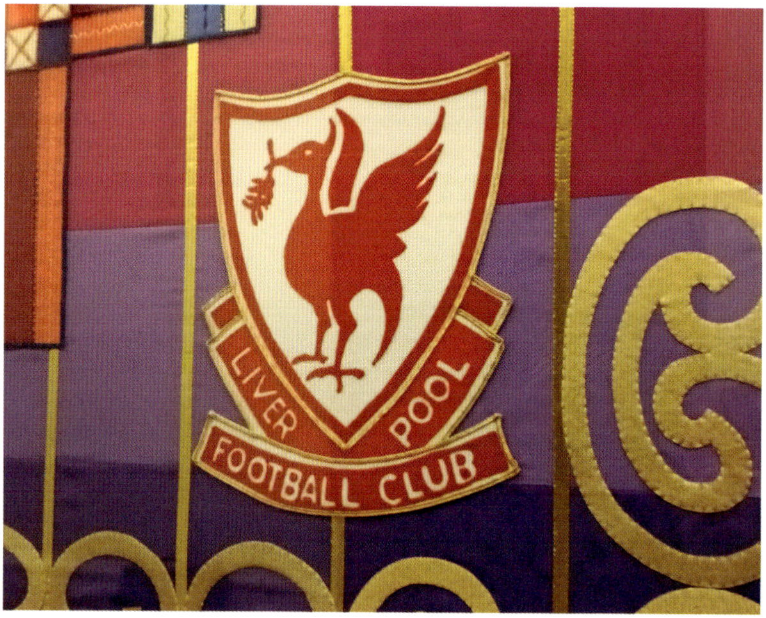

Mighty threads

While many people are invariably drawn towards the eternal flame of the Hillsborough Memorial at Anfield, there are other poignant tributes to the 97 in the heart of Liverpool.

One is a beautiful tapestry formerly located in the foyer of Millennium House, once council premises on Victoria Street, and now on display in St George's Hall, the city's grandest building, opposite Lime Street Station.

At the top are the words of the club anthem: 'YOU'LL NEVER WALK ALONE'. Below: 'HILLSBOROUGH 15th APRIL 1989'. Liver Birds appear either side with the city motto and the club crest.

The following details appears on a nearby plaque: 'The Hillsborough Memorial Tapestry was commissioned by the residing Lord Mayor (Councillor Dorothy Gavin) in 1990 in memory of the Hillsborough disaster that took place on 15 April 1989.

'The work was designed by Mrs Sheila Shepherd and made by Miss Alice and Miss Cecily Taggart of the Metropolitan Cathedral Art Studio and is a symbol of suffering and hope.

'The deep blue colours depict the River Mersey, while the dark colours above portray the grief and sorrow for those who died. The gold and cream indicate the souls rising to heaven and there is a cross for every person who lost their life [96 at the time].

'The Shankly Gates represent the love of Liverpool Football Club. The tapestry is on public display as a tribute to the 96 people that died and all those who suffered as a result of the tragedy'.

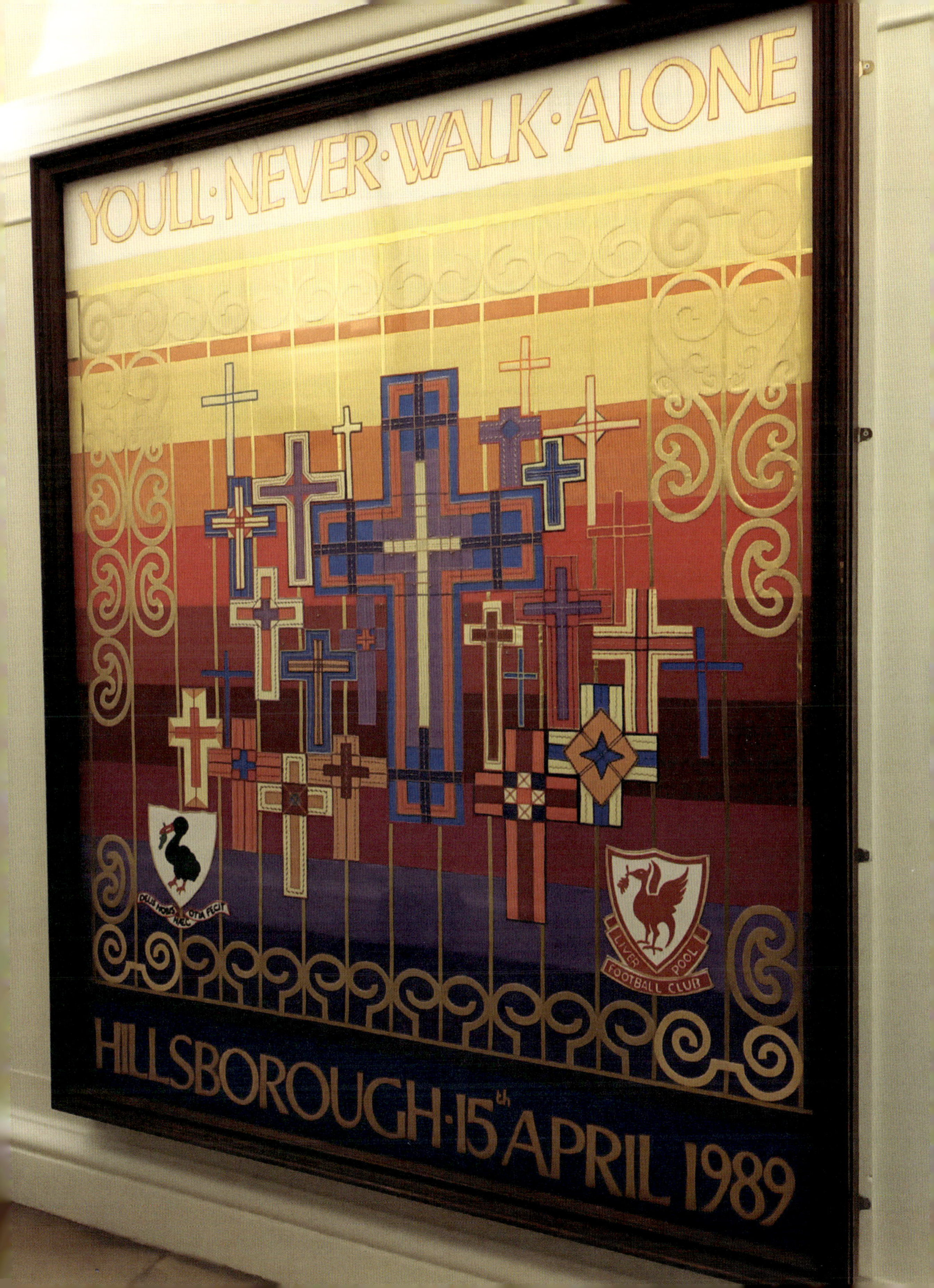

YOU'LL · NEVER · WALK · ALONE
DEUS NOBIS HAEC OTIA FECIT
LIVER POOL
FOOTBALL CLUB
HILLSBOROUGH · 15th APRIL 1989

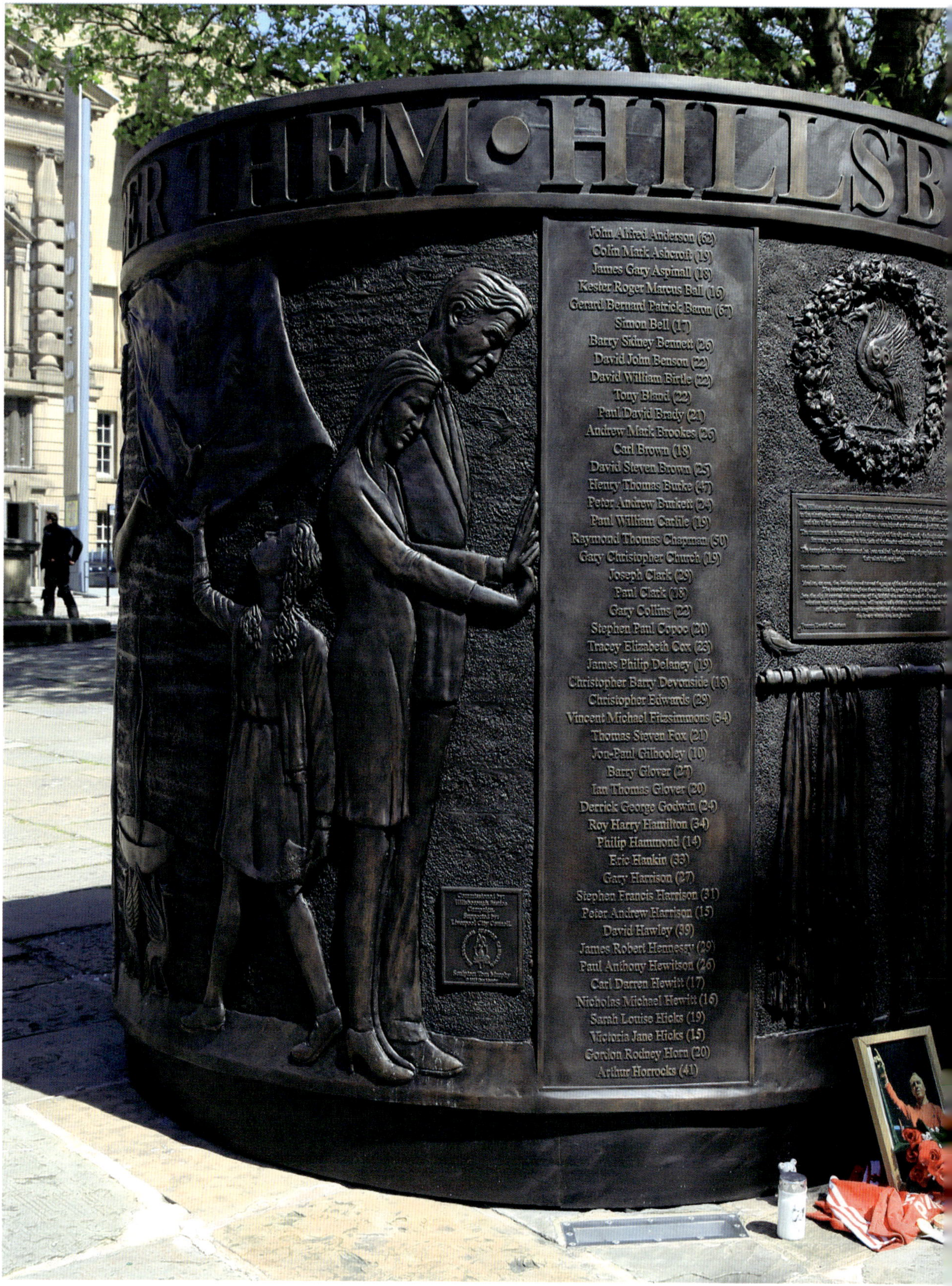
ER THEM • HILLSB
MUSEUM
John Alfred Anderson (62)
Colin Mark Ashcroft (19)
James Gary Aspinall (18)
Kester Roger Marcus Ball (16)
Gerard Bernard Patrick Baron (67)
Simon Bell (17)
Barry Sidney Bennett (26)
David John Benson (22)
David William Birtle (22)
Tony Bland (22)
Paul David Brady (21)
Andrew Mark Brookes (26)
Carl Brown (18)
David Steven Brown (25)
Henry Thomas Burke (47)
Peter Andrew Burkett (24)
Paul William Carlile (19)
Raymond Thomas Chapman (50)
Gary Christopher Church (19)
Joseph Clark (29)
Paul Clark (18)
Gary Collins (22)
Stephen Paul Copoc (20)
Tracey Elizabeth Cox (23)
James Philip Delaney (19)
Christopher Barry Devonside (18)
Christopher Edwards (29)
Vincent Michael Fitzsimmons (34)
Thomas Steven Fox (21)
Jon-Paul Gilhooley (10)
Barry Glover (27)
Ian Thomas Glover (20)
Derrick George Godwin (24)
Roy Harry Hamilton (34)
Philip Hammond (14)
Eric Hankin (33)
Gary Harrison (27)
Stephen Francis Harrison (31)
Peter Andrew Harrison (15)
David Hawley (39)
James Robert Hennessy (29)
Paul Anthony Hewitson (26)
Carl Darren Hewitt (17)
Nicholas Michael Hewitt (16)
Sarah Louise Hicks (19)
Victoria Jane Hicks (15)
Gordon Rodney Horn (20)
Arthur Horrocks (41)

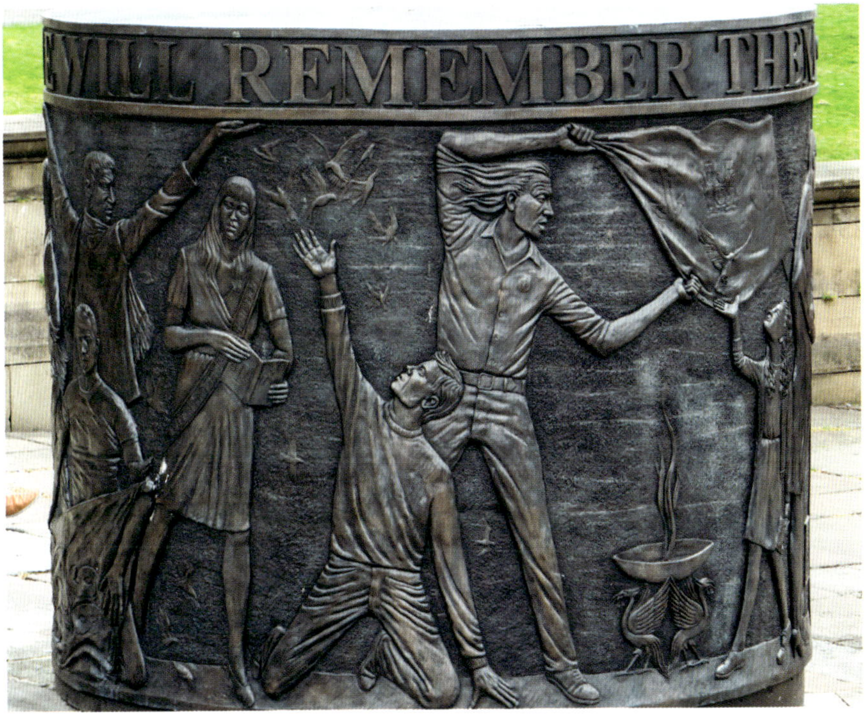

At the back of St George's Hall, near St John's Gardens in the city's Old Haymarket, a circular memorial to Hillsborough was unveiled in April 2013, in the same week that a magnificent mahogany clock in the council chamber of Liverpool's Town Hall was permanently stopped at 3.06pm.

Commissioned by the Hillsborough Justice Campaign, the 7ft high bronze monument was sculpted by Tom Murphy (of Shankly statue renown) and inscribed with the names of the victims and the words: 'Hillsborough Disaster – we will remember them'.

Tom has described the people depicted in the design as "the guardians of the memory" while other figures "represent justice, hope and loss. The setting is a beautiful and quiet place, which may help us to think about the characters and individual personalities of those who died. The people who passed away are represented by the birds who fly freely throughout the work."

Everton FC's badge is also included on the memorial to highlight that both clubs and their sets of fans have stood together over the years in support of those we lost and those who survived.

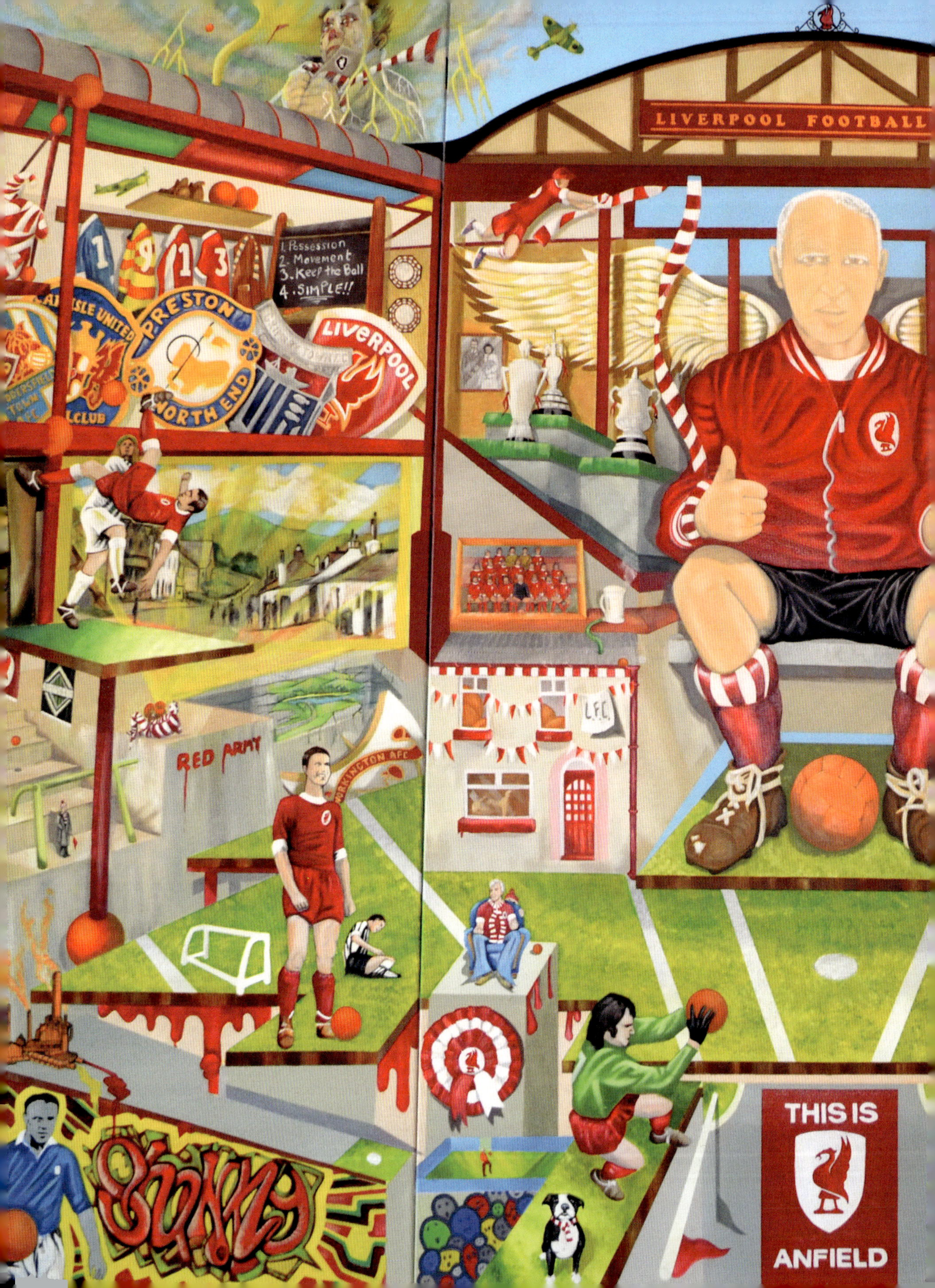
LIVERPOOL FOOTBALL
1. Possession
2. Movement
3. Keep the Ball
4. SIMPLE!!
PRESTON NORTH END
LIVERPOOL
RED ARMY
L.F.C.
THIS IS
ANFIELD

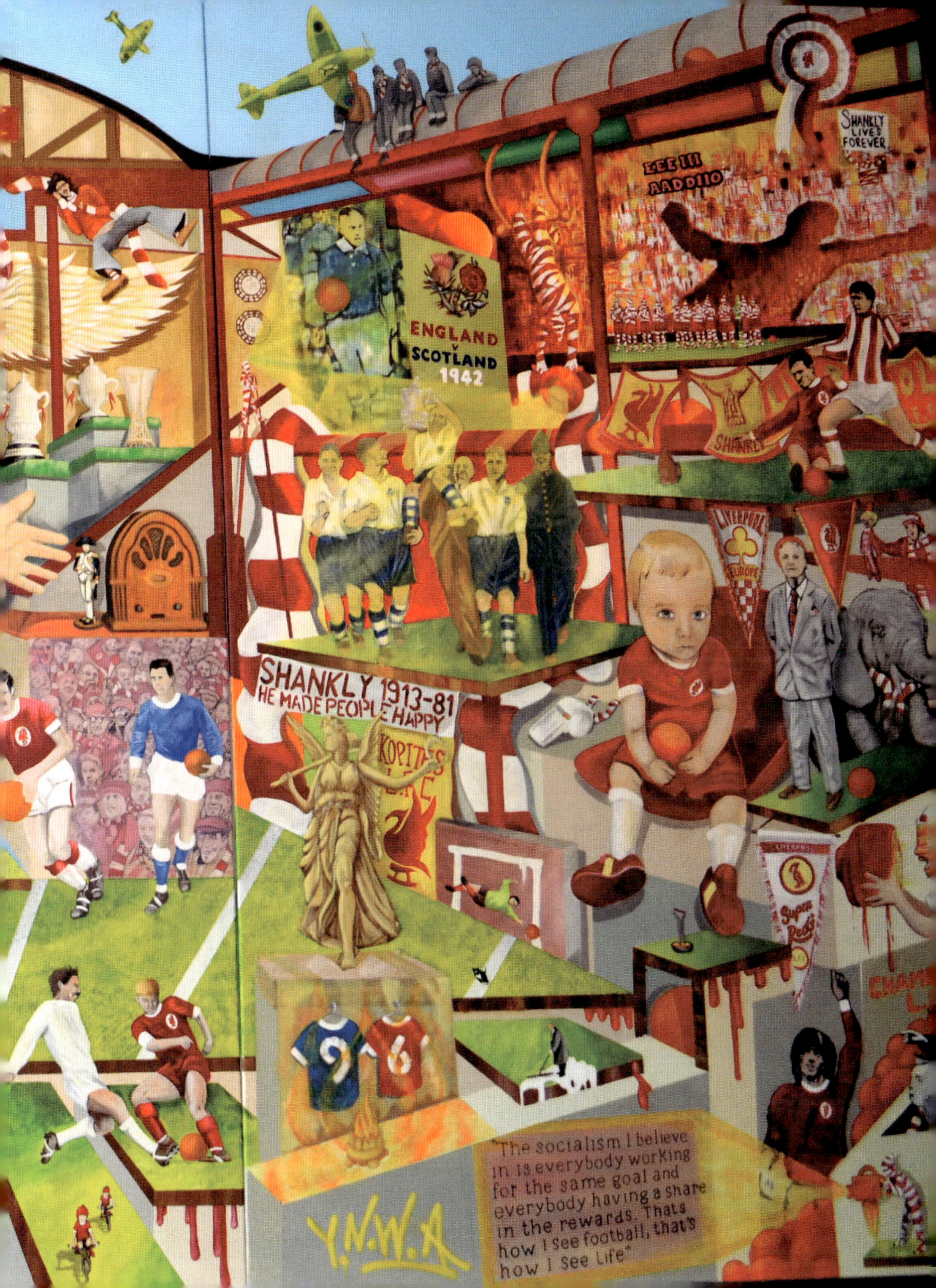
SHANKLY LIVES FOREVER
EEE III AADDIIO
ENGLAND v SCOTLAND 1942
SHANKLY
SHANKLY 1913-81
HE MADE PEOPLE HAPPY
LIVERPOOL
EUROPE
Super Reds
Y.N.W.A
"The socialism I believe in is everybody working for the same goal and everybody having a share in the rewards. Thats how I see football, that's how I see Life"

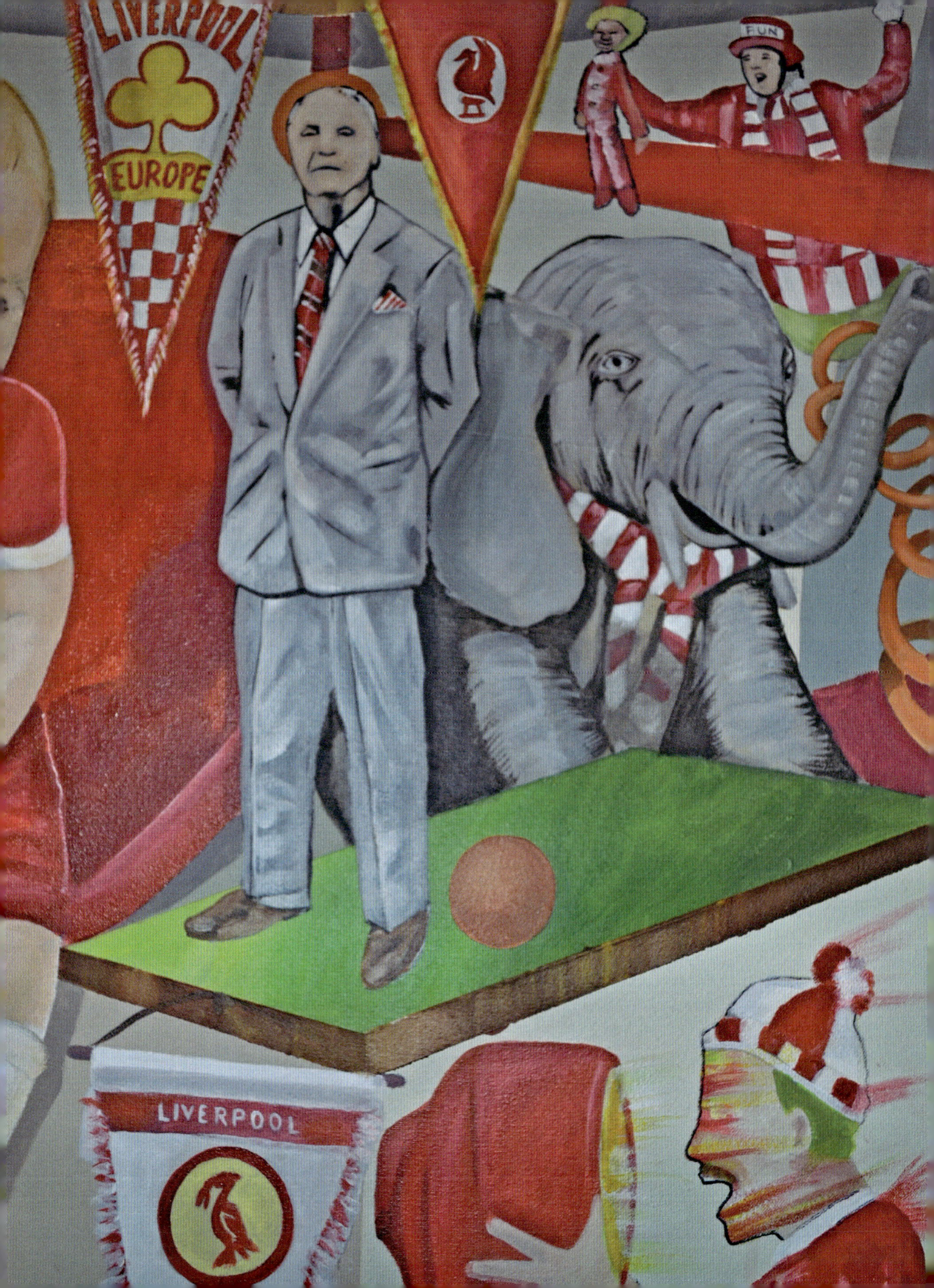
LIVERPOOL
EUROPE
FUN
LIVERPOOL

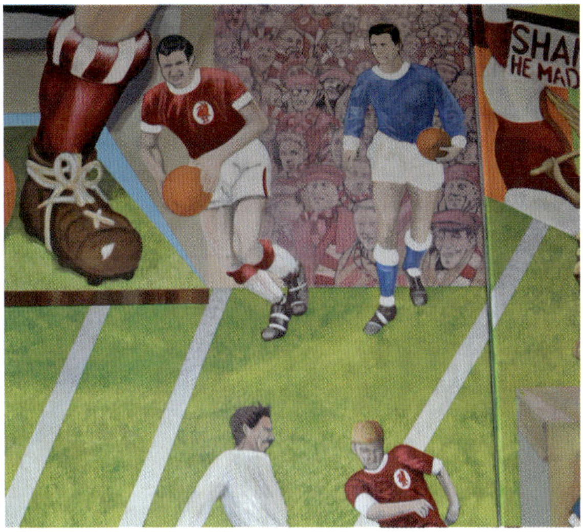

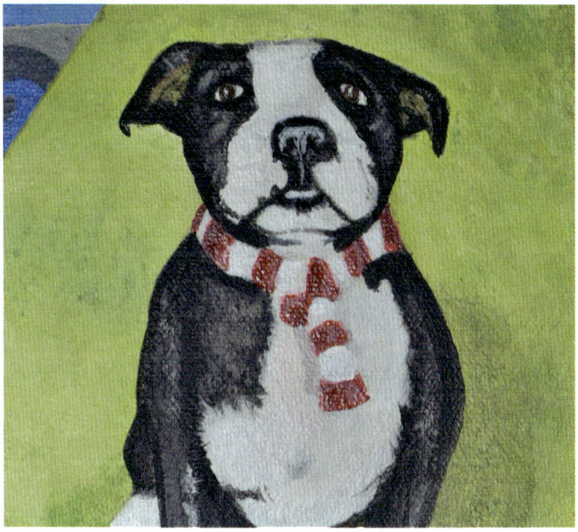

Hotel Bill

Alan Murray is a self-taught artist who hails from Liverpool 8 and has taught youngsters life and communication skills through the medium of art. His own critically-acclaimed style is highly original and thought-provoking, and his magnificent mural inside the Bill Shankly Hotel on Liverpool's Victoria Street is well worth a visit.

Shanks of course is the centre-piece of the mural – complete with angel's wings – but all around him are reminders of his Scottish roots, his footballing journey, Liverpool FC and the adopted city he loved during his tenure as manager. Players, supporters, the stadium, the trophies...they're all there.

The luxury city-centre hotel also boasts a Shankly museum and its director Chris Carline is Bill's grandson. He reveals: "When Nessie, my nan, passed away we had to clear the house and inside it we found about 90 per cent of the memorabilia on display here. Thanks to her it has allowed us to create the museum and I'm made-up that we've got so much of it on display in the hotel. It's a part of football history that should be available for people to see.

"Liverpool's first game when we opened was in 2015 and [former European Cup-winning defender] Alan Kennedy popped in to meet fans before they headed up to Anfield. We've even had Liverpool fans come in who have felt so emotional at seeing the pictures and the memorabilia that they've cried which, in a strange way, was nice as it showed the strength of feeling people still have for him."

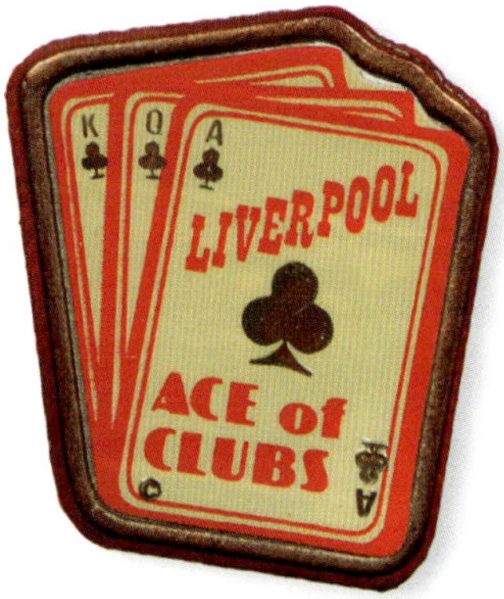
K
Q
A
LIVERPOOL
ACE of
CLUBS

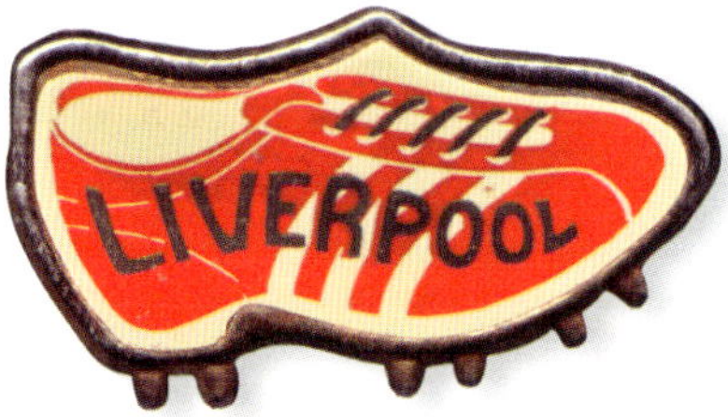
LIVERPOOL

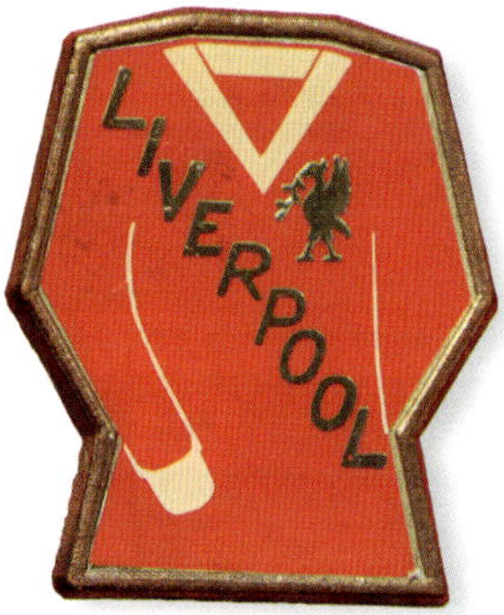
LIVERPOOL

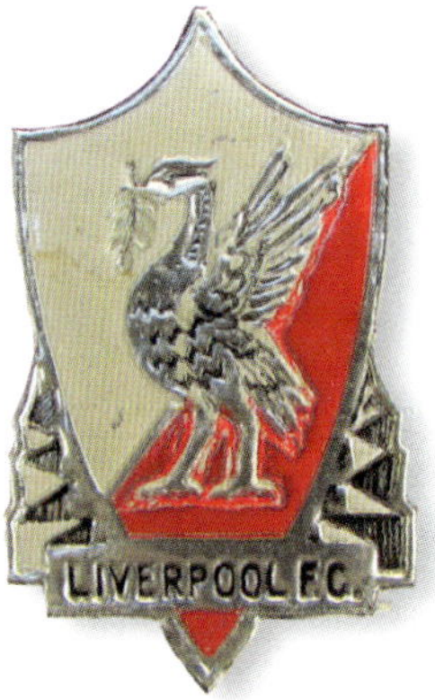
LIVERPOOL F.C.

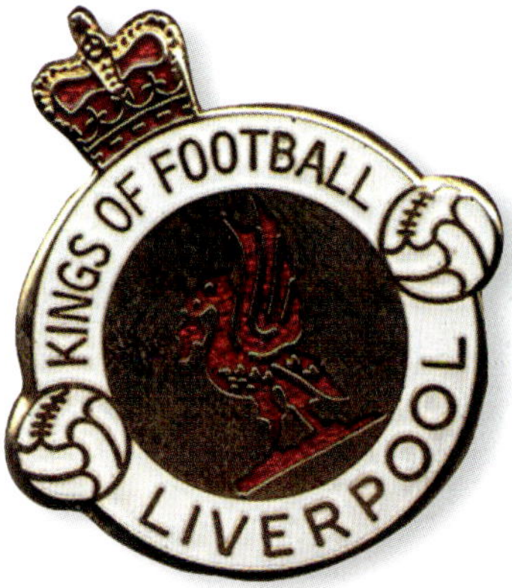
KINGS OF FOOTBALL
LIVERPOOL

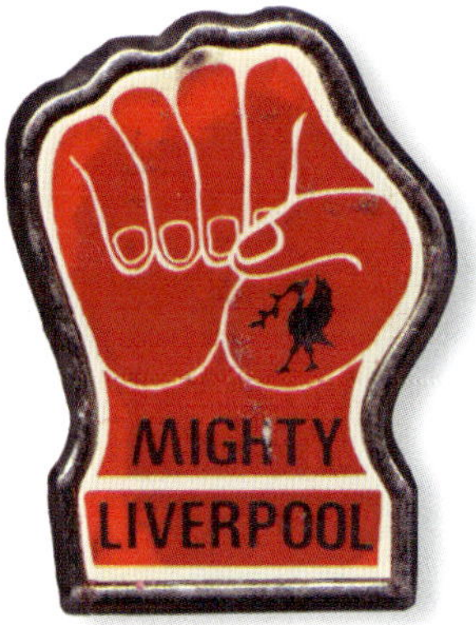
MIGHTY
LIVERPOOL

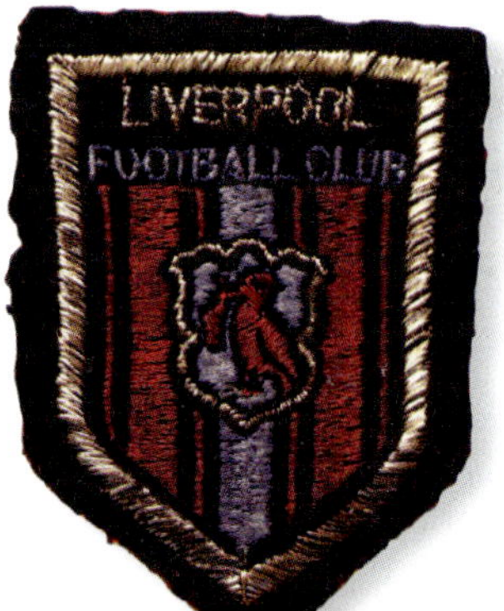
LIVERPOOL
FOOTBALL CLUB

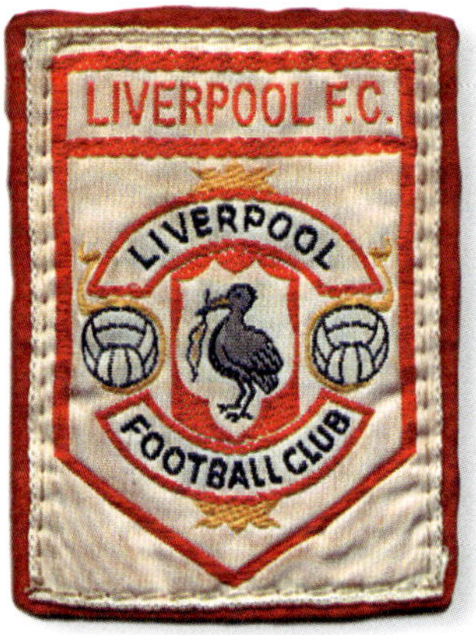
LIVERPOOL F.C.
LIVERPOOL
FOOTBALL CLUB

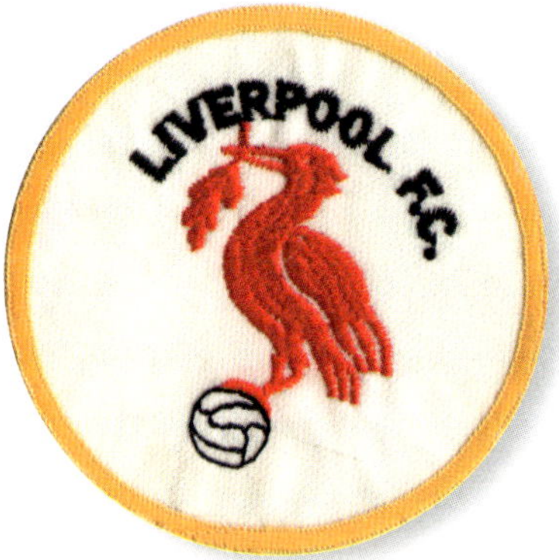
LIVERPOOL F.C.

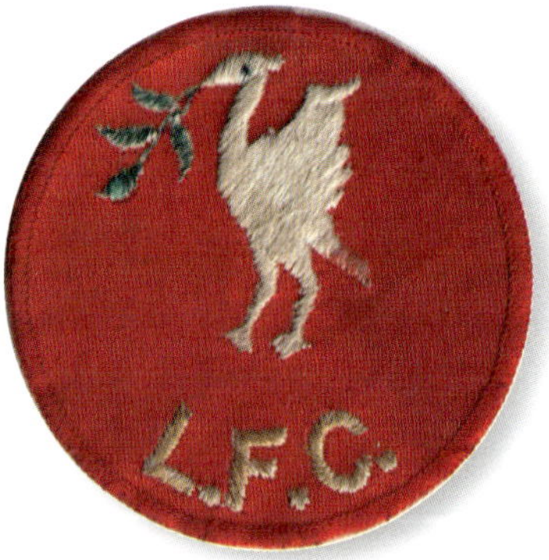
L.F.C.

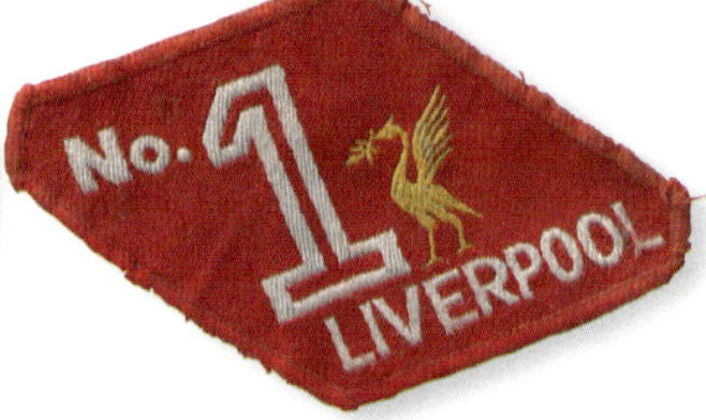
No. 1
LIVERPOOL

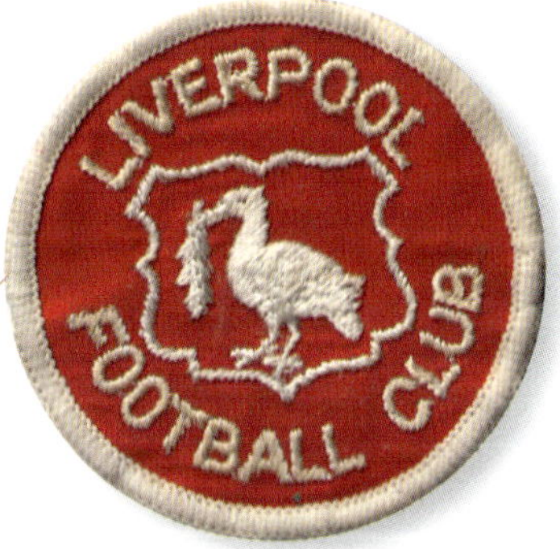
LIVERPOOL
FOOTBALL CLUB

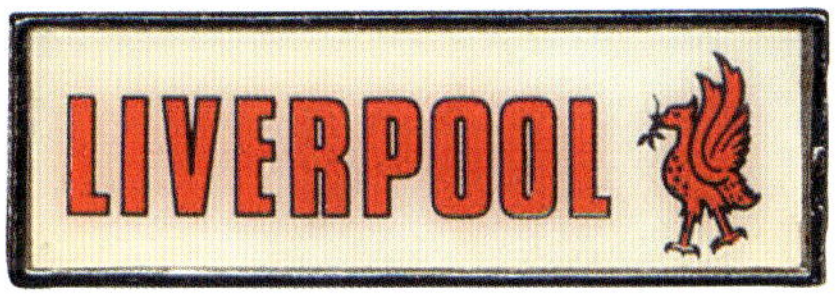

Scouse power

Denim waistcoats or white overalls? That was the ultimate sartorial dilemma for the best-dressed Kopites back in the early Seventies.

Among the more nostalgic curios in the possession of The Liverpool FC Story museum is just such a denim waistcoat belonging to fan Karl Marinas and covered with sew-on LFC patches. "Just gathering dust in my attic," he explained, "so I wondered if the club museum would be interested in having it."

The museum additionally has a collection of patches donated by another fan, Phillip Leece, amassed during his Reds-supporting travels since 1966.

Back in the day, colourful and creative patches embroidered with often improvised (and unofficial) LFC crests were sewn all over lucky hats, caps and scarves.

Another adornment was the metal pin-badge – still collected by many supporters and worn on match-going scarves or hats to this day. In the Seventies and Eighties they were ever-more-inventive, with designs in the shape of Che Guevara-style clenched fists, football kits and boots and playing cards.

Also in the Anfield museum's stewardship are two stupendous LFC-themed boiler-suits created by Reds supporters Ray Buck and Arthur Milton again in the early 1970s – turn the page to see their Kop craftsmanship.

A few years ago Ray told the club's matchday programme: "I worked at [electrical lighting company] Thorn Colour Tubes in Skelmersdale and we were issued with these overalls about every six months. Mysteriously I lost about 15 pairs of them just before the 1974 FA Cup final, about the same time that I had a mysterious illness too.

"I spent hours and hours painting the overalls and making hats to go with them. We wore them for the final, but before the game we took them down to see Shanks at Melwood. He stopped training and lined the players up and they all signed mine.

"The hats [long since lost] were quite an engineering feat. Inside each one was a false bottom which you could open to get out a plastic bag to protect the hats when it rained. One of them even had butties in it!"

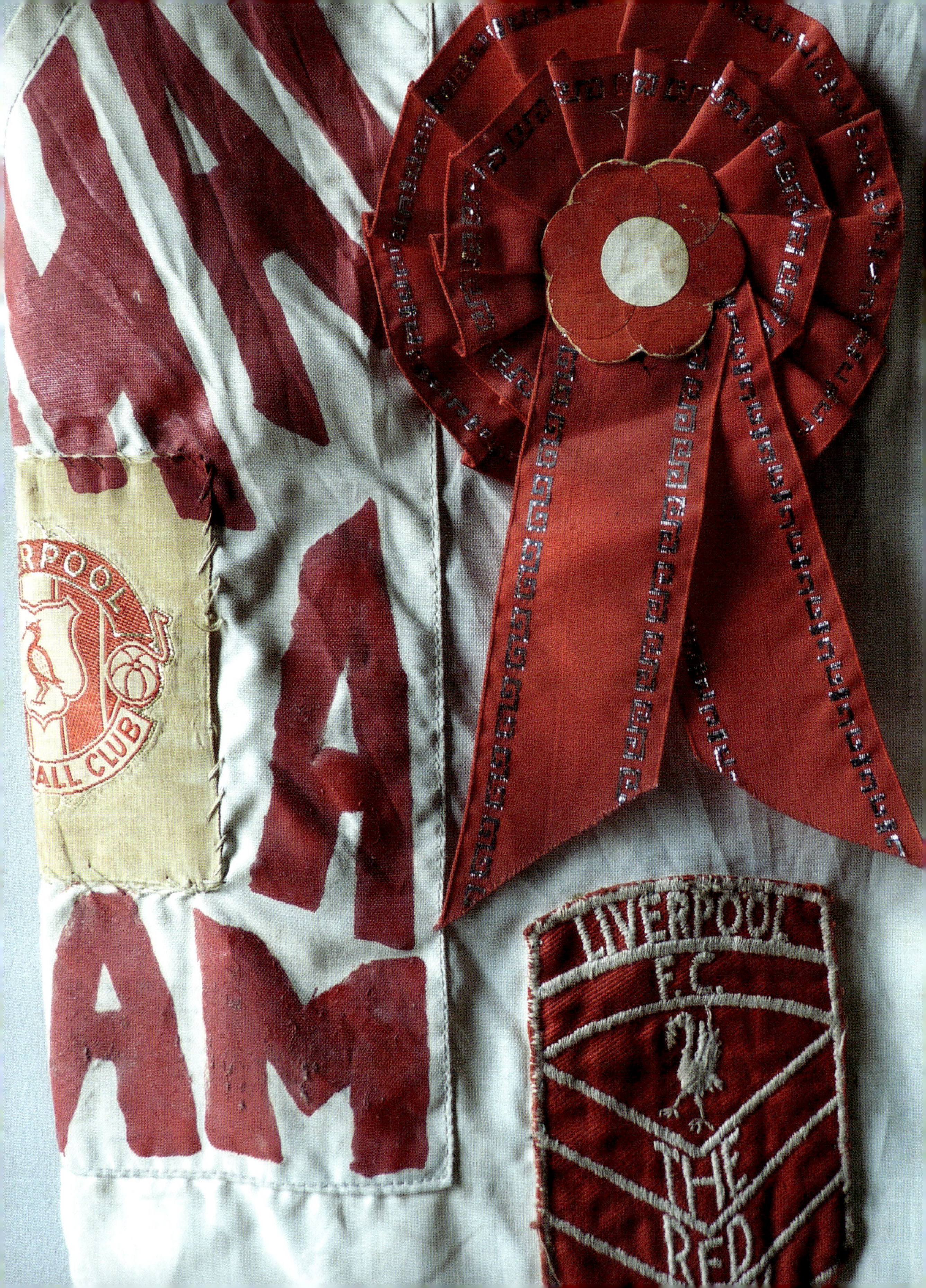
LIVERPOOL
F.C.

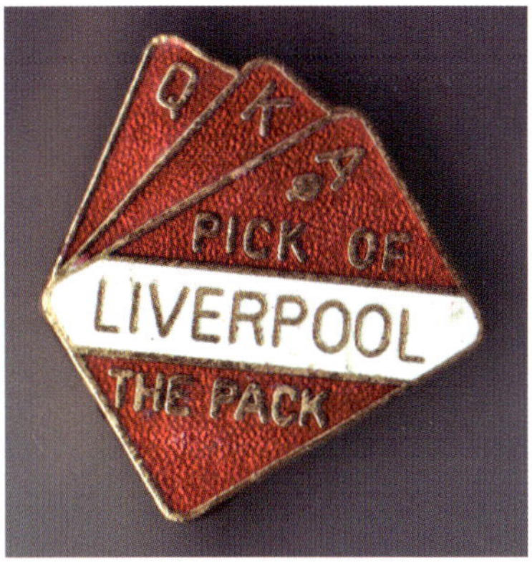
Q
K
A
PICK OF
LIVERPOOL
THE PACK
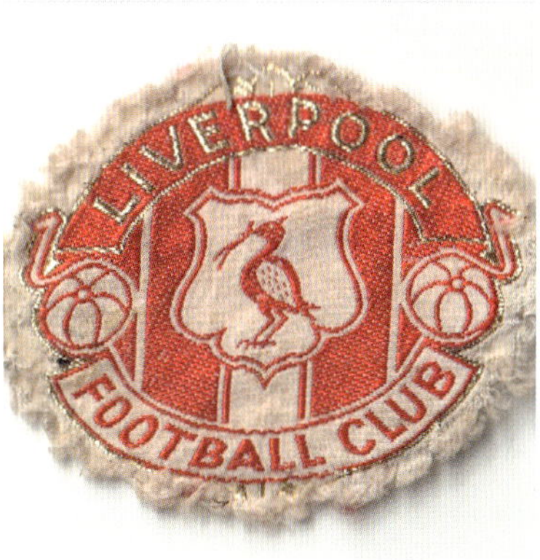
LIVERPOOL
FOOTBALL CLUB
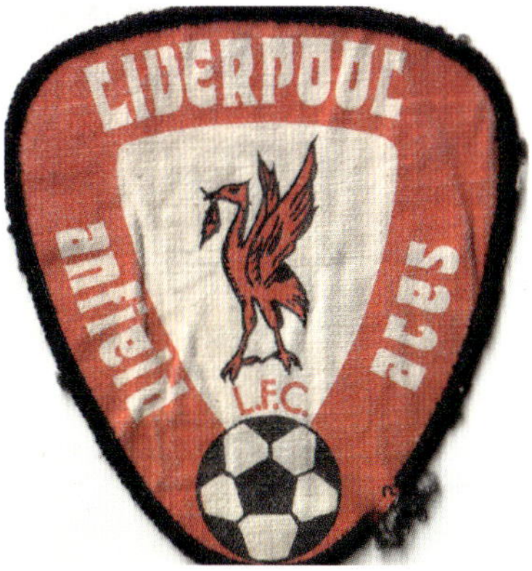
LIVERPOOL
anfield
aces
L.F.C.
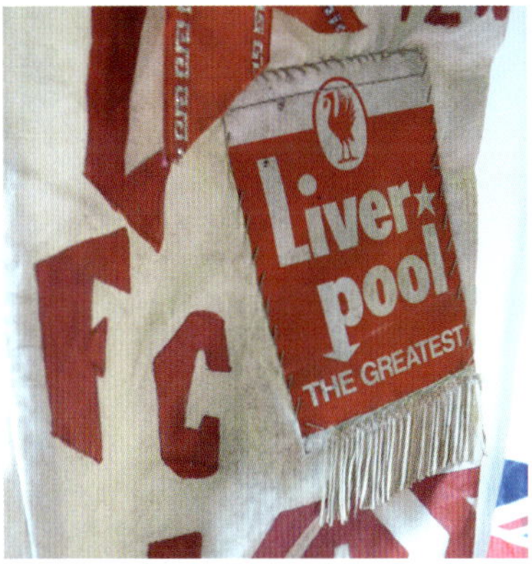
Liver
pool
THE GREATEST
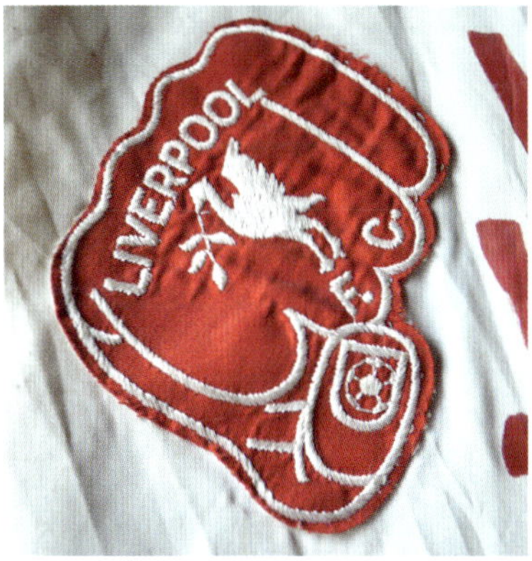
LIVERPOOL
F.C.
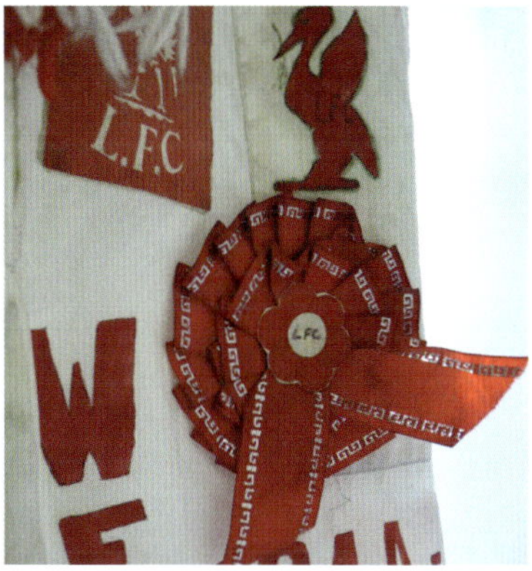
L.F.C
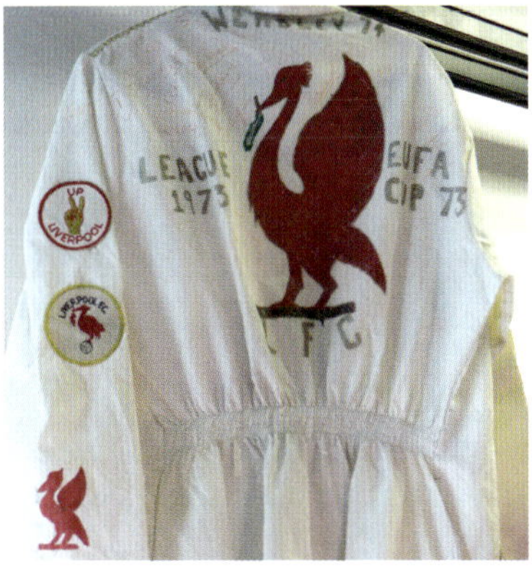
LEAGUE
1973
UEFA
CUP 73
L F C
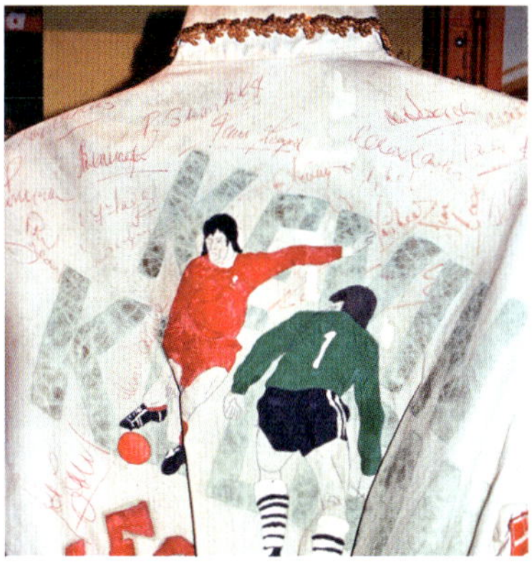
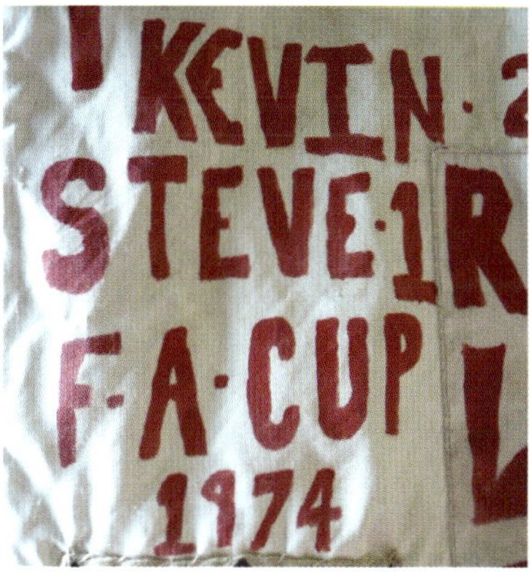
KEVIN ·
STEVE · 1
F · A · CUP
1974
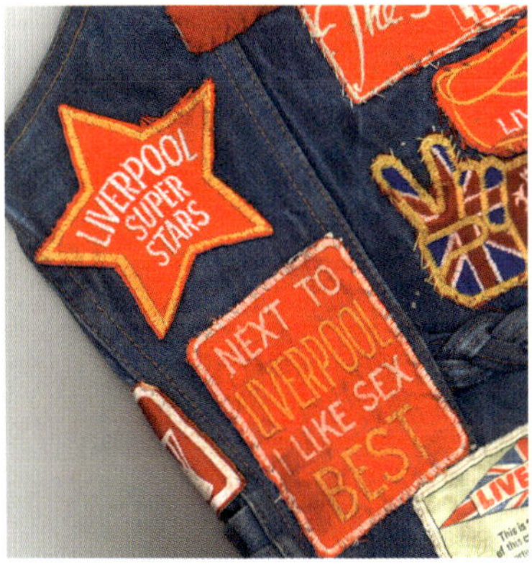
LIVERPOOL SUPER STARS
NEXT TO LIVERPOOL I LIKE SEX BEST
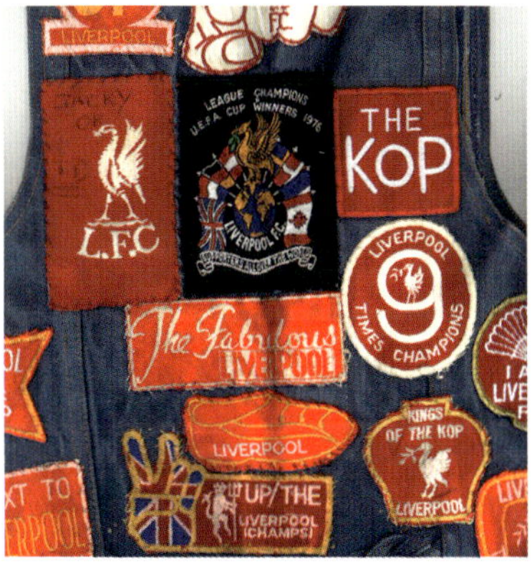
LIVERPOOL
L.F.C
LEAGUE CHAMPIONS UEFA CUP WINNERS 1976
THE KOP
LIVERPOOL 9 TIMES CHAMPIONS
The Fabulous LIVERPOOL
LIVERPOOL
KINGS OF THE KOP LIVERPOOL
UP THE LIVERPOOL CHAMPS
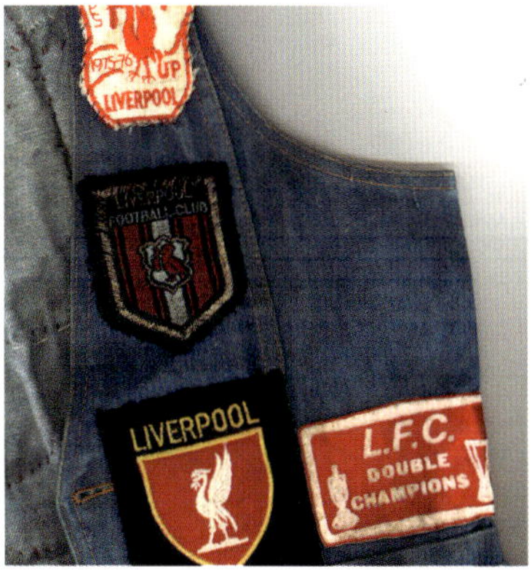
UP LIVERPOOL
LIVERPOOL
L.F.C. DOUBLE CHAMPIONS

Cover stories

Plenty of front covers from Liverpool FC's matchday programme have gone down in history – not least the issue for the now-legendary UEFA Champions League semi-final second leg against Barcelona at Anfield in May 2019. It featured the European Cup trophy made from colourful mosaics inspired by the famous Gaudi architecture of the Catalan capital – an instant, hugely sought-after collector's item.

European nights have always given the programme's designers an opportunity to take their creativity to another level, with covers causing a stir online and among the Anfield crowd in the build-up to big matches.

The Europa League group game against Rubin Kazan in October 2015 was Jürgen Klopp's first home fixture in charge and was commemorated by a Barack Obama 'Hope'-style image on the cover.

The subsequent round-of-16 first leg with arch rivals Manchester United in March 2016 was promoted in the manner of a heavyweight boxing poster; while the edition for the quarter-final second leg against Borussia Dortmund marked the anniversary of Hillsborough in Kop sheet-mosaic fashion.

The 2020/21 season saw a matchday programme first: an issue for a competitive home game on foreign soil, with the Reds 'hosting' RB Leipzig in the second leg of the Champions League round-of-16 in Budapest's Puskas Arena in March 2021. On the cover: a view of Anfield from the window of a passenger jet!

On the front cover for the second leg of the Champions League knockout tie with Inter Milan in March 2022 was La Scala, the legendary Italian opera house, with Anfield as its stage. For the semi-final first leg against Villarreal that same season there were two submarines in homage to the Spanish side's nickname and of course Liverpool's musical Fab Four.

In the Premier League era there have been many matchday programme highlights in recent seasons, not least the cover for the game against Chelsea in July 2020 when the Reds were crowned champions (the fastest-selling issue of all-time at Anfield). The cover for the final issue of 2021/22, for Liverpool v Wolverhampton Wanderers on 22 May 2022, said it all: 'THESE ARE THE DAYS'.

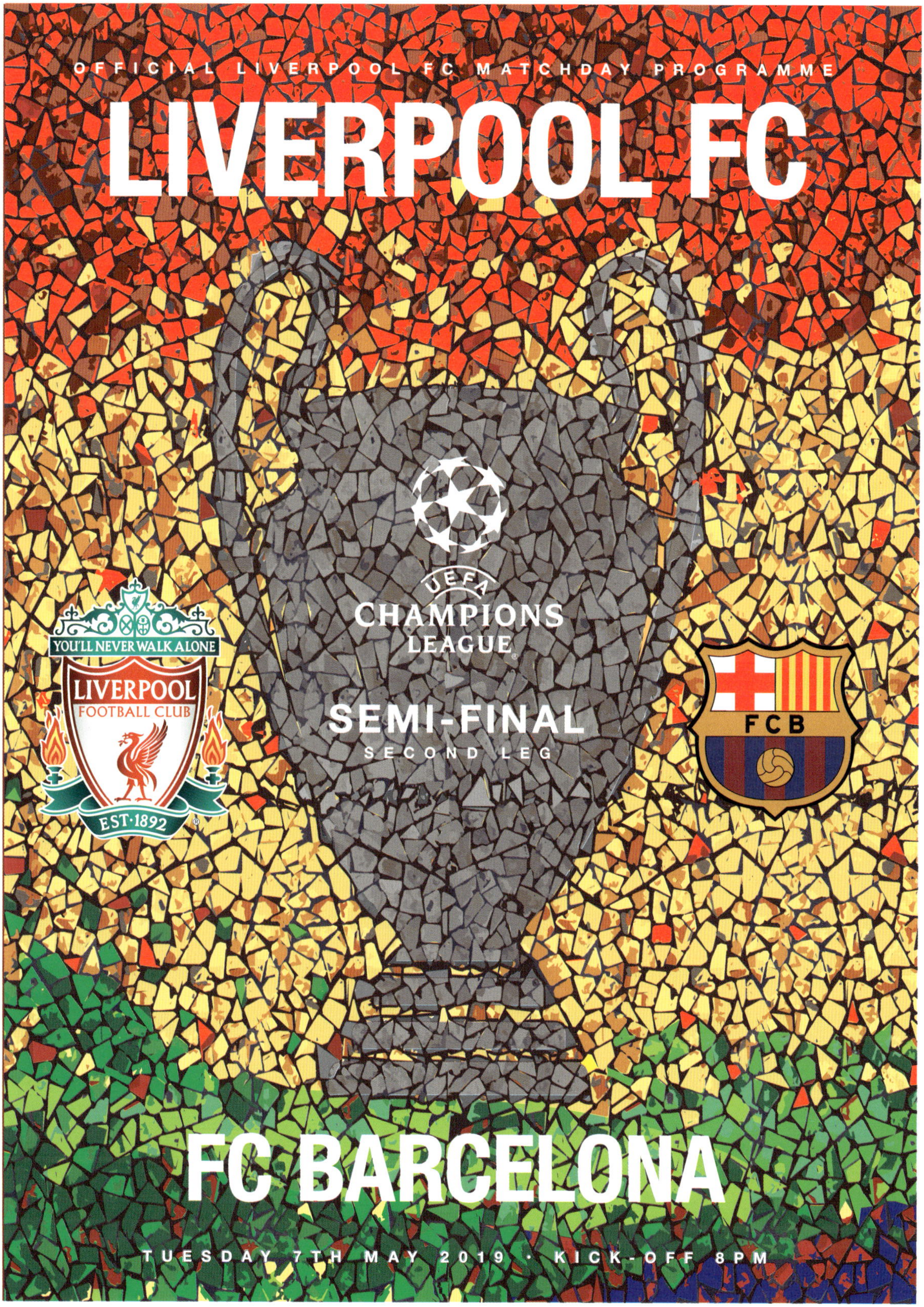

OFFICIAL LIVERPOOL FC MATCHDAY PROGRAMME
LIVERPOOL FC
UEFA CHAMPIONS LEAGUE
SEMI-FINAL
SECOND LEG
YOU'LL NEVER WALK ALONE
LIVERPOOL FOOTBALL CLUB
EST·1892
FCB
FC BARCELONA
TUESDAY 7TH MAY 2019 · KICK-OFF 8PM

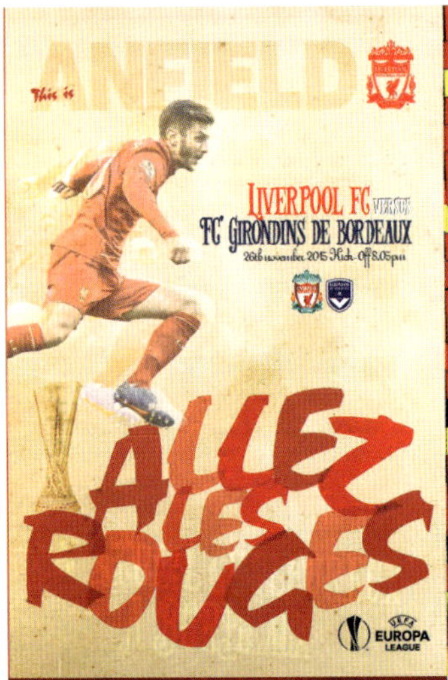
This is
ANFIELD
LIVERPOOL FC versus
FC GIRONDINS DE BORDEAUX
26th November 2015 Kick Off 8.05pm
ALLEZ LES ROUGES
EUROPA LEAGUE

THIS IS
ANFIELD
96
LIVERPOOL FC
V BORUSSIA DORTMUND
QUARTER-FINAL 2ND LEG 14.04.16 KICK-OFF 8.05PM
EUROPA LEAGUE

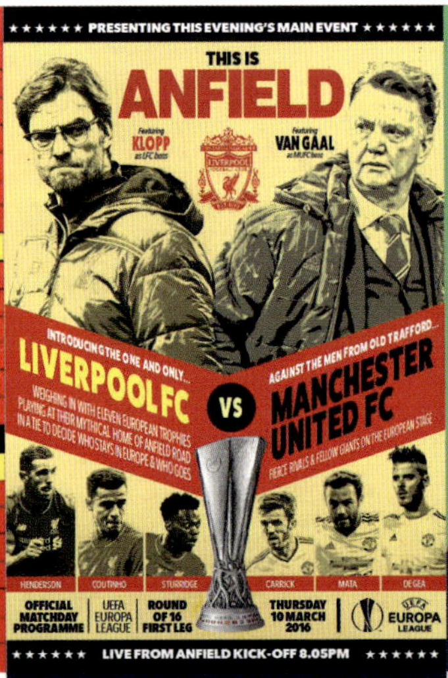
PRESENTING THIS EVENING'S MAIN EVENT
THIS IS
ANFIELD
KLOPP
VAN GAAL
INTRODUCING THE ONE AND ONLY...
LIVERPOOL FC
VS
AGAINST THE MEN FROM OLD TRAFFORD...
MANCHESTER UNITED FC
HENDERSON
COUTINHO
STURRIDGE
CARRICK
MATA
DE GEA
OFFICIAL MATCHDAY PROGRAMME
UEFA EUROPA LEAGUE
ROUND OF 16 FIRST LEG
THURSDAY 10 MARCH 2016
EUROPA LEAGUE
LIVE FROM ANFIELD KICK-OFF 8.05PM

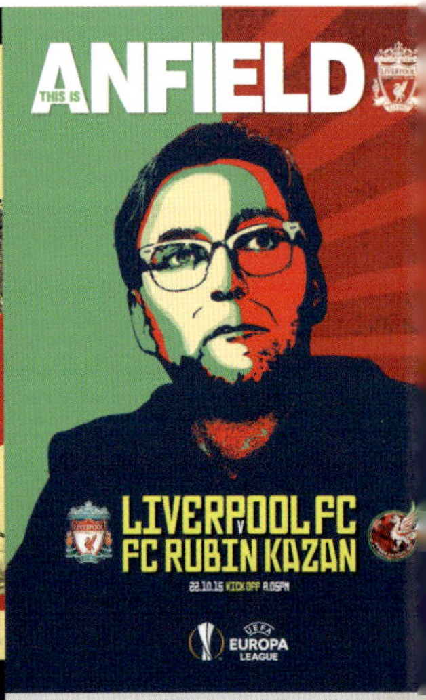
THIS IS
ANFIELD
LIVERPOOL FC
V
FC RUBIN KAZAN
22.10.15 KICK OFF 8.05PM
EUROPA LEAGUE

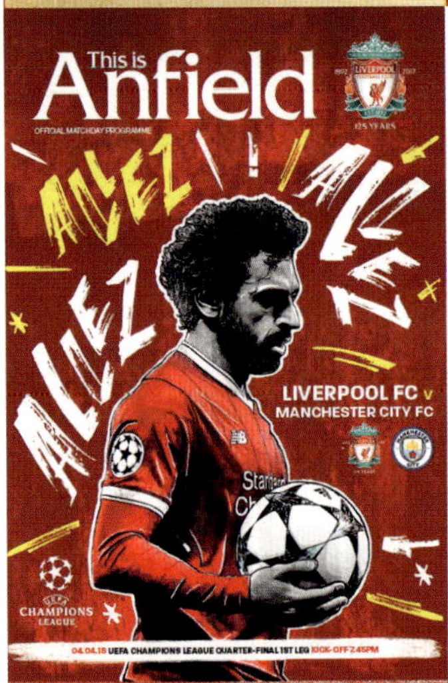
This is
Anfield
OFFICIAL MATCHDAY PROGRAMME
125 YEARS
ALLEZ ALLEZ ALLEZ
LIVERPOOL FC v
MANCHESTER CITY FC
CHAMPIONS LEAGUE
04.04.18 UEFA CHAMPIONS LEAGUE QUARTER-FINAL 1ST LEG KICK-OFF 7.45PM

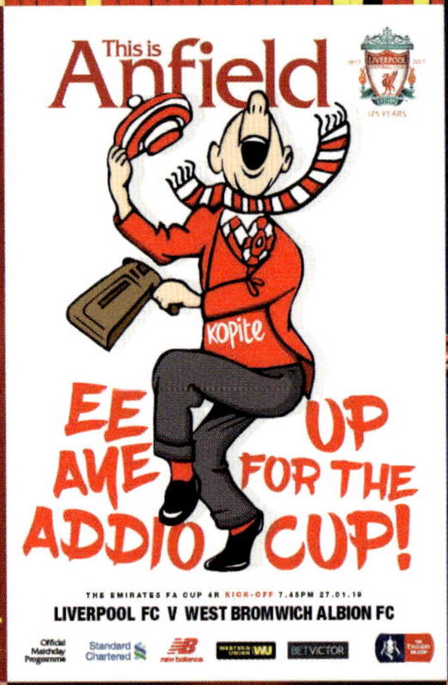
This is
Anfield
125 YEARS
Kopite
EE AYE ADDIO UP FOR THE CUP!
THE EMIRATES FA CUP 4R KICK-OFF 7.45PM 27.01.18
LIVERPOOL FC V WEST BROMWICH ALBION FC
Official Matchday Programme
Standard Chartered
new balance
WESTERN UNION WU
BETVICTOR

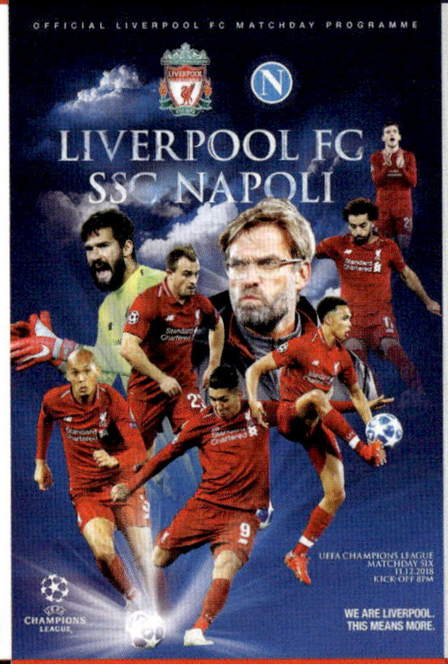
OFFICIAL LIVERPOOL FC MATCHDAY PROGRAMME
LIVERPOOL FC
SSC NAPOLI
UEFA CHAMPIONS LEAGUE
MATCHDAY SIX
11.12.2018
KICK-OFF 8PM
CHAMPIONS LEAGUE
WE ARE LIVERPOOL.
THIS MEANS MORE.

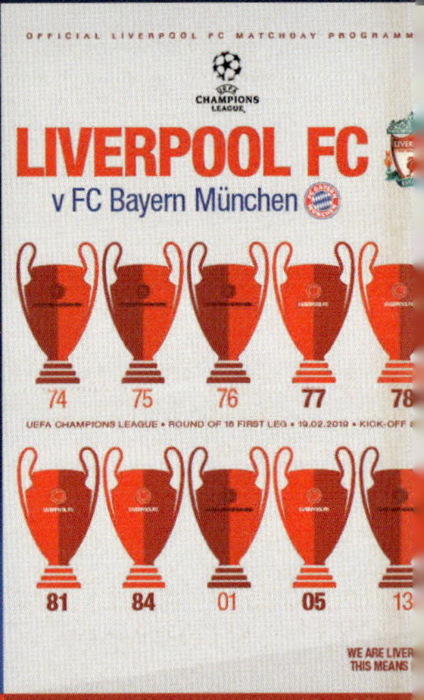
OFFICIAL LIVERPOOL FC MATCHDAY PROGRAMME
CHAMPIONS LEAGUE
LIVERPOOL FC
v FC Bayern München
74
75
76
77
78
UEFA CHAMPIONS LEAGUE • ROUND OF 16 FIRST LEG • 19.02.2019 • KICK-OFF
81
84
01
05
13
WE ARE LIVER
THIS MEANS

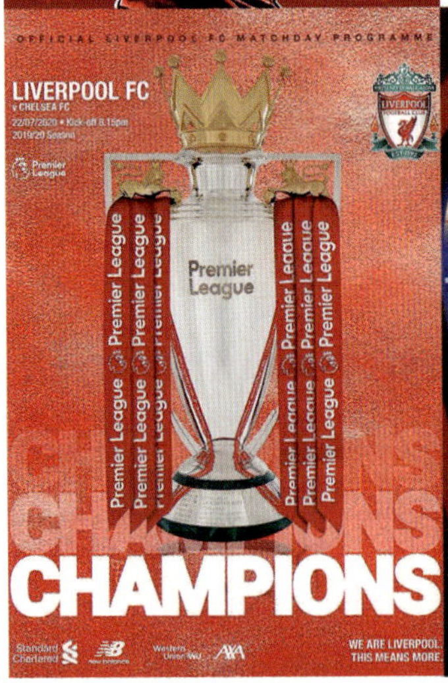
OFFICIAL LIVERPOOL FC MATCHDAY PROGRAMME
LIVERPOOL FC
v CHELSEA FC
22/07/2020 • Kick-off 8.15pm
2019/20 Season
Premier League
CHAMPIONS
WE ARE LIVERPOOL
THIS MEANS MORE.

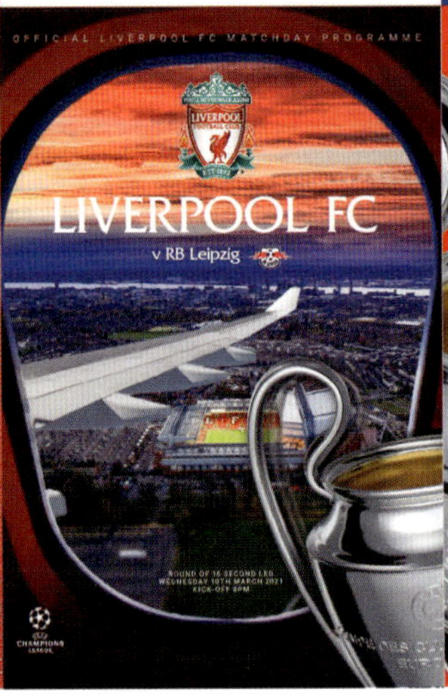
OFFICIAL LIVERPOOL FC MATCHDAY PROGRAMME
LIVERPOOL FC
v RB Leipzig
ROUND OF 16 SECOND LEG
WEDNESDAY 10TH MARCH 2021
KICK-OFF 8PM
CHAMPIONS LEAGUE

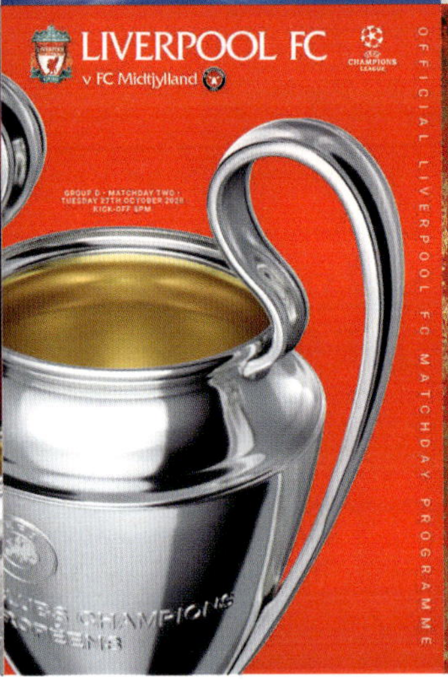
LIVERPOOL FC
v FC Midtjylland
CHAMPIONS LEAGUE
OFFICIAL LIVERPOOL FC MATCHDAY PROGRAMME

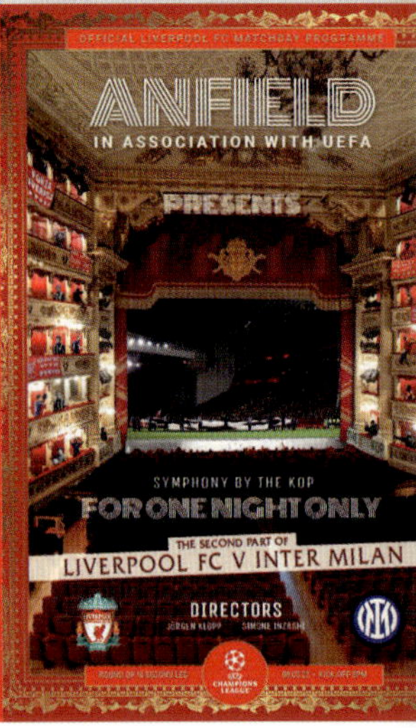
OFFICIAL LIVERPOOL FC MATCHDAY PROGRAMME
ANFIELD
IN ASSOCIATION WITH UEFA
PRESENTS
SYMPHONY BY THE KOP
FOR ONE NIGHT ONLY
THE SECOND PART OF
LIVERPOOL FC V INTER MILAN
DIRECTORS

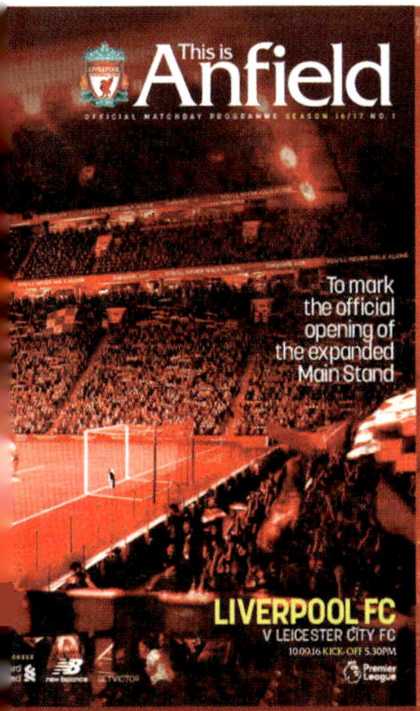
This is Anfield
To mark the official opening of the expanded Main Stand
LIVERPOOL FC
V LEICESTER CITY FC

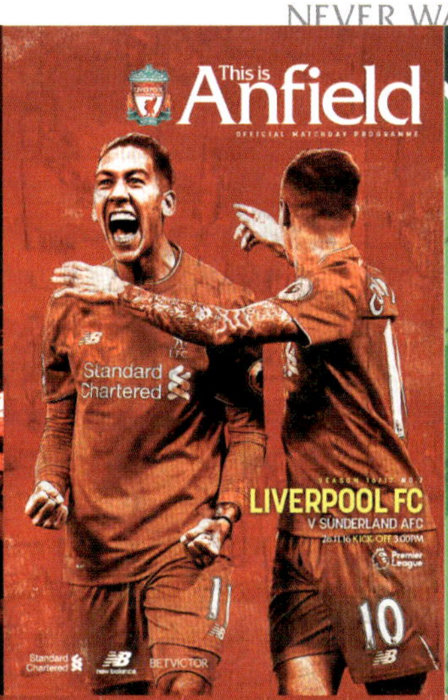
This is Anfield
OFFICIAL MATCHDAY PROGRAMME
Standard Chartered
LIVERPOOL FC
V SUNDERLAND AFC

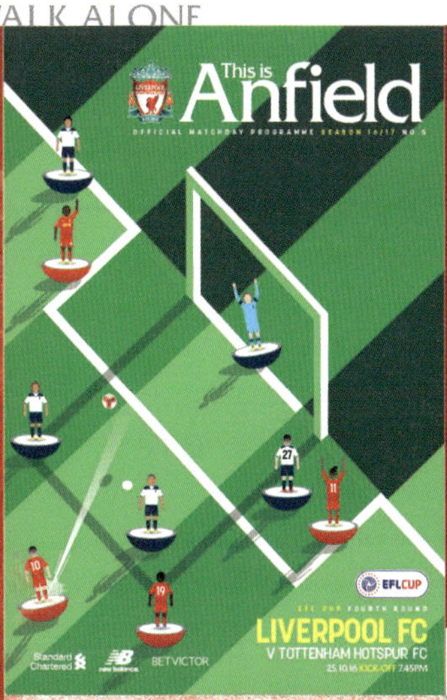
This is Anfield
EFL CUP
LIVERPOOL FC
V TOTTENHAM HOTSPUR FC

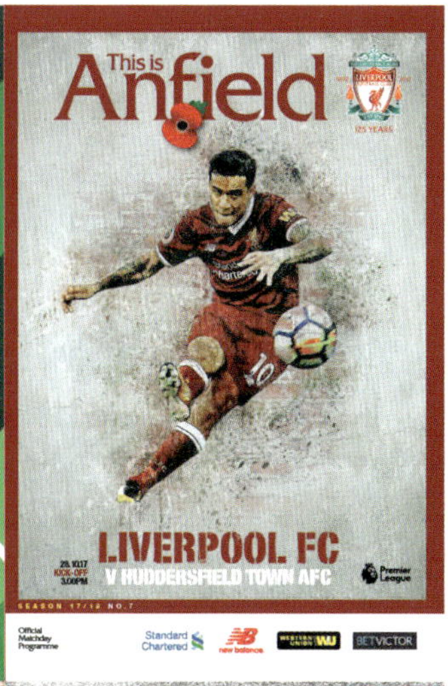
This is Anfield
125 YEARS
LIVERPOOL FC
V HUDDERSFIELD TOWN AFC

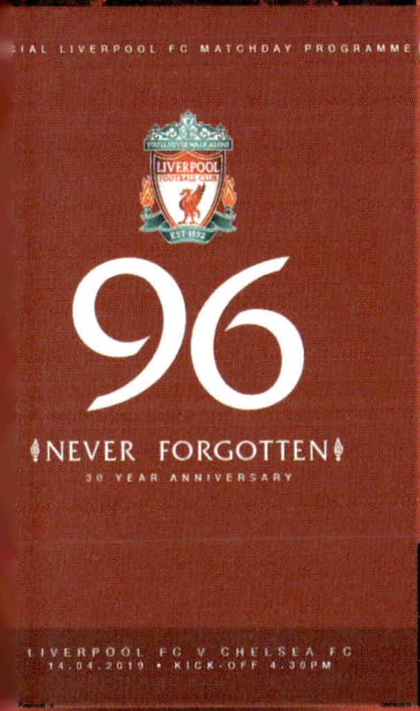
96
NEVER FORGOTTEN
30 YEAR ANNIVERSARY
LIVERPOOL FC V CHELSEA FC
14.04.2019 • KICK-OFF 4.30PM

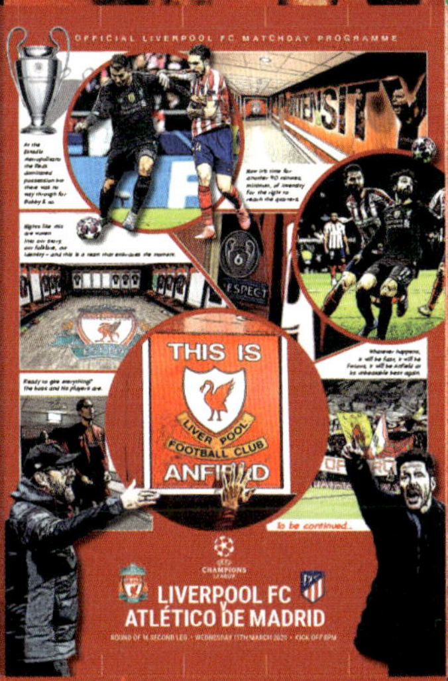
OFFICIAL LIVERPOOL FC MATCHDAY PROGRAMME
THIS IS ANFIELD
LIVERPOOL FC
ATLÉTICO DE MADRID

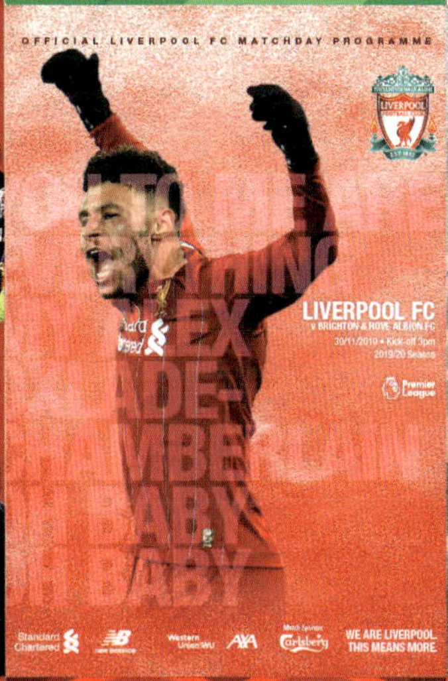
OFFICIAL LIVERPOOL FC MATCHDAY PROGRAMME
LIVERPOOL FC
WE ARE LIVERPOOL THIS MEANS MORE

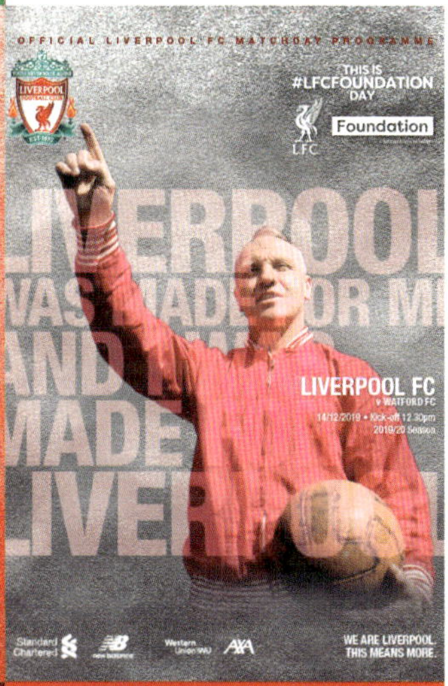
OFFICIAL LIVERPOOL FC MATCHDAY PROGRAMME
THIS IS #LFCFOUNDATION DAY
Foundation
LIVERPOOL FC
WE ARE LIVERPOOL THIS MEANS MORE

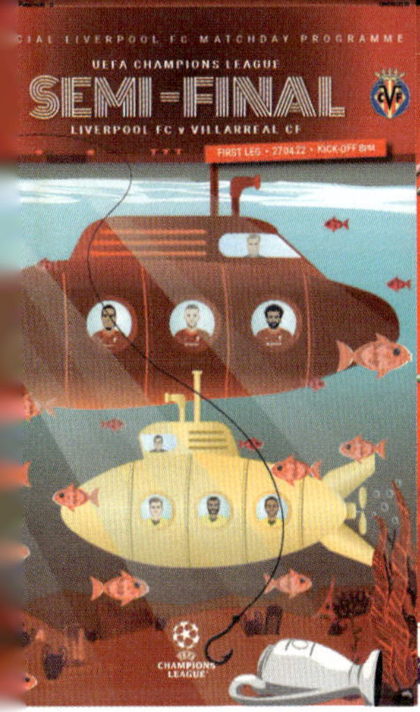
OFFICIAL LIVERPOOL FC MATCHDAY PROGRAMME
UEFA CHAMPIONS LEAGUE
SEMI-FINAL
LIVERPOOL FC v VILLARREAL CF

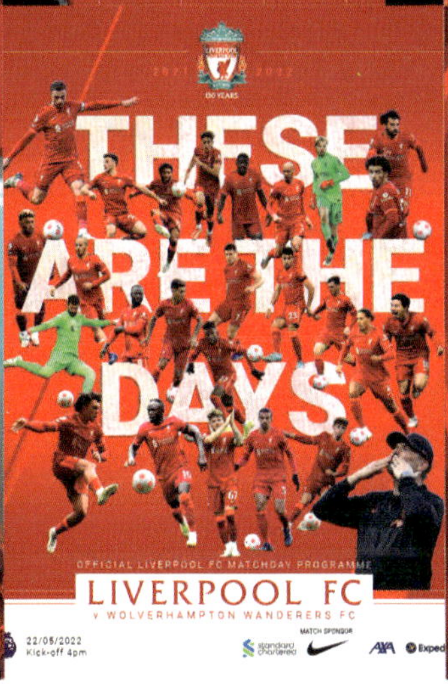
THESE ARE THE DAYS
OFFICIAL LIVERPOOL FC MATCHDAY PROGRAMME
LIVERPOOL FC
v WOLVERHAMPTON WANDERERS FC

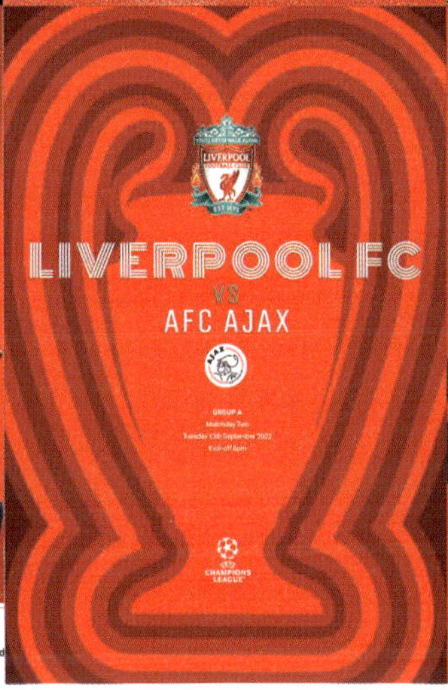
LIVERPOOL FC
VS
AFC AJAX

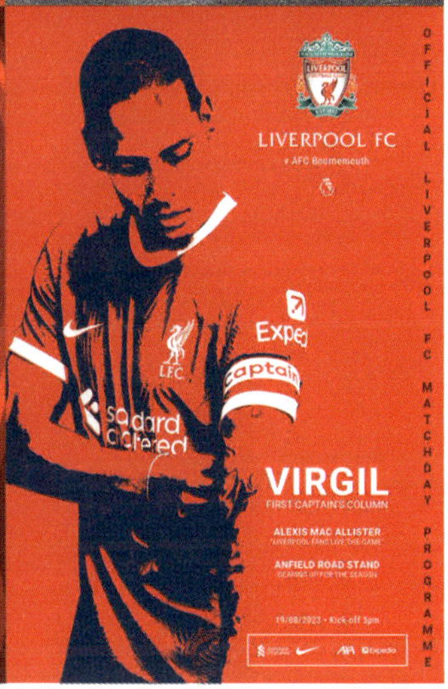
OFFICIAL LIVERPOOL FC MATCHDAY PROGRAMME
LIVERPOOL FC
v AFC Bournemouth
VIRGIL
FIRST CAPTAIN'S COLUMN
ALEXIS MAC ALLISTER
ANFIELD ROAD STAND

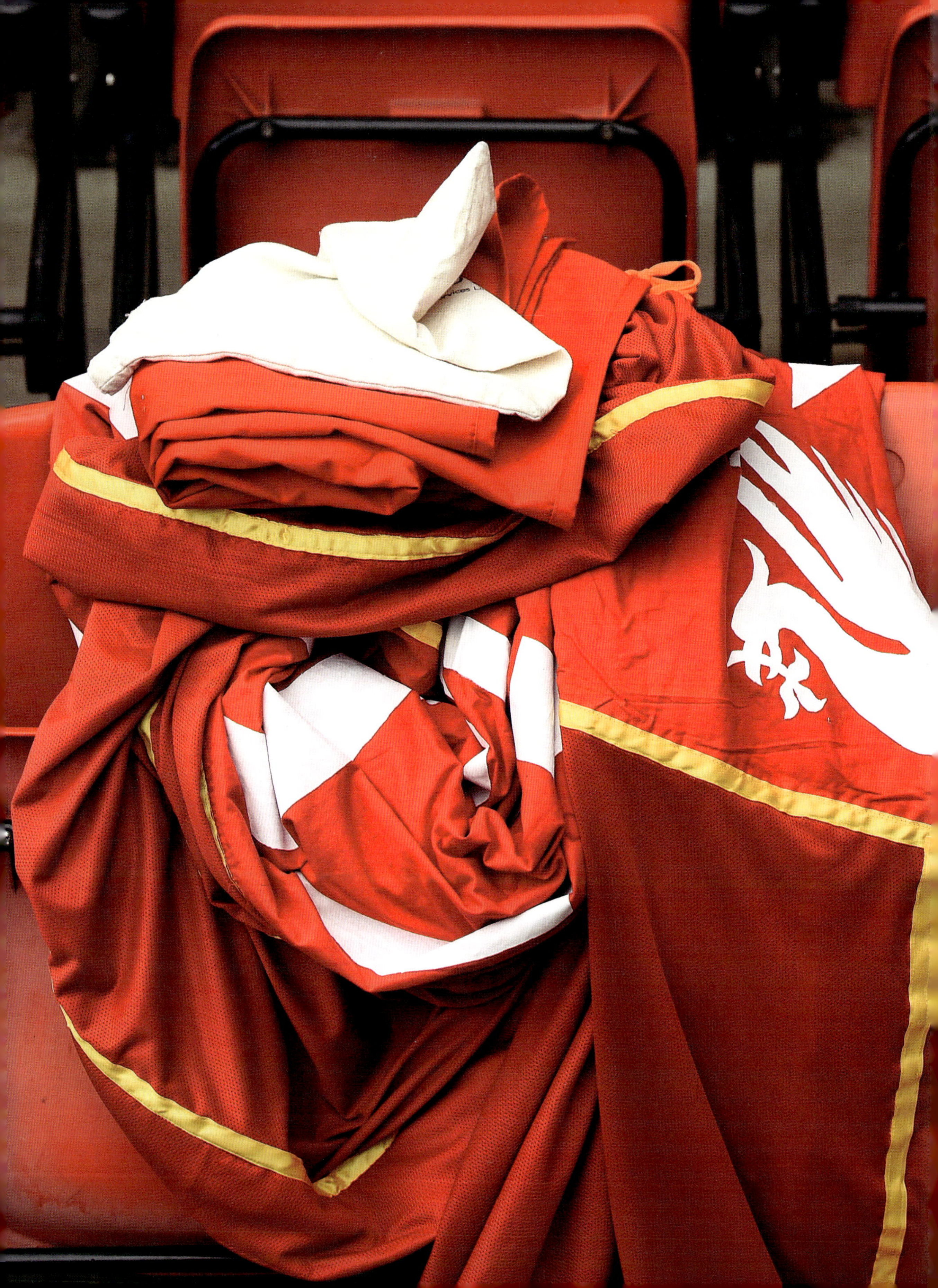